Applied Artificial Higher Order Neural Networks for Control and Recognition

Ming Zhang
Christopher Newport University, USA

A volume in the Advances in Computational
Intelligence and Robotics (ACIR) Book Series

Information Science
REFERENCE
An Imprint of IGI Global

Published in the United States of America by
    Information Science Reference (an imprint of IGI Global)
    701 E. Chocolate Avenue
    Hershey PA, USA 17033
    Tel: 717-533-8845
    Fax: 717-533-8661
    E-mail: cust@igi-global.com
    Web site: http://www.igi-global.com

Library of Congress Cataloging-in-Publication Data

Names: Zhang, Ming, 1949 July 29- editor.
Title: Applied artificial higher order neural networks for control and
  recognition / Ming Zhang, editor.
Description: Hershey PA : Information Science Reference (an imprint of IGI
  Global), [2016] | Includes bibliographical references and index.
Identifiers: LCCN 2015051300| ISBN 9781522500636 (hc) | ISBN 9781522500643
  (eISBN)
Subjects: LCSH: Automatic control--Data processing. | Pattern recognition
  systems--Data processing. | Neural networks (Computer science)
Classification: LCC TJ223.M53 A665 2016 | DDC 629.8/95632--dc23 LC record available at http://lccn.loc.
gov/2015051300

This book is published in the IGI Global book series Advances in Computational Intelligence and Robotics (ACIR) (ISSN: 2327-0411; eISSN: 2327-042X).

British Cataloguing in Publication Data
A Cataloguing in Publication record for this book is available from the British Library.

For electronic access to this publication, please contact: eresources@igi-global.com.

Advances in Computational Intelligence and Robotics (ACIR) Book Series

Ivan Giannoccaro
University of Salento, Italy

ISSN: 2327-0411
EISSN: 2327-042X

MISSION

While intelligence is traditionally a term applied to humans and human cognition, technology has progressed in such a way to allow for the development of intelligent systems able to simulate many human traits. With this new era of simulated and artificial intelligence, much research is needed in order to continue to advance the field and also to evaluate the ethical and societal concerns of the existence of artificial life and machine learning.

The **Advances in Computational Intelligence and Robotics (ACIR) Book Series** encourages scholarly discourse on all topics pertaining to evolutionary computing, artificial life, computational intelligence, machine learning, and robotics. ACIR presents the latest research being conducted on diverse topics in intelligence technologies with the goal of advancing knowledge and applications in this rapidly evolving field.

COVERAGE

- Computer Vision
- Intelligent control
- Synthetic Emotions
- Cognitive Informatics
- Fuzzy Systems
- Agent technologies
- Machine Learning
- Neural Networks
- Artificial Life
- Cyborgs

IGI Global is currently accepting manuscripts for publication within this series. To submit a proposal for a volume in this series, please contact our Acquisition Editors at Acquisitions@igi-global.com or visit: http://www.igi-global.com/publish/.

Titles in this Series

For a list of additional titles in this series, please visit: www.igi-global.com

Handbook of Research on Generalized and Hybrid Set Structures and Applications for Soft Computing
Sunil Jacob John (National Institute of Technology Calicut, India)
Information Science Reference • copyright 2016 • 607pp • H/C (ISBN: 9781466697980) • US $375.00 (our price)

Handbook of Research on Modern Optimization Algorithms and Applications in Engineering and Economics
Pandian Vasant (Universiti Teknologi Petronas, Malaysia) Gerhard-Wilhelm Weber (Middle East Technical University, Turkey) and Vo Ngoc Dieu (Ho Chi Minh City University of Technology, Vietnam)
Engineering Science Reference • copyright 2016 • 960pp • H/C (ISBN: 9781466696440) • US $325.00 (our price)

Problem Solving and Uncertainty Modeling through Optimization and Soft Computing Applications
Pratiksha Saxena (Gautam Buddha University, India) Dipti Singh (Gautam Buddha University, India) and Millie Pant (Indian Institute of Technology - Roorkee, India)
Information Science Reference • copyright 2016 • 403pp • H/C (ISBN: 9781466698857) • US $225.00 (our price)

Emerging Technologies in Intelligent Applications for Image and Video Processing
V. Santhi (VIT University, India) D. P. Acharjya (VIT University, India) and M. Ezhilarasan (Pondichery Engineering College, India)
Information Science Reference • copyright 2016 • 518pp • H/C (ISBN: 9781466696853) • US $235.00 (our price)

Handbook of Research on Design, Control, and Modeling of Swarm Robotics
Ying Tan (Peking University, China)
Information Science Reference • copyright 2016 • 854pp • H/C (ISBN: 9781466695726) • US $465.00 (our price)

Handbook of Research on Emerging Perspectives in Intelligent Pattern Recognition, Analysis, and Image Processing
Narendra Kumar Kamila (C.V. Raman College of Engineering, India)
Information Science Reference • copyright 2016 • 477pp • H/C (ISBN: 9781466686540) • US $255.00 (our price)

Handbook of Research on Advanced Hybrid Intelligent Techniques and Applications
Siddhartha Bhattacharyya (RCC Institute of Information Technology, India) Pinaki Banerjee (Goldstone Infratech Limited, India) Dipankar Majumdar (RCC Institute of Information Technology, India) and Paramartha Dutta (Visva-Bharati University, India)
Information Science Reference • copyright 2016 • 653pp • H/C (ISBN: 9781466694743) • US $285.00 (our price)

Research Advances in the Integration of Big Data and Smart Computing
Pradeep Kumar Mallick (Institute for Research and Development, India)
Information Science Reference • copyright 2016 • 374pp • H/C (ISBN: 9781466687370) • US $210.00 (our price)

www.igi-global.com

701 E. Chocolate Ave., Hershey, PA 17033
Order online at www.igi-global.com or call 717-533-8845 x100
To place a standing order for titles released in this series, contact: cust@igi-global.com
Mon-Fri 8:00 am - 5:00 pm (est) or fax 24 hours a day 717-533-8661

Editorial Advisory Board

Table of Contents

Section 1
Artificial Higher Order Neural Networks for Control

Section 2
Artificial Higher Order Neural Networks for Recognition

Section 3
Artificial Higher Order Neural Networks for Simulation and Predication

Section 4
Artificial Higher Order Neural Network Models and Applications

Detailed Table of Contents

Section 1
Artificial Higher Order Neural Networks for Control

This chapter develops a new nonlinear model, Ultra high frequency Polynomial and Trigonometric Higher Order Neural Networks (UPT-HONN), for control signal generator. UPT-HONN includes UPS-HONN (Ultra high frequency Polynomial and Sine function Higher Order Neural Networks) and UPC-HONN (Ultra high frequency Polynomial and Cosine function Higher Order Neural Networks). UPS-HONN and UPC-HONN model learning algorithms are developed in this chapter. UPS-HONN and UPC-HONN models are used to build nonlinear control signal generator. Test results show that UPS-HONN and UPC-HONN models are better than other Polynomial Higher Order Neural Network (PHONN) and Trigonometric Higher Order Neural Network (THONN) models, since UPS-HONN and UPC-HONN models can generate control signals with error approaching 0.0000%.

This chapter is a summarizing study of Higher Order Neural Units featuring the most common learning algorithms for identification and adaptive control of most typical representatives of plants of single-input single-output (SISO) nature in the control engineering field. In particular, the linear neural unit (LNU, i.e., 1st order HONU), quadratic neural unit (QNU, i.e. 2nd order HONU), and cubic neural unit (CNU, i.e. 3rd order HONU) will be shown as adaptive feedback controllers of typical models of linear plants in control including identification and control of plants with input time delays. The investigated and compared learning algorithms for HONU will be the step-by-step Gradient Descent adaptation with the study of known modifications of learning rate for improved convergence, the batch Levenberg-Marquardt algorithm, and the Resilient Back-Propagation algorithm. The theoretical achievements will be summarized and discussed as regards their usability and the real issues of control engineering tasks.

Chapter 3

Cyril Oswald, Czech Technical University in Prague, Czech Republic
Matous Cejnek, Czech Technical University in Prague, Czech Republic
Jan Vrba, Czech Technical University in Prague, Czech Republic
Ivo Bukovsky, Czech Technical University in Prague, Czech Republic

With focus on Higher Order Neural Units (HONUs), this chapter reviews two recently introduced adaptive novelty detection algorithms based on supervised learning of HONU with extension to adaptive monitoring of existing control loops. Further, the chapter also introduces a novel approach for novelty detection via local model monitoring with Self-organizing Map (SOM) and HONU. Further, it is discussed how these principles can be used to distinguish between external and internal perturbations of identified plant or control loops. The simulation result will demonstrates the potentials of the algorithms for single-input plants as well as for some representative of multiple-input plants and for the improvement of their control.

Section 2
Artificial Higher Order Neural Networks for Recognition

Chapter 4

Ming Zhang, Christopher Newport University, USA

This chapter develops a new nonlinear model, Ultra high frequency siGmoid and Trigonometric Higher Order Neural Networks (UGT-HONN), for data pattern recognition. UGT-HONN includes Ultra high frequency siGmoid and Sine function Higher Order Neural Networks (UGS-HONN) and Ultra high frequency siGmoid and Cosine functions Higher Order Neural Networks (UGC-HONN). UGS-HONN and UGC-HONN models are used to recognition data patterns. Results show that UGS-HONN and UGC-HONN models are better than other Polynomial Higher Order Neural Network (PHONN) and Trigonometric Higher Order Neural Network (THONN) models, since UGS-HONN and UGC-HONN models to recognize data pattern with error approaching 0.0000%.

Chapter 5

Ming Zhang, Christopher Newport University, USA

This chapter develops a new nonlinear model, Ultra high frequency SINC and Trigonometric Higher Order Neural Networks (UNT-HONN), for Data Classification. UNT-HONN includes Ultra high frequency siNc and Sine Higher Order Neural Networks (UNS-HONN) and Ultra high frequency siNc and Cosine Higher Order Neural Networks (UNC-HONN). Data classification using UNS-HONN and UNC-HONN models are tested. Results show that UNS-HONN and UNC-HONN models are better than other Polynomial Higher Order Neural Network (PHONN) and Trigonometric Higher Order Neural Network (THONN) models, since UNS-HONN and UNC-HONN models can classify the data with error approaching 0.0000%.

Chapter 6

José Carlos Palomares-Salas, University of Cadiz, Spain
Juan José González de la Rosa, University of Cadiz, Spain
José María Sierra-Fernández, University of Cadiz, Spain
Agustín Agüera-Pérez, University of Cadiz, Spain
Álvaro Jiménez-Montero, University of Cadiz, Spain
Rosa Piotrkowski, National University of General San Martín, Argentina

Higher-order statistics demonstrate their innovative features to characterize power quality events, beyond the traditional and limited Gaussian perspective, integrating time-frequency features and within the frame of a Higher-Order Neural Network (HONN). With the massive advent of smart measurement equipment in the electrical grid (Smart Grid), and in the frame of high penetration scenarios of renewable energy resources, the necessity dynamic power quality monitoring is gaining even more importance in order to identify the suspicious sources of the perturbation, which are nonlinear and unpredictable in nature. This eventually would satisfy the demand of intelligent instruments, capable not only of detecting the type of perturbation, but also the source of its origin in a scenario of distributed energy resources.

Section 3
Artificial Higher Order Neural Networks for Simulation and Predication

Chapter 7

Sarat Chandra Nayak, Veer Surendra Sai University of Technology, India
Bijan Bihari Misra, Silicon Institute of Technology, India
Himansu Sekhar Behera, Veer Surendra Sai University of Technology, India

This chapter presents two higher order neural networks (HONN) for efficient prediction of stock market behavior. The models include Pi-Sigma, and Sigma-Pi higher order neural network models. Along with the traditional gradient descent learning, how the evolutionary computation technique such as genetic algorithm (GA) can be used effectively for the learning process is also discussed here. The learning process is made adaptive to handle the noise and uncertainties associated with stock market data. Further, different prediction approaches are discussed here and application of HONN for time series forecasting is illustrated with real life data taken from a number of stock markets across the globe.

Chapter 8

Saeed Panahian, Universiti Sains, Malaysia
Zarita Zainuddin, Universiti Sains, Malaysia

One of the most important problems in the theory of approximation functions by means of neural networks is universal approximation capability of neural networks. In this study, we investigate the theoretical analyses of the universal approximation capability of a special class of three layer feedforward higher order neural networks based on the concept of approximate identity in the space of continuous multivariate functions. Moreover, we present theoretical analyses of the universal approximation capability of the networks in the spaces of Lebesgue integrable multivariate functions. The methods used in proving our results are based on the concepts of convolution and epsilon-net. The obtained results can be seen as an attempt towards the development of approximation theory by means of neural networks.

Chapter 9

Ming Zhang, Christopher Newport University, USA

This chapter develops two new nonlinear artificial higher order neural network models. They are Sine and Sine Higher Order Neural Networks (SIN-HONN) and Cosine and Cosine Higher Order Neural Networks (COS-HONN). Financial data prediction using SIN-HONN and COS-HONN models are tested. Results show that SIN-HONN and COS-HONN models are good models for financial data prediction compare with Polynomial Higher Order Neural Network (PHONN) and Trigonometric Higher Order Neural Network (THONN) models.

Chapter 10

Ming Zhang, Christopher Newport University, USA

New open box and nonlinear model of Cosine and Sigmoid Higher Order Neural Network (CS-HONN) is presented in this paper. A new learning algorithm for CS-HONN is also developed from this study. A time series data simulation and analysis system, CS-HONN Simulator, is built based on the CS-HONN models too. Test results show that average error of CS-HONN models are from 2.3436% to 4.6857%, and the average error of Polynomial Higher Order Neural Network (PHONN), Trigonometric Higher Order Neural Network (THONN), and Sigmoid polynomial Higher Order Neural Network (SPHONN) models are from 2.8128% to 4.9077%. It means that CS-HONN models are 0.1174% to 0.4917% better than PHONN, THONN, and SPHONN models.

Chapter 11

Sarat Chandra Nayak, Veer Surendra Sai University of Technology, India
Bijan Bihari Misra, Silicon Institute of Technology, India
Himansu Sekhar Behera, Veer Surendra Sai University of Technology, India

Multilayer neural networks are commonly and frequently used technique for mapping complex nonlinear input-output relationship. However, they add more computational cost due to structural complexity in architecture. This chapter presents different functional link networks (FLN), a class of higher order neural network (HONN). FLNs are capable to handle linearly non-separable classes by increasing the dimensionality of the input space by using nonlinear combinations of input signals. Usually such network is trained with gradient descent based back propagation technique, but it suffers from many drawbacks. To overcome the drawback, here a natural chemical reaction inspired metaheuristic technique called as artificial chemical reaction optimization (ACRO) is used to train the network. As a case study, forecasting of the stock index prices of different stock markets such as BSE, NASDAQ, TAIEX, and FTSE are considered here to compare and analyze the performance gain over the traditional techniques.

Section 4
Artificial Higher Order Neural Network Models and Applications

Chapter 12

    Zongyuan Zhao, University of Tasmania, Australia
    Shuxiang Xu, University of Tasmania, Australia
    Byeong Ho Kang, University of Tasmania, Australia
    Mir Md Jahangir Kabir, University of Tasmania, Australia
    Yunling Liu, China Agricultural University, China
    Rainer Wasinger, University of Tasmania, Australia

Artificial Neural Network has shown its impressive ability on many real world problems such as pattern recognition, classification and function approximation. An extension of ANN, higher order neural network (HONN), improves ANN's computational and learning capabilities. However, the large number of higher order attributes leads to long learning time and complex network structure. Some irrelevant higher order attributes can also hinder the performance of HONN. In this chapter, feature selection algorithms will be used to simplify HONN architecture. Comparisons of fully connected HONN with feature selected HONN demonstrate that proper feature selection can be effective on decreasing number of inputs, reducing computational time, and improving prediction accuracy of HONN.

    Hiromi Miyajima, Kagoshima University, Japan
    Shuji Yatsuki, Yatsuki Information System, Inc., Japan
    Noritaka Shigei, Kagoshima University, Japan
    Hirofumi Miyajima, Kagoshima University, Japan

Higher order neural networks (HONNs) have been proposed as new systems. In this paper, we show some theoretical results of associative capability of HONNs. As one of them, memory capacity of HONNs is much larger than one of the conventional neural networks. Further, we show some theoretical results on homogeneous higher order neural networks (HHONNs), in which each neuron has identical weights. HHONNs can realize shift-invariant associative memory, that is, HHONNs can associate not only a memorized pattern but also its shifted ones.

    Michel Lopez-Franco, CINVESTAV, Unidad Guadalajara, Mexico
    Edgar N. Sanchez, CINVESTAV, Unidad Guadalajara, Mexico
    Alma Y. Alanis, CUCEI, Universidad de Guadalajara, Mexico
    Carlos Lopez-Franco, CUCEI, Universidad de Guadalajara, Mexico
    Nancy Arana-Daniel, CUCEI, Universidad de Guadalajara, Mexico

This chapter presents a new approach to multi-agent control of complex systems with unknown parameters and dynamic uncertainties. A key strategy is to use of neural inverse optimal control. This approach consists in synthesizing a suitable controller for each subsystem, which is approximated by an identifier based on a recurrent high order neural network (RHONN), trained with an extended Kalman filter (EKF) algorithm. On the basis of this neural model and the knowledge of a control Lyapunov function, then an inverse optimal controller is synthesized to avoid solving the Hamilton Jacobi Bellman (HJB) equation. We have adopted an omnidirectional mobile robot, KUKA youBot, as robotic platform for our experiments. Computer simulations are presented which confirm the effectiveness of the proposed tracking control law.

Financial market creates a complex and ever changing environment in which population of investors are competing for profit. Predicting the future for financial gain is a difficult and challenging task, however at the same time it is a profitable activity. Hence, the ability to obtain the highly efficient financial model has become increasingly important in the competitive world. To cope with this, we consider functional link artificial neural networks (FLANNs) trained by particle swarm optimization (PSO) for stock index prediction (PSO-FLANN). Our strong experimental conviction confirms that the performance of PSO tuned FLANN model for the case of lower number of ahead prediction task is promising. In most cases LMS updated algorithm based FLANN model proved to be as good as or better than the RLS updated algorithm based FLANN but at the same time RLS updated FLANN model for the prediction of stock index system cannot be ignored.

Preface

Artificial Neural Networks (ANNs) are known to excel in control signal generating, pattern recognition, pattern matching and mathematical function approximation. However they suffer from several well known limitations – they can often become stuck in local, rather than global minima, as well as taking unacceptably long times to converge in practice. Of particular concern, especially from the perspective of control and recognition areas, is their inability to handle non-smooth, discontinuous training data, and complex mappings (associations). Another limitation of ANN is a 'black box' nature – meaning that explanations (reasons) for their decisions are not immediately obvious, unlike techniques such as Decision Trees. This then is the motivation for developing artificial Higher Order Neural Networks (HONNs), since HONNs are 'open-box' models and each neuron and weight are mapped to function variable and coefficient.

In recent years, researchers use HONNs for control signal generating, pattern recognition, nonlinear recognition, classification, and prediction in the control and recognition areas. The results show that HONNs are always faster, more accurate, and easier to explain. This is the second motivation for using HONNs in control and recognition areas, since HONNs can automatically select the initial coefficients, even automatically select the model for applications in control and recognition area.

Giles & Maxwell (1987) published the first paper on HONN. Bengtsson (1990) wrote the first book in the higher order (or higher-order, consistency) neural network area. Higher order correlations in the training data require more complex neuron activation functions (Barron, Gilstrap & Shrier, 1987; Giles & Maxwell, 1987; Psaltis, Park & Hong, 1988). Neurons which include terms up to and including degree-k are referred to as kth-order neurons (Lisboa & Perantonis, 1991). In addition, the increased computational load resulting from the large increase in network weights means that the complex input-output mappings normally only achievable in multi-layered networks can now be realized in a single HONN layer (Zhang & Fulcher, 2004). Currently the output of a kth-order single-layer HONN neuron will be a non-linear function comprising polynomials of up to kth-order. Moreover, since no hidden layers are involved, both Hebbian and Perceptron learning rules can be employed (Shin & Ghosh, 1991).

Several different HONN models have been developed by Zhang and Fulcher, during the past decade or so. A more comprehensive coverage, including derivations of weight update equations, is presented in Zhang & Fulcher (2004). The Neuron-Adaptive HONN (and NAHONN group) leads to faster convergence, much reduced network size and more accurate curve fitting, compared with P(T)HONNs (Zhang, Xu & Fulcher, 2002). Each element of the NAHONN group is standard multi-layer HONN comprising adaptive neurons, but which employs locally bounded, piecewise continuous (rather than polynomial) activation functions and thresholds. Now as with the earlier HONN groups, it is possible to provide a similar general result to that found previously by Hornik (1991) for ANNs – namely that

NAHONN groups are capable of approximating any kind of piecewise continuous function, to any degree of accuracy (a proof is provided in Zhang, Xu & Fulcher, 2002). Moreover, these models are capable of automatically selecting not only the optimum model for a particular time series, but also the appropriate model order and coefficients.

This is the first book which introduces HONNs to people working in the fields of control and recognition. This is the first book which introduces to researchers in the control and recognition areas that HONNs is an open box neural networks tool compare to traditional artificial neural networks. This is the first book which provides opportunities for millions of people working in the control and recognition areas to know what HONNs are, and how to use HONNs in control and recognition areas. This book explains why HONNs can approximate any nonlinear data to any degree of accuracy, and allows researchers to understand why HONNs are much easier to use, and HONNs can have better nonlinear data recognition accuracy than SAS nonlinear (NLIN) procedures. This book introduces the HONN group models and adaptive HONNs, and allows the people working in the control and recognition areas to understand HONN group models and adaptive HONN models, which can simulate not only nonlinear data, but also discontinuous and unsmooth nonlinear data.

Millions of people who are using artificial neural networks and who are doing control and recognition research, in particular, professors, graduate students, and senior undergraduate students in the department related to the control and recognition, as well as the professionals and researchers in the areas related to control and recognition, which should include computer science, computer engineering, information science, information technology, economics, business, materials, mathematics, and so on.

Chapter 1, "Ultra High Frequency Polynomial and Trigonometric Higher Order Neural Networks for Control Signal Generator", delivers a new nonlinear model, Ultra high frequency Polynomial and Trigonometric Higher Order Neural Networks (UPT-HONN), for control signal generator. UPT-HONN includes UPS-HONN (Ultra high frequency Polynomial and Sine function Higher Order Neural Networks) and UPC-HONN (Ultra high frequency Polynomial and Cosine function Higher Order Neural Networks). UPS-HONN and UPC-HONN model learning algorithms are developed in this chapter. UPS-HONN and UPC-HONN models are used to build nonlinear control signal generator. Test results show that UPS-HONN and UPC-HONN models are better than other Polynomial Higher Order Neural Network (PHONN) and Trigonometric Higher Order Neural Network (THONN) models, since UPS-HONN and UPC-HONN models can generate control signals with error approaching 0.0000%.

Chapter 2, "HONU and Supervised Learning Algorithms in Adaptive Feedback Control Peter Mark Benes", is a summarizing study of Higher Order Neural Units featuring the most common learning algorithms for identification and adaptive control of most typical representatives of plants of single-input single-output (SISO) nature in the control engineering field. In particular, the linear neural unit (LNU, i.e., 1st order HONU), quadratic neural unit (QNU, i.e. 2nd order HONU), and cubic neural unit (CNU, i.e. 3rd order HONU) will be shown as adaptive feedback controllers of typical models of linear plants in control including identification and control of plants with input time delays. The investigated and compared learning algorithms for HONU will be the step-by-step Gradient Descent adaptation with the study of known modifications of learning rate for improved convergence, the batch Levenberg-Marquardt algorithm, and the Resilient Back-Propagation algorithm. The theoretical achievements will be summarized and discussed as regards their usability and the real issues of control engineering tasks.

Chapter 3, "Novelty Detection in System Monitoring and Control with HONU Cyril Oswald", reviews two recently introduced adaptive novelty detection algorithms based on supervised learning of HONU with extension to adaptive monitoring of existing control loops. Further, the chapter also introduces a novel approach for novelty detection via local model monitoring with Self-organizing Map (SOM) and HONU. Further, it is discussed how these principles can be used to distinguish between external and internal perturbations of identified plant or control loops. The simulation result will demonstrate the potentials of the algorithms for single-input plants as well as for some representative of multiple-input plants and for the improvement of their control.

Chapter 4, "Ultra High Frequency Sigmoid and Trigonometric Higher Order Neural Networks for Data Pattern Recognition", develops a new nonlinear model, Ultra high frequency siGmoid and Trigonometric Higher Order Neural Networks (UGT-HONN), for data pattern recognition. UGT-HONN includes Ultra high frequency siGmoid and Sine function Higher Order Neural Networks (UGS-HONN) and Ultra high frequency siGmoid and Cosine functions Higher Order Neural Networks (UGC-HONN). UGS-HONN and UGC-HONN models are used to recognition data patterns. Results show that UGS-HONN and UGC-HONN models are better than other Polynomial Higher Order Neural Network (PHONN) and Trigonometric Higher Order Neural Network (THONN) models, since UGS-HONN and UGC-HONN models to recognize data pattern with error approaching 0.0000%.

Chapter 5, "Ultra High Frequency SINC and Trigonometric Higher Order Neural Networks for Data Classification, creates a new nonlinear model, Ultra high frequency SINC and Trigonometric Higher Order Neural Networks (UNT-HONN), for Data Classification. UNT-HONN includes Ultra high frequency siNc and Sine Higher Order Neural Networks (UNS-HONN) and Ultra high frequency siNc and Cosine Higher Order Neural Networks (UNC-HONN). Data classification using UNS-HONN and UNC-HONN models are tested. Results show that UNS-HONN and UNC-HONN models are better than other Polynomial Higher Order Neural Network (PHONN) and Trigonometric Higher Order Neural Network (THONN) models, since UNS-HONN and UNC-HONN models can classify the data with error approaching 0.0000%.

Chapter 6, "Integration of higher-order time-frequency statistics and neural networks: Application for power quality surveillance", is focus on that Higher-order statistics demonstrate their innovative features to characterize power quality events, beyond the traditional and limited Gaussian perspective, integrating time-frequency features and within the frame of a Higher-Order Neural Network (HONN). With the massive advent of smart measurement equipment in the electrical grid (Smart Grid), and in the frame of high penetration scenarios of renewable energy resources, the necessity dynamic power quality monitoring is gaining even more importance in order to identify the suspicious sources of the perturbation, which are nonlinear and unpredictable in nature. This eventually would satisfy the demand of intelligent instruments, capable not only of detecting the type of perturbation, but also the source of its origin in a scenario of distributed energy resources.

Chapter 7, "Adaptive Hybrid Higher Order Neural Networks for Prediction of Stock Market Behavior", establishes two higher order neural networks (HONN) for efficient prediction of stock market behavior. The models include Pi-Sigma, and Sigma-Pi higher order neural network models. Along with the traditional gradient descent learning, how the evolutionary computation technique such as genetic algorithm (GA) can be used effectively for the learning process is also discussed here. The learning process is made adaptive to handle the noise and uncertainties associated with stock market data. Further, different prediction approaches are discussed here and application of HONN for time series forecasting is illustrated with real life data taken from a number of stock markets across the globe.

Chapter 8, "Theoretical analyses of the universal approximation capability of a class of higher order neural networks based on approximate identity", studies one of the most important problems in the theory of approximation functions by means of neural networks is universal approximation capability of neural networks. In this study, the chapter investigates the theoretical analyses of the universal approximation capability of a special class of three layer feedforward higher order neural networks based on the concept of approximate identity in the space of continuous multivariate functions. Moreover, the chapter presents theoretical analyses of the universal approximation capability of the networks in the spaces of Lebesgue integrable multivariate functions. The methods used in proving our results are based on the concepts of convolution and epsilon-net. The obtained results can be seen as an attempt towards the development of approximation theory by means of neural networks.

Chapter 9, "Artificial Sine and Cosine Trigonometric Higher Order Neural Networks for Financial Data Prediction", addresses two new nonlinear artificial higher order neural network models. They are Sine and Sine Higher Order Neural Networks (SIN-HONN) and Cosine and Cosine Higher Order Neural Networks (COS-HONN). Financial data prediction using SIN-HONN and COS-HONN models are tested. Results show that SIN-HONN and COS-HONN models are good models for financial data prediction compare with Polynomial Higher Order Neural Network (PHONN) and Trigonometric Higher Order Neural Network (THONN) models.

Chapter 10, "Cosine and Sigmoid Higher Order Neural Networks for Data Simulations", studies new open box and nonlinear model of Cosine and Sigmoid Higher Order Neural Network (CS-HONN). A new learning algorithm for CS-HONN is also developed from this study. A time series data simulation and analysis system, CS-HONN Simulator, is built based on the CS-HONN models too. Test results show that average error of CS-HONN models are from 2.3436% to 4.6857%, and the average error of Polynomial Higher Order Neural Network (PHONN), Trigonometric Higher Order Neural Network (THONN), and Sigmoid polynomial Higher Order Neural Network (SPHONN) models are from 2.8128% to 4.9077%. It means that CS-HONN models are 0.1174% to 0.4917% better than PHONN, THONN, and SPHONN models.

Chapter 11, "Improving Performance of Higher Order Neural Network using Artificial Chemical Reaction Optimization: A Case Study on Stock Market Forecasting", discusses Multilayer neural networks are commonly and frequently used technique for mapping complex nonlinear input-output relationship. However, they add more computational cost due to structural complexity in architecture. This chapter presents different functional link networks (FLN), a class of higher order neural network (HONN). FLNs are capable to handle linearly non separable classes by increasing the dimensionality of the input space by using nonlinear combinations of input signals. Usually such network is trained with gradient descent based back propagation technique, but it suffers from many drawbacks. To overcome the drawback, here a natural chemical reaction inspired metaheuristic technique called as artificial chemical reaction optimization (ACRO) is used to train the network. As a case study, forecasting of the stock index prices of different stock markets such as BSE, NASDAQ, TAIEX, and FTSE are considered here to compare and analyze the performance gain over the traditional techniques.

Chapter 12, "Artificial Higher Order Neural Network Models", introduces the background of HONN model developing history and overview 24 applied artificial higher order neural network models. This chapter provides 24 HONN models and uses a single uniform HONN architecture for ALL 24 HONN models. This chapter also uses a uniform learning algorithm for all 24 HONN models and uses a uniform weight update formulae for all 24 HONN models. In this chapter, Polynomial HONN, Trigonometric HONN, Sigmoid HONN, SINC HONN, and Ultra High Frequency HONN structure and models are overviewed too.

Chapter 13, "A Theoretical Framework for Parallel Implementation of Deep Higher Order Neural Networks", proposes a theoretical framework for parallel implementation of Deep Higher Order Neural

Networks (HONNs). First, the chapter develops a new partitioning approach for mapping HONNs to individual computers within a master-slave distributed system (a local area network). This will use a network of computers (rather than a single computer) to train a HONN to drastically increase its learning speed: all of the computers will be running the HONN simultaneously (parallel implementation). Next, the chapter develops a new learning algorithm so that it can be used for HONN learning in a distributed system environment. Finally, the chapter proposes to improve the generalization ability of the new learning algorithm as used in a distributed system environment. Theoretical analysis of the proposal is thoroughly conducted to verify the soundness of the new approach. Experiments will be performed to test the new algorithm in the future.

Chapter 14, "Ant Colony Optimization Applied to the Training of a High Order Neural Network with Adaptable Exponential Weights", studies that high order neural networks (HONN) are neural networks which employ neurons that combine their inputs non-linearly. The HONEST (High Order Network with Exponential SynapTic links) network is a HONN that uses neurons with product units and adaptable exponents. The output of a trained HONEST network can be expressed in terms of the network inputs by a polynomial-like equation. This makes the structure of the network more transparent and easier to interpret. This study adapts ACO_R, an Ant Colony Optimization algorithm, to the training of an HONEST network. Using a collection of 10 widely-used benchmark datasets, we compare ACO_R to the well-known gradient-based Resilient Propagation (R-Prop) algorithm, in the training of HONEST networks. We find that our adaptation of ACO_R has better test set generalization than R-Prop, though not to a statistically significant extent.

Chapter 15, "Utilizing Feature Selection on Higher Order Neural Networks", is concerned that Artificial Neural Network has shown its impressive ability on many real world problems such as pattern recognition, classification and function approximation. An extension of ANN, higher order neural network (HONN), improves ANN's computational and learning capabilities. However, the large number of higher order attributes leads to long learning time and complex network structure. Some irrelevant higher order attributes can also hinder the performance of HONN. In this chapter, feature selection algorithms will be used to simplify HONN architecture. Comparisons of fully connected HONN with feature selected HONN demonstrate that proper feature selection can be effective on decreasing number of inputs, reducing computational time, and improving prediction accuracy of HONN.

Chapter 16, "Some Properties on The Capability of Associative Memory for Higher Order Neural Networks", describes that higher order neural networks (HONNs) have been proposed as new systems. This paper shows some theoretical results of associative capability of HONNs. As one of them, memory capacity of HONNs is much larger than one of the conventional neural networks. Further, the chapter shows some theoretical results on homogeneous higher order neural networks (HHONNs), in which each neuron has identical weights. HHNNs can realize shift-invariant associative memory, that is, HHONNs can associate not only a memorized pattern but also its shifted ones.

Chapter 17, "Discrete-time decentralized inverse optimal higher order neural network control for a multi-agent omnidirectional mobile robot", presents a new approach to multi- agent control of complex systems with unknown parameters and dynamic uncertainties. A key strategy is to use of neural inverse optimal control. This approach consists in synthesizing a suitable controller for each subsystem, which is approximated by an identifier based on a recurrent high order neural network (RHONN), trained with an extended Kalman filter (EKF) algorithm. On the basis of this neural model and the knowledge of a control Lyapunov function, then an inverse optimal controller is synthesized to avoid solving the Hamilton Jacobi Bellman (HJB) equation. We have adopted an omnidirectional mobile robot, KUKA youBot, as robotic platform for our experiments. Computer simulations are presented which confirm the effectiveness of the proposed tracking control law.

Chapter 18, "Higher Order Neural Network for Financial Modeling and Simulation", concentrates that financial market creates a complex and ever changing environment in which population of investors are competing for profit. Predicting the future for financial gain is a difficult and challenging task, however at the same time it is a profitable activity. Hence, the ability to obtain the highly efficient financial model has become increasingly important in the competitive world. To cope with this, we consider functional link artificial neural networks (FLANNs) trained by particle swarm optimization (PSO) for stock index prediction (PSO-FLANN). Our strong experimental conviction confirms that the performance of PSO tuned FLANN model for the case of lower number of ahead prediction task is promising. In most cases LMS updated algorithm based FLANN model proved to be as good as or better than the RLS updated algorithm based FLANN but at the same time RLS updated FLANN model for the prediction of stock index system cannot be ignored.

Let millions of people working in the control and recognition areas know that HONNs are much easier to use and can have better recognition results than SAS Nonlinear models, and understand how to successfully use HONNs models for nonlinear data control, recognition, and prediction. HONNs will challenge traditional artificial neural network products and change the research methodology that people are currently using in control and recognition areas for the control signal generating, pattern recognition, nonlinear recognition, classification, and prediction.

Currently no book has been published in the control and recognition areas using HONNs. This book will be the first book which collects chapters on HONNs for control and recognition.

After this book has been published, more people in control and recognition can use HONNs for control signal generating, patter recognition, nonlinear recognition, and system control. More researchers in the control, recognition, economics and business areas can use HONNs for control signal generating, data recognition, and data prediction.

Artificial neural network research is one of the new directions for new generation computers. Current research suggests that open box artificial HONNs play an important role in this new direction. Since HONNs are open box models they can be easily accepted and used by the people working in the information science, information technology, management, economics, and business areas. Researchers in the control, recognition, information systems, and economics and business areas can use HONNs in their studies.

Acknowledgment

The editor would like to acknowledge the help of all involved in the collation and the review process of the book, without whose support the project could not have been satisfactorily completed. Deep appreciation and gratitude are due to the Christopher Newport University, for providing research funding to support my research.

I would like to thank my supervisor, Dr. Rod Scofield, retired Senior Scientist of National Oceanic and Atmospheric Administration (NOAA), Washington DC, USA for supporting my artificial neural network research and awarding me USA National Research Council Postdoctoral Fellow (1991-1992) and Senior USA National Research Council Research Associate (1999-2000). I would like to thank Dr. John Fulcher, retired Professor of University of Wollongong in Australia, for a long time of research collaboration in the artificial neural network area since 1992.

I would like to thank Professor Kuang, Dingbo, Fellow of Chinese Academy of Sciences, and Senior Scientist of Shanghai Institute of Technical Physics, Shanghai, China. Thank you for being my postdoctoral advisor from 1989 to 1991, when I was a postdoctoral researcher. I would like to thank Professor Gong, Huixing, Fellow of Chinese Academy of Engineering, and Senior Scientist of Shanghai Institute of Technical Physics, Shanghai, China. Thank you for inspiring me in research from 1989 to 1991, when I was a postdoctoral researcher.

I want to thank all Editorial Advisory Board members for their excellent advising and great help to this book. I also want to thank all of the authors for their insights and excellent contributions to this book. Most of the authors of chapters included in this book also served as referees for chapters written by other authors. Thanks go to all the reviewers who provided constructive and comprehensive reviews and suggestions.

Special thanks also go to the publishing team at IGI Global, whose contributions throughout the whole process from inception of the initial idea to final publication have been invaluable.

Special thanks go to my family for their continuous support and encouragement, in particular, to my wife, Zhao Qing Zhang, for her unfailing support and encouragement during the years it took to give birth to this book.

Dr. Ming Zhang
Christopher Newport University, USA

Section 1
Artificial Higher Order Neural Networks for Control

Chapter 1
Ultra High Frequency Polynomial and Trigonometric Higher Order Neural Networks for Control Signal Generator

Ming Zhang
Christopher Newport University, USA

ABSTRACT

This chapter develops a new nonlinear model, Ultra high frequency Polynomial and Trigonometric Higher Order Neural Networks (UPT-HONN), for control signal generator. UPT-HONN includes UPS-HONN (Ultra high frequency Polynomial and Sine function Higher Order Neural Networks) and UPC-HONN (Ultra high frequency Polynomial and Cosine function Higher Order Neural Networks). UPS-HONN and UPC-HONN model learning algorithms are developed in this chapter. UPS-HONN and UPC-HONN models are used to build nonlinear control signal generator. Test results show that UPS-HONN and UPC-HONN models are better than other Polynomial Higher Order Neural Network (PHONN) and Trigonometric Higher Order Neural Network (THONN) models, since UPS-HONN and UPC-HONN models can generate control signals with error approaching 0.0000%.

INTRODUCTION

The perspective of this chapter will be: introduce the background of HONNs with the applications of HONNs in control area; develop a new HONN model called UPT-HONN for ultra-high frequency control signal generator; provide the UPT-HONN learning algorithm and weight update formulae; applications of UPT-HONN model for control signals.

This chapter is organized as follows: Section background gives the background knowledge of HONNs in control area. Section UPT-HONN models introduces UPT-HONN structure and different modes of the UPT-HONN model. Section learning algorithm of UPT-HONN models provides the UPT-HONN model update formula, learning algorithms, and convergence theories of HONN. Section UPT-HONN testing describes UPT-HONN computer software system and testing results.

DOI: 10.4018/978-1-5225-0063-6.ch001

BACKGROUND

Neural Networks for Control Signals and Control Systems

Artificial Neural Networks have been widely used in the control area. Studies found that artificial neural networks are good tools for system control and control signal generating. Narendra and Parthasarathy (1990) develop identification and control techniques of dynamical systems using artificial neural networks. Arai, Kohon, and Imai (1991) study an adaptive control of neural network with variable function of a unit and its application. Chen and Khalil (1992) develop an adaptive control of nonlinear systems using neural networks. Hu and Shao (1992) show the neural network adaptive control systems. Yamada and Yabuta (1992) investigate a neural network controller which uses an auto-tuning method for nonlinear functions. Campolucci, Capparelli, Guarnieri, Piazza, and Uncini (1996) learn neural networks with adaptive spline activation function. Lewis, Yesildirek, and Liu, (1996) design Multilayer neural-net robot controller with guaranteed tracking performance. Polycarpou (1996) applies stable adaptive neural control scheme for nonlinear systems. Lewis, Jagannathan, and Yesildirek (1998) build neural network control for robot manipulators and non-linear systems.

Norgaard, Ravn, Poulsen, and Hansen (2000) generate neural networks for modelling and control of dynamic systems. Poznyak, Sanchez, and Yu (2000) investigate differential neural networks for robust nonlinear control. Chen and Narendra (2002) present nonlinear adaptive control using neural networks and multiple models. Diao and Passino (2002) examine adaptive neural/fuzzy control for interpolated nonlinear systems. Holubar, Zani, Hager, Froschl, Radak, Braun (2002) explore advanced controlling of anaerobic digestion by means of hierarchical neural networks. Plett (2003) inspects adaptive inverse control of linear and nonlinear systems using dynamic neural networks. Ge, Zhang, and Lee (2004) probe adaptive neural network control for a class of MIMO nonlinear systems with disturbances in discrete-time. Shi and Li (2004) contribute a novel control of a small wind turbine driven generator based on neural networks. Bukovsky, Bila, and Gupta (2005) analyze linear dynamic neural units with time delay for identification and control. Yih, Wei, and Tsu (2005) experiment observer-based direct adaptive fuzzy-neural control for nonffine nonlinear systems. Farrell and Polycarpou (2006) indicate adaptive approximation based control by unifying neural, fuzzy and traditional adaptive approximation approaches. Boutalis, Theodoridis, and Christodoulou (2009) suppose a new neuro FDS definition for indirect adaptive control of unknown nonlinear systems using a method of parameter hopping. Hou, Cheng, and Tan (2009) supply decentralized robust adaptive control for the multiagent system consensus problem using neural networks. Alanis, Sanchez, Loukianov, and Perez-Cisneros (2010) seek real-time discrete neural block control using sliding modes for electric induction motors. Weidong, Yubing, and Xingpei (2010) offer short-term forecasting of wind turbine power generation based on genetic neural network. Kumar, Panwar, Sukavanam, Sharma, and Borm (2011) run neural network-based nonlinear tracking control of kinematically redundant robot manipulators. Pedro, and Dahunsi (2011) grant neural network based feedback linearization control of a servo-hydraulic vehicle suspension system. All of the studies above suggest that artificial neural networks are powerful tools for control signals and control systems

Higher Order Neural Networks for Control Signals and Control Systems

Artificial Higher Order Neural Networks (HONNs) have been widely used in the control area too. Studies also found that artificial higher order neural networks are good tools for system control and generating control signal Lee, Lee, and Park (1992) pilot neural controller of nonlinear dynamic systems using higher order neural networks. Rovithakis, Kosmatopoulos, and Christodoulou (1993) look at robust adaptive control of unknown plants using recurrent high order neural networks-application to mechanical systems. Rovithakis, Gaganis, Perrakis, and Christodoulou (1996) obtain a recurrent neural network model to describe manufacturing cell dynamics. Rovithakis and Chistodoulou (2000) disclose adaptive control with recurrent high -order neural networks. Li, Chen, and Yuan (2002) create simple recurrent neural network-based adaptive predictive control for nonlinear systems. Campos, Loukianov, and Sanchez (2003) deliver synchronous motor VSS control using recurrent high order neural networks. Alanis, Sanchez, and Loukianov (2006) test discrete-time recurrent neural induction motor control using Kalman learning. Butt and Shafiq (2006) examine higher-order neural network based root-solving controller for adaptive tracking of stable nonlinear plants. Sanchez, Alanis and Loukianov (2008) produce discrete time high order neural control trained with Kalman filtering. Baruch, Galvan-Guerra, Nenkova (2008) achieve centralized indirect control of an anaerobic digestion bioprocess using recurrent neural identifier. Theodoridis, Boutalis, and Christodoulou (2009) expand a new neuro-fuzzy dynamical system definition based on high order neural network function approximators. All of the researches above indicate that artificial higher order neural networks are usefultools for control signals and control systems.

Detail Examples of Artificial Higher Order Neural Networks for Control

Yu (2010) scans robust adaptive control using higher order neural networks and projection, and presents a novel robust adaptive approach for a class of unknown nonlinear systems. Firstly, the neural networks are designed to identify the nonlinear systems. Dead-zone and projection techniques are applied to weights training, in order to avoid singular cases. Secondly, a linearization controller is proposed based on the neuro identifier. Since the approximation capability of the neural networks is limited, four types of compensators are addressed. This chapter also proposes a robust neuro-observer, which has an extended Luenberger structure. Its weights are learned on-line by a new adaptive gradient-like technique. The control scheme is based on the proposed neuro-observer. The final structure is composed by two parts: the neuro-observer and the tracking controller. The simulations of a two-link robot show the effectiveness of the proposed algorithm.

Karnavas (2010) values electric machines excitation control via higher order neural networks, and is demonstrating a practical design of an intelligent type of controller using higher order neural network (HONN) concepts, for the excitation control of a practical power generating system. This type of controller is suitable for real time operation, and aims to improve the dynamic characteristics of the generating unit by acting properly on its original excitation system. The modeling of the power system under study consists of a synchronous generator connected via a transformer and a transmission line to an infinite bus. For comparison purposes and also for producing useful data in order for the demonstrating neural network controllers to be trained, digital simulations of the above system are performed using fuzzy logic control (FLC) techniques, which are based on previous work. Then, two neural network controllers are designed and applied by adopting the HONN architectures. The first one utilizes a single pi-sigma neural network (PSNN) and the significant advantages over the standard multi layered perceptron (MLP) are discussed. Secondly, an enhanced controller is designed, leading to a ridge polynomial neural network (RPNN) by combining multiple PSNNs if needed. Both controllers used, can be pre-trained rapidly from the corresponding FLC output signal and act as model dynamics capturers. The dynamic performances of the fuzzy logic controller (FLC) along with those of the two demonstrated controllers are presented by comparison using the well-known integral square error criterion (ISE). The latter controllers, show excellent convergence properties and accuracy for function approximation. Typical transient responses of the system are shown for comparison in order to demonstrate the effectiveness of the designed controllers. The computer simulation results obtained show clearly that the performance of the developed controllers offers competitive damping effects on the synchronous generator's oscillations, with respect to the associated ones of the FLC, over a wider range of operating conditions, while their hardware implementation is apparently much easier and the computational time needed for real-time applications is drastically reduced.

Theodoridis, Christodoulou, and Boutalis (2010) inspect neuro–fuzzy Control schemes based on high order neural network function approximators, and study the control schemes. The indirect or direct adaptive regulation of unknown nonlinear dynamical systems is considered in this chapter. Since the plant is considered unknown, this chapter first proposes its approximation by a special form of a fuzzy dynamical system (FDS) and in the sequel the fuzzy rules are approximated by the appropriate HONNFs. The system is regulated to zero adaptivity by providing weight updating laws for the involved HONNFs, which guarantee that both the identification error and the system states reach zero exponentially fast. At the same time, all signals in the closed loop are kept bounded. The existence of the control signal is always assured by introducing a novel method of parameter hopping, which is incorporated in the weight updating laws. The indirect control scheme is developed for square systems (number of inputs equal to the number of states) as well as for systems in Brunovsky canonical form. The direct control scheme is developed for systems in square form. Simulations illustrate the potency of the method and comparisons with conventional approaches on benchmarking systems are given.

Das, Lewis, and Subbarao (2010) discover back-stepping control of quadrotor by a dynamically tuned higher order like neural network approach, and revise the control of quadrotor. The dynamics of a quadrotor is a simplified form of helicopter dynamics that exhibit the same basic problems of strong coupling, multi-input/multi-output design, and unknown nonlinearities. The Lagrangian model of a typical quadrotor that involves four inputs and six outputs results in an underactuated system. There are several design techniques are available for nonlinear control of mechanical underactuated system. One of the most popular among them is backstepping. Backstepping is a well known recursive procedure where underactuation characteristic of the system is resolved by defining 'desired' virtual control and virtual state variables. Virtual control variables is determined in each recursive step assuming the corresponding subsystem is Lyapunov stable and virtual states are typically the errors of actual and desired virtual control variables. The application of the backstepping even more interesting when a virtual control law is applied to a Lagrangian subsystem. The necessary information to select virtual control and state variables for these systems can be obtained through model identification methods. One of these methods includes Neural Network approximation to identify the unknown parameters of the system. The unknown parameters may include uncertain aerodynamic force and moment coefficients or unmodeled dynamics. These aerodynamic coefficients generally are the functions of higher order state polynomials. This chapter discusses how can implement linear in parameter first order neural network approximation methods to identify these unknown higher order state polynomials in every recursive step of the backstepping. Thus the first order neural network eventually estimates the higher order state polynomials which is in fact a higher order like neural net (HOLNN). Moreover, when these artificial Neural Networks placed into a control loop, they become dynamic artificial Neural Network whose weights are tuned only. Due to the inherent characteristics of the quadrotor, the Lagrangian form for the position dynamics is bilinear in the controls, which is confronted using a bilinear inverse kinematics solution. The result is a controller of intuitively appealing structure having an outer kinematics loop for position control and an inner dynamics loop for attitude control. The stability of the control law is guaranteed by a Lyapunov proof. The control approach described in this chapter is robust since it explicitly deals with un-modeled state dependent disturbances without needing any prior knowledge of the same. A simulation study validates the results such as decoupling, tracking etc. obtained in the paper.

Das and Lewis (2013) bestow distributed adaptive control for multi-agent systems with pseudo higher order neural net, and suggest that the idea of using multi-agent systems is getting popular every day. It not only saves time and resource but also eliminates the requirement of large human coordination. These ideas are especially effective in combating zone where multiple unmanned aerial vehicles are required to control for achieving multiple simultaneous objectives or targets. The evolution of distributed control has started with simple integrator systems and then gradually different control methodologies have been adopted for more and more complex nonlinear systems. Also, from practical standpoint, the dynamics of the agents involved in networked control architecture might not be identical. Therefore an ideal distributed control should accommodate multiple agents which are nonlinear systems associated with unknown dynamics. In this chapter, a distributed control methodology has been presented, where nonidentical nonlinear agents communicate among themselves following directed graph topology. In addition, the nonlinear dynamics are considered unknown. While the pinning control strategy has been adopted to distribute the input command among the agents, a Pseudo Higher Order Neural Net (PHONN) based identification strategy is introduced for identifying the unknown dynamics. These two strategies are combined beautifully such that the stability of the system is assured even with minimum interaction among the agents. A detailed stability analysis is presented based on Lyapunov theory and a simulation study is performed to verify the theoretical claims.

Chen and Lewis (2013) afford cooperative control of unknown networked Lagrange systems using higher order neural networks, and explore the cooperative control problem for a group of Lagrange systems with a target system to be tracked. The development is suitable for the case that the desired trajectory of the target node is only available to a portion of the networked systems. All the networked systems can have different dynamics. The dynamics of the networked systems, as well as the target system, are all assumed unknown. A higher-order neural network is used at each node to approximate the distributed unknown dynamics. A distributed adaptive neural network control protocol is proposed so that the networked systems synchronize to the motion of the target node. The theoretical analysis shows that the synchronization error can be made arbitrarily small by appropriately tuning the design parameters.

UPT-HONN MODELS

Nyquist Rule says that a sampling rate must be at least twice as fast as the fastest frequency (Synder 2006). In simulating and predicting time series data, the new nonlinear models of UPT-HONN should have twice as high frequency as that of the ultra-high frequency of the time series data. To achieve this purpose, a new model should be developed to enforce high frequency of HONN in order to make the simulation and prediction error close to zero. The new HONN model, Ultra High Frequency Polynomial and Trigonometric Higher Order Neural Network (UPT-HONN), includes two different models base on the different neuron functions. Ultra high frequency Polynomial and Sine Trigonometric Higher Order Neural Network (UPS-HONN) has neurons with polynomial and sine functions. Ultra high frequency Polynomial and Cosine Trigonometric Higher Order Neural Network (UPC-HONN) has neurons with polynomial and cosine functions. Except for the functions in the neuron all other parts of these two models are the same.

UPS-HONN Model and UPC-HONN Model

UPS-HONN Model Structure can be seen in Figure 1. UPC-HONN Model Structure can be seen in Figure 2.

Figure 1. UPS-HONN Architecture

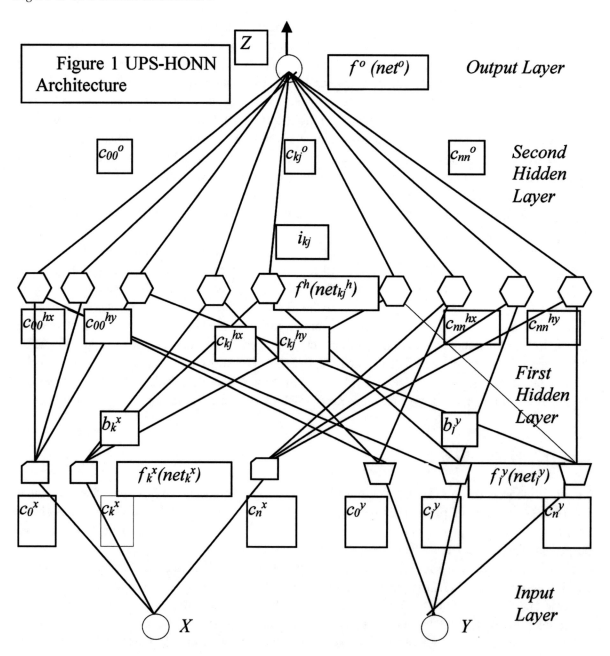

Figure 2.

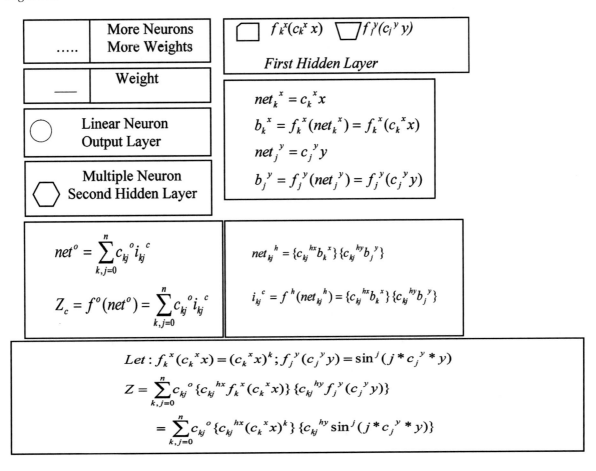

The Nyquist–Shannon sampling theorem, after Harry Nyquist and Claude Shannon, in the literature more commonly referred to as the Nyquist sampling theorem or simply as the sampling theorem, is a fundamental result in the field of information theory, in particular telecommunications and signal processing. Shannon's version of the theorem states:[Shannon, 1998]

If a function x(t) contains no frequencies higher than B hertz, it is completely determined by giving its ordinates at a series of points spaced 1/(2B) seconds apart.

In other words, a band limited function can be perfectly reconstructed from a countable sequence of samples if the band limit, B, is no greater than ½ the sampling rate (samples per second).

In simulating and predicting time series data, the new nonlinear models of UPT-HONN should have twice as high frequency as that of the ultra-high frequency of the time series data. To achieve this purpose, a new model should be developed to enforce high frequency of HONN in order to make the simulation and prediction error close to zero.

The different types of UPS-HONN models are shown as follows. Formula (1) (2) and (3) are for UPS-HONN model 2, 1 and 0 respectively. Model 2 has three layers of weights changeable, Model 1 has two layers of weights changeable, and model 0 has one layer of weights changeable. For models 2, 1 and 0, Z is the output while x and y are the inputs of UPS-HONN. c_{kj}^{o} is the weight for the output layer, c_{kj}^{hx} and c_{kj}^{hy} are the weights for the second hidden layer, and c_k^x and a_j^y are the weights for the first hidden

Figure 3. UPC-HONN Architecture

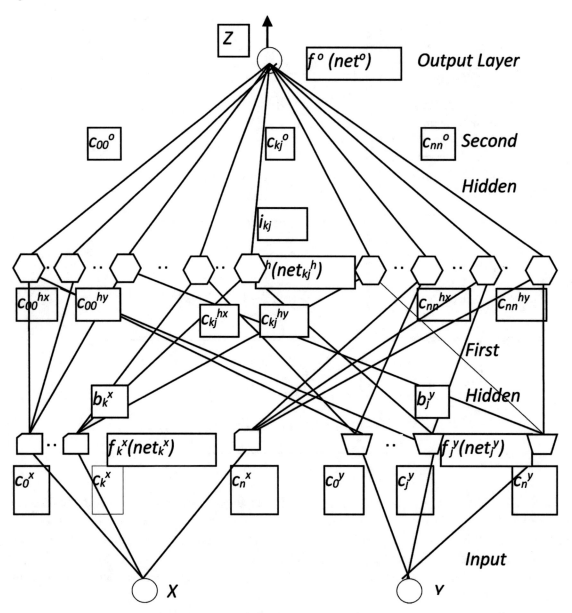

layer. Functions cosine and sine are the first and second hidden layer nodes of UPS-HONN. The output layer node of UPS-HONN is a linear function of $f^o(net^o) = net^o$, where net^o equals the input of output layer node. UPS-HONN is an open neural network model, each weight of HONN has its corresponding coefficient in the model formula, and each node of UPS-HONN has its corresponding function in the

Figure 4.

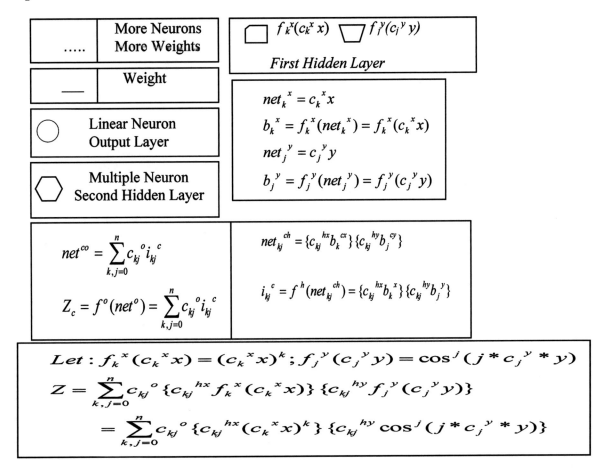

model formula. The structure of UPS-HONN is built by a nonlinear formula. It means, after training, there is rationale for each component of UPS-HONN in the nonlinear formula.

$UPS - HONN \qquad Model \qquad 2:$

$$Z = \sum_{k,j=0}^{n} (c_{kj}^{\ o})\{c_{kj}^{\ hx}(c_k^{\ x}x)^k\} \{c_{kj}^{\ hy} \sin^j(j * c_j^{\ y}y)\} \qquad (1)$$

$UPS - HONN \qquad Model \qquad 1:$

$$z = \sum_{k,j=0}^{n} c_{kj}^{\ o} \ (c_k^{\ x}x)^k \sin^j(j * c_j^{\ y}y)$$

$where: \qquad (c_{kj}^{\ hx}) = (c_{kj}^{\ hy}) = 1 \qquad (2)$

UPS – HONN   Model   0:

$$z = \sum_{k,j=0}^{n} c_{kj}^{\;o}\;(x)^k \sin^j(j*y)$$

where: $(c_{kj}^{\;hx}) = (c_{kj}^{\;hy}) = 1$

and $c_k^{\;x} = c_j^{\;y} = 1$ (3)

For formula 1, 2, and 3, values of k and j ranges from 0 to n, where n is an integer. The UPS-HONN model can simulate ultra-high frequency time series data, when n increases to a big number. This property of the model allows it to easily simulate and predicate ultra-high frequency time series data, since both k and j increase when there is an increase in n.

The following is an expansion of model UPS-HONN order two. This model is used in later sections to predict the exchange rates.

$$z = c_{00}^{\;o}\, c_{00}^{\;hx}\, c_{00}^{\;hy} \sin^0(0*c_0^{\;y}y)$$

$$+ c_{01}^{\;o}\, c_{01}^{\;hx}\, c_{01}^{\;hy} \sin(1*c_1^{\;y}\, y)$$

$$+ c_{02}^{\;o}\, c_{02}^{\;hx}\, c_{02}^{\;hy} \sin^2(2*c_2^{\;y}\, y)$$

$$+ c_{10}^{\;o}\, c_{10}^{\;hx}\, c_{10}^{\;hy} (c_1^{\;x}\, x)\, \sin^0(0*c_0^{\;y}y)$$

$$+ c_{11}^{\;o}\, c_{11}^{\;hx}\, c_{11}^{\;hy} (c_1^{\;x}\, x)\, \sin(1*c_1^{\;y}\, y)$$

$$+ c_{12}^{\;o}\, c_{12}^{\;hx}\, c_{12}^{\;hy} (c_1^{\;x}\, x)\, \sin^2(2*c_2^{\;y}\, y)$$

$$+ c_{20}^{\;o}\, c_{20}^{\;hx}\, c_{20}^{\;hy} (c_2^{\;x}\, x)^2\, \sin^0(0*c_0^{\;y}y)$$

$$+ c_{21}^{\;o}\, c_{21}^{\;hx}\, c_{21}^{\;hy} (c_2^{\;x}\, x)^2\, \sin(1*c_1^{\;y}\, y)$$

$$+ c_{22}^{\;o}\, c_{22}^{\;hx}\, c_{22}^{\;hy} (c_2^{\;x}\, x)^2\, \sin^2(2*c_2^{\;y}\, y) \qquad (4)$$

The "UPS-HONN Architecture" is shown. This model structure is used to develop the model learning algorithm, which make sure the convergence of learning. This allows the deference between desired output and real output of UPS-HONN close to zero.

UPC-HONN Model

The UPC-HONN models replace the sine functions from UPS-HONN with cosine functions models, and the UPC-HONN models are defined as follows.

UPCHONN   Model   2 :

$$Z = \sum_{k,j=0}^{n} (c_{kj}^{\ o}) \{c_{kj}^{\ hx} (c_k^{\ x} x)^k\} \{c_{kj}^{\ hy} \cos^j (j * c_j^{\ y} y)\} \qquad (5)$$

UPCHONN   Model   1 :

$$z = \sum_{k,j=0}^{n} c_{kj}^{\ o} (c_k^{\ x} x)^k \cos^j (j * c_j^{\ y} y)$$

where : $(c_{kj}^{\ hx}) = (c_{kj}^{\ hy}) = 1$ \qquad (6)

UPCHONN   Model   0 :

$$z = \sum_{k,j=0}^{n} c_{kj}^{\ o} (x)^k \cos^j (j * y)$$

where : $(c_{kj}^{\ hx}) = (c_{kj}^{\ hy}) = 1$

and $c_k^{\ x} = c_j^{\ y} = 1$ \qquad (7)

LEARNING ALGORITHM OF UPT-HONN MODELS

Learning Algorithm of UPS-HONN Model

Output Neurons in HONN Model (model 0, 1, and 2)

The output layer weights are updated according to:

$$c_{kj}^{\ o}(t+1) = c_{kj}^{\ o}(t) - \eta(\partial E \ / \partial c_{kj}^{\ o}) \qquad (A.1)$$

where = learning rate (positive and usually < 1)

c_{kj} = weight; index k an j = input index

(k, j=0, 1, 2,...,n means one of n*n input neurons from the second hidden layer)

E = error

t = training time

o = output layer

The output node equations are:

$$net^o = \sum_{k,j=1}^{n} c_{kj}{}^o i_{kj}$$

$$z = f^o(net^o) = \sum_{k,j=1}^{n} c_{kj}{}^o i_{kj} \qquad (A.2)$$

where i_{kj} = input to the output neuron (= output from 2nd hidden layer)

z = actual output from the output neuron

f^o = output neuron activity function

The error at a particular output unit (neuron) will be:

$$\delta = (d - z) \qquad (A.3)$$

where d = desired output value
The total error is the error of output unit, namely:

$$E = 0.5 * \delta^2 = 0.5 * (d - z)^2 \qquad (A.4)$$

The derivatives $f^o{}'(net^o)$ are calculated as follows:
The output neuron function is linear function ($f^o(net^o) = net^o$):

$$f^o{}'(net^o) = \partial f^o / \partial(net)^o = \partial(net^o) / \partial(net^o) = 1 \qquad (A.5)$$

Gradients are calculated as follows:

$$\partial E / \partial c_{kj}{}^o = (\partial E / \partial z)(\partial z / \partial(net^o))(\partial(net^o) / \partial c_{kj}{}^o) \qquad (A.6)$$

$$\partial E / \partial z = \partial(0.5 * (d - z)^2) / \partial z) = 0.5 * (-2(d - z)) = -(d - z) \qquad (A.7)$$

$$\partial z / \partial(net^o) = \partial f^o / \partial(net^o) = f^o{}'(net^o) \qquad (A.8)$$

$$\partial(net^o) / \partial_{kj}{}^o = \partial(\sum_{k,j=0}^{n} c_{kj}{}^o i_{kj}) / \partial c_{kj}{}^o = i_{kj}$$

Combining Eqns. A.6 through A.9, the negative gradient is:

$$-\partial E \ / \ \partial c_{kj}{}^o = (d - z)f^{o\,\prime}(net^o)i_{kj} \qquad (A.10)$$

For a linear output neuron, this becomes, by combining Eqns. A.10 and A.5:

$$-\partial E \ / \ \partial c_{kj}{}^o = (d - z)f^{o\,\prime}(net^o)i_{kj}$$
$$= (d - z)(1)i_{kj} = (d - z)i_{kj} \qquad (A.11)$$

The weight update equations are formulated as follows: for linear output neurons, let:

$$\delta^{ol} = (d - z) \qquad (A.12)$$

Combining Formulae A.1, A.11, and A.12:

$$c_{kj}{}^o(t+1) = c_{kj}{}^o(t) - \eta(\partial E \ / \ \partial a_{kj}{}^o)$$
$$= c_{kj}{}^o(t) + \eta(d - z)f^{o\,\prime}(net^o)i_{kj}$$
$$= a_{kj}{}^o(t) + \eta\delta^{ol}i_{kj}$$
$$where:$$
$$\delta^{ol} = (d - z)$$
$$f^{o\,\prime}(net^o) = 1 \qquad (linear \qquad neuron) \qquad (A.13)$$

Second-Hidden Layer Neurons in HONN Model (Model 2)

The second hidden layer weights are updated according to:

$$c_{kj}{}^{hx}(t+1) = c_{kj}{}^{hx}(t) - \eta(\partial E \ / \ \partial c_{kj}{}^{hx}) \qquad (B.1)$$

where = learning rate (positive & usually < 1)

k, j = input index (k, j = 0, 1, 2, …,n means one of 2*n*n input combinations from the first hidden layer)

E = error

t = training time

hx = hidden layer, related to x input

$c_{kj}{}^{hx}$ = hidden layer weight related to x input

The equations for the 2nd hidden layer node are:

$$net_{kj}{}^{h} = \{c_{kj}{}^{hx}b_{k}{}^{x}\}\{c_{kj}{}^{hy}b_{j}{}^{y}\}$$
$$i_{kj} = f^{h}(net_{kj}{}^{h}) \qquad\qquad (B.2)$$

where i_{kj} = output from 2nd hidden layer (= input to the output neuron)

$_{bk}x_{and\,bj}{}^{y}$ = input to 2nd hidden layer neuron

(= output from the 1st hidden layer neuron)

f^{h} = hidden neuron activation function

hy = hidden layer, related to y input

$c_{kj}{}^{hy}$ = hidden layer weight related to y input

We call the neurons at the second layer multiple neurons. Their activity function is linear and their inputs are the multiplication of two outputs of the first layer neuron output and their weights.

The error of a single output unit will be:

$$\delta = (d-z) \qquad\qquad (B.3)$$

where d = desired output value of output layer neuron

z = actual output value of output layer neuron

The total error is the sum of the squared errors across all output units, namely:

$$E_{p} = 0.5 * \delta^{2} = 0.5 * (d-z)^{2}$$
$$= 0.5 * (d - f^{o}(net^{o}))^{2}$$
$$= 0.5 * (d - f_{k}^{o}(\sum_{j} c_{kj}{}^{o}i_{kj}))^{2} \qquad\qquad (B.4)$$

The derivatives $f^{h\prime}(net^{h}{}_{pj})$ are calculated as follows, for a linear function of second layer neurons:

$$i_{kj} = f^h(net_{kj}{}^h) = net_{kj}{}^h$$

$$f^{h\,\prime}(net_{kj}{}^h) = 1 \qquad\qquad (B.5)$$

The gradient ($E/c_{kj}{}^{hx}$) is given by:

$$\partial E \;/\; \partial c_{kj}{}^{hx} = \partial(0.5*(d-z)^2)\,/\,\partial c_{kj}{}^{hx}$$

$$= (\partial(0.5*(d-z)^2)\,/\,\partial z\,)(\partial z\,/\,\partial(net^o))$$

$$(\partial(net^o)\,/\,\partial i_{kj})(\partial i_{kj}\,/\,\partial(net_{kj}{}^h))(\partial(net_{kj}{}^h)\,/\,\partial c_{kj}{}^{hx}) \qquad\qquad (B.6)$$

$$\partial(0.5*(d-z)^2)\,/\,\partial z = -(d-z) \qquad\qquad (B.7)$$

$$\partial z\,/\,\partial(net^o) = \partial f^o\,/\,\partial(net^o) = f_k^o\,{}'(net^o) \qquad\qquad (B.8)$$

$$\partial(net^o)\,/\,\partial i_{kj} = \partial(\sum_{k,j=1}^{n}(c_{kj}{}^o i_{kj}))\,/\,\partial i_{kj} = c_{kj}{}^o \qquad\qquad (B.9)$$

$$\partial i_{kj}\,/\,\partial(net_{kj}{}^h) = \partial(f^h(net_{kj}{}^h))\,/\,\partial(net_{kj}{}^h) = f^{h\,\prime}(net_{kj}{}^h) \qquad\qquad (B.10)$$

$$\partial(net_{kj}{}^h)\,/\,\partial c_{kj}{}^{hx} = \partial(\{c_{kj}{}^{hx}b_k{}^x\}\{c_{kj}{}^{hy}b_j{}^y\})\,/\,\partial c_{kj}{}^{hx}$$

$$= b_k{}^x c_{kj}{}^{hy} b_j{}^y = \delta_{kj}{}^{hx} b_k{}^x$$

$$where: \delta_{kj}{}^{hx} = c_{kj}{}^{hy} b_j{}^y \qquad\qquad (B.11)$$

Combining Eqns. B.6 through B.11, the negative gradient is:

$$-\partial E\,/\,\partial c_{kj}{}^{hx} = (d-z)f^{o\,\prime}(net^o)c_{kj}{}^o f^{h\,\prime}(net_{kj}{}^h)\delta^{hx}b_k{}^x \qquad\qquad (B.12)$$

The weight update equations are formulated as follows:

- let output neuron is a linear neuron:

$$\delta^{ol} = (d-z)f^o{}_k\,{}'(net^o) = (d-z) \qquad\qquad (B.13)$$

Also let the second layer neurons be linear neurons, combining Formulae B.1, B.5, B.12 and B.13:

$$c_{kj}{}^{hx}(t+1) = c_{kj}{}^{hx}(t) - \eta(\partial E / \partial c_{kj}{}^{hx})$$

$$= c_{kj}{}^{hx}(t) + \eta((d-z)f^{o}{}'(net^{o})c_{kj}{}^{o}f^{h}{}'(net_{kj}{}^{hx})c_{kj}{}^{hy}b_{j}{}^{y}b_{k}{}^{x})$$

$$= c_{kj}{}^{hx}(t) + \eta(\delta^{ol}c_{kj}{}^{o}\delta_{kj}{}^{hx}b_{k}{}^{x})$$

$$where: \qquad \delta^{ol} = (d-z)$$

$$\delta_{kj}{}^{hx} = c_{kj}{}^{hy}b_{j}{}^{y}$$

$$f^{o}{}'(net^{o}) = 1 \qquad (linear \qquad neuron)$$

$$f^{h}{}'(net_{kj}{}^{hx}) = 1 \qquad (linear \qquad neuron) \qquad (B.14)$$

Use the same rules, the weight update question for y input neurons is:

$$c_{kj}{}^{hy}(t+1) = c_{kj}{}^{hy}(t) - \eta(\partial E / \partial c_{kj}{}^{hy})$$

$$= c_{kj}{}^{hy}(t) + \eta((d-z)f^{o}{}'(net^{o})c_{kj}{}^{o}f^{h}{}'(net_{kj}{}^{hy})c_{kj}{}^{hx}b_{k}{}^{x}b_{j}{}^{y})$$

$$= c_{kj}{}^{hy}(t) + \eta(\delta^{ol}c_{kj}{}^{o}\delta_{kj}{}^{hy}b_{j}{}^{y})$$

$$where: \qquad \delta^{ol} = (d-z)$$

$$\delta_{kj}{}^{hy} = c_{kj}{}^{hx}b_{k}{}^{x}$$

$$f^{o}{}'(net^{o}) = 1 \qquad (linear \qquad neuron)$$

$$f^{h}{}'(net_{kj}{}^{hy}) = 1 \qquad (linear \qquad neuron) \qquad (B.15)$$

First Hidden Layer Neurons in UPS-HONN (Model 1 and Model 2)

The 1st hidden layer weights are updated according to:

$$c_{k}{}^{x}(t+1) = c_{k}{}^{x}(t) - \eta(\partial E_{p} / \partial c_{k}{}^{x}) \qquad (C.1)$$

where:

$c_{k}{}^{x}$ = 1st hidden layer weight for input x; k = kth neuron of first hidden layer

= learning rate (positive & usually < 1)

E = error

t = training time

The equations for the kth or j^{th} node in the first hidden layer are:

$$net_k{}^x = c_k{}^x * x$$
$$b_k{}^x = f_k{}^x (net_k{}^x)$$
or
$$net_j{}^y = c_j{}^y * y$$
$$b_j{}^y = f_j{}^y (net_j{}^y) \qquad (C.2)$$

where:

i_{kj} = output from 2nd hidden layer (= input to the output neuron)

$b_k{}^x$ and $b_j{}^y$ = output from the 1st hidden layer neuron (= input to 2nd hidden layer neuron)

$f_k{}^x$ and $f_j{}^y$ =1st hidden layer neuron activation function

x and y = input to 1st hidden layer

The total error is the sum of the squared errors across all hidden units, namely:

$$E_p = 0.5 * \delta^2 = 0.5 * (d - z)^2$$
$$= 0.5 * (d - f^o (net^o))^2$$
$$= 0.5 * (d - f^o (\sum_j c_{kj}{}^o i_{kj}))^2 \qquad (C.3)$$

The gradient $(\partial E_p / \partial c_k{}^x)$ is given by:

$$\partial E_p / \partial c_k{}^x = \partial(0.5 * (d - z)^2) / \partial c_k{}^x$$
$$= (\partial(0.5 * (d - z)^2) / \partial z)(\partial z / \partial(net^o))$$
$$(\partial(net^o) / \partial i_{kj})(\partial i_{kj} / \partial(net_{kj}{}^h))(\partial(net_{kj}{}^h) / \partial b_k{}^x)$$
$$(\partial b_k{}^x / \partial(net_k{}^x))(\partial(net_k{}^x) / \partial c_k{}^x) \qquad (C.4)$$

$$\partial(0.5 * (d - z)^2 / \partial z = -(d - z) \qquad (C.5)$$

$$\partial z / \partial(net^o) = \partial f^o / \partial(net^o) = f^o{}'(net^o) \qquad (C.6)$$

$$\partial(net^o) / \partial i_{kj} = \partial(\sum_{k,j=1}^{l} (c_{kj}{}^o i_{kj})) / \partial i_{kj} = c_{kj}{}^o \qquad (C.7)$$

$$\partial i_{kj} / \partial(net_{kj}{}^{h}) = \partial(f^{h}(net_{kj}{}^{h})) / \partial(net_{kj}{}^{h}) = f^{h}{}'(net_{kj}{}^{h}) \qquad (C.8)$$

$$\partial net_{kj}{}^{h} / \partial b_{k}{}^{x} = \partial((c_{kj}{}^{hx} * b_{k}{}^{x}) * (c_{kj}{}^{hy} * b_{j}{}^{y})) / \partial b_{k}{}^{x} = c_{kj}{}^{hx} * c_{kj}{}^{hy} * b_{j}{}^{y}$$
$$= \delta_{kj}{}^{hx} c_{kj}{}^{hx}$$
$$where : \delta_{kj}{}^{hx} = c_{kj}{}^{hy} * b_{j}{}^{y} \qquad (C.9)$$

$$\partial b_{k}{}^{x} / \partial(net_{k}{}^{x}) = f_{x}{}'(net_{k}{}^{x}) \qquad (C.10)$$

$$\partial(net_{k}{}^{x}) / \partial c_{k}{}^{x} = \partial(c_{k}{}^{x} * x) / \partial c_{k}{}^{x} = x \qquad (C.11)$$

Combining Formulae C.5 through C.11 the negative gradient is:

$$-\partial E_{p} / \partial c_{k}{}^{x} = (d-z)f^{o}{}'(net^{o})c_{kj}{}^{o} * f^{h}{}'(net_{kj}{}^{h})\delta_{kj}{}^{hx} c_{kj}{}^{hx} f_{x}{}'(net_{k}{}^{x})x \qquad (C.12)$$

The weight update equations are calculated as follows.
For linear output neurons:

$$f^{o}{}'(net^{o}) = 1$$
$$\delta^{ol} = (d-z)f^{o}{}'(net^{o}) = (d-z) \qquad (C.13)$$

For linear neurons of second hidden layer:

$$f^{h}{}'(net_{kj}{}^{h}) = 1 \qquad (C.14)$$

The negative gradient is:

$$-\partial E_{p} / \partial c_{k}{}^{x} = (d-z)f^{o}{}'(net^{o})c_{kj}{}^{o} * f^{h}{}'(net_{kj}{}^{h})\delta_{kj}{}^{hx} c_{kj}{}^{hx} f_{x}{}'(net_{k}{}^{x})x$$
$$= \delta^{ol} * c_{kj}{}^{o} * \delta_{kj}{}^{hx} * c_{kj}{}^{hx} * f_{x}{}'(net_{k}{}^{x}) * x \qquad (C.15)$$

By combining Formulae C.1, C.4, and C.16, for a linear 1st hidden layer neuron:

For a polynomial function of x input side:

$$b_{k}{}^{x} = f_{k}{}^{x}(net_{k}{}^{x}) = (net_{k}{}^{x})^{k} = (c_{k}{}^{x} * x)^{k}$$
$$f_{x}{}'(net_{k}{}^{x}) = \partial b_{k}{}^{x} / \partial(net_{k}{}^{x})$$
$$= \partial(net_{k}{}^{x})^{k}) / \partial(net_{k}{}^{x})$$
$$= k(net_{k}{}^{x})^{k-1} = k * (c_{k}{}^{x} * x)^{k-1} \qquad (C.16)$$

$$c_k^{\ x}(t+1) = c_k^{\ x}(t) - \eta(\partial E_p / \partial c_k^{\ x})$$

$$= c_k^{\ x}(t) + \eta(d-z)f^{o}{}'(net^{o})c_{kj}^{\ o} * f^{h}{}'(net_{kj}^{\ h})\delta_{kj}^{\ hx}c_{kj}^{\ hx}f_x{}'(net_k^{\ x})x$$

$$= c_k^{\ x}(t) + \eta * \delta^{\ ol} * c_{kj}^{\ o} * \delta^{\ hx} * c_{kj}^{\ hx} * k * (c_k^{\ x} * x)^{k-1} * x$$

$$= c_k^{\ x}(t) + \eta * \delta^{\ ol} * c_{kj}^{\ o} * \delta^{\ hx} * c_{kj}^{\ hx} * \delta^{\ x} * x$$

where :

$$\delta^{\ ol} = (d-z)f^{o}{}'(net^{o}) = d-z \qquad (linear \qquad neuron)$$

$$\delta^{\ hx} = f^{h}{}'(net_{kj}^{\ h})c_{kj}^{\ hy}b_j^{\ y} \quad = c_{kj}^{\ hy}b_j^{\ y} \qquad (linear \qquad neuron)$$

$$\delta^{\ x} = f_x{}'(net_k^{\ x}) = k * (net_k^{\ x})^{k-1} = k * (c_k^{\ x} * x)^{k-1} \qquad (C.17)$$

For a sine function of y input part:

$$b_j^{\ y} = f_j^{\ y}(net_j^{\ y}) = \sin^j(j * net_j^{\ y}) = \sin^j(j * c_j^{\ y} * y)$$

$$f_y{}'(net_j^{\ y}) = \partial b_j^{\ y} / \partial(net_j^{\ y})$$

$$= \partial(\sin^j(j * net_j^{\ y})) / \partial(net_j^{\ y})$$

$$= j\sin^{j-1}(j * net_j^{\ y}) * \cos(j * net_j^{\ y}) * j$$

$$= j^2 * \sin^{j-1}(j * net_j^{\ y}) * \cos(j * net_j^{\ y})$$

$$= j^2 * \sin^{j-1}(j * c_j^{\ y} * y) * \cos(j * c_j^{\ y} * y) \qquad (C.18)$$

Using the above procedure:

$$c_j^{\ y}(t+1) = c_j^{\ y}(t) - \eta(\partial E_p / \partial c_j^{\ y})$$

$$= c_j^{\ y}(t) + \eta(d-z)f^{o}{}'(net^{o})c_{kj}^{\ o} * f^{h}{}'(net_{kj}^{\ h})\delta_{kj}^{\ hy}c_{kj}^{\ hy}f_y{}'(net_j^{\ y})y$$

$$= c_j^{\ y}(t) + \eta * \delta^{\ ol} * c_{kj}^{\ o} * \delta^{\ hy} * c_{kj}^{\ hy} * (j^2)\sin^{j-1}(j * c_j^{\ y} * y)\cos(j * c_j^{\ y} * y) * y$$

$$= c_j^{\ y}(t) + \eta * \delta^{\ ol} * c_{kj}^{\ o} * \delta^{\ hy} * c_{kj}^{\ hy} * \delta^{\ y} * y$$

where :

$$\delta^{\ ol} = (d-z)f^{o}{}'(net^{o}) = d-z \qquad (linear \qquad neuron)$$

$$\delta^{\ hy} = f^{h}{}'(net_{kj}^{\ hy})c_{kj}^{\ hx}b_k^{\ x} \quad = c_{kj}^{\ hx}b_k^{\ x} \qquad (linear \qquad neuron)$$

$$\delta^{\ y} = f_y{}'(net_j^{\ y}) = (j^2)\sin^{j-1}(j * c_j^{\ y} * y)\cos(j * c_j^{\ y} * y) \qquad (C.19)$$

First Hidden Layer Neurons in UPC-HONN (Model 1 and Model 2)

The 1st hidden layer weights are updated according to:

$$c_k^{x}(t+1) = c_k^{x}(t) - \eta(\partial E_p / \partial c_k^{x}) \qquad (D.1)$$

Where:

c_k^{x} = 1st hidden layer weight for input x; $k = k^{th}$ neuron of first hidden layer

= learning rate (positive & usually < 1)

E = error

t = training time

The equations for the kth or j^{th} node in the first hidden layer are:

$$net_k^{x} = c_k^{x} * x$$
$$b_k^{x} = f_k^{x}(net_k^{x})$$
or
$$net_j^{y} = c_j^{y} * y$$
$$b_j^{y} = f_j^{y}(net_j^{y}) \qquad (D.2)$$

Where:

i_{kj} = output from 2nd hidden layer (= input to the output neuron)

b_k^{x} and b_j^{y} = output from the 1st hidden layer neuron (= input to 2nd hidden layer neuron)

f_k^{x} and f_j^{y} =1st hidden layer neuron activation function

x and y = input to 1st hidden layer

The total error is the sum of the squared errors across all hidden units, namely:

$$E_p = 0.5 * \delta^2 = 0.5 * (d - z)^2$$
$$= 0.5 * (d - f^{o}(net^{o}))^2$$
$$= 0.5 * (d - f^{o}(\sum_j c_{kj}^{o} i_{kj}))^2 \qquad (D.3)$$

For a polynomial and cosine function:
The gradient ($\partial E_p / \partial c_k{}^x$) is given by:

$$\partial E_p / \partial c_k{}^x = \partial(0.5*(d-z)^2) / \partial c_k{}^x$$
$$= (\partial(0.5*(d-z)^2) / \partial z)(\partial z / \partial(net^o))$$
$$(\partial(net^o) / \partial i_{kj})(\partial i_{kj} / \partial(net_{kj}{}^h))(\partial(net_{kj}{}^h) / \partial b_k{}^x)$$
$$(\partial b_k{}^x / \partial(net_k{}^x))(\partial(net_k{}^x) / \partial c_k{}^x) \qquad (D.4)$$

$$\partial(0.5*(d-z)^2 / \partial z = -(d-z) \qquad (D.5)$$

$$\partial z / \partial(net^o) = \partial f^o / \partial(net^o) = f^o{}'(net^o) \qquad (D.6)$$

$$\partial(net^o) / \partial i_{kj} = \partial(\sum_{k,j=1}^{L} (c_{kj}{}^o i_{kj})) / \partial i_{kj} = c_{kj}{}^o \qquad (D.7)$$

$$\partial i_{kj} / \partial(net_{kj}{}^h) = \partial(f^h(net_{kj}{}^h)) / \partial(net_{kj}{}^h) = f^h{}'(net_{kj}{}^h) \qquad (D.8)$$

$$\partial net_{kj}{}^h / \partial b_k{}^x = \partial((c_{kj}{}^{hx}*b_k{}^x)*(c_{kj}{}^{hy}*b_j{}^y)) / \partial b_k{}^x = c_{kj}{}^{hx}*c_{kj}{}^{hy}*b_j{}^y$$
$$= \delta_{kj}{}^{hx} c_{kj}{}^{hx}$$
$$where: \delta_{kj}{}^{hx} = c_{kj}{}^{hy}*b_j{}^y \qquad (D.9)$$

$$\partial b_k{}^x / \partial(net_k{}^x) = f_x{}'(net_k{}^x) \qquad (D.10)$$

$$\partial(net_k{}^x) / \partial c_k{}^x = \partial(c_k{}^x*x) / \partial c_k{}^x = x \qquad (D.11)$$

Combining Formulae D.5 through D.11 the negative gradient is:

$$-\partial E_p / \partial c_k{}^x = (d-z)f^o{}'(net^o)c_{kj}{}^o * f^h{}'(net_{kj}{}^h)\delta_{kj}{}^{hx}c_{kj}{}^{hx}f_x{}'(net_k{}^x)x \qquad (D.12)$$

The weight update equations are calculated as follows.
For linear output neurons:

$$f^o{}'(net^o) = 1$$
$$\delta^{ol} = (d-z)f^o{}'(net^o) = (d-z) \qquad (D.13)$$

For linear neurons of second hidden layer:

$$f^{h}{}'(net_{kj}{}^{h}) = 1 \qquad (D.14)$$

The negative gradient is:

$$-\partial E_{p} / \partial c_{k}{}^{x} = (d-z)f^{o}{}'(net^{o})c_{kj}{}^{o} * f^{h}{}'(net_{kj}{}^{h})\delta_{kj}{}^{hx}c_{kj}{}^{hx}f_{x}{}'(net_{k}{}^{x})x$$
$$= \delta^{ol} * c_{kj}{}^{o} * \delta_{kj}{}^{hx} * c_{kj}{}^{hx} * f_{x}{}'(net_{k}{}^{x}) * x \qquad (D.15)$$

For polynomial function of x input part:

$$b_{k}{}^{x} = f_{x}(net_{k}{}^{x}) = (net_{k}{}^{x})^{k} = (c_{k}{}^{x} * x)^{k}$$
$$f_{x}{}'(net_{k}{}^{x}) = \partial b^{x}{}_{k} / \partial(net_{k}{}^{x})$$
$$= \partial(net_{k}{}^{x})^{k}) / \partial(net_{k}{}^{x})$$
$$= k(net_{k}{}^{x})^{k-1} = k * (c_{k}{}^{x} * x)^{k-1} \qquad (D.16)$$

By combining Formulae D.1, D.15, and D.16, for a linear 1st hidden layer neuron:

$$c_{k}{}^{x}(t+1) = c_{k}{}^{x}(t) - \eta(\partial E_{p} / \partial c_{k}{}^{x})$$
$$= c_{k}{}^{x}(t) + \eta(d-z)f^{o}{}'(net^{o})c_{kj}{}^{o} * f^{h}{}'(net_{kj}{}^{h})\delta_{kj}{}^{hx}c_{kj}{}^{hx}f_{x}{}'(net_{k}{}^{x})x$$
$$= c_{k}{}^{x}(t) + \eta * \delta^{ol} * c_{kj}{}^{o} * \delta^{hx} * c_{kj}{}^{hx} * k * (c_{k}{}^{x} * x)^{k-1} * x$$
$$= c_{k}{}^{x}(t) + \eta * \delta^{ol} * c_{kj}{}^{o} * \delta^{hx} * c_{kj}{}^{hx} * \delta^{x} * x$$
$$where:$$
$$\qquad \delta^{ol} = (d-z)f^{o}{}'(net^{o}) = d-z \qquad (linear \qquad neuron)$$
$$\qquad \delta^{hx} = f^{h}{}'(net_{kj}{}^{h})c_{kj}{}^{hy}b_{j}{}^{y} \qquad = c_{kj}{}^{hy}b_{j}{}^{y} \qquad (linear \qquad neuron)$$
$$\qquad \delta^{x} = f_{x}{}'(net_{k}{}^{x}) = k * (net_{k}{}^{x})^{k-1} = k * (c_{k}{}^{x}*x)^{k-1} \qquad (D.17)$$

For cosine function of y input part:

$$b_{j}{}^{y} = f_{y}(net_{j}{}^{y}) = \cos^{j}(j * net_{j}{}^{y}) = \cos^{j}(j * c_{j}{}^{y} * y)$$
$$f_{y}{}'(net_{j}{}^{y}) = \partial b^{y}{}_{j} / \partial(net_{j}{}^{y})$$
$$= \partial(\cos^{j}(j * net_{j}{}^{y})) / \partial(net_{j}{}^{y})$$
$$= j\cos^{j-1}(j * net_{j}{}^{y}) * (-\sin(j * net_{j}{}^{y})) * j$$
$$= -j^{2} * \cos^{j-1}(j * net_{j}{}^{y}) * \sin(j * net_{j}{}^{y})$$
$$= -j^{2} * \cos^{j-1}(j * c_{j}{}^{y} * y) * \sin(j * c_{j}{}^{y} * y) \qquad (D.18)$$

Using the above procedure:

$$c_j^{\ y}(t+1) = c_j^{\ y}(t) - \eta(\partial E_p / \partial c_j^{\ y})$$

$$= c_j^{\ y}(t) + \eta(d-z)f^{o\ '}(net^{\ o})c_{kj}^{\ o} * f^{h\ '}(net_{kj}^{\ h})\delta_{kj}^{\ hy}c_{kj}^{\ hy}f_y^{\ '}(net_j^{\ y})y$$

$$= c_j^{\ y}(t) + \eta * \delta^{\ ol} * c_{kj}^{\ o} * \delta^{\ hy} * c_{kj}^{\ hy} * (-j^2) * \cos^{j-1}(j*c_j^{\ y}*y)*\sin(j*c_j^{\ y}*y)*y$$

$$= c_j^{\ y}(t) + \eta * \delta^{\ ol} * c_{kj}^{\ o} * \delta^{\ hy} * c_{kj}^{\ hy} * \delta^{\ y} * y$$

where :

$$\delta^{\ ol} = (d-z)f^{o\ '}(net^{\ o}) = d-z \qquad (linear \qquad neuron)$$

$$\delta^{\ hy} = f^{h\ '}(net_{kj}^{\ hy})c_{kj}^{\ hx}b_k^{\ x} \qquad = c_{kj}^{\ hx}b_k^{\ x} \qquad (linear \qquad neuron)$$

$$\delta^{\ y} = f_y^{\ '}(net_j^{\ y}) = (-j^2)*\cos^{j-1}(j*c_j^{\ y}*y)*\sin(j*c_j^{\ y}*y) \qquad (D.19)$$

UPT-HONN TESTING

UPS-HONN model is used to generate the control signals. The test results are shown in Table 1 and Figure 3. Next, test results for the control signals generated by UPC-HONN model are shown in Table 2 and Figure 4.

In Table 1, UPS-HONN model 0 has been used. The order number for UPS-HONN model is 6. In the first table of Table 1, the "No." column shows a total of 19 points are chosen. The "UPS-HONN x" column displays the input x values, which are all "1"s. The "UPS-HONN y" column displays the input y values, which are 0, 0.1, 0.2, 0.3, 0.4, 05, 0.7, 0.8, 0.9, 1, 2, 3, 4, 5, 6, 7 and 8. The "UPS-HONN z" column displays the output z values. The "Desired Signal" column displays the desired signal values. The "Absolute Desired Signal" column displays the absolute values for desired signal. The "Difference" column shows the difference between UPS-HONN output z and the desired signal (UPS-HONN z - Desired Signal). The "Absolute Difference" column shows the absolute difference between UPS-HONN output z and the desired signal (|UPS-HONN z - Desired Signal|). The "UPS-HONN Error %" column gives the error percentage for UPS-HONN Model (UPS-HONN error % = absolute difference / Absolute Desired Signal * 100%). The average UPS-HONN error is 0.00002383%, which is much closer to zero. After training UPS-HONN model by using desired signal values, in the second table of Table 1, the coefficients for UPS-HONN are displayed. For examples, $c_{00}^{\ o}= 0.7082$, $c_{01}^{\ o}= 0.1200$, and $c_{10}^{\ o}= -0.5910$. In the third table of Table 1, gives the values for $c_{kj}^{\ o}*(x)^k*sin^j(j*y)$, when $x=1$, $y=0.1$, $k=0,1,2,3,4,5,6$, and $j=0,1,2,3,4,5,6$. For example, $c_{01}^{\ o}*(1)^0*sin^1(1*0.1)=0.01198001$, $c_{02}^{\ o}*(1)^0*sin^2(2*0.1)=0.01736370$, and $c_{03}^{\ o}*(1)^0*sin^3(3*0.1)=-0.11646451$. And $z=\sum c_{kj}^{\ o}*(x)^k*sin^j(j*y)=\sum c_{kj}^{\ o}*(1)^k*sin^j(j*0.1)=-0.43642320$.

In Figure 3, UPS-HONN signal generator results are shown. Designed signals are shown by solid line. And UPS-HONN generated signals are shown by using dashed line. Evidence from Figure 3 suggeststhat UPS-HONN signal generator can match the desired signals well, since the average error percentage is close to 0.0000%.

Table 1. UPS-HONN signal generator (n=6, Model 0)

No.	UPS-HONN x	UPS-HONN y	UPS-HONN z	Desired Signal	Absolute Desired Signal	Difference	Absolute Difference	UPS-HONN Error %
1	1	0	0.00000000	0.000000	0.000000	0.00000000	0.00000000	0.000000%
2	1	0.1	-0.43642320	-0.436423	0.436423	-0.00000020	0.00000020	0.000019%
3	1	0.2	-0.81959500	-0.819595	0.819595	0.00000000	0.00000000	0.000000%
4	1	0.3	-1.10813896	-1.108139	1.108139	0.00000004	0.00000004	0.000004%
5	1	0.4	-1.28106187	-1.281062	1.281062	0.00000013	0.00000013	0.000012%
6	1	0.5	-1.34052178	-1.340522	1.340522	0.00000022	0.00000022	0.000021%
7	1	0.6	-1.30817427	-1.308174	1.308174	-0.00000027	0.00000027	0.000026%
8	1	0.7	-1.21630469	-1.216305	1.216305	0.00000031	0.00000031	0.000030%
9	1	0.8	-1.09648320	-1.096483	1.096483	-0.00000020	0.00000020	0.000020%
10	1	0.9	-0.96919948	-0.969199	0.969199	-0.00000048	0.00000048	0.000047%
11	1	1	-0.83763532	-0.837635	0.837635	-0.00000032	0.00000032	0.000031%
13	1	2	2.21472087	2.214721	2.214721	-0.00000013	0.00000013	0.000013%
14	1	3	-0.71285477	-0.712855	0.712855	0.00000023	0.00000023	0.000023%
15	1	4	-1.18563471	-1.185634	1.185634	-0.00000071	0.00000071	0.000069%
16	1	5	0.27836556	0.278366	0.278366	-0.00000044	0.00000044	0.000043%
17	1	6	1.06742608	1.067426	1.067426	0.00000008	0.00000008	0.000008%
18	1	7	-1.19736842	-1.197368	1.197368	-0.00000042	0.00000042	0.000041%
19	1	8	1.58517276	1.585173	1.585173	-0.00000024	0.00000024	0.000023%
Average					1.0363933		0.0000002470	0.00002383%

c_{kj}^{o}	k=0	k=1	k=2	k=3	k=4	k=5	k=6
j=0	0.7082	-0.5910	-0.7788	-0.6533	-1.3808	-0.6622	1.2421
j=1	0.1200	0.2814	-0.2746	-0.1233	0.1021	0.4677	-0.2658
j=2	0.0874	0.0153	-0.0034	-0.6101	-0.1802	0.0611	-0.3341
j=3	-0.3941	-0.0935	-0.8050	0.0872	0.3306	-0.1748	0.0299
j=4	-0.9193	0.7422	-0.3561	0.0324	-0.0043	0.2020	0.9701
j=5	-0.5921	0.3590	0.6168	0.4320	0.1921	-0.7954	-0.6462
j=6	0.4562	-0.1482	0.7517	-0.8923	-0.3717	-0.4859	0.6441

x=1, y=0.1 $c_{kj}^{o}*(x)^{k}*\sin^{j}(j*y)$	k = 0	k = 1	k = 2	k = 3	k = 4	k = 5	k = 6
j = 0	0.00000000	0.00000000	0.00000000	0.00000000	0.00000000	0.00000000	0.00000000
j = 1	0.01198001	0.02809312	-0.02741426	-0.01230946	0.01019299	0.04669209	-0.02653572
j = 2	0.01736370	0.00303964	-0.00067548	-0.12120816	-0.03580021	0.01213870	-0.06637542
j = 3	-0.11646451	-0.02763114	-0.23789377	0.02576936	0.09769898	-0.05165693	0.00883605
j = 4	-0.35799228	0.28902629	-0.13867187	0.01261715	-0.00167450	0.07866251	0.37777473
j = 5	-0.28386786	0.17211377	0.29570967	0.20711183	0.09209765	-0.38133507	-0.30980478
j = 6	0.25758990	-0.08368001	0.42444175	-0.50383048	-0.20987761	-0.27435978	0.36368622
Subtotal	-0.47139105	0.38096167	0.31549605	-0.39184975	-0.04736270	-0.56985849	0.34758108
$z = \Sigma c_{kj}^{o}*(x)^{k}*\sin^{j}(j*y)$		(k= 0, 1, 2 ,3, 4, 5, 6		j = 0, 1, 2, 3, 4, 5, 6) =			-0.43642320

Table 2. UPC-HONN signal generator (n=6, Model 0)

No.	UPC-HONN x	UPC-HONN y	UPC-HONN z	Desired Signal	Absolute Desired Signal	Difference	Absolute Difference	UPC-HONN Error %
1	1	0	-1.37456000	-1.374560	1.374560	0.00000000	0.00000000	0.000000%
2	1	0.1	-1.65434689	-1.654347	1.654347	0.00000011	0.00000011	0.000006%
3	1	0.2	-2.06259599	-2.062596	2.062596	0.00000001	0.00000001	0.000001%
4	1	0.3	-2.35404267	-2.354043	2.354043	0.00000033	0.00000033	0.000017%
5	1	0.4	-2.31009427	-2.310094	2.310094	-0.00000027	0.00000027	0.000014%
6	1	0.5	-0.92883259	-0.928833	0.928833	0.00000041	0.00000041	0.000021%
7	1	0.6	0.18761830	0.187618	0.187618	0.00000030	0.00000030	0.000016%
8	1	0.7	-1.21630469	-1.216305	1.216305	0.00000031	0.00000031	0.000016%
9	1	0.8	1.27246117	1.272461	1.272461	0.00000017	0.00000017	0.000009%
10	1	0.9	2.08134375	2.081344	2.081344	-0.00000025	0.00000025	0.000013%
11	1	1	2.46216605	2.462166	2.462166	0.00000005	0.00000005	0.000002%
13	1	2	-1.52657837	-1.526578	1.526578	-0.00000037	0.00000037	0.000019%
14	1	3	5.66527952	5.66528	5.665280	-0.00000048	0.00000048	0.000025%
15	1	4	-3.01334336	-3.0133433	3.013343	-0.00000006	0.00000006	0.000003%
16	1	5	3.11207179	3.112072	3.112072	-0.00000021	0.00000021	0.000011%
17	1	6	-2.26932211	-2.269322	2.269322	-0.00000011	0.00000011	0.000006%
18	1	7	0.37953036	0.37953	0.379530	0.00000036	0.00000036	0.000019%
19	1	8	0.32413459	0.324135	0.324135	-0.00000041	0.00000041	0.000022%
Average					1.8997015		0.0000002339	0.00001231%

$c_{kj}{}^{o}$	k=0	k=1	k=2	k=3	k=4	k=5	k=6
j=0	1.4159	-1.6558	-0.3245	-1.0977	0.7113	-0.8844	1.3532
j=1	0.9866	0.8369	-0.9190	-0.4566	0.3243	0.5788	-1.0435
j=2	0.1429	0.4597	-0.3367	-0.8323	-0.2913	0.8388	-1.0007
j=3	-0.8385	-0.1268	-1.0272	0.1983	1.1013	-0.8414	0.1854
j=4	-1.2526	0.9644	-0.4672	0.1435	-0.6709	0.7575	1.4145
j=5	-0.8143	0.4701	0.3945	1.0986	0.7476	-0.6394	-0.9793
j=6	0.5673	-0.3724	1.0850	-0.3367	-0.9272	-0.1525	0.4217

x=1, y=0.1	k =	k =	k =	k =	k =	k =	k =
$c_{kj}{}^{o}*(x)^{k}*cos^{j}(j*y)$	0	1	2	3	4	5	6
j = 0	1.41590000	-1.65576000	-0.32450000	-1.09770000	0.71130000	-0.88440000	1.35320000
j = 1	0.98167111	0.83271899	-0.91440883	-0.45431890	0.03237598	0.57590841	-1.03828685
j = 2	0.14005151	0.45053661	-0.32998842	-0.81570941	-0.05787238	0.82207985	-0.98075262
j = 3	-0.80104965	-0.12113667	-0.98132164	0.18944323	0.32545640	-0.80382012	0.17711939
j = 4	-1.15372100	0.88827122	-0.43031970	0.13217225	-0.26126077	0.69770370	1.30284078
j = 5	-0.71461548	0.41255156	0.34620632	0.96411220	0.35841853	-0.56112629	-0.85941660
j = 6	0.46821289	-0.30735498	0.89548914	-0.27789050	-0.52353650	-0.12586368	0.34804403
Subtotal	0.33644939	0.49982673	-1.73884312	-1.35989114	0.58488127	-0.27951813	0.30274812
$z = \Sigma c_{kj}{}^{o}*(x)^{k}*cos^{j}(j*y)$			(k= 0, 1, 2 ,3, 4, 5, 6		j = 0, 1, 2, 3, 4, 5, 6) =		-1.65434689

Based on the training of UPS-HONN model, UPS-HONN signal generator has the following formula:

$z = \sum c_{kj}{}^{o} * (x)^k * \sin^j(j*y)$ *(k, j = 0,1,2,3,4,5,6,)*

$= c_{00}{}^{o}*(x)^0*\sin^0(0*y) + c_{10}{}^{o}*(x)^1*\sin^0(0*y) + c_{20}{}^{o}*(x)^2*\sin^0(0*y) + c_{30}{}^{o}*(x)^3*\sin^0(0*y)$

$+ c_{40}{}^{o}*(x)^4*\sin^0(0*y) + c_{50}{}^{o}*(x)^5*\sin^0(0*y) + c_{60}{}^{o}*(x)^6*\sin^0(0*y)$

$+ c_{01}{}^{o}*(x)^0*\sin^1(1*y) + c_{11}{}^{o}*(x)^1*\sin^1(1*y) + c_{21}{}^{o}*(x)^2*\sin^1(1*y) + c_{31}{}^{o}*(x)^3*\sin^1(1*y)$

$+ c_{41}{}^{o}*(x)^4*\sin^1(1*y) + c_{51}{}^{o}*(x)^5*\sin^1(1*y) + c_{61}{}^{o}*(x)^6*\sin^1(1*y)$

$+ c_{02}{}^{o}*(x)^0*\sin^2(2*y) + c_{12}{}^{o}*(x)^1*\sin^2(2*y) + c_{22}{}^{o}*(x)^2*\sin^2(2*y) + c_{32}{}^{o}*(x)^3*\sin^2(2*y)$

$+ c_{42}{}^{o}*(x)^4*\sin^2(2*y) + c_{52}{}^{o}*(x)^5*\sin^2(2*y) + c_{62}{}^{o}*(x)^6*\sin^2(2*y)$

$+ c_{03}{}^{o}*(x)^0*\sin^3(3*y) + c_{13}{}^{o}*(x)^1*\sin^3(3*y) + c_{23}{}^{o}*(x)^2*\sin^3(3*y) + c_{33}{}^{o}*(x)^3*\sin^3(3*y)$

$+ c_{43}{}^{o}*(x)^4*\sin^3(3*y) + c_{53}{}^{o}*(x)^5*\sin^3(3*y) + c_{63}{}^{o}*(x)^6*\sin^3(3*y)$

$+ c_{04}{}^{o}*(x)^0*\sin^4(4*y) + c_{14}{}^{o}*(x)^1*\sin^4(4*y) + c_{24}{}^{o}*(x)^2*\sin^4(4*y) + c_{34}{}^{o}*(x)^3*\sin^4(4*y)$

$+ c_{44}{}^{o}*(x)^4*\sin^4(4*y) + c_{54}{}^{o}*(x)^5*\sin^4(4*y) + c_{64}{}^{o}*(x)^6*\sin^4(4*y)$

$+ c_{05}{}^{o}*(x)^0*\sin^5(5*y) + c_{15}{}^{o}*(x)^1*\sin^5(5*y) + c_{25}{}^{o}*(x)^2*\sin^5(4*y) + c_{35}{}^{o}*(x)^3*\sin^5(5*y)$

$+ c_{45}{}^{o}*(x)^4*\sin^5(5*y) + c_{55}{}^{o}*(x)^5*\sin^5(5*y) + c_{65}{}^{o}*(x)^6*\sin^5(5*y)$

$+ c_{06}{}^{o}*(x)^0*\sin^6(6*y) + c_{16}{}^{o}*(x)^1*\sin^6(6*y) + c_{26}{}^{o}*(x)^2*\sin^6(6*y) + c_{36}{}^{o}*(x)^3*\sin^6(6*y)$

$+ c_{46}{}^{o}*(x)^4*\sin^6(6*y) + c_{56}{}^{o}*(x)^5*\sin^6(6*y) + c_{66}{}^{o}*(x)^6*\sin^6(6*y)$

$= 0.7082*(x)^0*\sin^0(0*y) + (-0.5910)*(x)^1*\sin^0(0*y) + (-0.7788)*(x)^2*\sin^0(0*y)$

$+ (-0.6533)*(x)^3*\sin^0(0*y) + (-1.3808)*(x)^4*\sin^0(0*y)$

$+ (-0.6622)*(x)^5*\sin^0(0*y) + 1.2421*(x)^6*\sin^0(0*y)$

$+ 0.1200*(x)^0*\sin^1(1*y) + 0.2814*(x)^1*\sin^1(1*y) + (-0.2746)*(x)^2*\sin^1(1*y)$

$+ (-0.1233)*(x)^3*\sin^1(1*y) + 0.1021*(x)^4*\sin^1(1*y)$

$+ 0.4677*(x)^5*\sin^1(1*y) + (-0.2658)*(x)^6*\sin^1(1*y)$

$+ 0.0874*(x)^0*\sin^2(2*y) + 0.0153*(x)^1*\sin^2(2*y) + (-0.0034)*(x)^2*\sin^2(2*y)$

$+ (-0.6101)*(x)^3*\sin^2(2*y) + (-0.1802)*(x)^4*\sin^2(2*y)$

$+ 0.0611*(x)^{5}*\sin^2(2*y)+ (-0.3341)*(x)^6*\sin^2(2*y)$

$+ (-0.3941)*(x)^0*\sin^3(3*y)+ (-0.0935)*(x)^1*\sin^3(3*y)+ (-0.8050)*(x)^2*\sin^3(3*y)$

$+ 0.0872*(x)^3*\sin^3(3*y) + 0.3306*(x)^4*\sin^3(3*y)$

$+ (-0.1748)*(x)^5*\sin^3(3*y)+ 0.0299*(x)^6*\sin^3(3*y)$

$+(-0.9193)*(x)^0*\sin^4(4*y)+ 0.7422*(x)^1*\sin^4(4*y)+ (-0.3561)*(x)^2*\sin^4(4*y)$

$+ 0.0324*(x)^3*\sin^4(4*y) + (-0.0043)*(x)^4*\sin^4(4*y)$

$+ 0.2020*(x)^5*\sin^4(4*y)+ 0.9701*(x)^6*\sin^4(4*y)$

$+(-0.5921)*(x)^0*\sin^5(5*y)+ 0.3590*(x)^1*\sin^5(5*y)+ 0.6168*(x)^2*\sin^5(4*y)$

$+ 0.4320*(x)^3*\sin^5(5*y) + 0.1921*(x)^4*\sin^5(5*y)$

$+ (-0.7954)*(x)^5*\sin^5(5*y)+ (-0.6462)*(x)^6*\sin^5(5*y)$

$+0.4562*(x)^0*\sin^6(6*y)+ (-0.1482)*(x)^1*\sin^6(6*y)+ 0.7517*(x)^2*\sin^6(6*y)$

$+ (-0.8923)*(x)^3*\sin^6(6*y) + (-0.3717)*(x)^4*\sin^6(6*y)$

$+ (-0.4859)*(x)^5*\sin^6(6*y)+ 0.6441*(x)^6*\sin^6(6*y)$

In Table 2, UPC-HONN model 0 has been used. The order number for UPC-HONN model is 6. In the first table of Table 1, the "No." column shows total 19 points are chosen. The "UPC-HONN x" column displays the input x values, which are all "1" has been used. The "UPC-HONN y" column displays the input y values, which are 0, 0.1, 0.2, 0.3, 0.4, 05, 0.7, 0.8, 0.9, 1, 2, 3, 4, 5, 6, 7 and 8. The "UPC-HONN z" column displays the output z values. The "Desired Signal" column displays the desired signal values. The "Absolute Desired Signal" column displays the absolute values for desired signal. The "Difference" column shows the difference between UPC-HONN output z and the desired signal (UPC-HONN z - Desired Signal). The "Absolute Difference" column shows the absolute difference between UPC-HONN output z and the desired signal (|UPC-HONN z - Desired Signal|). The "UPC-HONN Error %" column gives the error percentage for UPC-HONN Model (UPC-HONN error % = absolute difference / Absolute Desired Signal * 100%). The average UPC-HONN error is 0.00001231%, which is very close to zero. After training UPC-HONN model by using desired signal values, in the second table of Table 2, the UPC-HONN all coefficients are displayed. For examples, $c_{00}{}^o= 1.4159$, $c_{01}{}^o= 0.9866$, and $c_{10}{}^o= -1.6558$. In the third table of Table 2, gives the values for $c_{kj}{}^o*(x)^k*\cos^j(j*y)$, when $x=1, y=0.1, k=0,1,2,3,4,5,6$, and $j=0,1,2,3,4,5,6$. For examples, $c_{01}{}^o*(1)^0*\cos^1(1*0.1)=0.98167111$, $c_{02}{}^o*(1)^0*\cos^2(2*0.1)=0.14005151$, and $c_{03}{}^o*(1)^0*\cos^3(3*0.1)=-0.80104965$. And $z=\sum c_{kj}{}^o*(x)^k*\cos^j(j*y)=\sum c_{kj}{}^o*(1)^k*\cos^j(j*0.1)=-1.65434689$.

In Figure 4, UPC-HONN signal generator results are shown. Designed signals are shown by solid line. And UPC-HONN generated signals are shown by using dashed line. Figure 4 presents the results that UPC-HONN signal generator can match the desired signals well, since the average error percentage is close to 0.0000%.

Based on the training of UPC-HONN model, UPC-HONN signal generator has the following formula:

$$z = \sum c_{kj}{}^{o} * (x)^k * \cos^j(j*y) \ (k, j = 0,1,2,3,4,5,6,)$$

$$= c_{00}{}^{o} * (x)^0 * \cos^0(0*y) + c_{10}{}^{o} * (x)^1 * \cos^0(0*y) + c_{20}{}^{o} * (x)^2 * \cos^0(0*y) + c_{30}{}^{o} * (x)^3 * \cos^0(0*y)$$

$$+ c_{40}{}^{o} * (x)^4 * \cos^0(0*y) + c_{50}{}^{o} * (x)^5 * \cos^0(0*y) + c_{60}{}^{o} * (x)^6 * \cos^0(0*y)$$

$$+ c_{01}{}^{o} * (x)^0 * \cos^1(1*y) + c_{11}{}^{o} * (x)^1 * \cos^1(1*y) + c_{21}{}^{o} * (x)^2 * \cos^1(1*y) + c_{31}{}^{o} * (x)^3 * \cos^1(1*y)$$

$$+ c_{41}{}^{o} * (x)^4 * \cos^1(1*y) + c_{51}{}^{o} * (x)^5 * \cos^1(1*y) + c_{61}{}^{o} * (x)^6 * \cos^1(1*y)$$

$$+ c_{02}{}^{o} * (x)^0 * \cos^2(2*y) + c_{12}{}^{o} * (x)^1 * \cos^2(2*y) + c_{22}{}^{o} * (x)^2 * \cos^2(2*y) + c_{32}{}^{o} * (x)^3 * \cos^2(2*y)$$

$$+ c_{42}{}^{o} * (x)^4 * \cos^2(2*y) + c_{52}{}^{o} * (x)^5 * \cos^2(2*y) + c_{62}{}^{o} * (x)^6 * \cos^2(2*y)$$

$$+ c_{03}{}^{o} * (x)^0 * \cos^3(3*y) + c_{13}{}^{o} * (x)^1 * \cos^3(3*y) + c_{23}{}^{o} * (x)^2 * \cos^3(3*y) + c_{33}{}^{o} * (x)^3 * \cos^3(3*y)$$

$$+ c_{43}{}^{o} * (x)^4 * \cos^3(3*y) + c_{53}{}^{o} * (x)^5 * \cos^3(3*y) + c_{63}{}^{o} * (x)^6 * \cos^3(3*y)$$

$$+ c_{04}{}^{o} * (x)^0 * \cos^4(4*y) + c_{14}{}^{o} * (x)^1 * \cos^4(4*y) + c_{24}{}^{o} * (x)^2 * \cos^4(4*y) + c_{34}{}^{o} * (x)^3 * \cos^4(4*y)$$

$$+ c_{44}{}^{o} * (x)^4 * \cos^4(4*y) + c_{54}{}^{o} * (x)^5 * \cos^4(4*y) + c_{64}{}^{o} * (x)^6 * \cos^4(4*y)$$

$$+ c_{05}{}^{o} * (x)^0 * \cos^5(5*y) + c_{15}{}^{o} * (x)^1 * \cos^5(5*y) + c_{25}{}^{o} * (x)^2 * \cos^5(4*y) + c_{35}{}^{o} * (x)^3 * \cos^5(5*y)$$

$$+ c_{45}{}^{o} * (x)^4 * \cos^5(5*y) + c_{55}{}^{o} * (x)^5 * \cos^5(5*y) + c_{65}{}^{o} * (x)^6 * \cos^5(5*y)$$

$$+ c_{06}{}^{o} * (x)^0 * \cos^6(6*y) + c_{16}{}^{o} * (x)^1 * \cos^6(6*y) + c_{26}{}^{o} * (x)^2 * \cos^6(6*y) + c_{36}{}^{o} * (x)^3 * \cos^6(6*y)$$

$$+ c_{46}{}^{o} * (x)^4 * \cos^6(6*y) + c_{56}{}^{o} * (x)^5 * \cos^6(6*y) + c_{66}{}^{o} * (x)^6 * \cos^6(6*y)$$

$$= 1.4159 * (x)^0 * \cos^0(0*y) + (-1.6558) * (x)^1 * \cos^0(0*y) + (-0.3245) * (x)^2 * \cos^0(0*y)$$

$$+ (-1.0977) * (x)^3 * \cos^0(0*y) + 0.7113 * (x)^4 * \cos^0(0*y)$$

$$+ (-0.8844) * (x)^5 * \cos^0(0*y) + 1.3532 * (x)^6 * \cos^0(0*y)$$

$$+ 0.9866 * (x)^0 * \cos^1(1*y) + 0.8369 * (x)^1 * \cos^1(1*y) + (-0.9190) * (x)^2 * \cos^1(1*y)$$

$$+ (-0.4566) * (x)^3 * \cos^1(1*y) + 0.3243 * (x)^4 * \cos^1(1*y)$$

$+ 0.5788*(x)^5*\cos^1(1*y)+ (-1.0435)*(x)^6*\cos^1(1*y)$

$+0.1429*(x)^0*\cos^2(2*y)+ 0.4597*(x)^1*\cos^2(2*y)+ (-0.3367)*(x)^2*\cos^2(2*y)$

$+ (-0.8323)*(x)^3*\cos^2(2*y) + (-0.2913)*(x)^4*\cos^2(2*y)$

$+ 8388*(x)^5*\cos^2(2*y)+ (-1.0007)*(x)^6*\cos^2(2*y)$

$+ (-0.8385)*(x)^0*\cos^3(3*y)+ (-0.1268)*(x)^1*\cos^3(3*y)+ (-1.0272)*(x)^2*\cos^3(3*y)$

$+ 0.1983*(x)^3*\cos^3(3*y) + 1.1013*(x)^4*\cos^3(3*y)$

$+ (-0.8414)*(x)^5*\cos^3(3*y)+ 0.1854*(x)^6*\cos^3(3*y)$

$+(-1.2526)*(x)^0*\cos^4(4*y)+ 0.9644*(x)^1*\cos^4(4*y)+ (-0.4672)*(x)^2*\cos^4(4*y)$

$+ 0.1435*(x)^3*\cos^4(4*y) + (-0.6709)*(x)^4*\cos^4(4*y)$

$+ 0.7575*(x)^5*\cos^4(4*y)+ 1.4145*(x)^6*\cos^4(4*y)$

$+(-0.8143)*(x)^0*\cos^5(5*y)+ 0.4701*(x)^1*\cos^5(5*y)+ 0.3945*(x)^2*\cos^5(4*y)$

$+ 1.0986*(x)^3*\cos^5(5*y) + 0.7476*(x)^4*\cos^5(5*y)$

$+ (-0.6394)*(x)^5*\cos^5(5*y)+ (-0.9793)*(x)^6*\cos^5(5*y)$

$+0.5673*(x)^0*\cos^6(6*y)+ (-0.3724)*(x)^1*\cos^6(6*y)+ 1.0850*(x)^2*\cos^6(6*y)$

$+ (-0.3367)*(x)^3*\cos^6(6*y) + (-0.9272)*(x)^4*\cos^6(6*y)$

$+ (-0.1525)*(x)^5*\cos^6(6*y)+ 0.4217*(x)^6*\cos^6(6*y)$

FUTHER RESEARCH DIRECTIONS

As the next step of HONN model research, more HONN models for different data control will be built to increase the pool of HONN models. Theoretically, the adaptive HONN models can be built and allow the computer automatically choose the best model, order, and coefficients. Thus, making the adaptive HONN models easier to use is one of the future research topics.

HONNs can automatically select the initial coefficients for nonlinear data analysis. The next step of this study will also focus on how to allow people working in the control area to understand that HONNs are much easier to use and can have better results. Moreover, further research will develop HONNs software packages for people working in the control area. HONNs will challenge classic procedures and change the research methodology that people are currently using in the control areas for the nonlinear data control application.

Figure 5. UPS-HONN signal generator

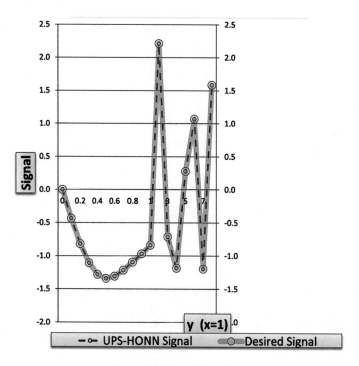

Figure 6. UPC-HONN signal generator

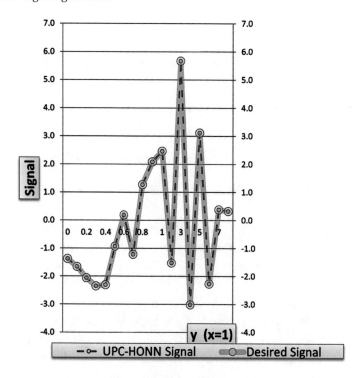

CONCLUSION

Two nonlinear neural network models, UPS-HONN and UPC-HONN, that are part of the Ultra High Frequency Polynomial and Trigonometric Higher Order Neural Networks (UPT-HONN), are developed. Based on the structures of UPT-HONN, this chapter provides two model learning algorithm formulae. This chapter tests the UPS-HONN model using ultra high frequency signals. Experimental results show that UPT-HONN models can generate any nonlinear signals with average error of 0.0000%.

One of the topics for future research is to continue building models using UPT-HONN for different data series. The coefficients of the higher order models will be studied not only using artificial neural network techniques, but also statistical methods. Using nonlinear functions to model and analyze time series data will be a major goal in the future.

REFERENCES

Alanis, A. Y., Sanchez, E. N., & Loukianov, A. G. (2006). Discrete- Time Recurrent Neural Induction Motor Control using Kalman Learning. *Proceedings of International Joint Conference on Neural Networks*, Vancouver, Canada (pp. 1993 – 2000). doi:10.1109/IJCNN.2006.246946

Alanis, A. Y., Sanchez, E. N., Loukianov, A. G., & Perez-Cisneros, M. A. (2010). Real-Time Discrete Neural Block Control Using Sliding Modes for Electric Induction Motors. *IEEE Transactions on Control Systems Technology*, *18*(1), 11–21. doi:10.1109/TCST.2008.2009466

Arai, M., Kohon, R., & Imai, H. (1991). Adaptive control of a neural network with a variable function of a unit and its application. *Transactions of the Institute of Electronics, Information and Communication Engineers, J74-A*, 551–559.

Baruch, I. S., Galvan-Guerra, R., & Nenkova, B. (2008). Centralized Indirect Control of an Anaerobic Digestion Bioprocess Using Recurrent Neural Identifier. Artificial Intelligence: Methodology, sytems and applications, *LNCS* (Vol. *5253*, pp. 297–310). doi:10.1007/978-3-540-85776-1_25

Boutalis, Y. S., Theodoridis, D. C., & Christodoulou, M. A. (2009). A new Neuro FDS definition for indirect adaptive control of unknown nonlinear systems using a method of parameter hopping. *IEEE Transactions on Neural Networks*, *20*(4), 609–625. doi:10.1109/TNN.2008.2010772 PMID:19273046

Bukovsky, I., Bila, J., & Gupta, M. M. (2005). Linear Dynamic Neural Units with Time Delay for Identification and Control (in Czech). *Automatizace*, 48(10), 628-635.

Butt, N. R., & Shafiq, M. (2006). Higher-Order Neural Network Based Root-Solving Controller for Adaptive Tracking of Stable Nonlinear Plants. *Proceedings of IEEE International Conference on Engineering of Intelligent Systems,* Islamabad, Pakistan (pp. 1–6). doi:10.1109/ICEIS.2006.1703175

Campolucci, P., Capparelli, F., Guarnieri, S., Piazza, F., & Uncini, A. (1996). Neural networks with adaptive spline activation function. *Proceedings of IEEE MELECON '96,* Bari, Italy (pp. 1442-1445). doi:10.1109/MELCON.1996.551220

Campos, J., Loukianov, A. G., & Sanchez, E. N. (2003). Synchronous motor VSS control using recurrent high order neural networks. *Proceedings of 42nd IEEE Conference on Decision and Control*, Maui, Hawaii, USA (Vol. 4, pp. 3894–3899). doi:10.1109/CDC.2003.1271757

Chen, F. C., & Khalil, H. K. (1992). Adaptive control of nonlinear systems using neural networks. *International Journal of Control*, 55(6), 1299–1317. doi:10.1080/00207179208934286

Chen, G., & Lewis, F. L. (2013). Cooperative Control of Unknown Networked Lagrange Systems Using Higher Order Neural Networks. In M. Zhang (Ed.), Artificial Higher Order Neural Networks for Modeling and Simulation (pp. 214-236). Hershey, PA, USA: IGI Global.

Chen, L., & Narendra, K. S. (2002, June). Nonlinear Adaptive Control Using Neural Networks and Multiple Models. *Proceedings of the 2000 American Control Conference*, Chicago, Illinois (pp. 4199-4203).

Das, A., & Lewis, F. (2013). Distributed Adaptive Control for Multi-Agent Systems with Pseudo Higher Order Neural Net. In M. Zhang (Ed.), Artificial Higher Order Neural Networks for Modeling and Simulation (pp. 194-213). Hershey, PA, USA: IGI Global.

Das, A., Lewis, F. L., & Subbarao, K. (2010). Back-Stepping Control of Quadrotor: A Dynamically Tuned Higher Order Like Neural Network Approach. In M. Zhang (Ed.), Artificial Higher Order Neural Networks for Computer Science and Engineering – Trends for Emerging Applications (pp. 484-513). Hershey, PA, USA: IGI Global.

Diao, Y., & Passino, K. M. (2002). Adaptive Neural/Fuzzy Control for Interpolated Nonlinear Systems. *IEEE Transactions on Fuzzy Systems*, 10(5), 583–595. doi:10.1109/TFUZZ.2002.803493

Farrell, J. A., & Polycarpou, M. M. (2006). *Adaptive approximation Based Control: Unifying Neural, Fuzzy and Traditional Adaptive Approximation Approaches*. N. Y., USA: John Wiley and Sons. doi:10.1002/0471781819

Ge, S. S., Zhang, J., & Lee, T. H. (2004). Adaptive neural network control for a class of MIMO nonlinear systems with disturbances in discrete-time. *IEEE Transactions on Systems, Man, and Cybernetics*, 34, 1630-1634. PMID:15462431

Holubar, P., Zani, L., Hager, M., Froschl, W., Radak, Z., & Braun, R. (2002). Advanced controlling of anaerobic digestion by means of hierarchical neural networks. *Water Research*, 36(10), 2582–2588. doi:10.1016/S0043-1354(01)00487-0 PMID:12153025

Hou, Z. G., Cheng, L., & Tan, M. (2009). Decentralized robust adaptive control for the multiagent system consensus problem using neural networks. *IEEE Transactions on Systems, Man, and Cybernetics. Part B, Cybernetics*, 39(3), 636–647. doi:10.1109/TSMCB.2008.2007810 PMID:19174350

Hu, Z., & Shao, H. (1992). The study of neural network adaptive control systems. *Control and Decision*, 7, 361–366.

Karnavas, Y. L. (2010). Electrical Machines Excitation Control via Higher Order Neural Networks, In M. Zhang (Ed.), Artificial Higher Order Neural Networks for Computer Science and Engineering – Trends for Emerging Applications (pp. 366-396). Hershey, PA, USA: IGI Global.

Kumar, N., Panwar, V., Sukavanam, N., Sharma, S. P., & Borm, J. H. (2011). Neural Network-Based Nonlinear Tracking Control of Kinematically Redundant Robot Manipulators. *Mathematical and Computer Modelling*, *53*(9), 1889–1901. doi:10.1016/j.mcm.2011.01.014

Lee, M., Lee, S. Y., & Park, C. H. (1992). Neural controller of nonlinear dynamic systems using higher order neural networks. *Electronics Letters*, *28*(3), 276–277. doi:10.1049/el:19920170

Leu, Y.-G., Wang, W.-Y., & Lee, T.-T. (2005). Observer-based direct adaptive fuzzy-neural control for nonaffine nonlinear systems. *IEEE Transactions on Neural Networks*, *16*(4), 853–861. doi:10.1109/TNN.2005.849824 PMID:16121727

Lewis, F. L., Jagannathan, S., & Yesildirek, A. (1998). *Neural Network Control of Robot Manipulators and Non-Linear Systems*. New York: Taylor & Francis.

Lewis, F. L., Yesildirek, A., & Liu, K. (1996). Multilayer neural-net robot controller with guaranteed tracking performance. *IEEE Transactions on Neural Networks*, *7*(2), 388–399. doi:10.1109/72.485674 PMID:18255592

Li, X., Chen, Z. Q., & Yuan, Z. Z. (2002). Simple Recurrent Neural Network-Based Adaptive Predictive Control for Nonlinear Systems. *Asian Journal of Control*, *4*(2), 31–239.

Narendra, K. S., & Parthasarathy, K. (1990). Identification and Control of Dynamical Systems Using Neural Networks. *IEEE Transactions on Neural Networks*, *1*(1), 4–27. doi:10.1109/72.80202 PMID:18282820

Narendra, S., & Parthasarathy, K. (1990). Identification and control of dynamical systems using neural networks. *IEEE Transactions on Neural Networks*, *1*(1), 4–27. doi:10.1109/72.80202 PMID:18282820

Norgaard, M., Ravn, O., Poulsen, N. K., & Hansen, L. K. (2000). *Neural Networks for Modelling and Control of Dynamic Systems: A practitioner's Handbook*. London, Great Britain: Springer-Verlag. doi:10.1007/978-1-4471-0453-7

Pedro, J., & Dahunsi, O. (2011). Neural Network Based Feedback Linearization Control of a Servo-Hydraulic Vehicle Suspension System. *International Journal of Applied Mathematics and Computer Science*, *21*(1), 137–147. doi:10.2478/v10006-011-0010-5

Plett, G. L. (2003). Adaptive Inverse Control of Linear and Nonlinear Systems Using Dynamic Neural Networks. *IEEE Transactions on Neural Networks*, *14*(2), 360–376. doi:10.1109/TNN.2003.809412 PMID:18238019

Polycarpou, M. M. (1996). Stable adaptive neural control scheme for nonlinear systems. *IEEE Transactions on Automatic Control*, *41*(3), 447–451. doi:10.1109/9.486648

Poznyak, A. S., Sanchez, E. N., & Yu, W. (2000). *Differential Neural Networks for Robust Nonlinear Control*. USA: World Scientific.

Rovithakis, G., Gaganis, V., Perrakis, S., & Christodoulou, M. (1996). A recurrent neural network model to describe manufacturing cell dynamics. *Proceedings of the 35th IEEE Conference on Decision and Control*, Kobe, Japan (Vol. 2, pp.1728 – 1733). doi:10.1109/CDC.1996.572808

Rovithakis, G. A., & Chistodoulou, M. A. (2000). *Adaptive Control with Recurrent High -Order Neural Networks*. Berlin, Germany: Springer Verlag. doi:10.1007/978-1-4471-0785-9

Rovithakis, G. A., Kosmatopoulos, E. B., & Christodoulou, M. A. (1993). Robust adaptive control of unknown plants using recurrent high order neural networks-application to mechanical systems. In *Proceedings of International Conference on Systems, Man and Cybernetics,* Le Touquet, France (Vol. 4, pp. 57 – 62). doi:10.1109/ICSMC.1993.390683

Sanchez, E. N., Alanis, A. Y., & Loukianov, A. G. (2008). *Discrete Time High Order Neural Control Trained with Kalman Filtering*. Germany: Springer-Verlag. doi:10.1007/978-3-540-78289-6

Shannon, C. E. (1998, February). Communication in the presence of noise. *Proceedings of the IEEE, 86*(2).

Shi, K. L., & Li, H. (2004). A Novel Control of a Small Wind Turbine Driven Generator Based on Neural Networks. *IEEE Power Engineering Society General Meeting, 2,* 1999-2005.

Theodoridis, D. C., Boutalis, Y. S., & Christodoulou, M. A. (2009, August 23 – 26). A new Neuro-Fuzzy Dynamical System Definition Based on High Order Neural Network Function Approximators. *Proceedings of the European Control Conference ECC-09,* Budapest, Hungary (pp. 3305-3310).

Theodoridis, D. C., Christodoulou, M. A., & Boutalis, Y. S. (2010). Neuro-Fuzzy Control Schemes Based on High Order Neural Network Function Approximators. In M. Zhang (Ed.), Artificial Higher Order Neural Networks for Computer Science and Engineering – Trends for Emerging Applications (pp. 450-383). Hershey, PA, USA: IGI Global.

Weidong, X., Yubing, L., & Xingpei, L. (2010). Short-Term Forecasting of Wind Turbine Power Generation Based on Genetic Neural Network. *Proceedings of Eighth World Congress on Intelligent Control and Automation,* Jinan, China (pp. 5943-5946).

Yamada, T., & Yabuta, T. (1992). Remarks on a neural network controller which uses an auto-tuning method for nonlinear functions. *IJCNN, 2,* 775–780.

Yu, W. (2010). Robust Adaptive Control Using Higher Order Neural Networks and Projection. In M. Zhang (Ed.), Artificial Higher Order Neural Networks for Computer Science and Engineering – Trends for Emerging Applications (pp. 99-137). Hershey, PA, USA: IGI Global.

Chapter 2
HONU and Supervised Learning Algorithms in Adaptive Feedback Control

Peter Mark Benes
Czech Technical University in Prague, Czech Republic

Martin Vesely
Czech Technical University in Prague, Czech Republic

Miroslav Erben
Czech Technical University in Prague, Czech Republic

Ondrej Liska
Technical University of Kosice, Slovakia

Ivo Bukovsky
Czech Technical University in Prague, Czech Republic

ABSTRACT

This chapter is a summarizing study of Higher Order Neural Units featuring the most common learning algorithms for identification and adaptive control of most typical representatives of plants of single-input single-output (SISO) nature in the control engineering field. In particular, the linear neural unit (LNU, i.e., 1st order HONU), quadratic neural unit (QNU, i.e. 2nd order HONU), and cubic neural unit (CNU, i.e. 3rd order HONU) will be shown as adaptive feedback controllers of typical models of linear plants in control including identification and control of plants with input time delays. The investigated and compared learning algorithms for HONU will be the step-by-step Gradient Descent adaptation with the study of known modifications of learning rate for improved convergence, the batch Levenberg-Marquardt algorithm, and the Resilient Back-Propagation algorithm. The theoretical achievements will be summarized and discussed as regards their usability and the real issues of control engineering tasks.

INTRODUCTION

Due to the ever-growing complexity of our technological society, adaptive control has become a rapidly growing area of study in the field of modern engineering and computational science. Stretching back through the last several decades, the industry has proven that further optimisation and increased efficiency has grown to not only become a desirable feature, but a necessity to keep up with factors associated with increase in production rates, technological changes and further demands for increase in flexibility. The

DOI: 10.4018/978-1-5225-0063-6.ch002

works from Alexandrov and Palenov (2014) highlight the trend in our modern industry for application of adaptively tuned Proportional-Integral-Derivative (PID) controllers as many processes indeed feature certain non-stationary parameters which can tend to drift in association with time. In this day various PID controllers manufactured within the industry incorporate a form of adaptive control, namely, the ABB-COMMANDER 351, Honeywell – UDC series and Foxboro – 700 series controllers. Their employed algorithms are classified under two key terms. Direct methods, are those where the controller parameters are immediately updated via a law that is in dependence of the controlled systems state, namely logical or rule-based, or further fuzzy logic based methods for updating the PID controller parameters. The latter, being an indirect approach where the engineering system or plant is parameterised with respect to a vector of unknown parameters, solved by on-line identification. The ultimate goal across both approaches is to retune the controller coefficients in order to preserve the desired controller objective or desired behaviour, even when certain non-stationary phenomena may be incorporated in a form of new or novel dynamics within an engineering system. In our day a leading trend in adaptive PID algorithms can be found in frequency adaptive control, here two approaches may be employed. The first features a sent single harmonic input test signal through the process. With application of a Fourier filter, the process dynamics may be singled out. The second approach, features two harmonic test signals, with the ultimate goal being an estimation of the model parameters, which may be further used for computation of the new PID controller coefficients.

Since as early as the 1960s, adaptive control has taken big leaps not only in the sense of adaptive tuning methods for conventional forms of industrial controllers, but also the conception of entirely different architectures of adaptive control methods. The motivation for such complex and advanced methods due largely to the necessity for control of processes featuring non-linear dynamics and furthermore non-linear uncertainties at their inputs. Pioneered by H. P. Whitaker and P. V. Osborn from the Massachusetts Institute of Technology, USA. Model Reference Adaptive Control (MRAC) particularly has featured an ever-growing increase in regards to its areas of application within the engineering field, with extensive studies focussing on not only theoretical but also practical application of newly proposed methods for controller parameter adjustment. In this current time, more emphasis in research has been pushed towards utilising soft computing techniques as such that of fuzzy and neural network based methods of MRAC adaptive control, however research in MRAC design with variable structures and advanced controller adjustment technique, whether they be directly or indirectly applied to the process are readily being extended to this field. With the design of model reference based adaptive control (MRAC) techniques, stability is key in ensuring convergence of the prescribed adaptive parameters as well as the process output value to its desirable set point. Several key works necessary to mention are from Patino and Liu (2000) and Wu, Wu, Luo, Zhu, and Guan (2012), these works encompass MRAC controller design via Lyapunov function based criteria as part of their respective adaptive control laws as a means of ensuring stability of convergence of the applied adaptive parameters. However, one drawback that can lead from such methods is the amount of adaptive parameters necessary to employ the control algorithm, which can increase the complexity and overall computational demand of such form for real time implementation.

In terms of alternative soft computing methods, advantages may be drawn in fuzzy logic based MRAC controller design. An advantage of using fuzzy based methods are the conversion of the control parameters from a more quantitatively based approach into that of a more qualitatively based approach. The reader may refer to the work of Lee, Hyun, Kim, and Park (2006) where a Takagi-Sugeno (T-S) fuzzy model is employed to represent the process dynamics for MRAC control of a discrete-time chaotic system. The adaptive control law itself backboned on a gradient descent based algorithm to adaptively tune the respective controller gains such to stabilise the employed error criterion. With regards to more practical engineering applications in Yang, Zhou, and Ren (2003) a fuzzy based form of adaptive control is used for control of a ship steering system. Here a Mamdani type fuzzy logic based system is used to approximate unknown non-linearities associated with the dynamics of the ship steering mechanism. In this method only one adaptive parameter is incorporated, its adaptation of which is achieved via a Lyapunov function based rule. A further example may also be drawn in (Kumar, Subba Rao, & Babu, 2008), where adaptive control of a DC motor is presented. Here a Model Reference Fuzzy Adaptive Controller (MRFAC) highlights its optimisation performance in reduction of steady state error in comparison to a conventionally derived form of MRAC controller.

Apart from fuzzy control based forms of MRAC control, a further discipline of MRAC control which has received particularly rapid growth in theoretical studies as well as positive applications in the engineering field is the use of polynomial function based neural networks (PNN) and Higher-Order-Neural-Networks (HONNs) furthermore Higher-Order-Neural-Units (HONUs) as fundamental non-linear feedback controllers. Some early works the reader may refer to regarding polynomial function based neural networks and higher-order-neural-networks may be found in the works of Ivakhnenko (1971), Softky and Kammen (1991) and Taylor and Coombes (1993). Furthermore, several more recent publications devoted to PNN concepts are that of the works by N.Y. Nikolaev and Iba (2003, 2007) while more recent works framed within the scope of HONNs can be found in Zhang (2008). The essence of this chapter is focussed on providing the reader with an introductory overview for the use of HONUs as a form of MRAC feedback control for the most typical engineering plants, i.e. from the first order of dynamics to third order plants including delayed systems. For readers interested primarily in control rather than in HONU, this chapter provides an overview of one alternative approach for linear and non-linear feedback controller tuning featuring the most popular learning algorithms in the neural networks field. The advantage of standalone HONUs is clear customizable non-linearity of input-output mapping via its polynomial order while these neural architectures being linear in parameters, and furthermore, every neural weight is unique in its function within HONU structure, contrary to layered networks. The conception of HONU as standalone neural units was predominantly introduced in Bukovsky, Hou, Bila, and Gupta (2007), Bukovsky et al., (2007) and M. Solo (2012). Some of the first works on HONU as standalone neural controllers appeared in publications from Song, Redlapalli, and Gupta (2003). In these works a comparison was drawn between the uses of conventional neural networks as such that of MLP architecture and the use of HONUs. A drawback that may be ascertained from using MLP architectures as a means of system modelling or extension to control is their necessity to use rather complex training algorithms in lieu with longer training runs to achieve adequate convergence to a minimal square error. In contrast to this, the approximation strength of such conventional neural networks may be improved by adding more neurons or even additional layers, which can provide better approximation for non-linear systems. However, as can be seen in the work (Bukovsky, Redlapalli, & Gupta, 2003), for efficient real time learning algorithms as such that of the gradient descent algorithm (GD) (Williams & Zipser, 1989) and the Levenberg-Marquardt (L-M) (Werbos, 1990) batch training algorithm, HONUs are computationally faster in achieving adequate convergence in square error whilst achieving desirable control performance for both non-linear unknown systems as well as linear systems of SISO structure. Some more recent applications of HONUs for real-time adaptive control may be found in the works Benes and Bukovsky (2014) and Bukovsky, Benes, and Slama (2015) where HONUs were applied in extension to the previously employed conventional control loops for successful optimisation on various SISO engineering processes.

In this chapter, the proposed derivations are accompanied by simulation examples with comparison of performance of three fundamental learning algorithms. Also, some real control examples are shown to provide an evidence of the real usability of the approach. In this work, the order of a plant usually relates to the order of dynamics, while the order of HONU relates to the polynomial order of mapping non-linearity of HONU. In all presented simulations, constant sampling is considered. The presence of capital letters denote matrices, small bold letters stand for vectors and small italic ones denotes scalars. The meaning of the most frequent notation and symbols is given in the nomenclature with the remaining being evident at first appearance.

HIGHER ORDER NEURAL UNITS

The general form of a HONU as a model of a SISO dynamical system is given as

$$\tilde{y} = f_r(\mathbf{W}, \mathbf{x})$$

where $\tilde{y}$ is the neural output, $\mathbf{W}$ is r-dimensional array of neural weights and $\mathbf{x}$ being defined in terms of a vector of recent n_y samples of the controlled variable $\mathbf{y}$, and $\mathbf{u}$ being the vector of recent n_u samples of the control input u, as follows

$$\mathbf{x} = \begin{bmatrix} x_o = 1 \\ x_1 \\ : \\ x_{n_x} \end{bmatrix} = \begin{bmatrix} 1 \\ y \\ u \end{bmatrix}$$

Here $x_o = 1$ is an augmenting unit that allows HONU for neural bias, i..e for the weight ; also $x_o = 1$ allows lower-order HONUs be subsets of higher-order HONUs. Thus, the length of vector $\mathbf{x}$ in is defined as

$$n_x = 1 + n_y + n_u$$

The mapping function in is the r-th order multivariate polynomial; thus, HONUs of a general r^{th} polynomial order can be expressed and implemented either in the classical notation or in a more efficient form for its computation and mathematical derivations. The classical notation of HONUs is the summation of multiplication terms that is for the example of QNU, i.e. HONU for $r=2$, as follows

$$\tilde{y} = \sum_{i=0}^{n_x} \sum_{j=i}^{n_x} \mathbf{W}_{i,j} . x_i . x_j ,$$

and for CNU, i.e. HONU for $=3$, it is extended as follows

$$\tilde{y} = \sum_{i=0}^{n_x} \sum_{j=i}^{n_x} \sum_{k=j}^{n_x} \mathrm{W}_{i,j,k}.x_i.x_j.x_k,$$

Because neural weights are in $\mathbf{W}$ that is a multidimensional array in or, it is more practical to express HONUs of general order r in a long-vector multiplication form, as used e.g. in (Bukovsky et al., 2007), as follows

$$\tilde{y} = f_r(\mathbf{W}.\mathbf{x}) = \mathbf{w}.\mathbf{colx},$$

where all neural weights are now in $\mathbf{w}$ that is the long-vector, i.e. flattened representation of the otherwise multidimensional array $\mathbf{W}$, and the augmented input vector of neural inputs $\mathbf{x}$ yields a long-column vector form $\mathbf{colx}$ that is for the example of a QNU as follows

$$r = 2 \Rightarrow \mathbf{colx} = [x_i.x_j]; i = 0..n_x, j = i..n_x, x_o = 1$$

and for the example of CNU as follows

$$r = 3 \Rightarrow \mathbf{colx} = [x_i.x_j.x_k]; i = 0..n_x, j = i...n_x, k = j...n_x, x_o = 1$$

Notice that the introduced long-vector form of HONUs, as shown for clarity for QNU and CNU via - demonstrates the inner-parameter linearity of HONU that is important feature of HONU in comparison to other types of neural networks. Furthermore, the form allows HONUs for general form of learning rules (GD, L-M, Rprop) for plant identification as indicated in Table 1 and for adjusting polynomial order of controllers as indicated later in the processing section.

Table 1shows details of three fundamental supervised learning algorithms, where $\mathbf{J}$ is Jacobian matrix, $\mathbf{I}$ is the identity matrix. ε is the training epoch index, and e denotes neural error that is here defined as

$$e(k) = y(k) - \tilde{y}(k)$$

The weight update system is generally a recurrent dynamical system as follows

$$\mathbf{w} \leftarrow \mathbf{w} + \Delta\mathbf{w}; \Delta\mathbf{w} = \Delta\mathbf{w}(\mathbf{w}).$$

First, in practice it is helpful to improve the convergence (i.e. the stability) of by normalizing (or standardizing) the data, e.g. by Z-scoring, to lower magnitudes around the origin, where a stable region can be more likely expected (rather than when data are larger and thus performs far from the origin where the instability region is more likely to be expected).

Second, another known improvement for the stability of the weight update system that has been found by the authors for practical applications is the normalization of the learning rate for GD learning. Being inspired by the learning rate normalization in linear adaptive filters (Widrow & Stearns, 1985), (Mandic

Table 1. Details of fundamental learning algorithms of HONU (for plant identification)

Weight Updates of HONU			Order of HONU
			$r=1$ (LNU), $r=2$ (QNU), $r=3$ (CNU),... (higher orders)
Learning	Sample-by-Sample Adaptation	Gradient Descent (GD)	$$\Delta\mathbf{w} = \mu.e(k).\mathbf{colx}^T$$
	Batch Training	Levenberg-Marquardt (L-M)	$$\Delta\mathrm{w} = (J^T.J + \frac{1}{\mu}.I)^{-1}.J^T.e$$ $$J(k,:) = \mathbf{colx}^T$$
		Resilient BP (Rprop)	$$\Delta\mathbf{w}(\varepsilon) = \begin{cases} -\Delta(\varepsilon) & if \quad \nabla E(\varepsilon) > 0 \\ +\Delta(\varepsilon) & if \quad \nabla E(\varepsilon) < 0 \\ 0 & if \quad \nabla E(\varepsilon) = 0 \end{cases}$$ $$\Delta\mathbf{w}(\varepsilon) = \begin{cases} \eta^+.\Delta(\varepsilon-1) & if \quad \nabla E(\varepsilon-1).\nabla E(\varepsilon) > 0 \\ \eta^-.\Delta(\varepsilon-1) & if \quad \nabla E(\varepsilon-1).\nabla E(\varepsilon) < 0 \\ \Delta(\varepsilon-1) & if \quad \nabla E(\varepsilon-1).\nabla E(\varepsilon) = 0 \end{cases}$$ $$\nabla E = -\sum_k e(k)\mathbf{colx}(k,:)$$

& Goh, 2009) and based on the authors experience with modifications of GD learning rate for HONU (Bukovsky et al., 2015) & (Bukovsky, Oswald, Cejnek, & Benes, 2014), it can be recommend that the learning rate normalization with squared Euclidean norm is given as follows

$$\mu \leftarrow \frac{\mu}{\|\mathbf{colx}\|^2}$$

where x_o in **colx** functions as the regularization term in the denominator (to avoid zero division).

With regards to batch learning, the ARPROP (Advanced RProp) algorithm (Aristoklis D Anastasiadis, 2003) handles evolution of square error criteria as follows

$$\Delta\mathrm{w}(\varepsilon+1) = \mathrm{w}(\varepsilon) - \frac{1}{2^q}.\Delta\mathrm{w}(\varepsilon-1) \; if \; E(\varepsilon) > E(\varepsilon-1),$$

where q is a midpoint-reduction factor applied when learning starts diverging. The authors have found the principle in also in practice it is useful for HONUs when trained with the Levenberg-Marquardt as well; thus, the authors kindly encourage readers to implement for batch training of HONU with L-M algorithm as an alternative to otherwise increasing and decreasing learning rate that is more common for L-M algorithm.

A general HONU for plant identification can be then implemented as:

- The static HONU if vector **y** in contains recent history of measured values y,
- The dynamical (recurrent) HONU if vector **y** in contains recent history of neural outputs $\tilde{y}$.

The performance of dynamical QNU was presented for time series prediction e.g. in (M. Solo, 2012) and for control of a SISO non-linear plant in (Bukovsky et al., 2010). As regards HONU as the feedback controller, the dynamical HONU would add integrating character to control; nevertheless, this chapter focuses on static HONUs as a controller in the proceeding section.

NOISE EFFECT ON ADAPTIVE PLANT IDENTIFICATION

An important aspect of successful control loop design is proper choice of sampling for the plant identification and controller tuning and thus also for real hardware implementation of the control loop. Because, the impact of the noise to learning capability of adaptive systems is not often discussed in literature, in this chapter the impact of the noise in measured data on the plant identification is introduced with an experimental conclusion into the relationship between the size of sampling and level of noise and order of HONU, in this subsection.

As a concrete example of a typical second-order engineering system, the following theoretical plant described by the below linear differential equation is chosen.

$$y''(t) + y'(t) + y(t) + 0.2 = u(t)$$

giving the following plant transfer function

$$G_{YU(s)} = \frac{1}{s^2 + s + 1}$$

Figure 1. The adaptive identification of the dynamics of a plant (usually before controller tuning measured y, d are z-scored)

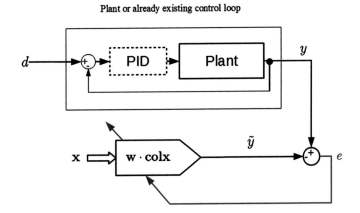

On analysing the resulting characteristic equation of $G_{YU(s)}$ the reader may find the resulting roots corresponding to the system poles of the plant correspond to $s_{1,2} = 0.5 \pm 0.87$. It is thus apparent that this system features an oscillatory component in its dynamical behaviour. This may be seen in the following illustration in Figure 2 where the initial system response can be analysed under an applied repeated staircase sequence at its input, furthermore a comparison of the systems response both with and without the introduction of white noise at the output of the system.

Further to this, the reader may also note that the time constant of this plant τ is equal to 2 seconds. In practice if the ratio of the plant time constant τ with the chosen sampling interval length Δt, for modelling of a discrete difference equation this order should be no greater than x10^2 Should the order of this ratio be greater than x10^3 the nature of sampling leads into the continuous time zone where the modelling theory is beyond the concepts discussed in this chapter. On analysing this ratio for the plant as per, it can be found that on a sampling interval of 0.02 seconds the ratio of $\tau/\Delta t$ would yield the order x10^2 and thus serves as a borderline for sampling in the sense of a discrete HONU model. Given this two sampling intervals of 0.005 and 0.01 in the bordering region of sampling for a HONU discrete model and two sampling intervals within the more, well defined discrete zone being 0.05 and 0.1 seconds are chosen. Therefore, a systematic assessment in the performance of the plant in is tested and analysed via the Mean Square Error (MSE) performance criteria. In all experiments a LNU, QNU and CNU (HONU $r=i$, where $i=1, 2, 3$ respectively).

For each order of HONUs used, the same fundamental input vector **x** featuring 5 previous samples of the previously identified neural unit outputs and 15 previous samples of the real system inputs, is chosen as follows

$$\mathbf{x} = [1, y(k-1), y(k-2), ..y(k-5), u(k-1), u(k-2), .., u(k-15)]^T$$

Figure 2. System response of theoretical 2-nd order system with noise

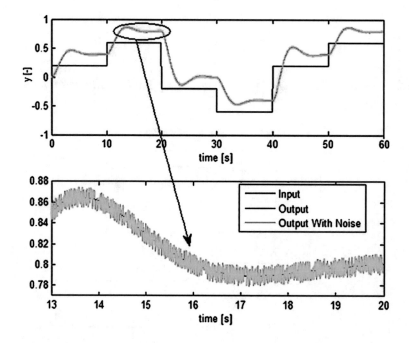

For each HONU model of plant the performance of an incremental GD algorithm for identification of the plant data is tested, where the output signal is under the influence of additional noise proceeding with a comparison of a batch form of training the HONU model neural weights via the L-M equation. Following this, the next phase is to assess both types of the above discussed learning algorithms under the same experimental setup without additional noise influencing the plant output signal. Moreover, to conclude the role that the sampling interval plays in accuracy of plant identification, furthermore, which learning algorithm is more advantageous for systems with additional noise in their respective output data.

The first simulation investigated was the performance of all three respective architectures of HONUs with respect to the minimized MSE of the GD algorithm under training data with noise at the output signal. From Table 2 it is clear that the most optimal performance was achieved via the simplest HONU of $r=1$ being the LNU model under a sampling rate of 0.005. Where, following investigation the reader may find that the neural model is still able to effectively learn the training data within the borderline of too high sampling. On a general overview the reader will tend to find that for the given noised data, as the sampling interval is increased the HONU model is not able to capture the intermediate deviations in the data caused by the fluctuations of noise. As a result such model trained via the GD algorithm is better able to learn the precise shape of the system data influenced by noise but worse in defining a smoother model incorporating the overall system dynamics. Should too high sampling be used, i.e. with a $\tau/\Delta t$ ratio in the order of $\times 10^3$, the tendency towards continuous time modelling becomes more suitable. As a result the performance of such HONU can be diminished.

In comparison with Table 3, the reader can see that for the same amount of training epochs, employing the L-M form of batch training is able to reduce the MSE in all four tests of different sampling intervals to a much lower order, where the CNU particularly deemed to be the most optimal performer at 0.01 seconds of sampling, on assessment of the MSE where the error is given as $(y_{noise} - y_{HONU})$, which is contrary to the performance obtained above via the GD algorithm. However, on comparison of the MSE criteria with the ideal plant data excluding noise i.e. $e = (y_{ideal} - y_{HONU})$, we may find that for all tested sampling intervals the LNU with 0.01 seconds of sampling was the best performer. Another interesting

Table 2. Comparison of MSE for HONUs with GD training on Noised Data

	Sample Time [s]			
	0.005	0.01	0.05	0.1
LNU	5.8172E-005	5.6445E-005	8.8605E-005	0.0001409069
QNU	0.0001107569	0.0002956502	0.00023466	0.0004949558
CNU	0.0008093955	0.0007942155	0.0007587475	0.0006841876

Table 3. Comparison of MSE for HONUs with L-M training on Noised Data

	Sample Time [s]			
	0.005	0.01	0.05	0.1
LNU	4.0371E-005	4.15E-005	4.0721E-005	0.000043942
QNU	3.9956E-005	4.0649E-005	3.6612E-005	3.5395E-005
CNU	3.7907E-005	3.7746E-005	0.000028666	0.000018998

notion is the tendency of the L-M algorithm to focus on the main governing law of the training data dynamics as opposed to the contemporary behaviour introduced by the influence of noise allowing the HONU model to better model the overall dynamics of the system response even with the contamination of noise in its measured output signal. Further to this, by training the HONU neural weights in batches over the training data as opposed to each individual samples, the overall reduction in MSE is more pronounced over each epoch in comparison to the GD algorithm.

Table 4depicts the second scenario of the exampled plant data, where the output signal measured by the sensor is without the influence of noise, in practice this may be due to the introduction of an additional filter at the process output. On testing the GD algorithm over the various chosen sampling intervals, the reader can deduce that the LNU at a sampling interval of 0.005 yields the highest accuracy in comparison to all other architectures. Where as in Table 5 it is the CNU with L-M training at 0.005 seconds of sampling that yields the largest reduction in MSE over all other architectures tested. However, on comparison of this result to a MSE criteria incorporating e $=(y_{ideal} - y_{HONU})$, the LNU architecture across all sampling intervals performed best against the higher order forms of HONU architectures tested. Furthermore, in an environment where the sampling interval is still bordering within a well fined discrete zone of sampling. The shorter the sampling interval is, yields the more information and hence data history that may be processed through the HONU model, and thus an enhanced ability to capture the intermediate dynamics of the system. Furthermore, as drawn from the results in Table 3 the L-M algorithm is able to achieve overall better accuracy in the modelling of the system data without the effect of noise.

On looking at the MSE produced over the various architectures of HONUs for both platforms of training algorithms, furthermore, under the influence of both with and without noise. Figure 3 illustrates the responses of all best performing architectures derived in Table 2-Table 5.

From this overview a general conclusion may be drawn that the batch form of neural weight training via the L-M equation tends to reduce MSE to lower orders in a fewer amount of epochs as compared to the incremental GD based algorithm. For process data influenced by noise at is output, the L-M algorithm can be more advantageous in modelling the main governing law of the system dynamics as opposed to

Table 4. Comparison of MSE of HONUs with GD training on Data without Noise

	Sample Time [s]			
	0.005	0.01	0.05	0.1
LNU	1.9842E-011	6.096E-010	2.0127E-008	2.8469E-008
QNU	6.2811E-011	2.0819E-009	6.464E-007	8.2084E-007
CNU	3.4876E-008	4.9168E-009	0.000000191	0.000000463

Table 5. Comparison of MSE for HONUs with L-M training on data without noise

	Sample Time [s]			
	0.005	0.01	0.05	0.1
LNU	3.1554E-011	4.4130E-011	3.5938E-010	4.9307E-010
QNU	2.9367E-011	5.2497E-011	3.6790E-010	5.0365E-010
CNU	1.6721E-012	2.7847E-012	1.2433E-011	1.3173E-011

Figure 3. Comparison of identified HONU models with various sample intervals

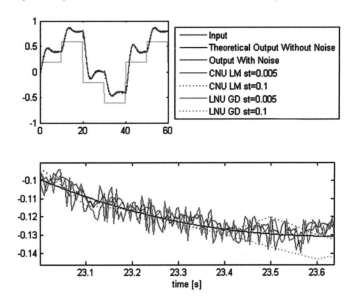

learning the contemporary dynamics induced by the influence of output noise. Furthermore, within a reasonable range respecting the time constant of the dynamic system, the tendency towards faster sampling yields a model which more closely defines the intermediate data shape, due to the more information and hence data history that the model is processed with and able to register during its learning. However, with a longer interval of sampling especially via the L-M form of weight training, the overall model is a smoother curve representation of the main governing dynamics of the engineering system and may also be computationally better for processing real-time sample calculation. The reader may also encounter that identification of dynamic systems with varying levels of noise, yields that with higher amplitudes of noise a longer sampling interval is necessary for the model to well define the dynamics of the system data. As seen in the above experimental results, though the model will have a higher MSE with respect to the noised data, a comparison to the ideal signal of the system without noise yields a better-defined model capturing the system dynamics as opposed to its influence by noise.

With regards to the various architectures of the HONU models used, it yields that the GD algorithm tends to achieve better accuracy in MSE reduction with an LNU as compared to higher order models, however on looking at the results produced by the L-M algorithm, a tendency towards higher order models yields in an overall more accurate model for this particular plant both in data tested with and without noise, where the MSE criteria incorporates the error as $(y_{noise} - y_{HONU})$. However, a tendency towards lowers order models namely the LNU with an MSE criteria incorporating, $e = (y_{ideal} - y_{HONU})$ can be shown to be the better solution. From this result, we may draw that in cases where the ideal plant signal without the effect of noise is known, a MSE incorporating $e = (y_{ideal} - y_{HONU})$ is the most appropriate criteria to choose, however in systems where the ideal signal is not known, a MSE where the error is chosen as $(y_{noise} - y_{HONU})$ would yield the only criteria for evaluation of the HONU modelling capability. Further to this, another concluding notion that can be drawn is that although for this plant the LNU under a GD based algorithm deemed to better model the plant data, that this is not always a general rule, but rather case dependant. A model of higher order, incorporating feature extraction techniques or further tuning with different learning parameter setting may yield to be an overall better model, especially in cases where there is a high linearity between the plant variables, yielding to a faster reduction of square error via the GD algorithm in other cases. Thus, the designer may find that even the simplest platform of a HONU being the LNU can result in the most optimal performance in terms of adequate reduction of MSE along with computational simplicity which overall may be most desirable for real time dynamic modelling and further adaptive control purposes. However, due to the complexities of an investigated system e.g. a system with non-linear dynamics, may lead to a further higher order neural model being the better choice.

HONU AS AN ADAPTIVE FEEDBACK

Following successful identification of the plant, the second phase of the control loop design is to extend the notions of section two into the design of an adaptive feedback controller. In this section HONUs as an adaptive feedback controller as a class of adaptive control known commonly as Model Reference based Adaptive Control (MRAC), where by the controller adjustment mechanism will be the derived HONU as an adaptive feedback controller setup, is presented.

Here two types of configurations may be employed. The first is illustrated in Figure 4, here two HONUs are used in the adaptive feedback controller loop. The role of the first HONU is to model the dynamic system which may be either a model of the plant directly or of the already existing control loop employed on the engineering system under analysis. Following the outputs of the HONU model of the engineering system, the next task is to compose the input vector and update rule of the HONU feedback controller. Similarly to equations & the output value computed by the HONU feedback controller q is

Figure 4. For adaptive weight tuning of the controller, one HONU works as a plant model and the second HONU as a controller

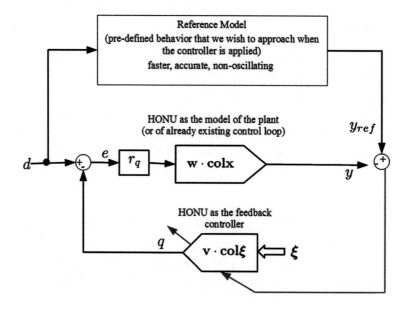

given by a summation of multiplication terms thus for a QNU, i.e. HONU for $r=2$, the HONU controller output may be denoted as follows

$$q = \sum_{i=0}^{n_{xi}} \sum_{j=i}^{n_{xi}} \mathbf{V}_{i,j} . \xi_i . \xi_j,$$

or for a CNU, i.e. HONU for $r=3$ we may denote the HONU controller output as follows

$$q = \sum_{i=0}^{n_x} \sum_{j=i}^{n_x} \sum_{k=j}^{n_x} \mathbf{V}_{i,j,k} . x_i . x_j . x_k,$$

where $\mathbf{V}$ represents the r-dimensional array of neural weights corresponding to the HONU feedback controller. However, as per equation we may express this HONU controller output in a long-vector multiplication form as follows

$$q = f_r(\mathbf{V} . \xi_i) = \mathbf{v} . \mathbf{col}\xi,$$

where $\mathbf{col}\xi$ now comprises of the variables ξ_i, ξ_j in the sense of a QNU or further ξ_k in the sense of a CNU. These terms thus being the previous outputs of the identified HONU plant model or the difference between the reference model and output of the real engineering system $(y_{ref} - y)$, denoted in short as e_{ref}. Further to this, the new inputs u that are fed into the existing plant controller (e.g. a PID controller) are thus as follows

$$u = r_q e - y = r_q (d - q) - y$$

where r_q denotes a proportional gain a the plant controllers desired set-point.

Regarding the parameter update rule of the HONU controller, the neural weight update rule of the HONU feedback controller can be analogically derive as follows

$$\Delta \mathbf{v} = \mu . e_{ref}(k) . \frac{\partial e_{ref}(k)}{\partial v_i} = \mu . e_{ref}(k) . \frac{\partial (y_{ref} - \tilde{y})}{\partial v_i}$$

From here $\Delta \mathbf{v}$ can be simplified to

$$\Delta \mathbf{v} = -\mu . e_{ref}(k) . \frac{\partial \tilde{y}}{\partial v_i}$$

via the chain rule it results that

$$\frac{\partial \tilde{y}}{\partial v_i} = \mathbf{w} . \frac{\partial x}{\partial v_i} = -\mathbf{w} . \frac{\partial q}{\partial v_i}$$

Therefore yielding to the final expression of the HONU feedback controller incremental weight update Δv for an LNU (HONU, r=1) as follows

$$\mathbf{\Delta v} = \mu.e_{ref}(k).\mathbf{w}.\frac{\partial q}{\partial v_i}$$

Or for a QNU (HONU, r=2) feedback controller as

$$\Delta \mathbf{v} = \mu.e_{ref}(k).\mathbf{colw}.\frac{\partial q}{\partial v_i}$$

However, $\Delta \mathbf{v}$ may be updated over every batch of the experimental data. In this case, the L-M algorithm according to Table 1 can be employed, where the Jacobian matrix of partial derivatives is now equal to the expression denoted in equation. On establishing the HONU feedback controller weight update mechanism, it is clear that whether employing a sample by sample update rule or batch form of training the overall weight update rule yields to be as follows

$$\mathbf{v} \leftarrow \mathbf{v} + \Delta \mathbf{v}; \Delta \mathbf{v} = \Delta \mathbf{v}(\mathbf{v})$$

where the parameter $\mathbf{v}$ denotes the HONU feedback controllers neural weights. The schematic in Figure 4may thus be used to test and identify various architectures and learning algorithms of the respectively employed HONUs and deduce which of these various tested architectures best perform as a feedback controller.

The configuration per Figure 5 may be applied in this manner as a feedback controller of constant parameters, with the neural weights $\mathbf{v}$ that have been tuned offline via the update rule as per equation -. Where the individual components of **colξ** are now fed directly form the plant as opposed to the output of the identified HONU plant model. However, the scheme as shown in Figure 4 can also be employed to adaptively tune the HONU feedback controller weights online during a real time run of the engineering system. In this case, the vector $\mathbf{w}$ may either be offline tuned or pre-trained before being further updated

Figure 5. HONU as a controller with constant weights that has been adaptively tuned offline

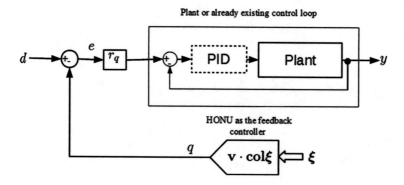

online, with the feedback controller weights **v** being adaptively tuned online via the training algorithms depicted in Table 1.

HONU Adaptive Control for Classical Dynamics Systems

To draw a more intuitive connection in the application of HONU controllers to physical engineering systems, this subsection aims to illustrate the capabilities of namely the LNU, QNU and CNU in controller optimization for control of several key, classical dynamic systems as illustrated per Table 6. Using the previously derived methodologies two kinds of learning algorithms are compared and analysed in their performance to optimize a previously applied proportional-integral-derivative (PID) controller to the original dynamic process.

As the first example an integral process with time-delay is considered, where $K=1$ and $Td=1$. As an initial controller a proportional-integral controller is chosen tuned via the SIMC method as discussed in the work (Di Ruscio, 2010), delivering already good performance in terms of minimization of steady state error as well as in its rate of convergence. Following experimental testing Table 7 denotes the used HONU parameters delivering the best optimization performance across their respective forms of training algorithms and chosen architecture. The process data is re-sampled to feature every 25th sample, with a LNU plant of ny=7, nu=7 used as the basis for a HONU process model.

From Figure 6 the reader may compare all three types of tested HONU architectures and the performance of their respective training algorithms on an integral process with time delay. In all tested cases the HONU feedback controller is able to optimise the performance of the already well-tuned initial PID controlled system, delivering faster speed of convergence in terms of the desired behaviour and adhesion towards the desired steady state. The reader may note that particularly as the order of the HONU architecture is increased with similar parameters across from LNU (r=1) to CNU(r=3) that the rate of convergence is increased. Furthermore, on comparison of the two tested learning algorithms GD and

Table 6. Summary of Classical Dynamic Systems

Characteristic Transfer Function	Variables
Integral Process with Time-Delay $$G(s) = \frac{K}{s} e^{-T_d s}$$	K=Process Gain, Td = Delay time
First-Order Process with Input Time Delay $$G(s) = \frac{K.e^{-sTd}}{T_1 s + 1}$$	K=Process Gain, T_1=Process time constant Td = Delay time
Second-Order Process $$G(s) = \frac{K.w_n^2}{s^2 + 2\xi w_n s + w_n^2}$$	K=Process Gain, w_n=Natural frequency of the process ξ= Damping Ratio
Second-Order Integral Process with Time Delay $$G(s) = \frac{K.e^{-sTd}}{s(T_1 s + 1)}$$	K=Process Gain, T_1=Process time constant Td = Delay time

Table 7. HONU Parameter Settings for Optimisation of Integral Process with Time-Delay

HONU Type	Training Method	No. HONU Model Outputs	No. of Desired Value Inputs	Learning Rate (without normalisation)	Feedback Gain r_o	Epochs
LNU	GD	7	7	0.001	1.0	1500
QNU	GD	7	7	0.001	1.0	1500
CNU	GD	7	7	0.001	1.0	500
LNU	LM	7	7	0.005	1.0	220
QNU	LM	7	7	0.0015	1.0	300
CNU	LM	7	7	0.0015	1.0	300

Figure 6. Integral Process with Time-Delay Optimized via HONU Adaptive Control

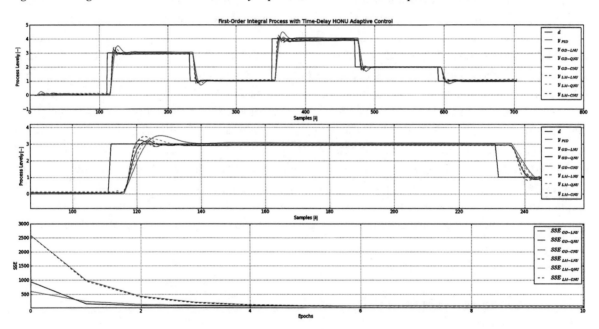

L-M, across all tested architectures the L-M neural weight training method yields the most rapid rate of minimisation of sum of square errors (SSE) yielding a desirable controller response in few epochs as compared to the GD incremental form of neural weight training.

Following tests on an integral process with time-delay, the next process to analyse as per Table 6 is that of a first-order process with time-delay, where $K=1$, $T_i=1$ and $Td=0.5$. As an initial controller a PID controller is chosen tuned via the IAE method as discussed in the work (Tan, Liu, Chen, & Marquez, 2006) from all tested methods on this dynamic system, the IAE tuning method deems to deliver the most optimal performance in comparison of its error criteria to other tested methods. Following experimentation Table 8 denotes the used HONU parameters delivering the best optimization performance across their respective forms of training algorithms and chosen architectures. The process data is re-sampled to feature every 20th sample, with a LNU plant of ny=4, nu=7 used as the basis for a HONU process model.

Table 8. HONU Parameter Settings for Optimisation First-Order Process with Time-Delay

HONU Type	Training Method	No. HONU Model Outputs	No. of Desired Value Inputs	Learning Rate (without normalization)	Feedback Gain r_o	Epochs
LNU	GD	4	7	0.001	1.0	3000
QNU	GD	4	7	0.001	1.0	3000
CNU	GD	4	7	0.001	1.0	3000
LNU	LM	4	7	0.5	1.0	100
QNU	LM	4	7	0.5	1.0	100
CNU	LM	4	7	0.5	1.0	100

Figure 7. First-Order Process with Time-Delay Optimised via HONU Adaptive Control

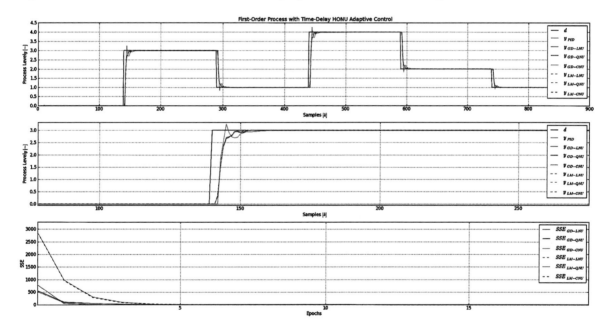

From Figure 7 the reader may analyse the performance of all three types of tested HONU architectures and their respective training algorithms on a first-order process with time delay. In all tested cases the HONU feedback controller is able to optimise the performance of the adequately tuned initial PID controlled system, with faster speed of convergence in terms of the desired behaviour and adhesion towards the desired steady state as well as gentler transition in the vicinity of the steady-state set point with no overshoot. On this system all architectures perform similarly in terms of their rate of convergence towards the steady state, which may be reasoned due to the complexity of this dynamic system being of lower order. Similarly the L-M, across all tested architectures yields the most rapid rate of minimisation of sum of square errors (SSE) yielding a desirable controller response in the order of 100 epochs as compared to the GD incremental form of neural weight training being in the order of thousands.

Following HONU adaptive controller optimisation for first-order dynamic processes, the next stage as per Table 6, is to analyse second-order based processes. In the proceeding example a second-order process is chosen, where $K=0.75$, $w_n=0.44$ and $\xi=1.25$. As an initial controller a PID controller tuned via the Ziegler-Nichols method is chosen, delivering already good control quality in terms of its error criteria in lieu with its speed of convergence and adhesion to the desired set-point. Following experimentation Table 9 denotes the used HONU parameters delivering the best optimization performance across their respective forms of training algorithms and chosen architectures. The process data is re-sampled to feature every 20th sample, with a LNU plant of ny=4, nu=7 used as the basis for a HONU process model.

In Figure 8 all three types of tested HONU architectures and their respective training algorithms are tested on a higher order process of second order. In all tested cases the HONU feedback controller optimises the performance of the adequately tuned initial PID controlled system, with much faster speed of convergence in terms of the desired behaviour and adhesion towards the desired steady state as well as reduced overshoot in the vicinity of the steady-state set point. On this system all architectures perform similarly in terms of their rate of convergence towards the steady state, however, the reader may note a

Table 9. HONU Parameter Settings for Optimisation of Second-Order Process

HONU Type	Training Method	No. HONU Model Outputs	No. of Desired Value Inputs	Learning Rate (without normalization)	Feedback Gain r_o	Epochs
LNU	GD	4	7	0.001	1.0	1000
QNU	GD	4	7	0.001	1.0	1000
CNU	GD	4	7	0.001	1.0	1000
LNU	LM	4	7	0.5	1.0	100
QNU	LM	4	7	0.5	1.0	100
CNU	LM	4	7	0.5	1.0	100

Figure 8. Second-Order Process Optimised via HONU Adaptive Control

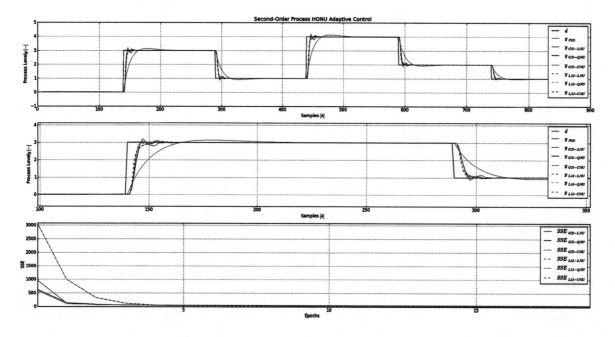

particular superiority in terms of the QNU and furthermore, CNU architecture with L-M neural weight training, delivering the most rapid rate of convergence to the desired set point as well as minimised overshoot. As noted on the previous tests with first-order processes the L-M, across all tested architectures yields the most rapid rate of minimisation in terms of sum of square errors (SSE) yielding a similar order in its final SSE value after 100 epochs as compared to the GD incremental form of neural weight training being in the order of 1000 epochs of training.

Following tests on a second-order process, a further investigation is to analyse the behaviour of HONU adaptive control for optimisation of a second-order integral process with time-delay, where $K=1$, $T_I=6$ and $Td=1.5$. As an initial controller a PID controller is chosen tuned via the SIMC method as discussed in the work (Skogestad, 2003), which yields to deliver the adequate performance in terms of steady state convergence and adhesion to the desired set-point. Following experimentation Table 10 denotes the used HONU parameters delivering the best optimization performance across their respective forms of training algorithms and chosen architectures. The process data is re-sampled to feature every 30th sample, with a QNU plant of ny=10, nu=15 used as the basis for a HONU process model.

Table 10. HONU Parameter Settings for Second-Order Integral Process with Time-Delay

HONU Type	Training Method	No. HONU Model Outputs	No. of Desired Value Inputs	Learning Rate (without normalization)	Feedback Gain r_o	Epochs
QNU	GD	3	15	0.001	0.5	100
CNU	GD	3	15	0.001	0.5	100
QNU	LM	3	15	5.0	0.5	10
CNU	LM	3	15	5.0	0.5	10

Figure 9. Second-Order Integral Process Optimised via HONU Adaptive Control

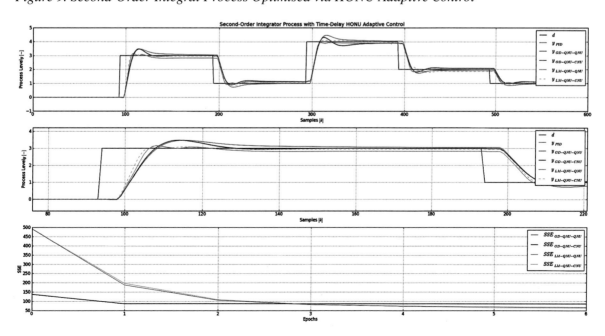

In Figure 9 the final system as per Table 6 is analysed, which is that of an integral process of second order with time delay. Here due to the larger degree of complexity and non-linearity induced with a considerable time delay value a QNU is used to provide adequate plant identification followed by tests of the QNU and CNU as a feedback controller. Following test across all prescribed architecture and learning algorithms as per Table 10, the reader may find that the L-M training method yields the most optimal performance with the CNU architecture primarily being the most superior in terms of rate of convergence, reduced overshoot and minimisation of steady state error as compared with all previously tested HONU feedback controllers. As may be compared to all previous tests the L-M training method, across all tested architectures yields the most rapid rate of minimisation in terms of sum of square errors (SSE) yielding an even further reduced order in its final SSE value after 10 epochs as compared to the GD incremental form of neural weight training being in the order of 100 epochs of training.

Hydraulic-Pneumatic Cascade Tank System

As a concrete example of a single-input-single-output (SISO) engineering system, this chapter presents a real example of a hydraulic-pneumatic cascade tank system. The goal behind this section is to illustrate the design principles and performance behind the various HONU architectures as employed on a real time engineering system. From this the authors also aim to provide the reader with a better intuition into the procedure behind design and testing of a HONU as an adaptive feedback controller, as well as to clearly highlight the advantages behind this methodology of adaptive control.

Figure 10. Hydraulic-pneumatic cascade tank system

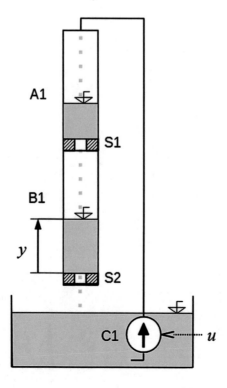

As illustrated in Figure 10, a water stream controlled by an input voltage u to the water pump C1 feeds the upper tank A1. An orifice S1 located at the bottom of tank A1 allows the contained water to trickle into the lower tank B1, where the water level held within the tank B1 is the process output y. A third orifice S2 completes the water passage way back into the holding tank. The process output y is measured via a differential pressure sensor where its level is a function of pressure in k Pa. A further overfilling reservoir is located at the top of the system, where the water may flow through valve K1R should the flow rate in tank A1 be too high such to cause overfilling. Given this system setup, the design of an adaptive controller capable of maintaining the desired set point of the water level in tank B1 may now be investigated. As a further component of investigation an initial proportional controller is implemented via means of a software algorithm to provide an initial element of control on the hydraulic-pneumatic cascade tank system. Thus for a more illustrative schematic of the adaptive controller setup, the reader may refer to Figure 5.

Following measurements of the hydraulic-pneumatic cascade tank system under control of a proportional controller, the first stage of our design is to establish a suitable input vector which will be used for adaptive identification of the plant model for this system. For simplicity, the same input vector is chosen to represent the HONU feedback controllers input samples. Thus, choosing a model featuring 5 previous samples of the neural model output along with 8 samples of the desired behaviour alone would yield the following HONU plant model input vector **w**.

$$\mathbf{x} = [1, y(k), y(k-1),..y(k-4), d(k), d(k-1),.., d(k-7)]^T$$

For an LNU (HONU, *r=1*) plant model, the reader can expect to train 14 neural unit weights such to model the dynamical behaviour of the hydraulic-pneumatic cascade tank system with minimum error to the actual measurements of the system output. In the sense of a QNU model design, it can be expected that the number of weights would be 105 as the reader may verify, for a HONU, *r=2* the number of weights respect the following general relation $0.5.(nx^2+nx)$. Given this, it may then be established that the update rule for the neural weights of the LNU plant model of each sample as follows

$$\mathbf{w} = \mathbf{w} + \mu.e(k).\mathbf{x}^T$$

Or via the L-M equation over training in batches of the system data as follows

$$\Delta \mathrm{w} = (J^T.J + \frac{1}{\mu}.I)^{-1}.J^T.e$$

where the Jacobian matrix of partial derivatives may be given as follows

$$J(:,k) = \mathbf{x}^T$$

Therefore the resulting LNU plant model may be computed over each sample of the measured experimental data as follows

$$\tilde{y} = \sum_{i=0}^{n_x} W_i . x_i = \mathbf{w}.\mathbf{x}$$

After identifying an adequate system model the second phase is to design a HONU feedback controller capable of optimizing the performance of the existing proportional controller employed on the hydraulic-pneumatic cascade tank system. Similarly to the input vector ξ corresponding to the HONU feedback controller is chosen as follows

$$\xi = [1, y(k), y(k-1), .. y(k-4), d(k), d(k-1), .., d(k-7)]^T$$

Therefore, the resulting output of the HONU feedback controller as an LNU will be as follows

$$q = \sum_{i=0}^{n_{xi}} \mathbf{V}_i . \xi_i = \mathbf{w}.\xi^{\mathbf{T}}$$

Considering equation the weight update mechanism in the sense of the incremental GD algorithm, can be obtained. In this case, the partial derivative *dq/dv* will result in a vector of equal dimension to the number of weights of the HONU plant model. The reader may verify that only the 8 last terms of this vector holds non-zero terms regarding its derivative with respect to the neural weights v. Moreover, that the value of these partial derivatives further simplifies to give the input vector ξ at the *k-th* sample. Thus, the resulting incremental weight update rule via GD algorithm of the HONU feedback controller may be analogically computed according to equations -. Or via a batch form of updating the respective neural weights applying the notions of the L-M algorithm illustrated in Table 1.

Following the theoretical design of a HONU adaptive control loop in extension to the existing control loop belonging to the hydraulic-pneumatic cascade tank system, the resulting response of the each derived configuration of a HONU feedback controller may be analysed. In the presented experiment, two kinds of learning algorithms are compared, the first being the incremental GD algorithm and the later being the L-M batch form of training. Each training method is exampled with two combinations of architectures. The first architecture investigated is a LNU plant model with a LNU feedback controller. The second architecture presented is an LNU plant model with a QNU feedback controller. In the presented experiments all training of the neural weights for both the plant model and adaptive controller respectively are offline trained, with application of the controller provided online as a feedback controller of constant parameters.

Figure 11depicts the output response of the hydraulic-pneumatic cascade tank system following the extension of an adaptive HONU feedback controller. Here the both architectures are trained offline via the GD algorithm over 400 epochs of the system data, with respect to both plant model and feedback controller weight identification. Here as per equation, 5 previous samples of the neural model output along with 8 samples of the desired behaviour alone were used as an input vector **w** for successful dynamic modelling of the hydraulic-pneumatic cascade tank system. With regards to the applied feedback controller as per equation, 5 previous samples of the real plant output along with 8 samples of the desired behaviour alone were used as an input vector **v**.

Figure 11. Adaptive control via GD training and identified LNU (HONU, r=1) plant model

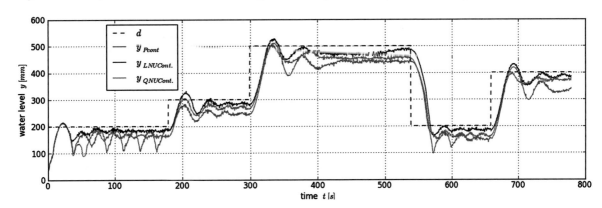

Following real-time experimentation of the respective architectures of LNU and the QNU as an adaptive feedback controller of constant parameters, Figure 11 illustrates the combination of plant modelling via an LNU followed by a LNU feedback controller yields the best performance under offline training via GD. As may be seen, the original proportional controller response is optimized in both applied architectures, adhering closer to the desired water level set-point as compared with the initial control of the hydraulic-pneumatic cascade tank system. As may be drawn, though tests of an adaptive controller employing an LNU plant model with a LNU feedback controller of constant parameters yields adequate control performance, there is still a small degree of steady state error. This steady state error is especially in larger deviation with the desired set-point values for higher working ranges of the water level in tank B1. Thus, the next consideration is to investigate a different weight update rule on the measured experimental data.

Figure 12thus depicts the hydraulic-pneumatic cascade tank system response with the extension of a HONU feedback controller identified via a batch form of training the plant model and feedback controller neural weights, being the L-M algorithm. In this design, the plant model is trained over 300 epochs of the initial experimental data via an LNU as per, featuring 5 previous samples of the neural model output along with 8 samples of the desired behaviour alone used as the input vector **w**. Follow-

Figure 12. Adaptive control via L-M training and Identified LNU (HONU, r=1) plant model

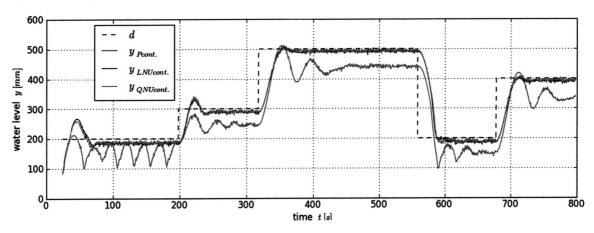

ing the successful plant identification, the HONU feedback controller is offline tuned over 300 epochs via the L-M algorithm. Here as per, 5 previous samples of the real plant output along with 8 samples of the desired behaviour alone were used as an input vector **v**. From Figure 12 the reader may draw that both the LNU and QNU HONU feedback controllers trained via the L-M algorithm yield better control performance as compared with the same adaptive controller setup under incremental GD form of training. On all desired water levels, the system response yields less overshooting beyond the desired set-point along with better minimization of the steady state error. This result may be rather intriguing for the reader however, as seen in section two the application of the L-M algorithm to systems with noise at their output, features the desirable property of focusing on the main governing law of the dynamics of the engineering system during each epoch of training, as opposed to the individual samples of noise which contaminate the measured data. Furthermore, due to the batch form of updating the HONU weights, as seen in the previous section a quicker reduction of sum of squared errors can be achieved with respect to the overall training epochs necessary for training the neural weights of the HONU as compared to the incremental training methods, resulting in more adequate control performance for such systems as the hydraulic-pneumatic cascade tank system investigated above.

CONCLUSION

This chapter summarized the design and usage of HONUs for adaptive dynamic system modelling and control, in the sense of an adaptive feedback controller as a class of MRAC based design. Following both theoretical as well as real time experimental tests the following remarks becomes apparent. HONU architectures namely the LNU, QNU and CNU (HONU of $r=i$, where $i=1,2,3$ respectively) are an efficient mechanism for dynamical system identification, with the use of efficient training algorithms such as the GD and L-M algorithm yielding desirable performance on both linear and non-linear system modelling, as well as exhibiting comparable if not better performance as compared to conventional neural networks, along with desirable computational efficiency. On application of HONUs as a plant model, it follows that designer must respect the correct sampling during both the software and hardware phase of system implementation, as well as enough data history (especially for systems featuring time-delays) within the chosen model design, such to best capture the overall system dynamics. The L-M algorithm can be particularly advantageous for engineering systems featuring noise, as well as achieving faster reduction of the sum of squared errors over each epoch of the training data. Therefore, on extension of HONUs as an adaptive feedback controller, this chapter highlights the most common learning algorithms and HONU architectures, however it is up to the designer to test the various combinations of HONU architectures for both modelling and control and compare which configuration best provides an adequate level of control performance on their engineering system under analysis.

REFERENCES

Alexandrov, A. G., & Palenov, M. V. (2014). Adaptive PID controllers: State of the art and development prospects. *Automation and Remote Control, 75*(2), 188–199. doi:10.1134/S0005117914020027

Aristoklis D Anastasiadis, G. D. M. (2003). *An efficient improvement of the Rprop algorithm.* 10.13140/2.1.5157.7282

Benes, P., & Bukovsky, I. (2014). Neural network approach to hoist deceleration control. *Proceedings of the 2014 International Joint Conference on Neural Networks (IJCNN)* (pp. 1864–1869). IEEE. Retrieved from http://ieeexplore.ieee.org/xpls/abs_all.jsp?arnumber=6889831

Bukovsky, I., Benes, P., & Slama, M. (2015). Laboratory Systems Control with Adaptively Tuned Higher Order Neural Units. In R. Silhavy, R. Senkerik, Z. K. Oplatkova, Z. Prokopova, & P. Silhavy (Eds.), *Intelligent Systems in Cybernetics and Automation Theory* (pp. 275–284). Springer International Publishing; doi:10.1007/978-3-319-18503-3_27

Bukovsky, I., Hou, Z.-G., Bila, J., & Gupta, M. M. (2007). Foundation of Notation and Classification of Nonconventional Static and Dynamic Neural Units. *Proceedings of the6th IEEE International Conference on Cognitive Informatics* (pp. 401–407). http://doi.org/ doi:10.1109/COGINF.2007.4341916

Bukovsky, I., Oswald, C., Cejnek, M., & Benes, P. M. (2014). Learning entropy for novelty detection a cognitive approach for adaptive filters. In *Sensor Signal Processing for Defence* (pp. 1–5). SSPD. doi:10.1109/SSPD.2014.6943329

Bukovsky, I., Redlapalli, S., & Gupta, M. M. (2003). Quadratic and cubic neural units for identification and fast state feedback control of unknown nonlinear dynamic systems. *Proceedings of theFourth International Symposium on Uncertainty Modeling and Analysis, 2003. ISUMA 2003* (pp. 330–334). http://doi.org/ doi:10.1109/ISUMA.2003.1236182

Di Ruscio, D. (2010). On Tuning PI Controllers for Integrating Plus Time Delay Systems. Retrieved from https://teora.hit.no/handle/2282/1044

Ivakhnenko, A. G. (1971). Polynomial Theory of Complex Systems. *IEEE Transactions on Systems, Man, and Cybernetics, SMC-1*(4), 364–378. doi:10.1109/TSMC.1971.4308320

Kumar, A. S., Subba Rao, M., & Babu, Y. S. K. (2008). Model reference linear adaptive control of DC motor using fuzzy controller. Proceedings of the 2008 IEEE Region 10 Conference TENCON '08 (pp. 1–5). doi:10.1109/TENCON.2008.4766484

Lee, W.-K., Hyun, C.-H., Kim, E., & Park, M. (2006). Adaptive Synchronization of Discrete-Time T-S Fuzzy Chaotic Systems Using Output Tracking Control. *Proceedings of theInternational Joint ConferenceSICE-ICASE '06* (pp. 3816–3820). http://doi.org/ doi:10.1109/SICE.2006.314668

Mandic, D., & Goh, V. S. L. (2009). *Complex Valued Nonlinear Adaptive Filters: Noncircularity, Widely Linear and Neural Models.* Wiley Publishing. doi:10.1002/9780470742624

Milone, D. H. (2007). Adaptive learning of polynomial networks, genetic programming, backpropagation and Bayesian methods, series on genetic and evolutionary computation. *Genetic Programming and Evolvable Machines, 8*(3), 289–291. doi:10.1007/s10710-007-9034-x

Nikolaev, N. Y., & Iba, H. (2003). Learning polynomial feedforward neural networks by genetic programming and backpropagation. *IEEE Transactions on Neural Networks, 14*(2), 337–350. doi:10.1109/TNN.2003.809405 PMID:18238017

Nikolaev, N. Y., & Iba, H. (2006). Adaptive learning of polynomial networks genetic programming, backpropagation and Bayesian methods. New York: Springer. Retrieved from http://public.eblib.com/choice/publicfullrecord.aspx?p=303002

Patino, H. D., & Liu, D. (2000). Neural network-based model reference adaptive control system. *IEEE Transactions on Systems, Man, and Cybernetics. Part B, Cybernetics*, *30*(1), 198–204. doi:10.1109/3477.826961 PMID:18244743

Skogestad, S. (2003). Simple analytic rules for model reduction and PID controller tuning. *Journal of Process Control*, *13*(4), 291–309. doi:10.1016/S0959-1524(02)00062-8

Softky, W. R., & Kammen, D. M. (1991). Correlations in high dimensional or asymmetric data sets: Hebbian neuronal processing. *Neural Networks*, *4*(3), 337–347. doi:10.1016/0893-6080(91)90070-L

M. Solo, G. (2012). Fundamentals of Higher Order Neural Networks for Modeling and Simulation. *Artificial Higher Order Neural Networks for Modeling and Simulation*. 10.4018/978-1-4666-2175-6.ch006

Tan, W., Liu, J., Chen, T., & Marquez, H. J. (2006). Comparison of some well-known PID tuning formulas. *Computers & Chemical Engineering*, *30*(9), 1416–1423. doi:10.1016/j.compchemeng.2006.04.001

Taylor, J. G., & Coombes, S. (1993). Learning higher order correlations. *Neural Networks*, *6*(3), 423–427. doi:10.1016/0893-6080(93)90009-L

Werbos, P. J. (1990). Backpropagation through time: What it does and how to do it. *Proceedings of the IEEE*, *78*(10), 1550–1560. doi:10.1109/5.58337

Widrow, B., & Stearns, S. D. (1985). *Adaptive signal processing*. Retrieved from http://adsabs.harvard.edu/abs/1985ph...book.....W

Williams, R. J., & Zipser, D. (1989). A Learning Algorithm for Continually Running Fully Recurrent Neural Networks. *Neural Computation*, *1*(2), 270–280. doi:10.1162/neco.1989.1.2.270

Wu, X., Wu, X., Luo, X., Zhu, Q., & Guan, X. (2012). Neural network-based adaptive tracking control for nonlinearly parameterized systems with unknown input nonlinearities. *Neurocomputing*, *82*, 127–142. doi:10.1016/j.neucom.2011.10.019

Yang, Y., Zhou, C., & Ren, J. (2003). Model reference adaptive robust fuzzy control for ship steering autopilot with uncertain nonlinear systems. *Applied Soft Computing*, *3*(4), 305–316. doi:10.1016/j.asoc.2003.05.001

Zhang, M. (2008). Artificial Higher Order Neural Networks for Economics and Business. Hershey, PA, USA: IGI Global.

Chapter 3
Novelty Detection in System Monitoring and Control with HONU

Cyril Oswald
Czech Technical University in Prague, Czech Republic

Jan Vrba
Czech Technical University in Prague, Czech Republic

Matous Cejnek
Czech Technical University in Prague, Czech Republic

Ivo Bukovsky
Czech Technical University in Prague, Czech Republic

ABSTRACT

With focus on Higher Order Neural Units (HONUs), this chapter reviews two recently introduced adaptive novelty detection algorithms based on supervised learning of HONU with extension to adaptive monitoring of existing control loops. Further, the chapter also introduces a novel approach for novelty detection via local model monitoring with Self-organizing Map (SOM) and HONU. Further, it is discussed how these principles can be used to distinguish between external and internal perturbations of identified plant or control loops. The simulation result will demonstrates the potentials of the algorithms for single-input plants as well as for some representative of multiple-input plants and for the improvement of their control.

INTRODUCTION

The novelty detection in the control loop is important to detect system perturbations as well as to detect system states for which neural network models and controllers has not been properly trained and thus unexpected behavior of a control loop may occur. Such a detection can serve for an early indication of an action to avoid unstable or unpredicted situation in a controlled system.

In principle, novelty carried through measured samples of data may be evaluated either, via probability based approaches as exampled in Markou and Singh (2003a) or, via learning system based approaches, as in the work Markou and Singh (2003b). The first of these streams, i.e. probabilistic, is represented by the statistical approaches of novelty measures and by probabilistic approaches for evaluation of entropy.

DOI: 10.4018/978-1-5225-0063-6.ch003

The Sample Entropy (SampEn) and the Approximate Entropy (ApEn) are very typical and very relevant examples to be mentioned (Pincus, 1991; Richman & Moorman, 2000). These approaches are closely related to the multi-scale evaluation of fractal measures, where further case studies utilizing SampEn, ApEn, and Multiscale Entropy (MSE) can be found in Costa, Goldberger, and Peng (2002) and Yin and Zhou (2012). Further to this, probabilistic entropy approach to the concept shift (sometimes the concept drift) detection in sensory data is reported in Vorburger and Bernstein (2006). The second of the mentioned streams is represented by the utilization of learning systems, such as neural networks and fuzzy-neural systems, and this is also the main area of focus, for the presented work in this paper. During the last three decades of 20th century, the works that were focused in regards to learning systems are that of(Willsky (1976) and Frank (1990) and for incremental learning approach can be referenced for example also the work (Widmer & Kubat, 1996). Then, a particularly focused approach toward the utilization of learning systems, has been rising with works (Polycarpou & Trunov, 2000; Trunov & Polycarpou, 2000). Where, nonlinear estimators and learning algorithm were utilized for the fault detection via the proposed utilization of a fault function that evaluates behavior of residuals of a learning system. Currently, significant research that shall also be referenced is adaptive concept drift detectors, proposed in Alippi, Boracchi, and Roveri (2013). Some readers might also see some analogies of the proposed approach in this paper to the Adaptive Resonance Theory (Grossberg, 2013). Another approach to novelty detection is based on utilization of adaptive parameters of incrementally learning models (neural networks), i.e. the Adaptation Plot (Ivo Bukovsky & Bila, 2010) that has been recently enhanced with multi-scale approach (I. Bukovsky, Kinsner, & Bila, 2012). A most recent method is the Learning Entropy, i.e., a multiscale approach to evaluation of unusual behavior of adaptive parameters of a learning model is introduced in (I. Bukovsky, Oswald, Cejnek, & Benes, 2014).

From recent studies of Bukovsky et al it appears that HONUs are suitable for fast and instant sample-by-sample detection of novel information that each individual sample of data carries. Further, it will be discussed how these principles can be used to distinguish between external and internal perturbations of identified plant or control loops. The simulation result will demonstrates the potentials of the algorithms for single-input plants as well as for some representative of multiple-input plants and for the improvement of their control.

With focus on Higher Order Neural Units (HONUs), this chapter reviews two recently introduced adaptive novelty detection algorithms based on supervised learning of HONU with extension to adaptive monitoring of existing control loops. Further, the chapter also introduces a novel approach for novelty detection in more complex systems via adaptive monitoring of local models with Self-organizing map (SOM) and HONU.

The first adaptive novelty detection algorithm (Cejnek, Benes, & Bukovsky, 2014) is based on gradient descent learning and it incorporates both learning increments as well as actual prediction error. Its extensions will be made for adaptive identification and control loops of plants. Contrary to I. Bukovsky et al., (2012) and Ivo Bukovsky (2013), this approach operates only on parameter space of incrementally learning systems, and it does not use the multi-scale approach for detection sensitivity.

The second adaptive novelty detection algorithm (I. Bukovsky et al., 2014) does not depend, in its principle, on prediction error and evaluates the actual learning effort of adaptive system.

The third approach is newly introduced in this chapter, the Self-organizing map (SOM) with HONU, is the method able to classify the observed system operating conditions and detect the novel operating states of the system.

For all equations in this chapter we will use the following notation: bold ($\mathbf{x}$, $\mathbf{w}$,...) for vectors, italic for scalars (y, e,...) and bold capitals for matrices ($\mathbf{R}$).

HONU AS PLANT OR CLOSED LOOP ADAPTIVE MODEL

This section utilizes static (feed-forward) and dynamical (recurrent) HONU as input-output models of plant or the whole control loops for novelty detection from using set-point and output variable. For brief review, the multiple-input HONU can be defined as follows

$$\tilde{y}(k) = \mathbf{w} \cdot \mathbf{colx},$$

where $\mathbf{colx}$ stands for input and the general form is defined as follows

$$\mathbf{colx} = \{x_{i_1} \cdot \ldots x_{i_r}; i_1 = 0 \ldots n_x, i_2 = i_1 \ldots n_x, \ldots i_r = i_{r-1} \ldots n_x\},$$

where $i_1 < i_2 < \ldots < i_r$ and $x_0 = 1$.

The r is the order of neural unit, x_0 is bias of neural unit and $\mathbf{w}$ is a long vector of all neural weights of HONU with indexing according to the actual order of HONU as follows

$$\mathbf{w} = \begin{bmatrix} w_{0,0,\ldots,0} & w_{0,0,\ldots,1} & \cdots & w_{i_1,i_2,\ldots,i_r} & \cdots & w_{n_x,n_x,\ldots,n_x} \end{bmatrix}$$

where $i_1 < i_2 < \ldots < i_r$

For example of second order HONU (QNU)

$$\mathbf{colx} = \{x_i \cdot x_j; i = 0 \ldots n_x, j = i \ldots n_x\},$$

and

$$\mathbf{w} = \begin{bmatrix} w_{0,0} & w_{0,1} & \cdots & w_{i,j} & \cdots & w_{n_x},n_x \end{bmatrix}$$

or for third order HONU (CNU)

$$\mathbf{colx} = \{x_i \cdot x_j \cdot x_k; i = 0 \ldots n_x, j = i \ldots n_x, \kappa = j \ldots n_x\}.$$

and

$$\mathbf{w} = \begin{bmatrix} w_{0,0,0} & w_{0,0,1} & \cdots & w_{i,j,\kappa} & \cdots & w_{n_x,n_x,n_x}, i < j < \kappa. \end{bmatrix}$$

The long-vector is composed of a unit-augmented vector that contains external (control) inputs and state feedbacks. Thus, for HONU as for the plant model, it is as follows

$$\mathbf{x} = \begin{bmatrix} 1 \\ \mathbf{u} \\ \mathbf{y} \end{bmatrix} = \begin{bmatrix} 1 \\ x_0 \\ x_1 \\ \vdots \\ x_{n_x} \end{bmatrix}$$

where $\mathbf{u}$ is the vector of external plant inputs and their step delays (the details of configuration of $\mathbf{u}$ are given in the previous chapter in this book) and $\mathbf{y}$ is the vector of state feedbacks that is defined for static HONU as follows

$$\mathbf{x} = \begin{bmatrix} y(k-1) \\ y(k-2) \\ \vdots \\ y(k-n_y) \end{bmatrix}$$

while for dynamical HONU $\mathbf{x}$ it yields

$$\mathbf{x} = \begin{bmatrix} 1 \\ \mathbf{u} \\ \tilde{\mathbf{y}} \end{bmatrix}$$

where

$$\tilde{\mathbf{y}} = \begin{bmatrix} \tilde{y}(k-1) \\ \tilde{y}(k-2) \\ \vdots \\ \tilde{y}(k-n_y) \end{bmatrix}$$

For HONU as adaptive model of already existing closed loop, the augmented input vector $\mathbf{x}$ into (dynamical) HONU involves the step delay vector $\mathbf{sp}$ of sps as follows

$$\mathbf{x} = \begin{bmatrix} 1 \\ \mathbf{sp} \\ \tilde{\mathbf{y}} \end{bmatrix}.$$

Then, for example the general GD adaptation rule is defined for HONU (Madan M. Gupta, Ivo Bukovsky, Noriyasu Homma, Ashu M. G. Solo, & Zeng-Guang Hou, 2013) for any polynomial order as follows

$$\mathbf{w}(k+1) = \mathbf{w}(k) + \Delta\mathbf{w}(k),$$

where increments $\Delta\mathbf{w}(k)$ of adaptive weights is calculated as follows

$$\Delta\mathbf{w}(k) = \mu \cdot e(k) \cdot \mathbf{colx}^T,$$

where μ is the learning rate and the error (e) is defined as follows

$$e(k) = y(k) - \tilde{y}(k).$$

For study on learning rate modifications particularly for HONU, please refer to (I. Bukovsky et al., 2014). Except learning rate normalization, which is discussed in following section, the stability of the learning should be improved by data normalization.

NOVELTY DETECTION TECHNIQUES WITH HONU

We tested supposed methods on highly nonlinear system which is described by following equation

$$2\tau(t) \cdot y''(t) + (\tau(t) + 2) \cdot y'(t) + y(t) = 3K(t) \cdot u(t),$$

where τ is the time constant and K the system sensitivity. The equation describing changes of time constant in time is as follows

$$\tau(t) = \tau_0(t) + \frac{1}{1 - e^{y(t)+\tau_0}}$$

and equation describing changes of system sensitivity in time is as follows

$$K(t) = K_0(t) + \frac{1}{1 - e^{y(t)+K_0}}.$$

Parameters τ and K_0 are also changing in time step-wise manner, as it is shown in Figure 2. At time $k=540$ [s] there is first perturbation in parameter K_0, at time $k=1080$ [s] there is perturbation in parameter τ_0 and finally at time $k=1620$ [s] the values of parameters K_0 and τ_0 revert back to original values.

Figure 1. Closed-loop system block diagram

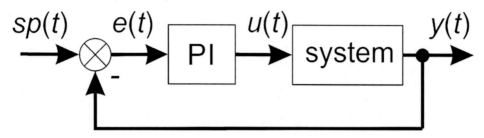

The supposed system is controlled by PI controller as is shown in Figure 1. Assume the PI controller in the form

$$u(t) = k_p e(t) + k_i \int_0^t u(\tau)d\tau + u(0)$$

Figure 2. Data obtained from system model

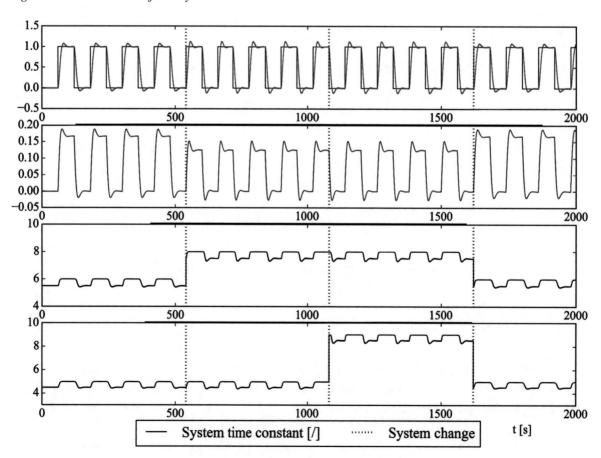

so we can describe this closed-loop system as follows

$$2\tau'(t)y''(t) + 2\tau(t)y'''(t) + 2y''(t) + \tau'(t)y'(t) + \tau(t)y''(t) + y'(t) =$$
$$3K'(t)k_p sp(t) + 3K(t)k_p sp'(t) + 3K(t)k_p sp'(t) - 3K'(t)k_p y(t) -$$
$$3K(t)k_p y'(t) + 3K'(t)k_i \int_0^t (sp(t) - y(t)\tau)d\tau + 3K(t)k_i(sp(t) - y(t)).$$

The k_i is integration constant, k_p is proportional constant and *sp* is desired value (set point).

In next subsection, there are results of introduced methods, which are tested on the suggested closed-loop system.

ADAPTIVE NOVELTY DETECTION WITH LEAST-SQUARES METHODS

This method of novelty detection, implemented with GD and HONU was recently introduced for time series in (Cejnek et al., 2014) and it is extended in this chapter for novelty detection in SISO control loops. The method utilizes an adaptive prediction model and shows one of the possibilities how to detect perturbations within measured data in every new sample. The adaptation technique is applied to the predictive model, adapted with Least-square method. In this subsection it will be this method introduced on following online feed-forward adaptive methods

- Gradient Descent (GD (Widrow & Stearns, 1985) - also known as stochastic gradient.
- Normalized Gradient Descent (Widrow & Stearns, 1985) - also known as Normalized Least Mean Squares (NLMS).
- Recursive Least Squares (RLS) (Hayes, 1996).

In general for novelty detection estimation at every new sample in discrete time k, we use the product of absolute values of the prediction error $e(k)$ and adaptive weight $\Delta w_i(k)$ changes according to equation, as follows

$$\mathbf{nd}(k) = \left| e(k) \cdot \Delta \mathbf{w}(k) \right|.$$

The $\mathbf{nd}(k)$ is vector of values describing how much novelty is recognized for every single adaptive weight w_i. The equation presents the main principle behind this introduced method of novelty detection of every new sample according to temporary system dynamics.

For some applications could be desirable to describe novelty in data just with single value of for every sample. As a good practice how to achieve that, it is reduction of this vector $\mathbf{nd}(k)$ to scalar as follows

$$nd(k) = \max(\mathbf{nd}(k)).$$

The novelty detection rule, is computationally easy to use. Its implementation for GD adaptation method is simple as follows

$$\mathbf{nd}(k) = \left| e(k) \cdot \Delta \mathbf{w}(k) \right| = \left| e(k)^2 \cdot \mathbf{x}(k) \cdot \mu \right|$$

Sometimes there is a need for use of Normalized Least Mean Squares NLMS (I. Bukovsky et al., 2014) instead of classical GD because of demand to increase the stability (convergence) for given application. In that case the learning rate μ is replaced in GD with normalized learning rate η, what could be obtained as follows

$$\eta = \frac{\mu}{\epsilon + \| \mathbf{x} \|_2^2},$$

where ϵ is a regularization term that can be adaptable when some more sophisticated adaptive learning rates would be used (as modified for HONUs in (I. Bukovsky et al., 2014)) and for HONU with already augmented input vector $\mathbf{x}$ it can be $\epsilon = 0$. According to our experience with learning rate normalization for HONU as by, the initial learning rate than can be selected in range $\mu \in (1, 0.1)$. In the case of NLMS algorithm the estimation of novelty in data will look as follows

$$\mathbf{nd}(k) = \Big| e(k) \cdot \Delta \mathbf{w}(k) \Big| = \Big| e(k)^2 \cdot \mathbf{x}(k) \cdot \eta \Big| = \Big| \frac{e(k)^2 \cdot \mathbf{x}(k) \cdot \mu}{\epsilon + \mathbf{x}(k))^T \cdot \mathbf{x}(k)} \Big|,$$

For demonstration of this method with GD adaptation, we will use a linear based adaptive model also sometimes called Linear Neural Unit (LNU) or first-order HONU (Madan M. Gupta et al., 2013). The Novelty detection is used on this example for detection of changes in system - plant model sensitivity and model time constant. Result is displayed in Figure 3. The squared prediction error or the presented novelty detection method produce visible high coefficients for samples where the system changes occur. So the coefficients could be used for visual or even automated detection of system changes. Also it is obvious, that for this particular case (given system and GD adaptation) the produced coefficients of novelty $\mathbf{nd}$ does not provide different information than squared error e^2. What does not apply always, as it is proven on next algorithm.

Figure 3. Example demonstration of ND ability to recognize a change in plant model sensitivity or model time constant according to prediction with GD

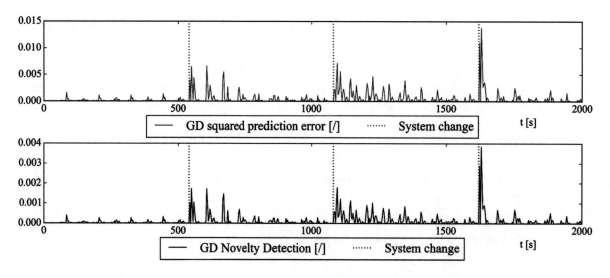

Other algorithm on which we will demonstrate the Novelty Detection is Recursive Least Squares (RLS). For this method the adaptive weights are calculated as follows

$$\mathbf{w}(k+1) = \mathbf{w}(k) + \mathbf{R}^{-1}(k)\mathbf{x}(k)e(k)$$

where the matrix $\mathbf{R}^{-1}(k)$ is inverse of the autocorrelation matrix with size $n \times n$, where n is amount of adaptive weights $\mathbf{w}(k)$. The $\mathbf{R}^{-1}(k+1)$ matrix is obtained as follows

$$\mathbf{R}^{-1}(k) = \frac{1}{\mu}\left(\mathbf{R}^{-1}(k-1) - \frac{\mathbf{R}^{-1}(k-1)\mathbf{x}(k)\mathbf{x}^{T}(k)\mathbf{R}^{-1}(k-1)}{\mu + \mathbf{x}^{T}(k)\mathbf{R}^{-1}(k-1)\mathbf{x}(k)}\right).$$

The initial value of matrix $\mathbf{R}^{-1}$ is set as follows

$$\mathbf{R}^{-1}(0) = \frac{1}{\delta}\mathbf{I} = \begin{bmatrix} \dfrac{1}{\delta} & & \\ & \ddots & \\ & & \dfrac{1}{\delta} \end{bmatrix},$$

where initialization parameter δ stands for small positive constant. According to the adaptation rule, we can describe novelty detection with RLS as follows

$$\mathbf{nd}(k) = \left| e(k) \cdot \Delta\mathbf{w}(k) \right| = \left| e^{2}(k)\mathbf{R}^{-1}(k)\mathbf{x}(k) \right|.$$

This method was tested on the same data as GD based Novelty detection approach. Results of the RLS novelty detection example are displayed on Figure 3. On this results is possible to see, that introduced technique could produce different and better information about novelty in data than just squared error of prediction e^{2}.

Adaptive Novelty Detection with Learning Entropy

The principle of Learning Entropy (LE) (Ivo Bukovsky, 2013; Ivo Bukovsky & Cyril Oswald, 2015) is extendable to incrementally learning dynamical systems in general as the LE algorithm evaluates weight increments of an adaptive model regardless its mathematical structure. For a general incremental learning rule, which is recalled in the form

$$\mathbf{w}(k+1) = \mathbf{w}(k) + \Delta\mathbf{w},$$

$\Delta\mathbf{w}$ is a vector of learning increments of all adaptable parameters calculated by actually applied learning rule for an input-output system such a plant or a whole control loop. The Learning Entropy can

Figure 4. Example demonstration of ND ability to recognize a change in plant model sensitivity or model time constant according to prediction with RLS

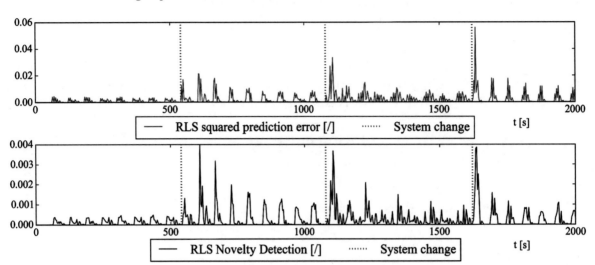

be practically calculated as the Approximate Individual Sample Learning Entropy (AISLE) (Ivo Bukovsky, 2013) that is the ratio of learning increments of unusually large magnitude in respect to the recent learning history. AISLE for the model is given as follows

$$E_A(k) = \frac{1}{n_\alpha \cdot n_w} \sum_{\alpha_{min}}^{\alpha_{max}} \sum_{i=0}^{n_w} h_\alpha(|\Delta w_i| \triangleright |\overline{\Delta w_i}|)$$

where h_α (TRUE) = 1, h_α (FALSE) = 0 and $\alpha = [\alpha_{min},...,\alpha_{max}]$ is vector of length n_α, that stands for detection sensitivities to overcome the otherwise single-scale nature of the detection (Demetriou & Polycarpou, 1998), (Ivo Bukovsky, 2013) and the recently average magnitude of each learning increment at time k is here calculated as

$$|\overline{\Delta w_i}| = \frac{1}{M} \sum_{\kappa=k-M}^{k-1} |\Delta w_i(\kappa)|$$

where M (i.e. m in (Ivo Bukovsky, 2013)) is the number of samples of considered recent learning history for LE. Contrary to (Ivo Bukovsky, 2013), (I. Bukovsky et al., 2012), it shall be highlighted that formula applies to adaptive models with time indexing according to.

Figure 5 displays result of Novelty Detection with Learning Entropy tested on system.

Adaptive Novelty Detection with SOM and HONU

In the control engineering, linear mathematical models of complex non-linear systems are often utilized for the controller design. These linear mathematical models are derived from non-linear mathematical

Figure 5. Data obtained from system model

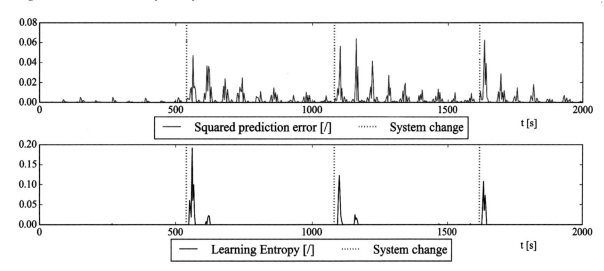

models of the controlled system by a linearizing at a system operating point. This approach is usually sufficient if majority of controlled systems running in steady operating points for a long period.

As mentioned in section 2, the HONU can be used as the controlled plant mathematical model in the operating point approximation. Let suppose that each novelty in the controlled system behavior can be considered as an operating point change. This change can be caused either by change in a measured system input or by unobserved change in the system operating conditions. Both require the HONU retraining for a new operating point. Gradually, it is possible to obtain a set of models defined by the HONU weights for all operating points achieved during a controlled system observation. The novelty of new weight vector acquired by HONU training can be assessed against a set of already gathered weight vectors of appropriates operating points.

A method introduced here utilizes Self-organizing Maps (SOMs) to store and evaluate obtained information about the controlled system operating point in form of trained HONU weight vectors. The SOM is a neural network which produces a smooth nonlinear mapping from high-dimensional input space onto a low dimensional 1D or 2D lattice. The resulted map then capture the latent structure of the input space data onto previously defined topology (Kohonen, 1990). The SOM learning is based on an unsupervised competitive learning. All neurons in the map are defined by their coordinates in the lattice and by a weight vector. During the learning period the SOM folds itself to fit input data by updating neurons weigh vectors which represents neurons position in the input data space, so the neurons groups are made in areas with high input data density (Su, Zhao, & Lee, 2004). Detail information about the theory of SOM is presented in (Kohonen, 1990).

In presented adaptive novelty method, the HONU is used as input-output model of the illustrational plant simulation model mentioned above. Particularly, the QNU defined by equations, and is utilize in following example. In each time step, the QNU is well trained by sliding window mode of Levenberg-Marquardt (LM) algorithm according to the equation

$$\Delta \mathbf{w}^{\text{HONU}}(k) = \left[\mathbf{J}^{T}(k)\mathbf{J}(k) + \frac{1}{\mu}\mathbf{I} \right]^{-1} \mathbf{J}^{T}(k)\mathbf{e}_{i}(k),$$

where $\Delta\mathbf{w}_i^{\text{HONU}}(k)$ is HONU weights update in particular training epoch i, k is the current time step, μ is the learning rate, $\mathbf{I}$ is the identity matrix and $\mathbf{J}(k)$ is the Jacobian matrix. $\mathbf{e}_i(k)$ is the HONU model error in training epoch i calculated as

$$\mathbf{e}_i(k) = \widetilde{\mathbf{y}}_i(k) - \mathbf{y}(k),$$

where $\mathbf{y}(k)$ is the output vector defined as

$$\mathbf{y}(k) = \begin{bmatrix} y(k-N) \\ y(k-N+1) \\ \vdots \\ y(k) \end{bmatrix}$$

where N is the sliding window length and $\widetilde{\mathbf{y}}_i(k)$ is the HONU model output in training epoch i determined by equation

$$\widetilde{\mathbf{y}}_i(k) = \mathbf{w}_i^{\text{HONU}}(k)\mathbf{X}(k).$$

In, $\mathbf{w}_i^{\text{HONU}}$ is the HONU weights vector in training epoch i. $\mathbf{X}(k)$ is the inputs matrix where inputs of all time steps included in current sliding window are sorted by columns. Using the definition of the input vector by the equation, $\mathbf{X}(k)$ can be written as

$$\mathbf{X}(k) = \begin{bmatrix} \mathbf{colx}(k-N) & \mathbf{colx}(k-N+1) & \cdots & \mathbf{colx}(k) \end{bmatrix}.$$

New weights vector is then calculated in each training epoch by equation

$$\mathbf{w}_{i+1}^{\text{HONU}}(k) = \mathbf{w}_i^{\text{HONU}}(k) + \Delta\mathbf{w}_i^{\text{HONU}}(k).$$

The HONU, or the QNU in this particular example, is trained in each time step for a predetermined number of epoch or until the error falls below a specified threshold. After a current time step HONU training period, the result weight vector is submitted to the SOM for training. The SOM is designed as 2D lattice with the SOM neurons in nodes. Each j-th SOM neuron has same number of weights in the j-th SOM neuron weight vector $\mathbf{w}_j^{\text{SOM}}(k)$ as the used HONU. As a first step, $\mathbf{w}_j^{\text{SOM}}(k)$ of each SOM neuron is considered as HONU weight vector and the sum of errors

$$\sum_{m=1}^{N} e_{m,j}(k) = \sum_{m=1}^{N} \widetilde{y}_{m,j}(k) - y_m(k),$$

is used as distance of each SOM neuron from current input data. The SOM neuron with lowest sum of errors is marked as a winner in current time step.

The SOM neuron weight vector update is for all SOM neurons then calculated by update rule

$$\Delta \mathbf{w}_{n,j}^{\mathrm{SOM}} - \left(\mathbf{w}^{\mathrm{HONU}}(k) - \mathbf{w}_{n,j}^{\mathrm{SOM}}(k), \right) \eta_n T_{n,(j,I(n))}(k),$$

where n. mean a number of SOM teaching iteration, $\eta(k)$ is the SOM learning rate

$$\eta_n = \eta(0) \exp\left(-\frac{n}{\lambda_\eta} \right),$$

which decreases with increases number of training iterations. $T_{n,(j,I(k))}(k)$ is so called the neighborhood function determining the learning impact to j-th SOM neuron depending on its lattice distance from the winner neuron as follows

$$T_{n,(j,I(k))}(k) = \exp\left(-\frac{S_{n,(j,I(k))}^2}{2\sigma_n^2} \right)$$

where $I(k)$ is the SOM winning neuron in time step k the function

$$\sigma_n = \sigma(0) \exp\left(-\frac{n}{\lambda_\sigma} \right)$$

ensures a learning influenced radius around the winner is decreasing with increasing number of training iterations.

The new j-th SOM neuron weights vector is then calculated as

$$\mathbf{w}_{j,i+1}^{\mathrm{SOM}}(k) = \mathbf{w}_{j,i}^{\mathrm{SOM}}(k) + \Delta \mathbf{w}_{j,i}^{\mathrm{SOM}}(k).$$

During the off-line pre-training period, the training data are segmented to individual sliding windows, and these sliding windows are presented to above described SOM with HONU in a random order in a sufficient number of iterations (from thousands to hundreds of thousands).

After the pre-training period, the SOM with HONU is switched to an on-line validation period. In each time step of on-line validation the HONU is trained, and the SOM winner neuron is found, same way as in pre-training period. Then the distance between $\mathbf{w}_{I(k)}^{\mathrm{SOM}}(k)$ and $\mathbf{w}^{\mathrm{HONU}}(k)$ is evaluated as squared Euclidian distance by equation

$$D_{I(k)}(k) = \left\| \mathbf{w}^{\mathrm{HONU}}(k) - \mathbf{w}_{I(k)}^{\mathrm{SOM}}(k) \right\|_2^2.$$

The novelty in presented input data can be evaluated from the value of the distance $D_{I(k)}(k)$, when larger distance mean more unknown system operating state.

The results of application of this SOM with HONU approach on closed-loop system presented in section 3 are in Figure 6 depicted. Data from 0 to 1000 seconds are used for pre-training period, that mean the SOM with HONU were taught to two variants of closed-loop systems. The closed-loop system variant between parameters changes in time 1080 [s] and 1620 [s] is completely unknown for the trained SOM with HONU. In Figure 6 is clearly seen the $D_{I(k)}(k)$ significantly increase around the first parameter change in time 540 [s], which indicates a transition of the system between two operating points a between parameters changes in time 1080 [s] and 1620 [s] $D_{I(k)}(k)$ indicates that the current operating point is unknown.

In Figure 7 are depicted the SOM with HONU distance map for four different time steps as representatives of four data sections. In maps are depicted distances between $\mathbf{w}^{\mathrm{HONU}}(k)$ and all $\mathbf{w}_j^{\mathrm{SOM}}(k)$. The distance is lower for darker color and the winner is presented by white square with black cross. The unknown closed-system state in data section 3 is in Figure 7, too.

Figure 6. Distance of trained HONU and SOM winner neuron. Increasing value of distance indicates more unknown system state. SOM with HONU was trained for data from 0 to 1000 seconds.

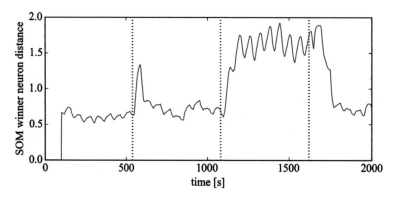

Figure 7. SOM distance maps for four different input data sections. Section 1 is represented by window at time 250 [s], Section 2 at time 650 [s], Section 3 at 1250 [s] and Section 4 at 1750 [s]. The distance is lower for darker color and the winner is presented by white square with black cross.

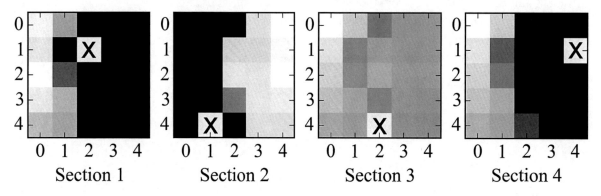

In Figure 8 the variant of SOM with HONU with on-line retraining on the same closed-loop system is shown. The SOM is retrained to unknown system state during the on-line validation. The retraining is triggered on when the distance $D_{I(k)}(k)$ is over given level for given time longer than usual system transition time. In this particular example the level, indicated by strong line in the figure, was set to 1.1.

The SOM with HONU was able to learn a new system state during the on-line validation period which is clearly seen on Figure 9, too.

SUMMARY

In this chapter we bring in three methods for detection of novelty in measured data. The methods were derived and presented on example data, obtained by model simulation.

Figure 8. Distance of trained HONU and SOM winner neuron with on-line validation retraining. Increasing value of distance indicates more unknown system state. SOM with HONU was trained for data from 0 to 1000 seconds. Strong line indicates the level for retraining start. Green color mean known state, blue mean unknown state without retraining and red mean retraining period.

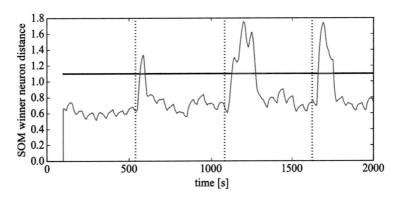

Figure 9. SOM with on-line validation retraining distance maps for four different input data sections. Section 1 is represented by window at time 250 [s], Section 2 at time 650 [s], Section 3 at 1250 [s] and Section 4 at 1750 [s]. The distance is lower for darker color and the winner is presented by white square with black cross.

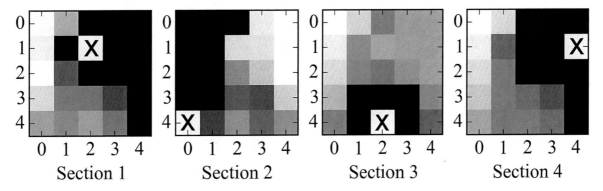

First introduced method - estimation of novelty detection coefficient (or coefficient vector) is based just on product of current value of adaptive weights and error of predictor. That makes this method low computationally complex and implementable on various online adaptive algorithms. However, this method in general produce lower accuracy than other presented, more sophisticated methods.

Second method, the novelty detection using Learning Entropy is built on evaluation of adaptive weight increments. This method is applicable for various model structures.

Both mentioned methods works just with actual or recent predictor information. In other words, these methods does not necessarily need to predict system accurately (it could have high prediction error), and still it could provide valuable information about novelty in data.

Last method is different. It is using SOM architecture and it is based on classification of system operation points. That means, that this method needs to be able to learn system behavior (unlike previously mentioned methods), otherwise it does not work correctly. When the method learns the system behavior, it is able to detect, whether the actual model state is new or if it was already measured in past.

REFERENCES

Alippi, C., Boracchi, G., & Roveri, M. (2013). Just-In-Time Classifiers for Recurrent Concepts. *IEEE Transactions on Neural Networks and Learning Systems*, *24*(4), 620–634. doi:10.1109/TNNLS.2013.2239309 PMID:24808382

Bukovsky, I. (2013). Learning Entropy: Multiscale Measure for Incremental Learning. *Entropy*, *15*(10), 4159–4187. doi:10.3390/e15104159

Bukovsky, I., & Bila, J. (2010). Adaptive Evaluation of Complex Dynamical Systems Using Low-Dimensional Neural Architectures. In Y. Wang, D. Zhang, & W. Kinsner (Eds.), Advances in Cognitive Informatics and Cognitive Computing (Vol. 323, pp. 33–57). Berlin, Heidelberg: Springer Berlin Heidelberg; Retrieved from http://link.springer.com/10.1007/978-3-642-16083-7_3 doi:10.1007/978-3-642-16083-7_3

Bukovsky, I., Kinsner, W., & Bila, J. (2012). Multiscale analysis approach for novelty detection in adaptation plot. In *Sensor Signal Processing for Defence* (pp. 1–6). SSPD; doi:10.1049/ic.2012.0114

Bukovsky, I., & Oswald, C. (2015). *Case Study of Learning Entropy for Adaptive Novelty Detection in Solid-fuel Combustion Control*. Advances in Intelligent Systems and Computing.

Bukovsky, I., Oswald, C., Cejnek, M., & Benes, P. M. (2014). Learning entropy for novelty detection a cognitive approach for adaptive filters. In *Sensor Signal Processing for Defence* (pp. 1–5). SSPD; doi:10.1109/SSPD.2014.6943329

Cejnek, M., Benes, P. M., & Bukovsky, I. (2014). Another Adaptive Approach to Novelty Detection in Time Series. In Computer Science & Information Technology (Vol. 4, pp. 341–351). Academy & Industry Research Collaboration Center (AIRCC). http://doi.org/ doi:10.5121/csit.2014.4229

Costa, M., Goldberger, A. L., & Peng, C.-K. (2002). Multiscale Entropy Analysis of Complex Physiologic Time Series. *Physical Review Letters*, *89*(6), 068102. doi:10.1103/PhysRevLett.89.068102 PMID:12190613

Demetriou, M. A., & Polycarpou, M. M. (1998). Incipient fault diagnosis of dynamical systems using online approximators. *IEEE Transactions on Automatic Control, 43*(11), 1612–1617. doi:10.1109/9.728881

Frank, P. M. (1990). Fault diagnosis in dynamic systems using analytical and knowledge-based redundancy: A survey and some new results. *Automatica, 26*(3), 459–474. doi:10.1016/0005-1098(90)90018-D

Grossberg, S. (2013). Adaptive Resonance Theory: How a Brain Learns to Consciously Attend, Learn, and Recognize a Changing World. *Neural Networks, 37*, 1–47. doi:10.1016/j.neunet.2012.09.017 PMID:23149242

Gupta, M. M., Bukovsky, I., Homma, N., Solo, A. M. G., & Hou, Z.-G. (2013). Fundamentals of Higher Order Neural Networks for Modeling and Simulation. In M. Zhang (Ed.), Artificial Higher Order Neural Networks for Modeling and Simulation (pp. 103–133). Hershey, PA, USA: IGI Global. Retrieved from http://services.igi-global.com/resolvedoi/resolve.aspx?doi=10.4018/978-1-4666-2175-6.ch006 doi:10.4018/978-1-4666-2175-6.ch006

Hayes, M. H. (1996). Recursive least squares. *Statistical Digital Signal Processing and Modeling*, 541.

Kohonen, T. (1990). The self-organizing map. *Proceedings of the IEEE, 78*(9), 1464–1480. doi:10.1109/5.58325

Markou, M., & Singh, S. (2003a). Novelty detection: a review—part 1: statistical approaches. *Signal Processing, 83*(12), 2481–2497. doi:10.1016/j.sigpro.2003.07.018

Markou, M., & Singh, S. (2003b). Novelty detection: a review—part 2: neural network based approaches. *Signal Processing, 83*(12), 2499–2521. doi:10.1016/j.sigpro.2003.07.019

Pincus, S. M. (1991). Approximate entropy as a measure of system complexity. *Proceedings of the National Academy of Sciences of the United States of America, 88*(6), 2297–2301. doi:10.1073/pnas.88.6.2297 PMID:11607165

Polycarpou, M. M., & Trunov, A. B. (2000). Learning approach to nonlinear fault diagnosis: Detectability analysis. *IEEE Transactions on Automatic Control, 45*(4), 806–812. doi:10.1109/9.847127

Richman, J. S., & Moorman, J. R. (2000). Physiological time-series analysis using approximate entropy and sample entropy. *American Journal of Physiology. Heart and Circulatory Physiology, 278*(6), H2039–H2049. PMID:10843903

Su, M.-C., Zhao, Y.-X., & Lee, J. (2004). SOM-based optimization. *Proceedings of the 2004 IEEE International Joint Conference on Neural Networks, 2004. Proceedings* (Vol. 1, p. -786). http://doi.org/doi:<ALIGNMENT.qj></ALIGNMENT>10.1109/IJCNN.2004.1380019

Trunov, A. B., & Polycarpou, M. M. (2000). Automated fault diagnosis in nonlinear multivariable systems using a learning methodology. *IEEE Transactions on Neural Networks, 11*(1), 91–101. doi:10.1109/72.822513 PMID:18249742

Vorburger, P., & Bernstein, A. (2006). Entropy-based Concept Shift Detection. *Proceedings of the Sixth International Conference on Data Mining, 2006. ICDM '06* (pp. 1113–1118). http://doi.org/doi:<ALIGNMENT.qj></ALIGNMENT>10.1109/ICDM.2006.66

Widmer, G., & Kubat, M. (1996). Learning in the presence of concept drift and hidden contexts. *Machine Learning*, *23*(1), 69–101. doi:10.1007/BF00116900

Widrow, B., & Stearns, S. D. (1985). *Adaptive signal processing*. Englewood Cliffs, N.J: Prentice Hall.

Willsky, A. S. (1976). A survey of design methods for failure detection in dynamic systems. *Automatica*, *12*(6), 601–611. doi:10.1016/0005-1098(76)90041-8

Yin, L., & Zhou, L. (2012). Function Based Fault Detection for Uncertain Multivariate Nonlinear Non-Gaussian Stochastic Systems Using Entropy Optimization Principle. *Entropy*, *15*(1), 32–52. doi:10.3390/e15010032

Section 2
Artificial Higher Order Neural Networks for Recognition

Chapter 4

Ultra High Frequency Sigmoid and Trigonometric Higher Order Neural Networks for Data Pattern Recognition

Ming Zhang
Christopher Newport University, USA

ABSTRACT

This chapter develops a new nonlinear model, Ultra high frequency siGmoid and Trigonometric Higher Order Neural Networks (UGT-HONN), for data pattern recognition. UGT-HONN includes Ultra high frequency siGmoid and Sine function Higher Order Neural Networks (UGS-HONN) and Ultra high frequency siGmoid and Cosine functions Higher Order Neural Networks (UGC-HONN). UGS-HONN and UGC-HONN models are used to recognition data patterns. Results show that UGS-HONN and UGC-HONN models are better than other Polynomial Higher Order Neural Network (PHONN) and Trigonometric Higher Order Neural Network (THONN) models, since UGS-HONN and UGC-HONN models to recognize data pattern with error approaching 0.0000%.

INTRODUCTION

The contributions of this chapter will be:

- Introduce the background of HONNs with the pattern recognition of HONNs.
- Develop a new UGT-HONN model for ultra-high frequency data pattern recognition.
- Provide the UGT-HONN learning algorithm and weight update formulae.
- Applications of UGT-HONN model for data pattern recognition.

This chapter is organized as follows: Section "BACKGROUND" gives the background knowledge of HONNs and pattern recognition applications using HONNs. Section "UGT-HONN MODELS" in-

DOI: 10.4018/978-1-5225-0063-6.ch004

troduces UGT-HONN structure and different modes of the UGT-HONN model. Section LEARNING ALGORITHM OF UGT-HONN MODELS provides the UGT-HONN model update formula, learning algorithms, and convergence theories of HONN. Section "UGT-HONN TESTING" describes UGT-HONN computer software system and testing results for data pattern recognition.

BACKGROUND

Artificial Neural Network (ANN) techniques had been widely used in the pattern recognition area. Sankar and Mammone (1991) study speaker independent vowel recognition using neural tree networks. Sethi and Jan (1991) analyze decision tree performance enhancement using an artificial neural networks implementation. Yao, Freeman, Burke, and Yang (1991) experiment pattern recognition by a distributed neural network.

Artificial Higher Order Neural Network (HONN) had been widely used in the pattern recognition area too. Reid, Spirkovska, and Ochoa (1989) show rapid training of higher-order neural networks for invariant pattern recognition. Spirkovska and Reid (1990) suggest connectivity strategies for higher-order neural networks applied to pattern recognition. Lisboa and Perantonis (1991) display the invariant pattern recognition using third-order networks and zernlike moments. Kanaoka, Chellappa, Yoshitaka, and Tomita (1992) built an artificial higher order neural network for distortion un-variant pattern recognition. Perantonis and Lisboa (1992) test the rotation and scale invariant pattern recognition by high-order neural networks and moment classifiers. Schmidt and Davis (1993) check the pattern recognition properties of various feature spaces for higher order neural networks. Spirkovska and Reid (1994) try higher order neural networks to apply 2D and 3D object recognition. He, and Siyal (1999) operate Improvement on higher-order neural networks for invariant object recognition. Park, Smith, and Mersereau (2000) employ target recognition based on directional filter banks and higher-order neural network. Kaita, Tomita, and Yamanaka (2002) research on a higher-order neural network for distortion invariant pattern recognition. Voutriaridis, Boutalis, and Mertzios (2003) seek ridge polynomial networks in pattern recognition. Foresti and Dolso (2004) look into an adaptive high-order neural tree for pattern recognition. Artyomov and Yadid-Pecht (2005) provide modified high-order neural network for invariant pattern recognition.

Selviah (2009) focuses on high speed optical higher order neural networks for discovering data trends and patterns in very large database. Selviah describes the progress in using optical technology to construct high-speed artificial higher order neural network systems. The chapter reviews how optical technology can speed up searches within large databases in order to identify relationships and dependencies between individual data records, such as financial or business time-series, as well as trends and relationships within them. Two distinct approaches in which optics may be used are reviewed. In the first approach, the chapter reviews current research replacing copper connections in a conventional data storage system, such as a several terabyte RAID array of magnetic hard discs, by optical waveguides to achieve very high data rates with low crosstalk interference. In the second approach, the chapter reviews how high speed optical correlators with feedback can be used to realize artificial higher order neural networks using Fourier Transform free space optics and holographic database storage.

Wang, Liu, and Liu (2009) investigate on complex artificial higher order neural networks for dealing with stochasticity, jumps and delays. This research deals with the analysis problem of the global exponential stability for a general class of stochastic artificial higher order neural networks with multiple mixed time delays and Markovian jumping parameters. The mixed time delays under consideration comprise both the discrete time-varying delays and the distributed time-delays. The main purpose of this chapter is to establish easily verifiable conditions under which the delayed high-order stochastic jumping neural network is exponentially stable in the mean square in the presence of both the mixed time delays and Markovian switching. By employing a new Lyapunov-Krasovskii functional and conducting stochastic analysis, a linear matrix nequality (LMI) approach is developed to derive the criteria ensuring the exponential stability. Furthermore, the criteria are dependent on both the discrete time-delay and distributed time-delay, hence less conservative. The proposed criteria can be readily checked by using some standard numerical packages such as the Matlab LMI Toolbox. A simple example is provided to demonstrate the effectiveness and applicability of the proposed testing criteria.

Zhang (2010) learn the rainfall estimation using neuron-adaptive higher order neural networks for rainfall estimation. Real world data is often nonlinear, discontinuous and may comprise high frequency, multi-polynomial components. Not surprisingly, it is hard to find the best models for modeling such data. Classical neural network models are unable to automatically determine the optimum model and appropriate order for data approximation. In order to solve this problem, Neuron-Adaptive Higher Order Neural Network (NAHONN) Models have been introduced. Definitions of one-dimensional, two-dimensional, and n-dimensional NAHONN models are studied. Specialized NAHONN models are also described. NAHONN models are shown to be "open box". These models are further shown to be capable of automatically finding not only the optimum model but also the appropriate order for high frequency, multi-polynomial, discontinuous data. Rainfall estimation experimental results confirm model convergence. This chapter further demonstrates that NAHONN models are capable of modeling satellite data. When the Xie and Scofield (1989) technique was used, the average error of the operator-computed IFFA rainfall estimates was 30.41%. For the Artificial Neural Network (ANN) reasoning network, the training error was 6.55% and the test error 16.91%, respectively. When the neural network group was used on these same fifteen cases, the average training error of rainfall estimation was 1.43%, and the average test error of rainfall estimation was 3.89%. When the neuron-adaptive artificial neural network group models was used on these same fifteen cases, the average training error of rainfall estimation was 1.31%, and the average test error of rainfall estimation was 3.40%. When the artificial neuron-adaptive higher order neural network model was used on these same fifteen cases, the average training error of rainfall estimation was 1.20%, and the average test error of rainfall estimation was 3.12%.

Murata (2010) presents the analysis and improvement of function approximation capabilities of pi-sigma higher order neural networks. Murata finds that A Pi-Sigma higher order neural network (Pi-Sigma HONN) is a type of higher order neural network, where, as its name implies, weighted sums of inputs are calculated first and then the sums are multiplied by each other to produce higher order terms that constitute the network outputs. This type of higher order neural networks have good function approximation capabilities. In this chapter, the structural feature of Pi-Sigma HONNs is discussed in contrast to other types of neural networks. The reason for their good function approximation capabilities is given based on pseudo-theoretical analysis together with empirical illustrations. Then, based on the analysis, an improved version of Pi-Sigma HONNs is proposed which has yet better functions approximation capabilities.

Ricalde, Sanchez, and Alanis (2010) propose recurrent higher order neural network control for output trajectory tracking with neural observers and constrained inputs. This study presents the design of an adaptive recurrent neural observer-controller scheme for nonlinear systems whose model is assumed to be unknown and with constrained inputs. The control scheme is composed of a neural observer based on Recurrent High Order Neural Networks which builds the state vector of the unknown plant dynamics and a learning adaptation law for the neural network weights for both the observer and identifier. These laws are obtained via control Lyapunov functions. Then, a control law, which stabilizes the tracking error dynamics Is developed using the Lyapunov and the inverse optimal control methodologies. Tracking error boundedness is established as a function of design parameters.

Fallahnezhad and Zaferanlouei (2013) produce a hybrid higher order neural structure for pattern recognition. This project considers that high order correlations of selected features next to the raw features of input can facilitate target pattern recognition. In artificial intelligence, this is usually addressed by Higher Order Neural Networks (HONNs). In general, HHON structures provide superior specifications (e.g. resolving dilemma of choosing number of neurons and layers of network, better fitting specs, lesser timing process and open-box specificity) to traditional neural networks. This chapter introduces a hybrid structure of higher order neural networks which can be generally applied in various branches of pattern recognition. Structure, learning algorithm, and network configuration are introduced and structure applied either as classifier (where is called HHONC) to different benchmark statistical data sets or as functional behavior approximation (where is called HHONN) to a heat and mass transfer dilemma. In each structure, results are compared with previous studies which imply on its superior performance next to other mentioned advantages.

UGT-HONN MODELS

The new HONN model, Ultra high frequency siGmoid and Trigonometric Higher Order Neural Network (UGT-HONN) has been developed. UGT-HONN includes two different models base on the different neuron functions. Ultra high frequency siGmoid and Sine Trigonometric Higher Order Neural Network (UGS-HONN) has neurons with sigmoid and sine functions. Ultra high frequency siGmoid and Cosine Trigonometric Higher Order Neural Network (UGC-HONN) has neurons with sigmoid and cosine functions. Except for the functions in the neuron all other parts of these three models are the same. The following section will discuss the UGS-HONN and UGC-HONN structures in detail.

UGT-HONN Model

UGS-HONN Model Structure can be seen in Figure 1. UGC-HONN Model Structure can be seen in Figure 2.

UGS-HONN Model

The Nyquist–Shannon sampling theorem, after Harry Nyquist and Claude Shannon, in the literature more commonly referred to as the Nyquist sampling theorem or simply as the sampling theorem, is a fundamental result in the field of information theory, in particular telecommunications and signal processing. Shannon's version of the theorem states:[Shannon, 1998]

If a function x(t) contains no frequencies higher than B hertz, it is completely determined by giving its ordinates at a series of points spaced 1/(2B) seconds apart.

In other words, a band limited function can be perfectly reconstructed from a countable sequence of samples if the band limit, B, is no greater than ½ the sampling rate (samples per second).

Figure 1. UGS-HONN Architecture

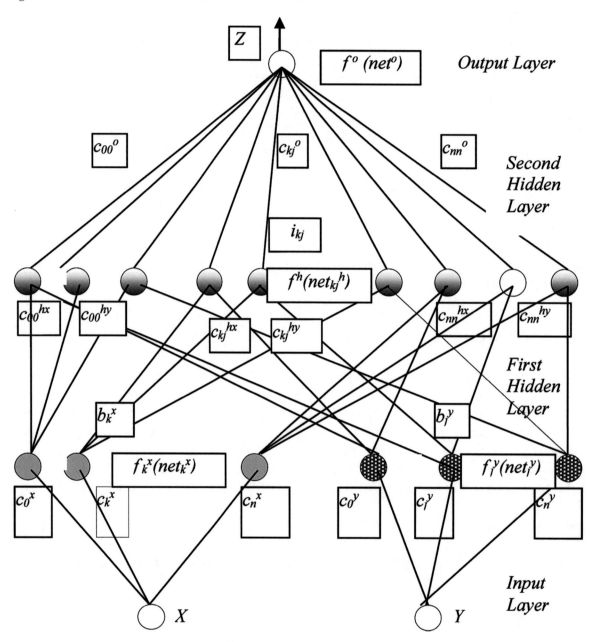

In simulating and predicting time series data, the new nonlinear models of UXS-HONN should have twice as high frequency as that of the ultra-high frequency of the time series data. To achieve this purpose, a new model should be developed to enforce high frequency of HONN in order to make the simulation and prediction error close to zero.

The different types of UGS-HONN models are shown as follows. Formula (1) (2) and (3) are for UGS-HONN model 2, 1 and 0 respectively. Model 2 has three layers of weights changeable, Model 1 has two layers of weights changeable, and model 0 has one layer of weights changeable. For models 2, 1

Figure 2.

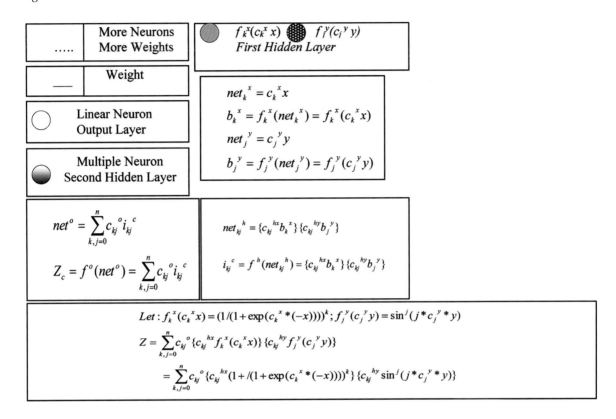

and 0, Z is the output while x and y are the inputs of UGS-HONN. c_{kj}^{o} is the weight for the output layer, c_{kj}^{hx} and c_{kj}^{hy} are the weights for the second hidden layer, and c_{k}^{x} and c_{j}^{y} are the weights for the first hidden layer. Functions cosine and sine are the first and second hidden layer nodes of UGS-HONN. The output layer node of UGS-HONN is a linear function of $f^{o}(net^{o}) = net^{o}$, where net^{o} equals the input of output layer node. UGS-HONN is an open neural network model, each weight of HONN has its corresponding coefficient in the model formula, and each node of UGS-HONN has its corresponding function in the model formula. The structure of UGS-HONN is built by a nonlinear formula. It means, after training, there is rationale for each component of UGS-HONN in the nonlinear formula.

$UGS - HONN \qquad Model \qquad 2:$

$$Z = \sum_{k,j=0}^{n} (c_{kj}^{o})\{c_{kj}^{hx}(1/(1+\exp(c_{k}^{x}*(-x))))^{k}\}\{c_{kj}^{hy}\sin^{j}(j*c_{j}^{y}y)\} \qquad (1)$$

$UGS - HONN \qquad Model \qquad 1:$

$$z = \sum_{k,j=0}^{n} c_{kj}^{o}\ (1/(1+\exp(c_{k}^{x}*(-x))))^{k}\sin^{j}(j*c_{j}^{y}y)$$

$where: \qquad (c_{kj}^{hx}) = (c_{kj}^{hy}) = 1 \qquad (2)$

$UGS - HONN \quad Model \quad 0:$

$$z = \sum_{k,j=0}^{n} c_{kj}^{\ o} \ (1 / (1 + \exp(-x)))^k \ \sin^j (j * y)$$
$where: \quad (c_{kj}^{\ hx}) = (c_{kj}^{\ hy}) = 1$
$\quad and \quad c_k^{\ x} = c_j^{\ y} = 1 \hspace{3cm} (3)$

For equations 1, 2, and 3, values of k and j ranges from 0 to n, where n is an integer. The UGS-HONN model can simulate ultra high frequency time series data, when n increases to a big number. This property of the model allows it to easily simulate and predicate ultra high frequency time series data, since both k and j increase when there is an increase in n.

The following is an expansion of model UGS-HONN order two.

$z = c_{00}^{\ o} \ c_{00}^{\ hx} \ c_{00}^{\ hy} \sin^0(0*c_0^{\ y}y)$

$+ c_{01}^{\ o} \ c_{01}^{\ hx} \ c_{01}^{\ hy} \sin(1*c_1^{\ y} y)$

$+ c_{02}^{\ o} \ c_{02}^{\ hx} \ c_{02}^{\ hy} \sin^2(2*c_2^{\ y} y)$

$+ c_{10}^{\ o} \ c_{10}^{\ hx} \ c_{10}^{\ hy} \ (1/(1+\exp(c_1^{\ x} (-x)))) \sin^0(0*c_0^{\ y}y)$

$+ c_{11}^{\ o} \ c_{11}^{\ hx} \ c_{11}^{\ hy} \ (1/(1+\exp(c_1^{\ x} (-x)))) \sin(1*c_1^{\ y} y)$

$+ c_{12}^{\ o} \ c_{12}^{\ hx} \ c_{12}^{\ hy} \ (1/(1+\exp(c_1^{\ x} (-x))) \sin^2(2*c_2^{\ y} y)$

$+ c_{20}^{\ o} \ c_{20}^{\ hx} \ c_{20}^{\ hy} \ (1/(1+\exp(c_2^{\ x} (-x))))^2 \sin^0(0*c_0^{\ y}y)$

$+ c_{21}^{\ o} \ c_{21}^{\ hx} \ c_{21}^{\ hy} \ (1/(1+\exp(c_2^{\ x} (-x))))^2 \sin(1*c_1^{\ y} y)$

$+ c_{22}^{\ o} \ c_{22}^{\ hx} \ c_{22}^{\ hy} \ (1/(1+\exp(c_2^{\ x} (-x))))^2 \sin^2(2*c_2^{\ y} y) \hspace{2cm} (4)$

The UGS-HONN Architecture is used to develop the model learning algorithm, which make sure the convergence of learning. This allows the deference between desired output and real output of UGS-HONN close to zero.

UGC-HONN Model

The UGC-HONN models replace the sine functions from UGS-HONN with cosine functions models, and the UGC-HONN models are defined as follows.

$UGCHONN \quad Model \quad 2:$

$$Z = \sum_{k,j=0}^{n} (c_{kj}^{\ o})\{c_{kj}^{\ hx}(1/(1+\exp(c_k^{\ x}*(-x))))^k\}\{c_{kj}^{\ hy}\cos^j(j*c_j^{\ y}y)\} \hspace{2cm} (5)$$

$UGCHONN \quad Model \quad 1:$

$$z = \sum_{k,j=0}^{n} c_{kj}{}^{o} \; (1 / (1 + \exp(c_{k}{}^{x} * (-x))))^{k} \cos^{j}(j * c_{j}{}^{y} y)$$

$where: \qquad (c_{kj}{}^{hx}) = (c_{kj}{}^{hy}) = 1 \qquad\qquad (6)$

$UGCHONN \quad Model \quad 0:$

$$z = \sum_{k,j=0}^{n} c_{kj}{}^{o} \; (1 / (1 + \exp(-x)))^{k} \cos^{j}(j * y)$$

$where: \qquad (c_{kj}{}^{hx}) = (c_{kj}{}^{hy}) = 1$

$\qquad and \qquad c_{k}{}^{x} = c_{j}{}^{y} = 1 \qquad\qquad (7)$

LEARNING ALGORITHM OF UGT-HONN MODELS

Learning Algorithm of UGS-HONN Model

Output Neurons in HONN Model (model 0, 1, and 2)

The output layer weights are updated according to:

$$c_{kj}{}^{o}(t + 1) = c_{kj}{}^{o}(t) - \eta(\partial E \; / \; \partial c_{kj}{}^{o}) \qquad\qquad (A.1)$$

where = learning rate (positive and usually < 1)

c_{kj} = weight; index k an j = input index

(k, j=0, 1, 2,…,n means one of n*n input neurons from the second hidden layer)

E = error

t = training time

o = output layer

The output node equations are:

$$net^o = \sum_{k,j=1}^{n} c_{kj}{}^o i_{kj}$$

$$z = f^o(net^o) = \sum_{k,j=1}^{n} c_{kj}{}^o i_{kj} \qquad (A.2)$$

where i_{kj} = input to the output neuron (= output from 2nd hidden layer)

z = actual output from the output neuron

f^o = output neuron activity function

The error at a particular output unit (neuron) will be:

$$\delta = (d - z) \qquad (A.3)$$

where d = desired output value
The total error is the error of output unit, namely:

$$E = 0.5 * \delta^2 = 0.5 * (d - z)^2 \qquad (A.4)$$

The derivatives $f^{o\prime}$(neto) are calculated as follows:
The output neuron function is linear function ($f^o(net^o) = net^o$):

$$f^{o\,\prime}(net^o) = \partial f^o / \partial(net^o) = \partial(net^o) / \partial(net^o) = 1 \qquad (A.5)$$

Gradients are calculated as follows:

$$\partial E \ / \partial c_{kj}{}^o = (\partial E / \partial z)(\partial z / \partial(net^o))(\partial(net^o) / \partial c_{kj}{}^o) \qquad (A.6)$$

$$\partial E \ / \partial z = (\partial(0.5 * (d - z)^2) / \partial z$$
$$= 0.5 * (-2(d - z)) = -(d - z) \qquad (A.7)$$

$$\partial z \ / \partial(net^o) = \partial f^o / \partial(net^o) = f^{o\,\prime}(net^o) \qquad (A.8)$$

$$\partial(net^o) / \partial_{kj}{}^o = \partial(\sum_{k,j=0}^{n} c_{kj}{}^o i_{kj}) / \partial c_{kj}{}^o = i_{kj} \qquad (A.9)$$

Combining Eqns. A.6 through A.9, the negative gradient is:

$$-\partial E \ / \ \partial c_{kj}{}^{o} = (d \ - z \ )f^{o} \ '(net^{o})i_{kj} \qquad\qquad (A.10)$$

For a linear output neuron, this becomes, by combining Eqns. A.10 and A.5:

$$-\partial E \ / \ \partial c_{kj}{}^{o} = (d \ - z \ )f^{o} \ '(net \ ^{o})i_{kj}$$
$$= (d \ - z \ )(1)i_{kj} = (d \ - z)i_{kj} \qquad\qquad (A.11)$$

The weight update equations are formulated as follows:for linear output neurons, let:

$$\delta^{ol} = (d - z) \qquad\qquad (A.12)$$

Combining Formulae A.1, A.11, and A.12:

$$c_{kj}{}^{o}(t + 1) = c_{kj}{}^{o}(t) - \eta(\partial E \ / \ \partial a_{kj}{}^{o})$$
$$= c_{kj}{}^{o}(t) + \eta(d \ - z \ )f^{o} \ '(net^{o})i_{kj}$$
$$= a_{kj}{}^{o}(t) + \eta\delta \ ^{ol}i_{kj}$$
$$where:$$
$$\delta^{ol} = (d - z)$$
$$f^{o'}(net^{o}) = 1 \qquad (linear \qquad neuron) \qquad\qquad (A.13)$$

Second-Hidden Layer Neurons in HONN Model (Model 2)

The second hidden layer weights are updated according to:

$$c_{kj}{}^{hx}(t + 1) = c_{kj}{}^{hx}(t) - \eta(\partial E \ / \ \partial c_{kj}{}^{hx}) \qquad\qquad (B.1)$$

where = learning rate (positive & usually < 1)

k,j = input index (k, j = 0, 1, 2, …,n means one of 2*n*n input combinations from the first hidden layer)

E = error

t = training time

hx = hidden layer, related to x input

$c_{kj}{}^{hx}$ = hidden layer weight related to x input

The equations for the 2nd hidden layer node are:

$$net_{kj}{}^h = \{c_{kj}{}^{hx}b_k{}^x\}\{c_{kj}{}^{hy}b_j{}^y\}$$
$$i_{kj} = f^h(net_{kj}{}^h) \qquad\qquad (B.2)$$

where i_{kj} = output from 2nd hidden layer (= input to the output neuron)

$b_k{}^x$ and $b_j{}^y$ = input to 2nd hidden layer neuron

(= output from the 1st hidden layer neuron)

f^h = hidden neuron activation function

hy = hidden layer, related to y input

$c_{kj}{}^{hy}$ = hidden layer weight related to y input

We call the neurons at the second layer multiple neurons. Their activity function is linear and their inputs are the multiplication of two outputs of the first layer neuron output times9 their weights.

The error of a single output unit will be:

$$\delta = (d - z) \qquad\qquad (B.3)$$

where d = desired output value of output layer neuron

z = actual output value of output layer neuron

The total error is the sum of the squared errors across all output units, namely:

$$E_p = 0.5 * \delta^2 = 0.5 * (d - z)^2$$
$$= 0.5 * (d - f^o(net^o))^2$$
$$= 0.5 * (d - f_k^o(\sum_j c_{kj}{}^o i_{kj}))^2 \qquad\qquad (B.4)$$

The derivatives f$^{h'}$(net$^h_{pj}$) are calculated as follows, for a linear function of second layer neurons:

$$i_{kj} = f^h(net_{kj}{}^h) = (net_{kj}{}^h)$$
$$f^h{}'(net_{kj}{}^h) = 1 \qquad\qquad (B.5)$$

The gradient (E/$c_{kj}{}^{hx}$) is given by:

$$\partial E \ / \partial c_{kj}{}^{hx} = \partial(0.5*(d-z)^2)/\partial c_{kj}{}^{hx}$$
$$= (\partial(0.5*(d-z)^2)/\partial z \ )(\partial z \ / \partial(net^{\,o}))$$
$$(\partial(net^{\,o})/\partial i_{kj})(\partial i_{kj} / \partial(net_{kj}{}^{h}))(\partial(net_{kj}{}^{h})/\partial c_{kj}{}^{hx}) \qquad\qquad (B.6)$$

$$\partial(0.5*(d-z)^2)/\partial z \ = 0.5*(-2(d-z)) = -(d-z) \qquad\qquad (B.7)$$

$$\partial z / \partial(net^{o}) = \partial f^{\,o} / \partial(net^{o}) = f_{k}^{\,o}\,{}'(net^{o}) \qquad\qquad (B.8)$$

$$\partial(net^{\,o})/\partial i_{kj} = \partial(\sum_{k,j=1}^{n}(c_{kj}{}^{o}i_{kj}))/\partial i_{kj} = c_{kj}{}^{o} \qquad\qquad (B.9)$$

$$\partial i_{kj} / \partial(net_{kj}{}^{h}) = \partial(f^{\,h}(net_{kj}{}^{h}))/\partial(net_{kj}{}^{h}) =)f^{\,h}\,{}'(net_{kj}{}^{h}) \qquad\qquad (B.10)$$

$$\partial(net_{kj}{}^{h})/\partial c_{kj}{}^{hx} = \partial(\{c_{kj}{}^{hx}b_{k}{}^{x}\}\{c_{kj}{}^{hy}b_{j}{}^{y}\})/\partial c_{kj}{}^{hx}$$
$$= b_{k}{}^{x}c_{kj}{}^{hy}b_{j}{}^{y} = \delta_{kj}{}^{hx}b_{k}{}^{x}$$
$$where: \delta_{kj}{}^{hx} = c_{kj}{}^{hy}b_{j}{}^{y} \qquad\qquad (B.11)$$

Combining Eqns. B.6 through B.11, the negative gradient is:

$$-\partial E \ / \partial c_{kj}{}^{hx} = (d-z)f^{\,o}\,{}'(net^{\,o})c_{kj}{}^{o}f^{\,h}\,{}'(net_{pj}{}^{h})\delta^{\,hx}b_{k}{}^{x} \qquad\qquad (B.12)$$

The weight update equations are formulated as follows:let output neuron is a linear neuron:

$$\delta^{ol} = (d-z)f^{\,o}{}_{k}\,{}'(net^{o}) = (d-z) \qquad\qquad (B.13)$$

And also let the second layer neurons be linear neurons. Combining Formulae B.1, B.5, B.12 and B.13:

$$c_{kj}{}^{hx}(t+1) = c_{kj}{}^{hx}(t) - \eta(\partial E / \partial c_{kj}{}^{hx})$$
$$= c_{kj}{}^{hx}(t) + \eta((d-z)f^{\,o}\,{}'(net^{\,o})c_{kj}{}^{o}f^{\,h}\,{}'(net_{kj}{}^{hx})c_{kj}{}^{hy}b_{j}{}^{y}b_{k}{}^{x})$$
$$= c_{kj}{}^{hx}(t) + \eta(\delta^{\,ol}c_{kj}{}^{o}\delta_{kj}{}^{hx}b_{k}{}^{x})$$
$$where: \qquad \delta^{\,ol} = (d-z)$$
$$\delta_{kj}{}^{hx} = c_{kj}{}^{hy}b_{j}{}^{y}$$
$$f^{\,o}\,{}'(net^{o}) = 1 \qquad (linear \qquad neuron)$$
$$f^{\,h}\,{}'(net_{kj}{}^{hx}) = 1 \qquad (linear \qquad neuron) \qquad\qquad (B.14)$$

Using the same rules, the weight update equation for y input neurons is:

$$c_{kj}^{hy}(t+1) = c_{kj}^{hy}(t) - \eta(\partial E / \partial c_{kj}^{hy})$$
$$= c_{kj}^{hy}(t) + \eta((d-z)f^{o'}(net^{o})c_{kj}^{o}f^{h'}(net_{kj}^{hy})c_{kj}^{hx}b_{k}^{x}b_{j}^{y})$$
$$= c_{kj}^{hy}(t) + \eta(\delta^{ol}c_{kj}^{o}\delta_{kj}^{hy}b_{j}^{y})$$

$$where: \quad \delta^{ol} = (d-z)$$
$$\delta_{kj}^{hy} = c_{kj}^{hx}b_{k}^{x}$$
$$f^{o'}(net^{o}) = 1 \quad (linear \quad neuron)$$
$$f^{h'}(net_{kj}^{hy}) = 1 \quad (linear \quad neuron) \quad\quad (B.15)$$

First Hidden Layer Neurons in HONN

First Hidden Layer Neurons in UGS-HONN (Model 1 and Model 2)

The 1st hidden layer weights are updated according to:

$$c_{k}^{x}(t+1) = c_{k}^{x}(t) - \eta(\partial E_{p} / \partial c_{k}^{x}) \quad\quad (C.1)$$

Where:

$c_{k}^{x} = 1^{st}$ hidden layer weight for input x; $k = k$th neuron of first hidden layer

= learning rate (positive & usually < 1)

E = error

t = training time

The equations for the kth or j^{th} node in the first hidden layer are:

$$net_{k}^{x} = c_{k}^{x} * x$$
$$b_{k}^{x} = f_{k}^{x}(net_{k}^{x})$$
$$or$$
$$net_{j}^{y} = c_{j}^{y} * y$$
$$b_{j}^{y} = f_{j}^{y}(net_{j}^{y}) \quad\quad (C.2)$$

Where: i_{kj} = output from 2nd hidden layer (= input to the output neuron) b_k^x and b_j^y = output from the 1st hidden layer neuron (= input to 2nd hidden layer neuron) f_k^x and f_j^y = 1st hidden layer neuron activation function x and y = input to 1st hidden layer

The total error is the sum of the squared errors across all hidden units, namely:

$$E_p = 0.5 * \delta^2 = 0.5 * (d - z)^2$$
$$= 0.5 * (d - f^o(net^o))^2$$
$$= 0.5 * (d - f^o(\sum_j c_{kj}^{\ o} i_{kj}))^2 \qquad (C.3)$$

The gradient $(\partial E_p / \partial c_k^x)$ is given by:

$$\partial E_p / \partial c_k^x = \partial(0.5 * (d-z)^2) / \partial c_k^x$$
$$= (\partial(0.5 * (d-z)^2) / \partial z)(\partial z / \partial(net^o))$$
$$(\partial(net^o) / \partial i_{kj})(\partial i_{kj} / \partial(net_{kj}^h))(\partial(net_{kj}^h) / \partial b_k^x)$$
$$(\partial b_k^x / \partial(net_k^x))(\partial(net_k^x) / \partial c_k^x) \qquad (C.4)$$

$$\partial(0.5 * (d-z)^2 / \partial z = -(d-z) \qquad (C.5)$$

$$\partial z / \partial(net^o) = \partial f^o / \partial(net^o) = f^o{}'(net^o) \qquad (C.6)$$

$$\partial(net^o) / \partial i_{kj} = \partial(\sum_{k,j=1}^{l} (c_{kj}^{\ o} i_{kj})) / \partial i_{kj} = c_{kj}^{\ o} \qquad (C.7)$$

$$\partial i_{kj} / \partial(net_{kj}^h) = \partial(f^h(net_{kj}^h)) / \partial(net_{kj}^h) = f^h{}'(net_{kj}^h) \qquad (C.8)$$

$$\partial net_{kj}^h / \partial b_k^x = \partial((c_{kj}^{hx} * b_k^x)*(c_{kj}^{hy} * b_j^y)) / \partial b_k^x = c_{kj}^{hx} * c_{kj}^{hy} * b_j^y$$
$$= \delta_{kj}^{hx} c_{kj}^{hx}$$
$$where : \delta_{kj}^{hx} = c_{kj}^{hy} * b_j^y \qquad (C.9)$$

$$\partial b_k^x / \partial(net_k^x) = f_x{}'(net_k^x) \qquad (C.10)$$

$$\partial(net_k^x) / \partial c_k^x = \partial(c_k^x * x) / \partial c_k^x = x \qquad (C.11)$$

Combining Formulae C.5 through C.11 the negative gradient is:

$$-\partial E_p / \partial c_k^{\,x} = (d-z)f^o{'}(net^o)c_{kj}^{\,o} * f^h{'}(net_{kj}^{\,h})\delta_{kj}^{\,hx}c_{kj}^{\,hx}f_x{'}(net_k^{\,x})x \qquad (C.12)$$

The weight update equations are calculated as follows.
For linear output neurons:

$$f^o{'}(net^o) = 1$$
$$\delta^{ol} = (d-z)f^o{'}(net^o) = (d-z) \qquad (C.13)$$

For linear neurons of second hidden layer:

$$f^h{'}(net_{kj}^{\,h}) = 1 \qquad (C.14)$$

The negative gradient is:

$$-\partial E_p / \partial c_k^{\,x} = (d-z)f^o{'}(net^o)c_{kj}^{\,o} * f^h{'}(net_{kj}^{\,h})\delta_{kj}^{\,hx}c_{kj}^{\,hx}f_x{'}(net_k^{\,x})x$$
$$= \delta^{ol} * c_{kj}^{\,o} * \delta_{kj}^{\,hx} * c_{kj}^{\,hx} * f_x{'}(net_k^{\,x}) * x \qquad (C.15)$$

By combining Formulae C.1, C.4, and C.16, for a linear 1st hidden layer neuron:

Let :
$$f_k^{\,j}(c_k^{\,j}x) = (1 / (1 + \exp(c_k^{\,x}(-x))))^k$$
$$f_j^{\,y}(c_j^{\,k}y) = \sin^j(j * c_j^{\,k}y)$$

For a sigmoid function of x input side:

$$b_k^{\,x} = f_k^{\,x}(net_k^{\,x}) = [1 / (1 + \exp(-net_k^{\,x}))]^k$$
$$\qquad = [1 / (1 + \exp(c_k^{\,x} * (-x)))]^k$$
$$f_x{'}(net_k^{\,x}) = \partial b_k^{\,x} / \partial(net_k^{\,x}) \qquad (UGS - HONN \qquad C.16)$$
$$= \partial[1 / (1 + \exp(-net_k^{\,x}))]^k / \partial(net_k^{\,x})$$
$$= k * [1 / (1 + \exp(-net_k^{\,x}))]^{k-1} * (1 + \exp(-net_k^{\,x}))^{-2} * \exp(-net_k^{\,x})$$
$$= k * [1 / (1 + \exp(-c_k^{\,x} * x))]^{k-1} * (1 + \exp(-c_k^{\,x} * x))^{-2} * \exp(-c_k^{\,x} * x)$$

$$c_k{}^x(t+1) = c_k{}^x(t) - \eta(\partial E_p \,/\, \partial c_k{}^x)$$

$$= c_k{}^x(t) + \eta(d-z)f^o{}'(net^o)c_{kj}{}^o * f^h{}'(net_{kj}{}^h)c_{kj}{}^{hy}b_j{}^y c_{kj}{}^{hx}f_x{}'(net_k{}^x)x$$

$$= c_k{}^x(t) + \eta * \delta^{ol} * c_{kj}{}^o * \delta^{hx} * c_{kj}{}^{hx} * f_x{}'(net_k{}^x) * x$$

$$= c_k{}^x(t) + \eta * \delta^{ol} * c_{kj}{}^o * \delta^{hx} * c_{kj}{}^{hx}$$

$$\qquad * [k * [1\,/\,(1+\exp(-c_k{}^x * x))]^{k-1} * (1+\exp(-c_k{}^x * x))^{-2} * \exp(-c_k{}^x * x)] * x$$

$$= c_k{}^x(t) + \eta * \delta^{ol} * c_{kj}{}^o * \delta^{hx} * c_{kj}{}^{hx} * \delta^x * x \qquad (UGS-HONN \qquad C.17)$$

where :

$$\delta^{ol} = (d-z)f^o{}'(net^o) = d-z \qquad (linear \qquad neuron \qquad f^o{}'(net^o) = 1)$$

$$\delta^{hx} = f^h{}'(net_{kj}{}^h)c_{kj}{}^{hy}b_j{}^y = c_{kj}{}^{hy}b_j{}^y \qquad (linear \qquad neuron \qquad f^h{}'(net_{kj}{}^h) = 1)$$

$$\delta^x = f_x{}'(net_k{}^x)$$

$$\qquad = k * [1\,/\,(1+\exp(-c_k{}^x * x))]^{k-1} * (1+\exp(-c_k{}^x * x))^{-2} * \exp(-c_k{}^x * x)$$

$$b_j{}^y = f_j{}^y(net_j{}^y) = \sin^j(j*net_j{}^y) = \sin^j(j*c_j{}^y*y)$$

$$f_y{}'(net_j{}^y) = \partial b_j{}^y \,/\, \partial(net_j{}^y)$$

$$= \partial(\sin^j(j*net_j{}^y))\,/\,\partial(net_j{}^y)$$

$$= j\sin^{j-1}(j*net_j{}^y)*\cos(j*net_j{}^y)*j$$

$$= j^2 * \sin^{j-1}(j*net_j{}^y)*\cos(j*net_j{}^y)$$

$$= j^2 * \sin^{j-1}(j*c_j{}^y*y)*\cos(j*c_j{}^y*y) \qquad (UGS-HONN \qquad C.18)$$

For an ultra-high frequency sine function of *y* input part:
Using the above procedure:

$$c_j{}^y(t+1) = c_j{}^y(t) - \eta(\partial E_p \,/\, \partial c_j{}^y)$$

$$= c_j{}^y(t) + \eta(d-z)f^o{}'(net^o)c_{kj}{}^o * f^h{}'(net_{kj}{}^h)c_{kj}{}^{hx}b_k{}^x c_{kj}{}^{hy}f_y{}'(net_j{}^y)y$$

$$= c_j{}^y(t) + \eta * \delta^{ol} * c_{kj}{}^o * \delta^{hy} * c_{kj}{}^{hy} * (j^2)\sin^{j-1}(j*c_j{}^y*y)\cos(j*c_j{}^y*y)*y$$

$$= c_j{}^y(t) + \eta * \delta^{ol} * c_{kj}{}^o * \delta^{hy} * c_{kj}{}^{hy} * \delta^y * y \qquad (UGS-HONN \qquad C.19)$$

where :

$$\delta^{ol} = (d-z)f^o{}'(net^o) = d-z \qquad (linear \qquad neuron \qquad f^o{}'(net^o) = 1)$$

$$\delta^{hy} = f^h{}'(net_{kj}{}^{hy})c_{kj}{}^{hx}b_k{}^x = c_{kj}{}^{hx}b_k{}^x \qquad (linear \qquad neuron \qquad f^h{}'(net_{kj}{}^{hy}) = 1)$$

$$\delta^y = f_y{}'(net_j{}^y) = (j^2)\sin^{j-1}(j*c_j{}^y*y)\cos(j*c_j{}^y*y)$$

First Hidden Layer Neurons in UGC-HONN (Model 1 and Model 2)

The 1st hidden layer weights are updated according to:

$$c_k^x(t+1) = c_k^x(t) - \eta(\partial E_p / \partial c_k^x) \qquad (D.1)$$

Where:

$c_k^x = 1^{st}$ hidden layer weight for input x; $k = k^{th}$ neuron of first hidden layer

η = learning rate (positive & usually < 1)

E = error

t = training time

The equations for the kth or j^{th} node in the first hidden layer are:

$$net_k^x = c_k^x * x$$
$$b_k^x = f_k^x(net_k^x)$$
$$or$$
$$net_j^y = c_j^y * y$$
$$b_j^y = f_j^y(net_j^y) \qquad (D.2)$$

Where:

i_{kj} = output from 2nd hidden layer (= input to the output neuron)

b_k^x and b_j^y = output from the 1st hidden layer neuron (= input to 2nd hidden layer neuron)

f_k^x and f_j^y = 1st hidden layer neuron activation function

x and y = input to 1st hidden layer

The total error is the sum of the squared errors across all hidden units, namely:

$$E_p = 0.5 * \delta^2 = 0.5 * (d - z)^2$$
$$= 0.5 * (d - f^o(net^o))^2$$
$$= 0.5 * (d - f^o(\sum_j c_{kj}^o i_{kj}))^2 \qquad (D.3)$$

For a polynomial and cosine function:
The gradient ($\partial E_p / \partial c_k^x$) is given by:

$$\partial E_p / \partial c_k^x = \partial(0.5 * (d-z)^2) / \partial c_k^x$$

$$= (\partial(0.5 * (d-z)^2) / \partial z)(\partial z / \partial(net^o))$$

$$(\partial(net^o) / \partial i_{kj})(\partial i_{kj} / \partial(net_{kj}^h))(\partial(net_{kj}^h) / \partial b_k^x)$$

$$(\partial b_k^x / \partial(net_k^x))(\partial(net_k^x) / \partial c_k^x) \qquad (D.4)$$

$$\partial(0.5 * (d-z)^2 / \partial z = -(d-z) \qquad (D.5)$$

$$\partial z / \partial(net^o) = \partial f^o / \partial(net^o) = f^o{}'(net^o) \qquad (D.6)$$

$$\partial(net^o) / \partial i_{kj} = \partial(\sum_{k,j=1}^{L}(c_{kj}^o i_{kj})) / \partial i_{kj} = c_{kj}^o \qquad (D.7)$$

$$\partial i_{kj} / \partial(net_{kj}^h) = \partial(f^h(net_{kj}^h)) / \partial(net_{kj}^h) = f^h{}'(net_{kj}^h) \qquad (D.8)$$

$$\partial net_{kj}^h / \partial b_k^x = \partial((c_{kj}^{hx} * b_k^x) * (c_{kj}^{hy} * b_j^y)) / \partial b_k^x = c_{kj}^{hx} * c_{kj}^{hy} * b_j^y$$

$$= \delta_{kj}^{hx} c_{kj}^{hx}$$

$$where : \delta_{kj}^{hx} = c_{kj}^{hy} * b_j^y \qquad (D.9)$$

$$\partial b_k^x / \partial(net_k^x) = f_x{}'(net_k^x) \qquad (D.10)$$

$$\partial(net_k^x) / \partial c_k^x = \partial(c_k^x * x) / \partial c_k^x = x \qquad (D.11)$$

Combining Formulae D.5 through D.11 the negative gradient is:

$$-\partial E_p / \partial c_k^x = (d-z)f^o{}'(net^o)c_{kj}^o * f^h{}'(net_{kj}^h)\delta_{kj}^{hx}c_{kj}^{hx}f_x{}'(net_k^x)x \qquad (D.12)$$

The weight update equations are calculated as follows.
For linear output neurons:

$$f^o{}'(net^o) = 1$$

$$\delta^{ol} = (d-z)f^o{}'(net^o) = (d-z) \qquad (D.13)$$

For linear neurons of second hidden layer:

$$f^{h}{}'(net_{kj}{}^{h}) = 1 \qquad (D.14)$$

The negative gradient is:

$$-\partial E_p / \partial c_k{}^{x} = (d-z)f^{o}{}'(net^{o})c_{kj}{}^{o} * f^{h}{}'(net_{kj}{}^{h})\delta_{kj}{}^{hx}c_{kj}{}^{hx}f_x{}'(net_k{}^{x})x$$
$$= \delta^{ol} * c_{kj}{}^{o} * \delta_{kj}{}^{hx} * c_{kj}{}^{hx} * f_x{}'(net_k{}^{x}) * x \qquad (D.15)$$

Let :
$$f_k{}^{j}(c_k{}^{j}x) = (1 / (1+\exp(c_k{}^{x}(-x))))^{k}$$
$$f_j{}^{y}(c_j{}^{k}y) = \cos^{j}(j * c_j{}^{k}y)$$

For a sigmoid function of x input side:

$$b_k{}^{x} = f_k{}^{x}(net_k{}^{x}) = [1 / (1+\exp(-net_k{}^{x}))]^{k}$$
$$= [1 / (1+\exp(c_k{}^{x} * (-x)))]^{k}$$
$$f_x{}'(net_k{}^{x}) = \partial b_k{}^{x} / \partial(net_k{}^{x}) \qquad (UGC-HONN \qquad D.16)$$
$$= \partial[1 / (1+\exp(-net_k{}^{x}))]^{k} / \partial(net_k{}^{x})$$
$$= k * [1 / (1+\exp(-net_k{}^{x}))]^{k-1} * (1+\exp(-net_k{}^{x}))^{-2} * \exp(-net_k{}^{x})$$
$$= k * [1 / (1+\exp(-c_k{}^{x} * x))]^{k-1} * (1+\exp(-c_k{}^{x} * x))^{-2} * \exp(-c_k{}^{x} * x)$$

$$c_k{}^{x}(t+1) = c_k{}^{x}(t) - \eta(\partial E_p / \partial c_k{}^{x})$$
$$= c_k{}^{x}(t) + \eta(d-z)f^{o}{}'(net^{o})c_{kj}{}^{o} * f^{h}{}'(net_{kj}{}^{h})c_{kj}{}^{hy}b_j{}^{y}c_{kj}{}^{hx}f_x{}'(net_k{}^{x})x$$
$$= c_k{}^{x}(t) + \eta * \delta^{ol} * c_{kj}{}^{o} * \delta^{hx} * c_{kj}{}^{hx} * f_x{}'(net_k{}^{x}) * x$$
$$= c_k{}^{x}(t) + \eta * \delta^{ol} * c_{kj}{}^{o} * \delta^{hx} * c_{kj}{}^{hx}$$
$$\qquad * [k * [1 / (1+\exp(-c_k{}^{x} * x))]^{k-1} * (1+\exp(-c_k{}^{x} * x))^{-2} * \exp(-c_k{}^{x} * x)] * x$$
$$= c_k{}^{x}(t) + \eta * \delta^{ol} * c_{kj}{}^{o} * \delta^{hx} * c_{kj}{}^{hx} * \delta^{x} * x \qquad (UGC-HONN \qquad D.17)$$
where :
$$\delta^{ol} = (d-z)f^{o}{}'(net^{o}) = d-z \qquad (linear \qquad neuron \qquad f^{o}{}'(net^{o}) = 1)$$
$$\delta^{hx} = f^{h}{}'(net_{kj}{}^{h})c_{kj}{}^{hy}b_j{}^{y} = c_{kj}{}^{hy}b_j{}^{y} \qquad (linear \qquad neuron \qquad f^{h}{}'(net_{kj}{}^{h}) = 1)$$
$$\delta^{x} = f_x{}'(net_k{}^{x})$$
$$\qquad = k * [1 / (1+\exp(-c_k{}^{x} * x))]^{k-1} * (1+\exp(-c_k{}^{x} * x))^{-2} * \exp(-c_k{}^{x} * x)$$

For an ultra-high frequency cosine function of y input part:

$$b_j^{\ y} = f_y\ (net_j^{\ y}) = \cos^j(j*net_j^{\ y}) = \cos^j(j*c_j^{\ y}*y)$$

$$f_y\ '(net_j^{\ y}) = \partial b_j^{\ y}\ /\ \partial(net_j^{\ y})$$

$$= \partial(\cos^j(j*net_j^{\ y}))\ /\ \partial(net_j^{\ y})$$

$$= j\cos^{j-1}(j*net_j^{\ y})*(-\sin(j*net_j^{\ y}))*j$$

$$= -j^2*\cos^{j-1}(j*net_j^{\ y})*\sin(j*net_j^{\ y})$$

$$= -j^2*\cos^{j-1}(j*c_j^{\ y}*y)*\sin(j*c_j^{\ y}*y) \qquad\qquad (UGC-HONN \qquad D.18)$$

Using the above procedure:

$$c_j^{\ y}(t+1) = c_j^{\ y}(t) - \eta(\partial E_p\ /\ \partial c_j^{\ y})$$

$$= c_j^{\ y}(t) + \eta(d-z)f^{o}\ '(net^{\ o})c_{kj}^{\ o}*f^{h}\ '(net_{kj}^{\ h})c_{kj}^{\ hx}b_k^{\ x}c_{kj}^{\ hy}f_y\ '(net_j^{\ y})y$$

$$= c_j^{\ y}(t) + \eta*\delta^{\ ol}*c_{kj}^{\ o}*\delta^{\ hy}*c_{kj}^{\ hy}*(-j^2)*\cos^{j-1}(j*c_j^{\ y}*y)*\sin(j*c_j^{\ y}*y)*y$$

$$= c_j^{\ y}(t) + \eta*\delta^{\ ol}*c_{kj}^{\ o}*\delta^{\ hy}*c_{kj}^{\ hy}*\delta^{\ y}*y \qquad\qquad (UGC-HONN \qquad D.19)$$

where :

$$\delta^{\ ol} = (d-z)f^{o}\ '(net^{\ o}) = d-z \qquad (linear \qquad neuron \qquad f^{o}\ '(net^{\ o}) = 1)$$

$$\delta^{\ hy} = f^{h}\ '(net_{kj}^{\ hy})c_{kj}^{\ hx}b_k^{\ x} = c_{kj}^{\ hx}b_k^{\ x} \qquad (linear \qquad neuron \qquad f^{h}\ '(net_{kj}^{\ hy}) = 1)$$

$$\delta^{\ y} = f_y\ '(net_j^{\ y}) = (-j^2)*\cos^{j-1}(j*c_j^{\ y}*y)*\sin(j*c_j^{\ y}*y)$$

UGT-HONN TESTING

UGS-HONN model is used to recognize the data pattern. Test results are shown in Table 1 and Figure 3A and Figure 3B. UPC-HONN model is used to recognize the data pattern too. Test results are shown in Table 2 and Figure 4A and Figure 4B.

In Table 1, UGS-HONN model 0 has been used. The order number for UGS-HONN model is 6. In the first table of Table 1, the "No." column shows total 19 points are chosen. The "UGS-HONN x" column displays the input x values, which are all "1" has been used. The "UGS-HONN y" column displays the input y values, which are 0, 0.1, 0.2, 0.3, 0.4, 05, 0.7, 0.8, 0.9, 1, 2, 3, 4, 5, 6, 7 and 8 are used. The "UGS-HONN z" column displays the output z values. The "Original Data" column displays the original data values. The "Absolute Original Data" column displays the absolute values for original data. The "Difference" column shows the difference between UGS-HONN output z and the original data (UPS-HONN z – Original Data). The "Absolute Difference" column shows the absolute difference between UGS-HONN output z and the original data (|UGS-HONN z – Original Data|). The "UGS-HONN Error %" column gives the error percentage for UGS-HONN Model (UGS-HONN error % = absolute difference / Absolute original Data * 100%). The average UGS-HONN error is 0.00005991%, which is very

Table 1. UGS-HONN data pattern recognition (n=6, Model 0)

No.	UGS-HONN x	UGS-HONN y	UGS-HONN z	Original Data	Absolute Original Data	Difference	Absolute Difference	UGS-HONN Error %
1	1	0	0.00000000	0.000000	0.000000	0.00000000	0.00000000	0.000000%
2	1	0.1	-0.01484859	-0.014849	0.014849	0.00000041	0.00000041	0.000084%
3	1	0.2	-0.06048644	-0.060486	0.060486	-0.00000044	0.00000044	0.000091%
4	1	0.3	-0.14886556	-0.148866	0.148866	0.00000044	0.00000044	0.000090%
5	1	0.4	-0.26167745	-0.261677	0.261677	-0.00000045	0.00000045	0.000093%
6	1	0.5	-0.35110658	-0.351107	0.351107	0.00000042	0.00000042	0.000086%
7	1	0.6	-0.35314432	-0.353144	0.353144	-0.00000032	0.00000032	0.000066%
8	1	0.7	-0.20927225	-0.209272	0.209272	-0.00000025	0.00000025	0.000052%
9	1	0.8	0.11084710	0.110847	0.110847	0.00000010	0.00000010	0.000021%
10	1	0.9	0.59367746	0.593678	0.593678	-0.00000054	0.00000054	0.000111%
11	1	1	1.17898893	1.178989	1.178989	-0.00000007	0.00000007	0.000013%
13	1	2	0.17275166	0.172752	0.172752	-0.00000034	0.00000034	0.000070%
14	1	3	-0.56122411	-0.561224	0.561224	-0.00000011	0.00000011	0.000022%
15	1	4	0.49855874	0.498559	0.498559	-0.00000026	0.00000026	0.000053%
16	1	5	-2.53172894	-2.531729	2.531729	0.00000006	0.00000006	0.000012%
17	1	6	0.13139118	0.131391	0.131391	0.00000018	0.00000018	0.000036%
18	1	7	-0.16800261	-0.168003	0.168003	0.00000039	0.00000039	0.000079%
19	1	8	1.47238249	1.472382	1.472382	0.00000049	0.00000049	0.000099%
Average					0.4899419		0.0000002935	0.00005991%

$c_{kj}{}^{o}$	k=0	k=1	k=2	k=3	k=4	k=5	k=6
j=0	0.6858	-0.4786	-0.6554	-0.5309	-1.2674	-0.5498	0.1297
j=1	0.9365	0.0579	-0.0401	-0.9998	0.9786	0.2332	-0.0313
j=2	0.7428	0.7707	-0.7688	-0.3755	-0.8456	0.7245	-0.0995
j=3	-0.9484	-0.6478	-0.4593	0.6315	0.9849	-0.7281	0.6732
j=4	-0.4525	0.5854	-0.8993	0.5756	-0.5475	0.7442	0.1133
j=5	-0.9242	0.7811	0.0489	0.8641	0.5242	-0.1275	-0.1783
j=6	0.7771	-0.3691	0.0726	-0.1132	-0.6926	-0.7067	0.9651

x=1, y=0.1	k = 0	k = 1	k = 2	k = 3	k = 4	k = 5	k = 6
j = 0	0.00000000	0.00000000	0.00000000	0.00000000	0.00000000	0.00000000	0.00000000
j = 1	0.09349399	0.00422578	-0.00213956	-0.03899829	0.02790550	0.00486144	-0.00047702
j = 2	0.14757158	0.11193563	-0.08162977	-0.02914723	-0.04798489	0.03005593	-0.00301764
j = 3	-0.28027136	-0.13995238	-0.07254174	0.07291503	0.08313579	-0.04493028	0.03036997
j = 4	-0.17621180	0.16665613	-0.18716531	0.08757774	-0.06089887	0.06051555	0.00673534
j = 5	-0.44308508	0.27376630	0.01252952	0.16186081	0.07178387	-0.01276416	-0.01304925
j = 6	0.43878367	-0.15235958	0.02190859	-0.02497333	-0.11170298	-0.08332389	0.08318766
Subtotal	-0.21971901	0.26427188	-0.30903827	0.22923472	-0.03776157	-0.04558541	0.10374907
$z = \Sigma c_{kj}{}^{o}*(1/(1+\exp(-x)))^{k}*\sin^{j}(j*y)$			(k= 0, 1, 2 ,3, 4, 5, 6		j = 0, 1, 2, 3, 4, 5, 6) =			-0.01484859

Figure 3. UGC-Honn Architecture

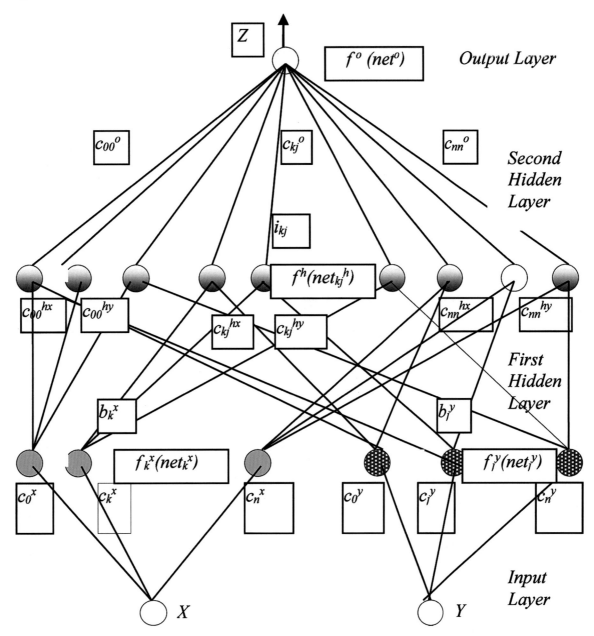

closed to zero. After training UGS-HONN model by using original data values, in the second table of Table 1, the UGS-HONN all coefficients are displayed. For examples, $c_{00}{}^o$= 0.6858, $c_{01}{}^o$= 0.9365, and $c_{10}{}^o$= -0.4786. In the third table of Table 1, gives the values for $c_{kj}{}^o*(1/(1+exp(-x)))^k*sin^j(j*y)$, when $x=1$, $y=0.1, k=0,1,2,3,4,5,6$, and $j=0,1,2,3,4,5,6$. For examples, $c_{01}{}^o*(1/(1+exp(-x)))^0*sin^1(1*0.1)=0.09349399$, $c_{02}{}^o*(1/(1+exp(-x)))^0*sin^2(2*0.1)=0.14757158$, and $c_{03}{}^o*(1/(1+exp(-x)))^0*sin^3(3*0.1)=-0.28027136$. And $z=\sum c_{kj}{}^o*(1/(1+exp(-x)))^k*sin^j(j*y)=\sum c_{kj}{}^o*(1)^k*sin^j(j*0.1)=-0.01484859$.

Table 2. UGC-HONN data pattern recognition (n=6, Model 0)

No.	UGC-HONN x	UGC-HONN y	UGC-HONN z	Original Data	Absolute Original Data	Difference	Absolute Difference	UGC-HONN Error %
1	1	0	-0.67901388	-0.679014	0.679014	0.00000012	0.00000012	0.000011%
2	1	0.1	-0.73321663	-0.733217	0.733217	0.00000037	0.00000037	0.000034%
3	1	0.2	-0.87717494	-0.877175	0.877175	0.00000006	0.00000006	0.000006%
4	1	0.3	-1.06038260	-1.060383	1.060383	0.00000040	0.00000040	0.000037%
5	1	0.4	-1.21528091	-1.215281	1.215281	0.00000009	0.00000009	0.000008%
6	1	0.5	-1.27727157	-1.277272	1.277272	0.00000043	0.00000043	0.000040%
7	1	0.6	-1.20433371	-1.204334	1.204334	0.00000029	0.00000029	0.000027%
8	1	0.7	-0.99075568	-0.990756	0.990756	0.00000032	0.00000032	0.000030%
9	1	0.8	-0.67113083	-0.671131	0.671131	0.00000017	0.00000017	0.000016%
10	1	0.9	-0.31345072	-0.313451	0.313451	0.00000028	0.00000028	0.000026%
11	1	1	-0.00309632	-0.003096	0.003096	-0.00000032	0.00000032	0.000030%
13	1	2	-2.56975825	-2.569758	2.569758	-0.00000025	0.00000025	0.000024%
14	1	3	-1.68937107	-1.689371	1.689371	-0.00000007	0.00000007	0.000007%
15	1	4	-1.91001454	-1.910015	1.910015	0.00000046	0.00000046	0.000043%
16	1	5	0.00849234	0.008492	0.008492	0.00000034	0.00000034	0.000032%
17	1	6	-1.02963976	-1.02964	1.029640	0.00000024	0.00000024	0.000023%
18	1	7	-0.94292615	-0.942926	0.942926	-0.00000015	0.00000015	0.000014%
19	1	8	-2.08157552	-2.0815756	2.081576	0.00000008	0.00000008	0.000007%
Average					1.0698271		0.0000002479	0.00002317%

$c_{kj}{}^o$	k=0	k=1	k=2	k=3	k=4	k=5	k=6
j=0	0.0315	-0.8243	-0.0011	-0.9866	-0.6021	-0.9955	0.5754
j=1	0.4933	0.5147	-0.5079	-0.4566	0.4354	0.7900	-0.5981
j=2	0.3107	0.3486	-0.3347	-0.6434	-0.4135	0.3924	-0.6674
j=3	-0.6295	-0.3269	-0.1384	0.3106	0.6630	-0.4072	0.3523
j=4	-0.2437	0.3766	-0.6805	0.3668	-0.3387	0.5354	0.9045
j=5	-0.8365	0.6934	0.9502	0.7764	0.4365	-0.0398	-0.0806
j=6	0.8902	-0.4825	0.1950	-0.5366	-0.7150	-0.8291	0.0885

x=1, y=0.1	k = 0	k = 1	k = 2	k = 3	k = 4	k = 5	k = 6
j = 0	0.03150000	-0.60261159	-0.00058789	-0.38547627	-0.17197976	-0.20787495	0.08783810
j = 1	0.49083555	0.37439604	-0.27008935	-0.17750776	0.12374340	0.16413941	-0.09084725
j = 2	0.30450669	0.24976705	-0.17531362	-0.24637303	-0.11575501	0.08030553	-0.09985156
j = 3	-0.60138432	-0.22830923	-0.07066377	0.11593494	0.18091668	-0.08123160	0.05137858
j = 4	-0.22446256	0.25358344	-0.33498154	0.13200010	-0.08910710	0.10297401	0.12717743
j = 5	-0.73409781	0.44486066	0.44566381	0.26621348	0.10941603	-0.00729343	-0.01079782
j = 6	0.73467250	-0.29112539	0.08601408	-0.17303653	-0.16855644	-0.14288887	0.01115031
Subtotal	0.00157004	0.20056098	-0.31995829	-0.46824506	-0.13132220	-0.09186989	0.07604779
$z = \Sigma c_{kj}{}^o*(1/(1+exp(-x)))^k*cos^j(j*y)$			(k= 0, 1, 2 ,3, 4, 5, 6		j = 0, 1, 2, 3, 4, 5, 6) =		-0.73321663

Figure 4.

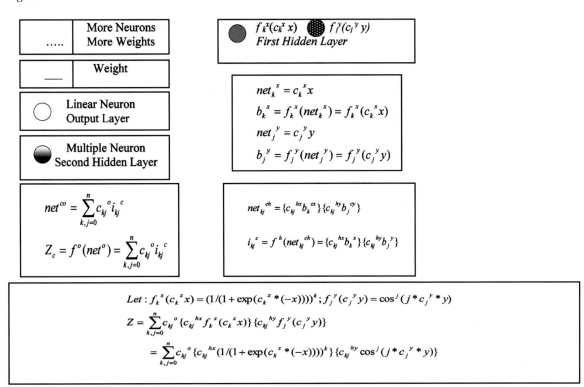

The pattern recognition results for UGS-HONN data are provided in Figure 3. Figure 3A shows the original data, while Figure 3B presents the data pattern results for UGS-HONN recognition. Results from Figure 3B suggestions that the UGS-HONN model can recognize data pattern very well, since the average error percentage is close to 0.0000%.

Based on the training of UGS-HONN model, UGS-HONN has the following formula to recognize the original data pattern:

$z = \sum c_{kj}{}^{o} *(1/(1+exp(-x)))^k *sin^j(j*y)$ $(k, j = 0,1,2,3,4,5,6,)$

$= c_{00}{}^{o} *(1/(1+exp(-x)))^0 *sin^0(0*y) + c_{10}{}^{o} *(1/(1+exp(-x)))^1 *sin^0(0*y)$

$+ c_{20}{}^{o} *(1/(1+exp(-x)))^2 *sin^0(0*y) + c_{30}{}^{o} *(1/(1+exp(-x)))^3 *sin^0(0*y)$

$+ c_{40}{}^{o} *(1/(1+exp(-x)))^4 *sin^0(0*y) + c_{50}{}^{o} *(1/(1+exp(-x)))^5 *sin^0(0*y)$

$+ c_{60}{}^{o} *(1/(1+exp(-x)))^6 *sin^0(0*y)$

$+ c_{01}{}^{o} *(1/(1+exp(-x)))^0 *sin^1(1*y) + c_{11}{}^{o} *(1/(1+exp(-x)))^1 *sin^1(1*y)$

$+ c_{21}{}^{o} *(1/(1+exp(-x)))^2 *sin^1(1*y) + c_{31}{}^{o} *(1/(1+exp(-x)))^3 *sin^1(1*y)$

$+ c_{41}{}^{o}*(1/(1+\exp(-x)))^{4}*\sin^{1}(1*y)+ c_{51}{}^{o}*(1/(1+\exp(-x)))^{5}*\sin^{1}(1*y)$

$+ c_{61}{}^{o}*(1/(1+\exp(-x)))^{6}*\sin^{1}(1*y)$

$+c_{02}{}^{o}*(1/(1+\exp(-x)))^{0}*\sin^{2}(2*y)+ c_{12}{}^{o}*(1/(1+\exp(-x)))^{1}*\sin^{2}(2*y)$

$+ c_{22}{}^{o}*(1/(1+\exp(-x)))^{2}*\sin^{2}(2*y)+ c_{32}{}^{o}*(1/(1+\exp(-x)))^{3}*\sin^{2}(2*y)$

$+ c_{42}{}^{o}*(1/(1+\exp(-x)))^{4}*\sin^{2}(2*y)+ c_{52}{}^{o}*(1/(1+\exp(-x)))^{5}*\sin^{2}(2*y)$

$+ c_{62}{}^{o}*(1/(1+\exp(-x)))^{6}*\sin^{2}(2*y)$

$+c_{03}{}^{o}*(1/(1+\exp(-x)))^{0}*\sin^{3}(3*y)+ c_{13}{}^{o}*(1/(1+\exp(-x00)^{1}*\sin^{3}(3*y)$

$+ c_{23}{}^{o}*(1/(1+\exp(-x)))^{2}*\sin^{3}(3*y)+ c_{33}{}^{o}*(1/(1+\exp(-x)))^{3}*\sin^{3}(3*y)$

$+ c_{43}{}^{o}*(1/(1+\exp(-x)))^{4}*\sin^{3}(3*y)+ c_{53}{}^{o}*(1/(1+\exp(-x)))^{5}*\sin^{3}(3*y)$

$+ c_{63}{}^{o}*(1/(1+\exp(-x)))^{6}*\sin^{3}(3*y)$

$+c_{04}{}^{o}*(1/(1+\exp(-x)))^{0}*\sin^{4}(4*y)+ c_{14}{}^{o}*(1/(1+\exp(-x)))^{1}*\sin^{4}(4*y)$

$+ c_{24}{}^{o}*(1/(1+\exp(-x)))^{2}*\sin^{4}(4*y)+ c_{34}{}^{o}*(1/(1+\exp(-x)))^{3}*\sin^{4}(4*y)$

$+ c_{44}{}^{o}*(1/(1+\exp(-x)))^{4}*\sin^{4}(4*y)+ c_{54}{}^{o}*(1/(1+\exp(-x)))^{5}*\sin^{4}(4*y)$

$+ c_{64}{}^{o}*(1/(1+\exp(-x)))^{6}*\sin^{4}(4*y)$

$+c_{05}{}^{o}*(1/(1+\exp(-x)))^{0}*\sin^{5}(5*y)+ c_{15}{}^{o}*(1/(1+\exp(-x)))^{1}*\sin^{5}(5*y)$

$+ c_{25}{}^{o}*(1/(1+\exp(-x)))^{2}*\sin^{5}(4*y)+ c_{35}{}^{o}*(1/(1+\exp(-x)))^{3}*\sin^{5}(5*y)$

$+ c_{45}{}^{o}*(1/(1+\exp(-x)))^{4}*\sin^{5}(5*y)+ c_{55}{}^{o}*(1/(1+\exp(-x)))^{5}*\sin^{5}(5*y)$

$+ c_{65}{}^{o}*(1/(1+\exp(-x)))^{6}*\sin^{5}(5*y)$

$+c_{06}{}^{o}*(1/(1+\exp(-x)))^{0}*\sin^{6}(6*y)+ c_{16}{}^{o}*(1/(1+\exp(-x)))^{1}*\sin^{6}(6*y)$

$+ c_{26}{}^{o}*(1/(1+\exp(-x)))^{2}*\sin^{6}(6*y)+ c_{36}{}^{o}*(1/(1+\exp(-x)))^{3}*\sin^{6}(6*y)$

$+ c_{46}{}^{o}*(1/(1+\exp(-x)))^{4}*\sin^{6}(6*y)+ c_{56}{}^{o}*(1/(1+\exp(-x)))^{5}*\sin^{6}(6*y)$

$+ c_{66}{}^{o}*(1/(1+\exp(-x)))^{6}*\sin^{6}(6*y)$

$= 0.6858*(1/(1+\exp(-x)))^{0}*\sin^{0}(0*y)+ (-0.4786) *(1/(1+\exp(-x)))^{1}*\sin^{0}(0*y)$

$+ (-0.6554)*(1/(1+\exp(-x)))^2*\sin^0(0*y)+ (-0.5309)*(1/(1+\exp(-x)))^3*\sin^0(0*y)$

$+ (-1.2674)*(1/(1+\exp(-x)))^4*\sin^0(0*y)+ (-0.5498)*(1/(1+\exp(-x)))^5*\sin^0(0*y)$

$+ 0.1297*(1/(1+\exp(-x)))^6*\sin^0(0*y)$

$+0.9365*(1/(1+\exp(-x)))^0*\sin^1(1*y)+ 0.0579*(1/(1+\exp(-x)))^1*\sin^1(1*y)$

$+ (-0.0401)*(1/(1+\exp(-x)))^2*\sin^1(1*y)+ (-0.9998)*(1/(1+\exp(-x)))^3*\sin^1(1*y)$

$+ 0.9786*(1/(1+\exp(-x)))^4*\sin^1(1*y)+ 0.2332*(1/(1+\exp(-x)))^5*\sin^1(1*y)$

$+ (-0.0313)*(1/(1+\exp(-x)))^6*\sin^1(1*y)$

$+0.7428*(1/(1+\exp(-x)))^0*\sin^2(2*y)+ 0.7707*(1/(1+\exp(-x)))^1*\sin^2(2*y)$

$+ (-0.7688)*(1/(1+\exp(-x)))^2*\sin^2(2*y)+ (-0.3755)*(1/(1+\exp(-x)))^3*\sin^2(2*y)$

$+(-0.8456)*(1/(1+\exp(-x)))^4*\sin^2(2*y)+ 0.7245*(1/(1+\exp(-x)))^5*\sin^2(2*y)$

$+ (-0.0995)*(1/(1+\exp(-x)))^6*\sin^2(2*y)$

$+(-0.9484)*(1/(1+\exp(-x)))^0*\sin^3(3*y)+ (-0.6478)*(1/(1+\exp(-x00)^1*\sin^3(3*y)$

$+ (-0.4593)*(1/(1+\exp(-x)))^2*\sin^3(3*y)+ 0.6315*(1/(1+\exp(-x)))^3*\sin^3(3*y)$

$+ 0.9849*(1/(1+\exp(-x)))^4*\sin^3(3*y)+ (-0.7281)*(1/(1+\exp(-x)))^5*\sin^3(3*y)$

$+ 0.6732*(1/(1+\exp(-x)))^6*\sin^3(3*y)$

$+(-0.4525)*(1/(1+\exp(-x)))^0*\sin^4(4*y)+ 0.5854*(1/(1+\exp(-x)))^1*\sin^4(4*y)$

$+ (-0.8993)*(1/(1+\exp(-x)))^2*\sin^4(4*y)+ 0.5756*(1/(1+\exp(-x)))^3*\sin^4(4*y)$

$+ (-0.5475)*(1/(1+\exp(-x)))^4*\sin^4(4*y)+ 0.7442*(1/(1+\exp(-x)))^5*\sin^4(4*y)$

$+ 0.1133*(1/(1+\exp(-x)))^6*\sin^4(4*y)$

$+(-0.9242)*(1/(1+\exp(-x)))^0*\sin^5(5*y)+ 0.7811*(1/(1+\exp(-x)))^1*\sin^5(5*y)$

$+ 0.0489*(1/(1+\exp(-x)))^2*\sin^5(4*y)+ 0.8641*(1/(1+\exp(-x)))^3*\sin^5(5*y)$

$+ 0.5242*(1/(1+\exp(-x)))^4*\sin^5(5*y)+ (-0.1275)*(1/(1+\exp(-x)))^5*\sin^5(5*y)$

$+ (-0.1783)*(1/(1+\exp(-x)))^6*\sin^5(5*y)$

$+0.7771*(1/(1+exp(-x)))^0*sin^6(6*y)+ (-0.3691)*(1/(1+exp(-x)))^1*sin^6(6*y)$

$+ 0.0726*(1/(1+exp(-x)))^2*sin^6(6*y)+ (-0.1132)*(1/(1+exp(-x)))^3*sin^6(6*y)$

$+ (-0.6926)*(1/(1+exp(-x)))^4*sin^6(6*y)+ (-0.7067)*(1/(1+exp(-x)))^5*sin^6(6*y)$

$+ 0.9651*(1/(1+exp(-x)))^6*sin^6(6*y)$

In Table 2, UGC-HONN model 0 has been used. The order number for UGC-HONN model is 6. In the first table of Table 2, the "No." column shows a total of 19 points are chosen. The "UGC-HONN x" column displays the input x values, which are all "1"s are used. The "UGC-HONN y" column displays the input y values, which are 0, 0.1, 0.2, 0.3, 0.4, 05, 0.7, 0.8, 0.9, 1, 2, 3, 4, 5, 6, 7 and 8 are used. The "UGC-HONN z" column displays the output z values. The "Original Data" column displays the original data values. The "Absolute Original Data" column displays the absolute values for original data. The "Difference" column shows the difference between UGC-HONN output z and the original data (UPC-HONN z – Original Data). The "Absolute Difference" column shows the absolute difference between UGC-HONN output z and the original data (|UGC-HONN z – Original Data|). The "UGC-HONN Error %" column gives the error percentage for UGC-HONN Model (UGC-HONN error % = absolute difference / Absolute original Data * 100%). The average UGC-HONN error is 0.00002317%, which is very closed to zero. After training UGC-HONN model by using original data values, in the second table of Table 2, all coefficients in the UGS-HONN model are displayed. For examples, $c_{00}{}^o= 0.0315$, $c_{01}{}^o= 0.4933$, and $c_{10}{}^o= -0.8243$. In the third table of Table 2, gives the values for $c_{kj}{}^o*(1/(1+exp(-x)))^k*cos^j(j*y)$, when $x=1$, $y=0.1, k=0,1,2,3,4,5,6$, and $j=0,1,2,3,4,5,6$. For examples, $c_{01}{}^o*(1/(1+exp(-x)))^0*cos^1(1*0.1)=0.49083555$, $c_{02}{}^o*(1/(1+exp(-x)))^0*cos^2(2*0.1)=0.30450669$, and $c_{03}{}^o*(1/(1+exp(-x)))^0*cos^3(3*0.1)=-0.60138432$. And $z=\sum c_{kj}{}^o*(1/(1+exp(-x)))^k*cos^j(j*y)=\sum c_{kj}{}^o*(1)^k*cos^j(j*0.1)=-0.73321663$.

The pattern recognition results for UGC-HONN data are provided Figure 4. The original data are displayed in Figure 4A, while Figure 4B presents the data pattern results for UGC-HONN recognition. Results from Figure 4B show that the UGC-HONN model can recognize data pattern very well, since the average error percentage is close to 0.0000%.

Based on the training of UGC-HONN model, UGC-HONN has the following formula to recognize the original data pattern:

$z=\sum c_{kj}{}^o*(1/(1+exp(-x)))^k*cos^j(j*y)$ $(k, j = 0,1,2,3,4,5,6,)$

$= c_{00}{}^o*(1/(1+exp(-x)))^0*cos^0(0*y)+ c_{10}{}^o*(1/(1+exp(-x)))^1*cos^0(0*y)$

$+ c_{20}{}^o*(1/(1+exp(-x)))^2*cos^0(0*y)+ c_{30}{}^o*(1/(1+exp(-x)))^3*cos^0(0*y)$

$+ c_{40}{}^o*(1/(1+exp(-x)))^4*cos^0(0*y)+ c_{50}{}^o*(1/(1+exp(-x)))^5*cos^0(0*y)$

$+ c_{60}{}^o*(1/(1+exp(-x)))^6*cos^0(0*y)$

$+c_{01}{}^o*(1/(1+exp(-x)))^0*cos^1(1*y)+ c_{11}{}^o*(1/(1+exp(-x)))^1*cos^1(1*y)$

$+ c_{21}{}^{o}*(1/(1+\exp(-x)))^2*\cos^1(1*y)+ c_{31}{}^{o}*(1/(1+\exp(-x)))^3*\cos^1(1*y)$

$+ c_{41}{}^{o}*(1/(1+\exp(-x)))^4*\cos^1(1*y)+ c_{51}{}^{o}*(1/(1+\exp(-x)))^5*\cos^1(1*y)$

$+ c_{61}{}^{o}*(1/(1+\exp(-x)))^6*\cos^1(1*y)$

$+c_{02}{}^{o}*(1/(1+\exp(-x)))^0*\cos^2(2*y)+ c_{12}{}^{o}*(1/(1+\exp(-x)))^1*\cos^2(2*y)$

$+ c_{22}{}^{o}*(1/(1+\exp(-x)))^2*\cos^2(2*y)+ c_{32}{}^{o}*(1/(1+\exp(-x)))^3*\cos^2(2*y)$

$+ c_{42}{}^{o}*(1/(1+\exp(-x)))^4*\cos^2(2*y)+ c_{52}{}^{o}*(1/(1+\exp(-x)))^5*\cos^2(2*y)$

$+ c_{62}{}^{o}*(1/(1+\exp(-x)))^6*\cos^2(2*y)$

$+c_{03}{}^{o}*(1/(1+\exp(-x)))^0*\cos^3(3*y)+ c_{13}{}^{o}*(1/(1+\exp(-x00)^1*\cos^3(3*y)$

$+ c_{23}{}^{o}*(1/(1+\exp(-x)))^2*\cos^3(3*y)+ c_{33}{}^{o}*(1/(1+\exp(-x)))^3*\cos^3(3*y)$

$+ c_{43}{}^{o}*(1/(1+\exp(-x)))^4*\cos^3(3*y)+ c_{53}{}^{o}*(1/(1+\exp(-x)))^5*\cos^3(3*y)$

$+ c_{63}{}^{o}*(1/(1+\exp(-x)))^6*\cos^3(3*y)$

$+c_{04}{}^{o}*(1/(1+\exp(-x)))^0*\cos^4(4*y)+ c_{14}{}^{o}*(1/(1+\exp(-x)))^1*\cos^4(4*y)$

$+ c_{24}{}^{o}*(1/(1+\exp(-x)))^2*\cos^4(4*y)+ c_{34}{}^{o}*(1/(1+\exp(-x)))^3*\cos^4(4*y)$

$+ c_{44}{}^{o}*(1/(1+\exp(-x)))^4*\cos^4(4*y)+ c_{54}{}^{o}*(1/(1+\exp(-x)))^5*\cos^4(4*y)$

$+ c_{64}{}^{o}*(1/(1+\exp(-x)))^6*\cos^4(4*y)$

$+c_{05}{}^{o}*(1/(1+\exp(-x)))^0*\cos^5(5*y)+ c_{15}{}^{o}*(1/(1+\exp(-x)))^1*\cos^5(5*y)$

$+ c_{25}{}^{o}*(1/(1+\exp(-x)))^2*\cos^5(4*y)+ c_{35}{}^{o}*(1/(1+\exp(-x)))^3*\cos^5(5*y)$

$+ c_{45}{}^{o}*(1/(1+\exp(-x)))^4*\cos^5(5*y)+ c_{55}{}^{o}*(1/(1+\exp(-x)))^5*\cos^5(5*y)$

$+ c_{65}{}^{o}*(1/(1+\exp(-x)))^6*\cos^5(5*y)$

$+c_{06}{}^{o}*(1/(1+\exp(-x)))^0*\cos^6(6*y)+ c_{16}{}^{o}*(1/(1+\exp(-x)))^1*\cos^6(6*y)$

$+ c_{26}{}^{o}*(1/(1+\exp(-x)))^2*\cos^6(6*y)+ c_{36}{}^{o}*(1/(1+\exp(-x)))^3*\cos^6(6*y)$

$+ c_{46}{}^{o}*(1/(1+\exp(-x)))^4*\cos^6(6*y)+ c_{56}{}^{o}*(1/(1+\exp(-x)))^5*\cos^6(6*y)$

$+ c_{66}{}^{o}*(1/(1+\exp(-x)))^6*\cos^6(6*y)$

$= 0.0315*(1/(1+exp(-x)))^0*cos^0(0*y)+ (-0.8243) *(1/(1+exp(-x)))^1*cos^0(0*y)$

$+ (-0.0011)*(1/(1+exp(-x)))^2*cos^0(0*y)+ (-0.9866)*(1/(1+exp(-x)))^3*cos^0(0*y)$

$+ (-0.6021)*(1/(1+exp(-x)))^4*cos^0(0*y)+ (-0.9955)*(1/(1+exp(-x)))^5*cos^0(0*y)$

$+ 0.5754*(1/(1+exp(-x)))^6*cos^0(0*y)$

$+0.4933*(1/(1+exp(-x)))^0*cos^1(1*y)+ 0.5147*(1/(1+exp(-x)))^1*cos^1(1*y)$

$+ (-0.5079)*(1/(1+exp(-x)))^2*cos^1(1*y)+ (-0.4566)*(1/(1+exp(-x)))^3*cos^1(1*y)$

$+ 0.4354*(1/(1+exp(-x)))^4*cos^1(1*y)+ 0.7900*(1/(1+exp(-x)))^5*cos^1(1*y)$

$+ (-0.5981)*(1/(1+exp(-x)))^6*cos^1(1*y)$

$+0.3107*(1/(1+exp(-x)))^0*cos^2(2*y)+ 0.3486*(1/(1+exp(-x)))^1*cos^2(2*y)$

$+ (-0.3347)*(1/(1+exp(-x)))^2*cos^2(2*y)+ (-0.6434)*(1/(1+exp(-x)))^3*cos^2(2*y)$

$+(-0.4135)*(1/(1+exp(-x)))^4*cos^2(2*y)+ 0.3924*(1/(1+exp(-x)))^5*cos^2(2*y)$

$+ (-0.6674)*(1/(1+exp(-x)))^6*cos^2(2*y)$

$+(-0.6295)*(1/(1+exp(-x)))^0*cos^3(3*y)+ (-0.3269)*(1/(1+exp(-x00)^1*cos^3(3*y)$

$+ (-0.1384)*(1/(1+exp(-x)))^2*cos^3(3*y)+ 0.3106*(1/(1+exp(-x)))^3*cos^3(3*y)$

$+ 0.6630*(1/(1+exp(-x)))^4*cos^3(3*y)+ (-0.4072)*(1/(1+exp(-x)))^5*cos^3(3*y)$

$+ 0.3523*(1/(1+exp(-x)))^6*cos^3(3*y)$

$+(-0.2437)*(1/(1+exp(-x)))^0*cos^4(4*y)+ 0.3766*(1/(1+exp(-x)))^1*cos^4(4*y)$

$+ (-0.6805)*(1/(1+exp(-x)))^2*cos^4(4*y)+ 0.3668*(1/(1+exp(-x)))^3*cos^4(4*y)$

$+ (-0.3387)*(1/(1+exp(-x)))^4*cos^4(4*y)+ 0.5354*(1/(1+exp(-x)))^5*cos^4(4*y)$

$+ 0.9045*(1/(1+exp(-x)))^6*cos^4(4*y)$

$+(-0.8365)*(1/(1+exp(-x)))^0*cos^5(5*y)+ 0.6934*(1/(1+exp(-x)))^1*cos^5(5*y)$

$+ 0.9502*(1/(1+exp(-x)))^2*cos^5(4*y)+ 0.7764*(1/(1+exp(-x)))^3*cos^5(5*y)$

$+ 0.4365*(1/(1+exp(-x)))^4*cos^5(5*y)+ (-0.0398)*(1/(1+exp(-x)))^5*cos^5(5*y)$

+ $(-0.0806)*(1/(1+\exp(-x)))^6*\cos^5(5*y)$

+ $0.8902*(1/(1+\exp(-x)))^0*\cos^6(6*y)$ + $(-0.4825)*(1/(1+\exp(-x)))^1*\cos^6(6*y)$

+ $0.1950*(1/(1+\exp(-x)))^2*\cos^6(6*y)$ + $(-0.5366)*(1/(1+\exp(-x)))^3*\cos^6(6*y)$

+ $(-0.7150)*(1/(1+\exp(-x)))^4*\cos^6(6*y)$ + $(-0.8291)*(1/(1+\exp(-x)))^5*\cos^6(6*y)$

+ $0.0885*(1/(1+\exp(-x)))^6*\cos^6(6*y)$

Figure 5. UGS-HONN data pattern recognition

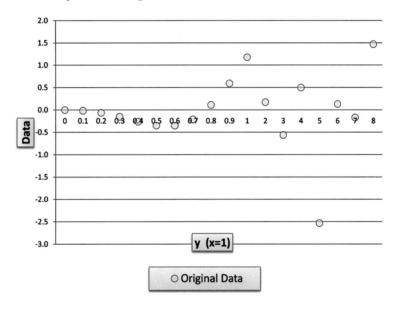

Figure 6. UGS-HONN data pattern recognition

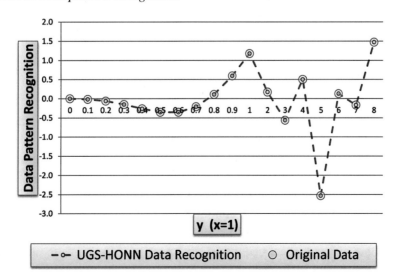

Figure 7. UGC-HONN data pattern recognition

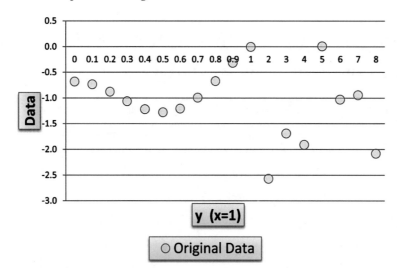

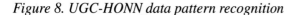

Figure 8. UGC-HONN data pattern recognition

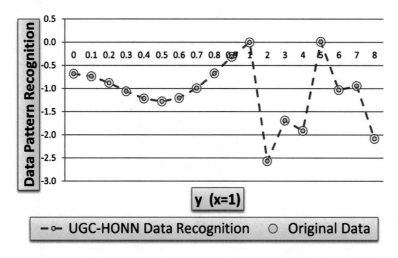

CONCLUSION

Two nonlinear neural network models, UGS-HONN, UGC-HONN, that are part of the Ultra High Frequency Sigmoid and Trigonometric Higher Order Neural Networks (UGT-HONN), are developed. Based on the structures of UGS-HONN and UGC-HONN, this chapter provides two model learning algorithm formulae. This chapter tests the UGS-HONN and UGC-HONN models to recognize the data patterns. Experimental results show that UGS-HONN and UGC-HONN models can recognize data pattern very well. Using the UGS-HONN and UGC-HONN models, the average error can reach 0.0000%.

One of the topics for future research is to continue building models using UGT-HONN for different data series. The coefficients of the higher order models will be studied not only using artificial neural network techniques, but also statistical methods. Using nonlinear functions to model and analyze time series data will be a major goal in the future.

REFERENCES

Artyomov, E., & Yadid-Pecht, O. (2005). Modified High-Order Neural Network for Invariant Pattern Recognition. *Pattern Recognition Letters*, 26(6), 843–851. doi:10.1016/j.patrec.2004.09.029

Fallahnezhad, M., & Zaferanlouei, S. (2013). A Hybrid Higher Order Neural Structure for Pattern Recognition. In M. Zhang (Ed.), Artificial Higher Order Neural Networks for Modeling and Simulation (pp. 364-387). Hershey, PA, USA: IGI Global.

Foresti, G. L., & Dolso, T. (2004). An adaptive high-order neural tree for pattern recognition. *IEEE Transactions on Systems, Man, and Cybernetics. Part B, Cybernetics*, 34(2), 988–996. doi:10.1109/TSMCB.2003.818538 PMID:15376845

He, Z., & Siyal, M. Y. (1999, August). Improvement on higher-order neural networks for invariant object recognition. *Neural Processing Letters*, 10(1), 49–55. doi:10.1023/A:1018610829733

Kaita, T., Tomita, S., & Yamanaka, J. (2002, June). On a higher-order neural network for distortion invariant pattern recognition. *Pattern Recognition Letters*, 23(8), 977 – 984, New York, NY, USA: Elsevier Science Inc.

Kanaoka, T., Chellappa, R., Yoshitaka, M., & Tomita, S. (1992). A Higher-order neural network for distortion unvariant pattern recognition. *Pattern Recognition Letters*, 13(12), 837–841. doi:10.1016/0167-8655(92)90082-B

Lisboa, P., & Perantonis, S. (1991). Invariant pattern recognition using third-order networks and zern-like moments. *Proceedings of the IEEE International Joint Conference on Neural Networks,* Singapore (Vol. II, pp. 1421-1425).

Murata, J. (2010). Analysis and Improvement of Function Approximation Capabilities of Pi-Sigma Higher Order Neural Networks. In M. Zhang (Ed.), Artificial Higher Order Neural Networks for Computer Science and Engineering – Trends for Emerging Applications (pp. 239-254). Hershey, PA, USA: IGI Global.

Pao, Y. H. (1989). *Adaptive Pattern Recognition and Neural Networks*. Reading, MA: Addison-Wesley.

Park, S., Smith, M. J. T., & Mersereau, R. M. (2000, October). Target Recognition Based on Directional Filter Banks and higher-order neural network. *Digital Signal Processing*, 10(4), 297–308. doi:10.1006/dspr.2000.0376

Perantonis, S. J., & Lisboa, P. J. G. (1992). Translation, rotation and scale invariant pattern recognition by high-order neural networks and moment classifiers. *IEEE Transactions on Neural Networks*, 3(2), 241–251. doi:10.1109/72.125865 PMID:18276425

Ragothaman, S., & Lavin, A. (2008). Restatements Due to Improper Revenue Recognition: A Neural Networks Perspective. *Journal of Emerging Technologies in Accounting*, 5(1), 129–142. doi:10.2308/jeta.2008.5.1.129

Reid, M. B., Spirkovska, L., & Ochoa, E. (1989). Rapid training of higher-order neural networks for invariant pattern recognition. *Proceedings of International Joint Conference on Neural Networks,* Washington, DC, USA (Vol.1, pp. 689-692).

Ricalde, L. J., Sanchez, E. N., & Alanis, A. Y. (2010). Recurrent Higher Order Neural Network Control for Output Trajectory Tracking with Neural Observers and Constrained Inputs. In M. Zhang (Ed.), Artificial Higher Order Neural Networks for Computer Science and Engineering – Trends for Emerging Applications (pp. 286-311). Hershey, PA, USA: IGI Global.

Sankar, A., & Mammone, R. J. (1991). Speaker Independent Vowel Recognition using Neural Tree Networks. *Proceedings of International Joint Conference on Neural Networks*, Seattle, WA (pp. 809-814).

Schmidt, W., & Davis, J. (1993). Pattern recognition properties of various feature spaces for higher order neural networks. *IEEE Transactions on Pattern Analysis and Machine Intelligence, 15*, 795–801.

Selviah, D. R. (2009). High Speed Optical Higher Order Neural Networks for Discovering Data Trends and Patterns in Very Large Databases. In M. Zhang (Ed.), Artificial Higher Order Neural Networks for Economics and Business (pp. 442-465). Hershey, PA, USA: IGI Global.

Sethi, I. K., & Jan, A. K. (1991). Decision Tree Performance Enhancement Using an Artificial Neural Networks Implementation. In *Artificial Neural Networks and Statistical Pattern Recognition* (pp. 71–88). Amsterdam, the Netherlands: Elsevier.

Shannon, C. E. (1998). Communication in the presence of noise, *Proceedings of IEEE, 86*(2).

Spirkovska, L., & Reid, M. B. (1990). Connectivity strategies for higher-order neural networks applied to pattern recognition. *Proceedings of International Joint Conference on Neural Networks,* San Diego, CA, USA (Vol. 1, pp. 21-26). doi:10.1109/IJCNN.1990.137538

Spirkovska L., & Reid, M. B. (1994, May). Higher-order neural networks applied to 2D and 3D object recognition. *Machine Learning, 15*(2), 169-199.

Voutriaridis, C., Boutalis, Y. S., & Mertzios, G. (2003). Ridge Polynomial Networks in pattern recognition. *Proceedings of 4th EURASIP Conference focused on Video/Image Processing and Multimedia Communications*, Croatia, Republic of Croatia (pp. 519-524).

Wang, Z., Liu, Y., & Liu, X. (2009). On Complex Artificial Higher Order Neural Networks: Dealing with Stochasticity Jumps and Delays. In M. Zhang (Ed.), Artificial Higher Order Neural Networks for Economics and Business (pp. 466-483). Hershey, PA, USA: IGI Global.

Yao, Y., Freeman, W. J., Burke, B., & Yang, Q. (1991). Pattern recognition by a distributed neural network: An industrial application. *Neural Networks, 4*(1), 103–121. doi:10.1016/0893-6080(91)90036-5

Zhang, M. (2010). Rainfall Estimation Using Neuron-Adaptive Artificial Higher Order Neural Networks. In M. Zhang (Ed.), Artificial Higher Order Neural Networks for Computer Science and Engineering – Trends for Emerging Applications (pp. 159-186). Hershey, PA, USA: IGI Global.

Chapter 5
Ultra High Frequency SINC and Trigonometric Higher Order Neural Networks for Data Classification

Ming Zhang
Christopher Newport University, USA

ABSTRACT

This chapter develops a new nonlinear model, Ultra high frequency SINC and Trigonometric Higher Order Neural Networks (UNT-HONN), for Data Classification. UNT-HONN includes Ultra high frequency siNc and Sine Higher Order Neural Networks (UNS-HONN) and Ultra high frequency siNc and Cosine Higher Order Neural Networks (UNC-HONN). Data classification using UNS-HONN and UNC-HONN models are tested. Results show that UNS-HONN and UNC-HONN models are better than other Polynomial Higher Order Neural Network (PHONN) and Trigonometric Higher Order Neural Network (THONN) models, since UNS-HONN and UNC-HONN models can classify the data with error approaching 0.0000%.

INTRODUCTION

The contributions of this chapter will be:

- Introduce the background of HONNs with the applications of HONNs in classification area.
- Develop a new HONN models called UNS-HONN and UNC-HONN for ultra- high frequency data classifications.
- Provide the UNS-HONN and UNC-HONN learning algorithm and weight update formulae.
- Compare UNS-HONN and UNC-HONN models with other HONN models.
- Applications of UNS-HONN and UNC-HONN models for classifications.

DOI: 10.4018/978-1-5225-0063-6.ch005

This chapter is organized as follows: the background section gives the background knowledge of HONN and HONN applications in classification area. Section HONN models introduces UNS-HONN and UNC-HONN structures. Section update formula provides the UNS-HONN and UNC-HONN model update formulae, learning algorithms, and convergence theories of HONN. Section test describes UNS-HONN and UNC-HONN testing results in the data classification area. Conclusions are presented in last section.

BACKGROUND

Artificial Neural Network (ANN) has been widely used in the classification areas. Lippman (1989) studies pattern classification using neural networks. Moon and Chang (1994) learn classification and prediction of the critical heat flux using fuzzy clustering and artificial neural networks. Lin and Cunningham (1995) develop a new approach to fuzzy-neural system modelling. Behnke and Karayiannis (1998) present a competitive Neural Trees for pattern classifications. Bukovsky, Bila, Gupta, Hou, and Homma (2010) provide foundation and classification of nonconventional neural units and paradigm of non-synaptic neural interaction.

Artificial Higher Order Neural Network (HONN) has been widely used in the classification area too. Reid, Spirkovska, and Ochoa (1989) research simultaneous position, scale, rotation invariant pattern classification using third-order neural networks. Shin (1991) investigate tThe Pi-Sigma network: an Efficient Higher-Order Neural Network for Pattern Classification and Function Approximation. Ghosh and Shin (1992) show efficient higher order neural networks for function approximation and classification. Shin, Ghosh, and Samani (1992) analyze computationally efficient invariant pattern classification with higher order Pi-Sigma networks. Husken and Stagge (2003) expand recurrent neural networks for time series classification. Fallahnezhad, Moradi, and Zaferanlouei (2011) contribute a hybrid higher order neural classifier for handling classification problems.

Shawash and Selviah (2010) test artificial higher order neural network training on limited precision processors, and investigate the training of networks using Back Propagation and Levenberg-Marquardt algorithms in limited precision achieving high overall calculation accuracy, using on-line training, a new type of HONN known as the Correlation HONN (CHONN), discrete XOR and continuous optical waveguide sidewall roughness datasets by simulation to find the precision at which the training and operation is feasible. The BP algorithm converged to a precision beyond which the performance did not improve. The results support previous findings in literature for Artificial Neural Network operation that discrete datasets require lower precision than continuous datasets. The importance of the chapter findings is that they demonstrate the feasibility of on-line, real-time, low-latency training on limited precision electronic hardware.

Sanchez, Urrego, Alanis, and Carlos-Hernandez (2010) focus on recurrent higher order neural observers for anaerobic processes, and propose the design of a discrete-time neural observer which requires no prior knowledge of the model of an anaerobic process, for estimate biomass, substrate and inorganic carbon which are variables difficult to measure and very important for anaerobic process control in a completely stirred tank reactor (CSTR) with biomass filter; this observer is based on a recurrent higher order neural network, trained with an extended Kalman filter based algorithm.

Boutalis, Christodoulou, and Theodoridis (2010) provide identification of nonlinear systems using a new neuro-fuzzy dynamical system definition based on high order neural network function approximators, and study the nonlinear systems. A new definition of Adaptive Dynamic Fuzzy Systems (ADFS) is presented in this chapter for the identification of unknown nonlinear dynamical systems. The proposed scheme uses the concept of Adaptive Fuzzy Systems operating in conjunction with High Order Neural Network Functions (HONNFs). Since the plant is considered unknown, this chapter first proposes its approximation by a special form of an adaptive fuzzy system and in the sequel the fuzzy rules are approximated by appropriate HONNFs. Thus the identification scheme leads up to a Recurrent High Order Neural Network, which however takes into account the fuzzy output partitions of the initial ADFS. Weight updating laws, for the involved HONNFs, are provided, which guarantee that the identification error reaches zero exponentially fast. Simulations illustrate the potency of the method and comparisons on well-known benchmarks are given.

Najarian, Hosseini, and Fallahnezhad (2010) explore artificial tactile sensing and robotic surgery using higher order neural networks, and introduce a new medical instrument, namely, the Tactile Tumor Detector (TTD) able to simulate the sense of touch in clinical and surgical applications. All theoretical and experimental attempts for its construction are presented. Theoretical analyses are mostly based on finite element method (FEM), artificial neural networks (ANN), and higher order neural networks (HONN). The TTD is used for detecting abnormal masses in biological tissue, specifically for breast examinations. This chapter presents a research work on ANN and HONN done on the theoretical results of the TTD to reduce the subjectivity of estimation in diagnosing tumor characteristics. This chapter uses HONN as a stronger open box intelligent unit than traditional black box neural networks (NN) for estimating the characteristics of tumor and tissue. The results show that by having an HONN model of our nonlinear input-output mapping, there are many advantages compared with ANN model, including faster running for new data, lesser RMS error and better fitting properties.

UNT-HONN MODELS

Nyquist Rule says that a sampling rate must be at least twice as fast as the fastest frequency (Shannon 1998). In classification, simulating and predicting data, the new nonlinear models of UNT-HONN should have twice as high frequency as that of the ultra-high frequency of data. To achieve this purpose, a new model should be developed to enforce high frequency of HONN in order to make the classification, simulation, and prediction error close to zero. The new HONN model, Ultra High Frequency SINC and Trigonometric Higher Order Neural Network (UNT-HONN), includes two different models base on the different neuron functions. Ultra high frequency siNc and Sine Trigonometric Higher Order Neural Network (UNS-HONN) has neurons with SINC and sine functions. Ultra high frequency siNc and Cosine Trigonometric Higher Order Neural Network (UNC-HONN) has neurons with SINC and cosine functions. Except for the functions in the neuron all other parts of these two models are the same. The following section will discuss the UNS-HONN and UNC models in detail.

UNS-HONN Model Structure can be seen in Figure 1. UNC-HONN Model Structure can be seen in Figure 2.

The Nyquist–Shannon sampling theorem, after Harry Nyquist and Claude Shannon, in the literature more commonly referred to as the Nyquist sampling theorem or simply as the sampling theorem, is a fundamental result in the field of information theory, in particular telecommunications and signal processing. Shannon's version of the theorem states:[Shannon 1998]

Figure 1. UNS-HON Architecture

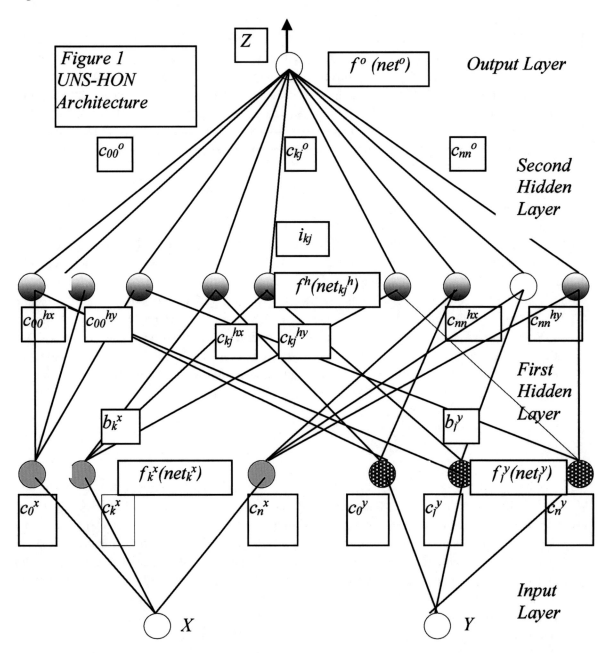

If a function x(t) contains no frequencies higher than B hertz, it is completely determined by giving its ordinates at a series of points spaced 1/(2B) seconds apart.

In other words, a band limited function can be perfectly reconstructed from a countable sequence of samples if the band limit, B, is no greater than ½ the sampling rate (samples per second).

In classification, simulating and predicting data, the new nonlinear models of UNS-HONN and UNC-HONN models should have twice as high frequency as that of the ultra-high frequency of the data. To

Figure 2.

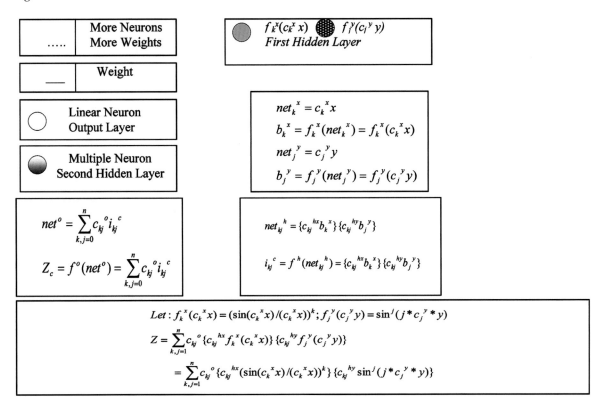

achieve this purpose, a new model should be developed to enforce high frequency of HONN in order to make the simulation and prediction error close to zero.

UNS-HONN Model

The different types of UNS-HONN models are shown as follows. Formula (1) (2) and (3) are for UNS-HONN model 2, 1 and 0 respectively. Model 2 has three layers of weights changeable, Model 1 has two layers of weights changeable, and model 0 has one layer of weights changeable. For models 2, 1 and 0, Z is the output while x and y are the inputs of UNS-HONN. c_{kj}^{o} is the weight for the output layer, c_{kj}^{hx} and c_{kj}^{hy} are the weights for the second hidden layer, and c_k^x and c_j^y are the weights for the first hidden layer. Functions SINC and sine are the first hidden layer nodes of UNS-HONN. The output layer node of UNS-HONN is a linear function of $f^o(net^o) = net^o$, where net^o equals the input of output layer node. UNS-HONN is an open neural network model, each weight of HONN has its corresponding coefficient in the model formula, and each node of UNS-HONN has its corresponding function in the model formula. The structure of UNS-HONN is built by a nonlinear formula. It means, after training, there is rationale for each component of UNS-HONN in the nonlinear formula.

UNS-HONN Model 2

$$Z = \sum_{k,j=1}^{n} (c_{kj}^{\ o})\{c_{kj}^{\ hx}(\sin(c_k^{\ x}x)/(c_k^{\ x}x))^k\}\{c_{kj}^{\ hy}\sin^j(j*c_j^{\ y}y)\} \quad . \tag{1}$$

$$UNS-HONN \qquad Model \qquad 1:$$

$$z = \sum_{k,j=1}^{n} c_{kj}^{\ o}\ (\sin(c_k^{\ x}x)/(c_k^{\ x}x))^k \sin^j(j*c_j^{\ y}y)$$

$$where: \qquad (c_{kj}^{\ hx}) = (c_{kj}^{\ hy}) = 1 \tag{2}$$

$$UNS-HONN \qquad Model \qquad 0:$$

$$z = \sum_{k,j=1}^{n} c_{kj}^{\ o}\ (\sin(x)/(x))^k \sin^j(j*y)$$

$$where: \qquad (c_{kj}^{\ hx}) = (c_{kj}^{\ hy}) = 1$$

$$and \qquad c_k^{\ x} = c_j^{\ y} = 1 \tag{3}$$

For equations 1, 2, and 3, values of k and j ranges from 0 to n, where n is an integer. The UNS-HONN model can classify ultra-high frequency data, when n increases to a big number. This property of the model allows it to easily classify, simulate and predicate ultra high frequency data, since both k and j increase when there is an increase in n.

The following is an expansion of model UNS-HONN order two.

$$z = c_{00}^{\ o}\ c_{00}^{\ hx}\ c_{00}^{\ hy}\ (\sin(c_0^{\ x}\ x)/\ c_0^{\ x}\ x)^0 \sin^0(0*c_0^{\ y}y)$$

$$+ c_{01}^{\ o}\ c_{01}^{\ hx}\ c_{01}^{\ hy}\ (\sin(c_0^{\ x}\ x)/\ c_0^{\ x}\ x)^0 \sin^1(1*c_1^{\ y}\ y)$$

$$+ c_{02}^{\ o}\ c_{02}^{\ hx}\ c_{02}^{\ hy}\ (\sin(c_0^{\ x}\ x)/\ c_0^{\ x}\ x)^0 \sin^2(2*c_2^{\ y}\ y)$$

$$+ c_{10}^{\ o}\ c_{10}^{\ hx}\ c_{10}^{\ hy}\ (\sin(c_1^{\ x}\ x)/\ c_1^{\ x}\ x)^1 \sin^0(0*c_0^{\ y}y)$$

$$+ c_{11}^{\ o}\ c_{11}^{\ hx}\ c_{11}^{\ hy}\ (\sin(c_1^{\ x}\ x)/\ c_1^{\ x}\ x)^1 \sin^1(1*c_1^{\ y}\ y)$$

$$+ c_{12}^{\ o}\ c_{12}^{\ hx}\ c_{12}^{\ hy}\ (\sin(c_1^{\ x}\ x)/\ c_1^{\ x}\ x)^1 \sin^2(2*c_2^{\ y}\ y)$$

$$+ c_{20}^{\ o}\ c_{20}^{\ hx}\ c_{20}^{\ hy}\ (\sin(c_2^{\ x}\ x)/\ c_2^{\ x}\ x)^2 \sin^0(0*c_0^{\ y}y)$$

$$+ c_{21}^{\ o}\ c_{21}^{\ hx}\ c_{21}^{\ hy}\ (\sin(c_2^{\ x}\ x)/\ c_2^{\ x}\ x)^2 \sin^1(1*c_1^{\ y}\ y)$$

$$+ c_{22}^{\ o}\ c_{22}^{\ hx}\ c_{22}^{\ hy}\ (\sin(c_2^{\ x}\ x)/\ c_2^{\ x}\ x)^2 \sin^2(2*c_2^{\ y}\ y) \tag{4}$$

The UNS-HONN Architecture is shown in Figure 1 and 1B. This model structure is used to develop the model learning algorithm, which make sure the convergence of learning. This allows the deference between desired output and real output of UNS-HONN close to zero.

UNC-HONN Model

The UNC-HONN models replace the sine functions from UNS-HONN with cosine functions. The UNC-HONN models are defined as follows.

UNCHONN   Model   2 :

$$Z = \sum_{k,j=0}^{n} (c_{kj}^{\ o})\{c_{kj}^{\ hx}(\sin(c_k^{\ x}x)/(c_k^{\ x}x))^k\}\{c_{kj}^{\ hy}\cos^j(j*c_j^{\ y}y)\} \tag{5}$$

UNCHONN   Model   1 :

$$z = \sum_{k,j=0}^{n} c_{kj}^{\ o}\ (\sin(c_k^{\ x}x)/(c_k^{\ x}x))^k \cos^j(j*c_j^{\ y}y)$$
$$where: \qquad (c_{kj}^{\ hx}) = (c_{kj}^{\ hy}) = 1 \tag{6}$$

UNCHONN   Model   0 :

$$z = \sum_{k,j=0}^{n} c_{kj}^{\ o}\ (\sin(x)/(x))^k \cos^j(j*y)$$
$$where: \qquad (c_{kj}^{\ hx}) = (c_{kj}^{\ hy}) = 1$$
$$and \qquad c_k^{\ x} = c_j^{\ y} = 1 \tag{7}$$

LEARNING ALGORITHM OF UPT-HONN MODELS

Output Neurons in HONN Model (model 0, 1, and 2)

The output layer weights are updated according to:

$$c_{kj}^{\ o}(t+1) = c_{kj}^{\ o}(t) - \eta(\partial E\ /\ \partial c_{kj}^{\ o}) \tag{A.1}$$

where = learning rate (positive and usually < 1)

c_{kj} = weight; index k an j = input index

(k, j=0, 1, 2,…,n means one of n*n input neurons from the second hidden layer)

E = error

t = training time

o = output layer

The output node equations are:

$$net^{o} = \sum_{k,j=1}^{n} c_{kj}{}^{o} i_{kj}$$

$$z = f^{o}(net^{o}) = \sum_{k,j=1}^{n} c_{kj}{}^{o} i_{kj} \qquad\qquad (A.2)$$

where i_{kj} = input to the output neuron (= output from 2nd hidden layer)

z = actual output from the output neuron

f^{o} = output neuron activity function

The error at a particular output unit (neuron) will be:

$$\delta = (d - z) \qquad\qquad (A.3)$$

where d = desired output value
The total error is the error of output unit, namely:

$$E = 0.5 * \delta^{2} = 0.5 * (d - z)^{2} \qquad\qquad (A.4)$$

The derivatives $f^{o\prime}(net^{o})$ are calculated as follows:
The output neuron function is linear function ($f^{o}(net^{o}) = net^{o}$):

$$f^{o}{}'(net^{o}) = \partial f^{o} / \partial(net)^{o} = \partial(net^{o}) / \partial(net^{o}) = 1 \qquad\qquad (A.5)$$

Gradients are calculated as follows:

$$\partial E \; / \partial c_{kj}{}^{o} = (\partial E / \partial z)(\partial z \; / \partial(net^{o}))(\partial(net^{o}) / \partial c_{kj}{}^{o}) \qquad\qquad (A.6)$$

$$\partial E \; / \partial z = \partial(0.5 * (d - z)^{2}) / \partial z) = 0.5 * (-2(d - z)) = -(d - z) \qquad\qquad (A.7)$$

$$\partial z / \partial (net^o) = \partial f^o / \partial (net^o) = f^o{}'(net^o) \qquad (A.8)$$

$$\partial (net^o) / \partial_{kj}{}^o = \partial (\sum_{k,j=0}^{n} c_{kj}{}^o i_{kj}) / \partial c_{kj}{}^o = i_{kj}$$

Combining Eqns. A.6 through A.9, the negative gradient is:

$$-\partial E / \partial c_{kj}{}^o = (d - z)f^o{}'(net^o)i_{kj} \qquad (A.10)$$

For a linear output neuron, this becomes, by combining Eqns. A.10 and A.5:

$$-\partial E / \partial c_{kj}{}^o = (d - z)f^o{}'(net^o)i_{kj}$$
$$= (d - z)(1)i_{kj} = (d - z)i_{kj} \qquad (A.11)$$

The weight update equations are formulated as follows:for linear output neurons, let:

$$\delta^{ol} = (d - z) \qquad (A.12)$$

Combining Formulae A.1, A.11, and A.12:

$$c_{kj}{}^o(t + 1) = c_{kj}{}^o(t) - \eta(\partial E / \partial a_{kj}{}^o)$$
$$= c_{kj}{}^o(t) + \eta(d - z)f^o{}'(net^o)i_{kj}$$
$$= a_{kj}{}^o(t) + \eta \delta^{ol} i_{kj}$$
$$where:$$
$$\delta^{ol} = (d - z)$$
$$f^{o'}(net^o) = 1 \qquad (linear \qquad neuron) \qquad (A.13)$$

Second-Hidden Layer Neurons in HONN Model (Model 2)

The second hidden layer weights are updated according to:

$$c_{kj}{}^{hx}(t + 1) = c_{kj}{}^{hx}(t) - \eta(\partial E / \partial c_{kj}{}^{hx}) \qquad (B.1)$$

Where = learning rate (positive & usually < 1)

k, j = input index (k, j = 0, 1, 2, ...,n means one of 2*n*n input combinations from the first hidden layer)

E = error

t = training time

hx = hidden layer, related to x input

$c_{kj}{}^{hx}$ = hidden layer weight related to x input

The equations for the 2nd hidden layer node are:

$$net_{kj}{}^{h} = \{c_{kj}{}^{hx}b_{k}{}^{x}\}\{c_{kj}{}^{hy}b_{j}{}^{y}\}$$
$$i_{kj} = f^{h}(net_{kj}{}^{h}) \qquad (B.2)$$

where i_{kj} = output from 2nd hidden layer (= input to the output neuron)

$b_{k}{}^{x}$ and $b_{j}{}^{y}$ = input to 2nd hidden layer neuron

(= output from the 1st hidden layer neuron)

f^{h} = hidden neuron activation function

hy = hidden layer, related to y input

$c_{kj}{}^{hy}$ = hidden layer weight related to y input

We call the neurons at the second layer multiple neurons. Their activity function is linear and their inputs are the multiplication of two outputs of the first layer neuron output and their weights.

The error of a single output unit will be:

$$\delta = (d - z) \qquad (B.3)$$

where d = desired output value of output layer neuron

z = actual output value of output layer neuron

The total error is the sum of the squared errors across all output units, namely:

$$E_{p} = 0.5 * \delta^{2} = 0.5 * (d - z)^{2}$$
$$= 0.5 * (d - f^{o}(net^{o}))^{2}$$
$$= 0.5 * (d - f_{k}^{o}(\sum_{j} c_{kj}{}^{o} i_{kj}))^{2} \qquad (B.4)$$

The derivatives $f^{h'}(net^h_{pj})$ are calculated as follows, for a linear function of second layer neurons:

$$i_{kj} = f^h(net_{kj}^{\ h}) = net_{kj}^{\ h}$$
$$f^h{'}(net_{kj}^{\ h}) = 1 \qquad\qquad (B.5)$$

The gradient $(E/c_{kj}^{\ hx})$ is given by:

$$\partial E \ / \ \partial c_{kj}^{\ hx} = \partial (0.5 * (d - z)^2) \ / \ \partial c_{kj}^{\ hx}$$
$$= (\partial (0.5 * (d - z)^2) \ / \ \partial z \ )(\partial z \ / \ \partial (net^o))$$
$$(\partial (net^o) \ / \ \partial i_{kj})(\partial i_{kj} \ / \ \partial (net_{kj}^{\ h}))(\partial (net_{kj}^{\ h}) \ / \ \partial c_{kj}^{\ hx}) \qquad\qquad (B.6)$$

$$\partial (0.5 * (d - z)^2) \ / \ \partial z = -(d - z) \qquad\qquad (B.7)$$

$$\partial z \ / \ \partial (net^o) = \partial f^o \ / \ \partial (net^o) = f_k^o{'}(net^o) \qquad\qquad (B.8)$$

$$\partial (net^o) \ / \ \partial i_{kj} = \partial (\sum_{k,j=1}^{n} (c_{kj}^{\ o} i_{kj})) \ / \ \partial i_{kj} = c_{kj}^{\ o} \qquad\qquad (B.9)$$

$$\partial i_{kj} \ / \ \partial (net_{kj}^{\ h}) = \partial (f^h(net_{kj}^{\ h})) \ / \ \partial (net_{kj}^{\ h}) = f^h{'}(net_{kj}^{\ h}) \qquad\qquad (B.10)$$

$$\partial (net_{kj}^{\ h}) \ / \ \partial c_{kj}^{\ hx} = \partial (\{c_{kj}^{\ hx} b_k^{\ x}\}\{c_{kj}^{\ hy} b_j^{\ y}\}) \ / \ \partial c_{kj}^{\ hx}$$
$$= b_k^{\ x} c_{kj}^{\ hy} b_j^{\ y} = \delta_{kj}^{\ hx} b_k^{\ x}$$
$$where : \delta_{kj}^{\ hx} = c_{kj}^{\ hy} b_j^{\ y} \qquad\qquad (B.11)$$

Combining Eqns. B.6 through B.11, the negative gradient is:

$$-\partial E \ / \ \partial c_{kj}^{\ hx} = (d - z) f^o{'}(net^o) c_{kj}^{\ o} f^h{'}(net_{kj}^{\ h}) \delta^{hx} b_k^{\ x} \qquad\qquad (B.12)$$

The weight update equations are formulated as follows:

- let output neuron is a linear neuron:

$$\delta^{ol} = (d - z) f^o_{\ k}{'}(net^o) = (d - z) \qquad\qquad (B.13)$$

Also let the second layer neurons be linear neurons, combining Formulae B.1, B.5, B.12 and B.13:

$$c_{kj}{}^{hx}(t+1) = c_{kj}{}^{hx}(t) - \eta(\partial E / \partial c_{kj}{}^{hx})$$

$$= c_{kj}{}^{hx}(t) + \eta((d-z)f^{o}{}'(net^{o})c_{kj}{}^{o}f^{h}{}'(net_{kj}{}^{hx})c_{kj}{}^{hy}b_{j}{}^{y}b_{k}{}^{x})$$

$$= c_{kj}{}^{hx}(t) + \eta(\delta^{ol}c_{kj}{}^{o}\delta_{kj}{}^{hx}b_{k}{}^{x})$$

$$where: \qquad \delta^{ol} = (d-z)$$

$$\delta_{kj}{}^{hx} = c_{kj}{}^{hy}b_{j}{}^{y}$$

$$f^{o}{}'(net^{o}) = 1 \qquad (linear \qquad neuron)$$

$$f^{h}{}'(net_{kj}{}^{hx}) = 1 \qquad (linear \qquad neuron) \qquad\qquad (B.14)$$

Use the same rules, the weight update question for y input neurons is:

$$c_{kj}{}^{hy}(t+1) = c_{kj}{}^{hy}(t) - \eta(\partial E / \partial c_{kj}{}^{hy})$$

$$= c_{kj}{}^{hy}(t) + \eta((d-z)f^{o}{}'(net^{o})c_{kj}{}^{o}f^{h}{}'(net_{kj}{}^{hy})c_{kj}{}^{hx}b_{k}{}^{x}b_{j}{}^{y})$$

$$= c_{kj}{}^{hy}(t) + \eta(\delta^{ol}c_{kj}{}^{o}\delta_{kj}{}^{hy}b_{j}{}^{y})$$

$$where: \qquad \delta^{ol} = (d-z)$$

$$\delta_{kj}{}^{hy} = c_{kj}{}^{hx}b_{k}{}^{x}$$

$$f^{o}{}'(net^{o}) = 1 \qquad (linear \qquad neuron)$$

$$f^{h}{}'(net_{kj}{}^{hy}) = 1 \qquad (linear \qquad neuron) \qquad\qquad (B.15)$$

First Hidden Layer Neurons in UNS-HONN (Model 1 and Model 2)

For the x input part, we have following formula as learning algorithm.
The 1st hidden layer weights are updated according to:

$$c_{k}{}^{x}(t+1) = c_{k}{}^{x}(t) - \eta(\partial E_{p} / \partial c_{k}{}^{x}) \qquad\qquad (C.1)$$

where:

$c_{k}{}^{x}$ = 1st hidden layer weight for input x; k = kth neuron of first hidden layer

= learning rate (positive & usually < 1)

E = error

t = training time

The equations for the kth or j^{th} node in the first hidden layer are:

$$net_k^{\,x} = c_k^{\,x} * x$$
$$b_k^{\,x} = f_k^{\,x}(net_k^{\,x})$$

or

$$net_j^{\,y} = c_j^{\,y} * y$$
$$b_j^{\,y} = f_j^{\,y}(net_j^{\,y}) \hspace{4cm} (C.2)$$

Where:

i_{kj} = output from 2nd hidden layer (= input to the output neuron)

$b_k^{\,x}$ and $b_j^{\,y}$ = output from the 1st hidden layer neuron (= input to 2nd hidden layer neuron)

$f_k^{\,x}$ and $f_j^{\,y}$ = 1st hidden layer neuron activation function

x and y = input to 1st hidden layer

The total error is the sum of the squared errors across all hidden units, namely:

$$E_p = 0.5 * \delta^2 = 0.5 * (d - z)^2$$
$$= 0.5 * (d - f^o(net^{\,o}))^2$$
$$= 0.5 * (d - f^o(\sum_j c_{kj}^{\,o} i_{kj}))^2 \hspace{3cm} (C.3)$$

The gradient is given by:

$$\partial E_p / \partial c_k^{\,x} = \partial(0.5 * (d - z)^2) / \partial c_k^{\,x}$$
$$= (\partial(0.5 * (d - z)^2) / \partial z)(\partial z / \partial(net^{\,o}))$$
$$(\partial(net^{\,o}) / \partial i_{kj})(\partial i_{kj} / \partial(net_{kj}^{\,h}))(\partial(net_{kj}^{\,h}) / \partial b_k^{\,x})$$
$$(\partial b_k^{\,x} / \partial(net_k^{\,x}))(\partial(net_k^{\,x}) / \partial c_k^{\,x}) \hspace{2cm} (C.4)$$

$$\partial(0.5 * (d - z)^2 / \partial z = -(d - z) \hspace{2cm} (C.5)$$

$$\partial z / \partial(net^{\,o}) = \partial f^o / \partial(net^o) = f^o{}'(net^o) \hspace{1.5cm} (C.6)$$

$$\partial(net^{\,o}) / \partial i_{kj} = \partial(\sum_{k,j=1}^{l} (c_{kj}^{\,o} i_{kj})) / \partial i_{kj} = c_{kj}^{\,o} \hspace{1.5cm} (C.7)$$

$$\partial i_{kj} \,/\, \partial(net_{kj}{}^{h}) = \partial(f^{h}(net_{kj}{}^{h})) \,/\, \partial(net_{kj}{}^{h}) = f^{h}{}'(net_{kj}{}^{h}) \qquad (C.8)$$

$$\partial net_{kj}{}^{h} \,/\, \partial b_{k}{}^{x} = \partial((c_{kj}{}^{hx} * b_{k}{}^{x}) * (c_{kj}{}^{hy} * b_{j}{}^{y})) \,/\, \partial b_{k}{}^{x} = c_{kj}{}^{hx} * c_{kj}{}^{hy} * b_{j}{}^{y}$$
$$= \delta_{kj}{}^{hx} c_{kj}{}^{hx}$$
$$where: \delta_{kj}{}^{hx} = c_{kj}{}^{hy} * b_{j}{}^{y} \qquad (C.9)$$

$$\partial b_{k}{}^{x} \,/\, \partial(net_{k}{}^{x}) = f_{x}{}'(net_{k}{}^{x}) \qquad (C.10)$$

$$\partial(net_{k}{}^{x}) \,/\, \partial c_{k}{}^{x} = \partial(c_{k}{}^{x} * x) \,/\, \partial c_{k}{}^{x} = x \qquad (C.11)$$

Combining Formulae C.5 through C.11 the negative gradient is:

$$-\partial E_{p} \,/\, \partial c_{k}{}^{x} = (d-z)f^{o}{}'(net^{o})c_{kj}{}^{o} * f^{h}{}'(net_{kj}{}^{h})\delta_{kj}{}^{hx} c_{kj}{}^{hx} f_{x}{}'(net_{k}{}^{x})x \qquad (C.12)$$

The weight update equations are calculated as follows.
For linear output neurons:

$$f^{o}{}'(net^{o}) = 1$$
$$\delta^{ol} = (d-z)f^{o}{}'(net^{o}) = (d-z) \qquad (C.13)$$

For linear neurons of second hidden layer:

$$f^{h}{}'(net_{kj}{}^{h}) = 1 \qquad (C.14)$$

The negative gradient is:

$$-\partial E_{p} \,/\, \partial c_{k}{}^{x} = (d-z)f^{o}{}'(net^{o})c_{kj}{}^{o} * f^{h}{}'(net_{kj}{}^{h})\delta_{kj}{}^{hx} c_{kj}{}^{hx} f_{x}{}'(net_{k}{}^{x})x$$
$$= \delta^{ol} * c_{kj}{}^{o} * \delta_{kj}{}^{hx} * c_{kj}{}^{hx} * f_{x}{}'(net_{k}{}^{x}) * x \qquad (C.15)$$

By combining Formulae C.1, C.4, and C.16, for a linear 1ˢᵗ hidden layer neuron:

$$Let:$$
$$f_{k}{}^{j}(c_{k}{}^{j}x) = (\sin(c_{k}{}^{x}x) \,/\, (c_{k}{}^{x}x))^{k}$$
$$f_{j}{}^{y}(c_{j}{}^{k}y) = \sin^{j}(j * c_{j}{}^{k}y)$$

For a SINC function of *x* input part:

$$b_k^{\ x} = f_k^{\ x}(net_k^{\ x}) = [\sin\ (net_k^{\ x})\,/\,(net_k^{\ x})]^k = [\sin\ (c_k^{\ x}x)\,/\,(c_k^{\ x}x)]^k$$

$$f_x{}'(net_k^{\ x}) = \partial b_k^{\ x}\,/\,\partial(net_k^{\ x})$$

$$= k[\sin\ (net_k^{\ x})\,/\,(net_k^{\ x})]^{k-1} * [\cos(net_k^{\ x})\,/\,(net_k^{\ x}) - \sin\ (net_k^{\ x})\,/\,(net_k^{\ x})^2]$$

$$= k[\sin\ (c_k^{\ x}x)\,/\,(c_k^{\ k}x)]^{k-1} * [\cos(c_k^{\ x}x)\,/\,(c_k^{\ x}x) - \sin\ (c_k^{\ x}x)\,/\,(c_k^{\ x}x)^2] \qquad (UNS-HONN \qquad C. \qquad 16)$$

$$c_k^{\ x}(t+1) = c_k^{\ x}(t) - \eta(\partial E_p\,/\,\partial c_k^{\ x})$$

$$= c_k^{\ x}(t) + \eta(d-z)f^o{}'(net^o)c_{kj}^{\ o} * f^h{}'(net_{kj}^{\ h})c_{kj}^{\ hy}b_j^{\ y}c_{kj}^{\ hx}f_x{}'(net_k^{\ x})x$$

$$= c_k^{\ x}(t) + \eta * \delta^{\,ol} * c_{kj}^{\ o} * \delta^{hx} * c_{kj}^{\ hx} * f_x{}'(net_k^{\ x}) * x$$

$$= c_k^{\ x}(t) + \eta * \delta^{\,ol} * c_{kj}^{\ o} * \delta^{hx} * c_{kj}^{\ hx}$$

$$\qquad * [k[\sin\ (c_k^{\ x}x)\,/\,(c_k^{\ k}x)]^{k-1} * [\cos(c_k^{\ x}x)\,/\,(c_k^{\ x}x) - \sin\ (c_k^{\ x}x)\,/\,(c_k^{\ k}x)^2]] * x$$

$$= c_k^{\ x}(t) + \eta * \delta^{\,ol} * c_{kj}^{\ o} * \delta^{hx} * c_{kj}^{\ hx} * \delta^x * x \qquad (UNC-HONN \qquad D. \qquad 17)$$

where :

$$\delta^{\,ol} = (d-z)f^o{}'(net^o) = (d-z) \qquad (linear \qquad neuron \qquad f^o{}'(net^o) = 1)$$

$$\delta^{hx} = f^h{}'(net_{kj}^{\ h})c_{kj}^{\ hy}b_j^{\ y} = c_{kj}^{\ hy}b_j^{\ y} \qquad (linear \qquad neuron \qquad f^h{}'(net_{kj}^{\ h}) = 1)$$

$$\delta^x = f_x{}'(net_k^{\ x})$$

$$\qquad = k[\sin\ (net_k^{\ x})\,/\,(net_k^{\ x})]^{k-1} * [\cos(net_k^{\ x})\,/\,(net_k^{\ x}) - \sin\ (net_k^{\ x})\,/\,(net_k^{\ x})^2]$$

$$\qquad = k[\sin\ (c_k^{\ x}x)\,/\,(c_k^{\ x}x)]^{k-1} * [\cos(c_k^{\ x}x)\,/\,(c_k^{\ x}x) - \sin\ (c_k^{\ x}x)\,/\,(c_k^{\ x}x)^2]$$

For an ultra-high frequency sine function of *y* input part:

$$b_j^{\ y} = f_j^{\ y}\ (net_j^{\ y}) = \sin^j(j*net_j^{\ y}) = \sin^j(j*c_j^{\ y}*y)$$

$$f_y{}'(net_j^{\ y}) = \partial b_j^{\ y}\,/\,\partial(net_j^{\ y})$$

$$= \partial(\sin^j(j*net_j^{\ y}))\,/\,\partial(net_j^{\ y})$$

$$= j\sin^{j-1}(j*net_j^{\ y})*\cos(j*net_j^{\ y})*j$$

$$= j^2*\sin^{j-1}(j*net_j^{\ y})*\cos(j*net_j^{\ y})$$

$$= j^2*\sin^{j-1}(j*c_j^{\ y}*y)*\cos(j*c_j^{\ y}*y) \qquad (UNS-HONN \qquad C. \qquad 18)$$

Using the above procedure:

$$c_j^{\ y}(t+1) = c_j^{\ y}(t) - \eta(\partial E_p\,/\,\partial c_j^{\ y})$$

$$= c_j^{\ y}(t) + \eta(d-z)f^o{}'(net^o)c_{kj}^{\ o} * f^h{}'(net_{kj}^{\ h})c_{kj}^{\ hx}b_k^{\ x}c_{kj}^{\ hy}f_y{}'(net_j^{\ y})y$$

$$= c_j^{\ y}(t) + \eta * \delta^{\,ol} * c_{kj}^{\ o} * \delta^{hy} * c_{kj}^{\ hy} * (j^2)\sin^{j-1}(j*c_j^{\ y}*y)\cos(j*c_j^{\ y}*y)*y$$

$$= c_j^{\ y}(t) + \eta * \delta^{\,ol} * c_{kj}^{\ o} * \delta^{hy} * c_{kj}^{\ hy} * \delta^y * y \qquad (UNS-HONN \qquad C. \qquad 19)$$

where :

$$\delta^{\,ol} = (d-z)f^o{}'(net^o) = d-z \qquad (linear \qquad neuron \qquad f^o{}'(net^o) = 1)$$

$$\delta^{hy} = f^h{}'(net_{kj}^{\ hy})c_{kj}^{\ hx}b_k^{\ x} = c_{kj}^{\ hx}b_k^{\ x} \qquad (linear \qquad neuron \qquad f^h{}'(net_{kj}^{\ hy}) = 1)$$

$$\delta^y = f_y{}'(net_j^{\ y}) = (j^2)\sin^{j-1}(j*c_j^{\ y}*y)\cos(j*c_j^{\ y}*y)$$

First Hidden Layer Neurons in UNC-HONN (Model 1 and Model 2)

The 1st hidden layer weights are updated according to:

$$c_j^y(t+1) = c_j^y(t) - \eta(\partial E_p / \partial c_j^y) \qquad (D.1)$$

where:

$C_j^y = $ 1st hidden layer weight for input y; $j = j$th neuron of first hidden layer

$=$ learning rate (positive & usually < 1)

$E =$ error

$t =$ training time

The equations for the kth or j^{th} node in the first hidden layer are:

$$net_k^x = c_k^x * x$$
$$b_k^x = f_k^x(net_k^x)$$
$$or$$
$$net_j^y = c_j^y * y$$
$$b_j^y = f_j^y(net_j^y) \qquad (D.2)$$

where:

$i_{kj} = $ output from 2nd hidden layer ($=$ input to the output neuron)

b_k^x and $b_j^y = $ output from the 1st hidden layer neuron ($=$ input to 2nd hidden layer neuron)

f_k^x and $f_j^y = $1st hidden layer neuron activation function

x and $y = $ input to 1st hidden layer

The total error is the sum of the squared errors across all hidden units, namely:

$$E_p = 0.5 * \delta^2 = 0.5 * (d - z)^2$$
$$= 0.5 * (d - f^o(net^o))^2$$
$$= 0.5 * (d - f^o(\sum_j c_{kj}^o i_{kj}))^2 \qquad (D.3)$$

The gradient is given by:

$$
\begin{aligned}
\partial E_p \,/\, \partial c_j^{\,y} &= \partial(0.5 * (d-z)^2) \,/\, \partial c_j^{\,y} \\
&= (\partial(0.5 * (d-z)^2) \,/\, \partial z)(\partial z \,/\, \partial(net^{\,o})) \\
&\quad (\partial(net^{\,o}) \,/\, \partial i_{kj})(\partial i_{kj} \,/\, \partial(net_{kj}^{\,h}))(\partial(net_{kj}^{\,h}) \,/\, \partial b_j^{\,y}) \\
&\quad (\partial b_j^{\,y} \,/\, \partial(net_j^{\,y}))(\partial(net_j^{\,y}) \,/\, \partial c_j^{\,y})
\end{aligned}
\tag{D.4}
$$

$$
\partial(0.5 * (d-z)^2 \,/\, \partial z \;=\; -(d-z)
\tag{D.5}
$$

$$
\partial z \,/\, \partial(net^{\,o}) = \partial f^{\,o} \,/\, \partial(net^{o}) = f^{\,o}{}'(net^{o})
\tag{D.6}
$$

$$
\partial(net^{\,o}) \,/\, \partial i_{kj} = \partial\!\left(\sum_{k,j=1}^{l} (c_{kj}^{\,o} i_{kj})\right) \,/\, \partial i_{kj} = c_{kj}^{\,o}
\tag{D.7}
$$

$$
\partial i_{kj} \,/\, \partial(net_{kj}^{\,h}) = \partial(f^{\,h}(net_{kj}^{\,h})) \,/\, \partial(net_{kj}^{\,h}) = f^{\,h}{}'(net_{kj}^{\,h})
\tag{D.8}
$$

$$
\begin{aligned}
\partial net_{kj}^{\,h} \,/\, \partial b_j^{\,y} &= \partial((c_{kj}^{\,hx} * b_k^{\,x}) * (c_{kj}^{\,hy} * b_j^{\,y})) \,/\, \partial b_j^{\,y} = c_{kj}^{\,hx} * c_{kj}^{\,hy} * b_k^{\,x} \\
&= \delta^{\,hy} c_{kj}^{\,hy} \\
where:\; \delta_{kj}^{\,hy} &= c_{kj}^{\,hy} * b_k^{\,x}
\end{aligned}
\tag{D.9}
$$

$$
\partial b_j^{\,y} \,/\, \partial(net_j^{\,y}) = f_y{}'(net_j^{\,y})
\tag{D.10}
$$

$$
\partial(net_j^{\,y}) \,/\, \partial c_j^{\,y} = \partial(c_j^{\,y} * y) \,/\, \partial c_j^{\,y} = y
\tag{D.11}
$$

Combining Formulae C.5 through C.11 the negative gradient is:

$$
-\partial E_p \,/\, \partial c_k^{\,x} = (d-z) f^{\,o}{}'(net^{\,o}) c_{kj}^{\,o} * f^{\,h}{}'(net_{kj}^{\,h}) \delta_{kj}^{\,hy} c_{kj}^{\,hy} f_y{}'(net_j^{\,y}) y
\tag{D.12}
$$

The weight update equations are calculated as follows.
For linear output neurons:

$$
\begin{aligned}
f^{\,o}{}'(net^{o}) &= 1 \\
\delta^{ol} &= (d-z) f^{\,o}{}'(net^{o}) = (d-z)
\end{aligned}
\tag{D.13}
$$

For linear neurons of second hidden layer:

$$f^{h}{}'(net_{kj}{}^{h}) = 1 \qquad (D.14)$$

The negative gradient is:

$$-\partial E_{p} / \partial c_{j}{}^{y} = (d-z)f^{o}{}'(net^{o})c_{kj}{}^{o} * f^{h}{}'(net_{kj}{}^{h})\delta_{kj}{}^{hy}c_{kj}{}^{hy}f_{y}{}'(net_{j}{}^{y})y$$

$$= \delta^{ol} * c_{kj}{}^{o} * \delta_{kj}{}^{hy} * c_{kj}{}^{hy} * f_{y}{}'(net_{j}{}^{y}) * y \qquad (D.15)$$

$Let:$

$$f_{k}{}^{j}(c_{k}{}^{j}x) = (\sin(c_{k}{}^{x}x) / (c_{k}{}^{x}x))^{k}$$

$$f_{j}{}^{y}(c_{j}{}^{k}y) = \cos^{j}(j * c_{j}{}^{k}y)$$

For a SINC function of x input part:

$$b_{k}{}^{x} = f_{k}{}^{x}(net_{k}{}^{x}) = [\sin (net_{k}{}^{x}) / (net_{k}{}^{x})]^{k} = [\sin (c_{k}{}^{x}x) / (c_{k}{}^{x}x)]^{k}$$

$$f_{x}{}'(net_{k}{}^{x}) = \partial b_{k}{}^{x} / \partial(net_{k}{}^{x})$$

$$= k[\sin (net_{k}{}^{x}) / (net_{k}{}^{x})]^{k-1} * [\cos(net_{k}{}^{x}) / (net_{k}{}^{x}) - \sin (net_{k}{}^{x}) / (net_{k}{}^{x})^{2}]$$

$$= k[\sin (c_{k}{}^{x}x) / (c_{k}{}^{k}x)]^{k-1} * [\cos(c_{k}{}^{x}x) / (c_{k}{}^{x}x) - \sin (c_{k}{}^{x}x) / (c_{k}{}^{x}x)^{2}] \qquad (UNC-HONN \quad D. \quad 16)$$

$$c_{k}{}^{x}(t+1) = c_{k}{}^{x}(t) - \eta(\partial E_{p} / \partial c_{k}{}^{x})$$

$$= c_{k}{}^{x}(t) + \eta(d-z)f^{o}{}'(net^{o})c_{kj}{}^{o} * f^{h}{}'(net_{kj}{}^{h})c_{kj}{}^{hy}b_{j}{}^{y}c_{kj}{}^{hx}f_{x}{}'(net_{k}{}^{x})x$$

$$= c_{k}{}^{x}(t) + \eta * \delta^{ol} * c_{kj}{}^{o} * \delta^{hx} * c_{kj}{}^{hx} * f_{x}{}'(net_{k}{}^{x}) * x$$

$$= c_{k}{}^{x}(t) + \eta * \delta^{ol} * c_{kj}{}^{o} * \delta^{hx} * c_{kj}{}^{hx}$$

$$* [k[\sin (c_{k}{}^{x}x) / (c_{k}{}^{x}x)]^{k-1} * [\cos(c_{k}{}^{x}x) / (c_{k}{}^{x}x) - \sin (c_{k}{}^{x}x) / (c_{k}{}^{k}x)^{2}]] * x$$

$$= c_{k}{}^{x}(t) + \eta * \delta^{ol} * c_{kj}{}^{o} * \delta^{hx} * c_{kj}{}^{hx} * \delta^{x} * x \qquad (UNC-HONN \quad D. \quad 17)$$

$where:$

$$\delta^{ol} = (d-z)f^{o}{}'(net^{o}) = (d-z) \qquad (linear \quad neuron \quad f^{o}{}'(net^{o}) = 1)$$

$$\delta^{hx} = f^{h}{}'(net_{kj}{}^{h})c_{kj}{}^{hy}b_{j}{}^{y} = c_{kj}{}^{hy}b_{j}{}^{y} \qquad (linear \quad neuron \quad f^{h}{}'(net_{kj}{}^{h}) = 1)$$

$$\delta^{x} = f_{x}{}'(net_{k}{}^{x})$$

$$= k[\sin (net_{k}{}^{x}) / (net_{k}{}^{x})]^{k-1} * [\cos(net_{k}{}^{x}) / (net_{k}{}^{x}) - \sin (net_{k}{}^{x}) / (net_{k}{}^{x})^{2}]$$

$$= k[\sin (c_{k}{}^{x}x) / (c_{k}{}^{x}x)]^{k-1} * [\cos(c_{k}{}^{x}x) / (c_{k}{}^{x}x) - \sin (c_{k}{}^{x}x) / (c_{k}{}^{x}x)^{2}]$$

For an ultra-high frequency cosine function of y input part:

$$b_j^{\ y} = f_y\ (net_j^{\ y}) = \cos^j(j * net_j^{\ y}) = \cos^j(j * c_j^{\ y} * y)$$

$$f_y\ '(net_j^{\ y}) = \partial b^y_{\ j} / \partial(net_j^{\ y})$$

$$= \partial(\cos^j(j * net_j^{\ y})) / \partial(net_j^{\ y})$$

$$= j\cos^{j-1}(j * net_j^{\ y}) * (-\sin(j * net_j^{\ y})) * j$$

$$= -j^2 * \cos^{j-1}(j * net_j^{\ y}) * \sin(j * net_j^{\ y})$$

$$= -j^2 * \cos^{j-1}(j * c_j^{\ y} * y) * \sin(j * c_j^{\ y} * y) \qquad (UNC - HONN \qquad D. \qquad 18)$$

Using the above procedure:

$$c_j^{\ y}(t+1) = c_j^{\ y}(t) - \eta(\partial E_p / \partial c_j^{\ y})$$

$$= c_j^{\ y}(t) + \eta(d - z)f^o\ '(net^o)c_{kj}^{\ o} * f^h\ '(net_{kj}^{\ h})c_{kj}^{\ hx}b_k^{\ x}c_{kj}^{\ hy}f_y\ '(net_j^{\ y})y$$

$$= c_j^{\ y}(t) + \eta * \delta^{ol} * c_{kj}^{\ o} * \delta^{hy} * c_{kj}^{\ hy} * (-j^2) * \cos^{j-1}(j * c_j^{\ y} * y) * \sin(j * c_j^{\ y} * y) * y$$

$$= c_j^{\ y}(t) + \eta * \delta^{ol} * c_{kj}^{\ o} * \delta^{hy} * c_{kj}^{\ hy} * \delta^{\ y} * y \qquad (UNC - HONN \qquad D. \qquad 19)$$

where :

$$\delta^{ol} = (d - z)f^o\ '(net^o) = d - z \qquad (linear \qquad neuron \qquad f^o\ '(net^o) = 1)$$

$$\delta^{hy} = f^h\ '(net_{kj}^{\ hy})c_{kj}^{\ hx}b_k^{\ x} = c_{kj}^{\ hx}b_k^{\ x} \qquad (linear \qquad neuron \qquad f^h\ '(net_{kj}^{\ hy}) = 1)$$

$$\delta^{\ y} = f_y\ '(net_j^{\ y}) = (-j^2) * \cos^{j-1}(j * c_j^{\ y} * y) * \sin(j * c_j^{\ y} * y)$$

UNS-HONN AND UNC-HONN MODELTESTING

This chapter uses UNS-HONN model to classify data. Test results are shown in Tables 1 and 2 and Figures 3A and 3B. Next, the UNC-HONN model is used to classify data. Results are provided in Tables 3 and 4 and Figures 4A and 4B.

The UNS-HONN model 0 is used in Table 1 of "UNS-HONN Data Classification 1",. The order number for UNS-HONN model is 6. In the first table of Table 1, the "No." column shows that a total of 19 points are chosen. The "UNS-HONN x" column displays the input x values, which are all "1"s. The "UNS-HONN y" column displays the input y values, which are 0, 0.1, 0.2, 0.3, 0.4, 05, 0.7, 0.8, 0.9, 1, 2, 3, 4, 5, 6, 7 and 8. The "UNS-HONN z" column displays the output z values. The "Original Data" column displays the original data values. The "Absolute Original Data" column displays the absolute values for original data. The "Difference" column shows the difference between UNS-HONN output z and the original data (UNS-HONN z – Original Data). The "Absolute Difference" column shows the absolute difference between UNS-HONN output z and the original data (|UNS-HONN z – Original Data|). The "UNS-HONN Error %" column gives the error percentage for UNS-HONN Model (UNS-HONN error %

Table 1. UNS-HONN Data Classification 1 (n=6, Model 0)

No.	UNS-HONN x	UNS-HONN y	UNS-HONN z	Original Data	Absolute Original Data	Difference	Absolute Difference	UNS-HONN Error %
1	1	0	0.00000000	0.000000	0.000000	0.00000000	0.00000000	0.000000%
2	1	0.1	0.13133595	0.131336	0.131336	-0.00000005	0.00000005	0.000006%
3	1	0.2	0.50814169	0.508142	0.508142	-0.00000031	0.00000031	0.000042%
4	1	0.3	1.11380489	1.113805	1.113805	-0.00000011	0.00000011	0.000015%
5	1	0.4	0.98063803	0.980638	0.980638	0.00000003	0.00000003	0.000004%
6	1	0.5	0.60215662	0.602157	0.602157	-0.00000038	0.00000038	0.000051%
7	1	0.6	0.75884561	0.758846	0.758846	-0.00000039	0.00000039	0.000052%
8	1	0.7	0.92516394	0.925164	0.925164	-0.00000006	0.00000006	0.000008%
9	1	0.8	0.78311983	0.78312	0.783120	-0.00000017	0.00000017	0.000023%
10	1	0.9	0.39932453	0.399325	0.399325	-0.00000047	0.00000047	0.000064%
11	1	1	0.51901116	0.519011	0.519011	0.00000016	0.00000016	0.000022%
13	1	2	1.17415686	1.174157	1.174157	-0.00000014	0.00000014	0.000020%
14	1	3	0.23994608	0.239946	0.239946	0.00000008	0.00000008	0.000011%
15	1	4	0.50750588	0.507506	0.507506	-0.00000012	0.00000012	0.000016%
16	1	5	-1.06444736	-1.064447	1.064447	-0.00000036	0.00000036	0.000049%
17	1	6	-1.10951452	-1.109515	1.109515	0.00000048	0.00000048	0.000066%
18	1	7	0.92533087	0.925331	0.925331	-0.00000013	0.00000013	0.000018%
19	1	8	1.48832443	1.488324	1.488324	0.00000043	0.00000043	0.000058%
Average				0.7350428			0.0000002151	0.00002926%

$c_{kj}{}^o$	k=0	k=1	k=2	k=3	k=4	k=5	k=6
j=0	0.3884	-0.1712	-0.3580	-0.2535	-0.9590	-0.2524	0.8223
j=1	0.9624	0.0838	-0.0760	-0.9257	0.9045	0.2691	-0.0672
j=2	0.9908	0.0399	-0.0250	-0.3347	-0.1048	0.0837	-0.3587
j=3	-0.5380	-0.2394	-0.0419	0.2238	0.5765	-0.3107	0.2658
j=4	-0.1784	0.4013	-0.7152	0.4915	-0.5638	0.6601	0.0392
j=5	-0.1825	0.9703	0.2072	0.2234	0.7835	-0.3868	-0.3376
j=6	0.3604	-0.9528	0.6653	-0.2069	-0.2853	-0.3984	0.5546

		k = 0	k = 1	k = 2	k = 3	k = 4	k = 5	k = 6
x=1, y=0.1								
j =	1	0.09607968	0.00703978	-0.00537239	-0.05506348	0.04527319	0.01133406	-0.00238166
j =	2	0.03910638	0.00132518	-0.00069868	-0.00787109	-0.00207386	0.00139374	-0.00502606
j =	3	-0.01388493	-0.00519906	-0.00076569	0.00344143	0.00745963	-0.00338297	0.00243529
j =	4	-0.00410261	0.00776558	-0.01164586	0.00673452	-0.00650051	0.00640429	0.00032003
j =	5	-0.00462241	0.02068002	0.00371598	0.00337137	0.00994950	-0.00413322	-0.00303559
j =	6	0.01167955	-0.02598257	0.01526642	-0.00399502	-0.00463553	-0.00544699	0.00638052
Subtotal		0.12425565	0.00562893	0.00049978	-0.05338227	0.04947242	0.00616892	-0.00130747
$z = \Sigma c_{kj}{}^o*(\sin(x)/x)^k*\sin^j(j*y)$			(k= 0, 1, 2 ,3, 4, 5, 6		j = 1, 2, 3, 4, 5, 6) =			0.13133595

Table 2. UNS-HONN Data Classification 2 (n=6, Model 0)

No.	UNS-HONN x	UNS-HONN y	UNS-HONN z	Original Data	Absolute Original Data	Difference	Absolute Difference	UNS-HONN Error %
1	1	0	0.00000000	0.000000	0.000000	0.00000000	0.00000000	0.000000%
2	1	0.1	0.06026689	0.060267	0.060267	-0.00000011	0.00000011	0.000015%
3	1	0.2	-0.23159418	-0.231594	0.231594	-0.00000018	0.00000018	0.000024%
4	1	0.3	0.02612711	0.026127	0.026127	0.00000011	0.00000011	0.000016%
5	1	0.4	0.47560577	0.475606	0.475606	-0.00000023	0.00000023	0.000031%
6	1	0.5	-0.11718982	-0.11719	0.117190	0.00000018	0.00000018	0.000025%
7	1	0.6	-0.42981324	-0.429813	0.429813	0.00000024	0.00000024	0.000033%
8	1	0.7	-0.71430141	-0.714301	0.714301	-0.00000041	0.00000041	0.000056%
9	1	0.8	-1.04031943	-1.040319	1.040319	-0.00000043	0.00000043	0.000058%
10	1	0.9	-0.34015426	-0.340154	0.340154	-0.00000026	0.00000026	0.000035%
11	1	1	0.29665747	0.296657	0.296657	0.00000047	0.00000047	0.000063%
13	1	2	1.35395383	1.353954	1.353954	-0.00000017	0.00000017	0.000023%
14	1	3	-0.00160868	-0.001609	0.001609	0.00000032	0.00000032	0.000044%
15	1	4	-1.13635617	-1.136356	1.136356	-0.00000017	0.00000017	0.000023%
16	1	5	-1.70555477	-1.705555	1.705555	0.00000023	0.00000023	0.000031%
17	1	6	-0.99931470	-0.999315	0.999315	0.00000030	0.00000030	0.000040%
18	1	7	-0.81816258	-0.818163	0.818163	0.00000042	0.00000042	0.000058%
19	1	8	1.59289786	1.592898	1.592898	-0.00000014	0.00000014	0.000019%
Average					0.6299932		0.0000002425	0.00003299%

$c_{kj}{}^o$	k=0	k=1	k=2	k=3	k=4	k=5	k=6
j=0	0.2896	-0.0624	-0.2592	-0.1347	-0.8502	-0.1496	0.7235
j=1	0.9747	0.0951	-0.0883	-0.9370	0.9148	0.2784	-0.0795
j=2	0.1245	0.1525	-0.1486	-0.4573	-0.2274	0.1063	-0.4713
j=3	-0.8645	-0.4651	-0.2776	0.4598	0.7022	-0.5463	0.4915
j=4	-0.4352	0.7681	-0.0720	0.7583	-0.8246	0.9273	0.3969
j=5	-0.7514	0.5173	0.8751	0.8913	0.3492	-0.9547	-0.0855
j=6	0.0493	-0.6317	0.3442	-0.9858	-0.2642	-0.2773	0.2373

x=1, y=0.1	k = 0	k = 1	k = 2	k = 3	k = 4	k = 5	k = 6
j = 1	0.09730763	0.00798906	-0.00624187	-0.05573564	0.04578874	0.01172576	-0.00281759
j = 2	0.00491395	0.00506490	-0.00415297	-0.01075425	-0.00449996	0.00177007	-0.00660380
j = 3	-0.02231139	-0.01010060	-0.00507294	0.00707046	0.00908613	-0.00594824	0.00450319
j = 4	-0.01000817	0.01486355	-0.00117240	0.01039020	-0.00950748	0.00899667	0.00324027
j = 5	-0.01903168	0.01102522	0.01569429	0.01345077	0.00443442	-0.01020160	-0.00076879
j = 6	0.00159767	-0.01722627	0.00789824	-0.01903476	-0.00429270	-0.00379129	0.00273007
Subtotal	0.05246803	0.01161586	0.00695236	-0.05461321	0.04100914	0.00255136	0.00028335
$z = \Sigma c_{kj}{}^o*(\sin(x)/x)^k*\sin^j(j*y)$		(k= 0, 1, 2 ,3, 4, 5, 6			j = 1, 2, 3, 4, 5, 6) =			0.06026689

Figure 3. UNC-HONN Architecture

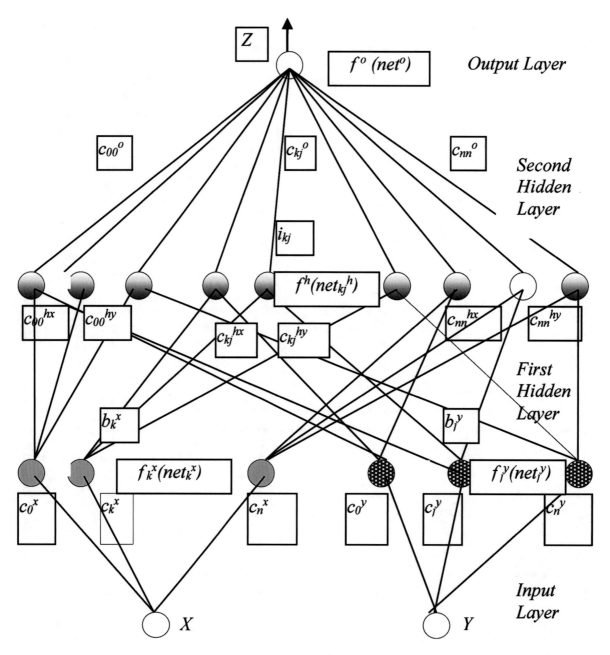

Table 3. UNC-HONN Data Classification 1 (n=6, Model 0)

No.	UNC-HONN x	UNC-HONN y	UNC-HONN z	Original Data	Absolute Original Data	Difference	Absolute Difference	UNC-HONN Error %
1	1	0	1.56288479	1.562885	1.562885	-0.00000021	0.00000021	0.000023%
2	1	0.1	0.93927060	0.939271	0.939271	-0.00000040	0.00000040	0.000044%
3	1	0.2	0.50395438	0.503954	0.503954	0.00000038	0.00000038	0.000042%
4	1	0.3	0.49922245	0.499222	0.499222	0.00000045	0.00000045	0.000050%
5	1	0.4	0.61472187	0.614722	0.614722	-0.00000013	0.00000013	0.000014%
6	1	0.5	0.98132019	0.981320	0.981320	0.00000019	0.00000019	0.000021%
7	1	0.6	0.72493825	0.724938	0.724938	0.00000025	0.00000025	0.000027%
8	1	0.7	0.83707694	0.837077	0.837077	-0.00000006	0.00000006	0.000006%
9	1	0.8	1.27132289	1.271323	1.271323	-0.00000011	0.00000011	0.000012%
10	1	0.9	1.36908792	1.369088	1.369088	-0.00000008	0.00000008	0.000009%
11	1	1	1.71589352	1.715894	1.715894	-0.00000048	0.00000048	0.000053%
13	1	2	-0.81211013	-0.812110	0.812110	-0.00000013	0.00000013	0.000014%
14	1	3	1.05732450	1.057325	1.057325	-0.00000050	0.00000050	0.000055%
15	1	4	-0.44306287	-0.443063	0.443063	0.00000013	0.00000013	0.000015%
16	1	5	0.95061990	0.95062	0.950620	-0.00000010	0.00000010	0.000011%
17	1	6	0.48989025	0.489890	0.489890	0.00000025	0.00000025	0.000027%
18	1	7	0.92299498	0.922995	0.922995	-0.00000002	0.00000002	0.000002%
19	1	8	0.67149105	0.671491	0.671491	0.00000005	0.00000005	0.000005%
Average				0.9092882			0.0000002176	0.00002394%

c_{kj}^{o}	k=0	k=1	k=2	k=3	k=4	k=5	k=6
j=0	0.2650	-0.0588	-0.2356	-0.1101	-0.8366	-0.1290	0.7099
j=1	0.7389	0.8593	-0.8425	-0.7912	0.7700	0.0356	-0.8337
j=2	0.7663	0.7943	-0.7804	-0.0991	-0.8692	0.7481	-0.0131
j=3	-0.1823	-0.8837	-0.6952	0.8774	0.1208	-0.9640	0.8191
j=4	-0.6116	0.9445	-0.2584	0.9347	-0.0066	0.1033	0.5724
j=5	-0.5156	0.3725	0.6393	0.6555	0.1156	-0.7189	-0.7697
j=6	0.6813	-0.2737	0.9862	-0.5278	-0.5062	-0.6193	0.8795

x=1, y=0.1	k = 0	k = 1	k = 2	k = 3	k = 4	k = 5	k = 6
j = 0	0.26500000	-0.04947849	-0.16682210	-0.06560014	-0.41944444	-0.05442337	0.25201828
j = 1	0.73520858	0.71946365	-0.59357158	-0.46906023	0.38412467	0.01494413	-0.29448934
j = 2	0.73605452	0.64199976	-0.53077042	-0.05671556	-0.41858866	0.30315626	-0.00446701
j = 3	-0.15894826	-0.64835535	-0.42919747	0.45581033	0.05280714	-0.35460255	0.25353674
j = 4	-0.44017061	0.57199821	-0.13168138	0.40081433	-0.00238152	0.03136531	0.14624737
j = 5	-0.26838166	0.16313496	0.23562584	0.20329657	0.03016854	-0.15787165	-0.14223166
j = 6	0.21533861	-0.07279431	0.22071244	-0.09939633	-0.08021623	-0.08258104	0.09868570
Subtotal	1.08410118	1.32596843	-1.39570466	0.36914897	-0.45353049	-0.30001290	0.30930008
$z = \Sigma c_{kj}^{o}*(\sin(x)/x)^{k}*\cos^{j}(j*y)$		(k= 0, 1, 2 ,3, 4, 5, 6		j = 0, 1, 2, 3, 4, 5, 6) =				0.93927060

Table 4. UNC-HONN Data Classification 2 (n=6, Model 0)

No.	UNC-HONN x	UNC-HONN y	UNC-HONN z	Original Data	Absolute Original Data	Difference	Absolute Difference	UNC-HONN Error %
1	1	0	-2.16502776	-2.165028	2.165028	0.00000000	0.00000000	0.000000%
2	1	0.1	-1.78433940	-1.78434	1.784340	0.00000060	0.00000060	0.000066%
3	1	0.2	-1.46798631	-1.46799	1.467990	0.00000369	0.00000369	0.000406%
4	1	0.3	-1.13496419	-1.134964	1.134964	-0.00000019	0.00000019	0.000021%
5	1	0.4	-0.97438327	-0.974383	0.974383	-0.00000027	0.00000027	0.000030%
6	1	0.5	-1.42257068	-1.422571	1.422571	0.00000032	0.00000032	0.000036%
7	1	0.6	-1.18117045	-1.181170	1.181170	-0.00000045	0.00000045	0.000050%
8	1	0.7	-0.52365606	-0.523656	0.523656	-0.00000006	0.00000006	0.000006%
9	1	0.8	-0.02415629	-0.024156	0.024156	-0.00000029	0.00000029	0.000032%
10	1	0.9	0.19021619	0.190216	0.190216	0.00000019	0.00000019	0.000021%
11	1	1	-0.20877411	-0.208774	0.208774	-0.00000011	0.00000011	0.000013%
13	1	2	-2.71593563	-2.715936	2.715936	0.00000037	0.00000037	0.000040%
14	1	3	-0.90161623	-0.901616	0.901616	-0.00000023	0.00000023	0.000025%
15	1	4	-1.78712533	-1.787125	1.787125	-0.00000033	0.00000033	0.000036%
16	1	5	-0.44375750	-0.443758	0.443758	0.00000050	0.00000050	0.000055%
17	1	6	-1.19241464	-1.192415	1.192415	0.00000036	0.00000036	0.000040%
18	1	7	-0.42963855	-0.429639	0.429639	0.00000045	0.00000045	0.000049%
19	1	8	-1.44245633	-1.442456	1.442456	-0.00000033	0.00000033	0.000036%
Average					1.1105663		0.0000004854	0.00005338%

c_{kj}^{o}	k=0	k=1	k=2	k=3	k=4	k=5	k=6
j=0	0.7228	-0.5156	-0.7924	-0.6779	-0.3934	-0.6828	0.2667
j=1	0.3068	0.4272	-0.4104	-0.3691	0.3489	0.6035	-0.4016
j=2	0.4454	0.4734	-0.4695	-0.7782	-0.5483	0.4272	-0.7922
j=3	-0.9734	-0.6749	-0.4864	0.6686	0.9110	-0.7552	0.6003
j=4	-0.5239	0.8568	-0.1607	0.8460	-0.9123	0.0156	0.4846
j=5	-0.6380	0.4959	0.7527	0.7789	0.2380	-0.8313	-0.8821
j=6	0.8158	-0.4072	0.1107	-0.7513	-0.7307	-0.8438	0.0038

x=1, y=0.1	k = 0	k = 1	k = 2	k = 3	k = 4	k = 5	k = 6
j = 0	0.72280000	-0.43386244	-0.56107738	-0.40390857	-0.19723816	-0.28806417	0.09467992
j = 1	0.30526728	0.35768052	-0.28914157	-0.21881968	0.17405338	0.25333658	-0.14185788
j = 2	0.42782028	0.38262959	-0.31931921	-0.44536883	-0.26404989	0.17311637	-0.27013501
j = 3	-0.84871219	-0.49516241	-0.30029006	0.34733849	0.39823925	-0.27779652	0.18581138
j = 4	-0.37705262	0.51888625	-0.08189318	0.36277835	-0.32919090	0.00473668	0.12381460
j = 5	-0.33209367	0.21720668	0.27742151	0.24156781	0.06211171	-0.18255487	-0.16300188
j = 6	0.25785005	-0.10830049	0.02477476	-0.14148628	-0.11579217	-0.11251716	0.00042639
Subtotal	0.15587913	0.43907770	-1.24952513	-0.25789872	-0.27186679	-0.42974310	-0.17026249
$z = \Sigma c_{kj}^{o}*(\sin(x)/x)^{k}*\cos^{j}(j*y)$		(k= 0, 1, 2 ,3, 4, 5, 6		j = 0, 1, 2, 3, 4, 5, 6) =				-1.78433940

Figure 4.

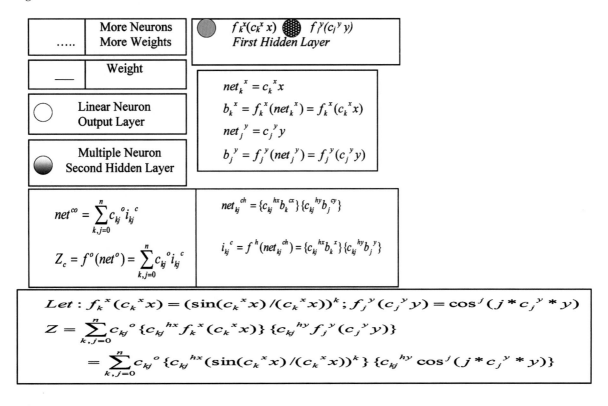

= absolute difference / Absolute original Data * 100%). The average UNS-HONN error is 0.00002926%, which is close to zero. After training UNS-HONN model by using original data values, the UNS-HONN all coefficients are displayed in the second table of Table 1. For examples, c_{00}^{o}= 0.3884, c_{01}^{o}= 0.9624, and c_{10}^{o}= -0.1712. In the third table of Table 1, the values for $c_{kj}^{o}*(sin(x)/x)^k*sin^j(j*y)$ *are provided* when $x=1, y=0.1, k=0,1,2,3,4,5,6,$ and $j=0,1,2,3,4,5,6.$ For examples, $c_{01}^{o}*(sin(x)/x)^0*sin^1(1*0.1)=0.09607968,$ $c_{02}^{o}*(sin(x)/x)^0*sin^2(2*0.1)=0.03910638,$ and $c_{03}^{o}*(sin(x)/x)^0*sin^3(3*0.1)=-0.01388493.$

And $z = \sum c_{kj}^{o}*(sin(x)/x)^k*sin^j(j*y) = \sum c_{kj}^{o}*(sin(1)/1)^k*sin^j(j*0.1)=0.13133595.$

In Table 2 of "UNS-HONN Data Classification 2", the UNS-HONN model 0 is used. The order number for UNS-HONN model is 6. In the first table of Table 2, the "No." column shows that a total of 19 points are chosen. The "UNS-HONN x" column displays the input x values, which are all "1"s. The "UNS-HONN y" column displays the input y values, which are 0, 0.1, 0.2, 0.3, 0.4, 05, 0.7, 0.8, 0.9, 1, 2, 3, 4, 5, 6, 7 and 8. The "UNS-HONN z" column displays the output z values. The "Original Data" column displays the original data values. The "Absolute Original Data" column displays the absolute values for the original data. The "Difference" column shows the difference between UNS-HONN output z and the original data (UNS-HONN z – Original Data). The "Absolute Difference" column shows the absolute difference between UNS-HONN output z and the original data (|UNS-HONN z – Original Data|). The "UNS-HONN Error %" column gives the error percentage for UNS-HONN Model (UNS-HONN error % = absolute difference / Absolute original Data * 100%). The average UNS-HONN error is 0.00002926%, which is close to zero. The UNS-HONN all coefficients are displayed in the second table of Table 2 after training UNS-HONN model by using original data values. For examples, $c_{00}{}^o = 0.2896$, $c_{01}{}^o = 0.9747$, and $c_{10}{}^o = -0.0624$. In the third table of Table 2, gives the values for $c_{kj}{}^o*(sin(x)/x)^k*sin^j(j*y)$, when $x=1$, $y=0.1$, $k=0,1,2,3,4,5,6$, and $j=0,1,2,3,4,5,6$. For examples, $c_{01}{}^o*(sin(x)/x)^0*sin^1(1*0.1)=0.09730763$, $c_{02}{}^o*(sin(x)/x)^0*sin^2(2*0.1)=0.00491395$, and $c_{03}{}^o*(sin(x)/x)^0*sin^3(3*0.1)=-0.02231139$.

And $z = \sum c_{kj}{}^o*(sin(x)/x)^k*sin^j(j*y) = \sum c_{kj}{}^o*(sin(1)/1)^k*sin^j(j*0.1)=0.106026689$.

In Figure 3, UNS-HONN data classification results are shown. Original Data are shown by Figure 3A. And UNS-HONN data classification results are shown by Figure 3B. In Figure 3, the data have been divided into two classifications. The Figure 3B also tells us the UNS-HONN model can classify data very well, since the average error percentage is close to 0.0000%.

Based on the training of UNS-HONN model, UNS-HONN has the following formula (see Table 1) to describe the data classification 1:

$z = \sum c_{kj}{}^o*(sin(x)/x)^k*sin^j(j*y)$ *(k, j = 0,1,2,3,4,5,6,)*

$= c_{00}{}^o*(sin(x)/x)^0*sin^0(0*y) + c_{10}{}^o*(sin(x)/x)^1*sin^0(0*y)$

$+ c_{20}{}^o*(sin(x)/x)^2*sin^0(0*y) + c_{30}{}^o*(sin(x)/x)^3*sin^0(0*y)$

$+ c_{40}{}^o*(sin(x)/x)^4*sin^0(0*y) + c_{50}{}^o*(sin(x)/x)^5*sin^0(0*y)$

$+ c_{60}{}^o*(sin(x)/x)^6*sin^0(0*y)$

$+ c_{01}{}^o*(sin(x)/x)^0*sin^1(1*y) + c_{11}{}^o*(sin(x)/x)^1*sin^1(1*y)$

$+ c_{21}{}^o*(sin(x)/x)^2*sin^1(1*y) + c_{31}{}^o*(sin(x)/x)^3*sin^1(1*y)$

$+ c_{41}{}^o*(sin(x)/x)^4*sin^1(1*y) + c_{51}{}^o*(sin(x)/x)^5*sin^1(1*y)$

$+ c_{61}{}^o*(sin(x)/x)^6*sin^1(1*y)$

$+ c_{02}{}^o*(sin(x)/x)^0*sin^2(2*y) + c_{12}{}^o*(sin(x)/x)^1*sin^2(2*y)$

$+ c_{22}{}^o*(sin(x)/x)^2*sin^2(2*y) + c_{32}{}^o*(sin(x)/x)^3*sin^2(2*y)$

$+ c_{42}{}^o*(sin(x)/x)^4*sin^2(2*y) + c_{52}{}^o*(sin(x)/x)^5*sin^2(2*y)$

$+ c_{62}{}^o*(sin(x)/x)^6*sin^2(2*y)$

$+ c_{03}{}^o*(sin(x)/x)^0*sin^3(3*y) + c_{13}{}^o*(sin(x)/x)^1*sin^3(3*y)$

$+ c_{23}{}^o*(sin(x)/x)^2*sin^3(3*y) + c_{33}{}^o*(sin(x)/x)^3*sin^3(3*y)$

$+ c_{43}{}^{o}*(sin(x)/x)^4*sin^3(3*y)+ c_{53}{}^{o}*(sin(x)/x)^5*sin^3(3*y)$

$+ c_{63}{}^{o}*(sin(x)/x)^6*sin^3(3*y)$

$+c_{04}{}^{o}*(sin(x)/x)^0*sin^4(4*y)+ c_{14}{}^{o}*(sin(x)/x)^1*sin^4(4*y)$

$+ c_{24}{}^{o}*(sin(x)/x)^2*sin^4(4*y)+ c_{34}{}^{o}*(sin(x)/x)^3*sin^4(4*y)$

$+ c_{44}{}^{o}*(sin(x)/x)^4*sin^4(4*y)+ c_{54}{}^{o}*(sin(x)/x)^5*sin^4(4*y)$

$+ c_{64}{}^{o}*(sin(x)/x)^6*sin^4(4*y)$

$+c_{05}{}^{o}*(sin(x)/x)^0*sin^5(5*y)+ c_{15}{}^{o}*(sin(x)/x)^1*sin^5(5*y)$

$+ c_{25}{}^{o}*(sin(x)/x)^2*sin^5(4*y)+ c_{35}{}^{o}*(sin(x)/x)^3*sin^5(5*y)$

$+ c_{45}{}^{o}*(sin(x)/x)^4*sin^5(5*y)+ c_{55}{}^{o}*(sin(x)/x)^5*sin^5(5*y)$

$+ c_{65}{}^{o}*(sin(x)/x)^6*sin^5(5*y)$

$+c_{06}{}^{o}*(sin(x)/x)^0*sin^6(6*y)+ c_{16}{}^{o}*(sin(x)/x)^1*sin^6(6*y)$

$+ c_{26}{}^{o}*(sin(x)/x)^2*sin^6(6*y)+ c_{36}{}^{o}*(sin(x)/x)^3*sin^6(6*y)$

$+ c_{46}{}^{o}*(sin(x)/x)^4*sin^6(6*y)+ c_{56}{}^{o}*(sin(x)/x)^5*sin^6(6*y)$

$+ c_{66}{}^{o}*(sin(x)/x)^6*sin^6(6*y)$

$= 0.3884*(sin(x)/x)^0*sin^0(0*y)+ (-0.1712) *(sin(x)/x)^1*sin^0(0*y)$

$+ (-0.3580)*(sin(x)/x)^2*sin^0(0*y)+ (-0.2535)*(sin(x)/x)^3*sin^0(0*y)$

$+ (-0.9590)*(sin(x)/x)^4*sin^0(0*y)+ (-0.2524)*(sin(x)/x)^5*sin^0(0*y)$

$+ 0.8223*(sin(x)/x)^6*sin^0(0*y)$

$+0.9624*(sin(x)/x)^0*sin^1(1*y)+ 0.0838*(sin(x)/x)^1*sin^1(1*y)$

$+ (-0.0760)*(sin(x)/x)^2*sin^1(1*y)+ (-0.9257)*(sin(x)/x)^3*sin^1(1*y)$

$+ 0.9045*(sin(x)/x)^4*sin^1(1*y)+ 0.2691*(sin(x)/x)^5*sin^1(1*y)$

$+ (-0.0672)*(sin(x)/x)^6*sin^1(1*y)$

$+0.9908*(sin(x)/x)^0*sin^2(2*y)+ 0.0399*(sin(x)/x)^1*sin^2(2*y)$

$+ (-0.0250)*(\sin(x)/x)^2*\sin^2(2*y)+ (-0.3347)*(\sin(x)/x)^3*\sin^2(2*y)$

$+(-0.1048)*(\sin(x)/x)^4*\sin^2(2*y)+ 0.0837*(\sin(x)/x)^5*\sin^2(2*y)$

$+ (-0.3587)*(\sin(x)/x)^6*\sin^2(2*y)$

$+(-0.5380)*(\sin(x)/x)^0*\sin^3(3*y)+ (-0.2394)*(\sin(x)/x)^1*\sin^3(3*y)$

$+ (-0.0419)*(\sin(x)/x)^2*\sin^3(3*y)+ 0.2238*(\sin(x)/x)^3*\sin^3(3*y)$

$+ 0.5765*(\sin(x)/x)^4*\sin^3(3*y)+ (-0.3017)*(\sin(x)/x)^5*\sin^3(3*y)$

$+ 0.2658*(\sin(x)/x)^6*\sin^3(3*y)$

$+(-0.1784)*(\sin(x)/x)^0*\sin^4(4*y)+ 0.4013*(\sin(x)/x)^1*\sin^4(4*y)$

$+ (-0.7152)*(\sin(x)/x)^2*\sin^4(4*y)+ 0.4915*(\sin(x)/x)^3*\sin^4(4*y)$

$+ (-0.5638)*(\sin(x)/x)^4*\sin^4(4*y)+ 0.6601*(\sin(x)/x)^5*\sin^4(4*y)$

$+ 0.0392*(\sin(x)/x)^6*\sin^4(4*y)$

$+(-0.1825)*(\sin(x)/x)^0*\sin^5(5*y)+ 0.9703*(\sin(x)/x)^1*\sin^5(5*y)$

$+ 0.2072*(\sin(x)/x)^2*\sin^5(4*y)+ 0.2234*(\sin(x)/x)^3*\sin^5(5*y)$

$+ 0.7835*(\sin(x)/x)^4*\sin^5(5*y)+ (-0.3868)*(\sin(x)/x)^5*\sin^5(5*y)$

$+ (-0.3376)*(\sin(x)/x)^6*\sin^5(5*y)$

$+0.3604*(\sin(x)/x)^0*\sin^6(6*y)+ (-0.9528)*(\sin(x)/x)^1*\sin^6(6*y)$

$+ 0.6653*(\sin(x)/x)^2*\sin^6(6*y)+ (-0.2069)*(\sin(x)/x)^3*\sin^6(6*y)$

$+ (-0.2853)*(\sin(x)/x)^4*\sin^6(6*y)+ (-0.3984)*(\sin(x)/x)^5*\sin^6(6*y)$

$+ 0.5546*(\sin(x)/x)^6*\sin^6(6*y)$

Based on the training of UNS-HONN model, UNS-HONN has the following formula (see Table 2) to describe the data classification 2:

$z=\sum c_{kj}{}^o*(\sin(x)/x)^k*\sin^j(j*y)$ *(k, j = 0,1,2,3,4,5,6,)*

$= c_{00}{}^o*(\sin(x)/x)^0*\sin^0(0*y)+ c_{10}{}^o*(\sin(x)/x)^1*\sin^0(0*y)$

$$+ c_{20}{}^{o}*(\sin(x)/x)^2*\sin^0(0*y)+ c_{30}{}^{o}*(\sin(x)/x)^3*\sin^0(0*y)$$

$$+ c_{40}{}^{o}*(\sin(x)/x)^4*\sin^0(0*y)+ c_{50}{}^{o}*(\sin(x)/x)^5*\sin^0(0*y)$$

$$+ c_{60}{}^{o}*(\sin(x)/x)^6*\sin^0(0*y)$$

$$+c_{01}{}^{o}*(\sin(x)/x)^0*\sin^1(1*y)+ c_{11}{}^{o}*(\sin(x)/x)^1*\sin^1(1*y)$$

$$+ c_{21}{}^{o}*(\sin(x)/x)^2*\sin^1(1*y)+ c_{31}{}^{o}*(\sin(x)/x)^3*\sin^1(1*y)$$

$$+ c_{41}{}^{o}*(\sin(x)/x)^4*\sin^1(1*y)+ c_{51}{}^{o}*(\sin(x)/x)^5*\sin^1(1*y)$$

$$+ c_{61}{}^{o}*(\sin(x)/x)^6*\sin^1(1*y)$$

$$+c_{02}{}^{o}*(\sin(x)/x)^0*\sin^2(2*y)+ c_{12}{}^{o}*(\sin(x)/x)^1*\sin^2(2*y)$$

$$+ c_{22}{}^{o}*(\sin(x)/x)^2*\sin^2(2*y)+ c_{32}{}^{o}*(\sin(x)/x)^3*\sin^2(2*y)$$

$$+ c_{42}{}^{o}*(\sin(x)/x)^4*\sin^2(2*y)+ c_{52}{}^{o}*(\sin(x)/x)^5*\sin^2(2*y)$$

$$+ c_{62}{}^{o}*(\sin(x)/x)^6*\sin^2(2*y)$$

$$+c_{03}{}^{o}*(\sin(x)/x)^0*\sin^3(3*y)+ c_{13}{}^{o}*(\sin(x)/x)^1*\sin^3(3*y)$$

$$+ c_{23}{}^{o}*(\sin(x)/x)^2*\sin^3(3*y)+ c_{33}{}^{o}*(\sin(x)/x)^3*\sin^3(3*y)$$

$$+ c_{43}{}^{o}*(\sin(x)/x)^4*\sin^3(3*y)+ c_{53}{}^{o}*(\sin(x)/x)^5*\sin^3(3*y)$$

$$+ c_{63}{}^{o}*(\sin(x)/x)^6*\sin^3(3*y)$$

$$+c_{04}{}^{o}*(\sin(x)/x)^0*\sin^4(4*y)+ c_{14}{}^{o}*(\sin(x)/x)^1*\sin^4(4*y)$$

$$+ c_{24}{}^{o}*(\sin(x)/x)^2*\sin^4(4*y)+ c_{34}{}^{o}*(\sin(x)/x)^3*\sin^4(4*y)$$

$$+ c_{44}{}^{o}*(\sin(x)/x)^4*\sin^4(4*y)+ c_{54}{}^{o}*(\sin(x)/x)^5*\sin^4(4*y)$$

$$+ c_{64}{}^{o}*(\sin(x)/x)^6*\sin^4(4*y)$$

$$+c_{05}{}^{o}*(\sin(x)/x)^0*\sin^5(5*y)+ c_{15}{}^{o}*(\sin(x)/x)^1*\sin^5(5*y)$$

$$+ c_{25}{}^{o}*(\sin(x)/x)^2*\sin^5(4*y)+ c_{35}{}^{o}*(\sin(x)/x)^3*\sin^5(5*y)$$

$$+ c_{45}{}^{o}*(\sin(x)/x)^4*\sin^5(5*y)+ c_{55}{}^{o}*(\sin(x)/x)^5*\sin^5(5*y)$$

$$+ c_{65}{}^{o}*(\sin(x)/x)^6*\sin^5(5*y)$$

$+c_{06}{}^{o}*(\sin(x)/x)^{0}*\sin^{6}(6*y)+ c_{16}{}^{o}*(\sin(x)/x)^{1}*\sin^{6}(6*y)$

$+ c_{26}{}^{o}*(\sin(x)/x)^{2}*\sin^{6}(6*y)+ c_{36}{}^{o}*(\sin(x)/x)^{3}*\sin^{6}(6*y)$

$+ c_{46}{}^{o}*(\sin(x)/x)^{4}*\sin^{6}(6*y)+ c_{56}{}^{o}*(\sin(x)/x)^{5}*\sin^{6}(6*y)$

$+ c_{66}{}^{o}*(\sin(x)/x)^{6}*\sin^{6}(6*y)$

$= 0.2896*(\sin(x)/x)^{0}*\sin^{0}(0*y)+ (-0.0624)*(\sin(x)/x)^{1}*\sin^{0}(0*y)$

$+ (-0.2592)*(\sin(x)/x)^{2}*\sin^{0}(0*y)+ (-0.1347)*(\sin(x)/x)^{3}*\sin^{0}(0*y)$

$+ (-0.8502)*(\sin(x)/x)^{4}*\sin^{0}(0*y)+ (-0.1496)*(\sin(x)/x)^{5}*\sin^{0}(0*y)$

$+ 0.7235*(\sin(x)/x)^{6}*\sin^{0}(0*y)$

$+0.9747*(\sin(x)/x)^{0}*\sin^{1}(1*y)+ 0.0951*(\sin(x)/x)^{1}*\sin^{1}(1*y)$

$+ (-0.0883)*(\sin(x)/x)^{2}*\sin^{1}(1*y)+ (-0.9370)*(\sin(x)/x)^{3}*\sin^{1}(1*y)$

$+ 0.9148*(\sin(x)/x)^{4}*\sin^{1}(1*y)+ 0.2784*(\sin(x)/x)^{5}*\sin^{1}(1*y)$

$+ (-0.0795)*(\sin(x)/x)^{6}*\sin^{1}(1*y)$

$+0.1245*(\sin(x)/x)^{0}*\sin^{2}(2*y)+ 0.1525*(\sin(x)/x)^{1}*\sin^{2}(2*y)$

$+ (-0.1486)*(\sin(x)/x)^{2}*\sin^{2}(2*y)+ (-0.4573)*(\sin(x)/x)^{3}*\sin^{2}(2*y)$

$+(-0.2274)*(\sin(x)/x)^{4}*\sin^{2}(2*y)+ 0.1063*(\sin(x)/x)^{5}*\sin^{2}(2*y)$

$+ (-0.4713)*(\sin(x)/x)^{6}*\sin^{2}(2*y)$

$+(-0.8645)*(\sin(x)/x)^{0}*\sin^{3}(3*y)+ (-0.4651)*(\sin(x)/x)^{1}*\sin^{3}(3*y)$

$+ (-0.2776)*(\sin(x)/x)^{2}*\sin^{3}(3*y)+ 0.4598*(\sin(x)/x)^{3}*\sin^{3}(3*y)$

$+ 0.7022*(\sin(x)/x)^{4}*\sin^{3}(3*y)+ (-0.5463)*(\sin(x)/x)^{5}*\sin^{3}(3*y)$

$+ 0.4915*(\sin(x)/x)^{6}*\sin^{3}(3*y)$

$+(-0.4352)*(\sin(x)/x)^{0}*\sin^{4}(4*y)+ 0.7681*(\sin(x)/x)^{1}*\sin^{4}(4*y)$

$+ (-0.0720)*(\sin(x)/x)^{2}*\sin^{4}(4*y)+ 0.7583*(\sin(x)/x)^{3}*\sin^{4}(4*y)$

$+ (-0.8246)*(\sin(x)/x)^{4}*\sin^{4}(4*y)+ 0.9273*(\sin(x)/x)^{5}*\sin^{4}(4*y)$

$+ 0.3969*(sin(x)/x)^6*sin^4(4*y)$

$+(-0.7514)*(sin(x)/x)^0*sin^5(5*y)+ 0.5173*(sin(x)/x)^1*sin^5(5*y)$

$+ 0.8751*(sin(x)/x)^2*sin^5(4*y)+ 0.8913*(sin(x)/x)^3*sin^5(5*y)$

$+ 0.3492*(sin(x)/x)^4*sin^5(5*y)+ (-0.9547)*(sin(x)/x)^5*sin^5(5*y)$

$+ (-0.0855)*(sin(x)/x)^6*sin^5(5*y)$

$+0.0493*(sin(x)/x)^0*sin^6(6*y)+ (-0.6317)*(sin(x)/x)^1*sin^6(6*y)$

$+ 0.3442*(sin(x)/x)^2*sin^6(6*y)+ (-0.9858)*(sin(x)/x)^3*sin^6(6*y)$

$+ (-0.2642)*(sin(x)/x)^4*sin^6(6*y)+ (-0.2773)*(sin(x)/x)^5*sin^6(6*y)$

$+ 0.2373*(sin(x)/x))^6*sin^6(6*y)$

In Table 3 of "UNC-HONN Data Classification 1", UNC-HONN model 0 has been used. The order number for UNC-HONN model is 6. In the first table of Table 3, the "No." column shows a total of 19 points. The "UNC-HONN x" column displays the input x values, which are all "1"s. The "UNC-HONN y" column displays the input y values, which are 0, 0.1, 0.2, 0.3, 0.4, 05, 0.7, 0.8, 0.9, 1, 2, 3, 4, 5, 6, 7 and 8. The "UNC-HONN z" column displays the output z values. The "Original Data" column displays the original data values. The "Absolute Original Data" column displays the absolute values for original data. The "Difference" column shows the difference between UNC-HONN output z and the original data (UNC-HONN z – Original Data). The "Absolute Difference" column shows the absolute difference between UNC-HONN output z and the original data (|UNC-HONN z – Original Data|). The "UNC-HONN Error %" column gives the error percentage for UNC-HONN Model (UNC-HONN error % = absolute difference / Absolute original Data * 100%). The average UNC-HONN error is 0.00002394%, which is close to zero. All of the coefficients for the UNC-HONN model are displayed in the second table of Table 3 after training UNC-HONN model by using original data values. For examples, $c_{00}{}^o = 0.2650$, $c_{01}{}^o = 0.7389$, and $c_{10}{}^o = -0.0588$. The third table of Table 3 provides the values for $c_{kj}{}^o*(sin(x)/x)^k*cos^j(j*y)$, when $x=1, y=0.1, k=0,1,2,3,4,5,6$, and $j=0,1,2,3,4,5,6$. For examples, $c_{01}{}^o*(sin(x)/x)^0*cos^1(1*0.1)=0.73520858$, $c_{02}{}^o*(sin(x)/x)^0*cos^2(2*0.1)=0.73605452$, and $c_{03}{}^o*(sin(x)/x)^0*cos^3(3*0.1)=-0.15894826$.

And $z = \sum c_{kj}{}^o*(sin(x)/x)^k*cos^j(j*y) = \sum c_{kj}{}^o*(sin(1)/1)^k*cos^j(j*0.1)=093927060.$

In Table 4 of "UNC-HONN Data Classification 2", UNC-HONN model 0 has been used. The order number for UNC-HONN model is 6. In the first table of Table 4, the "No." column shows total 19 points are chosen. The "UNC-HONN x" column displays the input x values, which are all "1"s. The "UNC-HONN y" column displays the input y values, which are 0, 0.1, 0.2, 0.3, 0.4, 05, 0.7, 0.8, 0.9, 1, 2, 3, 4, 5, 6, 7 and 8 are used. The "UNC-HONN z" column displays the output z values. The "Original Data" column displays the original data values. The "Absolute Original Data" column displays the absolute values for original data. The "Difference" column shows the difference between UNC-HONN output z and the original data (UNC-HONN z – Original Data). The "Absolute Difference" column shows the absolute difference between UNC-HONN output z and the original data (|UNC-HONN z – Original Data|). The "UNC-HONN Error %" column gives the error percentage for UNC-HONN Model (UNC-HONN error % = absolute difference / Absolute original Data * 100%). The average UNC-HONN error is 0.00005338%, which is much closed to zero. All the coefficients for UNC-HONN model are displayed in the second table of Table 4 after training UNC-HONN model by using original data values. For examples, $c_{00}{}^o$= 0.7228, $c_{01}{}^o$= 0.3068, and $c_{10}{}^o$= -0.5156. In the third table of Table 4, gives the values for $c_{kj}{}^o*(sin(x)/x)^k*cos^j(j*y)$, when $x=1$, $y=0.1$, $k=0,1,2,3,4,5,6$, and $j=0,1,2,3,4,5,6$. For examples, $c_{01}{}^o*(sin(x)/x)^0*cos^1(1*0.1)=0.30526728$, $c_{02}{}^o*(sin(x)/x)^0*cos^2(2*0.1)=0.42782028$, and $c_{03}{}^o*(sin(x)/x)^0*cos^3(3*0.1)=-0.84871219$.

And $z = \sum c_{kj}{}^o*(sin(x)/x)^k*cos^j(j*y) = \sum c_{kj}{}^o*(sin(1)/1)^k*cos^j(j*0.1)=-1.78433940$.

In Figure 4, UNC-HONN data classification results are shown. Original Data are shown in Figure 4A. UNC-HONN data classification results are shown in Figure 4B. In Figure 4, the data have been divided into two classifications. The Figure 4B presents the evidence that the UNC-HONN model can classify data very well, since the average error percentage is close to 0.0000%.

Based on the training of UNC-HONN model, UNC-HONN has the following formula (see Table 3) to describe the data classification 1:

$z=\sum c_{kj}{}^o*(sin(x)/x)^k*cos^j(j*y)$ $(k, j = 0,1,2,3,4,5,6,)$

$= c_{00}{}^o*(sin(x)/x)^0*cos^0(0*y)+ c_{10}{}^o*(sin(x)/x)^1*cos^0(0*y)$

$+ c_{20}{}^o*(sin(x)/x)^2*cos^0(0*y)+ c_{30}{}^o*(sin(x)/x)^3*cos^0(0*y)$

$+ c_{40}{}^o*(sin(x)/x)^4*cos^0(0*y)+ c_{50}{}^o*(sin(x)/x)^5*cos^0(0*y)$

$+ c_{60}{}^o*(sin(x)/x)^6*cos^0(0*y)$

$+c_{01}{}^o*(sin(x)/x)^0*cos^1(1*y)+ c_{11}{}^o*(sin(x)/x)^1*cos^1(1*y)$

$+ c_{21}{}^o*(sin(x)/x)^2*cos^1(1*y)+ c_{31}{}^o*(sin(x)/x)^3*cos^1(1*y)$

$+ c_{41}{}^o*(sin(x)/x)^4*cos^1(1*y)+ c_{51}{}^o*(sin(x)/x)^5*cos^1(1*y)$

$+ c_{61}{}^o*(sin(x)/x)^6*cos^1(1*y)$

$+c_{02}{}^o*(sin(x)/x)^0*cos^2(2*y)+ c_{12}{}^o*(sin(x)/x)^1*cos^2(2*y)$

$+ c_{22}{}^o*(sin(x)/x)^2*cos^2(2*y)+ c_{32}{}^o*(sin(x)/x)^3*cos^2(2*y)$

$+ c_{42}{}^o*(sin(x)/x)^4*cos^2(2*y)+ c_{52}{}^o*(sin(x)/x)^5*cos^2(2*y)$

$+ c_{62}{}^{o}*(\sin(x)/x)^6*\cos^2(2*y)$

$+c_{03}{}^{o}*(\sin(x)/x)^0*\cos^3(3*y)+ c_{13}{}^{o}*(\sin(x)/x)^1*\cos^3(3*y)$

$+ c_{23}{}^{o}*(\sin(x)/x)^2*\cos^3(3*y)+ c_{33}{}^{o}*(\sin(x)/x)^3*\cos^3(3*y)$

$+ c_{43}{}^{o}*(\sin(x)/x)^4*\cos^3(3*y)+ c_{53}{}^{o}*(\sin(x)/x)^5*\cos^3(3*y)$

$+ c_{63}{}^{o}*(\sin(x)/x)^6*\cos^3(3*y)$

$+c_{04}{}^{o}*(\sin(x)/x)^0*\cos^4(4*y)+ c_{14}{}^{o}*(\sin(x)/x)^1*\cos^4(4*y)$

$+ c_{24}{}^{o}*(\sin(x)/x)^2*\cos^4(4*y)+ c_{34}{}^{o}*(\sin(x)/x)^3*\cos^4(4*y)$

$+ c_{44}{}^{o}*(\sin(x)/x)^4*\cos^4(4*y)+ c_{54}{}^{o}*(\sin(x)/x)^5*\cos^4(4*y)$

$+ c_{64}{}^{o}*(\sin(x)/x)^6*\cos^4(4*y)$

$+c_{05}{}^{o}*(\sin(x)/x)^0*\cos^5(5*y)+ c_{15}{}^{o}*(\sin(x)/x)^1*\cos^5(5*y)$

$+ c_{25}{}^{o}*(\sin(x)/x)^2*\cos^5(4*y)+ c_{35}{}^{o}*(\sin(x)/x)^3*\cos^5(5*y)$

$+ c_{45}{}^{o}*(\sin(x)/x)^4*\cos^5(5*y)+ c_{55}{}^{o}*(\sin(x)/x)^5*\cos^5(5*y)$

$+ c_{65}{}^{o}*(\sin(x)/x)^6*\cos^5(5*y)$

$+c_{06}{}^{o}*(\sin(x)/x)^0*\cos^6(6*y)+ c_{16}{}^{o}*(\sin(x)/x)^1*\cos^6(6*y)$

$+ c_{26}{}^{o}*(\sin(x)/x)^2*\cos^6(6*y)+ c_{36}{}^{o}*(\sin(x)/x)^3*\cos^6(6*y)$

$+ c_{46}{}^{o}*(\sin(x)/x)^4*\cos^6(6*y)+ c_{56}{}^{o}*(\sin(x)/x)^5*\cos^6(6*y)$

$+ c_{66}{}^{o}*(\sin(x)/x)^6*\cos^6(6*y)$

$= 0.2650*(\sin(x)/x)^0*\cos^0(0*y)+ (-0.0588) *(\sin(x)/x)^1*\cos^0(0*y)$

$+ (-0.2356)*(\sin(x)/x)^2*\cos^0(0*y)+ (-0.1101)*(\sin(x)/x)^3*\cos^0(0*y)$

$+ (-0.8366)*(\sin(x)/x)^4*\cos^0(0*y)+ (-0.1290)*(\sin(x)/x)^5*\cos^0(0*y)$

$+ 0.7099*(\sin(x)/x)^6*\cos^0(0*y)$

$+0.7389*(\sin(x)/x)^0*\cos^1(1*y)+ 0.8593*(\sin(x)/x)^1*\cos^1(1*y)$

$+ (-0.8425)*(\sin(x)/x)^2*\cos^1(1*y)+ (-0.7912)*(\sin(x)/x)^3*\cos^1(1*y)$

$+ 0.7700*(sin(x)/x)^4*cos^1(1*y) + 0.0356*(sin(x)/x)^5*cos^1(1*y)$

$+ (-0.8337)*(sin(x)/x)^6*cos^1(1*y)$

$+0.7663*(sin(x)/x)^0*cos^2(2*y) + 0.7943*(sin(x)/x)^1*cos^2(2*y)$

$+ (-0.7804)*(sin(x)/x)^2*cos^2(2*y) + (-0.0991)*(sin(x)/x)^3*cos^2(2*y)$

$+(-0.8692)*(sin(x)/x)^4*cos^2(2*y) + 0.7481*(sin(x)/x)^5*cos^2(2*y)$

$+ (-0.0131)*(sin(x)/x)^6*cos^2(2*y)$

$+(-0.1823)*(sin(x)/x)^0*cos^3(3*y) + (-0.8837)*(sin(x)/-x)^1*cos^3(3*y)$

$+ (-0.6952)*(sin(x)/x)^2*cos^3(3*y) + 0.8774*(sin(x)/x)^3*cos^3(3*y)$

$+ 0.1208*(sin(x)/x)^4*cos^3(3*y) + (-0.9640)*(sin(x)/x)^5*cos^3(3*y)$

$+ 0.8191*(sin(x)/x)^6*cos^3(3*y)$

$+(-0.6116)*(sin(x)/x)^0*cos^4(4*y) + 0.9445*(sin(x)/x)^1*cos^4(4*y)$

$+ (-0.2584)*(sin(x)/x)^2*cos^4(4*y) + 0.9347*(sin(x)/x)^3*cos^4(4*y)$

$+ (-0.0066)*(sin(x)/x)^4*cos^4(4*y) + 0.1033*(sin(x)/x)^5*cos^4(4*y)$

$+ 0.5724*(sin(x)/x)^6*cos^4(4*y)$

$+(-0.5156)*(sin(x)/x)^0*cos^5(5*y) + 0.3725*(sin(x)/x)^1*cos^5(5*y)$

$+ 0.6393*(sin(x)/x)^2*cos^5(4*y) + 0.6555*(sin(x)/x)^3*cos^5(5*y)$

$+ 0.1156*(sin(x)/x)^4*cos^5(5*y) + (-0.7189)*(sin(x)/x)^5*cos^5(5*y)$

$+ (-0.7697)*(sin(x)/x)^6*cos^5(5*y)$

$+0.6813*(sin(x)/x)^0*cos^6(6*y) + (-0.2737)*(sin(x)/x)^1*cos^6(6*y)$

$+ 0.9862*(sin(x)/x)^2*cos^6(6*y) + (-0.5278)*(sin(x)/x)^3*cos^6(6*y)$

$+ (-0.5062)*(sin(x)/x)^4*cos^6(6*y) + (-0.6193)*(sin(x)/x)^5*cos^6(6*y)$

$+ 0.8795*(sin(x)/-x)^6*cos^6(6*y)$

Based on the training of UNC-HONN model, UNC-HONN has the following formula (see Table 4) to describe the data classification 2:

$$z = \sum c_{kj}{}^{o}{}^{+}(sin(x)/x)^{k}{}^{+}cos^{j}(j*y) \ (k, J = 0,1,2,3,4,5,6,)$$

$$= c_{00}{}^{o}*(sin(x)/x)^{0}*cos^{0}(0*y) + c_{10}{}^{o}*(sin(x)/x)^{1}*cos^{0}(0*y)$$

$$+ c_{20}{}^{o}*(sin(x)/x)^{2}*cos^{0}(0*y) + c_{30}{}^{o}*(sin(x)/x)^{3}*cos^{0}(0*y)$$

$$+ c_{40}{}^{o}*(sin(x)/x)^{4}*cos^{0}(0*y) + c_{50}{}^{o}*(sin(x)/x)^{5}*cos^{0}(0*y)$$

$$+ c_{60}{}^{o}*(sin(x)/x)^{6}*cos^{0}(0*y)$$

$$+ c_{01}{}^{o}*(sin(x)/x)^{0}*cos^{1}(1*y) + c_{11}{}^{o}*(sin(x)/x)^{1}*cos^{1}(1*y)$$

$$+ c_{21}{}^{o}*(sin(x)/x)^{2}*cos^{1}(1*y) + c_{31}{}^{o}*(sin(x)/x)^{3}*cos^{1}(1*y)$$

$$+ c_{41}{}^{o}*(sin(x)/x)^{4}*cos^{1}(1*y) + c_{51}{}^{o}*(sin(x)/x)^{5}*cos^{1}(1*y)$$

$$+ c_{61}{}^{o}*(sin(x)/x)^{6}*cos^{1}(1*y)$$

$$+ c_{02}{}^{o}*(sin(x)/x)^{0}*cos^{2}(2*y) + c_{12}{}^{o}*(sin(x)/x)^{1}*cos^{2}(2*y)$$

$$+ c_{22}{}^{o}*(sin(x)/x)^{2}*cos^{2}(2*y) + c_{32}{}^{o}*(sin(x)/x)^{3}*cos^{2}(2*y)$$

$$+ c_{42}{}^{o}*(sin(x)/x)^{4}*cos^{2}(2*y) + c_{52}{}^{o}*(sin(x)/x)^{5}*cos^{2}(2*y)$$

$$+ c_{62}{}^{o}*(sin(x)/x)^{6}*cos^{2}(2*y)$$

$$+ c_{03}{}^{o}*(sin(x)/x)^{0}*cos^{3}(3*y) + c_{13}{}^{o}*(sin(x)/x)^{1}*cos^{3}(3*y)$$

$$+ c_{23}{}^{o}*(sin(x)/x)^{2}*cos^{3}(3*y) + c_{33}{}^{o}*(sin(x)/x)^{3}*cos^{3}(3*y)$$

$$+ c_{43}{}^{o}*(sin(x)/x)^{4}*cos^{3}(3*y) + c_{53}{}^{o}*(sin(x)/x)^{5}*cos^{3}(3*y)$$

$$+ c_{63}{}^{o}*(sin(x)/x)^{6}*cos^{3}(3*y)$$

$$+ c_{04}{}^{o}*(sin(x)/x)^{0}*cos^{4}(4*y) + c_{14}{}^{o}*(sin(x)/x)^{1}*cos^{4}(4*y)$$

$$+ c_{24}{}^{o}*(sin(x)/x)^{2}*cos^{4}(4*y) + c_{34}{}^{o}*(sin(x)/x)^{3}*cos^{4}(4*y)$$

$$+ c_{44}{}^{o}*(sin(x)/x)^{4}*cos^{4}(4*y) + c_{54}{}^{o}*(sin(x)/x)^{5}*cos^{4}(4*y)$$

$$+ c_{64}{}^{o}*(sin(x)/x)^{6}*cos^{4}(4*y)$$

$+c_{05}{}^o*(\sin(x)/x)^0*\cos^5(5*y)+ c_{15}{}^o*(\sin(x)/x)^1*\cos^5(5*y)$

$+ c_{25}{}^o*(\sin(x)/x)^2*\cos^5(4*y)+ c_{35}{}^o*(\sin(x)/x)^3*\cos^5(5*y)$

$+ c_{45}{}^o*(\sin(x)/x)^4*\cos^5(5*y)+ c_{55}{}^o*(\sin(x)/x)^5*\cos^5(5*y)$

$+ c_{65}{}^o*(\sin(x)/x)^6*\cos^5(5*y)$

$+c_{06}{}^o*(\sin(x)/x)^0*\cos^6(6*y)+ c_{16}{}^o*(\sin(x)/x)^1*\cos^6(6*y)$

$+ c_{26}{}^o*(\sin(x)/x)^2*\cos^6(6*y)+ c_{36}{}^o*(\sin(x)/x)^3*\cos^6(6*y)$

$+ c_{46}{}^o*(\sin(x)/x)^4*\cos^6(6*y)+ c_{56}{}^o*(\sin(x)/x)^5*\cos^6(6*y)$

$+ c_{66}{}^o*(\sin(x)/x)^6*\cos^6(6*y)$

$= 0.7228*(\sin(x)/x)^0*\cos^0(0*y)+ (-0.5156) *(\sin(x)/x)^1*\cos^0(0*y)$

$+ (-0.7924)*(\sin(x)/x)^2*\cos^0(0*y)+ (-0.6779)*(\sin(x)/x)^3*\cos^0(0*y)$

$+ (-0.3934)*(\sin(x)/x)^4*\cos^0(0*y)+ (-0.6828)*(\sin(x)/x)^5*\cos^0(0*y)$

$+ 0.2667*(\sin(x)/x)^6*\cos^0(0*y)$

$+0.3068*(\sin(x)/x)^0*\cos^1(1*y)+ 0.4272*(\sin(x)/x)^1*\cos^1(1*y)$

$+ (-0.4104)*(\sin(x)/x)^2*\cos^1(1*y)+ (-0.3691)*(\sin(x)/x)^3*\cos^1(1*y)$

$+ 0.3489*(\sin(x)/x)^4*\cos^1(1*y)+ 0.6035*(\sin(x)/x)^5*\cos^1(1*y)$

$+ (-0.4016)*(\sin(x)/x)^6*\cos^1(1*y)$

$+0.4454*(\sin(x)/x)^0*\cos^2(2*y)+ 0.4734*(\sin(x)/x)^1*\cos^2(2*y)$

$+ (-0.4695)*(\sin(x)/x)^2*\cos^2(2*y)+ (-0.7782)*(\sin(x)/x)^3*\cos^2(2*y)$

$+(-0.5483)*(\sin(x)/x)^4*\cos^2(2*y)+ 0.4272*(\sin(x)/x)^5*\cos^2(2*y)$

$+ (-0.7922)*(\sin(x)/x)^6*\cos^2(2*y)$

$+(-0.9734)*(\sin(x)/x)^0*\cos^3(3*y)+ (-0.6749)*(\sin(x)/x)^1*\cos^3(3*y)$

$+ (-0.4864)*(\sin(x)/x)^2*\cos^3(3*y)+ 0.6686*(\sin(x)/x)^3*\cos^3(3*y)$

$+ 0.9110*(\sin(x)/x)^4*\cos^3(3*y)+ (-0.7552)*(\sin(x)/x)^5*\cos^3(3*y)$

$+ 0.6003*(\sin(x)/x)^6*\cos^3(3*y)$

$+(-0.5239)*(\sin(x)/x)^0*\cos^4(4*y)+ 0.8568*(\sin(x)/x)^1*\cos^4(4*y)$

$+ (-0.1607)*(\sin(x)/x)^2*\cos^4(4*y)+ 0.8460*(\sin(x)/x)^3*\cos^4(4*y)$

$+ (-0.9123)*(\sin(x)/x)^4*\cos^4(4*y)+ 0.0156*(\sin(x)/x)^5*\cos^4(4*y)$

$+ 0.4846*(\sin(x)/x)^6*\cos^4(4*y)$

$+(-0.6380)*(\sin(x)/x)^0*\cos^5(5*y)+ 0.4959*(\sin(x)/x)^1*\cos^5(5*y)$

$+ 0.7527*(\sin(x)/x)^2*\cos^5(4*y)+ 0.7789*(\sin(x)/x)^3*\cos^5(5*y)$

$+ 0.2380*(\sin(x)/x)^4*\cos^5(5*y)+ (-0.8313)*(\sin(x)/x)^5*\cos^5(5*y)$

$+ (-0.8821)*(\sin(x)/x)^6*\cos^5(5*y)$

$+0.8158*(\sin(x)/x)^0*\cos^6(6*y)+ (-0.4072)*(\sin(x)/x)^1*\cos^6(6*y)$

$+ 0.1107*(\sin(x)/x)^2*\cos^6(6*y)+ (-0.7513)*(\sin(x)/x)^3*\cos^6(6*y)$

$+ (-0.7307)*(\sin(x)/x)^4*\cos^6(6*y)+ (-0.8438)*(\sin(x)/x)^5*\cos^6(6*y)$

$+ 0.0038*(\mathrm{Sin}(x)/x)^6*\cos^6(6*y)$

FUTURE RESEARCH DIRECTIONS

As the next step of HONN model research, more HONN models for different data control will be built to increase the pool of HONN models. Theoretically, the adaptive HONN models can be built and allow the computer automatically choose the best model, order, and coefficients. Thus, making the adaptive HONN models easier to use is one of the future research topics.

HONNs can automatically select the initial coefficients for nonlinear data analysis. The next step of this study will also focus on how to allow people working in the prediction area to understand that HONNs are much easier to use and can have better results. Moreover, further research will develop HONNs software packages for people working in the prediction area. HONNs will challenge classic procedures and change the research methodology that people are currently using in the prediction areas for the nonlinear data control application.

CONCLUSION

Two nonlinear higher order neural network models, UNS-HONN and UNC-HONN, that are part of the Ultra High Frequency SINC and Trigonometric Higher Order Neural Networks (UNT-HONN), are

Figure 5.

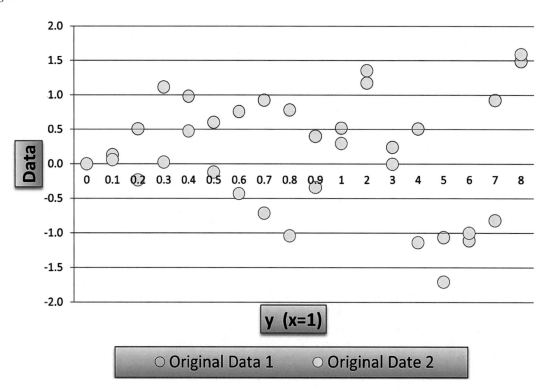

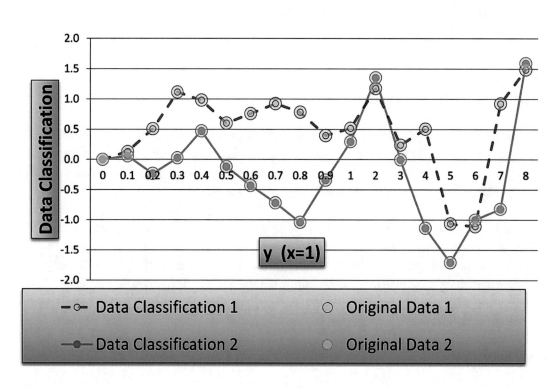

Figure 6.

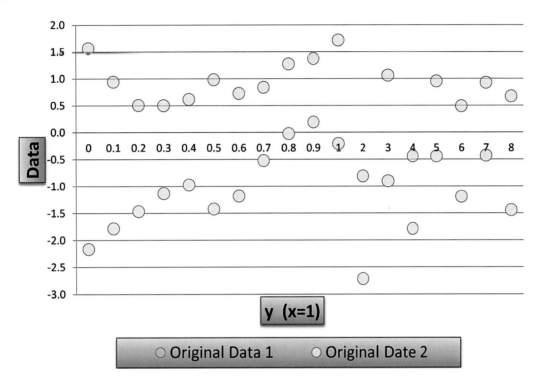

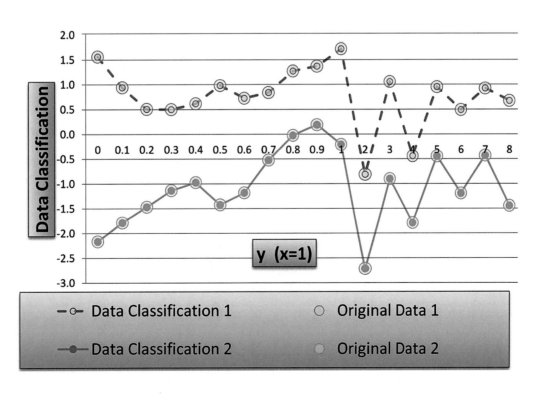

developed. Based on the structures of UNS-HONN and UNC-HONN, this paper provides two model learning algorithm formulae. This chapter tests the UNS-HONN and UNC-HONN models for ultra-high frequency data classifications. The running results show that UNS-HONN and UNC-HONN models are better than other Polynomial Higher Order Neural Network (PHONN) and Trigonometric Higher Order Neural Network (THONN) models, since UNS-HONN and UNC-HONN models can classify the data with error approaching 0.0000%.

One of the topics for future research is to continue building models using HONN for different data series. The coefficients of the higher order models will be studied not only using artificial neural network techniques, but also statistical methods. Using nonlinear functions to model and analyze time series data will be a major goal in the future.

REFERENCES

Behnke, S., & Karayiannis, N. B. (1998). CNeT: Competitive neural trees for pattern classifications. *IEEE Transactions on Neural Networks*, *9*(6), 1352–1369. doi:10.1109/72.728387 PMID:18255815

Boutalis, Y. S., Christodoulou, M. A., & Theodoridis, D. C. (2010). Identification of nonlinear systems using a new neuro-fuzzy dynamical system definition based on high order neural network function approximators. In M. Zhang (Ed.), *Artificial Higher Order Neural Networks for Computer Science and Engineering – Trends for Emerging Applications* (pp. 423–449). Hershey, PA, USA: IGI Global, Information Science Reference. doi:10.4018/978-1-61520-711-4.ch018

Bukovsky, I., Bila, J., & Gupta, M. M, Hou, Z-G., & Homma, N. (2010a). Foundation and classification of nonconventional neural units and paradigm of nonsynaptic neural interaction. In Y. Wang (Ed.), Discoveries and Breakthroughs in Cognitive Informatics and Natural Intelligence (pp.508-523). Hershey, PA, USA: IGI Publishing.

Fallahnezhad, M., Moradi, M. H., & Zaferanlouei, S. (2011). A hybrid higher order neural classifier for handling classification problems. *International Journal of Expert System and Application*, *38*(1), 386–393. doi:10.1016/j.eswa.2010.06.077

Ghosh, J., & Shin, Y. (1992). Efficient Higher-order Neural Networks for Function Approximation and Classification. *International Journal of Neural Systems*, *3*(4), 323–350. doi:10.1142/S0129065792000255

Husken, M., & Stagge, P. (2003). Recurrent neural networks for time series classification. *Neurocomputing*, *50*, 223–235. doi:10.1016/S0925-2312(01)00706-8

Lin, Y. H., & Cunningham, G. A. (1995). A new approach to fuzzy-neural system modelling. *IEEE Transactions on Fuzzy Systems*, *3*(2), 190–198. doi:10.1109/91.388173

Lippman, R. P. (1989). Pattern classification using neural networks. *IEEE Communications Magazine*, *27*(11), 47–64. doi:10.1109/35.41401

Moon, S., & Chang, S. H. (1994). Classification and prediction of the critical heat flux using fuzzy clustering and artificial neural networks. *Nuclear Engineering and Design*, *150*(1), 151–161. doi:10.1016/0029-5493(94)90059-0

Najarian, S., Hosseini, S. M., & Fallahnezhad, M. (2010). Artificial tactile sensing and robotic surgery using higher order neural networks. In M. Zhang (Ed.), *Artificial Higher Order Neural Networks for Computer Science and Engineering – Trends for Emerging Applications* (pp. 514–544). Hershey, PA, USA: IGI Global. doi:10.4018/978-1-61520-711-4.ch021

Reid, M. B., Spirkovska, L., & Ochoa, E. (1989). Simultaneous position, scale, rotation invariant pattern classification using third-order neural networks. *Int. J. Neural Networks*, *1*, 154–159.

Sanchez, E. N., Urrego, D. A., Alanis, A. Y., & Carlos-Hernandez, S. (2010). Recurrent higher order neural observers for anaerobic processes. In M. Zhang (Ed.), *Artificial Higher Order Neural Networks for Computer Science and Engineering – Trends for Emerging Applications* (pp. 333–365). Hershey, PA, USA: IGI Global. doi:10.4018/978-1-61520-711-4.ch015

Shannon, C. E. (1998, February). Communication in the presence of noise. In *Proceedings of Institute of Radio Engineers* (vol 37 (1), pp. 10–21, Jan. 1949). Reprint as classic paper in. *Proceedings of the IEEE*, *86*(2).

Shawash, J., & Selviah, D. R. (2010). Artificial higher order neural network training on limited precision processors. In M. Zhang (Ed.), *Artificial Higher Order Neural Networks for Computer Science and Engineering – Trends for Emerging Applications* (pp. 312–332). Hershey, PA, USA: IGI Global. doi:10.4018/978-1-61520-711-4.ch014

Shin, Y. (1991). The pi-sigma network: an efficient higher-order neural network for pattern classification and function approximation. *Proceedings of the International Joint Conference on Neural Networks*, Seattle, WA, USA (Vol. I, pp.13-18). doi:10.1109/IJCNN.1991.155142

Shin, Y., Ghosh, J., & Samani, D. (1992). Computationally efficient invariant pattern classification with higher-order pi-sigma networks. In Burke, & Shin (Ed.), Intelligent Engineering Systems through Artificial Neural Networks (Vol II, pp. 379-384). ASME Press.

Chapter 6
Integration of Higher–Order Time–Frequency Statistics and Neural Networks:
Application for Power Quality Surveillance

José Carlos Palomares-Salas
University of Cadiz, Spain

Agustín Agüera-Pérez
University of Cadiz, Spain

Juan José González de la Rosa
University of Cadiz, Spain

Álvaro Jiménez-Montero
University of Cadiz, Spain

José María Sierra-Fernández
University of Cadiz, Spain

Rosa Piotrkowski
National University of General San Martín, Argentina

ABSTRACT

Higher-order statistics demonstrate their innovative features to characterize power quality events, beyond the traditional and limited Gaussian perspective, integrating time-frequency features and within the frame of a Higher-Order Neural Network (HONN). With the massive advent of smart measurement equipment in the electrical grid (Smart Grid), and in the frame of high penetration scenarios of renewable energy resources, the necessity dynamic power quality monitoring is gaining even more importance in order to identify the suspicious sources of the perturbation, which are nonlinear and unpredictable in nature. This eventually would satisfy the demand of intelligent instruments, capable not only of detecting the type of perturbation, but also the source of its origin in a scenario of distributed energy resources.

INTRODUCTION

Power quality (PQ) is on the focus due to its influence over and from the loads which are connected to the modern Smart Grid (SG), provoking an unstoppable and unpredictable growth of the most complex system ever built. An adequate PQ ensures compatibility between equipment connected to the grid (Bollen et al., 2014), according to the following newly added concepts: sustainable power with low losses and high quality and security of supply and safety, being at the same time economically efficient, reliable and resilience ("Functionalities of smart grids," 2009; Xiao, 2012).

DOI: 10.4018/978-1-5225-0063-6.ch006

These preconditions are driving the development of emerging signal processing tools, capable of performing more detailed and precise detection of disturbances and events. One of the major requirements for PQ monitoring equipment is the detection of the electrical disturbances fixed in time, with the ability to detect both the initiation and end of the fault.

For these reasons, the role of smart meters in the smart grid is first being revised; and this research contributes via the integration of Artificial Neural Networks (ANNs) and advanced signal processing techniques based in Higher-Order Statistics with the goal of developing automated meters oriented to the detection and classification of PQ events in a SG with high renewable penetration.

The feature extraction stage from PQ disturbances is based on HOS, idea which has been proven to be efficient in several works former. Indeed, since PQ events are sudden changes in the power line signal, the higher-order estimators are potentially adequate to characterize each type of electrical anomaly both in the time and frequency domains. While the second order correlation products provide information regarding power fluctuations, the higher-order cumulants and their associated Fourier transforms (poly-spectra) characterize the instantaneous statistical distribution shape (symmetry and peakedness of the probability density curve).

According to this general idea, which situates the reader in a qualitative manner, the third-order cumulants provide information regarding the lack of symmetry in the time domain, and contribute to the detection of sags and swells. The fourth-order time domain cumulants characterize amplitude variability, and are conceived to target oscillatory and impulsive transients. In the frequency domain, the spectral kurtosis (based in the fourth-order Fourier transform) enables harmonic and transients detection.

As a novelty, the present research exploits the combination of time and frequency domain features, to deal with the inherent non-stationary associated to the electrical anomalies, and with the goal to improve the performance of the ANN, making at the same time feasible the integration or the computational guts into a hand-held smart meter, and therefore, facilitating the implementation in the future Smart Grid to guarantee compatibility of utilities and customers. The combined use of time and frequency features enhances detection of these non-stationary measurement sequences and offers interesting results for PQ disturbances classification.

In the following sections we summarize the main advances in the aforementioned field, paying special attention to the applications of ANNs for PQ automated analysis, based in the contribution of the HOS-based engine in the feature extraction stage and the internal architecture or the network.

BACKGROUND

The necessity to improve the performance in continuous electric signals PQ events monitoring devices has motivated the development of several techniques that have reached an acceptable tradeoff between computational complexity and performance.

Myriads of research papers have been produced regarding the wavelet-transform-based techniques for the purposes of detection of disturbances in electrical power systems. To cite, Nezih and Ece (Gerek & Ece, 2004a, 2004b) achieved good performance in second-order computing, using 2-D wavelets and compression techniques, finding despite the promising results, the limits of the procedure and quantifying its heavy and unaffordable computational cost. In line with this work, the researches Poisson et al. and Santoso et al. (Poisson et al., 2000; Santoso et al., 2000) also reported a wavelet-based method, finding the potential and the drawbacks of the technique so that to implement in an intelligent meter. There are also several techniques that make use of second-order information associated to the error signal, resulting from the subtraction of the fundamental component to the electric signal. The analysis of the error signal is an attractive and interesting solution to characterize the presence of disturbances; e.g., the techniques (Duque et al., 2005; Abdel-Galil et al., 2003) are very similar in the sense that all of them make use of second-order statistics of the error signal for the detection of the time occurrence of disturbances.

It is against that background of HOS applications in the field of the detection, in the time domain, several notable works are worthy to be mentioned, e.g., Nezih and Ece (Gerek & Ece, 2006) had been formerly performed the categorization of PQ anomalies, where they proved that HOS and quadratic classifiers notably improve the second-order-based methods (the results where depicted in bounded graphs, showing the detection zones). Bollen et al. introduced new advanced statistical features to PQ event detection (Bollen et al., 2007). In the same direction, Gu and Bollen (Gu & Bollen, 2000) found relevant characteristics associated to PQ events in the time and frequency domains. The work by Ribeiro et al. is also remarkable (Ribeiro et al., 2007), because they extracted new time-domain features based in cumulants, which work properly under controlled conditions. In addition, the same authors also performed the classification of single and multiple disturbances using HOS in the time domain and Bayes' theory-based techniques (Ribeiro & Pereira, 2007). HOS techniques and estimators have also been implemented to specifically detect sags and swells (Agüera-Pérez et al., 2011).

The direct predecessor of the present research is in the work by J.J.G. de la Rosa et al. (De la Rosa et al., 2013a), in which they confectioned an hybrid study involving the time-domain variance, the skewness, and the kurtosis; obtaining consequences in conjunction with the spectral kurtosis (SK), and over a set of real-life measurements, some of them containing mixed PQ perturbations. The same authors proposed a preliminary criterion for seven types of disturbances based on the former estimators (De la Rosa et al., 2013b). In a previous work (De la Rosa et al., 2012), they designed an offline case-based reasoning application based on time-domain HOS estimators. Furthermore, the authors used also HOS features in classification techniques for characterization of electrical PQ signals (Palomares-Salas et al., 2012).

Looking into the ANNs, as the scientific community knows, it have been broadly used for classification purposes in myriads of works and have proved the utility for a long time (Haykin, 1994). The novelty of this work, and perhaps the real and authentic guts of the ANN resides in the fact of combining time and frequency attributes. In fact, some former works had shown that the best detection performance for non-stationary signals was achieved by combining time and frequency characteristics obtained in the feature extraction stage via wavelet transforms (WT), on the hypotheses that WT performance is suitable for the analysis of transient signals with easy computation. More precisely, three works are worth to be cited as they are directly concerned with our research, involving ANN and PQ analysis. In the first one to mention, Angrisani et al. presented a wavelet network for automated transient detection; basically, it was based in an extended perceptron which incorporated wavelet nodes (Angrisani et al., 2001). They proposed a unique structure based on the introduction of wavelet nodes in the traditional ANN, in the neurons of the first layer, and was applied successfully to typical transients in the PQ analysis. The number of nodes was fixed to 12, and this number was related to the time location of the perturbation. The network has to be pre-conditioned in order to detect concrete transient signals.

Following the same procedure above, that is, using the WT as a preprocessing tool for ANN, the second work by Monedero et al. (Monedero et al., 2007) developed a neural perceptron-based (three hidden layers) real-time first system prototype, which was trained using a disturbance generator for pseudo-synthetic waveforms. They obtained a performance of 89% success combining simulated and real-time data structures. The perturbations were classified in frequency, voltage, and harmonics, and the topology of the ANN (number of hidden neurons and number of outputs) was highly moveable depending on the PQ event under study.

The third and most recent paper, by Martin Valtierra-Rodriguez et al. (Valtierra-Rodriguez et al., 2014) involves a new dual neural-network-based methodology to detect and classify single and combined PQ disturbances, consisting, on the one side, of an adaptive linear network for harmonic and inter-harmonic estimation that allowed computing the root-mean-square voltage and THD indices, from which it is possible to detect and classify sags, swells, outages, and harmonics. A complementary feed-forward neural network was used for pattern recognition using the horizontal and vertical histograms of a specific voltage waveform to classify spikes, notching, flicker, and oscillatory transients. The complementary action of these neural networks allows the detection and classification even if the integrate simultaneous electrical anomalies, both in noisy and noise less scenarios.

On the other hand, HOS with ANN to PQ classification has already been used. Liu et al. (Liu et al., 2014) propose a method based on the combination of SK and ANN. In particular, they proposed a new computation method of SK based on Butterworth distribution, where they chose the maximum, minimum, and average values of SK as the eigenvectors for the transient disturbance classification, which are the inputs into RBF neural network. The simulation results shown that the classification method proposed is efficient and feasible. In (De la Rosa et al., 2010), PQ event detection, classification and characterization using higher-order sliding cumulants (which were calculated over high-pass filtered signals to avoid the low-frequency 50-Hz sinusoidal), whose maxima and minima were the coordinates of two-dimensional feature vectors was proposed, and the classification strategy was based in competitive layers.

Apart from the difficulties in implementing a real-time processor in the smart grid frame, the main disadvantage of the above procedures lies in the fact that accuracy and repeatability are highly compromised by the second-order estimators (e.g., WT and V_{RMS}) used in the feature extraction stage. Indeed, drawbacks arise when the data are corrupted by noise; especially when the number of samples of the signal window is reduced, and the resolution and repeatability are degraded. These facts are dramatically increased if the tests are performed over synthetic signals of controlled-lab experiences, where predictability is tacitly supposed. In the real-world experiences, the system should be prepared for unpredictable phenomena, both in the time and in the frequency domains. As explained hereinafter, this goal is accomplished by statistical parameters of an order higher than two along with ANN due to it provide mathematical flexibility and high accuracy for real time applications.

INTEGRATION OF HOS AND ANN

The evaluation of the integration of HOS and ANN is developed following the structure shown in Fig. 1, where the main stages of the pre-processing actions are also outlined within the whole computing process.

One key stage in the frame of pattern recognition systems design is the extraction of features envisaging the improvement of the different classes' separation. The main goal of the feature extraction is to represent the dataset in a new feature space in which the probability to distinguish classes is higher than the one in the original space. Therefore, the identification of efficient pre-processing and feature extraction techniques is a key issue (Ferreira et al., 2011).

If the extracted features result in a feature space where the classes are well-enough separated, then it is said that there is a high probability that the designed classifier will demonstrate good performance. If not, the classifier will perform poorly no matter the technique used for the analysis.

Figure 1. Graphical abstract of the proposed procedure

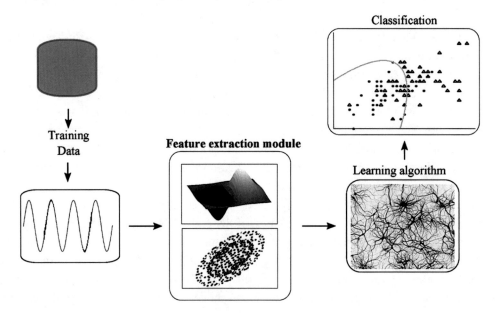

Another requirement for a good feature extraction-based technique is the ability to provide the required separation in a low-dimensional space (medium complexity). In pattern recognition problems, we aim to find a reduced number of features in order to make the classifier design feasible. If the feature extraction technique results in a high-dimensional space, the feature selection will play an important role in the system design. In order to select a feature extraction technique, good knowledge of the classification issues is required.

Features may directly be extracted from the original measurement either from some transformed domain or from the parameters of signals models. Feature extraction tools most used in the literature are based in Effective Value (RMS), Discrete Fourier Transform (DFT), S-transform, Hilbert Huang transform (HHT), Wavelet Transform (WT), Cumulants of Higher-Order Statistics, and Principal Component Analysis (PCA).

As said before, in the present research, a non-stationary signal processing with higher-order statistics in the time and frequency domains is postulates in order to extract a battery of features to be processed via ANNs with regression algorithms. Figure 2 shows a generic architecture, indicating how the input pattern is processed via the neurons to provide the output vector. This basic figure is thought to introduce the concrete architecture of the ANN in the present work.

The performance of the potential PQ monitoring system and consequently the ANN is directly related to the pre-processing and feature extraction techniques used. Convergence speed and accuracy of the ANN depends on the network architecture as well as noise in the signal.

PROPOSED METHODOLOGY: THE HOS-BASED ANN

The final objective of this work is the implementation of the prototype in the future *SG* to guarantee compatibility between all equipment connected. Data used in this work have been simulated using *MAT-*

Figure 2. Generic ANN structure which postulates the feature extraction stage previous to the ANN

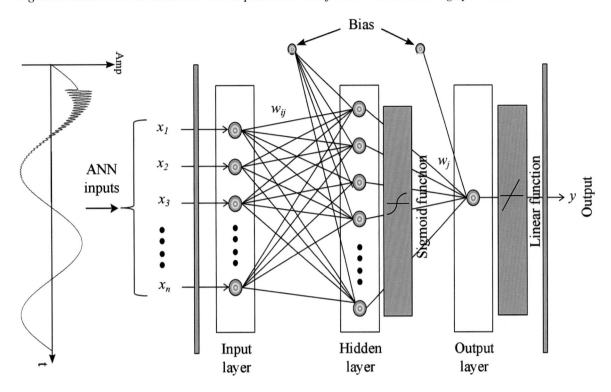

LAB^{*TM*} software. The dataset generated by the simulation consists of 550 samples including the different studied disturbance kinds, which cover the following disturbances: sag, swell, oscillatory transient, interruption, harmonic permanent distortion, harmonic temporal distortion, impulsive transient, and sag plus oscillatory transient. Each signal comprises a $20K$-point synthetic time-domain register with a duration of 1 s (corresponding to a 20 KHz sampling frequency). An additive normal noise process (1% of the amplitude of the signal) has been added in order to achieve a more realistic behavior, and to guarantee robust computation of the algorithm. Fig. 3 shows an example of these signals as well as healthy power-line sine wave that have been tested in this research.

Data used to realize the classification are based on representative coefficients obtained of the PQ disturbances referred to above. These coefficients are acquired by a process of feature extraction which is based on the combination of higher-order statistics in time and frequency domains. The HOS have been computed using a 400-points sliding window (which corresponds to a signal period), with a shift of 10 points over a vector of 20000 points. After the extraction stage, a number of 14 characteristic features are selected, nine of whom correspond to time domain and the remaining five to frequency domain. The coefficients selected in the first one correspond to the maxima, minima and the stable in the second-, third-, and fourth-order cumulants at zero lags (directly related to the variance, skewness and kurtosis). On the other hand, the coefficients selected in the second one correspond to the frequency of extreme value of *SK*, bandwidth of dome, extreme value of *SK*, number of peaks in *SK* and dome very targeted (between 0 and 1). Fig. 4 shows the modular graphic corresponding to the feature extraction module.

In order to illustrate the capability of the *SK* to discriminate *PQ* disturbances we have selected an illustrative example consisting of an oscillatory transient coupled to the power sine wave. The analysis

Figure 3. Example of healthy signal and different disturbances studied

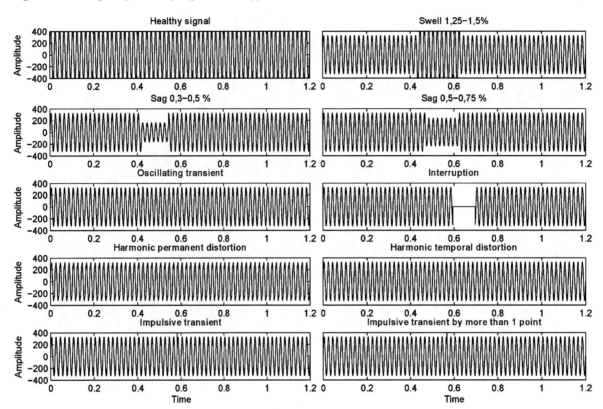

Figure 4. Procedure of the feature extraction stage. The lower subfigure forwards the reader the use of the spectral kurtosis, extracting the kurtosis of each frequency component

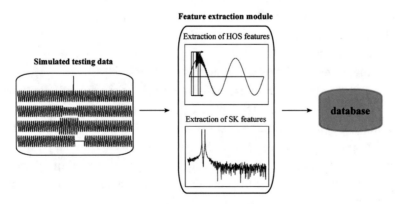

result is depicted in Fig. 5. The time-domain variance increases when it bumps into the transient; this behavior is independent of the transient frequency. Similarly, the time-domain skewness and kurtosis detect slight variations. The real detection takes place in the frequency domain; the *SK* produces a real enhancement in 2000 Hz, along with the high resolution bump (narrow peak).

Figure 5. An example of mixed analysis in the time and frequency domains

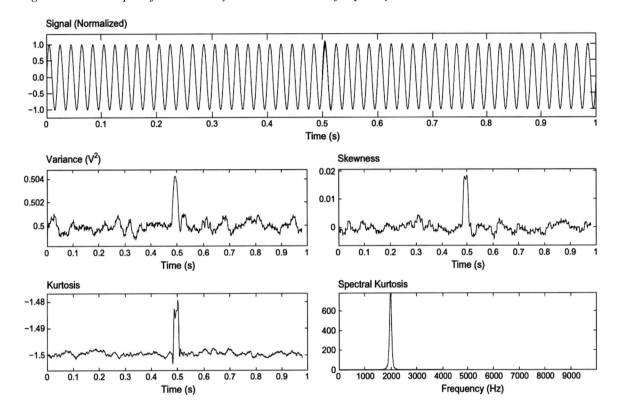

The resulting data after carrying out the feature extraction stage are included in a matrix with dimensions $ns \times f$, where ns is the number of samples (electrical signals recorded) and f is the number of selected features in each of them (HOS in time and frequency domains). Then, the classification algorithms are used to classify the PQ disturbances, as shown in Fig. 6.

Classification techniques used in this work are based on regression algorithms, each of which are briefly described as follows:

- **Adaptive Linear Neuron (LIN):** The fundamental characteristics are the absence of hidden layers and the use of the Widrow-Hoff rule to train weights and biases, minimizing the performance function.
- **Multilayer ANNs (BP1 and BP2):** The network is a dynamical system that changes with the learning rule, which sequentially finds the weights that codify the knowledge. The network will then have a generation capability that must be measured. The Levenberg-Marquardt algorithm has been chosen to optimize the network performance function according to the target outputs.
- **Radial Basis Function (RBF):** This network has similar form to that of a two-layer multilayer network. The fundamental difference arises on the hidden neurons, and operates on the distance between an input with respect to the synaptic vector (called centroid). The RBF neurons are localized response, because only respond with an appreciable intensity when presented input vector and the centroid of the neuron belonging to a nearby area in the input space. RBFs training com-

Figure 6. Design technique of the classification methods

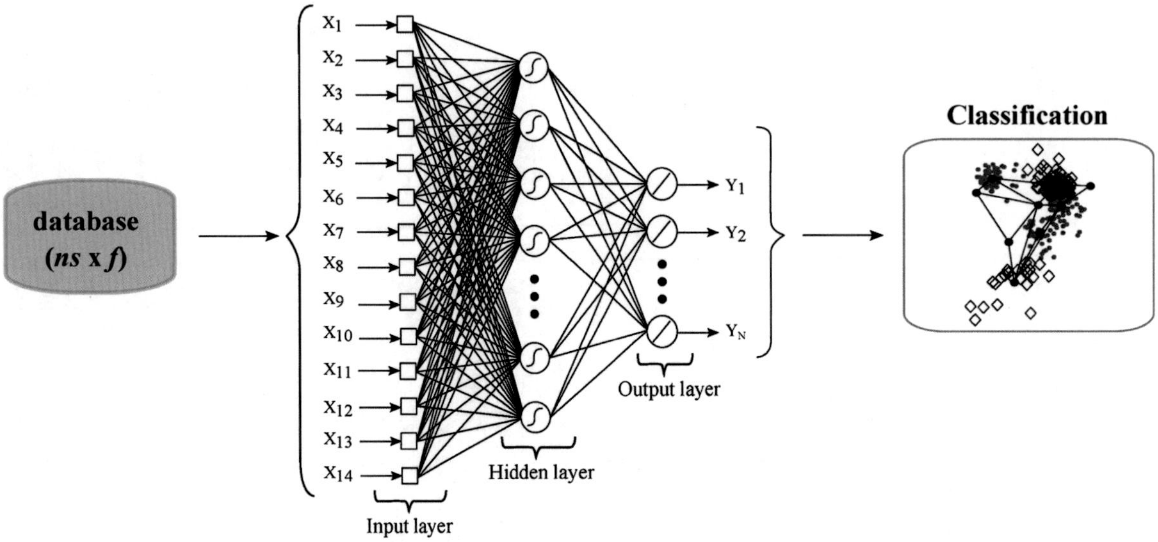

prises two stages. The first is unsupervised and accomplished by obtaining cluster centers of the training set inputs. The second consists of solving linear equations.

- **Exact Radial Basis (ERB):** It is similar to the radial basis network. The main drawback is that it produces a network with as many hidden neurons as the input vectors.
- **Generalized Regression Network (GRN):** It is similar to the radial basis network, but has a slightly different second layer (special linear layer).

The building of the models is performed by following two steps in order to efficiently classify the PQ disturbances, as detailed below:

1. **Normalization:** Data are normalized so that they are in the interval $[-1,1]$, and ensuring that all selected features represent the same dynamic range to achieve most efficient and faster calculations, which is by the way a desirable property when considering implementation issues.
2. **Datasets:** In order to design and test a classification algorithm, sets of samples from the patterns are required. Usually three datasets are used: training, validation and testing. The training dataset is used for system design during the classifier learning phase. The validation dataset is used in order to verify the classifier generalization performance. Finally, the test dataset is used to asses on the out-of-sample set the classification power of a model. If the error on the test set reaches a minimum at a significantly different iteration number than the validation set error, this might indicate a poor division of the dataset.

It is crucial for generalization purposes that the test dataset must not be used during the training phase of the classification algorithm because it is used to compare different models. However, this is not always possible if you have a limited-size dataset.

Each model has been intelligently adapted to meet the objective of PQ classification attending to their different characteristics. Table 1 shows the selected parameters corresponding to the architecture, activation function, and performance function of each used model. The optimization of these parameters has led to the final design the concerned models.

Acronyms: LM: Levenberg-Marquardt; WH: Widrow-Hoff; S: Sigmoid; G: Gaussian; L: Linear; *k*: *k*-means; TF: Transfer function; MSE: Mean square error.

Finally, the complete design of a classification system must include an evaluation of its performance, as this is an important step which could lead to the complete redesign of the system. The goal is to estimate the classification error of the designed system with a finite dataset available for the system design.

In this work, the classification criterion is based on the parameter hit rate (HR), which is defined as follows:

$$HR = \frac{N_C}{N_T} \times 100 \ \%$$

(1)

where N_C is the number of test samples and N_T is the number correct disturbance recognition.

This criterion is used to assess the capacity of classification to each model, providing a measure of comparison between them.

RESULTS

Once the assessed models were configured and optimized, they are used in the out-of-sample set. Because the database is small, we choose randomly two test sets, and in each of them, 100 experiments are launched by model. This is realized to achieve statistically meaningful results which rule out the random factors influencing the ANNs.

For each model, we have performed three analysis in function of the used features: HOS in the time domain (HOS_t), the SK, and the mixed (time and frequency domains) analysis $(HOS_t + SK)$. In all of them, the HR was calculated for each model on the 200 offline tests, observing the arithmetic mean. The number of models tested in this work amounts to more than 27000 configurations, attending to their

Table 1. Parameters of the ANNs

ANN	LIN	BP1	BP2	RBF	ERB	GRN
Hidden layers	-	1	2	1	1	1
Neurons hidden layer 1	-	[4 to 10]	[4 to 10]	[1 to 150]	[1 to 150]	[1 to 150]
Neurons hidden layer 2	-	-	[2 to 5]	-	-	-
Spread	-	-	-	[1 to 20]	[1 to 20]	[1 to 20]
TF	-	S	S	G	G	G
TF output	L	L	L	L	L	L
Training algorithm	WH	LM	LM	*k*	*k*	*k*
Performance function	MSE	MSE	MSE	MSE	MSE	MSE

typology, neurons of the layers, and selected features used in the simulations. The obtained results showing the percentage of effectiveness for classifying disturbances are presented in Tables 3-5. In most models, results obtained in the mixed analysis are better than in the other analyses except isolated results. These exceptions represent the 27.27% of the cases presented in these Tables, where the 14.28% of them correspond to HOS_t features, and the remaining 12.99% correspond to SK features.

Figure 7 and Table 6 show the global percentages associated to the different models attending to the three different analyses (and their respective sets of features) commented above. These percentages are obtained for each model as the average of the hit rates associated to each PQ disturbance.

Results show that the algorithms based on linear models are worse than those based on non-linear schemes. The best models both individually and collectively are ERB, GRN, and BP1, ranked according to their percentage of effectiveness.

FUTURE RESEARCH DIRECTIONS

Actually, the research team is developing new versions of the aforementioned HOS-based algorithms, paying special attention to the implementation in hand-held micro-controlled systems. The focus is

Table 3. Percentages of effectiveness considering HOS features in time domain $\left(HOS_t\right)$

PQ disturbance	LIN	BP1	BP2	RBF	ERB	GRN
Harmonic permanent distortion	0.00	59.88	49.61	52.87	83.22	1.83
Harmonic temporal distortion	0.00	60.73	59.91	53.02	79.71	33.77
Impulsive transient	0.00	53.23	56.37	19.85	80.38	10.00
Impulsive transient by more than one point	17.66	49.20	55.27	16.94	81.19	12.35
Oscillatory transient	98.58	24.12	25.81	45.02	79.55	95.39
Interruption	14.60	88.81	88.20	100.00	80.26	86.74
Sag 0.3% to 0.5%	38.88	54.49	59.02	60.64	79.76	14.52
Sag 0.5% to 0.75%	46.79	42.57	35.85	28.32	79.61	88.14
Swell 1.25% to 1.5%	17.92	76.86	84.36	39.42	80.36	50.42
Sag plus oscillatory	0.00	14.13	11.95	8.89	80.28	0.00
Healthy signal	0.00	12.07	25.20	0.00	95.28	0.00

Table 5. Global percentages considering different features

Features	LIN	BP1	BP2	RBF	ERB	GRN
$HOS_t + SK$	26,11	74,17	73,05	55,82	94,70	79,59
HOS_t	21,31	48,74	50,14	38,63	81,78	35,74
SK	18,17	48,98	48,00	48,75	83,64	23,66

Table 2. Percentages of effectiveness considering HOS features in time and frequency domains $\left(HOS_t + SK\right)$

PQ disturbance	LIN	BP1	BP2	RBF	ERB	GRN
Harmonic permanent distortion	0.00	85.89	78.03	54.94	100.00	69.39
Harmonic temporal distortion	10.54	74.56	70.00	42.17	93.00	48.41
Impulsive transient	53.40	82.84	81.44	38.59	96.39	100.00
Impulsive transient by more than one point	94.36	83.79	81.75	68.02	95.97	100.00
Oscillatory transient	5.99	75.23	77.29	83.60	96.93	90.16
Interruption	18.64	84.29	81.34	95.69	91.04	96.36
Sag 0.3% to 0.5%	40.51	67.49	69.70	38.93	90.11	64.80
Sag 0.5% to 0.75%	44.83	53.03	58.81	33.42	89.91	87.70
Swell 1.25% to 1.5%	18.89	84.02	78.64	40.06	99.66	94.90
Sag plus oscillatory	0.00	43.93	51.66	18.64	88.68	27.40
Healthy signal	0.00	80.83	74.91	99.98	100.00	96.35

Table 4. Percentages of effectiveness considering HOS features in frequency domain $\left(SK\right)$

PQ disturbance	LIN	BP1	BP2	RBF	ERB	GRN
Harmonic permanent distortion	0.00	88.00	70.00	100.00	100.00	0.00
Harmonic temporal distortion	1.30	17.12	24.82	1.79	80.58	0.00
Impulsive transient	3.82	56.52	55.42	42.22	82.55	0.00
Impulsive transient by more than one point	57.47	68.25	73.43	77.51	79.46	100.00
Oscillatory transient	3.22	52.14	58.24	39.01	79.84	2.90
Interruption	56.59	33.22	33.20	31.72	79.98	58.19
Sag 0.3% to 0.5%	21.23	29.60	33.37	23.49	78.38	39.83
Sag 0.5% to 0.75%	47.71	47.49	45.67	41.62	79.08	59.29
Swell 1.25% to 1.5%	8.57	43.56	45.18	27.85	79.50	0.00
Sag plus oscillatory	0.00	24.37	25.62	100.00	80.71	0.00
Healthy signal	0.00	78.50	63.00	51.00	100.00	0.00

twofold. By one side the algorithm has to be fast and with no dead-times. Secondly, the instrument should localize the origin or source of the perturbation along with the type of electrical anomaly. A transversal idea lies in the fact of satisfying the norm IEC-50160, and to make the appropriate transition to the higher-order estimators, developing a new power-quality index which would agglutinate not only the traditional second-order features, but also time and frequency domain higher-order measurements. The final user would have newly advanced features in the instrument display; this equipment would be conceived to be introduced in the smart grid.

Figure 7. Global percentages considering different features

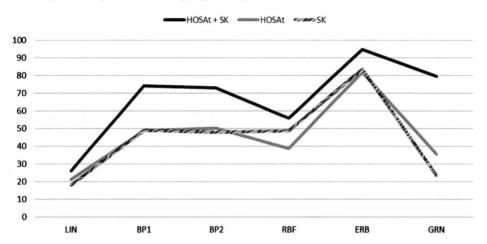

CONCLUSION

The complexity and variability of electrical signals demand new signal processing methods in order to distinguish each type of perturbation. This fact is even more precious in the modern smart grid, where distributed energy resources are connected asynchronously, in high penetration scenarios. For that reason, pattern recognition becomes an essential tool enabling the identification and control of the upcoming electric smart-grid environment, along with the physical localization of the fault.

In this chapter, six regression algorithms have been applied and compared for PQ disturbances classification. The novel aspect is the introduction of new representative coefficients based on HOS in time and frequency domains, which enhance pattern recognition due to the newly added statistical information (skewness and kurtosis). These coefficients are the inputs used in the classification algorithms to verify the occurrence or not of single or multiple disturbances in the electric signals.

The sets of signals used to test the proposed method were generated by the *MATLAB™* software. The considered PQ disturbances are the most common in the supply grid. As shown in the reported results, the best models are obtained implementing radial basis networks, generalized regression, and multilayer perceptron, both individually and collectively. The overall hit rates obtained for these configurations are 94.70%, 79.59%, and 74.17%, respectively. This is consistent with non-linearity in the used data and emphases of the ability of the HOS to work with these non-linearities.

In summary, it might be concluded that the proposed method can help to satisfactorily classify different types of PQ disturbances. Then, once their usefulness has been established, it is necessary to expand the experiment to find an ANN classifier with better characteristics than obtained in this research.

ACKNOWLEDGMENT

The authors would like to thank the Spanish Government for funding the research project TEC2010-19242-C03-03 (SIDER-HOSAPQ). This work is newly supported by the Spanish Ministry of Economy and Competitiveness in the frame of the Statal Plan of Excellency for Research, via the project TEC2013-

47316-C3-2-P (SCEMS-AD-TED-PQR). Our unforgettable thanks to the trust we have from the Andalusian Government for funding the Research Group PAIDI-TIC-168 in Computational Instrumentation and Industrial Electronics (ICEI).

REFERENCES

Abdel-Galil, T. K., El-Saadany, E. F., & Salama, M. M. A. (2003). Power quality event detection using adaline. *Electric Power Systems Research*, *64*(2), 137–144. doi:10.1016/S0378-7796(02)00173-6

Agüera-Pérez, A., Palomares-Salas, J. C., De la Rosa, J. J. G., Sierra-Fernández, J. M., Ayora-Sedeño, D., & Moreno-Muñoz, A. (2011). Characterization of electrical sags and swells using higher-order statistical estimators. *Journal of the International Measurement Confederation*, *44*(8), 1453–1460.

Angrisani, L., Daponte, P., & D'Apuzzo, M. (2001). Wavelet Network-based detection and classification of transients. *IEEE Transactions on Instrumentation and Measurement*, *50*(5), 1425–1435. doi:10.1109/19.963220

Bollen, M. H. J., Bahramirad, S., & Khodaei, A. (2014). Is there a place for power quality in the smart grid? *Proceedings of 2014 IEEE 16th International Conference on Harmonics and Quality of Power* Bucharest, Romania, University Politehnica of Bucharest (pp. 713-717). doi:10.1109/ICHQP.2014.6842865

Bollen, M.H.J., & Gu, I.Y.H., Axelber, P.G.V., & Styvaktakis, E. (2007). Classification of underlying causes of power quality disturbances: Deterministic versus statistical methods. *EURASIP Journal on Advances in Signal Processing*, *1*(1), 172.

De la Rosa, J. J. G., Agüera-Pérez, A., Palomares-Salas, J. C., Sierra-Fernández, J. M., & Moreno-Muñoz, A. (2012). A novel virtual instrument for power quality surveillance based in higher-order statistics and case-based reasoning. *Journal of the International Measurement Confederation*, *45*(7), 1824–1835.

De la Rosa, J. J. G., Lloret, I., Puntonet, C. G., & Górriz, J. M. (2004). Higher-order statistics to detect and characterize termite emissions. *Electronics Letters*, *40*(20), 1316–1317. doi:10.1049/el:20045664

De la Rosa, J. J. G., Moreno-Muñoz, A., Gallego, A., Piotrkowski, R., & Castro, E. (2010). Higher-order characterization of power quality transients and their classification using competitive layers. *Journal of the International Measurement Confederation*, *42*(3), 478–484.

De la Rosa, J. J. G., Sierra-Fernández, J. M., Agüera-Pérez, A., Palomares-Salas, J. C., Jiménez-Montero, A., & Moreno-Muñoz, A. (2013). Power quality events' measurement criteria based in higher-order statistics: towards new measurement indices.*Proceedings on the IEEE International Workshop on the Applied Measurements for Power Systems,*Aachen, Germany, RWTH Aachen University (pp. 73-79).

De la Rosa, J. J. G., Sierra-Fernández, J. M., Agüera-Pérez, A., Palomares-Salas, J. C., & Moreno-Muñoz, A. (2013). An application of the spectral kurtosis to characterize power quality events. *International Journal of Electrical Power & Energy Systems*, *49*, 386–398. doi:10.1016/j.ijepes.2013.02.002

Duque, C. A., Ribeiro, M. V., Ramos, F. R., & Szczupak, J. (2005). Power quality event detection based on the principle divided to conquer and innovation concept. *IEEE Transactions on Power Delivery*, *20*(4), 2361–2369. doi:10.1109/TPWRD.2005.855478

Ece, D. G., & Gerek, O. N. (2004). Power quality event detection using joint 2D wavelet subspaces. *IEEE Transactions on Instrumentation and Measurement*, *53*(4), 1040–1046. doi:10.1109/TIM.2004.831137

Ferreira, D. D., Marques, C. A. G., Seixas, J. M., Cerqueira, A. S., Ribeiro, M. V., & Duque, C. A. (2011). *Exploiting Higher-Order Statistics Information for Power Quality Monitoring*. Rijeka, Croatia: InTech Open Science.

Functionalities of smart grids and smart meters (2009). *European Union*. Retrieved from http://ec.europa.eu/energy/en/topics/markets-and-consumers/smartgrids-and-meters

Gerek, O. N., & Ece, D. G. (2004). 2-D analysis and compression of power quality event data. *IEEE Transactions on Power Delivery*, *19*(2), 791–798. doi:10.1109/TPWRD.2003.823197

Gerek, O. N., & Ece, D. G. (2006). Power-quality event analysis using higher order cumulants and quadratic classifiers. *IEEE Transactions on Power Delivery*, *21*(2), 883–889. doi:10.1109/TPWRD.2006.870989

Gu, I. Y. H., & Bollen, M. H. J. (2000). Time-frequency and time-scale domain analysis of voltage disturbances. *IEEE Transactions on Power Delivery*, *15*(4), 1279–1283. doi:10.1109/61.891515

Haykin, S. (1994). *Neural Networks*. Englewood Cliffs, NJ: Prentice Hall.

Jakubowski, J., Kwiatos, K., Chwaleba, A., & Osowski, S. (2002). Higher order statistics and neural network for tremor recognition. *IEEE Transactions on Bio-Medical Engineering*, *49*(2), 152–159. doi:10.1109/10.979354 PMID:12066882

Liu, Z., Zhang, Q., Han, Z., & Chen, G. (2014). A new classification method for transient power quality combining spectral kurtosis with neural network. *Neurocomputing*, *125*, 95–101. doi:10.1016/j.neucom.2012.09.037

Monedero, I., Leon, C., Ropero, J., Garcia, A., Elena, J. M., & Montano, J. C. (2007). Classification of electrical disturbances in real time using neural networks. *IEEE Transactions on Power Delivery*, *22*(3), 1288–1296. doi:10.1109/TPWRD.2007.899522

Palomares-Salas, J. C., De la Rosa, J. J. G., Agüera-Pérez, A., & Moreno-Muñoz, A. (2012). Intelligent methods for characterization of electrical power quality signals using higher order statistical features. *Przeglad Elektrotechniczny*, *8*, 236–243.

Poisson, O., Rioual, P., & Meunier, M. (2000). Detection and measurement of power quality disturbances using wavelet transform. *IEEE Transactions on Power Delivery*, *15*(3), 1039–1044. doi:10.1109/61.871372

Ribeiro, M. V., Marques, C. A. G., Duque, C. A., Cerqueira, A. S., & Pereira, J. L. R. (2007). Detection of disturbances in voltage signals for power quality analysis using HOS. *EURASIP Journal on Advances in Signal Processing*, *2007*(1), 1–13.

Ribeiro, M. V., & Pereira, J. L. R. (2007). Classification of single and multiple disturbances in electric signals. *EURASIP Journal on Advances in Signal Processing*, (1): 1–18.

Santoso, S., Grady, W. M., Powers, E. J., Lamoree, J., & Bhatt, S. C. (2000). Characterization of distribution power quality events with Fourier and wavelet transforms. *IEEE Transactions on Power Delivery*, *15*(1), 247–254. doi:10.1109/61.847259

Valtierra-Rodriguez, M., Romero-Troncoso, R. J., Osornio-Ríos, R. A., & García-Pérez, A. (2014). Detection and classification of single and combined power quality disturbances using neural networks. *IEEE Transactions on Industrial Electronics*, *61*(5), 2473–2482. doi:10.1109/TIE.2013.2272276

Xiao, Y. (2012). *Communication and networking in smart grids. Broken Sound Parkway NW*. USA: CRC Press. doi:10.1201/b11897

KEY TERMS AND DEFINITIONS

Feature Extraction: It is a process by which a sets of representative characteristics is obtained.
Higher-Order Statistics: It refers to functions which use higher power than two of a sample.
Power Quality: It is a measure of an ideal power supply system which allow to electrical systems to operate in rated operating conditions.

APPENDIX

The higher-order statistics are applicable when the process is non-Gaussian; several real-world applications are truly non-Gaussian. Under such circumstances the cumulants reveal important properties that cannot be revealed through low-order statistics. Cumulants have been used extensively to deduce newly statistical features from the data of non-Gaussian measurement time series.

Time-Domain HOS

Cumulants are estimated by using the well-known *Leonov-Shiryaev* formula, which expresses the compact relationship among the cumulants of stochastic signals and their moments (Agüera-Pérez et al., 2011). In this sense, the expressions for the second-, third-, and fourth-order cumulants for a real, random, and zero-mean (central cumulants) time series $x(t)$ can be estimated via:

$$C_{2,x}(\tau) = E\{x(t)\cdot x(t+\tau)\}$$
$$C_{3,x}(\tau_1,\tau_2) = E\{x(t)\cdot x(t+\tau_1)\cdot x(t+\tau_2)\}$$
$$C_{4,x}(\tau_1,\tau_2,\tau_3) = E\{x(t)\cdot x(t+\tau_1)\cdot x(t+\tau_2)\cdot x(t+\tau_3)\}$$

(2)

$$-C_{2,x}(\tau_1)C_{2,x}(\tau_2-\tau_3)$$
$$-C_{2,x}(\tau_2)C_{2,x}(\tau_3-\tau_1)$$
$$-C_{2,x}(\tau_3)C_{2,x}(\tau_1-\tau_2)$$

where $E\{\cdot\}$ is the expected value operator and τ is the lag. Then, looking at Equation 7, each cumulant is easily interpreted as a correlation between the original time series and its associated time-shifted versions, being the computational result of an rth-order cumulant is the rth degree of similarity among the aforementioned time series.

For a zero-mean stationary random sequence with a finite number of samples, the three unbiased estimates for the second-, third-, and fourth-order cumulants are:

$$\hat{C}_{2,x}(k) = \frac{1}{N}\sum_{n=0}^{N-1} x[n]x[n+k]$$

(3)

$$\hat{C}_{3,x}(k,l) = \frac{1}{N}\sum_{n=0}^{N-1} x[n]x[n+k]x[n+l]$$

(4)

$$\hat{C}_{4,x}(k,l,m) = \frac{1}{N}\sum_{n=0}^{N-1}x[n]x[n+k]x[n+l]x[n+m]$$

(5)

$$
\begin{aligned}
&-\hat{C}_{2,x}(k)\hat{C}_{2,x}(l-m)\\
&-\hat{C}_{2,x}(l)\hat{C}_{2,x}(m-k)\\
&-\hat{C}_{2,x}(m)\hat{C}_{2,x}(k-l)
\end{aligned}
$$

where $k,l,m \in [-\chi,\dots,-1,0,1,\dots,+\chi]$ and $n = 0,1,\dots,N-1$; χ is the index of the maximum time shift (lag) between samples of a record. The biased expressions are estimates over the real terms in the summations of expressions 3, 4, and 5. These expressions establish the correlation between the original signal and its time-shifted versions for the three orders of comparison. The second-order version is the classical auto-correlation, the third-order one account with the symmetry of the signal, and the fourth-order cumulant quantifies the impulsiveness in the time domain.

Avoided time shifting, $\tau_1 = \tau_2 = \tau_3 = 0$ in Equation 2, leads to the simplest computational expressions for cumulants, in Equation 6:

$$
\begin{aligned}
\gamma_{2,x} &= E\{x^2(t)\} = C_{2,x}(0)\\
\gamma_{3,x} &= E\{x^3(t)\} = C_{3,x}(0,0)\\
\gamma_{4,x} &= E\{x^4(t)\} - 3(\gamma_{2,x})^2 = C_{4,x}(0,0,0)
\end{aligned}
$$

(6)

The ensemble of Equation 6 constitutes indirect measurements of the variance, skewness, and kurtosis. If $x(t)$ is symmetrically distributed, its skewness is zero (but not *vice versa*, improbable situations); if $x(t)$ is Gaussian distributed, its kurtosis is necessarily zero (but not *vice versa*). Standardization (statistical normalization) makes estimators shift and scale invariant. Standardized quantities are defined as $\gamma_{4,x}/(\gamma_{2,x})^2$ and $\gamma_{3,x}/(\gamma_{2,x})^{3/2}$, for kurtosis and skewness, respectively.

Frequency-Domain HOS

Poly-spectra are defined to be the Fourier transforms of the higher-order cumulants sequences. The rth-order spectra are defined as the $(r-1)$-dimensional Fourier transforms of the rth-order cumulants, according to:

$$S_{r,x}(f_1,f_2,\dots,f_{r-1}) =$$

$$\sum_{\tau_1=-\infty}^{\tau_1=+\infty}\cdots\sum_{\tau_{r-1}=-\infty}^{\tau_{r-1}=+\infty}C_{r,x}(\tau_1,\tau_2,\dots,\tau_{r-1})\times exp\left[-j2\pi\left(f_1\tau_1 + f_2\tau_2 + \dots + f_{r-1}\tau_{r-1}\right)\right]$$

(7)

The power spectrum is the decomposition of the signal power in the frequency domain. When this concept is extended to higher orders, as suggested by Equation 7, the result is called a poly-spectrum. Power spectrum, bispectrum, and tri-spectrum are specific cases (particular poly-spectra) of Equation 7, with $r = 2, 3$, and 4, respectively. Only power spectrum is real, and the others are complex magnitudes.

The more common higher-order spectra are the bispectrum and the tri-spectrum. The first one identifies contributions to a signal's skewness as a function of frequency pairs, meanwhile the tri-spectrum refers to contributions to a signal's kurtosis as a function of frequency triplets. For this reason, poly-spectra output multidimensional data structures which comprise redundant information, distributed in multi-dimensional geometries, often called tensors. As a consequence, their computation may be impractical in many cases, and to extract the desired information, one-dimensional slices of cumulant sequences and spectra and bi-frequency planes are considered (Jakubowski et al., 2002; De la Rosa et al., 2004).

Ideally, the spectral kurtosis is a representation of the kurtosis of each frequency component of a process (or data from a measurement instrument x_i). For estimation issues, we will consider M realizations of the process; each realization containing N points; i.e., we consequently consider M measurement sweeps, each sweep with N points. The time spacing between points is the sampling period, T_s, of the data acquisition unit. The SK unbiased indirect estimator is given by Equation 8:

$$\hat{G}_{2,X}^{N,M} = \frac{M}{M-1} \left[\frac{(M+1)\sum_{i=1}^{M} \left| X_N^i(m) \right|^4}{\left(\sum_{i=1}^{M} \left| X_N^i(m) \right|^2 \right)^2} - 2 \right] \tag{8}$$

where m indicates the frequency index and $\hat{G}_{2,X}^{N,M}$ indicates the value of the kurtosis for this Fourier frequency. This expression offers an indirect calculation of the SK, as it is obtained directly from the Fourier transforms, and it supposes low computational burden. The graphical representation of the SK allows the identification of non-Gaussian frequency components. The higher the peak the more variable is the amplitude associated to this Fourier component.

Section 3
Artificial Higher Order Neural Networks for Simulation and Predication

Chapter 7
Adaptive Hybrid Higher Order Neural Networks for Prediction of Stock Market Behavior

Sarat Chandra Nayak
Veer Surendra Sai University of Technology, India

Bijan Bihari Misra
Silicon Institute of Technology, India

Himansu Sekhar Behera
Veer Surendra Sai University of Technology, India

ABSTRACT

This chapter presents two higher order neural networks (HONN) for efficient prediction of stock market behavior. The models include Pi-Sigma, and Sigma-Pi higher order neural network models. Along with the traditional gradient descent learning, how the evolutionary computation technique such as genetic algorithm (GA) can be used effectively for the learning process is also discussed here. The learning process is made adaptive to handle the noise and uncertainties associated with stock market data. Further, different prediction approaches are discussed here and application of HONN for time series forecasting is illustrated with real life data taken from a number of stock markets across the globe.

1. INTRODUCTION

The chapter gives a deep insight into the architecture, background, and applications of higher order neural networks to the area of data mining, control, as well as function approximation. Particularly, three HONNs have been developed and applied to the task of short and long term prediction of daily closing prices of five fast growing global stock market data. The concept of stock market prediction, problems involved with it, pitfalls of statistical methods, and application of HONN have been addressed by this chapter.

During the last two decades there are tremendous development in the areas of soft computing which include Artificial Neural Network (ANN), evolutionary algorithms, and fuzzy systems. This improve-

DOI: 10.4018/978-1-5225-0063-6.ch007

ment in computational intelligence capabilities has been enhanced the modeling of complex, dynamic and multivariate nonlinear systems. These soft computing methodologies have been applied successfully to the area data classification, financial forecasting, credit scoring, portfolio management, risk level evaluation etc. and are found to be producing better performance. The advantage of ANN applied to the area of stock market forecasting is that it incorporates prior knowledge in ANN to improve the prediction accuracy. It also allows the adaptive adjustment to the model and nonlinear description of the problems. ANNs are found to be good universal approximator which can approximate any continuous function to desired accuracy.

It has been found in most of the research work in financial forecasting area used ANN, particularly Multilayer Perceptron (MLP). The ability of MLP to perform complex nonlinear mappings and tolerance to noise in financial time series has been well established. Suffering from slow convergence, sticking to local minima are the two well-known lacunas of a MLP. In order to overcome the local minima, more number of nodes can be added to the hidden layers. Multiple hidden layers and more number of neurons in each layer also add more computational complexity to the network. Also, various feed forward and multilayer neural networks are found to be characterized with several drawbacks such as poor generalization, nonlinear input-output mapping capability as well as slow rate of learning capacity.

In the other hand, HONN are described as type of feed forward networks which provide nonlinear decision boundaries, hence offering better classification capability as compared to linear neuron by Guler and Sahin (1994). They are different from ordinary feed forward networks by the introduction of higher order terms into the network. HONN have fast learning properties, stronger approximation, greater storage capacity, higher fault tolerance capability and powerful mapping of single layer trainable weights as described by Wang et al. (2008). In most of the neural network models, neural inputs are combined using summing operation, where in HONN, not only summing units, but also units that find the product of weighted inputs called as higher order terms are present. Due to single layer of trainable weights needed to achieve nonlinear separability, they are simple in architecture and require less number of weights to capture the associated nonlinearity as suggested in Shin and Ghosh (1995), and Park et al. (2000). As compared to networks utilizing summation units only, higher order terms in HONN can increase the information capacity of the network. This representational power of higher order terms can help solving complex nonlinear problems with small networks as well as maintaining fast convergence capabilities discussed by Leerink et al. (1995).

Evolutionary training algorithms are capable of searching better than gradient descent based search techniques. The evolutionary hybrid networks received wide application in nonlinear forecasting due to its broad adaptive and learning ability discussed by Kwon and Moon (2007). The hybrid iterative evolutionary learning algorithm is more effective than the conventional algorithm in terms of learning accuracy and prediction accuracy as discussed by Yu and Zhang (2005).

With the increase in order of the network, there may exponential growth in tunable weights in HONN and hence more computation time. However, there is a special type of HONN called as Pi-Sigma neural network (PSNN) using less number of weights has been introduced by Shin and Ghosh (1991). The PSNN has been successfully employed solving several difficult problems including polynomial factorization by Perantonis et al. (1998), zeroing polynomials by Huang et al. (2005), classification by Shin and Ghosh (1992),and Epitropakis et al. (2010), and time series forecasting by Ghazali et al. (2012), and Ghazali et al. (2011).

Mining stock market trend is challenging due to the extreme nonlinearity, uncertainty and nonstationary characteristics of the stock market. The stock market is very complex and dynamic by nature, and has been a subject of study for modeling its characteristics by researchers. Factors such as gold rate, petrol rate, foreign exchange rate as well as the economic and political situation of the country, trader's expectation and investor's psychology are influencing the behavior of stock market. Hence, an accurate forecasting is both necessary and beneficial for all investors in the market including investment institutions as well as small individual investors. Hence there is a need to developing an automated forecasting model which can accurately estimate the risk level and the profit gained in return.

Conventional statistical methodologies can be applied on stationary data sets and can't be automated easily. At every stage it requires expert interpretation and development. They cannot be employed to mapping the nonlinearity and chaotic behavior of stock market. Tremendous development in the area of soft computing which includes artificial neural network (ANN), evolutionary algorithms, and fuzzy systems helps researchers to enhance the modeling of complex, dynamic and multivariate nonlinear systems. These soft computing methodologies have been applied successfully to the area data classification, financial forecasting, credit scoring, portfolio management, risk level evaluation etc. and are found to be producing better performance. The advantage of ANN applied to the area of stock market forecasting is that it incorporates prior knowledge in ANN to improve the prediction accuracy. It also allows the adaptive adjustment to the model and nonlinear description of the problems. ANNs are found to be good universal approximator which can approximate any continuous function to desired accuracy.

Evolutionary training algorithms such as GA, PSO etc. are capable of searching optimal solutions better than gradient descent based search techniques. The hybrid networks have been frequently applied in nonlinear forecasting due to their broad adaptive and learning abilities. The new hybrid iterative evolutionary learning algorithms are more effective than the conventional algorithms in terms of learning accuracy and prediction accuracy. Many researchers have adopted a neural network model, which is trained by GA and found to be effective.

In this chapter, a PSNN and a SPNN are considered for the task of short-term prediction of closing prices of some real stock market. The networks have been trained with two training methods. The PSNN and SPNN are first trained with the gradient descent based back propagation algorithm. For achieving better forecasting accuracy, the same network is trained again with an evolutionary search technique separately. All the forecasting models are trained adaptively; hence there is a significant reduction of training time.

The contribution of this chapter will be:

- A brief introduction to HONN
- Developing different adaptive HONN forecasting models
- Alleviating the lacunas of back propagation based learning using evolutionary technique
- Performances of the developed models compared with that of gradient descent based forecasting models
- Experimenting on global stock market data for short term forecasting

2. RELATED STUDIES TO HONN

To alleviate the well known drawbacks of traditional neural based models many researchers have turned their attention to various HONN based models. However, there exist only few studies using HONN, particularly in the areas of finance and economics. Ghazali (2005) developed a HONN based model for financial time series prediction and found that HONN performs superior as compared to conventional multilayer neural network based models. Another attempt by Knowles et al. (2005) used HONNs with Bayesian confidence measure for prediction of EUR/USD exchange rates and observed that the simulation results for HONNs are much better than multilayer approach based models. Some HONNs such as Higher Order Processing Unit Neural Network (HPUNN) by Giles and Maxwell (1987), Product Unit neural Network (PUNN) by Durbin and Rumelhart (1989) have been developed by the researchers in order to avoid the drawbacks of traditional neural models as well as better nonlinear mapping performance. However, there is exponential increase in the required higher order terms which may affect the network. But the PSNN developed by the authors Shin and Ghosh (1991) is able to avoid this increase in number of weight vectors along with the processing units. A novel application of Ridge polynomial neural network which is formed by adding different degrees of PSNNs has been proposed by Ghazali et al. (2006). The network has been applied for financial time series forecasting and able to find better nonlinearity mapping of various financial time series data with an appropriate generalization capability as well as learning speed. Yong Nie and Wei Deng (2008) proposed a hybrid genetic algorithm trained PSNN to resolve the function optimization problem. They concluded that the hybrid method can have better search capability and faster than genetic algorithm. Epitropakis et al. (2010) have been proposed a PSNN trained by distributed evolutionary algorithm which has superior performance. Another novel hybrid HONN has been proposed by authors Fallahnezhad et al. (2011) for the classification problem. This hybrid model exhibits good generalization capability and also improved classification accuracy. A Neuron-Adaptive Higher Order Neural-Network Model for automated financial data modeling has been suggested by Zhang et al. (2002). Their model shown to be "open box" and as such is more acceptable to financial experts than classical closed box neural networks. This model is further shown to be capable of automatically finding not only the optimum model, but also the appropriate order for specific financial data.

Back propagation based ANNs are very popular methods to predict stock market with better calculation, spreading abilities and stronger nonlinear mapping ability. Back propagation neural networks (BPNN), particularly the multilayer perceptron (MLP) has many shortcomings such as the slow learning rate, larger memory size, easy to get into local minimum, bigger randomicity and so on. This affects the predicted results of the stock price. Radial basis functional neural networks are also a very popular method to predict stock market, this network has better calculation and spreading abilities, also has stronger nonlinear mapped ability. But the stock market is not only with nonlinearity but also chaos, and it is a dynamic system related to time. Therefore the network for predicting itself is a dynamic system. These shortcomings force researchers toward developing hybrid models by combining linear and nonlinear models. These hybrid models that have been developed by many researchers combining nonlinear models such as ANN and evolutionary soft computing techniques such as Particle Swarm Optimization (PSO), Genetic Algorithm (GA) and other nature and bio-inspired search techniques, have better accuracies.

ANN and its hybridization with other soft computing techniques have been successfully applied to the potential corporate finance applications and found to be appropriate. Over the decades, a number of forecasting models based on soft computing techniques such as ANN by White (1998), and Chiang et al. (1996), fuzzy logic and its hybridization by Romahi and Shen (2000), and Abraham et al. (2001), and GA based ANN by Nayak et al. (2012a), Gurusen et al., (2011), and Nayak et al. (2012b) have been applied to the stock index forecasting. Several nature-inspired population based algorithms such as GA, PSO, differential evolution (DE), and evolutionary algorithms have been shown their promising ability as learning algorithm utilized for forecasting purpose. However, their performance may vary from one stock market to another. According to no free lunch theorem there is no single state-of-the-art constraint handling technique, which can outperform all others on every problem. Hence, choosing a suitable optimization technique for solving a particular problem involves a numerous trial-and-error method. The efficiency of these optimization techniques is characterized by tuning the parameters. Hence, an optimization technique requiring less parameters as well as good approximation capability may be the choice for achieving better forecasting accuracy. The authors Chauhan and Arya (2013) present an application of PSO for calculating the optimal coefficients of infinite-impulse response digital filters. The performance has been compared with other filter design tools and other heuristic methods such as simulated annealing (SA) and GA. Their proposed approach obtains higher performance. A brief literature review has been done by Yang and He (2013) for the recent advances and applications of Firefly Algorithm (FA) and concluded that FA can be an efficient searching strategy for higher dimensional optimization problem. A novel swarm optimizer for flexible flow shop scheduling has been proposed by the authors Singh et al. (2013). They proposed a PSO with chaotic mutation operator to avoid the problem of trapping the solution in local minima. An efficient Modified Invasive Weed Optimization (MIWO) approach has been proposed by Sharma et al. (2013) for solving the dynamic economic dispatch problem. The proposed MIWO algorithm implements a radical dual mutation strategy suitable for solving high dimensional problems and able to provide better solution.

3. ADAPTIVE HONN BASED FORECASTING MODELS

This section explains the architecture and adaptive based training of the two HONN based forecasting models. The two HONN based models are Pi-Sigma neural network (PSHONN) and Sigma-Pi neural network (SPHONN). The network parameters of both models have been selected by an evolutionary optimization technique called as genetic algorithm (GA).

3.1. Pi-Sigma HONN based Forecasting Model

The Pi-Sigma Neural Network has architecture of fully connected two-layered feed forward network. It is a class of HONN first introduced by Shin and Ghosh (1991). The two layers are termed as summing and product layer respectively. The input layers are connected to the summing layer and the output of this layer is feed to the product unit. The weight set between input and summing layer is trainable and the weight set between summing and product unit is non-trainable and set to unity. Hence, this network having only one tunable weight set reduces the training time of the network drastically. The summing units use a linear activation where as the product unit uses a nonlinear activation function to produce the output of the network. Incorporation of extra summing unit increases the order by one. The product units give the networks higher order capabilities by expanding input space into higher dimension space offering greater nonlinear separability without suffering the exponential increase in weights. Figure 1 shows the architecture of Pi-Sigma neural network forecasting model trained by GA.

As shown in Figure 1, the output at j^{th} summing unit in the hidden layer is computed by summation of product of each input x_i with the corresponding weight w_{ij} between i^{th} input and j^{th} hidden unit and represented by Eq. 1.

Figure 1. Pi-Sigma Neural Network Forecasting Model

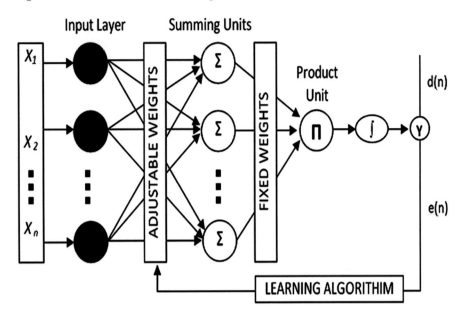

$$y_j = \sum_{i=1}^{n} w_{ij} * x_i \qquad (1)$$

Where n is the number of input signals, i.e. number of closing prices here. The output of the network is now computed by making the product of the output of each summing units in the hidden layer and then passing it to a nonlinear activation function i.e. sigmoid function here. The output *Y* is represented by Eq. 2.

$$Y = \sigma \left(\prod_{j=1}^{k} y_j \right) \qquad (2)$$

Where: *k* represents the order of the network same as the number of summing unit in the hidden layer.

In the first attempt the above PSNN model has been trained by gradient descent (GD) technique. In this case the weight and biases vectors of the model are optimized by the well known GD based technique. The high level GD based PSNN training is described by Algorithm 1.

Algorithm 1 GD-PSHONN Training

1. *Calculate the output **Y** of the model using Eq. 2.*
2. *Supply the desired output to compute the error signal by minimizing the error function computed as follows:*

$$E(n) = \frac{1}{N}\sum_{i=1}^{N}\left(d_n - Y(n)\right)^2$$

3. *Compute the weight changes by gradient descent method using following formula where learning rate is η.*

$$\Delta W = \eta\left(\prod_{j=1}^{k} y_j\right)X(n)$$

4. *Update the weight using change in weight and momentum factor α described as follows.*

$$W = W + \alpha\Delta W$$

5. *If stopping condition satisfies*
    Stop training
    else go to step 1.

Gradient descent based back propagation learning has been characterized with three well known pitfalls such as slow convergence capability, landing in local minima and over fitting. In order to avoid these drawbacks, in this study an evolutionary global learning technique, i.e. GA has been adopted to optimize the parameters of both PSHONN and SPHONN based forecasting model.

GA has been considered as a global search optimization technique. Its' capability has been well established by solving several complex real problems in the area of data mining. This work employed the GA in the learning phase of the PSNN network, as it is capable to search in a large search space. The hybridization of neural network and GA is able to select the optimal PSNN for prediction. The genetic algorithm performs search over the whole solution space, finds the optimal solution relatively easily, and it does not requires continuous differentiable objective functions. The problem of finding an optimal parameter set to train the model could be seen as a search problem into the space of all possible parameters. The fitness of the best and average individual (i.e. PSNN) in each generation increases towards a global optimum. It can be used as the tool for decision making in order to solve the complex nonlinear problems such as stock index prediction. The chromosome set of GA represent a set of potential PSNN models. Input data along with the chromosome values are fed to the set of PSNN models. The fitness is obtained from the absolute difference between the target and the estimated output. The less the fitness value of an individual, GA considers it better fit. The high level architecture of GA-PSNN forecasting model is shown by Figure 3. The high level algorithm of the GA based PSNN models can be summarized in Algorithm 2.

This study uses sliding window technique for selection of optimal number of input data for the model. The successive input vectors are selected by sliding the window one step forward for each time. In each sliding, only one new data has been included to the input vector and one old data has been discarded from the input vector. So there may be small difference in nonlinearity property of two adjacent windows. Therefore, instead of choosing a new weight and biases vector for each training set, the model uses the previously optimized parameter set. In this way the model trained adaptively and the training time reduces significantly. Figure 2 visualizes the adaptive GA-PSHONN based forecasting model.

Figure 3. Sigma-Pi Neural Network based Forecasting Model

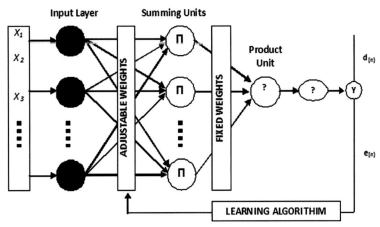

Figure 2. GA based adaptive PSNN forecasting model

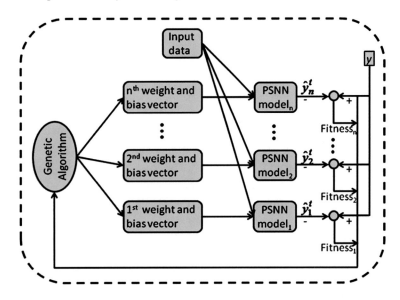

Algorithm 2 GA-PSHONN Training

1. *Setting training data, i.e. choosing number of closing prices as input vector for the network.*
2. *Random initialization of search spaces, i.e. populations.*
    Initialize each search space, i.e. chromosome with values from the domain [0, 1].
3. *While (termination criteria not met)*
    For each chromosome in the search space
    3.1. *Calculate the weighted sum at each summing unit node of hidden layer.*
    3.2. *Compute the product of output of summing unit at the output unit and passing it through a sigmoid transformation.*
    3.3. *Present the desired output, calculate the error signal and accumulate it.*

       3.4. *Fitness of the chromosome is equal to the accumulated error signal.*

End

Apply crossover operator.

Apply mutation operator.

Select better fit solutions.

End

4.   *Present the testing input vector, immediate to the training vectors.*

      Calculated the estimated signal and calculate the error value.

5.   *Repeat the steps 1-4 for all training and testing patterns, calculate the total error signals.*

3.2. Sigma-Pi HONN based Forecasting Model

The Sigma-Pi neural network is another HONN (SPHONN) which uses higher order terms of input signal at the hidden layer neurons. In SPHONN the hidden neuron calculates product of input signals and the output neuron uses the sum of product of input signals. Figure 3 presents the pictorial visualization of SPHONN based forecasting model. This model is also trained with GD based training as well as GA based training. The training algorithm of SPHONN is similar to that of PSHONN model except the computation at hidden neuron. For sake of space the training algorithm and adaptive model have been skipped.

4. SIMULATION RESULTS AND ANALYSIS

To validate the above developed HONN based forecasting models, daily closing indices of LSE, SSE and NIKKEI have been considered from 1st January 2014 to 31st December 2014. The data have been collected from their website for a period of one year. The raw data first pre-processed using min-max normalization method. Figure 4 represents the normalized closing indices of all the three data sets. MATLAB has been used for conducting all experiments.

Figure 4. Normalized closing indices of LSE, SSE and NIKKEI

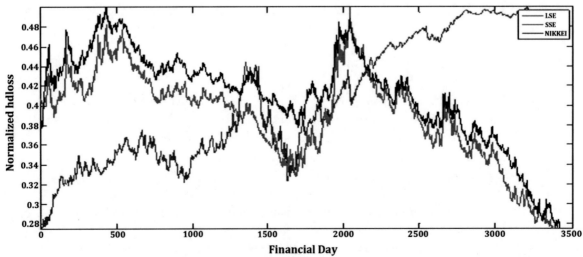

For input vector selection, sliding window technique is used. To avoid the biasness of results due to stochastic nature of neural based model, we simulate the model 10 times for each data set and the average value has been considered for the performance evaluation.

The mean absolute percentage error (MAPE) signal is used as the first performance metric throughout this study. Equation 3 represents the formula for measuring the MAPE.

$$MAPE = \frac{1}{N} \sum_{i=1}^{N} \frac{|x_i - \hat{x}_i|}{x_i} * 100\%$$ (3)

The second metric used is an important metric, particularly in the area of stock trend forecasting. The metric is called as prediction of change in direction (POCID) and can be represented as in Eq. 4 and Eq. 5. This is more important as compared to MAPE, because if the direction of stock trend can be predicted more accurately the investors may be guided better and monetary gain will be substantial.

$$POCID = \frac{\sum_{i=1}^{N} Trend_i}{N} * 100$$ (4)

where

$$Trend_i = \begin{cases} 1, if \left(x_i - x_{i-1}\right)\left(\hat{x}_i - \hat{x}_{i-1}\right) > 0 \\ 0, otherwise \end{cases}$$ (5)

This measure gives an account of number of correct directions when predicting the next closing prices in the financial time series. The ideal value of POCID for a perfect predictor is closer to 100 and the closer the values to 100 the more accurate is the prediction model.

The third evaluation measure is the Average Relative Variance (ARV). The ARV can be calculated as in Eq. 6.

$$\frac{\sum_{i=1}^{N} \left(\hat{x}_i - x_i\right)^2}{\sum_{i=1}^{N} \left(\hat{x}_i - \overline{X}\right)^2}$$ (6)

If the ARV value of the forecasting model is equal to 1, then it is same as considering the mean of the financial time series. The model is considered as performing worst as compared to mean if the ARV value is greater than 1. However, the model can be considered as performing better than simply calculating the mean if its ARV value is less than 1. Hence, the closer the value to 0, the forecasting model tends to be more accurate.

The fourth measure considered for evaluation of the models is U of Theil (UT) metric which compares the model performance with a random walk model. The metric can be calculated by using Eq. 7.

$$UofTheil = \frac{\sum_{i=1}^{N}\left(x_i - \hat{x}_i\right)^2}{\sum_{i=1}^{N}\left(x_i - x_{i+1}\right)^2} \tag{7}$$

If the value of this statistics is equal to 1, then the model has the same performance of the random walk model. If it is greater than 1, the model is considered performing worst as compared to a random walk model. The model is performing better than a random walk model if its U of Theil statistics is less than 1. Hence, the more closely the value to 0, the more perfect is the model.

4.1. Results from PSHONN Model

This subsection presents and analyzes the results obtained from GD-PSHONN and GA-PSHONN forecasting models experimented on the three data sets such as LSE, SSE and NIKKEI. Table 1 presents the MAPE values generated by both adaptive models.

It may be observed for Table 1 that the GA-PSHONN gives better performance as compared to GD-PSHONN in case of all data sets. The gain in performance is lowest for NIKKEI and the model achieves an average gain of 9.37% in performance. For obtaining more clarity on performance of these models the actual v/s estimated prices predicted by the models have been plotted. Figure 5 represents the plotting for LSE data set. Figure 6 presents plotting for SSE. Figure 7 represents the plotting for NIKKEI data set. Similarly, the POCID, ARV and U of Theil values for these forecasting models are examined and summarized in Table 2.

From Table 2 it may be observed that the GA-PSHONN based forecasting model obtained much better performances as compared to GD-PSHONN. Its POCID values for LSE and NIKKEI stock indices are above 90% which is an indication of stable forecasting system.

4.2. Results from SPHONN Model

Similarly, the SPHONN based forecasting models have been experimented on the same data sets considered earlier. The two models are GD based SPHONN (GD-SPHONN) and GA based SPHONN (GA-SPHONN). Table 3 summarizes the MAPE values obtained from the two models.

From Table 3 it can be observed that the GA based training of SPHONN outperforms GD based SPHONN for all indices. The gain in performance is maximum for SSE data set and minimum for NIKKEI data set. However the average gain % of GA-SPHONN over GD-SPHONN is 35%. Also the estimated closing prices have been plotted against actual prices for all the three data sets. Figure 8 presents the plotting from LSE data set. Figure 9 represents the plot obtained from SSE data set. Figure 10 presents the actual v/s estimated prices for NIKKEI data set. Similarly, the POCID, ARV and UT values obtained from these forecasting models are summarized in Table 4. Here also the GA-SPHONN based model achieves better performances over GD-SPHONN based forecasting model.

Table 1. MAPE from GD-PSHONN and GA-PSHONN

Stock Index	Forecasting Model		MAPE Reduction (%)
	GD-PSHONN	**GA-PSHONN**	
LSE	0.3502	0.3077	12.14
SSE	0.2086	0.1811	13.18
NIKKEI	0.4217	0.4099	2.8

Figure 5. Actual v/s estimated prices by PSHONN forecasting model from LSE data

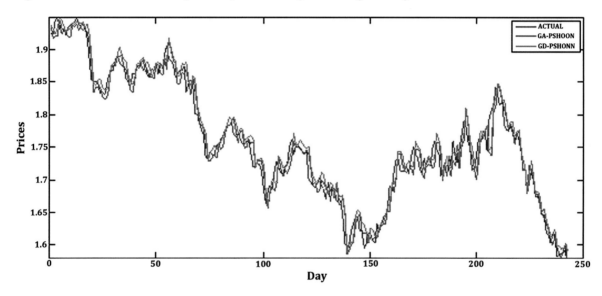

Figure 6. Actual v/s estimated prices by PSHONN forecasting model from SSE data

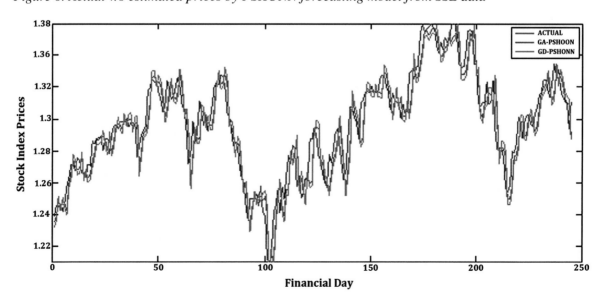

Figure 7. Actual v/s estimated prices by PSHONN forecasting model from NIKKEI data

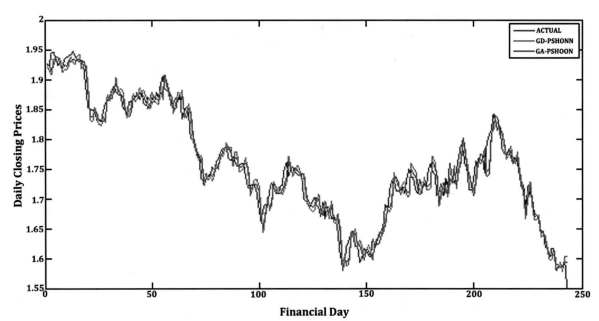

Table 2. POCID, ARV and UT values from GD-PSHONN and GA-PSHONN

Stock Index	Forecasting Model					
	GD-PSHONN			GA-PSHONN		
	POCID	ARV	UT	POCID	ARV	UT
LSE	67	0.0841	0.61	90.2	0.0082	0.425
SSE	66.5	0.1011	0.23	81.7	0.0624	0.099
NIKKEI	69.5	0.0652	0.095	93.3	0.0266	0.085

Table 3. MAPE from GD-SPHONN and GA-SPHONN

Stock Index	Forecasting Model		MAPE Reduction (%)
	GD-SPHONN	GA-SPHONN	
LSE	0.3387	0.3142	7.23
SSE	0.4408	0.2865	35.00
NIKKEI	0.4015	0.3774	6.00

Figure 8. Actual v/s estimated prices by SPHONN forecasting model from LSE data

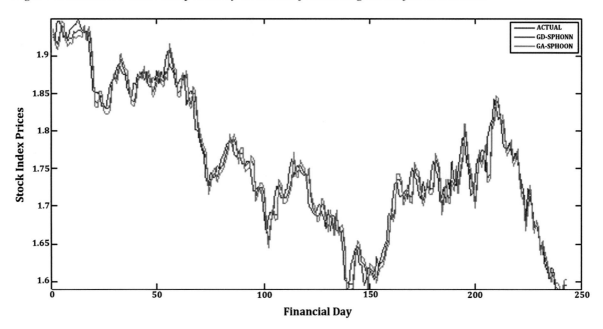

Figure 9. Actual v/s estimated prices by SPHONN forecasting model from SSE data

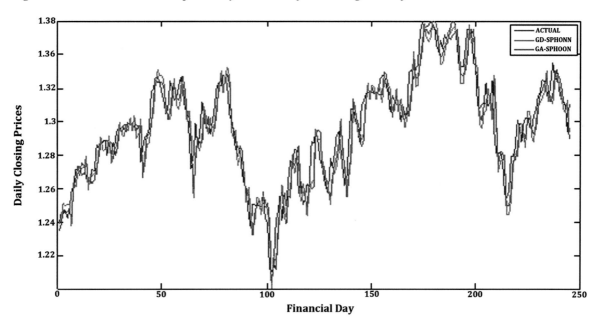

Table 4. POCID, ARV and UT values from GD-SPHONN and GA-SPHONN

Stock Index	Forecasting Model					
	GD-SPHONN			GA-SPHONN		
	POCID	ARV	UT	POCID	ARV	UT
LSE	66.5	0.052	0.66	85.5	0.0105	0.314
SSE	62.7	0.0543	0.54	86.8	0.0207	0.382
NIKKEI	71	0.0184	0.65	92.5	0.0142	0.525

Figure 10. Actual v/s estimated prices by SPHONN forecasting model from NIKKEI data

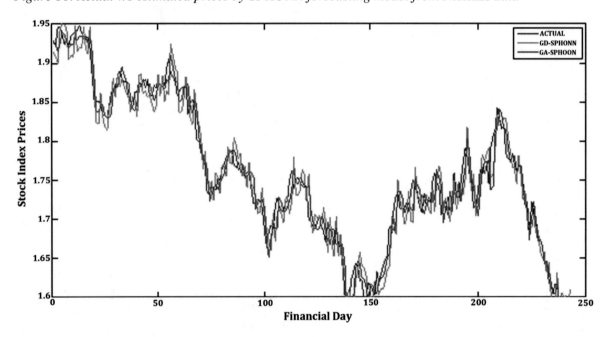

5. CONCLUSION AND FURTHER RESEARCH

With the objective of achieving better prediction accuracy, the higher order neural networks have been experimented in this chapter. Two HONN based networks such as PSNN and SPNN have been used as the base model. The models are first trained with the well known GD learning and the models are termed as GD-PSHONN and GD-SPHONN forecasting model respectively. To overcome the lacunas of GD based training, evolutionary algorithm based training has been adopted for both models. The models are termed as GA-PSHONN and GA-SPHONN respectively. The four models developed so far have been validated on three real stock indices. From extensive simulation studies it has been revealed that the HONN based forecasting models shows a consistent performance over all data sets. However, when GA based training has been adopted, the performances of the above models improve a lot. Also there is significant reduction in training time occurs as the models trained in an adaptive manner.

The study may be extended with some other higher order neural networks and other fast and robust evolutionary learning techniques.

REFERENCES

Abraham, A., Nath, B., & Mahanti, P. K. (2001). Hybrid intelligent systems for stock market analysis. In *Computational science-ICCS 2001* (pp. 337–345). Springer Berlin Heidelberg. doi:10.1007/3-540-45718-6_38

Babaei, M. (2013). A general approach to approximate solutions of nonlinear differential equations using particle swarm optimization. *Applied Soft Computing, 13*(7), 3354–3365. doi:10.1016/j.asoc.2013.02.005

Chauhan, R. S., & Arya, S. K. (2013). An application of swarm intelligence for the design of IIR digital filters. *International Journal of Swarm Intelligence, 1*(1), 3–18. doi:10.1504/IJSI.2013.055799

Chiang, W. C., Urban, T. L., & Baldridge, G. W. (1996). A neural network approach to mutual fund net asset value forecasting. *Omega, 24*(2), 205–215. doi:10.1016/0305-0483(95)00059-3

Durbin, R., & Rumelhart, D. E. (1989). Product units: A computationally powerful and biologically plausible extension to backpropagation networks. *Neural Computation, 1*(1), 133–142. doi:10.1162/neco.1989.1.1.133

Eberhart, R., Simpson, P., & Dobbins, R. (1996). *Computational intelligence PC tools*. Academic Press Professional, Inc.

Epitropakis, M. G., Plagianakos, V. P., & Vrahatis, M. N. (2010). Hardware-friendly higher-order neural network training using distributed evolutionary algorithms. *Applied Soft Computing, 10*(2), 398–408. doi:10.1016/j.asoc.2009.08.010

Fallahnezhad, M., Moradi, M. H., & Zaferanlouei, S. (2011). A hybrid higher order neural classifier for handling classification problems. *Expert Systems with Applications, 38*(1), 386–393. doi:10.1016/j.eswa.2010.06.077

Ghazali, R. (2007). *Higher order neural networks for financial time series prediction* [Doctoral dissertation]. Liverpool John Moores University.

Ghazali, R., Hussain, A., & El-Deredy, W. (2006, July). Application of ridge polynomial neural networks to financial time series prediction. *Proceedings of the International Joint Conference on Neural Networks IJCNN '06* (pp. 913-920). IEEE.

Ghazali, R., Hussain, A. J., & Liatsis, P. (2011). Dynamic Ridge Polynomial Neural Network: Forecasting the univariate non-stationary and stationary trading signals. *Expert Systems with Applications, 38*(4), 3765–3776. doi:10.1016/j.eswa.2010.09.037

Ghazali, R., Ismail, L. H., Husaini, N. A., & Samsuddin, N. A. (2012). *An Application of jordan pi-sigma neural network for the prediction of temperature time series signal*. INTECH Open Access Publisher. doi:10.5772/36026

Ghosh, J., & Shin, Y. (1992). Efficient higher-order neural networks for classification and function approximation. *International Journal of Neural Systems, 3*(04), 323–350. doi:10.1142/S0129065792000255

Giles, C. L., & Maxwell, T. (1987). Learning, invariance, and generalization in high-order neural networks. *Applied Optics, 26*(23), 4972–4978. doi:10.1364/AO.26.004972 PMID:20523475

Goldberg, D. E., & Holland, J. H. (1988). Genetic algorithms and machine learning. *Machine Learning, 3*(2), 95–99. doi:10.1023/A:1022602019183

Guler, M., & Sahin, E. (1994). A new higher-order binary-input neural unit: learning and generalizing effectively via using minimal number of monomials. *Proceedings of third Turkish symposium on artificial intelligence and neural networks* (pp. 51-60).

Guresen, E., Kayakutlu, G., & Daim, T. U. (2011). Using artificial neural network models in stock market index prediction. *Expert Systems with Applications, 38*(8), 10389–10397. doi:10.1016/j.eswa.2011.02.068

Holland, J. H. (1975). *Adaptation in natural and artificial systems: an introductory analysis with applications to biology, control, and artificial intelligence.* U Michigan Press.

Huang, D.S., Ip, H.H., Law, K.C.K., & Chi, Z. (2005). Zeroing polynomials using modified constrained neural network approach. *IEEE Transactions on* Neural Networks, *16*(3), 721–732.

Karci, A., & Arslan, A. (2002). Uniform population in genetic algorithms. *IU-Journal of Electrical & Electronics Engineering, 2*(2), 495–504.

Kennedy, J. (2011). Particle swarm optimization. In Encyclopedia of machine learning (pp. 760-766). Springer US.

Knowles, A., Hussein, A., Deredy, W., Lisboa, P., & Dunis, C. L. (2005). Higher-order neural networks with Bayesian confidence measure for prediction of EUR/USD exchange rate. In M. Zhang (Ed.), Artificial Higher Order Neural networks for Economics and Business (pp. 48-59). Hershey, PA, USA: Idea Group.

Kwon, Y. K., & Moon, B. R. (2007). A hybrid neurogenetic approach for stock forecasting. *IEEE Transactions on* Neural Networks, *18*(3), 851–864.

Leerink, L. R., Giles, C. L., Horne, B. G., & Jabri, M. A. (1995). Learning with Product Units. *Advances in Neural Information Processing Systems*, 1995, 537–544.

Nayak, S. C., Misra, B. B., & Behera, H. S. (2012). Stock index prediction with neuro-genetic hybrid techniques. *Int. J. Comput. Sci. Inform, 2*, 27–34.

Nayak, S. C., Misra, B. B., & Behera, H. S. (2012, February). Index prediction with neuro-genetic hybrid network: A comparative analysis of performance. *Proceedings of the 2012 International Conference on Computing Communication and Applications (ICCCA)* (pp. 1-6). IEEE. doi:10.1109/ICCCA.2012.6179215

Nie, Y., & Deng, W. (2008, October). A hybrid genetic learning algorithm for Pi-sigma neural network and the analysis of its convergence. *Proceedings of the Fourth International Conference on Natural Computation ICNC '08* (Vol. 3, pp. 19-23). IEEE. doi:10.1109/ICNC.2008.896

Park, S. I., Smith, M. J., & Mersereau, R. M. (2000). Target recognition based on directional filter banks and higher-order neural networks. *Digital Signal Processing, 10*(4), 297–308. doi:10.1006/dspr.2000.0376

Perantonis, S., Ampazis, N., Varoufakis, S., & Antoniou, G. (1998). Constrained learning in neural networks: Application to stable factorization of 2-D polynomials. *Neural Processing Letters, 7*(1), 5–14. doi:10.1023/A:1009655902122

Romahi, Y., & Shen, Q. (2000, May). Dynamic financial forecasting with automatically induced fuzzy associations. *Proceedings of the Ninth IEEE International Conference on Fuzzy Systems FUZZ '00* (Vol. 1, pp. 493-498). IEEE. doi:10.1109/FUZZY.2000.838709

Sharma, R., Nayak, S. K., Rout, P. K., & Krishnanand, K. R. (2013). Solution to dynamic economic dispatch problem using modified invasive weed optimisation with dual mutation strategy. *International Journal of Swarm Intelligence*, *1*(1), 70–90. doi:10.1504/IJSI.2013.055803

Shin, Y., & Ghosh, J. (1991, July). The pi-sigma network: An efficient higher-order neural network for pattern classification and function approximation. *Proceedings of the Seattle International Joint Conference on Neural Networks IJCNN '91* (Vol. 1, pp. 13-18). IEEE.

Shin, Y., & Ghosh, J. (1995). Ridge polynomial networks. *IEEE Transactions on* Neural Networks, *6*(3), 610–622.

Singh, M. R., Mahapatra, S. S., & Mishra, K. (2013). A novel swarm optimiser for flexible flow shop scheduling. *International Journal of Swarm Intelligence*, *1*(1), 51–69. doi:10.1504/IJSI.2013.055802

Wang, Z., Fang, J. A., & Liu, X. (2008). Global stability of stochastic high-order neural networks with discrete and distributed delays. *Chaos, Solitons, and Fractals*, *36*(2), 388–396. doi:10.1016/j.chaos.2006.06.063

White, H. (1988, July). Economic prediction using neural networks: The case of IBM daily stock returns. *Proceedings of the IEEE International Conference on Neural Networks '88* (pp. 451-458). IEEE.

Yang, X. S., & He, X. (2013). Firefly algorithm: Recent advances and applications. *International Journal of Swarm Intelligence*, *1*(1), 36–50. doi:10.1504/IJSI.2013.055801

Yu, L., & Zhang, Y. Q. (2005). Evolutionary fuzzy neural networks for hybrid financial prediction. *Proceedings of the IEEE Transactions on* Systems, Man, and Cybernetics, Part C: Applications and Reviews, *35*(2), 244–249.

Zhang, M., Xu, S., & Fulcher, J. (2002). Neuron-adaptive higher order neural-network models for automated financial data modeling. *IEEE Transactions on* Neural Networks, *13*(1), 188–204.

Chapter 8

Theoretical Analyses of the Universal Approximation Capability of a class of Higher Order Neural Networks based on Approximate Identity

Saeed Panahian
Universiti Sains, Malaysia

Zarita Zainuddin
Universiti Sains, Malaysia

ABSTRACT

One of the most important problems in the theory of approximation functions by means of neural networks is universal approximation capability of neural networks. In this study, we investigate the theoretical analyses of the universal approximation capability of a special class of three layer feedforward higher order neural networks based on the concept of approximate identity in the space of continuous multivariate functions. Moreover, we present theoretical analyses of the universal approximation capability of the networks in the spaces of Lebesgue integrable multivariate functions. The methods used in proving our results are based on the concepts of convolution and epsilon-net. The obtained results can be seen as an attempt towards the development of approximation theory by means of neural networks.

1. INTRODUCTION

The function approximation can be explained as follows: Let be a continuous function on a compact set. We intend to find a simple function g such that $\|f - g\| < \varepsilon$. This problem has attracted many researchers' attentions in the last century. According to Tikk et al. (2003), in 1900, Hilbert presented his 23 conjectures at the second international congress of mathematicians in Paris. Based on the 13th conjec-

DOI: 10.4018/978-1-5225-0063-6.ch008

ture, there exist continuous functions with multi variables which cannot be represented as the finite superposition of continuous functions with fewer variables. In 1957, Arnold rejected this conjecture. In the same year, Kolmogorov proved his representation theorem with a constructive proof. This theorem shows that a continuous function with multi variables can be decomposed as the finite superposition of continuous functions with one variable. In 1965, Sprecher improved the Kolmogorov's representation theorem. In 1966, Lorentz further improved this theorem.

In the approximation theory of artificial neural networks (ANNs) that problem reduces to find an artificial neural network such that approximate f, i.e. $\|f - ANNs\| < e$. In 1980, De Figueriedo generalized this theorem for multilayer feedforward artificial neural networks. In 1989, Poggio and Girosi showed that this theorem is irrelevant for artificial neural networks because in a Kolmogorov networks, nodes have wild and complex functions. Then, many researchers have been tried to solve the problem of approximation function by artificial neural networks such as Cybenko (1989), Funuhashi (1989), Park and Sandberg, (1991, 1993), Mhaskar, (1993), Leshno (1993), Suzuki (1998), Hahm and Hong, (2004), Li (2008), Ismailov (2012), Wang et al. (2012), Lin et al. (2013), and Arteaga and Marrero (2013).

The standard form of universal approximation capability of feedforward neural networks states that under what kind of conditions an arbitrary continuous function can be approximated by a single-hidden-layer feedforward neural networks to any degree of accuracy. Comprehensive surveys of the universal approximation capability of feedforward neural networks can be found in Nong (2013); Bouaziz et al. (2014); Wang (2010); Ismailov (2014); Arteaga and Marrero (2014), Costarelli (2014). Recently, the history of the development of universal approximation by artificial neural networks has been presented by Pricipe and Chen (2015).

In the present chapter, we are motivated to extend the scheme of the univariate universal approximation capability to the scheme of the multivariate universal approximation capability. In other words, the motivation of this chapter is to develop the theory of the universal approximation capability of a class of feedforward higher order neural networks based on approximate identity in multivariate functions spaces. We should address what we can expect from higher order neural networks based on approximate identity. In fact, higher order neural networks based on approximate identity are merging higher order neural networks and approximate identity neural networks.

Higher order neural networks extend standard feedforward neural networks by using a higher correlation of input neurons for better fitting properties. Higher order neural networks was first studied by Giles and Maxwell (1987) and further analysed by Pao (1989). The above networks have also been used in pattern recognition (Schmit & Davis, 1993), financial data simulation (Zhang et al., 2002). In recent years, universal approximation capability of different models of higher order neural networks have been investigated (Long et al., 2007; Long et al., 2007a).

Approximate identity neural networks are neural networks models which employ approximate identity as neuron activation functions. We briefly review the literature of this field of research. Turchetti et al. published the first paper on approximate identity neural networks (Turchetti, 1998). In recent years, universal approximation capability of several different types of approximate identity neural networks models have been investigated (Panahian & Zainuddin, 2013, 2014, 2012, 2014a, 2013a, 2014b, 2015, 2014c, 2014d).

The objective of this study is to describe an approximate representation of multivariate functions by a class of three layer feedforward higher order neural networks based on approximate identity in the space of continuous multivariate functions and in the spaces of Lebesgue integrable multivariate functions.

In other words, we aim to provide an answer to the question that what kind of three layer feedforward higher order neural networks are qualified to approximate continuous multivariate functions and Lebesgue integrable multivariate functions.

The method of the study can be explained as follows: first, we will prove a theorem that shows that the convolution of approximate identity and the continuous multivariate function f uniformly converges to f. Using this theorem, we will also prove a main theorem that shows that the universal approximation capability of higher order neural networks based on approximate identity in the space of continuous multivariate functions. Second, we will prove another theorem that shows the convolution of approximate identity and Lebesgue integrable multivariate function f uniformly converges to f. Using this theorem, we will prove a second main theorem that shows the universal approximation capability of the above networks in the spaces of Lebesgue integrable multivariate functions. The proofs of the main theorems are based on the notion of epsilon-net (Wu et al., 2007).

The study is organized as follows: In Section 2, we review some notations and basic definitions. In Section 3, we present a theorem on the uniform convergence in the space of continuous multivariate functions. Moreover, our first main theorem in this functions space is proved. In Section 4, we give a theorem on the uniform convergence in the spaces of Lebesgue integrable multivariate functions and our second main theorem in these functions spaces is established. In Section 5, we give our concluding remarks.

2. SOME NOTATIONS AND BASIC DEFINITIONS

In this section, some notations are reviewed. Let $C\left(\mathbb{R}^d\right)$ denotes the space of continuous multivariate functions, and let $L_p\left(\mathbb{R}^d\right)$ denotes the spaces of Lebesgue integrable multivariate functions. Moreover, the basic definitions of approximate identity, convolution, epsilon-net and finite epsilon-net are presented. First, we introduce the notion of approximate identity.

Definition1. (Turchetti et al., 1998) $\left\{\varphi_n\left(\boldsymbol{x}\right)\right\}_{n\in\mathbb{N}}$, $\varphi_n\left(\boldsymbol{x}\right): \mathbb{R}^d \to \mathbb{R}$ is said to be an approximate identity if the following properties hold:

1. $\int_{\mathbb{R}^d}\varphi_n\left(\boldsymbol{x}\right)d\boldsymbol{x}=1$

    Given ε and $\delta>0$, there exists N such that if $n\geq N$ then

$$\int_{|x|>\delta}\left|\varphi_n\left(\boldsymbol{x}\right)\right|d\boldsymbol{x}\leq\varepsilon.$$

The followings are two similar definitions. We define an epsilon-net in $C\left(\mathbb{R}^d\right)$ and in $L_p\left(\mathbb{R}^d\right)$ respectively.

Definition 2. (Lebedev, 1997) Let $\varepsilon>0$. A set $V_\varepsilon \subset C\left(\mathbb{R}^d\right)$ is called ε-net of a set V, if $\tilde{f}\in V_\varepsilon$ can be found for $\forall f\in V$ such that $\left\|f-\tilde{f}\right\|_{C\left(\mathbb{R}^d\right)}<\varepsilon$.

Definition 3. (Lebedev, 1997) Let $\varepsilon > 0$. A set $V_\varepsilon \subset L_P\left(\mathbb{R}^d\right)$ is called ε-net of a set V, if $\tilde{f} \in V_\varepsilon$ can be found for $\forall f \in V$ such that $\left\| f - \tilde{f} \right\|_{L_P\left(\mathbb{R}^d\right)} < \varepsilon$.

Now we define the notion of finite epsilon-net.

Definition 4. (Lebedev, 1997) The å -net is said to be finite if it is a finite set of elements.

In the next section, we present theoretical analyses of the universal approximation capability of a class of higher order neural networks based on approximate identity in the space of continuous multivariate functions.

3 THEORETICAL ANALYSES IN THE SPACE OF CONTINUOUS MULTIVARIATE FUNCTIONS

We begin with Theorem 1. The statement of Theorem 1 tells us that the convolution of approximate identity with every continuous multivariate function f converges uniformly to f on $\mathbb{R}^d$.

Theorem 1. Let $C\left(\mathbb{R}^d\right)$ be the linear space of all continuous functions on $\mathbb{R}^d$ with a compact support. Let $\{\varphi_n(x)\}_{n\in\mathbb{N}}$, $\varphi_n(x): \mathbb{R}^d \to \mathbb{R}$ be an approximate identity. Let $f \in C\left(\mathbb{R}^d\right)$. Then $\phi_n * f$ uniformly converges to f on $C\left(\mathbb{R}^d\right)$.

Proof. Let $x \in \mathbb{R}^n$ and $\varepsilon > 0$. There exists a $\delta > 0$ such that

$$\left| f(x) - f(y) \right| < \frac{\varepsilon}{2 \| \varphi \|_1} \text{ for all } y, |x - y| < \delta. \text{ Let us define } \{\varphi_n * f\}_{n\in\mathbb{N}} \text{ by}$$

$$\varphi_n(x) = n\varphi(nx). \text{ Then,}$$

$$\varphi_n * f(x) - f(x) = \int_{\mathbb{R}^d} n\varphi(ny)\{f(x-y) - f(y)\} dy$$

$$= \left(\int_{|y|<\delta} + \int_{|y|\geq\delta} \right) n\varphi(ny)\{f(x-y) - f(y)\} dy$$

$$= I_1 + I_2$$

we calculate I_1, I_2 as follows:

$$|I1| \leq \int_{|y|<\delta} n\left|\varphi(ny)\right|\{f(x-y) - f(y)\} dy$$

$$< \frac{\varepsilon}{2\|\varphi\|_1} \int_{|y|<\delta} n\left|\varphi(ny)\right| dy$$

$$= \frac{\varepsilon}{2\|\varphi\|_1} \int_{t<n\delta} \left|\varphi(t)\right| dt$$

$$\leq \frac{\varepsilon}{2\|\varphi\|_1} \int_{\mathbb{R}^d} \left|\varphi(t)\right| dt = \frac{\varepsilon}{2}.$$

For I_2, we have

$$\left|I_1\right| \leq 2\|f\|_{C(\mathbb{R}^d)} \int_{|y|\geq\delta} n\left|\varphi(ny)\right| dy$$

$$= 2\|f\|_{C(\mathbb{R}^d)} \int_{t\geq n\delta} \left|\varphi(t)\right| dt.$$

Since

$$\lim_{n\to\infty} \left|\varphi(t)\right| dt = 0,$$

There exist $n_0 \in \mathbb{N}$ such that for all $n \geq n_0$,

$$\int_{t\geq n\delta} \left|\varphi(t)\right| dt < \frac{\varepsilon}{2\|f\|_{C(\mathbb{R}^d)}}.$$

Combining I_1 and I_2 for $n \geq n_0$, we have

$$\left\|\varphi_n * f(x) - f(x)\right\|_{C(\mathbb{R}^d)} < \varepsilon$$

We use the above theorem in order to state a main result which shows universal approximation capability of three layer feedforward higher order neural networks based on approximate identity in $C\left(\mathbb{R}^d\right)$. The proof is based on the notion of epsilon-net.

Theorem 2. Let $C\left(\mathbb{R}^d\right)$ be the linear space of all continuous functions on $\mathbb{R}^d$ with a compact support and $V \subset C(\mathbb{R}^d)$. Let $\{\varphi_n(x)\}_{n\in\mathbb{N}}$, $\varphi_n(x): \mathbb{R}^d \to \mathbb{R}$ be an approximate identity. Let the family of functions $\{ \sum_{j=1}^{M} \lambda_j \varphi_j(x) \mid \lambda_j \in \mathbb{R}, x \in \mathbb{R}^d, M \in \mathbb{N} \}$ be dense in $C(\mathbb{R}^d)$, and given $\varepsilon > 0$. Then there exists $N \in \mathbb{N}$ which depends on V and ε but not on f, such that for any $f \in V$, there exist weights $c_k = c_k(f, V, \varepsilon)$ satisfying

$$\left\| f(x) - \sum_{i=1}^{N} c_k \varphi_k(x) \right\|_{C(\mathbb{R}^d)} < \varepsilon$$

Moreover, every c_k is a continuous function of $f \in V$.

Proof. Because V is compact, for any $\varepsilon > 0$, there is a finite $\frac{\varepsilon}{2}$-net $\{f^1, \ldots f^M\}$ for V. This implies that for any $f \in V$, there is an f^j such that $\left\| f - f^j \right\|_{C(\mathbb{R}^d)} < \frac{\varepsilon}{2}$. For any f^j, by assumption of the theorem, there are $\lambda_i^j \in \mathbb{R}, N_j \in \mathbb{N}$, and $\varphi_i^j(x)$ such that

$$\left\| f^j(x) - \sum_{i=1}^{N_j} \lambda_i^j \varphi_i^j(x) \right\|_{C(\mathbb{R}^d)} < \frac{\varepsilon}{2} \tag{1}$$

For any $f \in V$, we define

$$F_-(f) = \left\{ j \mid \left\| f - f^j \right\|_{C(\mathbb{R}^d)} < \frac{\varepsilon}{2} \right\}$$

$$F_0(f) = \left\{ j \mid \left\| f - f^j \right\|_{C(\mathbb{R}^d)} = \frac{\varepsilon}{2} \right\}$$

$$F_+(f) = \left\{ j \mid \left\| f - f^j \right\|_{C(\mathbb{R}^d)} > \frac{\varepsilon}{2} \right\}$$

Therefore, $F_-(f)$ is not empty according to the definition of $\frac{\varepsilon}{2}$-net. If $\tilde{f} \in V$ approaches f such that $\left\| \tilde{f} - f \right\|_{C(\mathbb{R}^d)}$ is small enough, then we have $F_-(f) \subset F_-(\tilde{f})$ and $F_+(f) \subset F_+(\tilde{f})$. Thus $F_-(\tilde{f}) \bigcap F_+(f) \subset F_-(\tilde{f}) \bigcap F_+(\tilde{f}) = \emptyset$, which implies $F_-(\tilde{f}) \subset F_-(f) \bigcup F_0(f)$. We finish with the following:

$$F_-(f) \subset F_-(\tilde{f}) \subset F_-(f) \bigcup F_0(f). \tag{2}$$

Define

$$d(f) = \left[\sum_{j \in F_-(f)} \left(\frac{\varepsilon}{2} - \left\| f - f^j \right\|_{C(\mathbb{R}^d)} \right) \right]^{-1}$$

and

$$f_h = \sum_{j \in F_-(f)} \sum_{i=1}^{N_j} d(f) \left(\frac{\varepsilon}{2} - \left\| f - f^j \right\|_{C(\mathbb{R}^d)} \right) \lambda_i^j \varphi_i^j (x) \tag{3}$$

Then $f_h \in \left\{ \sum_{i=1}^{M} \lambda_j \varphi_j (x) \right\}$ approximates f with accuracy ε:

$$\left\| f - f_h \right\|_{C(\mathbb{R}^d)}$$

$$= \left\| \sum_{j \in F_-(f)} d(f) \left(\frac{\varepsilon}{2} - f - f^j{}_{C(\mathbb{R}^d)} \right) \left(f - \sum_{i=1}^{N_j} \lambda_i^j \varphi_i^j (x) \right) \right\|_{C(\mathbb{R}^d)}$$

$$= \left\| \sum_{j \in F_-(f)} d(f) \left(\frac{\varepsilon}{2} - f - f^j{}_{C(\mathbb{R}^d)} \right) (f - f^j + f^j - \right.$$

$$\left. i = 1 N j \lambda i j \varphi i j (x)) C(\mathbb{R} \wedge d) \right.$$

$$\leq \sum_{j \in F_-(f)} d(f) \left(\frac{\varepsilon}{2} - \left\| f - f^j \right\|_{C(\mathbb{R}^d)} \right) \left(\left\| f - f^j \right\|_{C(\mathbb{R}^d)} + \left\| f^j - \sum_{i=1}^{N_j} \lambda_i^j \varphi_i^j (x) \right\|_{C(\mathbb{R}^d)} \right)$$

$$< \sum_{j \in F_-(f)} d(f) \left(\frac{\varepsilon}{2} - \left\| f - f^j \right\|_{C(\mathbb{R}^d)} \right) \left(\frac{\varepsilon}{2} + \frac{\varepsilon}{2} \right) = \varepsilon \tag{4}$$

In the following step, we prove the continuity of c_k. For the proof, we use (2) to obtain

$$\sum_{j \in F_-(f)} \left(\frac{\varepsilon}{2} - \left\| \tilde{f} - f^j \right\|_{C(\mathbb{R}^d)} \right)$$

$$\leq \sum_{j \in F_-(\tilde{f})} \left(\frac{\varepsilon}{2} - \left\| \tilde{f} - f^j \right\|_{C(\mathbb{R}^d)} \right)$$

$$\leq \sum_{j \in F_-(f)} \left(\frac{\varepsilon}{2} - \left\| \tilde{f} - f^j \right\|_{C(\mathbb{R}^d)} \right) +$$

$$\sum_{j \in F_0(f)} \left(\frac{\varepsilon}{2} - \left\| \tilde{f} - f^j \right\|_{C(\mathbb{R}^d)} \right) \tag{5}$$

Let $\tilde{f} \to f$ in (5), then we have

$$\sum_{j \in F_-(\tilde{f})} \left(\frac{\varepsilon}{2} - \left\| \tilde{f} - f^j \right\|_{C(\mathbb{R}^d)} \right) \to \sum_{j \in F_-(f)} \left(\frac{\varepsilon}{2} - \left\| f - f^j \right\|_{C(\mathbb{R}^d)} \right) \tag{6}$$

This obviously demonstrates that $d(\tilde{f}) \to d(f)$. Thus, $\tilde{f} \to f$ results

$$d(\tilde{f}) \left(\frac{\varepsilon}{2} - \left\| \tilde{f} - f^j \right\|_{C(\mathbb{R}^d)} \right) \lambda_i^j \to d(f) \left(\frac{\varepsilon}{2} - \left\| f - f^j \right\|_{C(\mathbb{R}^d)} \right) \lambda_i^j \tag{7}$$

Let $N = \sum_{j \in F_-(f)} N_j$ and define c_k in terms of

$$f_h = \sum_{j \in F_-(f)} \sum_{i=1}^{N_j} d(f) \left(\frac{\varepsilon}{2} - \left\| f - f^j \right\|_{C(\mathbb{R}^d)} \right) \lambda_i^j \varphi_i^j (x)$$

$$\equiv \sum_{k=1}^{N} c_k \varphi_k (x)$$

From (7), c_k is a continuous functional of f. This completes the proof.

4. THEORETICAL ANALYSES IN THE SPACE OF LEBESGUE INTEGRABLE MULTIVARIATE FUNCTIONS

This section explains how a class of three layer feedforward higher neural net-works based on approximate identity can be used to approximate a Lebesgue integrable multivariate function to any degree of accuracy. We begin with the theorem below which will be used to prove Theorem 4.

Theorem 3. (Jones, 1993) Assume $1 \le p \le +\infty$. If $f \in L_p\left(\mathbb{R}^d\right)$ then

$$lim_{x \to y} \left\| f(x) - f(y) \right\|_{L_P\left(\mathbb{R}^d\right)} = 0$$

Theorem 4 shows that the convolution of approximate identity with every Lebesgue integrable multivariate function f converges uniformly to f on $\mathbb{R}^d$.

Theorem 4. Let $L_p\left(\mathbb{R}^d\right)$ be the linear spaces of all Lebesgue integrable functions on $\mathbb{R}^d$ with a compact support. Let $\{\varphi_n(x)\}_{n \in \mathbb{N}}$, $\varphi_n(x) : \mathbb{R}^d \to \mathbb{R}$ be an approximate identity. Let $f \in L_p\left(\mathbb{R}^d\right)$. Then $\varphi * f$ converges uniformly to f on $L_p\left(\mathbb{R}^d\right)$.

Proof. Generalized Minkowski inequality implies

$$\left\| \varphi_n * f - f \right\|_{L_P\left(\mathbb{R}^d\right)} \le \int_{\mathbb{R}^d} \left\| f(x-y) - f(x) \right\|_{L_P\left(\mathbb{R}^d\right)} \left| \varphi_n(y) \right| dy \tag{8}$$

Using Theorem 3, for any $\varepsilon > 0$, there exists a $\delta > 0$ such that if $|y| < \delta$,

$$\left\| f(x-y) - f(x) \right\|_{L_P\left(\mathbb{R}^d\right)} \le \frac{\varepsilon}{2M} \tag{9}$$

Also the triangular inequality implies

$$\left\| f(x-y) - f(x) \right\|_{L_P\left(\mathbb{R}^d\right)} \le 2 \left\| f \right\|_{L_P\left(\mathbb{R}^d\right)} \tag{10}$$

By substituting the last two inequalities (9) and (10) in inequality (8), we obtain

$$\| \varphi_n * f - f \|_{L_P\left(\mathbb{R}^d\right)} \le \int_{|y|<\delta} \frac{\varepsilon}{2M} \left| \varphi_n(y) \right| dy + \int_{|y| \ge \delta} 2 \left\| f \right\|_{L_P\left(\mathbb{R}^d\right)} \left| \varphi_n(y) \right| dy \le$$
$$\frac{\varepsilon}{2M} \int_{|y|<\delta} \left| \varphi_n(y) \right| dy + 2 \left\| f \right\|_{L_P\left(\mathbb{R}^d\right)} \int_{|y| \ge \delta} \left| \varphi_n(y) \right| dy \tag{11}$$

By Definition 1, there exists an n such that for $n \ge N$

$$\int_{|y| \ge \delta} \left| \varphi_n(y) \right| dy \le \frac{\varepsilon}{4 \left\| f \right\|_{L_P\left(\mathbb{R}^d\right)}} \tag{12}$$

Using inequality (12) in (11), it follows that for $n \geq N$

$$\| \varphi_n * f - f \|_{L_p(\mathbb{R}^d)} \leq \frac{\varepsilon}{2M}.M + 2\|f\|_{L_p(\mathbb{R}^d)} \cdot \frac{\varepsilon}{4\|f\|_{L_p(\mathbb{R}^d)}} = \varepsilon$$

We need the above theorem to state another important main result. The following main result shows universal approximation capability of three layer feedforward higher order neural networks based on approximate identity in Lebesgue spaces $L_p(\mathbb{R}^d)$. The proof follows directly from Theorem 2.

Theorem 5. Let $L_p(\mathbb{R}^d)$ be the linear spaces of all Lebesgue integrable functions on $\mathbb{R}^d$ with a compact support and $V \subset L_p(\mathbb{R}^d)$. Let $\{\varphi_n(x)\}_{n \in \mathbb{N}}$, $\varphi_n(x): \mathbb{R}^d \to \mathbb{R}$ be an approximate identity. Let the family of functions $\{ \left\{ \sum_{j=1}^{M} \lambda_j \varphi_j(x) | \lambda_j \in \mathbb{R}, x \in \mathbb{R}^d, M \in \mathbb{N} \right\}$ be dense in $L_p(\mathbb{R}^d)$, and given $\varepsilon > 0$. Then there exists an $N \in \mathbb{N}$, which depends on V and ε but not on f, such that for any $f \in V$, there exist weights $c_k = c_k(f, V, \varepsilon)$ satisfying

$$\left\| f(x) - \sum_{i=1}^{N} c_k \varphi_k(x) \right\|_{L_p(\mathbb{R}^d)} < \varepsilon$$

Moreover, every c_k is a continuous function of $f \in V$.

Proof. Because V is compact, for any ε>0, there is a finite $\frac{\varepsilon}{2}$-net $\{f^1, \ldots f^M\}$ for V. This implies that for any $f \in V$, there is an f^j such that $\|f - f^j\|_{L_p(\mathbb{R}^d)} < \frac{\varepsilon}{2}$. For any f^j, by assumption of the theorem, there are $\lambda_i^j \in \mathbb{R}, N_j \in \mathbb{N}$, and $\varphi_i^j(x)$ such that

$$\left\| f^j(x) - \sum_{i=1}^{N_j} \lambda_i^j \varphi_i^j(x) \right\|_{L_p(\mathbb{R}^d)} < \frac{\varepsilon}{2} \tag{13}$$

For any $f \in V$, we define

$$F_-(f) = \left\{ j \mid \|f - f^j\|_{L_p(\mathbb{R}^d)} < \frac{\varepsilon}{2} \right\}$$

$$F_0(f) = \left\{ j \mid \|f - f^j\|_{L_p(\mathbb{R}^d)} = \frac{\varepsilon}{2} \right\}$$

$$F_+(f) = \left\{ j \mid \|f - f^j\|_{L_p(\mathbb{R}^d)} > \frac{\varepsilon}{2} \right\}$$

Therefore, $F_-(f)$ is not empty according to the definition of $\frac{\varepsilon}{2}$-net. If $\tilde{f} \in V$ approaches f such that $\|\tilde{f} - f\|_{L_p(\mathbb{R}^d)}$ is small enough, then we have $F_-(f) \subset F_-(\tilde{f})$ and $F_+(f) \subset F_+(\tilde{f})$. Thus $F_-(\tilde{f}) \bigcap F_+(f) \subset F_-(\tilde{f}) \bigcap F_+(\tilde{f}) = \varnothing$, which implies $F_-(\tilde{f}) \subset F_-(f) \bigcup F_0(f)$. We finish with the following.

$$F_-(f) \subset F_-(\tilde{f}) \subset F_-(f) \bigcup F_0(f) \tag{14}$$

Define

$$d(f) = \left[\sum_{j \in F_-(f)} \left(\frac{\varepsilon}{2} - \|f - f^j\|_{L_p(\mathbb{R}^d)} \right) \right]^{-1}$$

and

$$f_h = \sum_{j \in F_-(f)} \sum_{i=1}^{N_j} d(f) \left(\frac{\varepsilon}{2} - \|f - f^j\|_{L_p(\mathbb{R}^d)} \right) \lambda_i^j \varphi_i^j(x) \tag{15}$$

Then $f_h \in \left\{ \sum_{j=1}^{M} \lambda_j \varphi_j(x) \right\}$ approximates f with accuracy ε:

$$\|f - f_h\|_{L_p(\mathbb{R}^d)}$$

$$= \left\| \sum_{j \in F_-(f)} d(f) \left(\frac{\varepsilon}{2} - \|f - f^j\|_{L_p(\mathbb{R}^d)} \right) \left(f - \sum_{i=1}^{N_j} \lambda_i^j \varphi_i^j(x) \right) \right\|_{L_p(\mathbb{R}^d)}$$

$$= \left\| \sum_{j \in F_-(f)} d(f) \left(\frac{\varepsilon}{2} - \|f - f^j\|_{L_p(\mathbb{R}^d)} \right) (f - f^j + f^f - \right.$$

$$i = 1 N j \lambda i j \varphi(x)) L p(\mathbb{R} \wedge d)$$

$$\leq \sum_{j\in F_-(f)} d(f)\left(\frac{\varepsilon}{2}-\left\|f-f^j\right\|_{L_p(\mathbb{R}^d)}\right)\left(\left\|f-f^j\right\|_{L_p(\mathbb{R}^d)}+\left\|f^j-\sum_{i=1}^{N_j}\lambda_i^j\varphi_i^j(\boldsymbol{x})\right\|_{L_p(\mathbb{R}^d)}\right)$$

$$< \sum_{j\in F_-(f)} d(f)\left(\frac{\varepsilon}{2}-\left\|f-f^j\right\|_{L_p(\mathbb{R}^d)}\right)\left(\frac{\varepsilon}{2}+\frac{\varepsilon}{2}\right)=\varepsilon \tag{16}$$

In the following step, we prove the continuity of c_k. For the proof, we use (14) to obtain

$$\sum_{j\in F_-(f)}\left(\frac{\varepsilon}{2}-\left\|\tilde{f}-f^j\right\|_{L_p(\mathbb{R}^d)}\right)$$

$$\leq \sum_{j\in F_-(\tilde{f})}\left(\frac{\varepsilon}{2}-\left\|\tilde{f}-f^j\right\|_{L_p(\mathbb{R}^d)}\right)$$

$$\leq \sum_{j\in F_-(f)}\left(\frac{\varepsilon}{2}-\left\|\tilde{f}-f^j\right\|_{L_p(\mathbb{R}^d)}\right)+$$

$$\sum_{j\in F_0(f)}\left(\frac{\varepsilon}{2}-\left\|\tilde{f}-f^j\right\|_{L_p(\mathbb{R}^d)}\right) \tag{17}$$

Let $\tilde{f}\to f$ in (17), then we have

$$\sum_{j\in F_-(\tilde{f})}\left(\frac{\varepsilon}{2}-\left\|\tilde{f}-f^j\right\|_{L_p(\mathbb{R}^d)}\right)\to \sum_{j\in F_-(f)}\left(\frac{\varepsilon}{2}-\left\|f-f^j\right\|_{L_p(\mathbb{R}^d)}\right) \tag{18}$$

This obviously demonstrates $d(\tilde{f})\to d(f)$. Thus, $\tilde{f}\to f$ results

$$d(\tilde{f})\left(\frac{\varepsilon}{2}-\left\|\tilde{f}-f^j\right\|_{L_p(\mathbb{R}^d)}\right)\lambda_i^j \to d(f)\left(\frac{\varepsilon}{2}-\left\|f-f^j\right\|_{L_p(\mathbb{R}^d)}\right)\lambda_i^j \tag{19}$$

Let $N=\sum_{j\in F_-(f)}N_j$ and define c_k in terms of

$$f_h=\sum_{j\in F_-(f)}\sum_{i=1}^{N_j}d(f)\left(\frac{\varepsilon}{2}-\left\|f-f^j\right\|_{L_p(\mathbb{R}^d)}\right)\lambda_i^j\varphi_i^j(\boldsymbol{x})$$

$$\equiv \sum_{k=1}^{N} c_k \varphi_k \left(x \right)$$

From (19), c_k is a continuous functional of f. This completes the proof.

5. CONCLUSION

Multivariate function approximation arises in many problems such as statistics, physics and engineering. Multivariate function approximation also provides an accuracy stronger than univariate approximation. However, this topic is much less developed than univariate approximation. Future work is required to show the usefulness of the multivariate approximation. The overall aim of this study has been to develop a framework for universal approximation capability of feedforward neural networks. In this study, we have investigated the universal approximation capability of a special class of three layer feedforward higher order neural networks based on the notion of approximate identity. We have presented two main contributions. First, we have shown that the networks are universal approximators in the space of continuous multivariate functions. $C\left(\mathbb{R}^d \right)$. Second, we have also proved that the networks are universal approximators in the Lebesgue spaces $L_p\left(\mathbb{R}^d \right)$. The obtained theoretical analyses can be seen as an attempt to merge higher order neural networks and approximate identity neural networks towards the development of the approximation theory by means of artificial neural networks. It is important to mention that the proof of the main theorems provides only crude estimation for the upper bound of the error of approximations. Thus, for computational purposes, it would be interesting to establish results which state the tighter bound for good approximations to a given function f. Numerical examples of the proposed structures are in preparation.

ACKNOWLEDGMENT

We gratefully acknowledge the financial assistance provided by The Ministry of Education, Malaysia, under the Fundamental Research Grant Scheme (FRGS) and Universiti Sains Malaysia for postdoctoral research fellow program.

REFERENCES

Arteaga, C., & Marrero, I. (2013). Universal approximation by radial basis function networks of delsarte translates. *Neural Networks*, *46*, 299–305. doi:10.1016/j.neunet.2013.06.011 PMID:23876407

Arteaga, C., & Marrero, I. (2014). Approximation in weighted p-mean by RBF networks of Delsarte translates. *Journal of Mathematical Analysis and Applications*, *414*(1), 450–460. doi:10.1016/j.jmaa.2014.01.012

Bouaziz, S., Alimi, A. M., & Abraham, A. (2014) Universal approximation propriety of flexible beta basis function neural tree. *Proceedings of the International Joint Conference on Neural Networks (IJCNN)* (pp. 573-580). doi:10.1109/IJCNN.2014.6889671

Costarelli, D. (2014). Interpolation by neural network operators activated by ramp functions. *Journal of Mathematical Analysis and Applications, 419*(1), 574–582. doi:10.1016/j.jmaa.2014.05.013

Cybenko, G. (1989). Approximation by superpositions of a sigmoidal function. *Mathematics of Control, Signals, and Systems, 2*(4), 303–314. doi:10.1007/BF02551274

Funuhashi, K. (1989). On the approximate realization of continuous mapping by neural networks. *Neural Networks, 2*, 359–366.

Giles, L., & Maxwell, T. (1987). Learning, invariance and generalization in high order neural networks. *Applied Optics, 26*(23), 4972–4978. doi:10.1364/AO.26.004972 PMID:20523475

Hahm, N., & Hong, B. I. (2004). An approximation by neural networks with a fixed weight. *Computers & Mathematics with Applications (Oxford, England), 47*(12), 1897–1903. doi:10.1016/j.camwa.2003.06.008

Ismailov, V. E. (2012). Approximation by neural networks with weights varying on a finite set of directions. *Journal of Mathematical Analysis and Applications, 398*(1), 72–83. doi:10.1016/j.jmaa.2011.11.037

Ismailov, V. E. (2014). On the approximation by neural networks with bounded number of neurons in hidden layers. *Journal of Mathematical Analysis and Applications, 417*(2), 963–969. doi:10.1016/j.jmaa.2014.03.092

Jones, F. (1993). *Lebesgue integration on Euclidean space*. Jones and Bartlett.

Lebedev, V. (1997). *An introduction to functional analysis and computational mathematics*. Boston: Brikhauser.

Leshno, M., Pinkus, A., & Schocken, S. (1993). Multilayer feedforward neural networks with a polynomial activation function can approximate any function. *Neural Networks, 6*(6), 861–867. doi:10.1016/S0893-6080(05)80131-5

Li, F. (2008). Function approximation by neural networks. *Proceedings of the 5th International symposium on Neural Networks, LNCS* (Vol. 5263, pp. 384–390). doi:10.1007/978-3-540-87732-5_43

Lin, S., Guo, X., Cao, F., & Xu, Z. (2013). Approximation by neural networks with scattered data. *Applied Mathematics and Computation, 224*, 29–35. doi:10.1016/j.amc.2013.08.014

Long, J., Wu, W., & Nan, D. (2007). Lp approximation capabilities of sum-of-product and sigma-pi-sigma neural networks. *International Journal of Neural Systems, 17*(05), 419–424. doi:10.1142/S0129065707001251 PMID:18098373

Long, J., Wu, W., & Nan, D. (2007a). Uniform approximation capabilities of sum-of product and sigma-pi-sigma neural networks. In Advances in Neural Networks, *LNCS* (Vol. *4491*, pp. 1110–1116). doi:10.1007/978-3-540-72383-7_130

Mhaskar, H. N. (1993). Approximation properties of a multilayered feedforward artificial neural network. *Advances in Computational Mathematics, 1*(1), 61–80. doi:10.1007/BF02070821

Nong, J. (2013) Conditions for radial basis function neural networks to universal approximation and numerical experiments. *Proceedings of the 25th Chinese Control and Decision Conference CCDC '13* (pp. 2193-2197). IEEE. doi:10.1109/CCDC.2013.6561299

Panahian Fard, S., & Zainuddin, Z. (2013). On the universal approximation capability of flexible approximate identity neural networks. In Emerging technologies for Information systems, computing and management,*LNEE* (Vol. *236*, pp. 201–207). doi:10.1007/978-1-4614-7010-6_23

Panahian Fard, S., & Zainuddin, Z. (2013a). The universal approximation capabilities of Mellin approximate identity neural networks. In Advances in Neural Networks,*LNCS* (Vol. *7951*, pp. 205–213). doi:10.1007/978-3-642-39065-4_26

Panahian Fard, S., & Zainuddin, Z. (2014). Analyses for Lp[a, b]-norm approximation capability of flexible approximate identity neural networks. *Neural Computing & Applications*, *24*(1), 45–50. doi:10.1007/s00521-013-1493-9

Panahian Fard, S., & Zainuddin, Z. (2014a). The Universal Approximation Capability of Double Flexible Approximate Identity Neural Networks. In Computer Engineering and Networking, *LNEE* (Vol. *277*, pp. 125–133). doi:10.1007/978-3-319-01766-2_15

Panahian Fard, S., & Zainuddin, Z. (2014b) The universal approximation capabilities of pi-periodic approximate identity neural networks. *Proceedings of the 2013 International Conference on Information Science and Cloud Computing (ISCC)* (pp. 793-798). IEEE. doi:10.1007/s00500-014-1449-8

Panahian Fard, S., & Zainuddin, Z. (2014d). Toroidal approximate identity neural networks are universal approximators. In Neural Information Processing, *LNCS* (Vol. *8834*, pp. 135–142). doi:10.1007/978-3-319-12637-1_17

Panahian Fard, S., & Zainuddin, Z. (2015). The universal approximation capabilities of double periodic approximate identity neural networks. *Soft Computing*, *19*(10), 2883–2890. doi:10.1007/s00500-014-1449-8

Pao, Y. (1989) Adaptive Pattern Recognition and Neural Networks. Addison-Wesley, USA, ISBN: 0 201012584-6

Park, J., & Sandberg, I. W. (1991). Universal approximation using radial-basis-function networks. *Neural Computation*, *3*(2), 246–257. doi:10.1162/neco.1991.3.2.246

Park, J., & Sandberg, I. W. (1993). Approximation and radial-basis-functions networks. *Neural Computation*, *5*(2), 305–316. doi:10.1162/neco.1993.5.2.305

Principe, J. C., & Chen, B. (2015). Universal approximation with convex optimization: Gimmic or reality? *IEEE Computational Intelligence Magazine*, *10*, 68–77. doi:10.1109/MCI.2015.2405352

Schmidt, W. A. C., & Davis, J. P. (1993). Pattern recognition properties of various feature spaces for higher order neural networks. *IEEE Transactions on Pattern Analysis and Machine Intelligence*, 1993, 15.

Suzuki, S. (1998). Constructive function approximation by three-layer artificial neural networks. *Neural Networks*, *11*(6), 1049–1058. doi:10.1016/S0893-6080(98)00068-9 PMID:12662774

Tikk, D., Koczy, L. T., & Gedeon, T. D. (2003). A survey on universal approximation and its limits in soft computing techniques. *International Journal of Approximate Reasoning*, *33*(2), 185–202. doi:10.1016/S0888-613X(03)00021-5

Turchetti, C., Conti, M., Crippa, P., & Orcioni, S. (1998). On the approximation of stochastic processes by approximate identity neural networks. *IEEE Transactions on Neural Networks*, *9*(6), 1069–1085. doi:10.1109/72.728353 PMID:18255793

Wang, J., Chen, B., & Yang, C. (2012). Approximation of algebraic and trigonometric polynomials by feedforward neural networks. *Neural Computing & Applications*, *21*(1), 73–80. doi:10.1007/s00521-011-0617-3

Wang, J., & Xu, Z. (2010). New study on neural networks: The essential order of approximation. *Neural Networks*, *23*(5), 618–624. doi:10.1016/j.neunet.2010.01.004 PMID:20138734

Wu, W., Nan, D., Li, Z., & Long, J. (2007) Approximation to compact set of functions by feedforward neural networks.*Proceedings of the International Joint Conference on Neural Networks (Vol. 20*, pp. 1222-1225). doi:10.1109/IJCNN.2007.4371132

Zainuddin, Z., & Panahian Fard, S. (2012). Double approximate identity neural networks universal approximation in real Lebesgue space. In Neural Information Processing,*LNCS* (Vol. *7663*, pp. 409–415). doi:10.1007/978-3-642-34475-6_49

Zainuddin, Z., & Panahian Fard, S. (2014c) Spherical approximate identity neural networks are universal approximators. *Proceedings of the 10th International Conference on Natural Computation (ICNC)* (pp. 72-76). IEEE. doi:10.1109/ICNC.2014.6975812

Zhang, M., Xu, S., & Fulcher, J. (2002). Neuron-adaptive higher order neural-network models for automated financial data modeling. *IEEE Transactions on Neural Networks*, *13*(1), 188–204. doi:10.1109/72.977302 PMID:18244418

Chapter 9

Artificial Sine and Cosine Trigonometric Higher Order Neural Networks for Financial Data Prediction

Ming Zhang
Christopher Newport University, USA

ABSTRACT

This chapter develops two new nonlinear artificial higher order neural network models. They are Sine and Sine Higher Order Neural Networks (SIN-HONN) and Cosine and Cosine Higher Order Neural Networks (COS-HONN). Financial data prediction using SIN-HONN and COS-HONN models are tested. Results show that SIN-HONN and COS-HONN models are good models for financial data prediction compare with Polynomial Higher Order Neural Network (PHONN) and Trigonometric Higher Order Neural Network (THONN) models.

INTRODUCTION

The contributions of this chapter will be:

- Introduce the background of HONNs with the applications of HONNs in prediction area.
- Develop new HONN models called SIN-HONN and COS-HONN for financial data prediction.
- Provide the SIN-HONN and COS-HONN learning algorithm and weight update formulae.
- Compare SIN-HONN and COS-HONN with PHONN and THONN for data prediction.

This chapter is organized as follows: Section BACKGROUND gives the background knowledge of HONNs and introduction to applications using HONN in the data prediction area. Section SIN-HONN AND COS-HONN MODELS introduces both SIN-HONN structure and COS-HONN structure. Section LEARNING ALGORITHM OF SIN-HONN AND COS-HONN MODELS provides the SIN-HONN model and COS-HONN model update formula, learning algorithms, and convergence theories. Section FINANCIAL DATA PREDICTION USING HONN MODELS compares SIN-HONN and COS-HONN

DOI: 10.4018/978-1-5225-0063-6.ch009

models with other HONN models, and shows the results for data prediction using SIN-HONN and COS-HONN models.

BACKGROUND

Artificial Neural Network (ANN) has been widely used in prediction area. Durbin and Rumelhart (1989) study a computationally powerful and biologically plausible extension to backpropagation networks. Yapo, Embrechets, and Cathey (1992) analyze prediction of critical heat using a hybrid kohon-backpropagation neural network intelligent. Moon and Chang (1994) experiment classification and prediction of the critical heat flux using fuzzy clustering and artificial neural networks. Charitou and Charalambous (1996) show the prediction of earnings using financial statement information with logic models and artificial neural networks. Doulamis, Doulamis, and Kollias (2000) research recursive nonlinear models for online traffic prediction of VBR MPEG Coded video sources. Atiya (2001) seeks bankruptcy prediction for credit risk using neural networks. Su, Fukuda, Jia, and Morita (2002) look into application of an artificial neural network in reactor thermo hydraulic problem which related to prediction of critical heat flux. Doulamis, Doulamis, and Kollias, (2003) revise an adaptable neural network model for recursive nonlinear traffic prediction and modeling of MPEG video sources. Sanchez, Alanis, and Rico (2004) expose electric load demand prediction using neural networks trained by Kalman filtering. Shawver (2005) scrutinize merger premium predictions using neural network approach.

Vaziri, Hojabri, Erfani, Monsey, and Nilforooshan (2007) disclose critical heat flux prediction by using radial basis function and multilayer perceptron neural networks. Welch, Ruffing, and Venayagamoorthy (2009) display comparison of feed-forward and feedback neural network architectures for short term wind speed prediction.

Artificial Higher Order Neural Network (HONN) has been widly used in the prediction areas as well. Saad, Prokhorov, and Wunsch (1998) provide comparative study of stock trend prediction using time delay recurrent and probabilistic neural networks. Zhang and Fulcher (2004) grant higher order neural networks for satellite weather prediction. Fulcher, Zhang, and Xu (2006) demonstrate an application of higher-order neural networks to financial time series prediction.

Knowles, Hussain, Dereby, Lisboa, and Dunis (2009) develop higher order neural networks with Bayesian confidence measure for the prediction of the EUR/USD exchange rate. The higher order neural networks can be considered a 'stripped-down' version of MLPs, where joint activation terms are used, relieving the network of the task of learning the relationships between the inputs. The predictive performance of the network is tested with the EUR/USD exchange rate and evaluated using standard financial criteria including the annualized return on investment, showing an 8% increase in the return compared with the MLP. The output of the networks that give the highest annualized return in each category was subjected to a Bayesian based confidence measure.

Shi, Tan, and Ge (2009) expand automatically identifying predictor variables for stock return prediction and address nonlinear problem by developing a technique consisting of a top-down part using an artificial Higher Order Neural Network (HONN) model and a bottom-up part based on a Bayesian Network (BN) model to automatically identify predictor variables for the stock return prediction from a large financial variable set. Our study provides an operational guidance for using HONN and BN in selecting predictor variables from a large amount of financial variables to support the prediction of the stock return, including the prediction of future stock return value and future stock return movement trends.

Chen, Wu, and Wu (2009) focus foreign exchange rate forecasting using higher order flexible neural tree and establish that forecasting exchange rates is an important financial problem that is receiving increasing attention especially because of its difficulty and practical applications. In this chapter, we apply Higher Order Flexible Neural Trees (HOFNTs), which are capable of designing flexible Artificial Neural Network (ANN) architectures automatically, to forecast the foreign exchange rates. To demonstrate the efficiency of HOFNTs, we consider three different datasets in our forecast performance analysis. The data sets used are daily foreign exchange rates obtained from the Pacific Exchange Rate Service. The data comprises of the US dollar exchange rate against Euro, Great Britain Pound (GBP) and Japanese Yen (JPY). Under the HOFNT framework, we consider the Gene Expression Programming (GEP) approach and the Grammar Guided Genetic Programming (GGGP) approach to evolve the structure of HOFNT. The particle swarm optimization algorithm is employed to optimize the free parameters of the two different HOFNT models. This chapter briefly explains how the two different learning paradigms could be formulated using various methods and then investigates whether they can provide a reliable forecast model for foreign exchange rates. Simulation results are shown the effectiveness of the proposed methods.

Hussain, and Liatsis (2009) learn a novel recurrent polynomial neural network for financial time series prediction and this research is concerned with the development of a novel artificial higher-order neural networks architecture called the recurrent Pi-sigma neural network. The proposed artificial neural network combines the advantages of both higher-order architectures in terms of the multi-linear interactions between inputs, as well as the temporal dynamics of recurrent neural networks, and produces highly accurate one-step ahead of predictions of the foreign currency exchange rates, as compared to other feed-forward and recurrent structures.

Selviah, and Shawash (2009) generalize correlation higher order neural networks for financial time series prediction and develop a generalized correlation higher order neural network designs. Their performance is compared with that of first order networks, conventional higher order neural network designs, and higher order linear regression networks for financial time series prediction. The correlation higher order neural network design is shown to give the highest accuracy for prediction of stock market share prices and share indices. The simulations compare the performance for three different training algorithms, stationary versus non-stationary input data, different numbers of neurons in the hidden layer and several generalized correlation higher order neural network designs. Generalized correlation higher order linear regression networks are also introduced and two designs are shown by simulation to give good correct direction prediction and higher prediction accuracies, particularly for long-term predictions, than other linear regression networks for the prediction of inter-bank lending risk Libor and Swap interest rate yield curves. The simulations compare the performance for different input data sample lag lengths.

Onwubolu (2009) tests the artificial higher order neural networks in time series prediction and describes real world problems of nonlinear and chaotic processes, which make them hard to model and predict. This chapter first compares the neural network (NN) and the artificial higher order neural network (HONN) and then presents commonly known neural network architectures and a number of HONN architectures. The time series prediction problem is formulated as a system identification problem, where the input to the system is the past values of a time series, and its desired output is the future values of a time series. The polynomial neural network (PNN) is then chosen as the HONN for application to the time series prediction problem. This chapter presents the application of HONN model to the nonlinear time series prediction problems of three major international currency exchange rates, as well as two key U.S. interest rates—the Federal funds rate and the yield on the 5-year U.S. Treasury note. Empirical results indicate that the proposed method is competitive with other approaches for the exchange rate problem, and can be used as a feasible solution for interest rate forecasting problem. This implies that the HONN model can be used as a feasible solution for exchange rate forecasting as well as for interest rate forecasting.

Ghazali, and Al-Jumeily (2009) offer the application of Pi-Sigma neural networks and ridge polynomial neural networks to financial time series prediction and discuss the use of two artificial Higher Order Neural Networks (HONNs) models; the Pi-Sigma Neural Networks and the Ridge Polynomial Neural Networks, in financial time series forecasting. The networks were used to forecast the upcoming trends of three noisy financial signals; the exchange rate between the US Dollar and the Euro, the exchange rate between the Japanese Yen and the Euro, and the United States 10-year government bond. In particular, we systematically investigate a method of pre-processing the signals in order to reduce the trends in them. The performance of the networks is benchmarked against the performance of Multilayer Perceptrons. From the simulation results, the predictions clearly demonstrated that HONNs models, particularly Ridge Polynomial Neural Networks generate higher profit returns with fast convergence, therefore show considerable promise as a decision making tool. It is hoped that individual investor could benefit from the use of this forecasting tool.

Sanchez, Alanis, and Rico (2009) intent the electric load demand and electricity prices forecasting using higher order neural networks Trained by Kalman Filtering, and proposes the use of *Higher Order Neural Networks* (HONNs) trained with an *extended Kalman filter* based algorithm to predict the electric load demand as well as the electricity prices, with beyond a horizon of 24 hours. Due to the *chaotic behavior* of the electrical markets, it is not advisable to apply the traditional forecasting techniques used for time series; the results presented here confirm that HONNs can very well capture the complexity underlying electric load demand and electricity prices. The proposed neural network model produces very accurate next day predictions and also, prognosticates with very good accuracy, a week-ahead demand and price forecasts.

Eskander, and Atiya (2013) derive symbolic function network for the application to telecommunication networks prediction and introduce that Quality of Service (QoS) of telecommunication networks could be enhanced by applying predictive control methods. Such controllers rely on utilizing good and fast (real-time) predictions of the network traffic and quality parameters. Accuracy and recall speed of the traditional Neural Network models are not satisfactory to support such critical real-time applications. The Symbolic Function Network (SFN) is a HONN-like model that was originally motivated by the current needs of developing more enhanced and fast predictors for such applications. In this chapter, authors use the SFN model to design fast and accurate predictors for the telecommunication networks quality control applications. Three predictors are designed and tested for the network traffic, packet loss, and round trip delay. This chapter aims to open a door for researchers to investigate the applicability of SFN in other prediction tasks and to develop more accurate and faster predictors.

Ricalde, Catzin, Alanis, and Sanchez (2013) investigate time series forecasting via. higher order neural network trained with the extended Kalman filter for smart grid applications, and present the design of a neural network which combines higher order terms in its input layer and an Extended Kalman Filter (EKF) based algorithm for its training. The neural network based scheme is defined as a Higher Order Neural Network (HONN) and its applicability is illustrated by means of time series forecasting for three important variables present in smart grids: Electric Load Demand (ELD), Wind Speed (WS) and Wind Energy Generation (WEG). The proposed model is trained and tested using real data values taken from a microgrid system in the UADY School of Engineering. The length of the regression vector is determined via the Lipschitz quotients methodology.

SIN-HONN AND COS-HONN MODELS

Sine and Sine Trigonometric Higher Order Neural Network (SIN-HONN) and Cosine and Cosine Trigonometric Higher Order Neural Network (SIN-HONN) structures and model descriptions are shown as following. SIN-HONN model structure can be seen in Figure 1, while COS-HONN model structure can be seen in Figure 2.

Figure 1. SIN-HONN Architecture

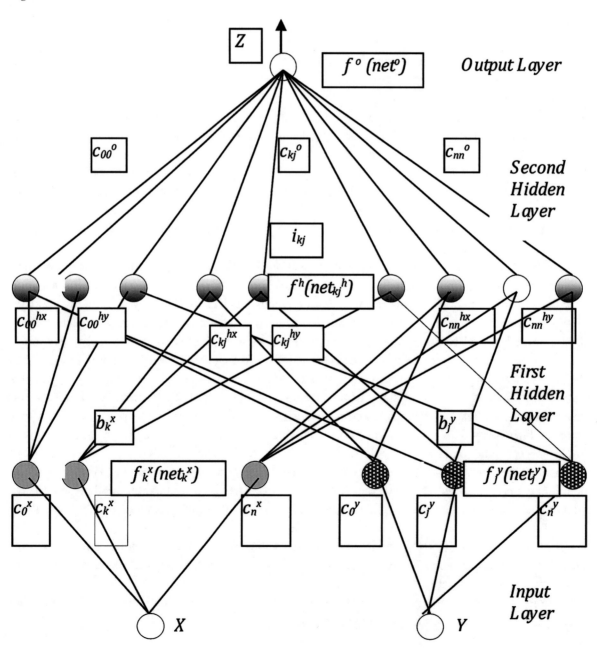

Figure 2.

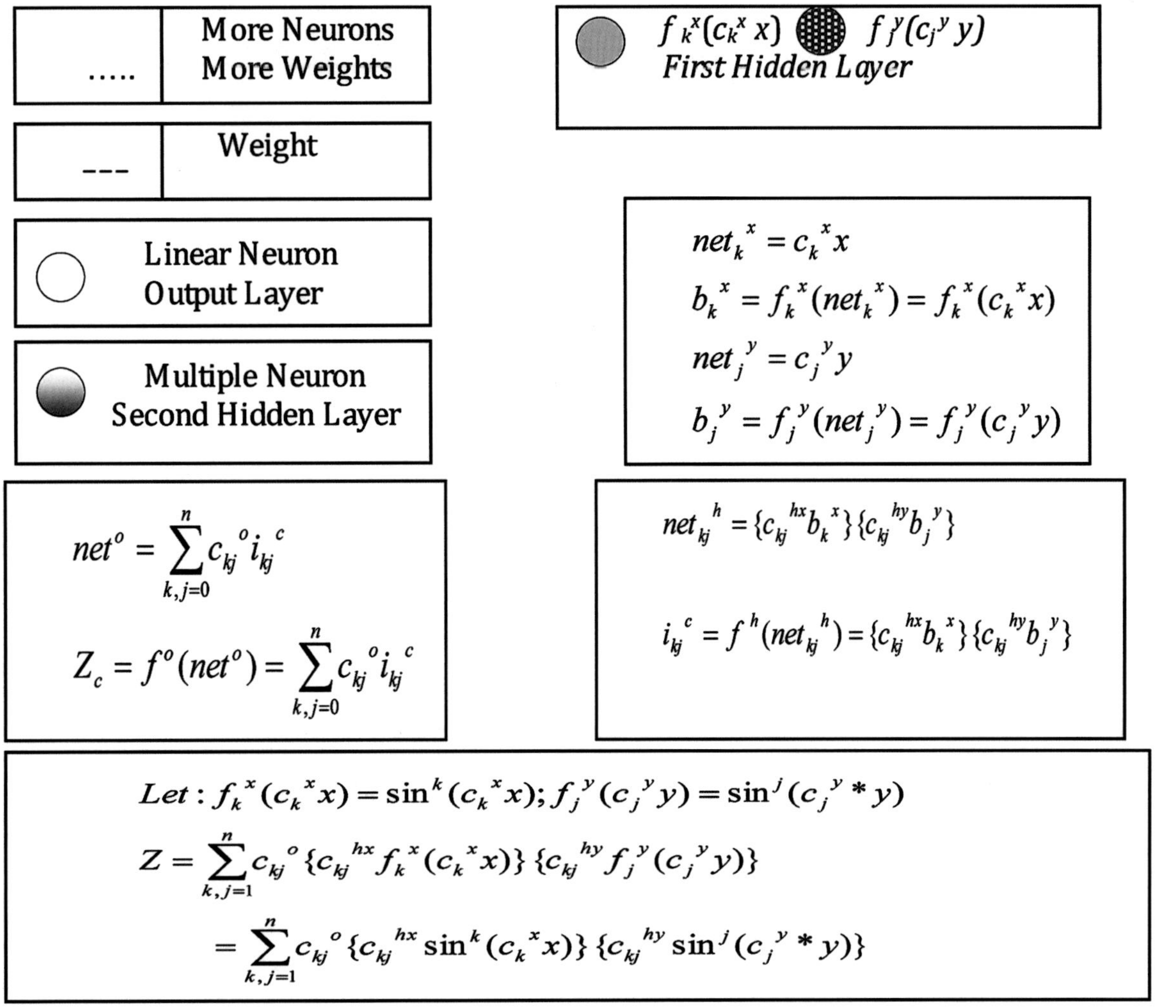

	More Neurons
.....	More Weights

	Weight

◯	Linear Neuron Output Layer

⬤	Multiple Neuron Second Hidden Layer

⬤	$f_k{}^x(c_k{}^x x)$ $f_j{}^y(c_j{}^y y)$ *First Hidden Layer*

$$net_k{}^x = c_k{}^x x$$
$$b_k{}^x = f_k{}^x(net_k{}^x) = f_k{}^x(c_k{}^x x)$$
$$net_j{}^y = c_j{}^y y$$
$$b_j{}^y = f_j{}^y(net_j{}^y) = f_j{}^y(c_j{}^y y)$$

$$net^o = \sum_{k,j=0}^{n} c_{kj}{}^o i_{kj}{}^c$$
$$Z_c = f^o(net^o) = \sum_{k,j=0}^{n} c_{kj}{}^o i_{kj}{}^c$$

$$net_{kj}{}^h = \{c_{kj}{}^{hx} b_k{}^x\}\{c_{kj}{}^{hy} b_j{}^y\}$$
$$i_{kj}{}^c = f^h(net_{kj}{}^h) = \{c_{kj}{}^{hx} b_k{}^x\}\{c_{kj}{}^{hy} b_j{}^y\}$$

$$Let : f_k{}^x(c_k{}^x x) = \sin^k(c_k{}^x x); f_j{}^y(c_j{}^y y) = \sin^j(c_j{}^y * y)$$
$$Z = \sum_{k,j=1}^{n} c_{kj}{}^o \{c_{kj}{}^{hx} f_k{}^x(c_k{}^x x)\}\{c_{kj}{}^{hy} f_j{}^y(c_j{}^y y)\}$$
$$= \sum_{k,j=1}^{n} c_{kj}{}^o \{c_{kj}{}^{hx} \sin^k(c_k{}^x x)\}\{c_{kj}{}^{hy} \sin^j(c_j{}^y * y)\}$$

SIN-HONN Model

Sine Higher Order Neural Network (SIN-HONN) model is as follows:

$Let :$
$$f_k{}^x(c_k{}^x x) = \sin^k(c_k{}^x x)$$
$$f_j{}^y(c_j{}^y y) = \sin^j(c_j{}^y y)$$

$SINHONN \quad Model \quad 0 :$

$$z = \sum_{k,j=0}^{n} c_{kj}{}^o \, \sin^k(x) \sin^j(y)$$
$$where: \quad (c_{kj}{}^{hx}) = (c_{kj}{}^{hy}) = 1$$
$$and \quad c_k{}^x = c_j{}^y = 1 \qquad (SIN-HONN \qquad 0)$$

SINHONN   *Model*   1:

$$z = \sum_{k,j=0}^{n} c_{kj}{}^{o} \, \sin^{k}(c_k{}^{x}x)\sin^{j}(c_j{}^{y}y)$$

where: $(c_{kj}{}^{hx}) = (c_{kj}{}^{hy}) = 1$ $(SIN-HONN$ $1)$

SINHONN   *Model*   2:

$$Z = \sum_{k,j=0}^{n} (c_{kj}{}^{o})\{c_{kj}{}^{hx} \sin^{k}(c_k{}^{x}x)\} \{c_{kj}{}^{hy} \sin^{j}(c_j{}^{y}y)\} \qquad (SIN-HONN \qquad 2)$$

COS-HONN Model

Cosine Higher Order Neural Network (COS-HONN) model is as follows:

Let:

$$f_k{}^{x}(c_k{}^{x}x) = \cos^{k}(c_k{}^{x}x)$$
$$f_j{}^{y}(c_j{}^{y}y) = \cos^{j}(c_j{}^{y}y)$$

COSHONN   *Model*   0:

$$z = \sum_{k,j=0}^{n} c_{kj}{}^{o} \, \cos^{k}(x)\cos^{j}(y)$$

where: $(c_{kj}{}^{hx}) = (c_{kj}{}^{hy}) = 1$

    and $c_k{}^{x} = c_j{}^{y} = 1$ $(COS-HONN \qquad 0)$

COSHONN   *Model*   1:

$$z = \sum_{k,j=0}^{n} c_{kj}{}^{o} \, \cos^{k}(c_k{}^{x}x)\cos^{j}(c_j{}^{y}y)$$

where: $(c_{kj}{}^{hx}) = (c_{kj}{}^{hy}) = 1$ $(COS-HONN \qquad 1)$

COSHONN   *Model*   2:

$$Z = \sum_{k,j=0}^{n} (c_{kj}{}^{o})\{c_{kj}{}^{hx} \cos^{k}(c_k{}^{x}x)\} \{c_{kj}{}^{hy} con^{j}(c_j{}^{y}y)\} \qquad (COS-HONN \qquad 2)$$

LEARNING ALGORITHM OF SIN-HONN AND COS-HONN MODELS

Learning Algorithm of HONN Model

Output Neurons in HONN Model (Model 0, 1, and 2)

The output layer weights are updated according to:

$$c_{kj}^{\ o}(t+1) = c_{kj}^{\ o}(t) - \eta(\partial E \ / \partial c_{kj}^{\ o}) \qquad (A.1)$$

where = learning rate (positive and usually < 1)

c_{kj} = weight; index k an j = input index

(k, j=0, 1, 2,...,n means one of n*n input neurons from the second hidden layer)

E = error

t = training time

o = output layer

The output node equations are:

$$net^{\ o} = \sum_{k,j=1}^{n} c_{kj}^{\ o} i_{kj}$$

$$z = f^{\ o}(net^{\ o}) = \sum_{k,j=1}^{n} c_{kj}^{\ o} i_{kj} \qquad (A.2)$$

where i_{kj} = input to the output neuron (= output from 2nd hidden layer)

z = actual output from the output neuron

f^{o} = output neuron activity function

The error at a particular output unit (neuron) will be:

$$\delta = (d - z) \qquad (A.3)$$

where d = desired output value

The total error is the error of output unit, namely:

$$E = 0.5 * \delta^{2} = 0.5 * (d - z)^{2} \qquad (A.4)$$

The derivatives $f^{o'}(net^o)$ are calculated as follows:

The output neuron function is linear function ($f^o(net^o) = net^o$):

$$f^o{}'(net^o) = \partial f^o / \partial(net)^o = \partial(net^o) / \partial(net^o) = 1 \qquad (A.5)$$

Gradients aore calculated as follows:

$$\partial E / \partial c_{kj}{}^o = (\partial E / \partial z)(\partial z / \partial(net^o))(\partial(net^o) / \partial c_{kj}{}^o) \qquad (A.6)$$

$$\partial E / \partial z = \partial(0.5*(d-z)^2) / \partial z) = 0.5*(-2(d-z)) = -(d-z) \qquad (A.7)$$

$$\partial z / \partial(net^o) = \partial f^o / \partial(net^o) = f^o{}'(net^o) \qquad (A.8)$$

$$\partial(net^o) / \partial_{kj}{}^o = \partial(\sum_{k,j=0}^{n} c_{kj}{}^o i_{kj}) / \partial c_{kj}{}^o = i_{kj}$$

Combining Eqns. A.6 through A.9, the negative gradient is:

$$-\partial E / \partial c_{kj}{}^o = (d-z)f^o{}'(net^o)i_{kj} \qquad (A.10)$$

For a linear output neuron, this becomes, by combining Eqns. A.10 and A.5:

$$-\partial E / \partial c_{kj}{}^o = (d-z)f^o{}'(net^o)i_{kj}$$
$$= (d-z)(1)i_{kj} = (d-z)i_{kj} \qquad (A.11)$$

The weight update equations are formulated as follows:for linear output neurons, let:

$$\delta^{ol} = (d-z) \qquad (A.12)$$

Combining Formulae A.1, A.11, and A.12:

$$c_{kj}{}^o(t+1) = c_{kj}{}^o(t) - \eta(\partial E / \partial a_{kj}{}^o)$$
$$= c_{kj}{}^o(t) + \eta(d-z)f^o{}'(net^o)i_{kj}$$
$$= a_{kj}{}^o(t) + \eta \delta^{ol} i_{kj}$$
$$where:$$
$$\delta^{ol} = (d-z)$$
$$f^{o'}(net^o) = 1 \qquad (linear \qquad neuron) \qquad (A.13)$$

Second-Hidden Layer Neurons in HONN Model (Model 2)

The second hidden layer weights are updated according to:

$$c_{kj}{}^{hx}(t+1) = c_{kj}{}^{hx}(t) - \eta(\partial E / \partial c_{kj}{}^{hx}) \qquad (B.1)$$

Where = learning rate (positive & usually < 1)

k, j = input index (k, j = 0, 1, 2, …,n means one of 2*n*n input combinations from the first hidden layer)

E = error

t = training time

hx = hidden layer, related to x input

$c_{kj}{}^{hx}$ = hidden layer weight related to x input

The equations for the 2nd hidden layer node are:

$$net_{kj}{}^{h} = \{c_{kj}{}^{hx}b_{k}{}^{x}\} \{c_{kj}{}^{hy}b_{j}{}^{y}\}$$
$$i_{kj} = f^{h}(net_{kj}{}^{h}) \qquad (B.2)$$

where i_{kj} = output from 2nd hidden layer (= input to the output neuron)

$b_{k}{}^{x}$ and $b_{j}{}^{y}$= input to 2nd hidden layer neuron

(= output from the 1st hidden layer neuron)

f^{h} = hidden neuron activation function

hy = hidden layer, related to y input

$c_{kj}{}^{hy}$ = hidden layer weight related to y input

We call the neurons at the second layer multiple neurons. Their activity function is linear and their inputs are the multiplication of two outputs of the first layer neuron output and their weights.
The error of a single output unit will be:

$$\delta = (d - z) \qquad (B.3)$$

where d = desired output value of output layer neuron

z = actual output value of output layer neuron

The total error is the sum of the squared errors across all output units, namely:

$$E_p = 0.5 * \delta^2 = 0.5 * (d-z)^2$$
$$= 0.5 * (d - f^o(net^o))^2$$
$$= 0.5 * (d - f_k^o(\sum_j c_{kj}^o i_{kj}))^2 \qquad (B.4)$$

The derivatives $f^{h'}(net^h_{pj})$ are calculated as follows, for a linear function of second layer neurons:

$$i_{kj} = f^h(net_{kj}^h) = net_{kj}^h$$
$$f^{h'}(net_{kj}^h) = 1 \qquad (B.5)$$

The gradient (E/c_{kj}^{hx}) is given by:

$$\partial E \ / \partial c_{kj}^{hx} = \partial(0.5 * (d-z)^2) / \partial c_{kj}^{hx}$$
$$= (\partial(0.5 * (d-z)^2) / \partial z)(\partial z \ / \partial(net^o))$$
$$(\partial(net^o) / \partial i_{kj})(\partial i_{kj} / \partial(net_{kj}^h))(\partial(net_{kj}^h) / \partial c_{kj}^{hx}) \qquad (B.6)$$

$$\partial(0.5 * (d-z)^2) / \partial z = -(d-z) \qquad (B.7)$$

$$\partial z / \partial(net^o) = \partial f^o / \partial(net^o) = f_k^{o'}(net^o) \qquad (B.8)$$

$$\partial(net^o) / \partial i_{kj} = \partial(\sum_{k,j=1}^n (c_{kj}^o i_{kj})) / \partial i_{kj} = c_{kj}^o \qquad (B.9)$$

$$\partial i_{kj} / \partial(net_{kj}^h) = \partial(f^h(net_{kj}^h)) / \partial(net_{kj}^h) = f^{h'}(net_{kj}^h) \qquad (B.10)$$

$$\partial(net_{kj}^h) / \partial c_{kj}^{hx} = \partial(\{c_{kj}^{hx} b_k^x\} \{c_{kj}^{hy} b_j^y\}) / \partial c_{kj}^{hx}$$
$$= b_k^x c_{kj}^{hy} b_j^y = \delta_{kj}^{hx} b_k^x$$
$$where: \delta_{kj}^{hx} = c_{kj}^{hy} b_j^y \qquad (B.11)$$

Combining Eqns. B.6 through B.11, the negative gradient is:

$$-\partial E \ / \partial c_{kj}^{hx} = (d-z)f^{o'}(net^o)c_{kj}^o f^{h'}(net_{kj}^h)\delta^{hx} b_k^x \qquad (B.12)$$

The weight update equations are formulated as follows:

- Let output neuron is a linear neuron:

$$\delta^{ol} = (d-z)f^{o}{}_{k}{}'(net^{o}) = (d-z) \qquad (B.13)$$

Also let the second layer neurons be linear neurons, combining Formulae B.1, B.5, B.12 and B.13:

$$c_{kj}{}^{hx}(t+1) = c_{kj}{}^{hx}(t) - \eta(\partial E / \partial c_{kj}{}^{hx})$$
$$= c_{kj}{}^{hx}(t) + \eta((d-z)f^{o}{}'(net^{o})c_{kj}{}^{o}f^{h}{}'(net_{kj}{}^{hx})c_{kj}{}^{hy}b_{j}{}^{y}b_{k}{}^{x})$$
$$= c_{kj}{}^{hx}(t) + \eta(\delta^{ol}c_{kj}{}^{o}\delta_{kj}{}^{hx}b_{k}{}^{x})$$

$$where: \qquad \delta^{ol} = (d-z)$$
$$\delta_{kj}{}^{hx} = c_{kj}{}^{hy}b_{j}{}^{y}$$
$$f^{o}{}'(net^{o}) = 1 \qquad (linear \qquad neuron)$$
$$f^{h}{}'(net_{kj}{}^{hx}) = 1 \qquad (linear \qquad neuron) \qquad (B.14)$$

Use the same rules, the weight update question for y input neurons is:

$$c_{kj}{}^{hy}(t+1) = c_{kj}{}^{hy}(t) - \eta(\partial E / \partial c_{kj}{}^{hy})$$
$$= c_{kj}{}^{hy}(t) + \eta((d-z)f^{o}{}'(net^{o})c_{kj}{}^{o}f^{h}{}'(net_{kj}{}^{hy})c_{kj}{}^{hx}b_{k}{}^{x}b_{j}{}^{y})$$
$$= c_{kj}{}^{hy}(t) + \eta(\delta^{ol}c_{kj}{}^{o}\delta_{kj}{}^{hy}b_{j}{}^{y})$$

$$where: \qquad \delta^{ol} = (d-z)$$
$$\delta_{kj}{}^{hy} = c_{kj}{}^{hx}b_{k}{}^{x}$$
$$f^{o}{}'(net^{o}) = 1 \qquad (linear \qquad neuron)$$
$$f^{h}{}'(net_{kj}{}^{hy}) = 1 \qquad (linear \qquad neuron) \qquad (B.15)$$

First Hidden Layer Neurons in HONN (Model 1 and Model 2)

For the x input part, we have following formula as learning algorithm.
The 1st hidden layer weights are updated according to:

$$c_{k}{}^{x}(t+1) = c_{k}{}^{x}(t) - \eta(\partial E_{p} / \partial c_{k}{}^{x}) \qquad (C.1)$$

where:

$c_k^x = 1^{st}$ hidden layer weight for input x; $k = k$th neuron of first hidden layer

η = learning rate (positive & usually < 1)

E = error

t = training time

The equations for the kth or j^{th} node in the first hidden layer are:

$$net_k^x = c_k^x * x$$
$$b_k^x = f_k^x(net_k^x)$$
or
$$net_j^y = c_j^y * y$$
$$b_j^y = f_j^y(net_j^y) \qquad\qquad (C.2)$$

where:

i_{kj} = output from 2nd hidden layer (= input to the output neuron)

b_k^x and b^y_j = output from the 1st hidden layer neuron (= input to 2nd hidden layer neuron)

f_k^x and f_j^y = 1st hidden layer neuron activation function

x and y = input to 1st hidden layer

The total error is the sum of the squared errors across all hidden units, namely:

$$E_p = 0.5 * \delta^2 = 0.5 * (d-z)^2$$
$$= 0.5 * (d - f^o(net^o))^2$$
$$= 0.5 * (d - f^o(\sum_j c_{kj}^o i_{kj}))^2 \qquad\qquad (C.3)$$

The gradient is given by:

$$\partial E_p / \partial c_k^x = \partial(0.5 * (d-z)^2) / \partial c_k^x$$
$$= (\partial(0.5 * (d-z)^2) / \partial z)(\partial z / \partial(net^o))$$
$$(\partial(net^o) / \partial i_{kj})(\partial i_{kj} / \partial(net_{kj}^h))(\partial(net_{kj}^h) / \partial b_k^x)$$
$$(\partial b_k^x / \partial(net_k^x))(\partial(net_k^x) / \partial c_k^x) \qquad\qquad (C.4)$$

$$\partial(0.5*(d-z)^2 / \partial z = -(d-z) \qquad (C.5)$$

$$\partial z / \partial(net^o) - \partial f^o / \partial(net^o) - f^{o\,\prime}(net^o) \qquad (C.6)$$

$$\partial(net^o) / \partial i_{kj} = \partial(\sum_{k,j=1}^{l}(c_{kj}^{\,o} i_{kj}) / \partial i_{kj} = c_{kj}^{\,o} \qquad (C.7)$$

$$\partial i_{kj} / \partial(net_{kj}^{\,h}) = \partial(f^h(net_{kj}^{\,h})) / \partial(net_{kj}^{\,h}) = f^{h\,\prime}(net_{kj}^{\,h}) \qquad (C.8)$$

$$\partial net_{kj}^{\,h} / \partial b_k^{\,x} = \partial((c_{kj}^{\,hx}*b_k^{\,x})*(c_{kj}^{\,hy}*b_j^{\,y})) / \partial b_k^{\,x} = c_{kj}^{\,hx}*c_{kj}^{\,hy}*b_j^{\,y}$$
$$= \delta_{kj}^{\,hx} c_{kj}^{\,hx}$$
$$where: \delta_{kj}^{\,hx} = c_{kj}^{\,hy}*b_j^{\,y} \qquad (C.9)$$

$$\partial b_k^{\,x} / \partial(net_k^{\,x}) = f_x^{\,\prime}(net_k^{\,x}) \qquad (C.10)$$

$$\partial(net_k^{\,x}) / \partial c_k^{\,x} = \partial(c_k^{\,x}*x) / \partial c_k^{\,x} = x \qquad (C.11)$$

Combining Formulae C.5 through C.11 the negative gradient is:

$$-\partial E_p / \partial c_k^{\,x} = (d-z)f^{o\,\prime}(net^o)c_{kj}^{\,o}*f^{h\,\prime}(net_{kj}^{\,h})\delta_{kj}^{\,hx}c_{kj}^{\,hx}f_x^{\,\prime}(net_k^{\,x})x \qquad (C.12)$$

The weight update equations are calculated as follows.
For linear output neurons:

$$f^{o\,\prime}(net^o) = 1$$
$$\delta^{ol} = (d-z)f^{o\,\prime}(net^o) = (d-z) \qquad (C.13)$$

For linear neurons of second hidden layer:

$$f^{h\,\prime}(net_{kj}^{\,h}) = 1 \qquad (C.14)$$

The negative gradient is:

$$-\partial E_p / \partial c_k^{\,x} = (d-z)f^{o\,\prime}(net^o)c_{kj}^{\,o}*f^{h\,\prime}(net_{kj}^{\,h})\delta_{kj}^{\,hx}c_{kj}^{\,hx}f_x^{\,\prime}(net_k^{\,x})x$$
$$= \delta^{ol}*c_{kj}^{\,o}*\delta_{kj}^{\,hx}*c_{kj}^{\,hx}*f_x^{\,\prime}(net_k^{\,x})*x \qquad (C.15)$$

By combining Formulae C.1, C.4, and C.15, for a linear 1st hidden layer neuron:

$$b_k^{\ x} = f_k^{\ x}\ (net_k^{\ x})$$
$$f_x\ '(net_k^{\ x}) = \partial b_k^{\ x} / \partial (net_k^{\ x})$$

For a function of x input side:

$$c_k^{\ x}(t+1) = c_k^{\ x}(t) - \eta(\partial E_p / \partial c_k^{\ x})$$
$$= c_k^{\ x}(t) + \eta(d-z)f^{\ o}\ '(net^{\ o})c_{kj}^{\ o} * f^{\ h}\ '(net_{kj}^{\ h})c_{kj}^{\ hy}b_j^{\ y}c_{kj}^{\ hx} f_x\ '(net_k^{\ x})x$$
$$= c_k^{\ x}(t) + \eta * \delta^{\ ol} * c_{kj}^{\ o} * \delta^{\ hx} * c_{kj}^{\ hx} * \delta^{\ x} * x$$
where :

$$\delta^{\ ol} = (d-z)f^{\ o}\ '(net^{\ o}) = d-z \qquad (linear \qquad neuron)$$
$$\delta^{\ hx} = f^{\ h}\ '(net_{kj}^{\ h})c_{kj}^{\ hy}b_j^{\ y} \qquad = c_{kj}^{\ hy}b_j^{\ y} \qquad (linear \qquad neuron)$$
$$\delta^{\ x} = f_x\ '(net_k^{\ x}) \qquad\qquad\qquad\qquad (C.17)$$

For the y input part, we have following formula as learning algorithm. The 1st hidden layer weights are updated according to:

$$c_j^{\ y}(t+1) = c_j^{\ y}(t) - \eta(\partial E_p / \partial c_j^{\ y}) \qquad\qquad (D.1)$$

Where:

$C_j^y = $ 1st hidden layer weight for input y; $j = j$th neuron of first hidden layer

$\eta = $ learning rate (positive & usually < 1)

$E = $ error

$t = $ training time

The equations for the kth or j^{th} node in the first hidden layer are:

$$net_k^{\ x} = c_k^{\ x} * x$$
$$b_k^{\ x} = f_k^{\ x}(net_k^{\ x})$$
or
$$net_j^{\ y} = c_j^{\ y} * y$$
$$b_j^{\ y} = f_j^{\ y}(net_j^{\ y}) \qquad\qquad (D.2)$$

where:

i_{kj} = output from 2nd hidden layer (= input to the output neuron)

$b_k{}^x$ and $b^y{}_j$ = output from the 1st hidden layer neuron (= input to 2nd hidden layer neuron)

$f_k{}^x$ and $f_j{}^y$ = 1st hidden layer neuron activation function

x and y = input to 1st hidden layer

The total error is the sum of the squared errors across all hidden units, namely:

$$E_p = 0.5 * \delta^2 = 0.5 * (d - z)^2$$
$$= 0.5 * (d - f^o(net^o))^2$$
$$= 0.5 * (d - f^o(\sum_j c_{kj}{}^o i_{kj}))^2 \qquad (D.3)$$

The gradient ($\partial E_p / \partial c_j{}^y$) is given by:

$$\partial E_p / \partial c_j{}^y = \partial(0.5 * (d - z)^2) / \partial c_j{}^y$$
$$= (\partial(0.5 * (d - z)^2) / \partial z)(\partial z / \partial(net^o))$$
$$(\partial(net^o) / \partial i_{kj})(\partial i_{kj} / \partial(net_{kj}{}^h))(\partial(net_{kj}{}^h) / \partial b_j{}^y)$$
$$(\partial b_j{}^y / \partial(net_j{}^y))(\partial(net_j{}^y) / \partial c_j{}^y) \qquad (D.4)$$

$$\partial(0.5 * (d - z)^2 / \partial z = -(d - z) \qquad (D.5)$$

$$\partial z / \partial(net^o) = \partial f^o / \partial(net^o) = f^o{}'(net^o) \qquad (D.6)$$

$$\partial(net^o) / \partial i_{kj} = \partial(\sum_{k,j=1}^{l} (c_{kj}{}^o i_{kj}) / \partial i_{kj} = c_{kj}{}^o \qquad (D.7)$$

$$\partial i_{kj} / \partial(net_{kj}{}^h) = \partial(f^h(net_{kj}{}^h)) / \partial(net_{kj}{}^h) = f^h{}'(net_{kj}{}^h) \qquad (D.8)$$

$$\partial net_{kj}{}^h / \partial b_j{}^y = \partial((c_{kj}{}^{hx} * b_k{}^x) * (c_{kj}{}^{hy} * b_j{}^y)) / \partial b_j{}^y = c_{kj}{}^{hx} * c_{kj}{}^{hy} * b_k{}^x$$
$$= \delta^{hy} c_{kj}{}^{hy}$$
$$where : \delta_{kj}{}^{hy} = c_{kj}{}^{hy} * b_k{}^x \qquad (D.9)$$

$$\partial b_j{}^y / \partial(net_j{}^y) = f_y{}'(net_j{}^y) \qquad (D.10)$$

$$\partial(net_j{}^y) / \partial c_j{}^y = \partial(c_j{}^y * y) / \partial c_j{}^y = y \qquad (D.11)$$

Combining Formulae C.5 through C.11 the negative gradient is:

$$-\partial E_p / \partial c_k{}^x = (d-z) f^o\ '(net\ ^o) c_{kj}{}^o * f^h\ '(net_{kj}{}^h) \delta_{kj}{}^{hy} c_{kj}{}^{hy} f_y\ '(net_j{}^y) y \qquad (D.12)$$

The weight update equations are calculated as follows.
For linear output neurons:

$$f^o\ '(net^o) = 1$$
$$\delta^{ol} = (d-z) f^o\ '(net^o) = (d-z) \qquad (D.13)$$

For linear neurons of second hidden layer:

$$f^h\ '(net_{kj}{}^h) = 1 \qquad (D.14)$$

The negative gradient is:

$$-\partial E_p / \partial c_j{}^y = (d-z) f^o\ '(net\ ^o) c_{kj}{}^o * f^h\ '(net_{kj}{}^h) \delta_{kj}{}^{hy} c_{kj}{}^{hy} f_y\ '(net_j{}^y) y$$
$$= \delta^{ol} * c_{kj}{}^o * \delta_{kj}{}^{hy} * c_{kj}{}^{hy} * f_y{}'(net_j{}^y) * y \qquad (D.15)$$

By combining Formulae D.1, D.4, and D.15, for a linear 1st hidden layer neuron:
For a function of *y* input part:

$$b_j{}^y = f_j{}^y (net_j{}^y)$$
$$f_y\ '(net_j{}^y) = \partial b_j{}^y / \partial(net_j{}^y) \qquad (D.16)$$

Using the above procedure:

$$c_j{}^y(t+1) = c_j{}^y(t) - \eta(\partial E_p / \partial c_j{}^y)$$
$$= c_j{}^y(t) + \eta(d-z) f^o\ '(net\ ^o) c_{kj}{}^o * f^h\ '(net_{kj}{}^h) c_{kj}{}^{hx} b_k{}^x c_{kj}{}^{hy} f_y\ '(net_j{}^y) y$$
$$= c_j{}^y(t) + \eta * \delta^{ol} * c_{kj}{}^o * \delta^{hy} * c_{kj}{}^{hy} * \delta^y * y$$

where:

$$\delta^{ol} = (d-z) f^o\ '(net\ ^o) = d-z \qquad (linear \quad neuron \quad f^o\ '(net\ ^o) = 1)$$
$$\delta^{hy} = f^h\ '(net_{kj}{}^h) c_{kj}{}^{hx} b_k{}^x \quad = c_{kj}{}^{hx} b_k{}^x \qquad (linear \quad neuron \quad f^h\ '(net_{kj}{}^h) = 1)$$
$$\delta^y = f_y\ '(net_j{}^y) \qquad\qquad (D.17)$$

SIN-HONN Model First Layer Neuron Weights Learning Formula

Sine Higher Order Neural Network (SIN-HONN) model is as follows:

For a sine function of x input side:

$$b_k^{\ x} = f_k^{\ x}\ (net_k^{\ x}) = \sin^k(net_k^{\ x}) = \sin^k(c_k^{\ x} * x)^k$$
$$f_x\ '(net_k^{\ x}) = \partial b_k^{\ x} / \partial(net_k^{\ x})$$
$$= \partial(\sin^k(net_k^{\ x})) / \partial(net_k^{\ x})$$
$$= k * \sin^{k-1}(net_k^{\ x}) * \cos(net_k^{\ x}) = k * \sin^{k-1}(c_k^{\ x} * x) * \cos(c_k^{\ x} * x) \qquad (SIN - HONN \qquad C. \qquad 16)$$

$$c_k^{\ x}(t+1) = c_k^{\ x}(t) - \eta(\partial E_p / \partial c_k^{\ x})$$
$$= c_k^{\ x}(t) + \eta(d - z)f^o\ '(net^o)c_{kj}^{\ o} * f^h\ '(net_{kj}^{\ h})c_{kj}^{\ hy}b_j^{\ y}c_{kj}^{\ hx}f_x\ '(net_k^{\ x})x$$
$$= c_k^{\ x}(t) + \eta * \delta^{\ ol} * c_{kj}^{\ o} * \delta^{hx} * c_{kj}^{\ hx} * k * \sin^{k-1}(c_k^{\ x} * x) * \cos(c_k^{\ x} * x) * x$$
$$= c_k^{\ x}(t) + \eta * \delta^{\ ol} * c_{kj}^{\ o} * \delta^{\ hx} * c_{kj}^{\ hx} * \delta^{\ x} * x \qquad (SIN - HONN \qquad C. \qquad 17)$$
where :
$$\delta^{\ ol} = (d - z)f^o\ '(net^o) = d - z \qquad (linear \qquad neuron \qquad f^o\ '(net^o) = 1)$$
$$\delta^{\ hx} = f^h\ '(net_{kj}^{\ h})c_{kj}^{\ hy}b_j^{\ y} \quad = c_{kj}^{\ hy}b_j^{\ y} \qquad (linear \qquad neuron \qquad f^h\ '(net_{kj}^{\ h}) = 1)$$
$$\delta^{\ x} = f_x\ '(net_k^{\ x}) = k * (net_k^{\ x})^{k-1} = k * \sin^{k-1}(c_k^{\ x} * x) * \cos(c_k^{\ x} * x)$$

For a sine function of y input part:

$$b_j^{\ y} = f_j^{\ y}\ (net_j^{\ y}) = \sin^j(net_j^{\ y}) = \sin^j(c_j^{\ y} * y)$$
$$f_y\ '(net_j^{\ y}) = \partial b_j^{\ y} / \partial(net_j^{\ y})$$
$$= \partial(\sin^j(net_j^{\ y})) / \partial(net_j^{\ y})$$
$$= j * \sin^{j-1}(net_j^{\ y}) * \cos(net_j^{\ y})$$
$$= j\ * \sin^{j-1}(c_j^{\ y} * y) * \cos(c_j^{\ y} * y) \qquad (SIN - HONN \qquad D. \qquad 16)$$

Using the above procedure:

$$c_j^{\ y}(t+1) = c_j^{\ y}(t) - \eta(\partial E_p / \partial c_j^{\ y})$$

$$= c_j^{\ y}(t) + \eta(d-z)f^{o}{}'(net^{o})c_{kj}^{\ o} * f^{h}{}'(net_{kj}^{\ h})c_{kj}^{\ hy}b_j^{\ y}c_{kj}^{\ hy}f_y{}'(net_j^{\ y})y$$

$$= c_j^{\ y}(t) + \eta * \delta^{ol} * c_{kj}^{\ o} * \delta^{hy} * c_{kj}^{\ hy} * j * \sin^{j-1}(c_j^{\ y} * y)\cos(c_j^{\ y} * y) * y$$

$$= c_j^{\ y}(t) + \eta * \delta^{ol} * c_{kj}^{\ o} * \delta^{hy} * c_{kj}^{\ hy} * \delta^{y} * y \qquad\qquad (SIN-HONN \qquad D. \qquad 17)$$

where :

$$\delta^{ol} = (d-z)f^{o}{}'(net^{o}) = d-z \qquad (linear \qquad neuron \qquad f^{o}{}'(net^{o}) = 1)$$

$$\delta^{hy} = f^{h}{}'(net_{kj}^{\ h})c_{kj}^{\ hx}b_k^{\ x} \qquad = c_{kj}^{\ hx}b_k^{\ x} \qquad (linear \qquad neuron \qquad f^{h}{}'(net_{kj}^{\ h}) = 1)$$

$$\delta^{y} = f_y{}'(net_j^{\ y}) = j * \sin^{j-1}(c_j^{\ y} * y) * \cos(c_j^{\ y} * y)$$

Cosine and Cosine Higher Order Neural Network (COS-HONN) model as follows:

Let :

$$f_k^{\ x}(c_k^{\ x}x) = \cos^{k}(c_k^{\ x}x)$$

$$f_j^{\ y}(c_j^{\ y}y) = \cos^{j}(c_j^{\ y}y)$$

For a cosine function of x input side:

$$b_k^{\ x} = f_k^{\ x}(net_k^{\ x}) = \cos^{k}(net_k^{\ x}) = \cos^{k}(c_k^{\ x} * x)$$

$$f_x{}'(net_k^{\ x}) = \partial b_k^{\ x} / \partial(net_k^{\ x})$$

$$= \partial(\cos^{k}(net_k^{\ x})) / \partial(net_k^{\ x})$$

$$= k * \cos^{k-1}(net_k^{\ x}) * (-\sin(net_k^{\ x}))$$

$$= (-k) * \cos^{k-1}(c_k^{\ x} * x) * \sin(c_k^{\ x} * x) \qquad\qquad (COS-HONN \qquad C. \qquad 16)$$

$$c_k^{\ x}(t+1) = c_k^{\ x}(t) - \eta(\partial E_p / \partial c_k^{\ x})$$

$$= c_k^{\ x}(t) + \eta(d-z)f^{o}{}'(net^{o})c_{kj}^{\ o} * f^{h}{}'(net_{kj}^{\ h})c_{kj}^{\ hy}b_j^{\ y}c_{kj}^{\ hx}f_x{}'(net_k^{\ x})x$$

$$= c_k^{\ x}(t) + \eta * \delta^{ol} * c_{kj}^{\ o} * \delta^{hx} * c_{kj}^{\ hx} * (-k) * \cos^{k-1}(c_k^{\ x} * x) * \sin(c_k^{\ x} * x) * x$$

$$= c_k^{\ x}(t) + \eta * \delta^{ol} * c_{kj}^{\ o} * \delta^{hx} * c_{kj}^{\ hx} * \delta^{x} * x \qquad\qquad (COS-HONN \qquad C. \qquad 17)$$

where :

$$\delta^{ol} = (d-z)f^{o}{}'(net^{o}) = d-z \qquad (linear \qquad neuron \qquad f^{o}{}'(net^{o}) = 1)$$

$$\delta^{hx} = f^{h}{}'(net_{kj}^{\ h})c_{kj}^{\ hy}b_j^{\ y} \qquad = c_{kj}^{\ hy}b_j^{\ y} \qquad (linear \qquad neuron \qquad f^{h}{}'(net_{kj}^{\ h}) = 1)$$

$$\delta^{x} = f_x{}'(net_k^{\ x}) = (-k) * \cos^{k-1}(net_k^{\ x}) * \sin(net_k^{\ x}) = (-k) * \cos^{k-1}(c_k^{\ x} * x) * \sin(c_k^{\ x} * x)$$

For cosine function of *y* input part:

$$b_i^y = f_v(net_i^y) = \cos^j(net_i^y) = \cos^j(c_j^y * y)$$

$$f_y'(net_j^y) = \partial b_j^y / \partial(net_j^y)$$

$$= \partial(\cos^j(net_j^y)) / \partial(net_j^y)$$

$$= j\cos^{j-1}(net_j^y) * (-\sin(net_j^y))$$

$$= (-j) * \cos^{j-1}(net_j^y) * \sin(net_j^y)$$

$$= (-j) * \cos^{j-1}(c_j^y * y) * \sin(c_j^y * y) \qquad (COS-HONN \qquad D. \qquad 16)$$

Using the above procedure:

$$c_j^y(t+1) = c_j^y(t) - \eta(\partial E_p / \partial c_j^y)$$

$$= c_j^y(t) + \eta(d-z)f^o{}'(net^o)c_{kj}^o * f^h{}'(net_{kj}^h)c_{kj}^{hx}b_k^x c_{kj}^{hy}f_y'(net_j^y)y$$

$$= c_j^y(t) + \eta * \delta^{ol} * c_{kj}^o * \delta^{hy} * c_{kj}^{hy} * (-j) * \cos^{j-1}(c_j^y * y) * \sin(c_j^y * y) * y$$

$$= c_j^y(t) + \eta * \delta^{ol} * c_{kj}^o * \delta^{hy} * c_{kj}^{hy} * \delta^y * y \qquad (COS-HONN \qquad D. \qquad 17)$$

where :

$$\delta^{ol} = (d-z)f^o{}'(net^o) = d-z \qquad (linear \qquad neuron \qquad f^o{}'(net^o) = 1)$$

$$\delta^{hy} = f^h{}'(net_{kj}^h)c_{kj}^{hx}b_k^x \quad = c_{kj}^{hx}b_k^x \qquad (linear \qquad neuron \qquad f^h{}'(net_{kj}^h) = 1)$$

$$\delta^y = f_y'(net_j^y) = (-j) * \cos^{j-1}(c_j^y * y) * \sin(c_j^y * y)$$

FINANCIAL DATA PREDICTION USING HONN MODELS

Time Series Data Prediction Simulation Test Using SIN-HONN

This test uses the monthly Australian dollar and USA dollar exchange rate from November 2003 to November 2004 as the test data for SIN-HONN models. In Table 1, the "Exchange Rates" are chosen from USA Federal Reserve Bank Data bank. The "Input1"data are the exchange rates for two months prior to the prediction date. The "Input 2" data are the exchange rates for one month before the prediction date. The "Output Data" are chosen from USA Federal Reserve Bank Data bank for prediction simulating. The values of "Exchange Rates", "Input 1 Data", "Input 2 Data", and "Output Data" are converted to a range from 0 to 1 and then used as inputs and output in the SIN-HONN model. SIN-HONN model 0, 1, and 2 are tested. The order number for SIN-HONN model is 6. The epochs numbers for the tests are 1000, 10000, and 100000. Table 2 shows the test results for exchange rate prediction simulation errors by using SIN-HONN models, PHONN models, and THONN models.

Table 1. Australia Dollars Vs US Dollars for SIN-HONN Models

Date	Exchange Rates 1AU$ = ? US$	Two Months before Input 1Data	One Month before Input 2 Data	Prediction Simulating Output Data
11/28/2003	0.7236			
12/31/2003	0.7520			
1/30/2004	0.7625	0.7236	0.7520	0.7625
2/27/2004	0.7717	0.7520	0.7625	0.7717
3/31/2004	0.7620	0.7625	0.7717	0.7620
4/30/2004	0.7210	0.7717	0.7620	0.7210
5/28/2004	0.7138	0.7620	0.7210	0.7138
6/30/2004	0.6952	0.7210	0.7138	0.6952
7/30/2004	0.7035	0.7138	0.6952	0.7035
8/31/2004	0.7071	0.6952	0.7035	0.7071
9/30/2004	0.7244	0.7035	0.7071	0.7244
10/29/2004	0.7468	0.7071	0.7244	0.7468
11/30/2004	0.7723	0.7244	0.7468	0.7723

Table 2. 2004 AU$ /US$ Exchange Rate Prediction Simulation Average Error

Models	Order 6 Epochs 1,000	Order 6 Epochs 10,000	Order 6 Epochs 100,000
SIN-HONN Model 0	7.3674%	6.0274%	4.4401%
PHONN Model 0	8.7080%	7.1142%	4.4457%
THONN Model 0	10.0366%	9.2834%	4.5712%
SIN-HONN Model 1	8.0236%	7.1892%	7.3012%
PHONN Model 1	9.5274%	8.3484%	7.8234%
THONN Model 1	10.8966%	7.3811%	7.3468%
SIN-HONN Model 2	14.2982%	9.0278%	6.6030%
PHONN Model 2	14.8800%	9.1474%	9.0276%
THONN Model 2	10.5600%	10.1914%	6.7119%

For example, in Table 1 of "AustralianDollar/USDollar Exchange Rate" and based on "Exchange Rates" column, AUD$1.00 = USD$0.7236 on 28-Nov-2003, and AUD$1.00 = USD$0.7520 on 31-Dec-2003. The value 0.7236 (AUD$1.00 = USD$0.7236 on 28-Nov-2003) has been used as Input 1 Data for 30-January-2004 row in the Column of "Two months before Input 1 Data". The value 0.7520 (AUD$1.00 = USD$0.7520 on 31-Dec-2003) has been used as Input 1 Data for 27-February-2004 row in the Column of "Two months before Input 1 Data", and has been used as Input 2 Data for 30-january-2004 row in the column of "One month before Input 2 Data".

In Table 2 of "2004 AU$/US$ Exchange Rate Prediction Simulation Error", The average errors of SIN-HONN Model 0, PHONN Model 0, and THONN Model 0 with Epochs 1000 are 7.3674%, 8.7080%, and 10.0366% respectively. The average errors of SIN-HONN Model 0, PHONN Model 0, and THONN

Model 0 with Epochs 10000 are 6.0274%, 7.1142%, and 9.2834% respectively. The average errors of SIN-HONN Model 0, PHONN Model 0, and THONN Model 0 with Epochs 100000 are 4.4401%, 4.4457%, and 4.5712% respectively.

In Table 2 of "2004 AU$/US$ Exchange Rate Prediction Simulation Error", The average errors of SIN-HONN Model 1, PHONN Model 1, and THONN Model 1 with Epochs 1000 are 8.0236%, 9.5274%, and 10.8966% respectively. The average errors of SIN-HONN Model 1, PHONN Model 1, and THONN Model 1 with Epochs 10000 are 7.1892%, 8.3484%, and 7.3811% respectively. The average errors of SIN-HONN Model 1, PHONN Model 1, and THONN Model 1 with Epochs 100000 are 7.3012%, 7.8234%, and 7.3468% respectively.

In Table 2 of "2004 AU$/US$ Exchange Rate Prediction Simulation Error", The average errors of SIN-HONN Model 2, PHONN Model 2, and THONN Model 2 with Epochs 1000 are 14.2982%, 14.8800%, and 10.5600% respectively. The average errors of SIN-HONN Model 2, PHONN Model 2, and THONN Model 2 with Epochs 10000 are 9.0278%, 9.1474%, and 10.1914% respectively. The average errors of SIN-HONN Model 2, PHONN Model 2, and THONN Model 2 with Epochs 100000 are 6.6030%, 9.0276%, and 6.7119% respectively.

The 2004 AU$/US$ exchange rate prediction simulation errors by chart is shown in Figure 3. Test results tell that SIN-HONN models are better when using these data shown in Table 1. Generally speaking, SIN-HONN Models should have similar test results compared with PHONN and THONN models.

COS-HONN Model Prediction for All Banks Deposits Repayable in Australia

The *COS-HONN* model (Model 2, Order 6) has been used to predict All Banks Deposits Repayable in Australia. In Table 3 of "All Banks Deposits Repayable in Australia ($Million)", Column 1 shows the "Month/Year". Column 2 shows "Total Deposit Certificates". Column 3 shows the COS-HONN training or prediction testing absolute error values. Column 4 of "Case" shows which data have been used for training the COS-HONN model, and which data have been used for prediction testing the COS-HONN model.

In Table 3, the data from 11/1994 to 06/1995 are used as training data. The data of 07/1995 and 08/1995 are used as testing cases for prediction. Prediction results shows that the average error of *COS-HONN* model is about 14.12%. Figure 4 of "All Banks Deposits Repayable in Australia ($Million) Training and Prediction |Error|%" shows the absolute error of training and prediction test for COS-HONN model (Model 2, Order 6).

COS-HONN Model Prediction for All Banks Credit Card Lending in Australia

The *COS-HONN* model (Model 2, Order 6) has been used to predict All Banks Credit Lending in Australia. In Table 4 of "All Banks Credit Card in Australia ($Million)", Column 1 shows the "Month/Year". Column 2 shows the "Limits Outstanding", while column 3 shows the COS-HONN training or prediction testing absolute error values. Column 4 of "Case" shows which data have been used for training the COS-HONN model, and which data have been used for prediction testing the COS-HONN model.

In Table 4, the data from 03/1994 to 11/1994 are used as training data. The data of 11/1994 and 12/1994 are used as testing cases for prediction. Prediction results showed that the average error of *COS-HONN* model is about 12.93%. Figure 5 of "All Banks Credit Lending in Australia ($Million) Training and Prediction |Error|%" shows the absolute error of training and prediction test for COS-HONN model (Model 2, Order 6).

Figure 3. COS-HONN Architecture

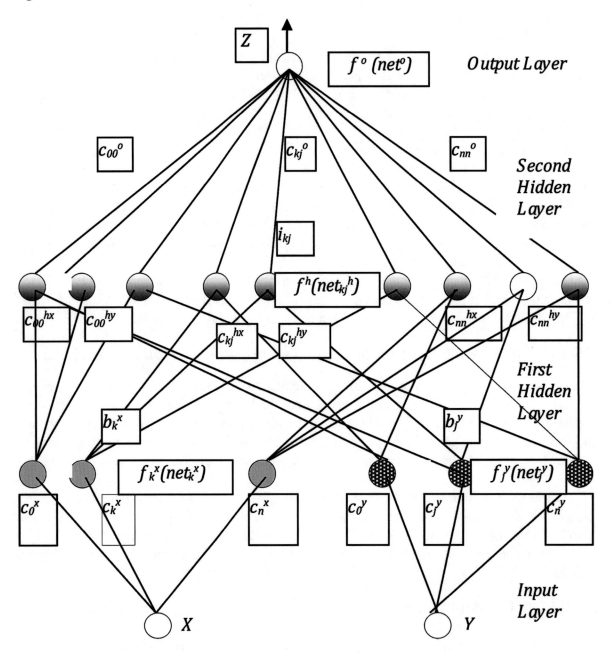

Table 3. All Banks Deposits Repayable in Australia ($Million)

Month/Year	Total Deposit Certificates	COS-HONN |Error|%	Case
11/1994	53011	12.85%	Training
12/1994	55867	12.81%	Training
01/1995	55449	6.83%	Training
02/1995	55594	19.45%	Training
03/1995	57366	6.74%	Training
04/1995	57548	0.73%	Training
05/1995	56798	19.19%	Training
06/1995	58197	12.65%	Training
07/1995 (Prediction)	59472	19.61%	Prediction Testing
08/1995 (Prediction)	59045	8.63%	Prediction Testing
Average Prediction |Error|		14.12%	

Reserve Bank of Australia Bulletin (August 1996, page s5)

Figure 4.

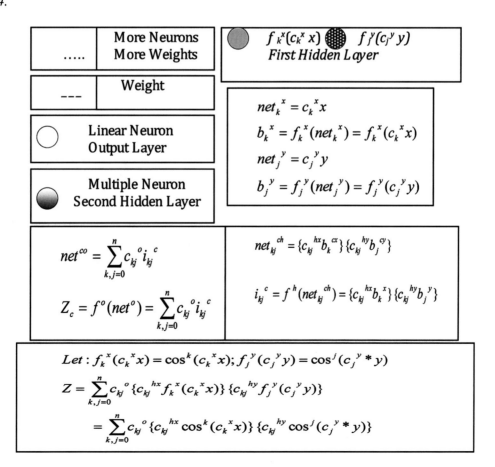

Table 4. All Banks Credit Card Lending ($million)

Month/Year	Limits Outstanding	COS-HONN |Error|%	Case
03/1994	18274	11.52%	Training
04/1994	18432	7.69%	Training
05/1994	18268	0.11%	Training
06/1994	18357	18.71%	Training
07/1994	18427	0.72%	Training
08/1994	18343	6.43%	Training
09/1994	18423	1.92%	Training
10/1994	18556	3.46%	Training
11/1994 (Prediction)	18450	13.13%	Prediction Testing
12/1994 (Prediction)	18925	12.72%	Prediction Testing
Average Prediction |Error|		12.93%	

Reserve Bank of Australia Bulletin (August 1996, page s18)

Figure 5. All banks' deposits repayable in Australia ($million); training and prediction [error]%

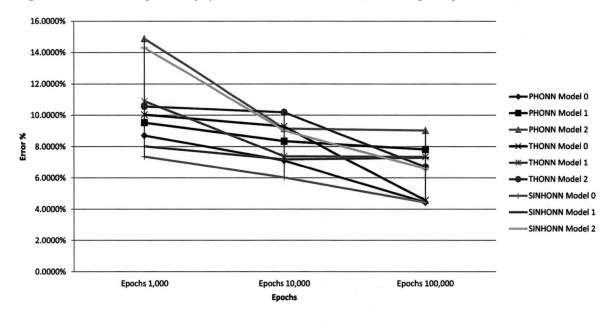

Figure 6. All banks' credit lending in Aistralia ($million); training and prediction [error]%

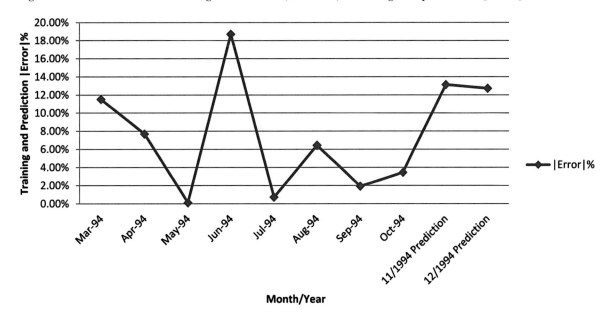

FUTURE RESEARCH DIRECTIONS

As the next step of HONN model research, more HONN models for different data control will be built to increase the pool of HONN models. Theoretically, the adaptive HONN models can be built and allow the computer automatically choose the best model, order, and coefficients. Thus, making the adaptive HONN models easier to use is one of the future research topics.

HONNs can automatically select the initial coefficients for nonlinear data analysis. The next step of this study will also focus on how to allow people working in the prediction area to understand that HONNs are much easier to use and can have better results. Moreover, further research will develop HONNs software packages for people working in the prediction area. HONNs will challenge classic procedures and change the research methodology that people are currently using in the prediction areas for the nonlinear data control application.

CONCLUSION

Two nonlinear neural network models, SIN-HONN, and COS-HONN models are developed. Based on the structures of SIN-HONN and COS-HONN models, this chapter provides model learning algorithm formulae. This chapter tests the SIN-HONN modes using nonlinear data for prediction simulation and the running results are compared with PHONN and PHONN models.

This chapter also tests the COS-HONN models using nonlinear data for prediction tests. Test results tell that, SIN-HONN models can do prediction simulation with similar or better results than PHONN and THONN models. Test results also tell that COS-HONN model can do nonlinear data prediction with around 10% error.

One of the topics for future research is to continue building HONN models for different data series. The coefficients of the higher order models will be studied not only using artificial neural network techniques, but also statistical methods. Using nonlinear functions to predict and analyze time series data will be a major goal in the future.

REFERENCES

Atiya, A.F. (2001). Bankruptcy prediction for credit risk using neural networks: A survey and new results. *IEEE Transactions on Neural Networks*, 12(4), 929-935.

Charitou, A., & Charalambous, C. (1996). The prediction of earnings using financial statement information: Empirical evidence with logit models and artificial neural networks. *Intelligent Systems in Accounting, Finance & Management*, 5(4), 199–215. doi:10.1002/(SICI)1099-1174(199612)5:4<199::AID-ISAF114>3.0.CO;2-C

Chen, Y., Wu, P., & Wu, Q. (2009). Foreign Exchange Rate Forecasting Using Higher Order Flexible Neural Tree. In M. Zhang (Ed.), Artificial Higher Order Neural Networks for Economics and Business (pp. 94-112). Hershey, PA, USA: IGI Global.

Doulamis, A. D., Doulamis, N. D., & Kollias, S. D. (2000). Recursive nonlinear models for online traffic prediction of VBR MPEG Coded video sources. Proceedings of IEEE-INNS-ENNS international joint conference on neural networks IJCNN, Como, Italy (pp. 114-119).

Doulamis, A. D., Doulamis, N. D., & Kollias, S. D. (2003). An adaptable neural network model for recursive nonlinear traffic prediction and modeling of MPEG video sources. *IEEE Transactions on Neural Networks*, 14(1), 150–166. doi:10.1109/TNN.2002.806645 PMID:18237998

Durbin, R., & Rumelhart, D. E. (1989). Product units: A computationally powerful and biologically plausible extension to backpropagation networks. *Neural Computation*, 1(1), 133–142. doi:10.1162/neco.1989.1.1.133

Eskander, G. S., & Atiya, A. (2013). Symbolic Function Networks: Application to Telecommunication Networks Prediction. In M. Zhang (Ed.), Artificial Higher Order Neural Networks for Modeling and Simulation (pp. 237-253). Hershey, PA, USA: IGI Global.

Fulcher, J., Zhang, M., & Shuxiang, Xu. (2006). Application of higher-order neural networks to financial time series prediction. In J. B. Kamruzzaman (Ed.), *Artificial neural networks in finance and manufacturing* (pp. 80-108). Hershey, PA, USA: IGI Global.

Ghazali, R., & Al-Jumeily, D. (2009). Application of Pi-Sigma Neural Networks and Ridge Polynomial Neural Networks to Financial Time Series Prediction. In M. Zhang (Ed.), Artificial Higher Order Neural Networks for Economics and Business (pp. 271-294). Hershey, PA, USA: IGI Global.

Hussain, A., & Liatsis, P. (2009). A Novel Recurrent Polynomial Neural Network for Financial Time Series Prediction. In M. Zhang (Ed.), Artificial Higher Order Neural Networks for Economics and Business (pp. 190-211). Hershey, PA, USA: IGI Global.

Knowles, A., & Hussain, A. Dereby, Wal El, Lisboa, P G. J. & Dunis, C L. (2009). Higher Order Neural Networks with Bayesian Confidence Measure for the Prediction of the EUR/USD Exchange Rate. In M. Zhang (Ed.), Artificial Higher Order Neural Networks for Economics and Business (pp. 48-59). Hershey, PA, USA: IGI Global.

Moon, S., & Chang, S. H. (1994). Classification and prediction of the critical heat flux using fuzzy clustering and artificial neural networks. *Nuclear Engineering and Design, 150*(1), 151–161. doi:10.1016/0029-5493(94)90059-0

Onwubolu, G. C. (2009). Artificial Higher Order Neural Networks in Time Series Prediction. In M. Zhang (Ed.), Artificial Higher Order Neural Networks for Economics and Business (pp. 250-270). Hershey, PA, USA: IGI Global.

Ricalde, L. J., Catzin, G. A., Alanis, A. Y., & Sanchez, E. N. (2013). Time Series Forecasting via a Higher Order Neural Network trained with the Extended Kalman Filter for Smart Grid Applications. In M. Zhang (Ed.), Artificial Higher Order Neural Networks for Modeling and Simulation (pp. 254-275). Information Science Reference, Hershey, PA, USA: IGI Global.

Saad, E. W., Prokhorov, D. V., & Wunsch, D. C. II. (1998). Comparative Study of Stock Trend Prediction Using Time Delay Recurrent and Probabilistic Neural Networks. *IEEE Transactions on Neural Networks, 9*(6), 1456–1470. doi:10.1109/72.728395 PMID:18255823

Sanchez, E. N., Alanis, A. Y., & Rico, J. (2004). Electric Load Demand Prediction Using Neural Networks Trained by Kalman Filtering. *Proceedings of the IEEE International Joint Conference on Neural Networks,* Budapest, Hungary (pp. 2771-2775). doi:10.1109/IJCNN.2004.1381093

Sanchez, E. N., Alanis, A. Y., & Rico, J. (2009). Electric Load Demand and Electricity Prices Forecasting Using Higher Order Networks Trained by Kalman Filtering. In M. Zhang (Ed.), Artificial Higher Order Neural Networks for Economics and Business (pp. 295-313). Hershey, PA, USA: IGI Global.

Selviah, D. R., & Shawash, J. (2009). Generalized Correlation Higher Order Neural Networks for Financial Time Series Prediction. In M. Zhang (Ed.), Artificial Higher Order Neural Networks for Economics and Business (pp. 212-249). Hershey, PA, USA: IGI Global.

Shawver, T. (2005). Merger premium predictions using neural network approach. *Journal of Emerging Technologies in Accounting, 1*(1), 61–72. doi:10.2308/jeta.2005.2.1.61

Shi, Da, Tan, Shaohua, & Ge Shuzhi Sam (2009). Automatically Identifying Predictor Variables for Stock Return Prediction. In M. Zhang (Ed.), *Artificial Higher Order Neural Networks for Economics and Business* (pp. 60-78). Hershey, PA, USA: IGI Global.

Su, G., Fukuda, K., Jia, D., & Morita, K. (2002). Application of an artificial neural network in reactor thermo hydraulic problem: Prediction of critical heat flux. *Journal of Nuclear Science and Technology, 39*(5), 564–571. doi:10.1080/18811248.2002.9715235

Vaziri, N., Hojabri, A., Erfani, A., Monsey, M., & Nilforooshan, N. (2007). Critical heat flux prediction by using radial basis function and multilayer perceptron neural networks: A comparison study. *Nuclear Engineering and Design, 237*(4), 377–385. doi:10.1016/j.nucengdes.2006.05.005

Welch, R. L., Ruffing, S. M., & Venayagamoorthy, G. K. (2009). Comparison of Feedforward and Feedback Neural Network Architectures for Short Term Wind Speed Prediction. *Paper presented at the IEEE International Joint Conference on Neural Networks,* Atlanta, Georgia, USA (pp. 3335-3340). doi:10.1109/IJCNN.2009.5179034

Yapo, T., Embrechets, S. T., & Cathey, S. T. (1992). Prediction of critical heat using a hybrid kohon-backpropagation neural network intelligent. Eng. *Systems through Artificial Neural Networks-proc. Artificial Neural Networks in Eng., 2,* 853–858.

Zhang, M., & Fulcher, J. (2004). Higher Order Neural Networks for Satellite Weather Prediction. In J. Fulcher, & L.C. Jain (Eds.), Applied Intelligent Systems (Vol. 153, pp. 17-57). Springer. doi:10.1007/978-3-540-39972-8_2

Chapter 10
Cosine and Sigmoid Higher Order Neural Networks for Data Simulations

Ming Zhang
Christopher Newport University, USA

ABSTRACT

New open box and nonlinear model of Cosine and Sigmoid Higher Order Neural Network (CS-HONN) is presented in this paper. A new learning algorithm for CS-HONN is also developed from this study. A time series data simulation and analysis system, CS-HONN Simulator, is built based on the CS-HONN models too. Test results show that average error of CS-HONN models are from 2.3436% to 4.6857%, and the average error of Polynomial Higher Order Neural Network (PHONN), Trigonometric Higher Order Neural Network (THONN), and Sigmoid polynomial Higher Order Neural Network (SPHONN) models are from 2.8128% to 4.9077%. It means that CS-HONN models are 0.1174% to 0.4917% better than PHONN, THONN, and SPHONN models.

INTRODUCTION

This chapter introduces a new Higher Order Neural Network (HONN) model. This new model is tested in the data simulation areas. The contributions of this chapter are:

- Present a new model – CS-HONN.
- Based on the CS-HONN models, build a time series simulation system – CS-HONN simulator.
- Develop the CS-HONN learning algorithm and weight update formulae.
- Shows that CS-HONN can do better than Polynomial Higher Order Neural Network (PHONN), Trigonometric Higher Order Neural Network (THONN), and Sigmoid Polynomial Higher Order Neural Network (SPHONN) models in the data simulation examples.

BACKGROUND

Many studies use traditional artificial neural network models. Blum and Li (1991) studied approximation by feed-forward networks. Gorr (1994) studied the forecasting behavior of multivariate time series using

DOI: 10.4018/978-1-5225-0063-6.ch010

neural networks. Barron, Gilstrap, and Shrier (1987) used polynomial neural networks for the analogies and engineering applications. However, all of the studies above use traditional artificial neural network models - black box models that did not provide users with a function that describe the relationship between the input and output. The first motivation of this paper is to develop nonlinear "open box" neural network models that will provide rationale for network's decisions, also provide better results.

Jiang, Gielen, and Wang (2010) investigated the combined effects of quantization and clipping on Higher Order function neural networks (HOFNN) and multilayer feedforward neural networks (MLF-NN). Statistical models were used to analyze the effects of quantization in a digital implementation This study established and analyzed the relationships for a true nonlinear neuron between inputs and outputs bit resolution, training and quantization methods, the number of network layers, network order and performance degradation, all based on statistical models, and for on-chip and off-chip training. The experimental simulation results verify the presented theoretical analysis.

Lu, Song, and Shieh (2010) studied the polynomial kernel higher order neural networks. As a general framework to represent data, the kernel method can be used if the interactions between elements of the domain occur only through inner product. As a major stride towards the nonlinear feature extraction and dimension reduction, two important kernel-based feature extraction algorithms, kernel principal component analysis and kernel Fisher discriminant, have been proposed. In an attempt to mitigate these drawbacks, this study focused on the application of the newly developed polynomial kernel higher order neural networks in improving the sparsity and thereby obtaining a succinct representation for kernel-based nonlinear feature extraction algorithms. Particularly, the learning algorithm is based on linear programming support vector regression, which outperforms the conventional quadratic programming support vector regression in model sparsity and computational efficiency.

Murata (2010) found that A Pi-Sigma higher order neural network (Pi-Sigma HONN) is a type of higher order neural network, where, as its name implies, weighted sums of inputs are calculated first and then the sums are multiplied by each other to produce higher order terms that constitute the network outputs. This type of higher order neural networks have good function approximation capabilities. In this study, the structural feature of Pi-Sigma HONNs is discussed in contrast to other types of neural networks. The reason for their good function approximation capabilities is given based on pseudo-theoretical analysis together with empirical illustrations.

Ghazali, Hussain, and Nawi (2010) proposed a novel Dynamic Ridge Polynomial Higher Order Neural Network (DRPHONN). The architecture of the new DRPHONN incorporates recurrent links into the structure of the ordinary Ridge Polynomial Higher Order Neural Network (RPHONN). RPHONN is a type of feed-forward Higher Order Neural Network (HONN) which implements a static mapping of the input vectors. In order to model dynamical functions of the brain, it is essential to utilize a system that is capable of storing internal states and can implement complex dynamic system. Neural networks with recurrent connections are dynamical systems with temporal state representations. The dynamic structure approach has been successfully used for solving varieties of problems, such as time series forecasting, approximating a dynamical system, forecasting a stream flow, and system control.

Granger and Bates (1981) researched the combination of forecasts. Granger and Weiss (1983) showed the importance of cointegration in the modeling of nonstationary economic series. Granger and Lee (1990) studied multicointegration. Granger and Swanson (1996) further developed multicointegration in studying of cointegrated variables. The second motivation of this paper is to develop a new nonstationary data analysis system by using new generation computer techniques that will improve the accuracy of the data simulation.

Psaltis, Park, and Hong (1988) studied higher order associative memories and their optical implementations. Redding, Kowalczyk, Downs (1993) developed constructive high-order network algorithm. Zhang, Murugesan, and Sadeghi (1995) developed a Polynomial Higher Order Neural Network (PHONN) model for data simulation. The idea first extended to PHONN Group models (Zhang, Fulcher, and Scofield, (1996)), then to Trigonometric Higher Order Neural Network (THONN) models for data simulation (Zhang, Zhang, and Keen, (1999)). Zhang, Zhang, and Fulcher (2000) studied HONN group model for data simulation. By utilizing adaptive neuron activation functions, Zhang, Xu, and Fulcher (2002) developed an neuron adaptive HONN. Zhang and Fulcher (2004) provide detail mathematics for THONN models. Zhang (2009A) published a HONN book, where all 22 chapters focused on artificial higher order neural networks for economics and business. Zhang (2009B) found that HONN can simulate non-continuous data with better accuracy than SAS NLIN (non-linear) models. Zhang (2009C) also developed Ultra High Frequency Trigonometric Higher Order Neural Networks, in which model details of UCSHONN (Ultra High Frequency Cosine and Sine Higher Order Neural Network) was given.

MODELS OF CS-HONN

CS-HONN model structure can be seen in Figure 1. Formula (1) (2) and (3) are for CS-HONN models 1b, 1 and 0 respectively. Model 1b has three layers of weights changeable, Model 1 has two layers of weights changeable, and model 0 has one layer of weights changeable. For models 1b, 1 and 0, Z is the output while x and y are the inputs of CS-HONN. $a_{kj}{}^{o}$ is the weight for the output layer, $a_{kj}{}^{hx}$ and $a_{kj}{}^{hy}$ are the weights for the second hidden layer, and $a_{k}{}^{x}$ and $a_{j}{}^{y}$ are the weights for the first hidden layer. Functions polynomial and sigmoid are the first hidden layer nodes of CS-HONN. The nodes of the second hidden layer are multiplication neurons. The output layer node of CS-HONN is a linear function of $f^{o}(net^{o}) = net^{o}$, where net^{o} equals the input of output layer node. CS-HONN is an open neural network model, each weight of HONN has its corresponding coefficient in the model formula, and each node of CS-HONN has its corresponding function in the model formula. The structure of CS-HONN is built by a nonlinear formula. It means, after training, there is rationale for each component of CS-HONC in the nonlinear formula.

For formula 1, 2, and 3, values of k and j ranges from 0 to n, where n is an integer. The CS-HONN model can simulate high frequency time series data, when n increases to a big number. This property of the model allows it to easily simulate and predicate high frequency time series data, since both k and j increase when there is an increase in n.

The CS-HONN Architecture was shown in Figure 1. This model structure is used to develop the model learning algorithm, which make sure the convergence of learning. This allows the deference between desired output and real output of CS-HONN close to zero. Formula 1:

$$CS - HONN \quad Model \quad 1b:$$

$$Z = \sum_{k,j=0}^{n} (c_{kj}{}^{o})\{c_{kj}{}^{hx} \cos^{k}(c_{k}{}^{x}x)\}\{c_{kj}{}^{hy}(1/(1+\exp(c_{j}{}^{y}(-y))))^{j}\}$$

Figure 1. CS-HONN Architecture

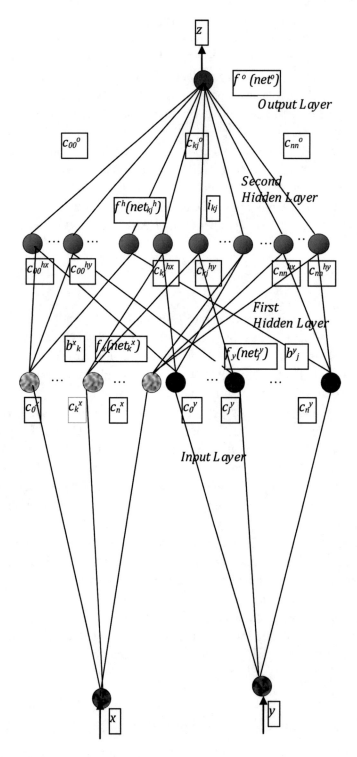

Formula 2:

$CS - HONN \qquad Model \qquad 1:$

$$z = \sum_{k,j=0}^{n} c_{kj}{}^{o} \cos^k(c_k{}^x x)(1/(1+\exp(c_j{}^y(-y))))^j$$

$where: \qquad (c_{kj}{}^{hx}) = (c_{kj}{}^{hy}) = 1$

Formula 3:

$CS - HONN \qquad Model \qquad 0:$

$$z = \sum_{k,j=0}^{n} c_{kj}{}^{o} \cos^k(x)(1/(1+\exp(-y)))^j$$

$where: \qquad (c_{kj}{}^{hx}) = (c_{kj}{}^{hy}) = 1$

$\qquad and \qquad c_k{}^x = c_j{}^y = 1$

CS-HONN TIME SERIES ANALYSIS SYSTEM

The CS-HONN simulator is written in C language, runs under X window on Sun workstation, based on previous work by Zhang, Fulcher, Scofield (1996). A user-friendly *GUI* (Graphical User Interface) system has also been incorporated. When you run the system, any step, data or calculation can be reviewed and modified from different windows during processing. Hence, changing data, network models and comparing results can be done very easily and efficiently.

LEARNING ALGORITHM OF CS-HONN

Learning Algorithm of CS-HONN Model can be described as followings.
    The 1st hidden layer weights are updated according to:

$$c_k{}^x(t+1) = c_k{}^x(t) - \eta(\partial E_p / \partial c_k{}^x)$$

$$c_j{}^y(t+1) = c_j{}^y(t) - \eta(\partial E_p / \partial c_j{}^y)$$

$$c_j{}^y(t+1) = c_j{}^y(t) - \eta(\partial E_p / \partial c_j{}^y)$$

Where:

$c_k{}^x = $ 1st hidden layer weight for input x

Figure 2. CS-HONN Architecture

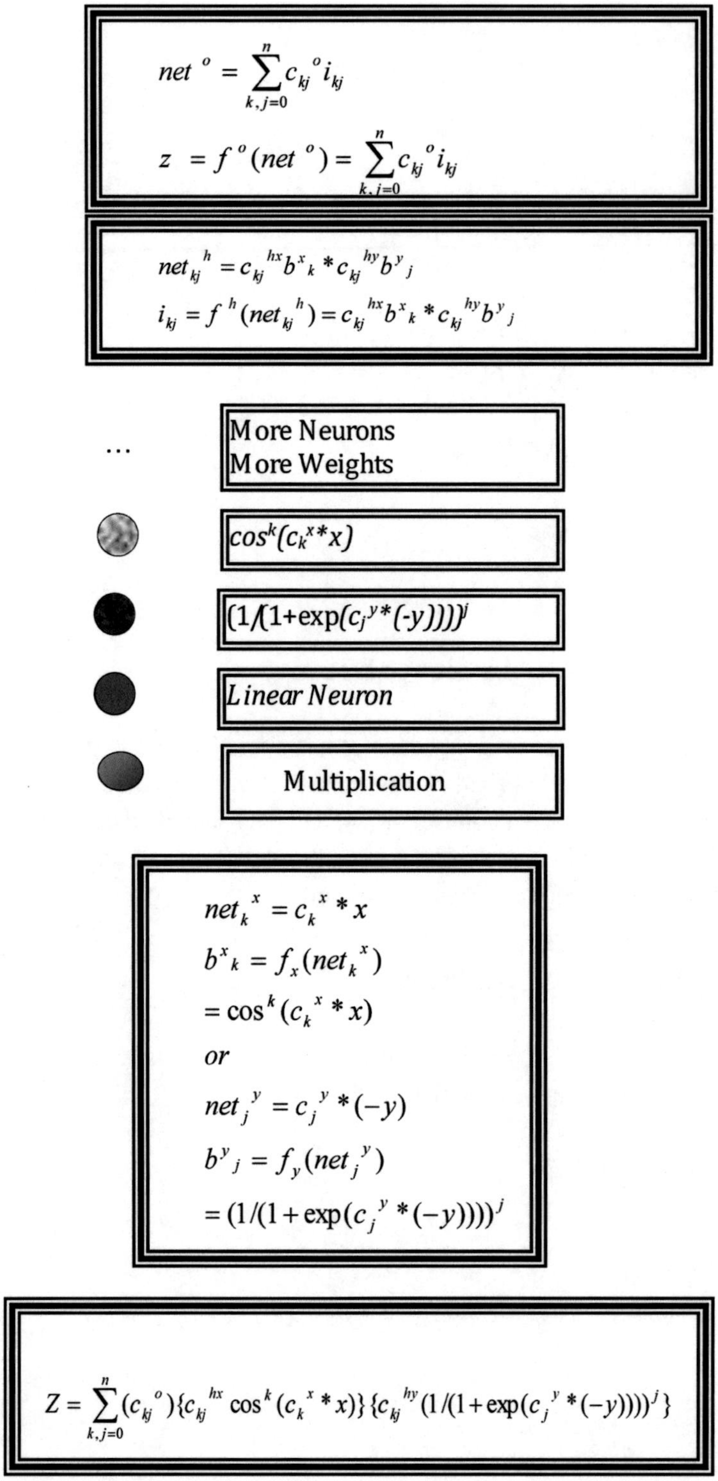

$$net^o = \sum_{k,j=0}^{n} c_{kj}{}^o i_{kj}$$

$$z = f^o(net^o) = \sum_{k,j=0}^{n} c_{kj}{}^o i_{kj}$$

$$net_{kj}{}^h = c_{kj}{}^{hx} b^x{}_k * c_{kj}{}^{hy} b^y{}_j$$

$$i_{kj} = f^h(net_{kj}{}^h) = c_{kj}{}^{hx} b^x{}_k * c_{kj}{}^{hy} b^y{}_j$$

... | More Neurons / More Weights

$cos^k(c_k{}^x*x)$

$(1/(1+exp(c_j{}^y*(-y))))^j$

Linear Neuron

Multiplication

$$net_k{}^x = c_k{}^x * x$$

$$b^x{}_k = f_x(net_k{}^x)$$

$$= \cos^k(c_k{}^x * x)$$

or

$$net_j{}^y = c_j{}^y * (-y)$$

$$b^y{}_j = f_y(net_j{}^y)$$

$$= (1/(1 + \exp(c_j{}^y * (-y))))^j$$

$$Z = \sum_{k,j=0}^{n} (c_{kj}{}^o)\{c_{kj}{}^{hx} \cos^k(c_k{}^x * x)\}\{c_{kj}{}^{hy}(1/(1+\exp(c_j{}^y*(-y))))^j\}$$

$k = k$th neuron of first hidden layer

$c_j^y = 1^{st}$ hidden layer weight for input y

$j = j$th neuron of first hidden layer

$\eta =$ learning rate (positive & usually < 1)

$E_p =$ error

$t =$ training time

The equations for the kth or jth node in the first hidden layer are:

$$net_k^x = c_k^x * x$$
$$b_k^x = f_x(net_k^x) = \cos^k(c_k^x * x)$$
or
$$net_j^y = c_j^y * (-y)$$
$$b_j^y = f_y(net_j^y) = (1/(1 + \exp(c_j^y * (-y))))^j$$

where:

b_k^x and $b_j^y =$ output from the 1st hidden layer neuron ($=$ input to 2nd hidden layer neuron)

f_x and $f_y = 1^{st}$ hidden layer neuron activation function

x and y $=$ input to 1st hidden layer

$$net_{kj}^h = c_{kj}^{hx} b_k^x * c_{kj}^{hy} b_j^y$$
$$i_{kj} = f^h(net_{kj}^h) = c_{kj}^{hx} b_k^x * c_{kj}^{hy} b_j^y$$

where:

$i_{kj} =$ output from 2nd hidden layer ($=$ input to the output neuron)

$$net^o = \sum_{k,j=0}^{n} c_{kj}^o i_{kj}$$

$$z = f^o(net^o) = \sum_{k,j=0}^{n} c_{kj}^o i_{kj}$$

where:

Z is output of HONN.

The total error is the sum of the squared errors across all hidden units, namely:

$$E_p = 0.5 * \delta^2 = 0.5 * (d - z)^2$$
$$= 0.5 * (d - f^o(net^o))^2$$
$$= 0.5 * (d - f^o(\sum_j c_{kj}{}^o i_{kj}))^2$$

where:

d is actual output of HONN

For polynomial function and sigmoid function as in the first layer of HONN:

$$b^x{}_k = f_x (net_k{}^x) = \cos^k(net_k{}^x)$$
$$f_x{}'(net_k{}^x) = \partial b^x{}_k / \partial(net_k{}^x)$$
$$= \partial(\cos^k(net_k{}^x)) / \partial(net_k{}^x)$$
$$= k\cos^{k-1}(net_k{}^x) * (-\sin(net_k{}^x))$$
$$= -k\,\cos^{k-1}(net_k{}^x)\sin(net_k{}^x)$$

$$b^y{}_j = f_y (net_j{}^y) = (1/(1+\exp(net_j{}^y)))^j$$
$$f_y{}'(net_j{}^y) = \partial b^y{}_j / \partial(net_j{}^y)$$
$$= \partial(1/(1+\exp(net_j{}^y)))^j / \partial(net_j{}^y)$$
$$= -j * \exp(net_j{}^y) * (1/(1+\exp(net_j{}^y)))^{j+1}$$

The gradient ($\partial E_p / \partial c_k{}^x$) is given by:

$$\partial E_p / \partial c_k{}^x = \partial(0.5 * (d-z)^2) / \partial c_k{}^x$$
$$= (\partial(0.5 * (d-z)^2) / \partial z)(\partial z / \partial(net^o))$$
$$(\partial(net^o) / \partial i_{kj})(\partial i_{kj} / \partial(net_{kj}{}^h))(\partial(net_{kj}{}^h) / \partial b^x{}_k)$$
$$(\partial b^x{}_k / \partial(net_k{}^x))(\partial(net_k{}^x) / \partial c_k{}^x)$$

$$\partial(0.5 * (d-z)^2 / \partial z = -(d-z)$$

$$\partial z / \partial(net^o) = \partial f^o / \partial(net^o) = f^o{}'(net^o)$$

$$\partial(net^{\,o}) / \partial i_{kj} = \partial(\sum_{k,j=1}^{L}(c_{kj}^{\,o}i_{kj})) / \partial i_{kj} = c_{kj}^{\,o}$$

$$\partial i_{kj} / \partial(net_{kj}^{\,h})$$
$$= \partial(f^{\,h}(net_{kj}^{\,h})) / \partial(net_{kj}^{\,h}) = f^{\,h}\,'(net_{kj}^{\,h})$$

$$\partial net_{kj}^{\,h} / \partial b_{k}^{\,x}$$
$$= \partial((c_{kj}^{\,hx} * b_{k}^{\,x}) * (c_{kj}^{\,hy} * b_{j}^{\,y})) / \partial b_{k}^{\,x} = c_{kj}^{\,hx} * c_{kj}^{\,hy} * b_{j}^{\,y}$$
$$= \delta_{kj}^{\,hx} c_{kj}^{\,hx}$$
$$where : \delta_{kj}^{\,hx} = c_{kj}^{\,hy} * b_{j}^{\,y}$$

$$\partial b_{k}^{\,x} / \partial(net_{k}^{\,x}) = f_{x}\,'(net_{k}^{\,x})$$

$$\partial(net_{k}^{\,x}) / \partial c_{k}^{\,x} = \partial(c_{k}^{\,x} * x) / \partial c_{k}^{\,x} = x$$

Combining Formulae the negative gradient is:

$$-\partial E_{p} / \partial c_{k}^{\,x}$$
$$= (d - z)f^{\,o}\,'(net^{\,o})c_{kj}^{\,o} * f^{\,h}\,'(net_{kj}^{\,h})\delta_{kj}^{\,hx} c_{kj}^{\,hx} f_{x}\,'(net_{k}^{\,x})x$$

The weight update equations are calculated as follows.
For linear output neurons:

$$f^{\,o}\,'(net^{\,o}) = 1$$
$$\delta^{\,ol} = (d - z)f^{\,o}\,'(net^{\,o}) = (d - z)$$

For linear neurons of second hidden layer:

$$f^{\,h}\,'(net_{kj}^{\,h}) = 1$$

The negative gradient is:

$$-\partial E_{p} / \partial c_{k}^{\,x}$$
$$= (d - z)f^{\,o}\,'(net^{\,o})c_{kj}^{\,o} * f^{\,h}\,'(net_{kj}^{\,h})\delta_{kj}^{\,hx} c_{kj}^{\,hx} f_{x}\,'(net_{k}^{\,x})x$$
$$= \delta^{\,ol} * c_{kj}^{\,o} * \delta_{kj}^{\,hx} * c_{kj}^{\,hx} * k * (net_{k}^{\,x})^{k-1} * x$$

By combining the above formulae, the learning algorithm for the 1st hidden layer weights of x input neuron:

$$c_k^{\,x}(t+1) = c_k^{\,x}(t) - \eta(\partial E_p / \partial c_k^{\,x})$$

$$= c_k^{\,x}(t) + \eta(d-z)f^{o\,\prime}(net^{\,o})c_{kj}^{\,o} * f^{h\,\prime}(net_{kj}^{\,h})\delta_{kj}^{\,hx}c_{kj}^{\,hx}f_x^{\,\prime}(net_k^{\,x})x$$

$$= c_k^{\,x}(t) -$$

$$\qquad \eta * \delta^{\,ol} * c_{kj}^{\,o} * \delta^{\,hx} * c_{kj}^{\,hx} * (k)\cos^{k-1}(net_k^{\,x})\sin(net_k^{\,x}) * x$$

$$= c_k^{\,x}(t) + \eta * \delta^{\,ol} * c_{kj}^{\,o} * \delta^{\,hx} * c_{kj}^{\,hx} * \delta^{\,x} * x$$

where:

$$\delta^{\,ol} = (d-z)f^{o\,\prime}(net^{\,o}) = d-z \qquad (linear)$$

$$\delta^{\,hx} = f^{h\,\prime}(net_{kj}^{\,h})c_{kj}^{\,hy}b^y_{\,j} \qquad = c_{kj}^{\,hy}b_j \qquad (linear)$$

$$\delta^{\,x} = f_x^{\,\prime}(net_k^{\,x}) = -(k)\cos^{k-1}(net_k^{\,x})\sin(net_k^{\,x})$$

Using the above procedure, the learning algorithm for the 1st hidden layer weights of y input neuron:

$$c_j^{\,y}(t+1) = c_j^{\,y}(t) - \eta(\partial E_p / \partial c_j^{\,y})$$

$$= c_j^{\,y}(t) + \eta(d-z)f^{o\,\prime}(net^{\,o})c_{kj}^{\,o} * f^{h\,\prime}(net_{kj}^{\,h})\delta_{kj}^{\,hy}c_{kj}^{\,hy}f_y^{\,\prime}(net_j^{\,y})y$$

$$= c_j^{\,y}(t) + \eta * \delta^{\,ol} * c_{kj}^{\,o} * \delta^{\,hy} * c_{kj}^{\,hy}$$

$$\qquad * (-j) * \exp(net_j^{\,y}) * (1/(1+\exp(net_j^{\,y})))^{j+1} * y$$

$$= c_j^{\,y}(t) + \eta * \delta^{\,ol} * c_{kj}^{\,o} * \delta^{\,hy} * c_{kj}^{\,hy} * \delta^{\,y} * y$$

where:

$$\delta^{\,ol} = (d-z)f^{o\,\prime}(net^{\,o}) = d-z \qquad (linear)$$

$$\delta^{\,hy} = f^{h\,\prime}(net_{kj}^{\,hy})c_{kj}^{\,hx}b^x_{\,k} \qquad = c_{kj}^{\,hx}b^x_{\,k} \qquad (linear)$$

$$\delta^{\,y} = f_y^{\,\prime}(net_j^{\,y}) = (-j) * \exp(net_j^{\,y}) * (1/(1+\exp(net_j^{\,y})))^{j+1}$$

TIME SERIES DATA TEST USING CS-HONN

This paper uses the monthly Switzerland Franc and USA dollar exchange rate from November 2008 to December 2009 (See Table 1 and 2) as the test data for CS-HONN models. This paper also uses the monthly New Zealand dollar and USA dollar exchange rate from November 2008 to December 2009 (See Table 3 and 4) as the test data for CS-HONN models. The rate and desired output data, R_t are from

USA Federal Reserve Bank Data bank. Input1, R_{t-2} are the data at time t-2. Input 2, R_{t-1} are the data at time t-1.The values of R_{t-2}, R_{t-1}, and R_t are converted to a range from 0 to 1 and then used as inputs and output in the CS-HONN model. CS-HONN model 1b is used for Table 1, 2, 3 and 4. The test data of CS-HONN orders 6 for using 10,000 epochs are shown on the tables.

In Table 1, "SwitzelandFranc/USDollar Exchange Rate CHF\$1.00 = USD\$0.8561 on 3-Nov-08", the average errors of PHONN, THONN, SPHONN, and CS-HONN are 2.7552%, 2.8547%, 2.8286%, and 2.6954% respectively. The average error of PHONN, THONN, and SPHONN is 2.8128%. So CS-HONN error is 0.1174% better than the average error of PHONN, THONN, and SPHONN models.

In Table 2, "SwitzelandFranc/USDollar Exchange Rate CHF\$1.00 = USD\$0.8220 on 28-Nov-08", the average errors of PHONN, THONN, SPHONN, and CS-HONN are 2.1962%, 3.5549%, 2.7549%, and 2.3436% respectively. The average error of PHONN, THONN, and SPHONN is 2.8353%. So CS-HONN error is 0.4917% better than the average error of PHONN, THONN, and SPHONN models.

In Table 3, "NewZealandDollar/USDollar Exchange Rate NZD\$1.00 = USD\$0.5975 on 3-Nov-09", the average errors of PHONN, THONN, SPHONN, and CS-HONN are 4.3653%, 5.6771%, 4.6806%, and 4.6857% respectively. The average error of PHONN, THONN, and SPHONN is 4.9077%. So CS-HONN error is 0.2220% better than the average error of PHONN, THONN, and SPHONN models.

Table 1. SwitzelandFranc/USDollar Exchange Rate

Original Data				HONN Output				HONN Error (% Percentage)			
Date	Rate Desired Output	Input1 2 month ago data	Input2 1 month ago data	PHONN	THONN	SPHONN	CS-HONN	PHONN	THONN	SPHONN	CS-HONN
11/3/08	0.8561										
12/1/08	0.8281										
1/2/09	0.9359	0.8561	0.8281	0.8812	0.8769	0.8755	0.8677	5.8430	6.3031	6.4530	7.2911
2/2/09	0.8591	0.8281	0.9359	0.8946	0.9074	0.8690	0.9267	4.1348	5.6271	1.1502	7.8697
3/2/09	0.8530	0.9359	0.8591	0.9317	0.9262	0.9475	0.8827	9.2218	8.5760	11.0770	3.4834
4/1/09	0.8722	0.8591	0.8530	0.8904	0.8874	0.8818	0.8510	2.0869	1.7424	1.0994	2.4305
5/1/09	0.8800	0.8530	0.8722	0.8928	0.8921	0.8797	0.8674	1.4608	1.3811	0.0303	1.4298
6/1/09	0.9356	0.8722	0.8800	0.9062	0.9030	0.8967	0.9187	3.1402	3.4828	4.1572	1.8121
7/1/09	0.9328	0.8800	0.9356	0.9292	0.9269	0.9115	0.9270	0.3914	0.6384	2.2919	0.6289
8/3/09	0.9454	0.9356	0.9328	0.9619	0.9518	0.9581	0.9361	1.7537	0.6836	1.3511	0.9771
9/1/09	0.9387	0.9328	0.9454	0.9659	0.9548	0.9576	0.9539	2.9019	1.7175	2.0163	1.6171
10/1/09	0.9593	0.9454	0.9387	0.9704	0.9593	0.9678	0.9532	1.1493	0.0008	0.8883	0.6373
11/2/09	0.9826	0.9387	0.9593	0.9754	0.9624	0.9645	0.9585	0.7378	2.0527	1.8387	2.4571
12/1/09	1.0016	0.9593	0.9826	0.9992	0.9811	0.9857	0.9845	0.2403	2.0503	1.5903	1.7111
Average Error (% Percentage)								2.7552	2.8547	2.8286	2.6954
Average Error pf PHONN, THONN, and SPHONN(% Percentage)								2.8128	CS-HONN Better		0.1174

CHF\$1.00 = USD\$0.8561 on 3-Nov-08, USA Federal Reserve Bank Data (CHF-USD2009-1.dat)

Table 2. SwitzelandFranc/USDollar Exchange Rate

	Original Data			HONN Output				HONN Error (% Percentage)			
Date	Rate Desired Output	Input1 2 month ago data	Input2 1 month ago data	PHONN	THONN	SPHONN	CS-HONN	PHONN	THONN	SPHONN	CS-HONN
11/28/08	0.8220										
12/31/08	0.9369										
1/30/09	0.8612	0.8220	0.9369	0.8811	0.9418	0.9446	0.9153	2.3101	9.3580	9.6816	6.2900
2/27/09	0.8568	0.9369	0.8612	0.9445	0.9396	0.8796	0.8853	10.237	9.6676	2.6646	3.3379
3/31/09	0.8776	0.8612	0.8568	0.8629	0.8718	0.8822	0.8604	1.6766	0.6562	0.5229	1.9525
4/30/09	0.8770	0.8568	0.8776	0.8701	0.8805	0.8978	0.8523	0.7881	0.3918	2.3658	2.8196
5/29/09	0.9353	0.8776	0.8770	0.8913	0.8790	0.8958	0.8912	4.7000	6.0191	4.2212	4.7106
6/30/09	0.9202	0.8770	0.9353	0.9249	0.9035	0.9390	0.9255	0.5037	1.8210	2.0391	0.5754
7/31/09	0.9374	0.9353	0.9202	0.9553	0.9314	0.9224	0.9287	1.9114	0.6362	1.6021	0.9228
8/31/09	0.9462	0.9202	0.9374	0.9531	0.9173	0.9365	0.9529	0.7342	3.0516	1.0219	0.7091
9/30/09	0.9639	0.9374	0.9462	0.9636	0.9369	0.9412	0.9525	0.0309	2.7975	2.3536	1.1806
10/30/09	0.9768	0.9462	0.9639	0.9708	0.9511	0.9532	0.9876	0.6073	2.6243	2.4104	1.1100
11/30/09	0.9950	0.9639	0.9768	0.9739	0.9799	0.9607	0.9562	2.1224	1.5225	3.4524	3.9009
12/31/09	0.9654	0.9768	0.9950	0.9725	1.0051	0.9724	0.9595	0.7329	4.1133	0.7226	0.6136
Average Error (% Percentage)								2.1962	3.5549	2.7549	2.3436
Average Error pf PHONN, THONN, and SPHONN(% Percentage)								2.8353	CS-HONN Better		0.4917

CHF$1.00 = USD$0.8220 on 28-Nov-08, USA Federal Reserve Bank Data (CHF-USD2009-2.dat)

In Table 4, "NewZealandDollar/USDollar Exchange RateNZD$1.00 = USD$0.5500 on 28-Nov-08", the average errors of PHONN, THONN, SPHONN, and CS-HONN are 4.2512%, 4.6730%, 5.1945%, and 4.3306% respectively. The average error of PHONN, THONN, and SPHONN is 4.7062%. So CS-HONN error is 0.3756% better than the average error of PHONN, THONN, and SPHONN models.

FUTURE RESEARCH DIRECTIONS

As the next step of HONN model research, more HONN models for different data control will be built to increase the pool of HONN models. Theoretically, the adaptive HONN models can be built and allow the computer automatically choose the best model, order, and coefficients. Thus, making the adaptive HONN models easier to use is one of the future research topics.

HONNs can automatically select the initial coefficients for nonlinear data analysis. The next step of this study will also focus on how to allow people working in the prediction area to understand that HONNs are much easier to use and can have better results. Moreover, further research will develop HONNs software packages for people working in the prediction area. HONNs will challenge classic

Table 3. NewZealandDollar/USDollar Exchange Rate

Original Data				HONN Output				HONN Error (% Percentage)			
Date	Rate Desired Output	Input1 2 month ago data	Input2 1 month ago data	PHONN	THONN	SPHONN	CS-HONN	PHONN	THONN	SPHONN	CS-HONN
11/3/08	0.5975										
12/1/08	0.5355										
1/2/09	0.5850	0.5975	0.5355	0.5706	0.5599	0.5914	0.5904	2.4682	4.2988	1.0934	0.9242
2/2/09	0.5026	0.5355	0.5850	0.5883	0.5867	0.5934	0.5516	17.0441	16.7252	18.0587	9.7552
3/2/09	0.4926	0.5850	0.5026	0.5486	0.5413	0.5668	0.5698	11.3602	9.8961	15.0575	15.6726
4/1/09	0.5635	0.5026	0.4926	0.5310	0.5474	0.5290	0.5245	5.7669	2.8580	6.1159	6.9175
5/1/09	0.5687	0.4926	0.5635	0.5629	0.5906	0.5649	0.5552	1.0178	3.8500	0.6719	2.3739
6/1/09	0.6509	0.5635	0.5687	0.5856	0.5745	0.5964	0.6119	10.0259	11.7383	8.3807	5.9887
7/1/09	0.6452	0.5687	0.6509	0.6449	0.6281	0.6377	0.6564	0.0401	2.6484	1.1580	1.7328
8/3/09	0.6683	0.6509	0.6452	0.6648	0.6484	0.6703	0.6591	0.5194	2.9829	0.2982	1.3775
9/1/09	0.6794	0.6452	0.6683	0.6825	0.6652	0.6780	0.6672	0.4502	2.0911	0.2039	1.7942
10/1/09	0.7168	0.6683	0.6794	0.6954	0.6877	0.6917	0.6578	2.9920	4.0592	3.5002	8.2364
11/2/09	0.7225	0.6794	0.7168	0.7271	0.7343	0.7110	0.7154	0.6389	1.6371	1.5895	0.9824
12/1/09	0.7285	0.7168	0.7225	0.7289	0.7674	0.7288	0.7251	0.0600	5.3400	0.0400	0.4726
Average Error (% Percentage)								4.3653	5.6771	4.6806	4.6857
Average Error pf PHONN, THONN, and SPHONN(% Percentage)								4.9077	CS-HONN Better		0.2220

NZD$1.00 = USD$0.5975 on 3-Nov-09, USA Federal Reserve Bank Data (NZD-USD2009-1.dat)

procedures and change the research methodology that people are currently using in the prediction areas for the nonlinear data control application

CONCLUSION

This paper develops the details of a open box and nonlinear higher order neural network models of CS-HONN. This paper also provides the learning algorithm formulae for CS-HONN, based on the structures of CS-HONN. This paper uses CS-HONN simulator and tests the CS-HONN models using high frequency data and the running results are compared with Polynomial Higher Order Neural Network (PHONN), Trigonometric Higher Order Neural Network (THONN), and Sigmoid Polynomial Higher Order Neural Network (SPHONN) models. Test results show that average error of CS-HONN models are from 2.3436% to 4.6857%, and the average error of Polynomial Higher Order Neural Network (PHONN), Trigonometric Higher Order Neural Network (THONN), and Sigmoid polynomial Higher Order Neural Network (SPHONN) models are from 2.8128% to 4.9077%. It means that CS-HONN models are 0.1174% to 0.4917% better than PHONN, THONN, and SPHONN models.

Table 4. NewZealandDollar/USDollar Exchange Rate

Original Data				HONN Output				HONN Error (% Percentage)			
Date	Rate Desired Output	Input1 2 month ago data	Input2 1 month ago	PHONN	THONN	SPHONN	CS-HONN	PHONN	THONN	SPHONN	CS-HONN
11/28/08	0.5500										
12/31/08	0.5815										
1/30/09	0.5084	0.5500	0.5815	0.5911	0.5974	0.5882	0.5453	16.2598	17.5013	15.6890	7.2636
2/27/09	0.5030	0.5815	0.5084	0.5390	0.5318	0.5655	0.5354	7.1663	5.7240	12.4309	6.4485
3/31/09	0.5692	0.5084	0.5030	0.5293	0.5269	0.5376	0.5307	7.0055	7.4388	5.5524	6.7720
4/30/09	0.5695	0.5030	0.5692	0.5758	0.5858	0.5638	0.5565	1.1114	2.8694	1.0033	2.2788
5/29/09	0.6370	0.5692	0.5695	0.5851	0.5860	0.5903	0.6690	8.1451	8.0084	7.3365	5.0224
6/30/09	0.6447	0.5695	0.6370	0.6400	0.6509	0.6221	0.6536	0.7347	0.9646	3.5030	1.3809
7/31/09	0.6605	0.6370	0.6447	0.6646	0.6572	0.6565	0.6536	0.6254	0.4950	0.6049	1.0476
8/31/09	0.6856	0.6447	0.6605	0.6792	0.6722	0.6681	0.6530	0.9316	1.9474	2.5506	4.7550
9/30/09	0.7233	0.6605	0.6856	0.7016	0.6958	0.6886	0.6823	3.0059	3.7983	4.8013	5.6676
10/30/09	0.7230	0.6856	0.7233	0.7265	0.7297	0.7206	0.7388	0.4863	0.9278	0.3366	2.1913
11/30/09	0.7151	0.7233	0.7230	0.7243	0.7275	0.7389	0.7495	1.2920	1.7283	3.3312	4.8089
12/31/09	0.7255	0.7230	0.7151	0.7227	0.7203	0.7349	0.7271	0.3900	0.7100	1.2900	0.2236
Average Error (% Percentage)								4.2513	4.6730	5.1945	4.3306
Average Error pf PHONN, THONN, and SPHONN(% Percentage)								4.7062	CS-HONN Better		0.3756

NZD$1.00 = USD$0.5500 on 28-Nov-08, USA Federal Reserve Bank Data (NZD-USD2009-2.dat)

One of the topics for future research is to continue building models of higher order neural networks for different data series. The coefficients of the higher order models will be studied not only using artificial neural network techniques, but also statistical methods.

REFERENCES

Barron, R., Gilstrap, L., & Shrier, S. (1987). Polynomial and neural networks: analogies and engineering applications. *Proceedings of International Conference of Neural Networks* New York, USA (Vol. 2, pp. 431-439).

Blum, E., & Li, K. (1991). Approximation theory and feed-forward networks. *Neural Networks*, *4*(4), 511–515. doi:10.1016/0893-6080(91)90047-9

Ghazali, R., Hussain, A., & Nawi, N. (2010). Dynamic ridge polynomial higher order neural network. In M. Zhang (Ed.), *Artificial Higher Order Neural Networks for Computer Science and Engineering* (pp. 255–268). Hershey, PA, USA: IGI Global.

Gorr, W. L. (1994). Research prospective on neural network forecasting. *International Journal of Forecasting, 10*(1), 1–4. doi:10.4018/978-1-61520-711-4.ch011

Granger, C. W. J. (1981). Some properties of time series data and their use in econometric model specification. *Journal of Econometrics, 16*(1), 121–130. doi:10.1016/0304-4076(81)90079-8

Granger, C. W. J., & Lee, T. H. (1990). Multicointegration. In G. F. Rhodes, Jr & T. B. Fomby (Eds.), Advances in Econometrics: Cointegration, Spurious Regressions and Unit Roots (pp. 17-84). New York, USA: JAI Press.

Granger, C. W. J., & Swanson, N. R. (1996). Further developments in study of cointegrated variables. *Oxford Bulletin of Economics and Statistics, 58*, 374–386.

Granger, C. W. J., & Weiss, A. A. (1983). Time series analysis of error-correction models. In S. Karlin, T. Amemiya & L. A. Goodman (Eds), Studies in Econometrics, Time Series and Multivariate Statistics (pp. 255-278). San Diego, USA: Academic Press. doi:10.1016/B978-0-12-398750-1.50018-8

Jiang, M., Gielen, G., & Wang, L. (2010). Analysis of quantization effects of higher order function and multilayer feedforward neural networks. In M. Zhang (Ed.), *Artificial Higher Order Neural Networks for Computer Science and Engineering* (pp. 187–222). Hershey, PA, USA: IGI Global. doi:10.4018/978-1-61520-711-4.ch008

Lu, Z., Song, G., & Shieh, L. (2010). Improving sparsity in kernelized nonlinear feature extraction algorithms by polynomial kernel higher order neural networks. In M. Zhang (Ed.), *Artificial Higher Order Neural Networks for Computer Science and Engineering* (pp. 223–238). Hershey, PA, USA: IGI Global. doi:10.4018/978-1-61520-711-4.ch009

Murata, J. (2010). Analysis and improvement of function approximation capabilities of pi-sigma higher order neural networks. In M. Zhang (Ed.), *Artificial Higher Order Neural Networks for Computer Science and Engineering* (pp. 239–254). Hershey, PA, USA: IGI Global. doi:10.4018/978-1-61520-711-4.ch010

Psaltis, D., Park, C., & Hong, J. (1988). Higher order associative memories and their optical implementations. *Neural Networks, 1*(2), 149–163. doi:10.1016/0893-6080(88)90017-2

Redding, N., Kowalczyk, A., & Downs, T. (1993). Constructive high-order network algorithm that is polynomial time. *Neural Networks, 6*(7), 997–1010. doi:10.1016/S0893-6080(09)80009-9

Zhang, M. (2009A). *Artificial higher order neural networks for economics and business*. Hershey, PA, USA: IGI Global. doi:10.4018/978-1-59904-897-0

Zhang, M. (2009B). Artificial higher order neural network nonlinear models: SAS NLIN or HONNs. In M. Zhang (Ed.), *Artificial higher order neural networks for economics and business* (pp. 1–47). Hershey, PA, USA: IGI Global. doi:10.4018/978-1-59904-897-0.ch001

Zhang, M. (2009C). Ultra high frequency trigonometric higher order neural networks. In M. Zhang (Ed.), *Artificial higher order neural networks for economics and business* (pp. 133–163). Hershey, PA, USA: IGI Global. doi:10.4018/978-1-59904-897-0.ch007

Zhang, M., & Fulcher, J. (2004). Higher order neural networks for satellite weather prediction. In J. Fulcher & L. C. Jain (Eds.), *Applied Intelligent Systems* (Vol. 153, pp. 17–57). New York, USA: Springer. doi:10.1007/978-3-540-39972-8_2

Zhang, M., Fulcher, J., & Scofield, R. A. (1996). Neural network group models for estimating rainfall from satellite images. *Proceedings of World Congress on Neural Networks,* San Diego, CA, USA (pp. 897-900).

Zhang, M., Murugesan, S., & Sadeghi, M. (1995). Polynomial higher order neural network for economic data simulation, *Proceedings of International Conference on Neural Information Processing,* Beijing, China (pp. 493-496).

Zhang, M., Xu, S., & Fulcher, J. (2002). Neuron-adaptive higher order neural network models for automated financial data modeling. *IEEE Transactions on Neural Networks, 13*(1), 188–204. doi:10.1109/72.977302 PMID:18244418

Zhang, M., Zhang, J. C., & Fulcher, J. (2000). Higher order neural network group models for data approximation. *International Journal of Neural Systems, 10*(2), 123–142. doi:10.1142/S0129065700000119 PMID:10939345

Zhang, M., Zhang, J. C., & Keen, S. (1999). Using THONN system for higher frequency non-linear data simulation & prediction, *Proceedings of IASTED, International Conference on Artificial Intelligence and Soft Computing,* Honolulu, Hawaii, USA (pp. 320-323).

Chapter 11

Improving Performance of Higher Order Neural Network using Artificial Chemical Reaction Optimization:
A Case Study on Stock Market Forecasting

Sarat Chandra Nayak
Veer Surendra Sai University of Technology, India

Bijan Bihari Misra
Silicon Institute of Technology, India

Himansu Sekhar Behera
Veer Surendra Sai University of Technology, India

ABSTRACT

Multilayer neural networks are commonly and frequently used technique for mapping complex nonlinear input-output relationship. However, they add more computational cost due to structural complexity in architecture. This chapter presents different functional link networks (FLN), a class of higher order neural network (HONN). FLNs are capable to handle linearly non-separable classes by increasing the dimensionality of the input space by using nonlinear combinations of input signals. Usually such network is trained with gradient descent based back propagation technique, but it suffers from many drawbacks. To overcome the drawback, here a natural chemical reaction inspired metaheuristic technique called as artificial chemical reaction optimization (ACRO) is used to train the network. As a case study, forecasting of the stock index prices of different stock markets such as BSE, NASDAQ, TAIEX, and FTSE are considered here to compare and analyze the performance gain over the traditional techniques.

DOI: 10.4018/978-1-5225-0063-6.ch011

INTRODUCTION

Artificial Neural Networks (ANN) are found to be good universal approximator which can approximate any continuous function to desired accuracy. It also allows the adaptive adjustment to the model and nonlinear description of the problems. Some earlier use of ANN for the financial forecasting purpose can be found in the research work carried out by Refenes et al. (1994), Schoeneburg (1990), Yoon et al. (1994), Yoon and Swales (1991), Choi et al. (1995), Gately (1996), and Drossu and Obradovic (1996). The ANNs have recently been applied to many areas such as data mining, stock market analysis, medical and many other fields. Gradient based methods are one of the most widely used error minimization methods used to train back propagation networks. Back propagation algorithm is a classical domain dependent technique for supervised training. It works by measuring the output error calculating the gradient of this error, and adjusting the ANN weights and biases in the descending gradient direction. Back propagation is the most commonly used and the simplest feed forward algorithm used for classification. Back propagation based ANNs are very popular methods to predict stock market with better calculation, spreading abilities and stronger nonlinear mapping ability.

It is observed that Multilayer Perceptron (MLP) has been adopted as the most frequently used ANN by the researchers for the task of forecasting. An MLP contains one or more hidden layer, and each layer can contain more than one neurons. The input pattern is applied to the input layer of the network and it propagates the signals through the network from one layer to other till it reaches the output layer. During the forward phase, the synaptic weights of the networks are fixed. In the backward phase, the weights are adjusted in accordance with the error correction rule popularly called as back propagation learning rule. Some forecasting applications of MLP are financial time series forecasting by Yu and Wang (2009), market trend analysis by Aiken and Bsat (1999), macroeconomic data forecasting by Aminian et al. (2006), stock exchange movement by Mohamed and Mostafa (2010), railway traffic forecasting by Zhuo et al. (2007), airline passenger traffic forecasting by Nam and Yi (1997), maritime traffic forecasting by Mohamed and Mostafa (2004), electric load forecasting by Darbellay and Slama (2000) and air pollution forecasting by Videnova et al. (2006). Though MLP is the most widely and frequently used technique, but it suffers from slow and non convergence. Calderon and Cheh (2002) argued that the standard MLP network is subject to problems of local minima. Again there is no formal guideline how to develop a network for the MLP technique as suggested in the work carried out by Swicegood and Clark (2001). It is suggested that to overcome the local minima problem, more number of nodes may be added to the hidden layers. But multiple hidden layers with large number of neurons in each layer make the network computationally inefficient. Finding an optimal structure of the network of MLP technique leads to a combinatorial problem. Defining a feasible architecture and parameters for MLP is very often a matter of trial and error which is also computationally very expensive. From the study of the existing literature on stock market index forecasting, it is observed that improved forecasting accuracy and adopting models with less computational complexities are important areas of present day research in the stock market. The research work by (Patra et al. 2009a), Kim et al.(2006), (Majhi et al., 2009a) proposed a trigonometric functional link network (FLN) using least mean squared (LMS) and recursive least square (RLS) to forecast both short and long term forecasting. The work concludes that FLN based stock market prediction model is an effective approach both computationally as well as performance wise to foresee the market levels both in short and medium terms future. There have been several applications of FLN including pattern classification and recognition by Mishra and Dehuri (2007), Mishra et al. (2008), (Dehuri and Cho, 2010a), (Dehuri and Cho, 2010b), (Majhi et al. 2009b), system identification and control by Majhi et al. (2012), Purwar et al.(2007), functional approximation by (Patra et al., 1999a), Lee and Jeng (1998), and digital communications channel equalization by Yang and Tseng (1996). The trigonometric expansion is chosen in many research works, because such expansion based models have been shown to provide improved performance for various applications such as by (Majhi et al., 2009c), (Patra et al., 1999c), Patra et al., (1994), and (Patra et al., 1999d).

Aiming with better forecasting accuracies, researchers moved toward adopting hybrid ANN models with large number of evolutionary optimization techniques. Optimization is one of the cornerstones in science and engineering. Most of the problems can be formulated in the form of optimization ranging from power generation scheduling in electrical engineering by AlRashidi and EI-Hawary (2009), DNA sequencing in biomedical science by Shin et al. (2005), to stock market trend prediction by Yu et al. (2009). In the recent past, the field of nature-inspired optimization techniques has grown incredibly fast. These algorithms are usually general-purpose and population-based. They are normally referred to as evolutionary algorithms because many of them are motivated by biological evolution. In a broad sense, evolutionary algorithms cover those which vary a group of solutions in iterations based on some nature-inspired operations. Examples include GA, memetic algorithm (MA), ant colony optimization (ACO), particle swarm optimization (PSO), differential evolution (DE), and harmony search (HS). Many of them are inspired by biological processes, varying in scale from the genetic level, e.g. GA, MA, and DE, to the creature level, e.g. ACO and PSO. Unlike the others, HS is motivated by the phenomenon of human activities in composing music. These algorithms are successful in solving many different kinds of optimization problems.

Newly research attempts to hybridize several artificial intelligence (AI) techniques to improve the prediction performance. The new hybrid iterative evolutionary learning algorithm is more effective than the conventional algorithm in terms of learning accuracy and prediction accuracy. Evolutionary training algorithms are capable of searching better than gradient descent based search techniques. Artificial chemical reaction optimization is a recently invented metaheuristic which mimics the nature of chemical reaction. The parameters of a network can be encoded into a form of reactants, a set of such reactants forming a population, which undergo a sequence of chemical reactions and finally obtaining an optimal set of reactants with least enthalpy (better fit). The algorithm requires less number of parameters, easy to implement as well as faster convergence characteristics. There are few applications of this technique into the area of data mining and financial forecasting.

The stock market is very complex and dynamic in nature, and has been a subject of study for modeling its characteristics by various researchers. Stock index forecasting is challenging due to the nonlinear and non-stationary characteristics of the stock market. Various economic factors such as oil prices, exchange rates, interest rates, stock price indexes in other countries, domestic/global economic situations, etc. affect the movement of a stock market. These factors have been employed on the study of stock price prediction and found to be important elements for influencing the market. An accurate forecasting is both necessary and beneficial for all investors in the market including investment institutions as well as small individual investors. Hence there is a need of developing an automated forecasting model which can accurately estimate the risk level and the profit gain in return as well as the direction of the stock market movement.

The traditional technical analysis approach that predicts stock prices based on historical data have been used by the stock investors to aid the investment decisions are found in Murphy (1999), Trippi and DeSieno (1992), Kryzanowski et al. (1993). There also found some prediction systems used by the financial experts, based on pure mathematical models and expert systems such as work done by

Han et al. (1998), John and Miller (1996). Several statistical techniques have been used extensively for stock market prediction. Among those statistical techniques employed in this regard, moving averages (MA), auto-regressive integrated moving average (ARIMA), auto-regressive heteroscedastic (ARCH), generalized ARCH (GARCH) received wide acceptance. Liu et al. (2009) investigated the influence of specification of return distribution on the performance of volatility forecasting using two Generalized Auto Regressive Conditional Heteroskedasticity (GARCH) models i.e. GARCH-N and GARCH-SGED. Their empirical results from Shanghai and Shenzhen composite stock indices indicated that the GARCH-SGED model is more accurate and superior to the GARCH-N model in forecasting the volatility of China stock market. Kung and Yu (2008) adopted the GM (1, 1) model to predict the rates of return of nine major index futures in the American and Eurasian market and compared the performance with GARCH/TGARCH. Their results findings revealed that the latter models perform better than the former in terms of forecasting capabilities. They have successfully applied to different engineering, economic and social applications. These traditionally statistical models can be applied on stationary data sets and can't be automated easily. At every stage it requires expert interpretation and development. These models were lacking with capturing the non-linearity of other types of time series, since they have developed to model certain types of problems. Due to the presence of noise and non-linearity in the financial time series, such traditional methods have seldom proved to be effective. They have poor capabilities to map the nonlinearity and chaotic behavior of the stock market. This paves the path of adopting nonlinear models such as soft and evolutionary computing methodologies which include artificial neural networks (ANN), fuzzy neural networks, rough set theory, genetic algorithm etc.

This chapter attempts to use and study the performance of FLN based forecasting models applied for prediction of daily closing prices of stock market. The FLN based forecasting models are trained with back propagation. In order to improve the prediction accuracies of these models a natural chemical reaction inspired optimization algorithm is used in place of back propagation based training. The weight and bias vectors of the model have been selected by artificial chemical reaction optimization during training process. These models are employed to forecast the one-day, one-week, and one-month-ahead closing prices of five global stock markets.

The contribution of this chapter will be:

- Introduction to FLN based HONN
- Developing different adaptive FLN based HONN forecasting models
- Performance improvement using ACRO
- Performances of the developed models are compared with that of gradient descent based forecasting models
- Experiment on global stock market data for short term, medium term and long term prediction.

1. HIGHER ORDER NEURAL NETWORK (HONN)

Higher Order Neural Networks (HONN) are type of feed forward networks which provide nonlinear decision boundaries, hence offering better classification capability as compared to linear neuron suggested by Guler and Sahin (1994). They are different from ordinary feed forward networks by the introduction of higher order terms into the network. In most of the neural network models, neural inputs are combined using summing operation, where in HONN, not only summing units, but also units that find the product of weighted inputs called as higher order terms are present. Due to single layer of trainable weights needed to achieve nonlinear separability, they are simple in architecture and require less number of weights to capture the associated nonlinearity as discussed by Guler and Sahin (1994), and Shin and Ghosh (1995). As compared to networks utilizing summation units only, higher order terms in HONN can increase the information capacity of the network. This representational power of higher order terms can help solving complex nonlinear problems with small networks as well as maintaining fast convergence capabilities described by Park et al. (2000). HONN have fast learning properties, stronger approximation, greater storage capacity, higher fault tolerance capability and powerful mapping of single layer trainable weights as discussed by Leerink et al. (1995), Wang et al. (2008).

To alleviate the well-known drawbacks of traditional neural based models many researchers have been turned their attention to various HONN based models. However, there exist only few studies using HONN, particularly in the areas of finance and economics. Ghazali (2005) developed a HONN based model for financial time series prediction and found that HONN performs superior as compared to conventional multilayer neural network based models. Another attempt by Knowles et al. (2005) used HONNs with Bayesian confidence measure for prediction of EUR/USD exchange rates and observed that the simulation results for HONNs are much better than multilayer approach based models. Some HONNs such as Higher Order Processing Unit Neural Network (HPUNN) by Giles and Maxwell (1987), Product Unit neural Network (PUNN) by Durbin and Rumelhart (1989) have been developed by the researchers in order to avoid the drawbacks of traditional neural models as well as better nonlinear mapping performance. However, there is exponential increase in the required higher order terms which may affect the network. But the PSNN developed by the authors Shin and Ghosh (1991) is able to avoid this increase in number of weight vectors along with the processing units. A novel application of Ridge polynomial neural network which is formed by adding different degrees of PSNNs has been proposed by Ghazali et al. (2006). The network has been applied for financial time series forecasting and able to find better nonlinearity mapping of various financial time series data with an appropriate generalization capability as well as learning speed. Yong Nie and Wei Deng (2008) proposed a hybrid genetic algorithm trained PSNN to resolve the function optimization problem. They concluded that the hybrid method can have better search capability and faster than genetic algorithm. Epitropakis et al. (2010) have been proposed a PSNN trained by distributed evolutionary algorithm which has superior performance. Another novel hybrid HONN has been proposed by authors Fallahnezhad et al. (2011) for the classification problem. This hybrid model exhibits good generalization capability and also improved classification accuracy. A Neuron-Adaptive Higher Order Neural-Network Model for automated financial data modeling has been suggested by Zhang et al. (2002). Their model shown to be "open box" and as such is more acceptable to financial experts than classical closed box neural networks. This model is further shown to be capable of automatically finding not only the optimum model, but also the appropriate order for specific financial data.

The FLN architecture was originally proposed by Pao et al. (1989). They have shown that, their proposed network may be conveniently used for function approximation and pattern classification with faster convergence rate and lesser computational load than the multilayer perceptron (MLP) structure as discussed by Pao and Takefuji (1992), Patra and Bos (2000), (Patra et al., 1999b). The FLN is basically a flat net and the need of the hidden layer is removed and hence, the learning algorithm used in this network becomes very simple. The functional expansion effectively increases the dimensionality of the input vector and hence the hyper plane generated by the FLN provides greater discrimination capability in the input pattern space. The FLN architecture uses a single layer feed forward neural network and to overcome the linear mapping, functionally expands the input vector.

Different nonlinear expansions may be employed. These are trigonometric (*sine* and *cosine*), Chebyshev *polynomial* function, *Lagurre polynomial* function, *Legendre polynomial* function and *power polynomial* function. In the functional expansion process each input signal to the model is nonlinearly expanded to generate several input values. The functional expansion component will generate a set of linearly independent functions with each closing value in the input vector taken as argument of the function. This nonlinearity to the input elements reduces the number of layers and hence lesser is the computational complexity.

The FLN model considered here is a single layer model with on trigonometric expansion. Let each element of the input pattern before expansion be represented as $z(i)$, $1<i<d$, where each element $z(i)$ is functionally expanded as $fn(z(i))$, $1<n<N$, where N is the number of expanded points for each input element. For designing the network, at the first instance a functional expansion (FE) unit expands each input attribute of the input data. Figure 1 represents the FE unit of the FLN based model.

The attributes of each input pattern is passed through the FE unit. Here a single output neuron is considered. This model does not contain any hidden layer other than the FE unit. Figure 2 shows the architecture of the FLN model.

The sum of the output signals of the FE units multiplied with weights is passed on to the sigmoidal activation function of the output unit. This estimated output is compared with the target output and error signal is obtained. This error signal is passed on to the training algorithm as its fitness function and the model having minimum error is considered as the best fit individual.

2. ARTIFICIAL CHEMICAL REACTION OPTIMIZATION (ACRO)

Artificial chemical reaction optimization (ACRO) is one of the recently established meta-heuristics for optimization proposed by Lam and Li (2010). It is an evolutionary optimization technique inspired by the nature of chemical reaction. In a short period of time, ACRO has been applied to solve many problems

Figure 1. Functional expansion (FE) unit

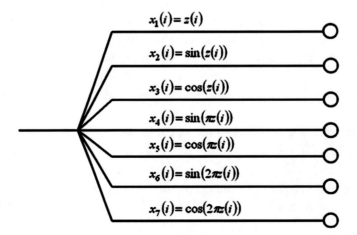

Figure 2. Basic architecture of a FLN model

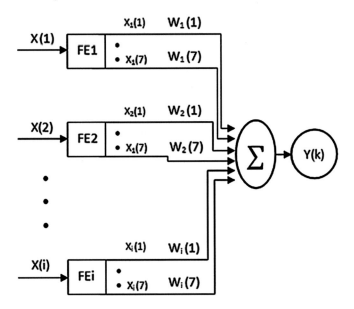

successfully, outperforming many existing evolutionary algorithms in most of the test cases. There are few applications of ACRO to multiple-sequence alignment, data mining, classification rule discovery and some benchmark functions and the efficiency has been demonstrated in Alatas (2011), and Alatas (2012). This optimization method does not need a local search method to refine the search and includes both local and global search capability. Unlike other optimization techniques, ACRO does not require many parameters that must be specified at beginning and only defining number of initial reactants is enough for implementation. As the initial reactants are distributed over feasible global search region, optimal solutions can be obtained with few iterations and hence significant reduction in computational time. The ACRO has been successfully used to solve many complex problems in recent years and found to be outperforming many other evolutionary population based algorithms. A complete guideline to help the readers implement ACRO for their optimization problem can be found in the tutorial introduced by Lam and Li (2012). The tutorial summarizes the basic characteristics as well as applications reported in the literature. A real coded version of chemical reaction optimization (RCCRO) has been proposed by Lam et al. (2012) to solve the continuous optimization problems. Also, they proposed an adaptive scheme for RCCRO for performance improvement. The performance of RCCRO has been compared with a large number of techniques experimented on a set of standard continuous benchmark functions. The results show the suitability of ACRO solving problems in the continuous domain. Chemical reaction optimization also successfully applied for population transition peer-to-peer live streaming by Lam et al. 2010). They employed chemical reaction optimization to maximize the probability of universal streaming by manipulating population transition probability matrix. Their simulation results show that ACRO outperforms many commonly used strategies for this problem. Minimizing the number of coding links of a network for a given target transmission rate to improve the network efficiency is a NP-hard problem. Pan et al. (2011) adopted chemical reaction optimization to develop an algorithm to solve this complex problem and found that the ACRO based framework outperforms other existing algorithms. The ACRO also has been successfully applied to grid scheduling problem by Xu et al. (2010) and task scheduling problem by Xu et al. (2011). The authors compared the efficiency of several versions of chemical reaction optimization with other algorithms such as genetic algorithm, simulated annealing, threshold accepting and particle swarm optimization and found superior. ACRO also used to replace the back propagation based training of ANN for classification problem by Yu et al. (2011). The simulation results show that the ACRO based ANN outperforms other optimization techniques such as GA, SVM etc. Allocating available channels to the unlicensed users in order to maximize the utility of radio channels is a complex task. An algorithm based on ACRO has been developed by (Lam & Li, 2010b) to solve this radio spectrum allocation problem which outperforms other evolutionary techniques. Two different types of chemical reaction optimization, named canonical CRO and super molecule based CRO (S-CRO) have been proposed by Xu et al. (2011) for the problem of stock portfolio selection and suggested that S-CRO is promising in handling the stock portfolio optimization problem. A special type of higher order neural network, called as Pi-Sigma neural network (PSNN) has been trained with ACRO forms a novel CRO-PSNN model by Nayak et al. (2015). The model performance has been tested with various benchmark data sets. The performance of their proposed model is found superior to PSNN, GA-PSNN and PSO-PSNN. A new chemical reaction optimization with greedy strategy algorithm (CROG) has been proposed by Truong et al. (2013) to solve the 0-1 knapsack problem. The article designed a new repair function integrating a greedy strategy and random selection is used to repair the infeasible solutions. The experimental results show the superiority of CROG over GA, ACO and quantum-inspired evolutionary algorithm.

2.1. Basics of Different Chemical Reactions

Chemical reactions are usually characterized by a chemical change. One or more products having properties different from reactants are produced. N different types of molecules or chemical reactants may take part in one or more of M types of chemical reactions. Many reactions are reversible. The observable properties and concentrations of all participants become constant when a chemical system reaches a state of equilibrium, i.e. rate of forward reaction = rate of backward reaction. In that state the solution becomes inert. Chemical reactions can be classified into the following categories:

a. Synthesis Reactions

A synthesis reaction is when two or more reactants combine to produce a single product. In generic terms, synthesis reactions look like the following:

Example: $2H_2 + O_2 \rightarrow 2H_2O$

$6CO_2 + 6H_2O \rightarrow C_6H_{12}O_6 + 6O_2$

b. Decomposition Reactions

When a single compound breaks down into two or more elements or compounds on application of some energy source such as heat, light, or electricity, the reaction is termed as decomposition reaction. In general decomposition reaction look like the following:

Example: $2H_2O \rightarrow 2H_2 + O_2$

$2KClO_3 \rightarrow 2KCl + 3O_2$

c. Single Displacement Reactions

In this reaction, one element trades places with another element in a compound. In general, single displacement reaction look like the following:

Example: $Cl + 2KBr \rightarrow 2KCl + Br_2$

d. Double Displacement Reactions

This is when the anions and cations of two different molecules switch places, forming two entirely different compounds. In generic terms, double replacement reactions look like the following:

Example: $NaCO_3 + BaCl_2 \rightarrow NaCl + BaCO_3$

e. Combustion Reactions

A combustion reaction is when oxygen combines a substance and releases energy in the form of heat and light.

Example: $CH_4 + O2 \rightarrow CO_2 + H_2O$

f. Redox Reactions

Redox reactions are the transfer of electrons from one reactant to another. The chemical which gains electrons is reduced and is called an oxidizing agent. The chemical which loses electrons is oxidized and is called the reducing agent.

Example: $Fe + Cu^{+2} \rightarrow Fe^{+2} + Cu$

g. Reversible Reactions

In reversible reactions, products of certain reactions can be converted back to the reactants. Thus, in reversible reactions the products can react with one another under suitable conditions to give back the reactants. In other words, in reversible reactions the reaction takes place in both the forward and backward directions.

Example: $CaCO3 \leftrightarrow CaO + CO2$

2.2. ACRO Algorithm

ACRO Algorithm (ACROA) begins with set of initial reactants in a solution. Then reactants are consumed and produced via chemical reactions. Algorithm is terminated when the termination criterion is met similar to the state when no more reactions can take place (inert solution).

The ACRO algorithm is discussed by Algorithm 2. The reactants are updated according to their enthalpy (fitness value).

Different chemical reactions are applied on the reactants to generate new reactants. If the newly generated reactants give a better function value, the new reactant set is included and the worse reactant is excluded similar to reversible chemical reactions. The reactant with best enthalpy values is used as the

Algorithm 1: Major steps of ACROA

Step 1: Problem and algorithm parameter initialization.
Step 2: Setting the initial reactants and evaluation.
Step 3: Applying chemical reactions.
Step 4: Reactants update.
Step 5: Termination criterion check.

Algorithm 2: Artificial Chemical Reaction Optimization

Set IterationNum = 0
/ Initialize Reactants of size **ReacNum** randomly from a uniform distribution */*
*Create molecules M_i of size **ReacNum** by uniform population.*
for *i = 1 to ReacNum* **do**
Calculate the enthalpy e (M_i)
end for
While *(termination criterion not met)* **do**
for *I = 1 to ReacNum* **do**
   /*Apply all reactions over the reactants of M_i */
      Get $rand_1$ randomly in interval [0,1]
         if$rand_1 \leq 0.5$then
            Get $rand_2$ randomly in interval [0, 1]
               if$rand_2 \leq 0.5$then
                  Decomposition *(M_i)*
               else
                  Redox1 *(M_i)*
               end if
         else
            Select another molecule M_j ($M_i \neq M_j$)
Get $rand_3$ randomly in interval [0, 1]
         if$0 \leq rand_3 \leq 0.33$then
            Synthesis *(M_i, M_j)*
         else if$0.33 \leq rand_3 \leq 0.66$then
            Displacement *(M_i, M_j)*
         else
            Redox$_2$ *(M_i, M_j)*
         end if
      end if
      *Apply**Reversible Reaction**for increased enthalpy to update reactants*
   end for
   IterationNum=IterationNum+1
end while
   Employ the reactant with best enthalpy as the optimal weight & biases set for the FLN model.

Algorithm 3: Reversible Reaction

```
/* Monomolecular Reactions*/
Let M₁ undergoes monomolecular reaction and produced the product M₂
ifenthalpy(M₂) < enthalpy(M₁)
Replace M₁ by M₂
end
/*Bimolecular Reactions */
ifM₁ and M₂ undergoes any bimolecular reactions and produced product Prod (Redox2 and Synthesis)
ifenthalpy(Prod) < enthalpy(M₁)
Replace M₁ by Prod
end
end
ifM₁ and M₂ undergoes bimolecular reaction and produced Prod₁ and Prod₂ (Displacement reaction)
ifenthalpy(Prod₁) < enthalpy(M₁)
Replace M₁ by Prod₁
end
ifenthalpy(Prod₂) < enthalpy(M₂)
Replace M₂ by Prod₂
end
end
```

optimal solution for the forecasting model. The algorithm for reversible reaction for increased enthalpy to update reactants is explained by Algorithm 3.

The reactants can be encoded by using real encoding or binary encoding. In this work we adopted the binary encoding system where each reactant is represented as an array of binary bits, i.e. 1 and 0. For more clarity in understanding the pseudo codes for the above mentioned chemical operators (reactions) in Algorithm 2 are presented as follows: Algorithm 4 presents Synthesis reaction, Algorithm 5 presents Displacement reaction, Algorithm 6 presents Redox1 reaction, Algorithm 7 explains Redox2 and Algorithm 8 presents Decomposition reaction.

Algorithm 4: Synthesis Reaction (Reac1, Reac2)

```
Input: Two reactants Reac₁ and Reac₂
newReac= Reac₁;
Flag = 0;
for i = 1: Length(Reac₁)
if Reac₁(i) != Reac₂(i) AND Flag = 0
newReac(i) = Reac₁(i);
Flag = 1;
else if Reac₁(i) != Reac₂(i) AND Flag = 1
newReac(i) = Reac₂(i);
Flag = 0;
end
end
Output: A new reactant newReac
```

Algorithm 5: Displacement Reaction (Reac1, Reac2)

Input: Two reactants $Reac_1$ and $Reac_2$
$mask$ = random binary string of $length(Reac_1)$;
for $i = 1$: $Length(Reac_1)$
if $mask = 1$
$newReac_1(i) = Reac_2(i)$;
$newReac_2(i) = Reac_1(i)$;
else
$newReac_1(i) = Reac_1(i)$;
$newReac_2(i) = Reac_2(i)$;
  end
end
Output: Two new reactants, $newReac_1$ and $newReac_2$

Algorithm 6: Redox1 Reaction (Reac1)

Input: A single reactant $Reac_1$
r_1 = one random integer from $[1, length(Reac_1)]$;
$newReac = Reac_1$;
  if $newReac(r_1) = 1$
$newReac(r_1) = 0$;
else
   $newReac(r_1) = 1$;
  end
Output: A new reactant $newReac$

Algorithm 7: Redox2 Reaction (Reac1, Reac2)

Input: Two reactants $Reac_1$ and $Reac_2$
r_1 = one random integer from $[1, length(Reac_1)]$;
r_2 = one random integer from $[1, length(Reac_1)]$;
$newReac_1 = Reac_1$;
$newReac_2 = Reac_2$;
$newReac_1(r_1: r_2) = Reac_2(r_1: r_2)$;
$newReac_2(r_1: r_2) = Reac_1(r_1: r_2)$;
Output: Two new reactants $newReac_1$ and $newReac_2$

Algorithm 8: Decomposition Reaction (Reac)

Input: A single reactant $Reac$
r_1 = one random integer from $[1, length(Reac)]$;
r_2 = one random integer from $[1, length(Reac)]$;
$newReac = Reac$
for $i = r_1$: r_2
if $Reac(i) = 1$
$newReac(i) = 0$;
else
$newReac(i) = 1$;
end
end
Output: A new reactant $newReac$

3. STOCK MARKET FORECASTING

3.1. Stock Market

A stock market is a public platform or market for the customer want to trade their share. It is also known as a trading market for the company's stocks and derivatives at an approved stock price. Stock market allows companies and individuals to sell or buy their shares. Stock market gets investors together to buy and sell shares in companies. Share market sets prices according to supply and demand. Hence, a stock that is highly in demand will increase in price, whereas a stock that is being heavily sold will decrease in price. Primary market deals with the new issues of securities directly from the company. An official prospectus is published under the corporation law that contains all the information about the company that is reasonably required by the investors to make an informed investment decisions. The existing securities are bought and sold in the secondary market among traders. A share is a document issued by a company, which entitles its holder to be one of the owners of the company. By owning a share one can earn a portion of the company's profit called dividend. Also, by selling the shares one gets the capital gain. However, there is a risk of making a capital loss, if selling price of the share is lower than the buying price. Stock is a collection or a group of shares. Stock Exchanges act as the clearing house for each transaction, that is, they collect and deliver the share, and guarantee payment to the seller of a security. The smooth functioning of all these activities facilitates business expansion, economic growth, employments and promotes production of goods and services. To be able to trade a security on a certain stock exchange, it has to be listed there. Listing requirements are the set of conditions imposed by a given stock exchange on companies that want to be listed. Stock brokers are licensed agents to trade shares. They have direct access to the share market to do share transactions. They charge a fee for this service. Traders buy and sell financial instruments such as stocks, bonds and derivatives. Traders are either professionals working in a financial institution or a corporation, or individual investors.

Stock exchanges have multiple roles in the economy; this may includes raising capital for businesses, mobilizing savings for investment, facilitating company growth, profit sharing, corporate governance, creating investment opportunities for small investors, government capital-raising for development projects, barometer of the economy. Listing requirements are the set of conditions imposed by a given stock exchange on companies that want to be listed on that exchange. Conditions sometimes include minimum number of shares outstanding, minimum market capitalization and minimum annual income.

An index is a statistical composite measure of the movement in the overall market or industry. Basically indices allow measuring the performance of a group of companies over a period of time. Companies are organized in an index according to two main methods or weighting as it is commonly termed. The movements of the prices in a market or section of a market are captured in price indices called stock market indices, e.g., the S&P, the FTSE and the Euro next indices. Such indices are usually market capitalization weighted, with the weights reflecting the contribution of the stock to the index. The constituents of the index are reviewed frequently to include/exclude stocks in order to reflect the changing business environment. There are two major classes of indexes in use: Equally weighted price index: The index is calculated by taking the average of the prices of a set of companies.

3.2. Stock Market Prediction

The process of predicting / forecasting the future index of a stock exchange based on the past performance or data aiming at high profit is called as stock market forecasting. Stock market forecasting is a cornerstone and challenging issue in economics and financial engineering. The successful forecasting of a stock market could yield significant profit and hence require an efficient automated prediction system for stock forecasting. Recently forecasting stock market return is gaining more attention, may be because of the fact that if the direction of the market is successfully predicted the investors may be better guided and also monetary rewards will be substantial. The stock market is a very complicated nonlinear dynamic system. It has both the high income and high risk properties. So the forecast of stock market trend has been always paid attention to by stockholders and invest organization. However, because of the high nonlinearity of the stock market, it is difficult to reveal the inside law by the traditional forecast methods. If any system which can consistently predict the trends of the dynamic stock market be developed, would make the owner of the system wealthy. In recent years, the rapid development of computer and artificial intelligence technology provide many new technology methods for the modeling and forecast of the stock market. With the rise of artificial intelligence technology and the growing interrelated markets of the last two decades offering unprecedented trading opportunities, technical analysis simply based on forecasting models is no longer enough. To meet the trading challenge in today's global market, technical analysis must be redefined.

4. ACRO BASED FLN FOR STOCK MARKET FORECASTING

4.1. Back Propagation Based Functional Link Network: FLN-BP

The FLN introduces higher order effects through nonlinear functional transforms via links rather than at nodes. The FLN architecture uses a single layer feed forward network without hidden layers. The functional expansion effectively increases the dimensionality of the input vector and hence the hyper plane generated by the FLN provides greater discrimination capability in the input pattern space.

For designing the network, at the first instance a functional expansion unit (FE) expands each input attribute of the input data. The simple trigonometric basis functions of *sine* and *cosine* are used here to expand the original input value into higher dimensions. An input value x_i expanded to several terms by using the trigonometric expansion functions. Equation 1 shows set of trigonometric basis functions used in this experimental study.

$$
\begin{cases}
c_1\left(x_i\right) = \left(x_i\right), \\
c_2\left(x_i\right) = \sin\left(x_i\right), \\
c_3\left(x_i\right) = \cos\left(x_i\right), \\
c_4\left(x_i\right) = \sin\left(\pi x_i\right), \\
c_5\left(x_i\right) = \cos\left(\pi x_i\right), \\
c_6\left(x_i\right) = \sin\left(2\pi x_i\right), \\
c_7\left(x_i\right) = \cos\left(2\pi x_i\right)
\end{cases}
\tag{1}
$$

Figure 3. Architecture of traditional FLN forecasting model

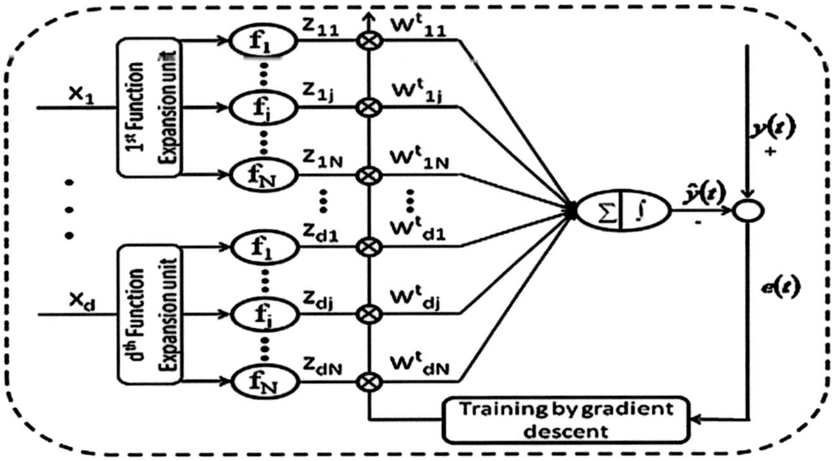

The attributes of each input pattern is passed through the FE unit. The sum of the output signals of the FE units multiplied with weights is passed on to the sigmoidal activation function of the output unit. The estimated output is compared with the target output and error signal is obtained. This error signal is used to train the model. Figure 3 shows the architecture of the FLN model. The FLN model obtains the optimal weight set W iteratively using gradient descent learning algorithm based on the training samples. The learning process of FLN can be explained as follows:

The estimated output of the FLN forecasting model is calculated as follows:

A fixed number of weight parameters W and a set of basis functions f are used to represent an approximating function $\varphi_w(X)$. Now the problem can be represented as *'find the optimal weight set W which provide the best possible approximation of f on the set of input-output samples'*. The FLN obtains this solution by updating W iteratively.

Let there are k training pattern to be applied to the FLN and denoted by $\langle X_i : Y_i \rangle, 1 \le i \le k$.

Let at i^{th} instant $(1 \le i \le k)$, the N-dimensional input- output pattern are given by $X_i = \langle x_{i1}, x_{i2}, \cdots, x_{iD} \rangle, \hat{Y}_i = [\hat{y}_i], 1 \le i \le k$. The dimension of the input signal is increased from N to N' by a set of basis functions . Equation 2 presents the set of basis functions.

$$\left. \begin{aligned} f(X_i) &= \left[f_1(x_{i1}), f_2(x_{i1}), \cdots, f_1(x_{i2}), f_2(x_{i2}), \cdots, f_1(x_{iN}), f_2(x_{iN}), \cdots \right] \\ &= \left[f_1(x_{i1}), f_2(x_{i2}), \cdots, f_N(x_{iN}) \right] \end{aligned} \right\} \tag{2}$$

$W = \left[W_1, W_2, \cdots, W_k \right]^T$ is the $k * N$ dimensional matrix, where W_i is the weight vector associated with the ith output and is given by $W_1 = \left[w_{i1}, w_{i2}, \cdots, w_{iN} \right]$. Equation 3 has been used to estimate the ith output of the model.

$$\hat{y}_i(t) = \varphi \left(\sum_{j=1}^{N'} f_j(x_{ij}) * w_{ij} \right) = \varphi \left(W_i * f^T(x_i) \right), \forall i \tag{3}$$

The error signal associated with the ith output is calculated by Equation 4.

$$e_i(t) = y_i(t) - \hat{y}_i(t) \tag{4}$$

The weights of the model can be updated using adaptive learning rule as given by Equation 5.

$$\left. \begin{array}{l} w_{ij}(t+1) = w_{ij}(t) + \mu * \Delta(t) \\ \Delta(t) = \delta(t) * f(x_i) \end{array} \right\} \tag{5}$$

Where $w_{ij}(t)$ is the weight for training set t, $w_{ij}(t+1)$ is the weight for training set t+1, $\Delta(t)$ is the change in weight value, $\delta(t) = [\delta_1(t), \delta_2(t), \cdots, \delta_k(t)]$, $\delta_i(t) = (1 - \hat{y}_i^2(t) * e_i(t))$ and μ is the learning parameter.

4.2. ACRO based Functional Link Network: FLN-CRO

Figure 4. represents the architecture of the proposed FLN-CRO based forecasting model. Here the weight and parameter set of FLN are optimized by the ACRO algorithm.

The binary ACRO technique is employed for FLN. This model generates a set of weight and bias vectors representing a set of FLN models. The input vector along with weights and bias values are passed on to the respective FLN model. The absolute difference between the target and the estimated output is treated as the fitness of the respective FLN models. Lower fitness value is considered as the better fit individuals for the purpose of selection of individual to the next generation by the CRO. The algorithm starts with assigning values for termination criteria (number of iteration or threshold error), length of reactant, *ReacNum*, i.e. total number of reactants in a population. A string of binary values has been

Figure 4. Architecture of FLN-CRO based forecasting model

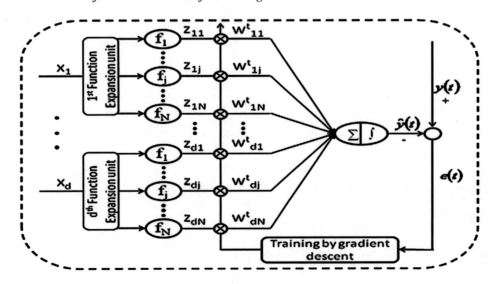

considered as an atom and set of such atoms represents one reactant which corresponds to a weight set of the FLN-CRO. The length of a reactant depends on number of input signal selected and number of functional expansions used (i.e. number of input X number of basis function). The reaction processes are simulated in iteration phase. The reactions can be monomolecular (i.e. *Redox1, Decomposition*) or bimolecular (i.e. *Redox2, Synthesis, Displacement*). The reactants are updated by applying reversible reactions. The fitness of a reactant is the enthalpy associated with it. The Mean absolute of error (MAE) is considered as fitness function of a reactant in this experimentation. The lower the value of enthalpy is the better the reactant. Figure 5 presents the adaptive FLN-CRO based forecasting model.

Figure 5. Adaptive FLN-CRO based forecasting model

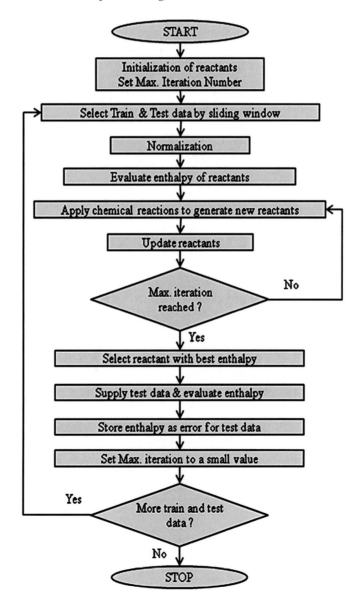

5. SIMULATION RESULTS AND PERFORMANCE ANALYSIS

To ascertain the performance of the suggested model, the daily closing price of different stock markets across the globe such as BSE, NASDAQ, TAIEX, and FTSE are considered for this experiment. Further to establish that the suggested model is unbiased and it can work for different types of trend in different economic/political scenario without much deviation in the capabilities of prediction, the daily closing prices are used for a period from 1st January 2000 to 31st December 2014.

Very often to train a model a large number of patterns are presented with large number of epochs to train the model for prediction. In some cases about 2/3rd data is presented as training set and the rest are used for testing. Here, though the objective is to design a generalized model, but very often it fails to track the financial market trend in general. Further the number of neurons in the input layer is also kept quite high, which also adds to the computation time. For this experiment, a sliding window concept is used which takes only five values for the input layer and only three patterns are presented to build a model.

It is a fact that as each time the sliding window moves one step ahead, closing price data at the beginning is dropped and one new closing price data at the end is included. Therefore two consecutive training sets possibly possess minimal change in the nonlinear behavior of the input-output mapping. To incorporate the minor change in input-output mapping in the new model, the optimized weight set of the predecessor model for the same dataset is considered and minimal epochs help in capturing the change in nonlinear mapping.

Further considering the requirements of the neural network, the input data needs to be normalized. Here sigmoidal function is used for this purpose as in Equation 6.

$$x_{norm} = \frac{1}{1 + e^{-\left(\frac{x_i - x_{min}}{x_{max} - x_{min}}\right)}} \qquad (6)$$

Where x_{norm} is the normalized price, x_i is the current day closing price, x_{min} is the minimum price, and x_{max} is the maximum price of the respective training set.

To establish the performance of the proposed model, two other forecasting models are considered here in this experimental study such as FLN-BP and Multiple Linear Regression (MLR). The normalized training sets and test sets presented to the proposed model are also presented to these three models to obtain the respective error in forecasting and these errors in forecasting are compared. The less the error the better is the performance of the model considered. Table 1 presents the parameters considered for experimentation of different models. NA stands for not applicable.

Table 1. Simulated parameters for FLN-CRO and FLN-BP forecasting models

Parameter	FLN-CRO	FLN-BP
Learning Rate (α)	NA	0.3
Momentum Factor (μ)	NA	0.5
No. of iteration for 1st training set	100	500
No. of iteration for subsequent training	10	20
Reactant Number	50	NA
Weight updated/found	ACRO	Gradient descent

Depending on the number of working days in a year, the total data obtained for each index may be different, accordingly different number of training and test sets are generated for the 15 year period considered for this experiment. Table 2 shows the number of training sets generated for each dataset and for each prediction category.

The error signals obtained from all the data sets out of MLR, FLN-BP and FLN-CRO for one-day-ahead, one-week-ahead and one-month-ahead forecasting are presented subsequently. Table 3 presents the results obtained from the three models for all data sets for one-day-ahead forecasting. Table 4 summarizes the results obtained from one-week-ahead forecasting. Table 5 presents the error signals generated by all three forecasting models for one-month-ahead forecasting.

In one-day-ahead forecasting, it is observed that the results of FLN-CRO are much better in comparison to FLN-BP and MLR technique in case of all the stock index data considered. Further significantly low standard deviation values of FLN-CRO also depicts that the variation in forecasting is also low and

Table 2. Number of windows generated for each category of prediction

Stock Indices	One-Day-Ahead	One-Week-Ahead	One-Month-Ahead
BSE	3738	3730	3707
NASDAQ	3771	3763	3740
FTSE	3904	3896	3873
TAIEX	3706	3698	3675

Table 3. Error Signals generated by FLN-CRO, FLN-BP and MLR forecasting models for one-day-ahead prediction

Stock Indices		FLN-CRO	FLN-BP	MLR
BSE	Minimum	0.000001	0.000201	0.000004
	Maximum	0.024535	0.028213	0.604622
	Average	**0.007640**	**0.020932**	**0.032537**
	Std. Deviation	0.001821	0.007014	0.185269
NASDAQ	Minimum	0.000074	0.000352	0.000005
	Maximum	0.0303631	0.286615	0.145339
	Average	**0.008478**	**0.042974**	**0.056570**
	Std. Deviation	0.002806	0.012705	0.299219
FTSE	Minimum	0.000001	0.000033	0.000008
	Maximum	0.028219	0.225782	0.279426
	Average	**0.003752**	**0.009671**	**0.052170**
	Std. Deviation	0.003638	0.070233	1.384871
TAIEX	Minimum	0.001166	0.000025	0.000003
	Maximum	0.039852	0.286401	0.128334
	Average	**0.006651**	**0.010445**	**0.380917**
	Std. Deviation	0.003810	0.070422	0.211121

Table 4. Error Signals generated by FLN-CRO, FLN-BP and MLR forecasting models for one-week-ahead prediction

Stock Indices		FLN-CRO	FLN-BP	MLR
BSE	Minimum	0.000002	0.001100	0.001509
	Maximum	0.252044	0.337627	0.258028
	Average	**0.021766**	**0.105256**	**0.318371**
	Std. Deviation	0.059013	0.058318	0.661832
NASDAQ	Minimum	0.000005	0.001003	0.000082
	Maximum	0.251055	0.310421	0.231468
	Average	**0.020818**	**0.100306**	**0.730785**
	Std. Deviation	0.059627	0.085170	0.317837
FTSE	Minimum	0.000215	0.000353	0.001048
	Maximum	0.254404	0.333771	0.025583
	Average	**0.007985**	**0.015275**	**0.873451**
	Std. Deviation	0.059643	0.082148	0.542483
TAIEX	Minimum	0.000001	0.001003	0.000015
	Maximum	0.256054	0.347520	0.413010
	Average	**0.032732**	**0.110249**	**0.440463**
	Std. Deviation	0.060122	0.082653	0.169659

Table 5. Error Signals generated by FLN-CRO, FLN-BP and MLR forecasting models for one-month-ahead prediction

Stock Indices		FLN-CRO	FLN-BP	MLR
BSE	Minimum	0.000007	0.000013	0.003536
	Maximum	0.027982	0.140161	0.704581
	Average	**0.090426**	**0.131675**	**0.506175**
	Std. Deviation	0.013706	0.122531	0.371826
NASDAQ	Minimum	0.000061	0.000037	0.002013
	Maximum	0.028736	0.427573	0.834681
	Average	**0.095755**	**0.147532**	**0.878752**
	Std. Deviation	0.062937	0.123604	0.078352
FTSE	Minimum	0.000051	0.000215	0.001048
	Maximum	0.280242	0.418102	0.025883
	Average	**0.020963**	**0.130065**	**0.908325**
	Std. Deviation	0.071305	0.120527	0.754352
TAIEX	Minimum	0.000032	0.000077	0.000015
	Maximum	0.024965	0.423725	0.813215
	Average	**0.098145**	**0.134824**	**0.830415**
	Std. Deviation	0.070700	0.121204	0.925403

the proposed model is consistent in its performance. The average results are made bold which are later used for further evaluation of performance.

As expected, the result of one-week-ahead prediction is slightly inferior to that of one-day-ahead prediction. But the results of FLN-CRO are much better than FLN-BP, RBFNN and MLR for all data sets as before. In some cases the standard deviation values of FLN-CRO is not good enough as in case of one-day-ahead prediction, but it is better than FLN-BP, MLR models, however RBFNN show slightly better standard deviation value for one-week-ahead forecasting.

The results of one-month-ahead forecasting are relatively inferior to that of the other two categories. But the prediction accuracy of FLN-CRO is better than FLN-BP and MLR models for all the data sets. However, the standard deviation values of FLN-CRO are much better than FLN-BP and MLR models.

It can be observed from Table III-V that, the proposed FLN-CRO forecasting model generates better prediction accuracy in comparison to FLN-BP and MLR for all data sets in one-day-ahead, one-week-ahead, and one-month-ahead prediction. Further, to find the quantum of gain in accuracy by FLN-CRO over FLN-BP and MLR, percentage gain in accuracy is evaluated by Eq. 7.

$$AccuracyGain = \frac{\left(MAEofexisting\ \mathrm{mod}\,el - MAEofFLNCRO\,\mathrm{mod}\,el \right)}{MAEofexisting\ \mathrm{mod}\,el} * 100\% \qquad (7)$$

The percentage gain in accuracy by FLN-CRO over FLN-BP and MLR for different data set is presented by following figures. Figure 6 presents gain in accuracy for one-day-ahead prediction. Figure 7 presents gain in accuracy for one-month-ahead forecasting. Figure 8 presents gain in accuracy for one-month-ahead forecasting.

From Figure 6, it can be revealed that the percentage gain in accuracy by FLN-CRO is significant over all other models and in case of all datasets with a minimum gain of 36.32% in TAIEX data for FLN-BP and maximum gain of 80.27% in case of NASDAQ data set. Over MLR model, the minimum gain is 76.51% in case of BSE data set and maximum of 98.25% in case of TAIEX data set.

Figure 7. shows that in case of one-week-ahead forecasting quite good percentage gain in accuracy is obtained like Figure 5 with a minimum gain of 47.72% in case of FTSE data for FLN-BP model and maximum gain of 79.32% in case of BSE data. Similarly, over MLR model the minimum gain is 92.56% in case of TAIEX and maximum of 99.08% in case of FTSE data set.

Figure 6. A comparison of percentage gain in accuracy by FLN-CRO over FLN-BP and MLR in short term prediction

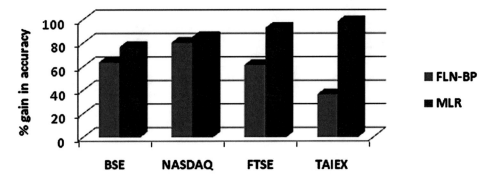

Figure 7. A comparison of percentage gain in accuracy by FLN-CRO over FLN-BP and MLR in medium term prediction

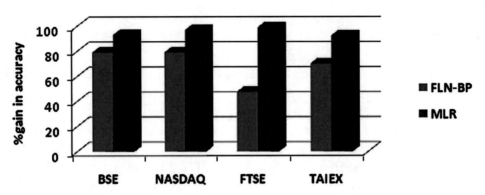

Figure 8. A comparison of percentage gain in accuracy by FLN-CRO over FLN-BP, RBFNN, and MLR in long term prediction

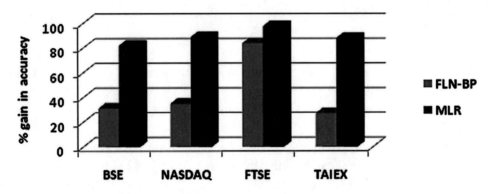

Figure 9. Comparison of average percentage gain in accuracy by FLN-CRO over FLN-BP and MLR for one-day-ahead, one-week-ahead and one-month-ahead prediction of stock index values

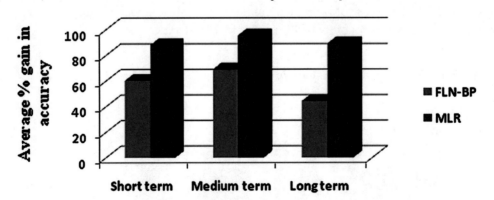

It can be revealed form Figure 8 that the percentage gain in accuracy by FLN-CRO over FLN-BP is minimal i.e. 27.20% in case of TAIEX and maximum gain is 83.88% in case of FTSE data set. As compared to the performance of MLP model, the minimum gain is of 82.13% for BSE and maximum of 97.69% for FTSE data set.

Figure 9. presents the average gain in accuracy by FLN-CRO over FLN-BP and MLR for four different stock indices. Average percentage gain in accuracy by FLN-CRO is quite good as compared to the performance of MLR. The FLN-CRO has the minimum average performance gain over FLN-BP in long term prediction.

6. CONCLUSION

This chapter presents and analyses the performances of HONN based forecasting models. Particularly, FLN based forecasting models have been developed and utilized for the prediction of stock closing prices. For case study original stock data for a period of 15 years collected from four fast growing stock exchanges and experimented. The higher order terms of original input signals have been achieved by expanding them with the use of seven trigonometric basis functions. These higher order terms helped to capture the high non-linearity and volatility associated with the stock data with better accuracies. The gradient descent based back propagation learning was used to train the FLN models. However, the performance of the FLN-BP model was not found satisfactory. In order to improve the prediction accuracies of FLN based models, a natural chemical reaction inspired optimization technique called ACRO has been employed to train the FLN model. The ACRO required less parameter, hence easy to implement. It was found that the use of ACRO in place of BP learning improves the prediction accuracies a lot.

REFERENCES

Aiken, M. W., & Bsat, M. (1999). Forecasting Market Trends with Neural Networks. *IS Management*, *16*(4), 1–7.

Alatas, B. (2011). ACROA: Artificial chemical reaction optimization algorithm for global optimization. *Expert Systems with Applications*, *38*(10), 13170–13180. doi:10.1016/j.eswa.2011.04.126

Alatas, B. (2012). A novel chemistry based metaheuristic optimization method for mining of classification rules. *Expert Systems with Applications*, *39*(12), 11080–11088. doi:10.1016/j.eswa.2012.03.066

AlRashidi, M. R., & El-Hawary, M. E. (2009). A survey of particle swarm optimization applications in electric power systems. *IEEE Transactions on* Evolutionary Computation, *13*(4), 913–918.

Aminian, F., Suarez, E. D., Aminian, M., & Walz, D. T. (2006). Forecasting economic data with neural networks. *Computational Economics*, *28*(1), 71–88. doi:10.1007/s10614-006-9041-7

Calderon, T. G., & Cheh, J. J. (2002). A roadmap for future neural networks research in auditing and risk assessment. *International Journal of Accounting Information Systems*, *3*(4), 203–236. doi:10.1016/S1467-0895(02)00068-4

Choi, J. H., Lee, M. K., & Rhee, M. W. (1995, June). Trading S&P 500 stock index futures using a neural network. *Proceedings of the third annual international conference on artificial intelligence applications on Wall Street* (pp. 63-72).

Chun Liu, H., Hsien Lee, Y., & Chih Lee, M. (2009). Forecasting China Stock Markets Volatility via GARCH Models Under Skewed-GED Distribution.

Darbellay, G. A., & Slama, M. (2000). Forecasting the short-term demand for electricity: Do neural networks stand a better chance? *International Journal of Forecasting, 16*(1), 71–83. doi:10.1016/S0169-2070(99)00045-X

Dehuri, S., & Cho, S. B. (2010a). Evolutionarily optimized features in functional link neural network for classification. *Expert Systems with Applications, 37*(6), 4379–4391. doi:10.1016/j.eswa.2009.11.090

Dehuri, S., & Cho, S. B. (2010b). A hybrid genetic based functional link artificial neural network with a statistical comparison of classifiers over multiple datasets. *Neural Computing & Applications, 19*(2), 317–328. doi:10.1007/s00521-009-0310-y

Drossu, R., & Obradovic, Z. (1996). Rapid design of neural networks for time series prediction. *Computational Science & Engineering, IEEE, 3*(2), 78–89. doi:10.1109/99.503317

Durbin, R., & Rumelhart, D. E. (1989). Product units: A computationally powerful and biologically plausible extension to backpropagation networks. *Neural Computation, 1*(1), 133–142. doi:10.1162/neco.1989.1.1.133

Epitropakis, M. G., Plagianakos, V. P., & Vrahatis, M. N. (2010). Hardware-friendly higher-order neural network training using distributed evolutionary algorithms. *Applied Soft Computing, 10*(2), 398–408. doi:10.1016/j.asoc.2009.08.010

Fallahnezhad, M., Moradi, M. H., & Zaferanlouei, S. (2011). A hybrid higher order neural classifier for handling classification problems. *Expert Systems with Applications, 38*(1), 386–393. doi:10.1016/j.eswa.2010.06.077

Gately, E. (1995). *Neural networks for financial forecasting*. John Wiley & Sons, Inc.

Ghazali, R. (2007). *Higher order neural networks for financial time series prediction* [Doctoral dissertation]. Liverpool John Moores University.

Ghazali, R., Hussain, A., & El-Deredy, W. (2006, July). Application of ridge polynomial neural networks to financial time series prediction. *Proceedings of the International Joint Conference on Neural Networks IJCNN '06* (pp. 913-920). IEEE.

Giles, C. L., & Maxwell, T. (1987). Learning, invariance, and generalization in high-order neural networks. *Applied Optics, 26*(23), 4972–4978. doi:10.1364/AO.26.004972 PMID:20523475

John, G. H., Miller, P., & Kerber, R. (1996). Stock selection using rule induction. *IEEE Intelligent Systems, 5*, 52–58.

Knowles, A., Hussein, A., Deredy, W., Lisboa, P., & Dunis, C. L. (2009). Higher-order neural networks with Bayesian confidence measure for prediction of EUR/USD exchange rate. In M. Zhang (Ed.), Artificial Higher Order Neural networks for Economics and Business (pp. 48-59). Hershey, PA, USA: IGI Global.

Kryzanowski, L., Galler, M., & Wright, D. W. (1993). Using artificial neural networks to pick stocks. *Financial Analysts Journal, 49*(4), 21–27. doi:10.2469/faj.v49.n4.21

Kung, L. M., & Yu, S. W. (2008). Prediction of index futures returns and the analysis of financial spillovers—A comparison between GARCH and the grey theorem. *European Journal of Operational Research, 186*(3), 1184–1200. doi:10.1016/j.ejor.2007.02.046

Lam, A., & Li, V. O. (2010). Chemical-reaction-inspired metaheuristic for optimization. *IEEE Transactions on* Evolutionary Computation, *14*(3), 381–399.

Lam, A., & Li, V. O. (2010, December). Chemical reaction optimization for cognitive radio spectrum allocation. *Proceedings of theGlobal Telecommunications Conference GLOBECOM '10* (pp. 1-5). IEEE. doi:10.1109/GLOCOM.2010.5684065

Lam, A., Li, V. O., & Yu, J. J. (2012). Real-coded chemical reaction optimization. *IEEE Transactions on* Evolutionary Computation, *16*(3), 339–353.

Lam, A., Xu, J., & Li, V. O. (2010, July). Chemical reaction optimization for population transition in peer-to-peer live streaming. *Proceedings of the 2010 IEEE Congress on Evolutionary Computation (CEC)* (pp. 1-8). IEEE. doi:10.1109/CEC.2010.5585933

Lam, A.Y., & Li, V.O. (2012). Chemical reaction optimization: A tutorial. *Memetic Computing, 4*(1), 3–17. doi:10.1007/s12293-012-0075-1

Lee, T. T., & Jeng, J. T. (1998). The Chebyshev-polynomials-based unified model neural networks for function approximation. *IEEE Transactions on* Systems, Man, and Cybernetics, Part B: Cybernetics, *28*(6), 925–935.

Leerink, L. R., Giles, C. L., Horne, B. G., & Jabri, M. A. (1995). Learning with product units, In G. Tesaro, D. Touretzky, & T. Leen (Eds.), Advances in Neural Information Processing Systems (Vol. 7, pp. 537-544). Cambridge, MA: MIT Press.

Lu, H., Han, J., & Feng, L. (1998, June). Stock movement prediction and n-dimensional inter-transaction association rules.*Proceedings of the ACM SIGMOD workshop on research issues in data mining and knowledge discovery* (p. 12).

Majhi, R., Majhi, B., & Panda, G. (2012). Development and performance evaluation of neural network classifiers for Indian internet shoppers. *Expert Systems with Applications, 39*(2), 2112–2118. doi:10.1016/j.eswa.2011.07.128

Majhi, R., Panda, G., & Sahoo, G. (2009a). Development and performance evaluation of FLANN based model for forecasting of stock markets. *Expert Systems with Applications, 36*(3), 6800–6808. doi:10.1016/j.eswa.2008.08.008

Majhi, R., Panda, G., & Sahoo, G. (2009b). Development and performance evaluation of FLANN based model for forecasting of stock markets. *Expert Systems with Applications*, *36*(3), 6800–6808. doi:10.1016/j.eswa.2008.08.008

Majhi, R., Panda, G., & Sahoo, G. (2009c). Development and performance evaluation of FLANN based model for forecasting of stock markets. *Expert Systems with Applications*, *36*(3), 6800–6808. doi:10.1016/j.eswa.2008.08.008

Mishra, B. B., Dehuri, S., Panda, G., & Dash, P. K. (2008). Fuzzy swarm net (FSN) for classification in data mining. *The CSI Journal of Computer Science and Engineering*, *5*(2 & 4 (b)), 1–8.

Misra, B. B., & Dehuri, S. (2007). Functional Link Artificial Neural Network for Classification Task in Data Mining 1.

Mostafa, M. M. (2004). Forecasting the Suez Canal traffic: A neural network analysis. *Maritime Policy & Management*, *31*(2), 139–156. doi:10.1080/0308883032000174463

Mostafa, M. M. (2010). Forecasting stock exchange movements using neural networks: Empirical evidence from Kuwait. *Expert Systems with Applications*, *37*(9), 6302–6309. doi:10.1016/j.eswa.2010.02.091

Murphy, J. J. (1999). *Technical analysis of the financial markets: A comprehensive guide to trading methods and applications*. Penguin.

Nam, K., Yi, J., & Prybutok, V. R. (1997). Predicting airline passenger volume. *The Journal of Business Forecasting*, *16*(1), 14.

Nayak, J., Naik, B., & Behera, H. S. (2015). A novel chemical reaction optimization based higher order neural network (CRO-HONN) for nonlinear classification. *Ain Shams Engineering Journal*, *6*(3), 1069–1091. doi:10.1016/j.asej.2014.12.013

Nie, Y., & Deng, W. (2008, October). A hybrid genetic learning algorithm for Pi-sigma neural network and the analysis of its convergence. *Proceedings of the Fourth International Conference on Natural Computation ICNC '08* (Vol. 3, pp. 19-23). IEEE. doi:10.1109/ICNC.2008.896

Pan, B., Lam, A., & Li, V. O. (2011, December). Network coding optimization based on chemical reaction optimization. *Proceedings of theGlobal Telecommunications Conference GLOBECOM '11* (pp. 1-5). IEEE.

Pao, Y. (1989). Adaptive pattern recognition and neural networks.

Pao, Y. H., & Takefji, Y. (1992). Functional-link net computing. *IEEE Computer Journal*, *25*(5), 76–79. doi:10.1109/2.144401

Park, S. I., Smith, M. J., & Mersereau, R. M. (2000). Target recognition based on directional filter banks and higher-order neural networks. *Digital Signal Processing*, *10*(4), 297–308. doi:10.1006/dspr.2000.0376

Patra, J. C., Lim, W., Meher, P. K., & Ang, E. L. (2006, July). Financial prediction of major indices using computational efficient artificial neural networks. *Proceedings of the International Joint Conference on Neural Networks IJCNN '06* (pp. 2114-2120). IEEE.

Patra, J. C., Pal, R. N., Baliarsingh, R., & Panda, G. (1999b). Nonlinear channel equalization for QAM signal constellation using artificial neural networks. *IEEE Transactions on* Systems, Man, and Cybernetics, Part B: Cybernetics, *29*(2), 262–271.

Patra, J. C., Pal, R. N., Baliarsingh, R., & Panda, G. (1999c). Nonlinear channel equalization for QAM signal constellation using artificial neural networks. *IEEE Transactions on* Systems, Man, and Cybernetics, Part B: Cybernetics, *29*(2), 262–271.

Patra, J. C., Pal, R. N., Chatterji, B. N., & Panda, G. (1999a). Identification of nonlinear dynamic systems using functional link artificial neural networks. *IEEE Transactions on* Systems, Man, and Cybernetics, Part B: Cybernetics, *29*(2), 254–262.

Patra, J. C., Pal, R. N., Chatterji, B. N., & Panda, G. (1999d). Identification of nonlinear dynamic systems using functional link artificial neural networks. *IEEE Transactions on* Systems, Man, and Cybernetics, Part B: Cybernetics, *29*(2), 254–262.

Patra, J. C., Panda, G., & Baliarsingh, R. (1994). Artificial neural network-based nonlinearity estimation of pressure sensors. *IEEE Transactions on* Instrumentation and Measurement, *43*(6), 874–881.

Patra, J. C., & Van den Bos, A. (2000). Modeling of an intelligent pressure sensor using functional link artificial neural networks. *ISA Transactions, 39*(1), 15–27. doi:10.1016/S0019-0578(99)00035-X PMID:10826282

Purwar, S., Kar, I. N., & Jha, A. N. (2007). On-line system identification of complex systems using Chebyshev neural networks. *Applied Soft Computing, 7*(1), 364–372. doi:10.1016/j.asoc.2005.08.001

Refenes, A. N., Zapranis, A., & Francis, G. (1994). Stock performance modeling using neural networks: A comparative study with regression models. *Neural Networks, 7*(2), 375–388. doi:10.1016/0893-6080(94)90030-2

Sahin, E. (1994). A New Higher-order Binary-input Neural Unit: Learning and Generalizing Effectively via Using Minimal Number of Monomials.

Schöneburg, E. (1990). Stock price prediction using neural networks: A project report. *Neurocomputing, 2*(1), 17–27. doi:10.1016/0925-2312(90)90013-H

Shin, S. Y., Lee, I. H., Kim, D., & Zhang, B. T. (2005). Multiobjective evolutionary optimization of DNA sequences for reliable DNA computing. *IEEE Transactions on* Evolutionary Computation, *9*(2), 143–158.

Shin, Y., & Ghosh, J. (1991, July). The pi-sigma network: An efficient higher-order neural network for pattern classification and function approximation. *Proceedings of the Seattle International Joint Conference on Neural Networks IJCNN '91* (Vol. 1, pp. 13-18). IEEE.

Shin, Y., & Ghosh, J. (1995). Ridge polynomial networks. *IEEE Transactions on* Neural Networks, *6*(3), 610–622.

Swicegood, P., & Clark, J. A. (2001). Off-site monitoring systems for predicting bank underperformance: A comparison of neural networks, discriminant analysis, and professional human judgment. *Intelligent Systems in Accounting, Finance & Management, 10*(3), 169–186. doi:10.1002/isaf.201

Trippi, R. R., & DeSieno, D. (1992). Trading equity index futures with a neural network. *Journal of Portfolio Management*, *19*(1), 27–33. doi:10.3905/jpm.1992.409432

Truong, T. K., Li, K., & Xu, Y. (2013). Chemical reaction optimization with greedy strategy for the 0–1 knapsack problem. *Applied Soft Computing*, *13*(4), 1774–1780. doi:10.1016/j.asoc.2012.11.048

Videnova, I., Nedialkov, D., Dimitrova, M., & Popova, S. (2006). Neural networks for air pollution nowcasting. *Applied Artificial Intelligence*, *20*(6), 493–506. doi:10.1080/08839510600753741

Wang, Z., Fang, J. A., & Liu, X. (2008). Global stability of stochastic high-order neural networks with discrete and distributed delays. *Chaos, Solitons, and Fractals*, *36*(2), 388–396. doi:10.1016/j.chaos.2006.06.063

Xu, J., Lam, A., & Li, V. O. (2010, May). Chemical reaction optimization for the grid scheduling problem. *Proceedings of the 2010 IEEE International Conference on Communications (ICC)* (pp. 1-5). IEEE. doi:10.1109/ICC.2010.5502406

Xu, J., Lam, A., & Li, V. O. (2011). Chemical reaction optimization for task scheduling in grid computing. *IEEE Transactions on* Parallel and Distributed Systems, *22*(10), 1624–1631.

Xu, J., Lam, A. Y., & Li, V. O. (2011, June). Stock portfolio selection using chemical reaction optimization. *Proceedings of the international conference on operations research and financial engineering, Paris, France.*

Yang, S. S., & Tseng, C. S. (1996). An orthogonal neural network for function approximation. *IEEE Transactions on* Systems, Man, and Cybernetics, Part B: Cybernetics, *26*(5), 779–785.

Yoon, Y., Guimaraes, T., & Swales, G. (1994). Integrating artificial neural networks with rule-based expert systems. *Decision Support Systems*, *11*(5), 497–507. doi:10.1016/0167-9236(94)90021-3

Yoon, Y., & Swales, G. (1991, January). Predicting stock price performance: A neural network approach. *Proceedings of the Twenty-Fourth Annual Hawaii International Conference onSystem Sciences* (Vol. 4, pp. 156-162). IEEE. doi:10.1109/HICSS.1991.184055

Yu, J. J., Lam, A., & Li, V. O. (2011, June). Evolutionary artificial neural network based on chemical reaction optimization. *Proceedings of the 2011 IEEE Congress on Evolutionary Computation (CEC)* (pp. 2083-2090). IEEE. doi:10.1109/CEC.2011.5949872

Yu, L., Chen, H., Wang, S., & Lai, K. K. (2009). Evolving least squares support vector machines for stock market trend mining. *IEEE Transactions on* Evolutionary Computation, *13*(1), 87–102.

Yu, L., Wang, S., & Lai, K. K. (2009). A neural-network-based nonlinear metamodeling approach to financial time series forecasting. *Applied Soft Computing*, *9*(2), 563–574. doi:10.1016/j.asoc.2008.08.001

Zhang, M., Xu, S., & Fulcher, J. (2002). Neuron-adaptive higher order neural-network models for automated financial data modeling. *IEEE Transactions on* Neural Networks, *13*(1), 188–204.

Zhuo, W., Li-Min, J., Yong, Q., & Yan-Hui, W. (2007). Railway passenger traffic volume prediction based on neural network. *Applied Artificial Intelligence*, *21*(1), 1–10. doi:10.1080/08839510600938409

Section 4
Artificial Higher Order Neural Network Models and Applications

Chapter 12
Artificial Higher Order Neural Network Models

Ming Zhang
Christopher Newport University, USA

ABSTRACT

This chapter introduces the background of HONN model developing history and overview 24 applied artificial higher order neural network models. This chapter provides 24 HONN models and uses a single uniform HONN architecture for ALL 24 HONN models. This chapter also uses a uniform learning algorithm for all 24 HONN models and uses a uniform weight update formulae for all 24 HONN models. In this chapter, Polynomial HONN, Trigonometric HONN, Sigmoid HONN, SINC HONN, and Ultra High Frequency HONN structure and models are overviewed too.

INTRODUCTION

The contributions of this chapter will be:

- Introduce the background of HONN models' developing history.
- Overview 24 applied artificial higher order neural network models.
- Provide 24 HONN Models learning algorithm and weight update formulae.
- Using a single uniform HONN architecture for ALL 24 HONN models.
- Using a uniform learning algorithm for all 24 HONN models
- Using a uniform weight update formulae for all 24 HONN models

This chapter is organized as follows: Section background gives the developing history of applied artificial higher order neural network (HONN) models. Section Higher Order Neural Network structure and Models introduces a single uniform structure for all 24 HONN modes. Section Learning Algorithm and Weight Update Formulae provides the uniform learning algorithm for all 24 HONN models and provides weight update formulae for all 24 HONN models. Section Future Research Directions predicts the future development direction in applied artificial higher order neural network area. Section Conclusion gives the summery of the 24 HONN models.

DOI: 10.4018/978-1-5225-0063-6.ch012

BACKGROUND

In 1995, Zhang, Murugesan, and Sadeghi (1995) develops very basic applied artificial higher order neural network model, called Polynomial Higher Order Neural Network (PHONN), for economic data simulation. PHONN can simulate data using higher order (order from 2 to 6) polynomial functions. In 1997, Zhang, Zhang, & Fulcher (1997) creates second very basic applied artificial higher order neural work model, called Trigonometric polynomial Higher Order Neural Network(THONN) models and THONN group models for financial prediction. PHONN models can model data by using higher order trigonometric functions, or by using groups of higher order trigonometric functions. In 1999, Zhang, Zhang, & Keen (1999) builds THONN system for analyzing higher frequency non-linear data simulation & prediction. The analyzing errors are always around from 1% to 5%.

Starting from 2000, new applied artificial higher order neural network models are developed, based on PHONN and THONN models. Lu, Qi, Zhang, & Scofield (2000) study the PT-HONN models for multi-polynomial function simulation. Zhang, Zhang, & Fulcher (2000) apply higher order neural network group models for financial simulation. Qi, Zhang, & Scofield (2001) use M-PHONN model for rainfall estimation. Zhang (2001) tests the financial data simulation using A-PHONN model. Zhang, & Lu, (2001) also use M-PHONN model in studying financial data simulation. A-PHONN Model is also used in rainfall estimation (Zhang, & Scofield 2001).

From 2002, adaptive higher order neural network models are studied. And new HONN models continue to be developed. Xu, and Zhang (2002) present an adaptive activation function for higher order neural networks. Based on the different data, HONN adaptively chose the best function(s) for the special data. Zhang (2002a) investigates the rainfall estimation by using PL-HONN model. Zhang (2002b) also researches the financial data simulation by using PL-HONN model. Zhang, Xu, & Fulcher (2002) suggest the neuron-adaptive higher order neural network models for automated financial data modeling. Zhang, & Crane (2004) operate rainfall estimation using SPHONN model. Zhang, & Fulcher (2004) examine higher order neural networks for weather prediction.

New HONN models are developed from 2005. Crane, and Zhang (2005) generate data simulation system by using SINCHONN model. Fulcher, & Zhang (2005) introduce different higher order neural network models in the system and processing areas. Zhang (2005) build a data simulation system using sinx/x and sinx polynomial higher order neural networks. Fulcher, Zhang, and Xu. (2006) overview the application of higher order neural networks to financial time series prediction. Zhang (2006) make a data simulation system using CSINC polynomial higher order neural networks. Zhang (2007) also build a data simulation system using YSINC polynomial higher order neural networks.

Starting from 2008, building new HONN models with the error approaching 0 became a hot research direction. Before 2008, the HONN error always is between 1% and 5%. For a lot of applications, error between 1% and 5% is acceptable. But for nonlinear and discontinued data simulation, errors close to zero are welcomed. To solve this problem, Zhang (2008) design a higher order neural network nonlinear model and find the new HONN modes has better running result than SAS software. The simulation data error is close to zero. Zhang (Ed.) (2009a) edit a book called *Artificial Higher Order Neural Networks for Economics and Business*, in which includes new HONN model with error close to zero. Zhang (2009b) compares the running result between artificial higher order neural networks and SAS software for economics and business. The research results show that HONN model is better than SAS software if both simulate nonlinear and discontinued data. Zhang, M. (2009c) develop an ultra-high frequency trigonometric higher order neural networks for time series data Analysis. The key point is that the newly developed HONN can actually simulate 2 times higher than ultra-high frequency real word data. And newly developed HONN can let the simulating error approach to E-6. Zhang (2009d) also tries the time series simulation using ultra high frequency cosine and cosine higher order neural networks.

After 2010, adaptive higher order neural network models, high order neural network group models, and ultra-high frequency high order neural network models are continually developed.

Zhang (Ed.) (2010a) collects the HONN models and applications in *computer science and engineering areas*. Zhang (2010b) proposed higher order neural network group-based adaptive tolerance tree models. Zhang (2010c) shows the rainfall estimation results by using neuron-adaptive higher order neural networks. Zhang (2010d) publishes the time series simulation results by using ultra high frequency sine and sine higher order neural network models. Zhang (2011) studies a sine and sigmoid higher order neural networks for data simulation. Zhang (2012) use the polynomial and sigmoid higher order neural networks for data simulations and prediction. Zhang (Ed.) (2013a) collects the higher order neural networks for modeling and simulation. Zhang (2013b) develops the artificial multi-polynomial higher order neural network models. Zhang (2013c) also studies the artificial polynomial and trigonometric higher order neural network group models. Zhang (2014a) develops a SINC and sigmoid higher order neural network for data modeling and simulation. Zhang (2014b) uses an ultra-high frequency polynomial and sine artificial higher order neural networks for control signal generator.

Starting from 2015, ultra-high frequency HONN and other HONN models are continually developed. Zhang (2016a) creates the ultra-high frequency polynomial and trigonometric higher order neural networks for control signal generator. Zhang (2016b) studies ultra-high frequency sigmoid and trigonometric higher order neural networks for data pattern recognition. Zhang (2016c) also develops artificial sine and cosine trigonometric higher order neural networks for financial data prediction. Zhang (2016d) researches the ultra-high frequency SINC and trigonometric higher order neural networks for data classification. Zhang, M. (2016e) uses cosine and sigmoid higher order neural networks for date simulations. Above research results are shown in the book of "Applied Artificial Higher Order Neural Networks for Control and Recognition" edited by Zhang, M. (Ed.) (2016g).

HIGHER ORDER NEURAL NETWORK ARCHITECTURE AND MODELS

HONN Model Structure can be seen in Figure 1.

1. PHONN Model

Zhang, Murugesan, and Sadeghi (1995) developed Polynomial Higher Order Neural Network (PHONN) model as follows:

Let :

$$f_k^x(c_k^x x) = (c_k^x x)^k$$
$$f_j^y(c_j^y y) = (c_j^y y)^j$$

Figure 1. HONN Architecture

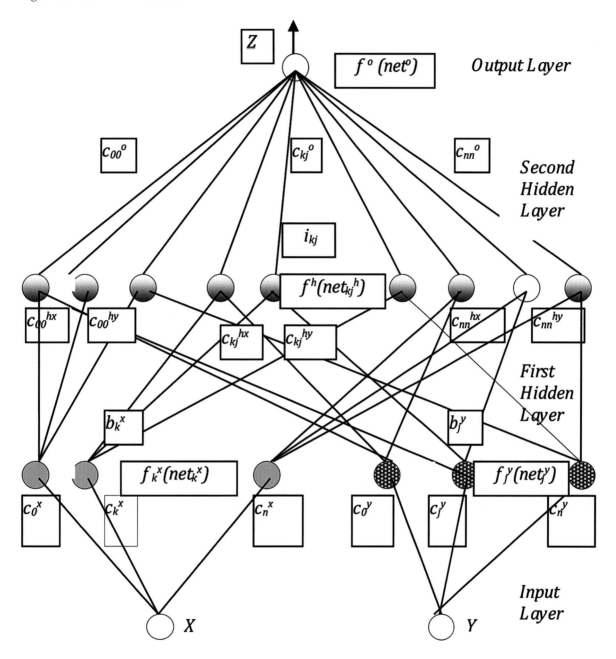

Figure 2.

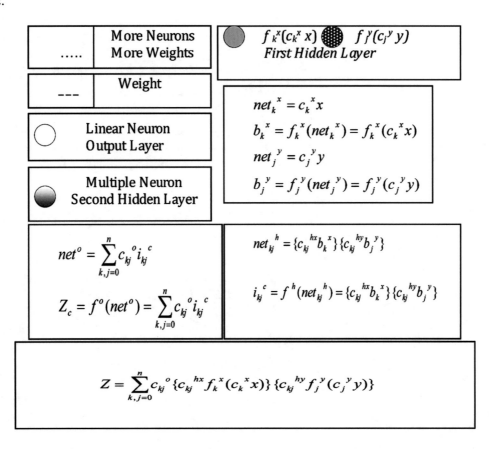

PHONN   Model   0:

$$z = \sum_{k,j=0}^{n} c_{kj}^{\ o}\ (x)^{k}(y)^{j}$$

where: $(c_{kj}^{\ hx}) = (c_{kj}^{\ hy}) = 1$

   and $c_{k}^{\ x} = c_{j}^{\ y} = 1$ (PHONN   0)

THONN   Model   1:

$$z = \sum_{k,j=0}^{n} c_{kj}^{\ o}\ \sin^{k}(c_{k}^{\ x}x)con^{j}(c_{j}^{\ y}y)$$

where: $(c_{kj}^{\ hx}) = (c_{kj}^{\ hy}) = 1$ (PHONN   1)

PHONN   Model   2:

$$Z = \sum_{k,j=0}^{n} (c_{kj}^{\ o})\{c_{kj}^{\ hx}(c_{k}^{\ x}x)^{k}\}\{c_{kj}^{\ hy}(c_{j}^{\ y}y)^{j}\}$$ (PHONN   2)

2. XSHONN Model

Polynomial and Sine Higher Order Neural Network (XSHONN) model as follows:

Let :

$$f_k^{\ x}(c_k^{\ x}x) = (c_k^{\ x}x)^k$$

$$f_j^{\ y}(c_j^{\ y}y) = \sin^j(c_j^{\ y}y)$$

XSHONN   Model   0 :

$$z = \sum_{k,j=0}^{n} c_{kj}^{\ o} \ (x)^k \sin^j(y)$$

where : $(c_{kj}^{\ hx}) = (c_{kj}^{\ hy}) = 1$

        and $c_k^{\ x} = c_j^{\ y} = 1$ (*XSHONN   0*)

XSHONN   Model   1 :

$$z = \sum_{k,j=0}^{n} c_{kj}^{\ o} \ (c_k^{\ x}x)^k \sin^j(c_j^{\ y}y)$$

where : $(c_{kj}^{\ hx}) = (c_{kj}^{\ hy}) = 1$ (*XSHONN   1*)

XSHONN   Model   2 :

$$Z = \sum_{k,j=0}^{n} (c_{kj}^{\ o})\{c_{kj}^{\ hx}(c_k^{\ x}x)^k\} \{c_{kj}^{\ hy} \sin^j(c_j^{\ y}y)\}$$ (*XSHONN   2*)

3. XCHONN Model

Polynomial and Cosine Higher Order Neural Network (XCHONN) model as follows:

Let :

$$f_k^{\ x}(c_k^{\ x}x) = (c_k^{\ x}x)^k$$

$$f_j^{\ y}(c_j^{\ y}y) = \cos^j(c_j^{\ y}y)$$

XCHONN   Model   0 :

$$z = \sum_{k,j=0}^{n} c_{kj}^{\ o} \ (x)^k \cos^j(y)$$

where : $(c_{kj}^{\ hx}) = (c_{kj}^{\ hy}) = 1$

        and $c_k^{\ x} = c_j^{\ y} = 1$ (*XCHONN   0*)

XCHONN   Model   1:

$$z = \sum_{k,j=0}^{n} c_{kj}{}^{o}\ (c_k{}^{x}x)^k \cos^j(c_j{}^{y}y)$$

$where:$ $(c_{kj}{}^{hx}) = (c_{kj}{}^{hy}) = 1$ *(XCHONN   1)*

XCHONN   Model   2:

$$Z = \sum_{k,j=0}^{n} (c_{kj}{}^{o})\{c_{kj}{}^{hx}(c_k{}^{x}x)^k\}\{c_{kj}{}^{hy}\cos^j(c_j{}^{y}y)\}$$ *(XCHONN   2)*

4. SIN-HONN Model

Zhang (2016c) develops artificial sine and cosine trigonometric higher order neural networks for financial data prediction. Sine Higher Order Neural Network (SINHONN) model as follows:

$Let:$

$$f_k{}^{x}(c_k{}^{x}x) = \sin^k(c_k{}^{x}x)$$

$$f_j{}^{y}(c_j{}^{y}y) = \sin^j(c_j{}^{y}y)$$

SINHONN   Model   0:

$$z = \sum_{k,j=0}^{n} c_{kj}{}^{o}\ \sin^k(x)\sin^j(y)$$

$where:$ $(c_{kj}{}^{hx}) = (c_{kj}{}^{hy}) = 1$

     and $c_k{}^{x} = c_j{}^{y} = 1$ *(SINHONN   0)*

SINHONN   Model   1:

$$z = \sum_{k,j=0}^{n} c_{kj}{}^{o}\ \sin^k(c_k{}^{x}x)\sin^j(c_j{}^{y}y)$$

$where:$ $(c_{kj}{}^{hx}) = (c_{kj}{}^{hy}) = 1$ *(SINHONN   1)*

SINHONN   Model   2:

$$Z = \sum_{k,j=0}^{n} (c_{kj}{}^{o})\{c_{kj}{}^{hx}\sin^k(c_k{}^{x}x)\}\{c_{kj}{}^{hy}\sin^j(c_j{}^{y}y)\}$$ *(SINHONN   2)*

5. COS-HONN Model

Zhang (2016c) develops artificial sine and cosine trigonometric higher order neural networks for financial data prediction. Cosine Higher Order Neural Network (COSHONN) model as follows:

Let :

$$f_k^x(c_k^x x) = \cos^k(c_k^x x)$$
$$f_j^y(c_j^y y) = \cos^j(c_j^y y)$$

COSHONN   Model   0 :

$$z = \sum_{k,j=0}^{n} c_{kj}^{\ o} \ \cos^k(x)\cos^j(y)$$

where : $(c_{kj}^{\ hx}) = (c_{kj}^{\ hy}) = 1$

   and $c_k^{\ x} = c_j^{\ y} = 1$ (*COSHONN*   0)

COSHONN   Model   1 :

$$z = \sum_{k,j=0}^{n} c_{kj}^{\ o} \ \cos^k(c_k^x x)\cos^j(c_j^y y)$$

where : $(c_{kj}^{\ hx}) = (c_{kj}^{\ hy}) = 1$ (*COSHONN*   1)

COSHONN   Model   2 :

$$Z = \sum_{k,j=0}^{n} (c_{kj}^{\ o})\{c_{kj}^{\ hx}\cos^k(c_k^x x)\} \{c_{kj}^{\ hy}con^j(c_j^y y)\}$$ (*COSHONN*   2)

6. THONN Model

Zhang, Zhang, and Fulcher (1997) and Zhang, Zhang, and Steve (1999) developed Trigonometric Higher Order Neural Network (THONN) model as follows:

Let :

$$f_k^x(c_k^x x) = \sin^k(c_k^x x)$$
$$f_j^y(c_j^y y) = \cos^j(c_j^y y)$$

THONN   *Model* 0:

$$z = \sum_{k,j=0}^{n} c_{kj}{}^{o} \ \sin^{k}(x)\cos^{j}(y)$$

where: $(c_{kj}{}^{hx}) = (c_{kj}{}^{hy}) = 1$

    and $c_{k}{}^{x} = c_{j}{}^{y} = 1$ *(THONN   0)*

THONN   *Model* 1:

$$z = \sum_{k,j=0}^{n} c_{kj}{}^{o} \ \sin^{k}(c_{k}{}^{x}x)\cos^{j}(c_{j}{}^{y}y)$$

where: $(c_{kj}{}^{hx}) = (c_{kj}{}^{hy}) = 1$ *(THONN   1)*

THONN   *Model* 2:

$$Z = \sum_{k,j=0}^{n} (c_{kj}{}^{o})\{c_{kj}{}^{hx} \sin^{k}(c_{k}{}^{x}x)\} \{c_{kj}{}^{hy} \cos^{j}(c_{j}{}^{y}y)\}$$ *(THONN   2)*

7. SPHONN Model

Zhang, & Crane (2004) developed Sigmoid Polynomial Higher Order Neural Network (SPHONN) model as follows:

Let:

$$f_{k}{}^{x}(c_{k}{}^{x}x) = (1/(1+\exp(c_{k}{}^{x}(-x))))^{k}$$
$$f_{j}{}^{y}(c_{j}{}^{y}y) = (1/(1+\exp(c_{j}{}^{y}(-y))))^{j}$$

SPHONN   *Model* 0:

$$z = \sum_{k,j=0}^{n} c_{kj}{}^{o} \ (1/(1+\exp(-x)))^{k} (1/(1+\exp(-y)))^{j}$$

where: $(c_{kj}{}^{hx}) = (c_{kj}{}^{hy}) = 1$

    and $c_{k}{}^{x} = c_{j}{}^{y} = 1$ *(SPHONN   0)*

SPHONN   *Model* 1:

$$z = \sum_{k,j=0}^{n} c_{kj}{}^{o} \ (1/(1+\exp(c_{k}{}^{x}(-x))))^{k} (1/(1+\exp(c_{j}{}^{y}(-y))))^{j}$$

where: $(c_{kj}{}^{hx}) = (c_{kj}{}^{hy}) = 1$ *(SPHONN   1)*

SPHONN   Model   2:

$$Z = \sum_{k,j=0}^{n} (c_{kj}{}^{o})\{c_{kj}{}^{hx}(1/(1+\exp(c_k{}^x(-x))))^k\}\{c_{kj}{}^{hy}(1/(1+\exp(c_j{}^y(-y))))^j\} \qquad (SPHONN \qquad 2)$$

8. SINCHONN Model

Crane, and Zhang (2005) develop SINC Higher Order Neural Network (SINCHONN) model as follows:

Let :

$$f_k{}^x(c_k{}^x x) = (\sin(c_k{}^x x)/(c_k{}^x x))^k$$
$$f_j{}^y(c_j{}^y y) = (\sin(c_j{}^y y)/(c_k{}^x y))^j$$

SINCHONN   Model   0:

$$z = \sum_{k,j=0}^{n} c_{kj}{}^{o} \ (\sin(x)/x)^k (\sin(y)/y)^j$$

where : $(c_{kj}{}^{hx}) = (c_{kj}{}^{hy}) = 1$

    and $c_k{}^x = c_j{}^y = 1$ $(SINCHONN \qquad 0)$

SINCHONN   Model   1:

$$z = \sum_{k,j=0}^{n} c_{kj}{}^{o} \ (\sin(c_k{}^x x)/(c_k{}^k x))^k (\sin(c_j{}^y y)/(c_j{}^y y))^j$$

where : $(c_{kj}{}^{hx}) = (c_{kj}{}^{hy}) = 1$ $(SINCHONN \qquad 1)$

SINHONN   Model   2:

$$Z = \sum_{k,j=0}^{n} (c_{kj}{}^{o})\{c_{kj}{}^{hx}(\sin(c_k{}^x x)/(c_k{}^x x))^k\}\{c_{kj}{}^{hy}(\sin(c_j{}^y y)/(c_j{}^y y))^j\} \qquad (SINCHONN \qquad 2)$$

9. SSINCHONN Model

Zhang (2005) developed Sine and SINC Higher Order Neural Network (SSINCHONN) model as follows:

Let :

$$f_k{}^x(c_k{}^x x) = (\sin(c_k{}^x x))^k$$
$$f_j{}^y(c_j{}^y y) = (\sin(c_j{}^y y)/(c_k{}^x y))^j$$

SSINCHONN   Model   0:

$$z = \sum_{k,j=0}^{n} c_{kj}{}^{o} \ (\sin(x))^{k} (\sin(y)/y)^{j}$$

where: $(c_{kj}{}^{hx}) = (c_{kj}{}^{hy}) = 1$

        and $c_{k}{}^{x} = c_{j}{}^{y} = 1$ (*SSINCHONN*   0)

SSINCHONN   Model   1:

$$z = \sum_{k,j=0}^{n} c_{kj}{}^{o} \ (\sin(c_{k}{}^{x}x))^{k} (\sin(c_{j}{}^{y}y)/(c_{j}{}^{y}y))^{j}$$

where: $(c_{kj}{}^{hx}) = (c_{kj}{}^{hy}) = 1$ (*SSINCHONN*   1)

SSINHONN   Model   2:

$$Z = \sum_{k,j=0}^{n} (c_{kj}{}^{o})\{c_{kj}{}^{hx}(\sin(c_{k}{}^{x}x))^{k}\} \{c_{kj}{}^{hy}(\sin(c_{j}{}^{y}y)/(c_{j}{}^{y}y))^{j}\}$$ (*SSINCHONN*   2)

10. CSINCHONN Model

Zhang (2006) developed Cosine and SINC Higher Order Neural Network (CSINCHONN) model as follows:

Let:

$$f_{k}{}^{x}(c_{k}{}^{x}x) = (\cos(c_{k}{}^{x}x))^{k}$$
$$f_{j}{}^{y}(c_{j}{}^{y}y) = (\sin(c_{j}{}^{y}y)/(c_{k}{}^{x}y))^{j}$$

CSINCHONN   Model   0:

$$z = \sum_{k,j=0}^{n} c_{kj}{}^{o} \ (\cos(x))^{k} (\sin(y)/y)^{j}$$

where: $(c_{kj}{}^{hx}) = (c_{kj}{}^{hy}) = 1$

        and $c_{k}{}^{x} = c_{j}{}^{y} = 1$ (*CSINCHONN*   0)

CSINCHONN   Model   1:

$$z = \sum_{k,j=0}^{n} c_{kj}{}^{o} \ (\cos(c_{k}{}^{x}x))^{k} (\sin(c_{j}{}^{y}y)/(c_{j}{}^{y}y))^{j}$$

where: $(c_{kj}{}^{hx}) = (c_{kj}{}^{hy}) = 1$ (*CSINCHONN*   1)

CSINHONN   Model   2:

$$Z = \sum_{k,j=0}^{n} (c_{kj}{}^{o})\{c_{kj}{}^{hx}(\cos(c_k{}^x x))^k\}\{c_{kj}{}^{hy}(\sin(c_j{}^y y)/(c_j{}^y y))^j\} \qquad (CSINCHONN \quad 2)$$

11. YSINCHONN Model

Zhang (2007) developed polynomial and SINC Higher Order Neural Network (YSINCHONN) model as follows:

Let :

$$f_k{}^x(c_k{}^x x) = (c_k{}^x x)^k$$

$$f_j{}^y(c_j{}^y y) = (\sin(c_j{}^y y)/(c_k{}^x y))^j$$

YSINCHONN   Model   0:

$$z = \sum_{k,j=0}^{n} c_{kj}{}^{o} \ (x)^k (\sin(y)/y)^j$$

where : $(c_{kj}{}^{hx}) = (c_{kj}{}^{hy}) = 1$

$\quad$ *and* $\quad c_k{}^x = c_j{}^y = 1$ $\qquad (YSINCHONN \quad 0)$

YSINCHONN   Model   1:

$$z = \sum_{k,j=0}^{n} c_{kj}{}^{o} \ (c_k{}^x x)^k (\sin(c_j{}^y y)/(c_j{}^y y))^j$$

where : $(c_{kj}{}^{hx}) = (c_{kj}{}^{hy}) = 1$ $\qquad (YSINCHONN \quad 1)$

YSINHONN   Model   2:

$$Z = \sum_{k,j=0}^{n} (c_{kj}{}^{o})\{c_{kj}{}^{hx}(c_k{}^x x)^k\}\{c_{kj}{}^{hy}(\sin(c_j{}^y y)/(c_j{}^y y))^j\} \qquad (YSINCHONN \quad 2)$$

12. UCSHONN Model

Zhang (2009c) developed Ultra High Frequency Trigonometric Higher Order Neural Network (UTHONN) models, which includes Ultra High Frequency Sine and Cosine Higher Order Neural Network (UC-SHONN) model as follows:

Let :

$$f_k^x(c_k^x x) = \cos^k(k * c_k^x x)$$
$$f_j^y(c_j^y y) = \sin^j(j * c_j^y y)$$

UCSHONN   Model   0 :

$$z = \sum_{k,j=0}^{n} c_{kj}^{o} \ \cos^k(k * x)\sin^j(j * y)$$

where : $(c_{kj}^{hx}) = (c_{kj}^{hy}) = 1$

    and $c_k^x = c_j^y = 1$ *(UCSHONN   0)*

UCSHONN   Model   1 :

$$z = \sum_{k,j=0}^{n} c_{kj}^{o} \ \cos^k(k * c_k^x x)\sin^j(j * c_j^y y)$$

where : $(c_{kj}^{hx}) = (c_{kj}^{hy}) = 1$ *(UCSHONN   1)*

UCSHONN   Model   2 :

$$Z = \sum_{k,j=0}^{n} (c_{kj}^{o})\{c_{kj}^{hx}\cos^k(k * c_k^x x)\}\{c_{kj}^{hy}\sin^j(j * c_j^y y)\}$$ *(UCSHONN   2)*

13. UCCHONN Model

Zhang (2009d) developed Ultra High Frequency Cosine and Cosine Higher Order Neural Network (UC-CHONN) model as follows:

Let :

$$f_k^x(c_k^x x) = \cos^k(k * c_k^x x)$$
$$f_j^y(c_j^y y) = \cos^j(j * c_j^y y)$$

UCCHONN   Model   0 :

$$z = \sum_{k,j=0}^{n} c_{kj}^{o} \ \cos^k(k * x)\cos^j(j * y)$$

where : $(c_{kj}^{hx}) = (c_{kj}^{hy}) = 1$

    and $c_k^x = c_j^y = 1$ *(UCCHONN   0)*

UCCHONN   Model   1:

$$z = \sum_{k,j=0}^{n} c_{kj}^{\ o} \ \cos^k (k * c_k^{\ x} x) \cos^j (j * c_j^{\ y} y)$$

$where: \qquad (c_{kj}^{\ hx}) = (c_{kj}^{\ hy}) = 1 \qquad\qquad (UCCHONN \qquad 1)$

UCCHONN   Model   2:

$$Z = \sum_{k,j=0}^{n} (c_{kj}^{\ o})\{c_{kj}^{\ hx} \cos^k (k * c_k^{\ x} x)\} \{c_{kj}^{\ hy} \cos^j (j * c_j^{\ y} y)\} \qquad (UCCHONN \qquad 2)$$

14. USSHONN Model

Zhang (2010d) developed Ultra High Frequency Sine and Sine Higher Order Neural Network (USS-HONN) model as follows:

Let:

$$f_k^{\ x}(c_k^{\ x} x) = \sin^k (k * c_k^{\ x} x)$$
$$f_j^{\ y}(c_j^{\ y} y) = \sin^j (j * c_j^{\ y} y)$$

USSHONN   Model   0:

$$z = \sum_{k,j=0}^{n} c_{kj}^{\ o} \ \sin^k (k * x) \sin^j (j * y)$$

$where: \qquad (c_{kj}^{\ hx}) = (c_{kj}^{\ hy}) = 1$

$\qquad and \qquad c_k^{\ x} = c_j^{\ y} = 1 \qquad\qquad (USSHONN \qquad 0)$

USSHONN   Model   1:

$$z = \sum_{k,j=0}^{n} c_{kj}^{\ o} \ \sin^k (k * c_k^{\ x} x) \sin^j (j * c_j^{\ y} y)$$

$where: \qquad (c_{kj}^{\ hx}) = (c_{kj}^{\ hy}) = 1 \qquad\qquad (USSHONN \qquad 1)$

USSHONN   Model   2:

$$Z = \sum_{k,j=0}^{n} (c_{kj}^{\ o})\{c_{kj}^{\ hx} \sin^k (k * c_k^{\ x} x)\} \{c_{kj}^{\ hy} \sin^j (j * c_j^{\ y} y)\} \qquad (USSHONN \qquad 2)$$

15. SS-HONN Model

Zhang (2011) developed Sine and Sigmoid Higher Order Neural Network (SS-HONN) model as follows:

Let :

$$f_k^{\ x}(c_k^{\ x}x) = \sin^k(c_k^{\ x}x)$$
$$f_j^{\ y}(c_j^{\ y}y) = (1/(1+\exp(c_j^{\ y}(-y))))^j$$

SS − HONN   Model   0 :

$$z = \sum_{k,j=0}^{n} c_{kj}^{\ o} \ \sin^k(x)(1/(1+\exp(-y)))^j$$
where : $(c_{kj}^{\ hx}) = (c_{kj}^{\ hy}) = 1$
      and $c_k^{\ x} = c_j^{\ y} = 1$ (*SS − HONN   0*)

SS − HONN   Model   1 :

$$z = \sum_{k,j=0}^{n} c_{kj}^{\ o} \ \sin^k(c_k^{\ x}x)(1/(1+\exp(c_j^{\ y}(-y))))^j$$
where : $(c_{kj}^{\ hx}) = (c_{kj}^{\ hy}) = 1$ (*SS − HONN   1*)

SS − HONN   Model   2 :

$$Z = \sum_{k,j=0}^{n} (c_{kj}^{\ o})\{c_{kj}^{\ hx} \sin^k(c_k^{\ x}x)\}\{c_{kj}^{\ hy}(1/(1+\exp(c_j^{\ y}(-y))))^j\}$$ (*SS − HONN   2*)

16. PS-HONN Model

Zhang (2012) developed Polynomial and Sigmoid Higher Order Neural Network (PS-HONN) model as follows:

Let :

$$f_k^{\ x}(c_k^{\ x}x) = (c_k^{\ x}x)^k$$
$$f_j^{\ y}(c_j^{\ y}y) = (1/(1+\exp(c_j^{\ y}(-y))))^j$$

SPHONN   Model   0 :

$$z = \sum_{k,j=0}^{n} c_{kj}{}^{o} \ (x)^{k} (1/(1+\exp(-y)))^{j}$$

where : $(c_{kj}{}^{hx}) = (c_{kj}{}^{hy}) = 1$

   and $c_{k}{}^{x} = c_{j}{}^{y} = 1$ (*PS – HONN*   0)

SPHONN   Model   1 :

$$z = \sum_{k,j=0}^{n} c_{kj}{}^{o} \ (c_{k}{}^{x}x)^{k} (1/(1+\exp(c_{j}{}^{y}(-y))))^{j}$$

where : $(c_{kj}{}^{hx}) = (c_{kj}{}^{hy}) = 1$ (*PS – HONN*   1)

SPHONN   Model   2 :

$$Z = \sum_{k,j=0}^{n} (c_{kj}{}^{o}) \{ c_{kj}{}^{hx} (c_{k}{}^{x}x)^{k} \} \{ c_{kj}{}^{hy} (1/(1+\exp(c_{j}{}^{y}(-y))))^{j} \}$$ (*PS – HONN*   2)

17. CS-HONN Model

Zhang (2016e) developed Cosine and Sigmoid Higher Order Neural Network (CS-HONN) model as follows:

Let :

$$f_{k}{}^{x}(c_{k}{}^{x}x) = \cos^{k}(c_{k}{}^{x}x)$$

$$f_{j}{}^{y}(c_{j}{}^{y}y) = (1/(1+\exp(c_{j}{}^{y}(-y))))^{j}$$

CS – HONN   Model   0 :

$$z = \sum_{k,j=0}^{n} c_{kj}{}^{o} \ \cos^{k}(x)(1/(1+\exp(-y)))^{j}$$

where : $(c_{kj}{}^{hx}) = (c_{kj}{}^{hy}) = 1$

   and $c_{k}{}^{x} = c_{j}{}^{y} = 1$ (*CS_HONN*   0)

CS – HONN   Model   1 :

$$z = \sum_{k,j=0}^{n} c_{kj}{}^{o} \ \cos^{k}(c_{k}{}^{x}x)(1/(1+\exp(c_{j}{}^{y}(-y))))^{j}$$

where : $(c_{kj}{}^{hx}) = (c_{kj}{}^{hy}) = 1$ (*CS – HONN*   1)

$CS - HONN \quad Model \quad 2:$

$$Z = \sum_{k,j=0}^{n} (c_{kj}{}^{o})\{c_{kj}{}^{hx} \cos^{k}(c_{k}{}^{x}x)\} \{c_{kj}{}^{hy}(1/(1+\exp(c_{j}{}^{y}(-y))))^{j}\} \qquad\qquad (CS - HONN \qquad 2)$$

18. NS-HONN Model

Zhang (2014a) developed SINC and Sigmoid Higher Order Neural Network (NS-HONN) model as follows:

$Let:$

$$f_{k}{}^{x}(c_{k}{}^{x}x) = (\sin(c_{k}{}^{x}x)/(c_{k}{}^{x}x))^{k}$$

$$f_{j}{}^{y}(c_{j}{}^{y}y) = (1/(1+\exp(c_{j}{}^{y}(-y))))^{j}$$

$NS - HONN \quad Model \quad 0:$

$$z = \sum_{k,j=0}^{n} c_{kj}{}^{o}\ (\sin(x)/(x))^{k}(1/(1+\exp(-y)))^{j}$$

$where: \qquad (c_{kj}{}^{hx}) = (c_{kj}{}^{hy}) = 1$

$\qquad and \qquad c_{k}{}^{x} = c_{j}{}^{y} = 1 \qquad\qquad\qquad (NS\_HONN \qquad 0)$

$NS - HONN \quad Model \quad 1:$

$$z = \sum_{k,j=0}^{n} c_{kj}{}^{o}\ (\sin(c_{k}{}^{x}*x)/(c_{k}{}^{x}*x))^{k}(1/(1+\exp(c_{j}{}^{y}(-y))))^{j}$$

$where: \qquad (c_{kj}{}^{hx}) = (c_{kj}{}^{hy}) = 1 \qquad\qquad (NS\_HONN \qquad 1)$

$NS - HONN \quad Model \quad 2:$

$$Z = \sum_{k,j=0}^{n} (c_{kj}{}^{o})\{c_{kj}{}^{hx}(\sin(c_{k}{}^{x}x)/(c_{k}{}^{x}x))^{k}\} \{c_{kj}{}^{hy}(1/(1+\exp(c_{j}{}^{y}(-y))))^{j}\} \qquad (NS - HONN \qquad 2$$

19. UPS-HONN Model

Ming Zhang (2016a) developed Ultra high frequency Polynomial and Sine Higher Order Neural Network (UPS-HONN) model as follows:

$Let:$

$$f_{k}{}^{x}(c_{k}{}^{x}x) = (c_{k}{}^{x}x)^{k}$$

$$f_{j}{}^{y}(c_{j}{}^{y}y) = \sin^{j}(j*c_{j}{}^{y}y)$$

$UPS - HONN \qquad Model \qquad 0:$

$$z = \sum_{k,j=0}^{n} (c_{kj}{}^{o} \ (x)^k (\sin^j(j*y)))$$

$where: \qquad (c_{kj}{}^{hx}) = (c_{kj}{}^{hy}) = 1$

$\qquad and \qquad c_k{}^x = c_j{}^y = 1 \qquad\qquad (UPS - HONN \qquad 0)$

$UPS - HONN \qquad Model \qquad 1:$

$$z = \sum_{k,j=0}^{n} (c_{kj}{}^{o} \ (c_k{}^x * x)^k (\sin^j(j * c_j{}^y y)))$$

$where: \qquad (c_{kj}{}^{hx}) = (c_{kj}{}^{hy}) = 1 \qquad\qquad (UPS - HONN \qquad 1)$

$UPS - HONN \qquad Model \qquad 2:$

$$Z = \sum_{k,j=0}^{n} (c_{kj}{}^{o})\{c_{kj}{}^{hx}(c_k{}^x * x)^k\} \{c_{kj}{}^{hy}(\sin^j(j * c_j{}^y y))\} \qquad (UPS - HONN \qquad 2)$$

20. UPC-HONN Model

Ming Zhang (2016a) developed Ultra high frequency Polynomial and Cosine Higher Order Neural Network (UPC-HONN) model as follows:

$Let:$

$$f_k{}^x(c_k{}^x x) = (c_k{}^x x)^k$$
$$f_j{}^y(c_j{}^y y) = \cos^j(j * c_j{}^y y)$$

$UPC - HONN \qquad Model \qquad 0:$

$$z = \sum_{k,j=0}^{n} (c_{kj}{}^{o} \ (x)^k (\cos^j(j*y)))$$

$where: \qquad (c_{kj}{}^{hx}) = (c_{kj}{}^{hy}) = 1$

$\qquad and \qquad c_k{}^x = c_j{}^y = 1 \qquad\qquad (UPC - HONN \qquad 0)$

$UPC - HONN \qquad Model \qquad 1:$

$$z = \sum_{k,j=0}^{n} (c_{kj}{}^{o} \ (c_k{}^x * x)^k (\cos^j(j * c_j{}^y y)))$$

$where: \qquad (c_{kj}{}^{hx}) = (c_{kj}{}^{hy}) = 1 \qquad\qquad (UPC - HONN \qquad 1)$

$UPC - HONN \qquad Model \qquad 2:$

$$Z = \sum_{k,j=0}^{n} (c_{kj}{}^{o})\{c_{kj}{}^{hx}(c_{k}{}^{x}*x)^{k}\}\{c_{kj}{}^{hy}(\cos^{j}(j*c_{j}{}^{y}y))\} \qquad\qquad (UPC - HONN \qquad 2)$$

21. UGS-HONN Model

Zhang (2016b) developed Ultra high frequency siGmoid and Sine and Higher Order Neural Network (UGS-HONN) model as follows:

$Let:$

$$f_{k}{}^{j}(c_{k}{}^{j}x) = (1/(1+\exp(c_{k}{}^{x}(-x))))^{k}$$

$$f_{j}{}^{y}(c_{j}{}^{k}y) = \sin^{j}(j*c_{j}{}^{k}y)$$

$UGS - HONN \qquad Model \qquad 0:$

$$z = \sum_{k,j=0}^{n} (c_{kj}{}^{o} \ (1/(1+\exp(-x)))^{k}(\sin^{j}(j*y)))$$

$where: \qquad (c_{kj}{}^{hx}) = (c_{kj}{}^{hy}) = 1$

$\qquad and \qquad c_{k}{}^{x} = c_{j}{}^{y} = 1$

$UGS - HONN \qquad Model \qquad 1:$

$$z = \sum_{k,j=0}^{n} (c_{kj}{}^{o} \ (1/(1+\exp(c_{k}{}^{x}(-x))))^{k}(\sin^{j}(j*c_{j}{}^{y}y)))$$

$where: \qquad (c_{kj}{}^{hx}) = (c_{kj}{}^{hy}) = 1 \qquad\qquad (UGS - HONN \qquad 1)$

$UGS - HONN \qquad Model \qquad 2:$

$Z =$

$$\sum_{k,j=0}^{n} (c_{kj}{}^{o})\{c_{kj}{}^{hx}(1/(1+\exp(c_{k}{}^{x}(-x))))^{k}\}\{c_{kj}{}^{hy}(\sin^{j}(j*c_{j}{}^{y}y))\} \qquad (UGS - HONN \qquad 2)$$

22. UGC-HONN Model

Zhang (2016b) developed Ultra high frequency siGmoid and Cosine and Higher Order Neural Network (UGC-HONN) model as follows:

Let :

$$f_k^{\ j}(c_k^{\ j}x) = (1/(1+\exp(c_k^{\ x}(-x))))^k$$

$$f_j^{\ y}(c_j^{\ k}y) = \cos^i(j * c_j^{\ k}y)$$

$UGC - HONN \qquad Model \qquad 0$:

$$z = \sum_{k,j=0}^{n} (c_{kj}^{\ o}\ (1/(1+\exp(-x)))^k (\cos^j(j*y)))$$

where : $\qquad (c_{kj}^{\ hx}) = (c_{kj}^{\ hy}) = 1$

$\qquad$ *and* $\qquad c_k^{\ x} = c_j^{\ y} = 1$ $\qquad\qquad$ $(UGC - HONN \qquad 0)$

$UGC - HONN \qquad Model \qquad 1$:

$$z = \sum_{k,j=0}^{n} (c_{kj}^{\ o}\ (1/(1+\exp(c_k^{\ x}(-x))))^k (\cos^j(j*c_j^{\ y}y)))$$

where : $\qquad (c_{kj}^{\ hx}) = (c_{kj}^{\ hy}) = 1$ $\qquad\qquad$ $(UGC - HONN \qquad 1)$

$UGC - HONN \qquad Model \qquad 2$:

$Z =$

$$\sum_{k,j=0}^{n} (c_{kj}^{\ o})\{c_{kj}^{\ hx}(1/(1+\exp(c_k^{\ x}(-x))))^k\}\{c_{kj}^{\ hy}(\cos^j(j*c_j^{\ y}y))\} \qquad (UGC - HONN \qquad 2)$$

23. UNS-HONN Model

Zhang (2016d) developed Ultra high frequency siNc and Sine and Higher Order Neural Network (UNS-HONN) model as follows:

Let :

$$f_k^{\ j}(c_k^{\ j}x) = (\sin(c_k^{\ x}x)/(c_k^{\ x}x))^k$$

$$f_j^{\ y}(c_j^{\ k}y) = \sin^j(j*c_j^{\ k}y)$$

$UNS - HONN \qquad Model \qquad 0$:

$$z = \sum_{k,j=0}^{n} (c_{kj}^{\ o}\ (\sin(x)/(x))^k (\sin^j(j*y)))$$

where : $\qquad (c_{kj}^{\ hx}) = (c_{kj}^{\ hy}) = 1$

$\qquad$ *and* $\qquad c_k^{\ x} = c_j^{\ y} = 1$ $\qquad\qquad$ $(UNS - HONN \qquad 0)$

UNS – HONN   *Model*   1:

$$z = \sum_{k,j=0}^{n} (c_{kj}^{\ o}\ (\sin(c_k^{\ x} * x) / (c_k^{\ x} * x))^k (\sin^j (j * c_j^{\ y} y)))$$

where: $(c_{kj}^{\ hx}) = (c_{kj}^{\ hy}) = 1$ (*UNS – HONN*   1)

UNS – HONN   *Model*   2:

$$Z = \sum_{k,j=0}^{n} (c_{kj}^{\ o}) \{c_{kj}^{\ hx} (\sin(c_k^{\ x} * x) / (c_k^{\ x} * x))^k\} \{c_{kj}^{\ hy} (\sin^j (j * c_j^{\ y} y))\}$$ (*UNS – HONN*   2)

24. UNC-HONN Model

Zhang (2016d) developed Ultra high frequency siNc and Cosine and Higher Order Neural Network (UNC-HONN) model as follows:

Let:

$$f_k^{\ j} (c_k^{\ j} x) = (\sin(c_k^{\ x} x) / (c_k^{\ x} x))^k$$
$$f_j^{\ y} (c_j^{\ k} y) = \cos^j (j * c_j^{\ k} y)$$

UNC – HONN   *Model*   0:

$$z = \sum_{k,j=0}^{n} (c_{kj}^{\ o}\ (\sin(x) / (x))^k (\cos^j (j * y)))$$

where: $(c_{kj}^{\ hx}) = (c_{kj}^{\ hy}) = 1$

   and $c_k^{\ x} = c_j^{\ y} = 1$ (*UNC – HONN*   0)

UNC – HONN   *Model*   1:

$$z = \sum_{k,j=0}^{n} (c_{kj}^{\ o}\ (\sin(c_k^{\ x} * x) / (c_k^{\ x} * x))^k (\cos^j (j * c_j^{\ y} y)))$$

where: $(c_{kj}^{\ hx}) = (c_{kj}^{\ hy}) = 1$ (*UNC – HONN*   1)

UNC – HONN   *Model*   2:

$$Z = \sum_{k,j=0}^{n} (c_{kj}^{\ o}) \{c_{kj}^{\ hx} (\sin(c_k^{\ x} * x) / (c_k^{\ x} * x))^k\} \{c_{kj}^{\ hy} (\cos^j (j * c_j^{\ y} y))\}$$ (*UNC – HONN*   2)

Models of UCSHONN, UCCHONN, USSHONN, UPS-HONN, UPC-HONN, UGS-HONN, UGC-HONN, UNS-HONN, and UNC-HONN are ultra-high frequency higher order neural networks. The key feature of these models is that these models all can simulate nonlinear data with error close to zero.

The Nyquist–Shannon sampling theorem, after Harry Nyquist and Claude Shannon, in the literature more commonly referred to as the Nyquist sampling theorem or simply as the sampling theorem, is a fundamental result in the field of information theory, in particular telecommunications and signal processing. Shannon's version of the theorem states:

If a function x(t) contains no frequencies higher than B hertz, it is completely determined by giving its ordinates at a series of points spaced 1/(2B) seconds apart.

In other words, a band limited function can be perfectly reconstructed from a countable sequence of samples if the band limit, B, is no greater than ½ the sampling rate (samples per second).

In simulating and predicting time series data, the nonlinear models of ultra-high frequency HONN should have twice as high frequency as that of the ultra-high frequency of the time series data. To achieve this purpose, a new model should be developed to enforce high frequency of HONN in order to make the simulation and prediction error close to zero.

The values of k and j ranges from 0 to n, where n is an integer. The ultra-high frequency HONN models can simulate ultra-high frequency time series data, when n increases to a big number. This property of the model allows it to easily simulate and predicate ultra-high frequency time series data, since both k and j increase when there is an increase in n.

GENERAL LEARNING ALGORITHM AND WEIGHT UPDATE FORMULAE

Output Neurons in HONN Model (model 0, 1, and 2)

The output layer weights are updated according to:

$$c_{kj}^{\ o}(t+1) = c_{kj}^{\ o}(t) - \eta(\partial E \ / \partial c_{kj}^{\ o}) \qquad (A.1)$$

where η = learning rate (positive and usually < 1)

c_{kj} = weight; index k an j = input index

(k, j=0, 1, 2,…,n means one of n*n input neurons from the second hidden layer)

E = error

t = training time

o = output layer

The output node equations are:

$$net^{\ o} = \sum_{k,j=1}^{n} c_{kj}^{\ o} i_{kj}$$

$$z = f^{\ o}(net^{\ o}) = \sum_{k,j=1}^{n} c_{kj}^{\ o} i_{kj} \qquad (A.2)$$

where i_{kj} = input to the output neuron (= output from 2nd hidden layer)

z = actual output from the output neuron

f^o = output neuron activity function

The error at a particular output unit (neuron) will be:

$$\delta = (d - z) \qquad (A.3)$$

where d = desired output value

The total error is the error of output unit, namely:

$$E = 0.5 * \delta^2 = 0.5 * (d - z)^2 \qquad (A.4)$$

The derivatives $f^{o'}(net^o)$ are calculated as follows:

The output neuron function is linear function ($f^o(net^o) = net^o$):

$$f^{o'}(net^o) = \partial f^o / \partial(net)^o = \partial(net^o) / \partial(net^o) = 1 \qquad (A.5)$$

Gradients are calculated as follows:

$$\partial E / \partial c_{kj}{}^o = (\partial E / \partial z)(\partial z / \partial(net^o))(\partial(net^o) / \partial c_{kj}{}^o) \qquad (A.6)$$

$$\partial E / \partial z = \partial(0.5 * (d - z)^2) / \partial z) = 0.5 * (-2(d - z)) = -(d - z) \qquad (A.7)$$

$$\partial z / \partial(net^o) = \partial f^o / \partial(net^o) = f^{o'}(net^o) \qquad (A.8)$$

$$\partial(net^o) / \partial_{kj}{}^o = \partial(\sum_{k,j=0}^{n} c_{kj}{}^o i_{kj}) / \partial c_{kj}{}^o = i_{kj}$$

Combining Eqns. A.6 through A.9, the negative gradient is:

$$-\partial E / \partial c_{kj}{}^o = (d - z) f^{o'}(net^o) i_{kj} \qquad (A.10)$$

For a linear output neuron, this becomes, by combining Eqns. A.10 and A.5:

$$-\partial E / \partial c_{kj}{}^o = (d - z) f^{o'}(net^o) i_{kj}$$
$$= (d - z)(1) i_{kj} = (d - z) i_{kj} \qquad (A.11)$$

The weight update equations are formulated as follows:for linear output neurons, let:

$$\delta^{ol} = (d - z) \qquad (A.12)$$

Combining Formulae A.1, A.11, and A.12:

$$c_{kj}{}^{o}(t+1) = c_{kj}{}^{o}(t) - \eta(\partial E / \partial a_{kj}{}^{o})$$
$$= c_{kj}{}^{o}(t) + \eta(d - z)f^{o}{}'(net^{o})i_{kj}$$
$$= a_{kj}{}^{o}(t) + \eta \delta^{ol} i_{kj}$$
$$where:$$
$$\delta^{ol} = (d - z)$$
$$f^{o'}(net^{o}) = 1 \qquad (linear \qquad neuron) \qquad (A.13)$$

Second-Hidden Layer Neurons in HONN Model (Model 2)

The second hidden layer weights are updated according to:

$$c_{kj}{}^{hx}(t+1) = c_{kj}{}^{hx}(t) - \eta(\partial E / \partial c_{kj}{}^{hx}) \qquad (B.1)$$

Where η = learning rate (positive & usually < 1)

k, j = input index (k, j = 0, 1, 2, …,n means one of 2*n*n input combinations from the first hidden layer)

E = error

t = training time

hx = hidden layer, related to x input

$c_{kj}{}^{hx}$ = hidden layer weight related to x input

The equations for the 2nd hidden layer node are:

$$net_{kj}{}^{h} = \{c_{kj}{}^{hx}b_{k}{}^{x}\}\{c_{kj}{}^{hy}b_{j}{}^{y}\}$$
$$i_{kj} = f^{h}(net_{kj}{}^{h}) \qquad (B.2)$$

where i_{kj} = output from 2nd hidden layer (= input to the output neuron)

$b_k{}^x$ and $b_j{}^y$ = input to 2nd hidden layer neuron (= output from the 1st hidden layer neuron)

f^h = hidden neuron activation function

hy = hidden layer, related to y input

$c_{kj}{}^{hy}$ = hidden layer weight related to y input

We call the neurons at the second layer multiple neurons. Their activity function is linear and their inputs are the multiplication of two outputs of the first layer neuron output and their weights.

The error of a single output unit will be:

$$\delta = (d - z) \qquad (B.3)$$

where d = desired output value of output layer neuron

z = actual output value of output layer neuron

The total error is the sum of the squared errors across all output units, namely:

$$E_p = 0.5 * \delta^2 = 0.5 * (d - z)^2$$
$$= 0.5 * (d - f^o(net^o))^2$$
$$= 0.5 * (d - f_k{}^o(\sum_j c_{kj}{}^o i_{kj}))^2 \qquad (B.4)$$

The derivatives $f^{h'}(net^h{}_{pj})$ are calculated as follows, for a linear function of second layer neurons:

$$i_{kj} = f^h(net_{kj}{}^h) = net_{kj}{}^h$$
$$f^{h'}(net_{kj}{}^h) = 1 \qquad (B.5)$$

The gradient $(E/c_{kj}{}^{hx})$ is given by:

$$\partial E / \partial c_{kj}{}^{hx} = \partial(0.5 * (d - z)^2) / \partial c_{kj}{}^{hx}$$
$$= (\partial(0.5 * (d - z)^2) / \partial z)(\partial z / \partial(net^o))$$
$$(\partial(net^o) / \partial i_{kj})(\partial i_{kj} / \partial(net_{kj}{}^h))(\partial(net_{kj}{}^h) / \partial c_{kj}{}^{hx}) \qquad (B.6)$$

$$\partial(0.5 * (d - z)^2) / \partial z = -(d - z) \qquad (B.7)$$

$$\partial z \,/\, \partial(net^{\,o}) = \partial f^{\,o} \,/\, \partial(net^{o}) = f_{k}^{\,o}\,'(net^{o}) \qquad\qquad (B.8)$$

$$\partial(net^{\,o}) \,/\, \partial i_{kj} = \partial(\sum_{k,j=1}^{n} (c_{kj}^{\,o} i_{kj})) \,/\, \partial i_{kj} = c_{kj}^{\,o} \qquad\qquad (B.9)$$

$$\partial i_{kj} \,/\, \partial(net_{kj}^{\,h}) = \partial(f^{h}(net_{kj}^{\,h})) \,/\, \partial(net_{kj}^{\,h}) = f^{\,h}\,'(net_{kj}^{\,h}) \qquad\qquad (B.10)$$

$$\partial(net_{kj}^{\,h}) \,/\, \partial c_{kj}^{\,hx} = \partial(\{c_{kj}^{\,hx} b_{k}^{\,x}\}\{c_{kj}^{\,hy} b_{j}^{\,y}\}) \,/\, \partial c_{kj}^{\,hx}$$
$$= b_{k}^{\,x} c_{kj}^{\,hy} b_{j}^{\,y} = \delta_{kj}^{\,hx} b_{k}^{\,x}$$
$$where: \delta_{kj}^{\,hx} = c_{kj}^{\,hy} b_{j}^{\,y} \qquad\qquad (B.11)$$

Combining Eqns. B.6 through B.11, the negative gradient is:

$$-\partial E \,/\, \partial c_{kj}^{\,hx} = (d-z) f^{\,o}\,'(net^{\,o}) c_{kj}^{\,o} f^{\,h}\,'(net_{kj}^{\,h}) \delta^{\,hx} b_{k}^{\,x} \qquad\qquad (B.12)$$

The weight update equations are formulated as follows:

- let output neuron is a linear neuron:

$$\delta^{\,ol} = (d-z) f_{\,k}^{\,o}\,'(net^{o}) = (d-z) \qquad\qquad (B.13)$$

Also let the second layer neurons be linear neurons, combining Formulae B.1, B.5, B.12 and B.13:

$$c_{kj}^{\,hx}(t+1) = c_{kj}^{\,hx}(t) - \eta(\partial E \,/\, \partial c_{kj}^{\,hx})$$
$$= c_{kj}^{\,hx}(t) + \eta((d-z) f^{\,o}\,'(net^{\,o}) c_{kj}^{\,o} f^{\,h}\,'(net_{kj}^{\,hx}) c_{kj}^{\,hy} b_{j}^{\,y} b_{k}^{\,x})$$
$$= c_{kj}^{\,hx}(t) + \eta(\delta^{\,ol} c_{kj}^{\,o} \delta_{kj}^{\,hx} b_{k}^{\,x})$$
$$where: \qquad \delta^{\,ol} = (d-z)$$
$$\delta_{kj}^{\,hx} = c_{kj}^{\,hy} b_{j}^{\,y}$$
$$f^{\,o}\,'(net^{o}) = 1 \qquad (linear \qquad neuron)$$
$$f^{\,h}\,'(net_{kj}^{\,hx}) = 1 \qquad (linear \qquad neuron) \qquad\qquad (B.14)$$

Use the same rules, the weight update question for y input neurons is:

$$c_{kj}{}^{hy}(t+1) = c_{kj}{}^{hy}(t) - \eta(\partial E / \partial c_{kj}{}^{hy})$$

$$= c_{kj}{}^{hy}(t) + \eta((d-z)f^o{}'(net^o)c_{kj}{}^o f^h{}'(net_{kj}{}^{hy})c_{kj}{}^{hx}b_k{}^x b_j{}^y)$$

$$= c_{kj}{}^{hy}(t) + \eta(\delta^{ol}c_{kj}{}^o \delta_{kj}{}^{hy}b_j{}^y)$$

$$where: \qquad \delta^{ol} = (d-z)$$

$$\delta_{kj}{}^{hy} = c_{kj}{}^{hx}b_k{}^x$$

$$f^o{}'(net^o) = 1 \qquad (linear \qquad neuron)$$

$$f^h{}'(net_{kj}{}^{hy}) = 1 \qquad (linear \qquad neuron) \qquad (B.15)$$

First Hidden Layer x Neurons in HONN (Model 1 and Model 2)

For the x input part, we have following formula as learning algorithm.

The 1st hidden layer weights are updated according to:

$$c_k{}^x(t+1) = c_k{}^x(t) - \eta(\partial E_p / \partial c_k{}^x) \qquad (C.1)$$

where:

$c_k{}^x = $ 1st hidden layer weight for input x; $k = k$th neuron of first hidden layer

$\eta = $ learning rate (positive & usually < 1)

$E = $ error

$t = $ training time

The equations for the kth or j^{th} node in the first hidden layer are:

$$net_k{}^x = c_k{}^x * x$$

$$b_k{}^x = f_k{}^x(net_k{}^x)$$

or

$$net_j{}^y = c_j{}^y * y$$

$$b_j{}^y = f_j{}^y(net_j{}^y) \qquad (C.2)$$

where:

i_{kj} = output from 2nd hidden layer (= input to the output neuron)

$b_k{}^x$ and $b^y{}_j$ = output from the 1st hidden layer neuron (= input to 2nd hidden layer neuron)

$f_k{}^x$ and $f_j{}^y$ = 1st hidden layer neuron activation function

x and y = input to 1st hidden layer

The total error is the sum of the squared errors across all hidden units, namely:

$$E_p = 0.5*\delta^2 = 0.5*(d-z)^2$$
$$= 0.5*(d-f^o(net^o))^2$$
$$= 0.5*\left(d-f^o\left(\sum_j c_{kj}{}^o i_{kj}\right)\right)^2 \tag{C.3}$$

The gradient is given by:

$$\partial E_p / \partial c_k{}^x = \partial(0.5*(d-z)^2)/\partial c_k{}^x$$
$$= (\partial(0.5*(d-z)^2)/\partial z)(\partial z/\partial(net^o))$$
$$(\partial(net^o)/\partial i_{kj})(\partial i_{kj}/\partial(net_{kj}{}^h))(\partial(net_{kj}{}^h)/\partial b_k{}^x)$$
$$(\partial b_k{}^x/\partial(net_k{}^x))(\partial(net_k{}^x)/\partial c_k{}^x) \tag{C.4}$$

$$\partial(0.5*(d-z)^2/\partial z = -(d-z) \tag{C.5}$$

$$\partial z/\partial(net^o) = \partial f^o/\partial(net^o) = f^o{}'(net^o) \tag{C.6}$$

$$\partial(net^o)/\partial i_{kj} = \partial(\sum_{k,j=1}^{l}(c_{kj}{}^o i_{kj}))/\partial i_{kj} = c_{kj}{}^o \tag{C.7}$$

$$\partial i_{kj}/\partial(net_{kj}{}^h) = \partial(f^h(net_{kj}{}^h))/\partial(net_{kj}{}^h) = f^h{}'(net_{kj}{}^h) \tag{C.8}$$

$$\partial net_{kj}{}^h/\partial b_k{}^x = \partial((c_{kj}{}^{hx}*b_k{}^x)*(c_{kj}{}^{hy}*b_j{}^y))/\partial b_k{}^x = c_{kj}{}^{hx}*c_{kj}{}^{hy}*b_j{}^y$$
$$= \delta_{kj}{}^{hx} c_{kj}{}^{hx}$$
$$where: \delta_{kj}{}^{hx} = c_{kj}{}^{hy}*b_j{}^y \tag{C.9}$$

$$\partial b_k^{\ x} / \partial(net_k^{\ x}) = f_x'(net_k^{\ x}) \qquad (C.10)$$

$$\partial(net_k^{\ x}) / \partial c_k^{\ x} = \partial(c_k^{\ x} * x) / \partial c_k^{\ x} = x \qquad (C.11)$$

Combining Formulae C.5 through C.11 the negative gradient is:

$$-\partial E_p / \partial c_k^{\ x} = (d-z)f^o{}'(net^o)c_{kj}^{\ o} * f^h{}'(net_{kj}^{\ h})\delta_{kj}^{\ hx}c_{kj}^{\ hx}f_x'(net_k^{\ x})x \qquad (C.12)$$

The weight update equations are calculated as follows.
For linear output neurons:

$$f^o{}'(net^o) = 1$$
$$\delta^{ol} = (d-z)f^o{}'(net^o) = (d-z) \qquad (C.13)$$

For linear neurons of second hidden layer:

$$f^h{}'(net_{kj}^{\ h}) = 1 \qquad (C.14)$$

The negative gradient is:

$$-\partial E_p / \partial c_k^{\ x} = (d-z)f^o{}'(net^o)c_{kj}^{\ o} * f^h{}'(net_{kj}^{\ h})\delta_{kj}^{\ hx}c_{kj}^{\ hx}f_x'(net_k^{\ x})x$$
$$= \delta^{ol} * c_{kj}^{\ o} * \delta_{kj}^{\ hx} * c_{kj}^{\ hx} * f_x'(net_k^{\ x}) * x \qquad (C.15)$$

By combining Formulae C.1, C.4, and C.15, for a linear 1st hidden layer neuron:
For a function of x input side:

$$b_k^{\ x} = f_k^{\ x}(net_k^{\ x})$$
$$f_x'(net_k^{\ x}) = \partial b_k^{\ x} / \partial(net_k^{\ x}) \qquad (C.16)$$

$$c_k^{\ x}(t+1) = c_k^{\ x}(t) - \eta(\partial E_p / \partial c_k^{\ x})$$
$$= c_k^{\ x}(t) + \eta(d-z)f^o{}'(net^o)c_{kj}^{\ o} * f^h{}'(net_{kj}^{\ h})c_{kj}^{\ hy}b_j^{\ y}c_{kj}^{\ hx}f_x'(net_k^{\ x})x$$
$$= c_k^{\ x}(t) + \eta * \delta^{ol} * c_{kj}^{\ o} * \delta^{hx} * c_{kj}^{\ hx} * \delta^x * x$$
$$where:$$
$$\delta^{ol} = (d-z)f^o{}'(net^o) = d-z \qquad (linear \qquad neuron)$$
$$\delta^{hx} = f^h{}'(net_{kj}^{\ h})c_{kj}^{\ hy}b_j^{\ y} \quad = c_{kj}^{\ hy}b_j^{\ y} \qquad (linear \qquad neuron)$$
$$\delta^x = f_x'(net_k^{\ x}) \qquad (C.17)$$

First Hidden Layer y Neurons in HONN (Model 1 and Model 2)
For the y input part, we have following formula as learning algorithm.
The 1st hidden layer weights are updated according to:

$$c_j^{\ y}(t+1) = c_j^{\ y}(t) - \eta(\partial E_p / \partial c_j^{\ y}) \qquad (D.1)$$

where:

$C_j^{\ y} = 1^{st}$ hidden layer weight for input y; $j = j$th neuron of first hidden layer

η = learning rate (positive & usually < 1)

E = error

t = training time

The equations for the kth or j^{th} node in the first hidden layer are:

$$net_k^{\ x} = c_k^{\ x} * x$$
$$b_k^{\ x} = f_k^{\ x}(net_k^{\ x})$$
$$or$$
$$net_j^{\ y} = c_j^{\ y} * y$$
$$b_j^{\ y} = f_j^{\ y}(net_j^{\ y}) \qquad (D.2)$$

where:

i_{kj} = output from 2nd hidden layer (= input to the output neuron)

$b_k^{\ x}$ and $b_j^{\ y}$ = output from the 1st hidden layer neuron (= input to 2nd hidden layer neuron)

$f_k^{\ x}$ and $f_j^{\ y}$ = 1st hidden layer neuron activation function

x and y = input to 1st hidden layer

The total error is the sum of the squared errors across all hidden units, namely:

$$E_p = 0.5 * \delta^2 = 0.5 * (d - z)^2$$
$$= 0.5 * (d - f^o(net^o))^2$$
$$= 0.5 * (d - f^o(\sum_j c_{kj}^{\ o} i_{kj}))^2 \qquad (D.3)$$

The gradient is given by:

$$\partial E_p / \partial c_j^{\ y} = \partial(0.5*(d-z)^2) / \partial c_j^{\ y}$$
$$= (\partial(0.5*(d-z)^2) / \partial z)(\partial z / \partial(net^{\ o}))$$
$$(\partial(net^{\ o}) / \partial i_{kj})(\partial i_{kj} / \partial(net_{kj}^{\ h}))(\partial(net_{kj}^{\ h}) / \partial b_j^{\ y})$$
$$(\partial b_j^{\ y} / \partial(net_j^{\ y}))(\partial(net_j^{\ y}) / \partial c_j^{\ y}) \qquad\qquad (D.4)$$

$$\partial(0.5*(d-z)^2 / \partial z = -(d-z) \qquad\qquad (D.5)$$

$$\partial z / \partial(net^{\ o}) = \partial f^{\ o} / \partial(net^o) = f^{\ o\ '}(net^o) \qquad\qquad (D.6)$$

$$\partial(net^{\ o}) / \partial i_{kj} = \partial(\sum_{k,j=1}^{l} (c_{kj}^{\ o} i_{kj})) / \partial i_{kj} = c_{kj}^{\ o} \qquad\qquad (D.7)$$

$$\partial i_{kj} / \partial(net_{kj}^{\ h}) = \partial(f^{\ h}(net_{kj}^{\ h})) / \partial(net_{kj}^{\ h}) = f^{\ h\ '}(net_{kj}^{\ h}) \qquad\qquad (D.8)$$

$$\partial net_{kj}^{\ h} / \partial b_j^{\ y} = \partial((c_{kj}^{\ hx}*b_k^{\ x})*(c_{kj}^{\ hy}*b_j^{\ y})) / \partial b_j^{\ y} = c_{kj}^{\ hx}*c_{kj}^{\ hy}*b_k^{\ x}$$
$$= \delta^{\ hy} c_{kj}^{\ hy}$$
$$where: \delta_{kj}^{\ hy} = c_{kj}^{\ hy}*b_k^{\ x} \qquad\qquad (D.9)$$

$$\partial b_j^{\ y} / \partial(net_j^{\ y}) = f_y^{\ '}(net_j^{\ y}) \qquad\qquad (D.10)$$

$$\partial(net_j^{\ y}) / \partial c_j^{\ y} = \partial(c_j^{\ y}*y) / \partial c_j^{\ y} = y \qquad\qquad (D.11)$$

Combining Formulae C.5 through C.11 the negative gradient is:

$$-\partial E_p / \partial c_k^{\ x} = (d-z)f^{\ o\ '}(net^{\ o})c_{kj}^{\ o}*f^{\ h\ '}(net_{kj}^{\ h})\delta_{kj}^{\ hy}c_{kj}^{\ hy}f_y^{\ '}(net_j^{\ y})y \qquad\qquad (D.12)$$

The weight update equations are calculated as follows.
For linear output neurons:

$$f^{\ o\ '}(net^o) = 1$$
$$\delta^{\ ol} = (d-z)f^{\ o\ '}(net^o) = (d-z) \qquad\qquad (D.13)$$

For linear neurons of second hidden layer:

$$f^{h}{}'(net_{kj}{}^{h}) = 1 \qquad (D.14)$$

The negative gradient is:

$$-\partial E_{p} / \partial c_{j}{}^{y} = (d-z)f^{o}{}'(net^{o})c_{kj}{}^{o} * f^{h}{}'(net_{kj}{}^{h})\delta_{kj}{}^{hy}c_{kj}{}^{hy}f_{y}{}'(net_{j}{}^{y})y$$
$$= \delta^{ol} * c_{kj}{}^{o} * \delta_{kj}{}^{hy} * c_{kj}{}^{hy} * f_{y}{}'(net_{j}{}^{y}) * y \qquad (D.15)$$

By combining Formulae D.1, D.4, and D.15, for a linear 1st hidden layer neuron:
For a function of y input part:

$$b_{j}{}^{y} = f_{j}{}^{y}(net_{j}{}^{y})$$
$$f_{y}{}'(net_{j}{}^{y}) = \partial b_{j}{}^{y} / \partial(net_{j}{}^{y}) \qquad (D.16)$$

Using the above procedure:

$$c_{j}{}^{y}(t+1) = c_{j}{}^{y}(t) - \eta(\partial E_{p} / \partial c_{j}{}^{y})$$
$$= c_{j}{}^{y}(t) + \eta(d-z)f^{o}{}'(net^{o})c_{kj}{}^{o} * f^{h}{}'(net_{kj}{}^{h})c_{kj}{}^{hx}b_{k}{}^{x}c_{kj}{}^{hy}f_{y}{}'(net_{j}{}^{y})y$$
$$= c_{j}{}^{y}(t) + \eta * \delta^{ol} * c_{kj}{}^{o} * \delta^{hy} * c_{kj}{}^{hy} * \delta^{y} * y$$

$where$:
$$\delta^{ol} = (d-z)f^{o}{}'(net^{o}) = d-z \qquad (linear \qquad neuron \qquad f^{o}{}'(net^{o}) = 1)$$
$$\delta^{hy} = f^{h}{}'(net_{kj}{}^{h})c_{kj}{}^{hx}b_{k}{}^{x} \qquad = c_{kj}{}^{hx}b_{k}{}^{x} \qquad (linear \qquad neuron \qquad f^{h}{}'(net_{kj}{}^{h}) = 1)$$
$$\delta^{y} = f_{y}{}'(net_{j}{}^{y}) \qquad (D.17)$$

24 HONN MODELS LEARNING ALGORITHM AND WEIGHT UPDATE FORMULAE

1. PHONN Model First Layer Neuron Weights Learning Formula

Let:
$$f_{k}{}^{x}(c_{k}{}^{x}x) = (c_{k}{}^{x}x)^{k}$$
$$f_{j}{}^{y}(c_{j}{}^{y}y) = (c_{j}{}^{y}y)^{j}$$

For a polynomial function of x input side:

$$b_k^{\ x} = f_k^{\ x}\ (net_k^{\ x}) = (net_k^{\ x})^k = (c_k^{\ x} * x)^k$$

$$f_x\ '(net_k^{\ x}) = \partial b_k^{\ x} / \partial(net_k^{\ x})$$

$$= \partial(net_k^{\ x})^k) / \partial(net_k^{\ x})$$

$$= k(net_k^{\ x})^{k-1} = k*(c_k^{\ x} * x)^{k-1} \qquad (PHONN \quad C. \quad 16)$$

$$c_k^{\ x}(t+1) = c_k^{\ x}(t) - \eta(\partial E_p / \partial c_k^{\ x})$$

$$= c_k^{\ x}(t) + \eta(d-z)f^o{}'(net^o)c_{kj}^{\ o} * f^h{}'(net_{kj}^{\ h})c_{kj}^{\ hy}b_j^{\ y}c_{kj}^{\ hx}f_x{}'(net_k^{\ x})x$$

$$= c_k^{\ x}(t) + \eta * \delta^{ol} * c_{kj}^{\ o} * \delta^{hx} * c_{kj}^{\ hx} * k*(c_k^{\ x} * x)^{k-1} * x$$

$$= c_k^{\ x}(t) + \eta * \delta^{ol} * c_{kj}^{\ o} * \delta^{hx} * c_{kj}^{\ hx} * \delta^x * x \qquad (PHONN \quad C. \quad 17)$$

where :

$$\delta^{ol} = (d-z)f^o{}'(net^o) = d-z \qquad (linear \quad neuron \quad f^o{}'(net^o) = 1)$$

$$\delta^{hx} = f^h{}'(net_{kj}^{\ h})c_{kj}^{\ hy}b_j^{\ y} \quad = c_{kj}^{\ hy}b_j^{\ y} \qquad (linear \quad neuron \quad f^h{}'(net_{kj}^{\ h}) = 1)$$

$$\delta^x = f_x{}'(net_k^{\ x}) = k*(net_k^{\ x})^{k-1} = k*(c_k^{\ x}*x)^{k-1}$$

For a polynomial function of *y* input part:

$$b_j^{\ y} = f_j^{\ y}\ (net_j^{\ y}) = (net_j^{\ y})^j = (c_j^{\ y} * y)^j$$

$$f_y\ '(net_j^{\ y}) = \partial b_j^{\ y} / \partial(net_j^{\ y})$$

$$= \partial(net_j^{\ y})^j) / \partial(net_j^{\ y})$$

$$= j*(net_j^{\ y})^{j-1} = j*(c_j^{\ y} * y)^{j-1} \qquad (PHONN \quad D. \quad 16)$$

Using the above procedure:

$$c_j^{\ y}(t+1) = c_j^{\ y}(t) - \eta(\partial E_p / \partial c_j^{\ y})$$

$$= c_j^{\ y}(t) + \eta(d-z)f^o{}'(net^o)c_{kj}^{\ o} * f^h{}'(net_{kj}^{\ h})c_{kj}^{\ hx}b_k^{\ x}c_{kj}^{\ hy}f_y{}'(net_j^{\ y})y$$

$$= c_j^{\ y}(t) + \eta * \delta^{ol} * c_{kj}^{\ o} * \delta^{hy} * c_{kj}^{\ hy} * j*(c_j^{\ y} * y)^{j-1} * y$$

$$= c_j^{\ y}(t) + \eta * \delta^{ol} * c_{kj}^{\ o} * \delta^{hy} * c_{kj}^{\ hy} * \delta^y * y \qquad (PHONN \quad D.17)$$

where :

$$\delta^{ol} = (d-z)f^o{}'(net^o) = d-z \qquad (linear \quad neuron \quad f^o{}'(net^o) = 1)$$

$$\delta^{hy} = f^h{}'(net_{kj}^{\ h})c_{kj}^{\ hx}b_k^{\ x} \quad = c_{kj}^{\ hx}b_k^{\ x} \qquad (linear \quad neuron \quad f^h{}'(net_{kj}^{\ h}) = 1)$$

$$\delta^y = f_y{}'(net_j^{\ y}) = j*(c_j^{\ y} * y)^{j-1}$$

2. XSHONN Model First Layer Neuron Weights Learning Formula

Polynomial and Sine Higher Order Neural Network (XSHONN) model as follows:

Let :

$$f_k^{\,x}(c_k^{\,x}x) = (c_k^{\,x}x)^k$$
$$f_j^{\,y}(c_j^{\,y}y) = \sin^j(c_j^{\,y}y)$$

For a polynomial function of *x* input side:

$$b_k^{\,x} = f_k^{\,x}\,(net_k^{\,x}) = (net_k^{\,x})^k = (c_k^{\,x} * x)^k$$
$$f_x\,{}'(net_k^{\,x}) = \partial b_k^{\,x} / \partial(net_k^{\,x})$$
$$= \partial(net_k^{\,x})^k) / \partial(net_k^{\,x})$$
$$= k(net_k^{\,x})^{k-1} = k * (c_k^{\,x} * x)^{k-1} \qquad\qquad (XSHONN \qquad C. \qquad 16)$$

$$c_k^{\,x}(t+1) = c_k^{\,x}(t) - \eta(\partial E_p / \partial c_k^{\,x})$$
$$= c_k^{\,x}(t) + \eta(d-z)f^{o}\,{}'(net^{o})c_{kj}^{\,o} * f^{h}\,{}'(net_{kj}^{\,h})c_{kj}^{\,hy}b_j^{\,y}c_{kj}^{\,hx}f_x\,{}'(net_k^{\,x})x$$
$$= c_k^{\,x}(t) + \eta * \delta^{ol} * c_{kj}^{\,o} * \delta^{hx} * c_{kj}^{\,hx} * k * (c_k^{\,x} * x)^{k-1} * x$$
$$= c_k^{\,x}(t) + \eta * \delta^{ol} * c_{kj}^{\,o} * \delta^{hx} * c_{kj}^{\,hx} * \delta^{x} * x \qquad\qquad (XSHONN \qquad C. \qquad 17)$$
where :

$$\delta^{ol} = (d-z)f^{o}\,{}'(net^{o}) = d-z \qquad (linear \qquad neuron \qquad f^{o}\,{}'(net^{o}) = 1)$$
$$\delta^{hx} = f^{h}\,{}'(net_{kj}^{\,h})c_{kj}^{\,hy}b_j^{\,y} \qquad = c_{kj}^{\,hy}b_j^{\,y} \qquad (linear \qquad neuron \qquad f^{h}\,{}'(net_{kj}^{\,h}) = 1)$$
$$\delta^{x} = f_x\,{}'(net_k^{\,x}) = k * (net_k^{\,x})^{k-1} = k * (c_k^{\,x} * x)^{k-1}$$

For a sine function of *y* input part:

$$b_j^{\,y} = f_j^{\,y}\,(net_j^{\,y}) = \sin^j(net_j^{\,y}) = \sin^j(c_j^{\,y} * y)$$
$$f_y\,{}'(net_j^{\,y}) = \partial b_j^{\,y} / \partial(net_j^{\,y})$$
$$= \partial(\sin^j(net_j^{\,y})) / \partial(net_j^{\,y})$$
$$= j * \sin^{j-1}(net_j^{\,y}) * \cos(net_j^{\,y})$$
$$= j \; * \sin^{j-1}(c_j^{\,y} * y) * \cos(c_j^{\,y} * y) \qquad\qquad (XSHONN \qquad D. \qquad 16)$$

Using the above procedure:

$$c_j^{\;y}(t+1) = c_j^{\;y}(t) - \eta(\partial E_p / \partial c_j^{\;y})$$
$$= c_j^{\;y}(t) + \eta(d-z)f^{o\,\prime}(net^{\,o})c_{kj}^{\;o} * f^{h\,\prime}(net_{kj}^{\;h})c_{kj}^{\;hx}b_k^{\;x}c_{kj}^{\;hy}f_y^{\;\prime}(net_j^{\;y})y$$
$$= c_j^{\;y}(t) + \eta * \delta^{\,ol} * c_{kj}^{\;o} * \delta^{\,hy} * c_{kj}^{\;hy} * j * \sin^{j-1}(c_j^{\;y} * y)\cos(c_j^{\;y} * y) * y$$
$$= c_j^{\;y}(t) + \eta * \delta^{\,ol} * c_{kj}^{\;o} * \delta^{\,hy} * c_{kj}^{\;hy} * \delta^{\,y} * y \qquad (XSHONN \qquad D. \qquad 17)$$

where :
$$\delta^{\,ol} = (d-z)f^{o\,\prime}(net^{\,o}) = d - z \qquad (linear \qquad neuron \qquad f^{o\,\prime}(net^{\,o}) = 1)$$
$$\delta^{\,hy} = f^{h\,\prime}(net_{kj}^{\;h})c_{kj}^{\;hx}b_k^{\;x} \quad = c_{kj}^{\;hx}b_k^{\;x} \qquad (linear \qquad neuron \qquad f^{h\,\prime}(net_{kj}^{\;h}) = 1)$$
$$\delta^{\,y} = f_y^{\;\prime}(net_j^{\;y}) = j * \sin^{j-1}(c_j^{\;y} * y)\cos(c_j^{\;y} * y)$$

3. XCHONN Model First Layer Neuron Weights Learning Formula

Polynomial and Cosine Higher Order Neural Network (XCHONN) model as follows:

Let :
$$f_k^{\;x}(c_k^{\;x}x) = (c_k^{\;x}x)^k$$
$$f_j^{\;y}(c_j^{\;y}y) = \cos^j(c_j^{\;y}y)$$

For a polynomial function of x input side:

$$b_k^{\;x} = f_k^{\;x}(net_k^{\;x}) = (net_k^{\;x})^k = (c_k^{\;x} * x)^k$$
$$f_x^{\;\prime}(net_k^{\;x}) = \partial b_k^{\;x} / \partial(net_k^{\;x})$$
$$= \partial(net_k^{\;x})^k) / \partial(net_k^{\;x})$$
$$= k(net_k^{\;x})^{k-1} = k * (c_k^{\;x} * x)^{k-1} \qquad (XCHONN \qquad C. \qquad 16)$$

$$c_k^{\;x}(t+1) = c_k^{\;x}(t) - \eta(\partial E_p / \partial c_k^{\;x})$$
$$= c_k^{\;x}(t) + \eta(d-z)f^{o\,\prime}(net^{\,o})c_{kj}^{\;o} * f^{h\,\prime}(net_{kj}^{\;h})c_{kj}^{\;hy}b_j^{\;y}c_{kj}^{\;hx}f_x^{\;\prime}(net_k^{\;x})x$$
$$= c_k^{\;x}(t) + \eta * \delta^{\,ol} * c_{kj}^{\;o} * \delta^{hx} * c_{kj}^{\;hx} * k * (c_k^{\;x} * x)^{k-1} * x$$
$$= c_k^{\;x}(t) + \eta * \delta^{\,ol} * c_{kj}^{\;o} * \delta^{\,hx} * c_{kj}^{\;hx} * \delta^{\,x} * x \qquad (XCHONN \qquad C. \qquad 17)$$
where :
$$\delta^{\,ol} = (d-z)f^{o\,\prime}(net^{\,o}) = d - z \qquad (linear \qquad neuron \qquad f^{o\,\prime}(net^{\,o}) = 1)$$
$$\delta^{\,hx} = f^{h\,\prime}(net_{kj}^{\;h})c_{kj}^{\;hy}b_j^{\;y} \quad = c_{kj}^{\;hy}b_j^{\;y} \qquad (linear \qquad neuron \qquad f^{h\,\prime}(net_{kj}^{\;h}) = 1)$$
$$\delta^{\,x} = f_x^{\;\prime}(net_k^{\;x}) = k * (net_k^{\;x})^{k-1} = k * (c_k^{\;x} * x)^{k-1}$$

For cosine function of y input part:

$$b_j^y = f_y(net_j^y) = \cos^j(net_j^y) = \cos^j(c_j^y * y)$$
$$f_y'(net_j^y) = \partial b_j^y / \partial(net_j^y)$$
$$= \partial(\cos^j(net_j^y)) / \partial(net_j^y)$$
$$= j\cos^{j-1}(net_j^y) * (-\sin(net_j^y))$$
$$= (-j) * \cos^{j-1}(net_j^y) * \sin(net_j^y)$$
$$= (-j) * \cos^{j-1}(c_j^y * y) * \sin(c_j^y * y) \qquad\qquad (XCHONN \qquad D. \qquad 16)$$

Using the above procedure:

$$c_j^y(t+1) = c_j^y(t) - \eta(\partial E_p / \partial c_j^y)$$
$$= c_j^y(t) + \eta(d-z)f^o{}'(net^o)c_{kj}^o * f^h{}'(net_{kj}^h)c_{kj}^{hx}b_k^x c_{kj}^{hy}f_y'(net_j^y)y$$
$$= c_j^y(t) + \eta * \delta^{ol} * c_{kj}^o * \delta^{hy} * c_{kj}^{hy} * (-j) * \cos^{j-1}(c_j^y * y) * \sin(c_j^y * y) * y$$
$$= c_j^y(t) + \eta * \delta^{ol} * c_{kj}^o * \delta^{hy} * c_{kj}^{hy} * \delta^y * y \qquad\qquad (XCHONN \qquad D. \qquad 17)$$

where :

$$\delta^{ol} = (d-z)f^o{}'(net^o) = d-z \qquad (linear \qquad neuron \qquad f^o{}'(net^o) = 1)$$
$$\delta^{hy} = f^h{}'(net_{kj}^h)c_{kj}^{hx}b_k^x = c_{kj}^{hx}b_k^x \qquad (linear \qquad neuron \qquad f^h{}'(net_{kj}^h) = 1)$$
$$\delta^y = f_y'(net_j^y) = (-j) * \cos^{j-1}(c_j^y * y) * \sin(c_j^y * y)$$

4. SINHONN Model First Layer Neuron Weights Learning Formula

Sine Higher Order Neural Network (SINHONN) model as follows:

Let :

$$f_k^x(c_k^x x) = \sin^k(c_k^x x)$$
$$f_j^y(c_j^y y) = \sin^j(c_j^y y)$$

For a sine function of x input side:

$$b_k^x = f_k^x(net_k^x) = \sin^k(net_k^x) = \sin^k(c_k^x * x)$$
$$f_x'(net_k^x) = \partial b_k^x / \partial(net_k^x)$$
$$= \partial(\sin^k(net_k^x)) / \partial(net_k^x)$$
$$= k * \sin^{k-1}(net_k^x) * \cos(net_k^x) = k * \sin^{k-1}(c_k^x * x) * \cos(c_k^x * x) \qquad (SINHONN \qquad C. \qquad 16)$$

$$c_k^{\ x}(t+1) = c_k^{\ x}(t) - \eta(\partial E_p / \partial c_k^{\ x})$$

$$= c_k^{\ x}(t) + \eta(d-z)f^{o}{}'(net^{o})c_{kj}^{\ o} * f^{h}{}'(net_{kj}^{\ h})c_{kj}^{\ hy}b_j^{\ y}c_{kj}^{\ hx}f_x{}'(net_k^{\ x})x$$

$$= c_k^{\ x}(t) + \eta * \delta^{ol} * c_{kj}^{\ o} * \delta^{hx} * c_{kj}^{\ hx} * k * \sin^{k-1}(c_k^{\ x} * x) * \cos(c_k^{\ x} * x) * x$$

$$= c_k^{\ x}(t) + \eta * \delta^{ol} * c_{kj}^{\ o} * \delta^{hx} * c_{kj}^{\ hx} * \delta^{x} * x \qquad (SINHONN \qquad C. \qquad 17)$$

where:

$$\delta^{ol} = (d-z)f^{o}{}'(net^{o}) = d-z \qquad (linear \qquad neuron \qquad f^{o}{}'(net^{o}) = 1)$$

$$\delta^{hx} = f^{h}{}'(net_{kj}^{\ h})c_{kj}^{\ hy}b_j^{\ y} \qquad = c_{kj}^{\ hy}b_j^{\ y} \qquad (linear \qquad neuron \qquad f^{h}{}'(net_{kj}^{\ h}) = 1)$$

$$\delta^{x} = f_x{}'(net_k^{\ x}) = k * (net_k^{\ x})^{k-1} = k * \sin^{k-1}(c_k^{\ x} * x) * \cos(c_k^{\ x} * x)$$

For a sine function of *y* input part:

$$b_j^{\ y} = f_j^{\ y}(net_j^{\ y}) = \sin^{j}(net_j^{\ y}) = \sin^{j}(c_j^{\ y} * y)$$

$$f_y{}'(net_j^{\ y}) = \partial b_j^{\ y} / \partial(net_j^{\ y})$$

$$= \partial(\sin^{j}(net_j^{\ y})) / \partial(net_j^{\ y})$$

$$= j * \sin^{j-1}(net_j^{\ y}) * \cos(net_j^{\ y})$$

$$= j * \sin^{j-1}(c_j^{\ y} * y) * \cos(c_j^{\ y} * y) \qquad (SINHONN \qquad D. \qquad 16)$$

Using the above procedure:

$$c_j^{\ y}(t+1) = c_j^{\ y}(t) - \eta(\partial E_p / \partial c_j^{\ y})$$

$$= c_j^{\ y}(t) + \eta(d-z)f^{o}{}'(net^{o})c_{kj}^{\ o} * f^{h}{}'(net_{kj}^{\ h})c_{kj}^{\ hy}b_j^{\ y}c_{kj}^{\ hy}f_y{}'(net_j^{\ y})y$$

$$= c_j^{\ y}(t) + \eta * \delta^{ol} * c_{kj}^{\ o} * \delta^{hy} * c_{kj}^{\ hy} * j * \sin^{j-1}(c_j^{\ y} * y)\cos(c_j^{\ y} * y) * y$$

$$= c_j^{\ y}(t) + \eta * \delta^{ol} * c_{kj}^{\ o} * \delta^{hy} * c_{kj}^{\ hy} * \delta^{y} * y \qquad (SINHONN \qquad D. \qquad 17)$$

where:

$$\delta^{ol} = (d-z)f^{o}{}'(net^{o}) = d-z \qquad (linear \qquad neuron \qquad f^{o}{}'(net^{o}) = 1)$$

$$\delta^{hy} = f^{h}{}'(net_{kj}^{\ h})c_{kj}^{\ hx}b_k^{\ x} \qquad = c_{kj}^{\ hx}b_k^{\ x} \qquad (linear \qquad neuron \qquad f^{h}{}'(net_{kj}^{\ h}) = 1)$$

$$\delta^{y} = f_y{}'(net_j^{\ y}) = j * \sin^{j-1}(c_j^{\ y} * y) * \cos(c_j^{\ y} * y)$$

5. COSHONN Model First Layer Neuron Weights Learning Formula

Cosine Higher Order Neural Network (COSHONN) model as follows:

Let :

$$f_k^{\ x}(c_k^{\ x}x) = \cos^k(c_k^{\ x}x)$$
$$f_j^{\ y}(c_j^{\ y}y) = \cos^j(c_j^{\ y}y)$$

For a cosine function of x input side:

$$b_k^{\ x} = f_k^{\ x}\ (net_k^{\ x}) = \cos^k(net_k^{\ x}) = \cos^k(c_k^{\ x} * x)$$
$$f_x\ '(net_k^{\ x}) = \partial b_k^{\ x}\ /\ \partial(net_k^{\ x})$$
$$= \partial(\cos^k(net_k^{\ x}))\ /\ \partial(net_k^{\ x})$$
$$= k * \cos^{k-1}(net_k^{\ x}) * (-\sin(net_k^{\ x}))$$
$$= (-k) * \cos^{k-1}(c_k^{\ x} * x) * \sin(c_k^{\ x} * x) \qquad\qquad (COSHONN \quad C. \quad 16)$$

$$c_k^{\ x}(t+1) = c_k^{\ x}(t) - \eta(\partial E_p\ /\ \partial c_k^{\ x})$$
$$= c_k^{\ x}(t) + \eta(d-z)f^o\ '(net^o)c_{kj}^{\ o} * f^h\ '(net_{kj}^{\ h})c_{kj}^{\ hy}b_j^{\ y}c_{kj}^{\ hx}f_x\ '(net_k^{\ x})x$$
$$= c_k^{\ x}(t) + \eta * \delta^{\ ol} * c_{kj}^{\ o} * \delta^{\ hx} * c_{kj}^{\ hx} * (-k) * \cos^{k-1}(c_k^{\ x} * x) * \sin(c_k^{\ x} * x) * x$$
$$= c_k^{\ x}(t) + \eta * \delta^{\ ol} * c_{kj}^{\ o} * \delta^{\ hx} * c_{kj}^{\ hx} * \delta^{\ x} * x \qquad\qquad (COSHONN \quad C. \quad 17)$$

$where$:

$$\delta^{\ ol} = (d-z)f^o\ '(net^o) = d-z \qquad (linear \qquad neuron \qquad f^o\ '(net^o) = 1)$$
$$\delta^{\ hx} = f^h\ '(net_{kj}^{\ h})c_{kj}^{\ hy}b_j^{\ y} \qquad = c_{kj}^{\ hy}b_j^{\ y} \qquad (linear \qquad neuron \qquad f^h\ '(net_{kj}^{\ h}) = 1)$$
$$\delta^{\ x} = f_x\ '(net_k^{\ x}) = (-k) * \cos^{k-1}(net_k^{\ x}) * \sin(net_k^{\ x}) = (-k) * \cos^{k-1}(c_k^{\ x} * x) * \sin(c_k^{\ x} * x)$$

For cosine function of y input part:

$$b_j^{\ y} = f_y\ (net_j^{\ y}) = \cos^j(net_j^{\ y}) = \cos^j(c_j^{\ y} * y)$$
$$f_y\ '(net_j^{\ y}) = \partial b^y_{\ j}\ /\ \partial(net_j^{\ y})$$
$$= \partial(\cos^j(net_j^{\ y}))\ /\ \partial(net_j^{\ y})$$
$$= j\cos^{j-1}(net_j^{\ y}) * (-\sin(net_j^{\ y}))$$
$$= (-j) * \cos^{j-1}(net_j^{\ y}) * \sin(net_j^{\ y})$$
$$= (-j) * \cos^{j-1}(c_j^{\ y} * y) * \sin(c_j^{\ y} * y) \qquad\qquad (COSHONN \quad D. \quad 16)$$

Using the above procedure:

$$c_j^y(t+1) = c_j^y(t) - \eta(\partial E_p / \partial c_j^y)$$
$$= c_j^y(t) + \eta(d-z)f^o{}'(net^o)c_{kj}^o * f^h{}'(net_{kj}^h)c_{kj}^{hx}b_k^x c_{kj}^{hy}f_y{}'(net_j^y)y$$
$$= c_j^y(t) + \eta * \delta^{ol} * c_{kj}^o * \delta^{hy} * c_{kj}^{hy} * (-j) * \cos^{j-1}(c_j^y * y) * \sin(c_j^y * y) * y$$
$$= c_j^y(t) + \eta * \delta^{ol} * c_{kj}^o * \delta^{hy} * c_{kj}^{hy} * \delta^y * y \qquad (COSHONN \qquad D. \qquad 17)$$

where :

$$\delta^{ol} = (d-z)f^o{}'(net^o) = d - z \qquad (linear \qquad neuron \qquad f^o{}'(net^o) = 1)$$
$$\delta^{hy} = f^h{}'(net_{kj}^h)c_{kj}^{hx}b_k^x \qquad = c_{kj}^{hx}b_k^x \qquad (linear \qquad neuron \qquad f^h{}'(net_{kj}^h) = 1)$$
$$\delta^y = f_y{}'(net_j^y) = (-j) * \cos^{j-1}(c_j^y * y) * \sin(c_j^y * y)$$

6. THONN Model First Layer Neuron Weights Learning Formula

Let :

$$f_k^x(c_k^x x) = \sin^k(c_k^x x)$$
$$f_j^y(c_j^y y) = \cos^j(c_j^y y)$$

For a sine function of x input side:

$$b_k^x = f_k^x(net_k^x) = \sin^k(net_k^x) = \sin^k(c_k^x * x)^k$$
$$f_x{}'(net_k^x) = \partial b_k^x / \partial(net_k^x)$$
$$= \partial(\sin^k(net_k^x)) / \partial(net_k^x)$$
$$= k * \sin^{k-1}(net_k^x) * \cos(net_k^x) = k * \sin^{k-1}(c_k^x * x) * \cos(c_k^x * x) \qquad (THONN \qquad C. \qquad 16)$$
$$c_k^x(t+1) = c_k^x(t) - \eta(\partial E_p / \partial c_k^x)$$
$$= c_k^x(t) + \eta(d-z)f^o{}'(net^o)c_{kj}^o * f^h{}'(net_{kj}^h)c_{kj}^{hy}b_j^y c_{kj}^{hx}f_x{}'(net_k^x)x$$
$$= c_k^x(t) + \eta * \delta^{ol} * c_{kj}^o * \delta^{hx} * c_{kj}^{hx} * k * \sin^{k-1}(c_k^x * x) * \cos(c_k^x * x) * x$$
$$= c_k^x(t) + \eta * \delta^{ol} * c_{kj}^o * \delta^{hx} * c_{kj}^{hx} * \delta^x * x \qquad (THONN \qquad C. \qquad 17)$$
where :

$$\delta^{ol} = (d-z)f^o{}'(net^o) = d - z \qquad (linear \qquad neuron \qquad f^o{}'(net^o) = 1)$$
$$\delta^{hx} = f^h{}'(net_{kj}^h)c_{kj}^{hy}b_j^y \qquad = c_{kj}^{hy}b_j^y \qquad (linear \qquad neuron \qquad f^h{}'(net_{kj}^h) = 1)$$
$$\delta^x = f_x{}'(net_k^x) = k * (net_k^x)^{k-1} = k * \sin^{k-1}(c_k^x * x) * \cos(c_k^x * x)$$

For cosine function of *y* input part:

$$b_j^y = f_y(net_j^y) = \cos^j(net_j^y) = \cos^j(c_j^y * y)$$
$$f_y'(net_j^y) = \partial b_j^y / \partial(net_j^y)$$
$$= \partial(\cos^j(net_j^y)) / \partial(net_j^y)$$
$$= j\cos^{j-1}(net_j^y) * (-\sin(net_j^y))$$
$$= (-j) * \cos^{j-1}(net_j^y) * \sin(net_j^y)$$
$$= (-j) * \cos^{j-1}(c_j^y * y) * \sin(c_j^y * y) \qquad (THONN \qquad D. \qquad 16)$$

Using the above procedure:

$$c_j^y(t+1) = c_j^y(t) - \eta(\partial E_p / \partial c_j^y)$$
$$= c_j^y(t) + \eta(d-z)f^o{}'(net^o)c_{kj}^o * f^h{}'(net_{kj}^h)c_{kj}^{hx}b_k^x c_{kj}^{hy}f_y'(net_j^y)y$$
$$= c_j^y(t) + \eta * \delta^{ol} * c_{kj}^o * \delta^{hy} * c_{kj}^{hy} * (-j) * \cos^{j-1}(c_j^y * y) * \sin(c_j^y * y) * y$$
$$= c_j^y(t) + \eta * \delta^{ol} * c_{kj}^o * \delta^{hy} * c_{kj}^{hy} * \delta^y * y \qquad (THONN \qquad D. \qquad 17)$$

where :

$$\delta^{ol} = (d-z)f^o{}'(net^o) = d-z \qquad (linear \qquad neuron \qquad f^o{}'(net^o) = 1)$$
$$\delta^{hy} = f^h{}'(net_{kj}^h)c_{kj}^{hx}b_k^x = c_{kj}^{hx}b_k^x \qquad (linear \qquad neuron \qquad f^h{}'(net_{kj}^h) = 1)$$
$$\delta^y = f_y'(net_j^y) = (-j) * \cos^{j-1}(c_j^y * y) * \sin(c_j^y * y)$$

7. SPHONN Model First Layer Neuron Weights Learning Formula

Let :

$$f_k^x(c_k^x x) = (1/(1+\exp(c_k^x(-x))))^k$$
$$f_j^y(c_j^y y) = (1/(1+\exp(c_j^y(-y))))^j$$

For a sigmoid function of *x* input side:

$$b_k^{\ x} = f_k^{\ x}(net_k^{\ x}) = [1/(1+\exp(-net_k^{\ x}))]^k$$

$$= [1/(1+\exp(c_k^{\ x}*(-x)))]^k$$

$$f_x'(net_k^{\ x}) = \partial b_k^{\ x}/\partial(net_k^{\ x}) \qquad (SPHONN \qquad C. \qquad 16)$$

$$= \partial[1/(1+\exp(-net_k^{\ x}))]^k/\partial(net_k^{\ x})$$

$$= k*[1/(1+\exp(-net_k^{\ x}))]^{k-1}*(1+\exp(-net_k^{\ x}))^{-2}*\exp(-net_k^{\ x})$$

$$= k*[1/(1+\exp(-c_k^{\ x}*x))]^{k-1}*(1+\exp(-c_k^{\ x}*x))^{-2}*\exp(-c_k^{\ x}*x)$$

$$c_k^{\ x}(t+1) = c_k^{\ x}(t) - \eta(\partial E_p/\partial c_k^{\ x})$$

$$= c_k^{\ x}(t) + \eta(d-z)f^o{}'(net^o)c_{kj}^{\ o}*f^h{}'(net_{kj}^{\ h})c_{kj}^{\ hy}b_j^{\ y}c_{kj}^{\ hx}f_x'(net_k^{\ x})x$$

$$= c_k^{\ x}(t) + \eta*\delta^{\ ol}*c_{kj}^{\ o}*\delta^{\ hx}*c_{kj}^{\ hx}*f_x'(net_k^{\ x})*x$$

$$= c_k^{\ x}(t) + \eta*\delta^{\ ol}*c_{kj}^{\ o}*\delta^{\ hx}*c_{kj}^{\ hx}$$

$$*[k*[1/(1+\exp(-c_k^{\ x}*x))]^{k-1}*(1+\exp(-c_k^{\ x}*x))^{-2}*\exp(-c_k^{\ x}*x)]*x$$

$$= c_k^{\ x}(t) + \eta*\delta^{\ ol}*c_{kj}^{\ o}*\delta^{\ hx}*c_{kj}^{\ hx}*\delta^x*x \qquad (SPHONN \qquad C. \qquad 17)$$

$$where:$$

$$\delta^{\ ol} = (d-z)f^o{}'(net^o) = d-z \qquad (linear \qquad neuron \qquad f^o{}'(net^o) = 1)$$

$$\delta^{\ hx} = f^h{}'(net_{kj}^{\ h})c_{kj}^{\ hy}b_j^{\ y} = c_{kj}^{\ hy}b_j^{\ y} \qquad (linear \qquad neuron \qquad f^h{}'(net_{kj}^{\ h}) = 1)$$

$$\delta^x = f_x'(net_k^{\ x})$$

$$= k*[1/(1+\exp(-c_k^{\ x}*x))]^{k-1}*(1+\exp(-c_k^{\ x}*x))^{-2}*\exp(-c_k^{\ x}*x)$$

For a sigmoid function of *y* input side:

$$b_j^{\ y} = f_j^{\ y}(net_j^{\ y}) = [1/(1+\exp(-net_j^{\ y}))]^j$$

$$= [1/(1+\exp(c_j^{\ y}*(-y)))]^j$$

$$f_y'(net_j^{\ y}) = \partial b_j^{\ y}/\partial(net_j^{\ y}) \qquad (SPHONN \qquad D. \qquad 16)$$

$$= \partial[1/(1+\exp(-net_j^{\ y}))]^k/\partial(net_j^{\ y})$$

$$= j*[1/(1+\exp(-net_j^{\ y}))]^{j-1}*(1+\exp(-net_j^{\ y}))^{-2}*\exp(-net_j^{\ y})$$

$$= j*[1/(1+\exp(-c_j^{\ y}*y))]^{j-1}*(1+\exp(-c_j^{\ y}*y))^{-2}*\exp(-c_j^{\ y}*y)$$

$$c_j^{\ y}(t+1) = c_j^{\ y}(t) - \eta(\partial E_p \ / \ \partial c_j^{\ y})$$

$$= c_j^{\ y}(t) + \eta(d-z)f^{o\ \prime}(net^{\ o})c_{kj}^{\ o} * f^{h\ \prime}(net_{kj}^{\ h})c_{kj}^{\ hx}b_k^{\ x}c_{kj}^{\ hy}f_y^{\ \prime}(net_j^{\ y})y$$

$$= c_j^{\ y}(t) + \eta * \delta^{\ ol} * c_{kj}^{\ o} * \delta^{hy} * c_{kj}^{\ hy} * f_y^{\ \prime}(net_j^{\ y}) * y$$

$$= c_j^{\ y}(t) + \eta * \delta^{\ ol} * c_{kj}^{\ o} * \delta^{hy} * c_{kj}^{\ hy}$$

$$* [j * [1 \ / \ (1 + \exp(-c_j^{\ y} * y))]^{j-1} * (1 + \exp(-c_j^{\ y} * y))^{-2} * \exp(-c_j^{\ y} * y)] * y$$

$$= c_j^{\ y}(t) + \eta * \delta^{\ ol} * c_{kj}^{\ o} * \delta^{hy} * c_{kj}^{\ hy} * \delta^y * y \qquad (SPHONN \qquad D. \qquad 17)$$

where :

$$\delta^{\ ol} = (d-z)f^{o\ \prime}(net^o) = d-z \qquad (linear \qquad neuron \qquad f^{o\ \prime}(net^o) = 1)$$

$$\delta^{hy} = f^{h\ \prime}(net_{kj}^{\ h})c_{kj}^{\ hx}b_k^{\ x} = c_{kj}^{\ hx}b_k^{\ x} \qquad (linear \qquad neuron \qquad f^{h\ \prime}(net_{kj}^{\ h}) = 1)$$

$$\delta^y = f_y^{\ \prime}(net_j^{\ y})$$

$$= j * [1 \ / \ (1 + \exp(-c_j^{\ y} * y))]^{j-1} * (1 + \exp(-c_j^{\ y} * y))^{-2} * \exp(-c_j^{\ y} * y)$$

8. SINCHONN Model First Layer Neuron Weights Learning Formula

Let :

$$f_k^{\ x}(c_k^{\ x}x) = (\sin(c_k^{\ x}x) \ / \ (c_k^{\ x}x))^k$$

$$f_j^{\ y}(c_j^{\ y}y) = (\sin(c_j^{\ y}y) \ / \ (c_k^{\ x}y))^j$$

For a SINC function of *x* input part:

$$b_k^{\ x} = f_k^{\ x}(net_k^{\ x}) = [\sin \ (net_k^{\ x}) \ / \ (net_k^{\ x})]^k = [\sin \ (c_k^{\ x}x) \ / \ (c_k^{\ x}x)]^k$$

$$f_x^{\ \prime}(net_k^{\ x}) = \partial b_k^{\ x} \ / \ \partial(net_k^{\ x})$$

$$= k[\sin \ (net_k^{\ x}) \ / \ (net_k^{\ x})]^{k-1} * [\cos(net_k^{\ x}) \ / \ (net_k^{\ x}) - \sin \ (net_k^{\ x}) \ / \ (net_k^{\ x})^2]$$

$$= k[\sin \ (c_k^{\ x}x) \ / \ (c_k^{\ k}x)]^{k-1} * [\cos(c_k^{\ x}x) \ / \ (c_k^{\ x}x) - \sin \ (c_k^{\ x}x) \ / \ (c_k^{\ x}x)^2] \qquad (SINCHONN \qquad C. \qquad 16)$$

$$c_k^{\ x}(t+1) = c_k^{\ x}(t) - \eta(\partial E_p \ / \ \partial c_k^{\ x})$$

$$= c_k^{\ x}(t) + \eta(d-z)f^{o\ \prime}(net^{\ o})c_{kj}^{\ o} * f^{h\ \prime}(net_{kj}^{\ h})c_{kj}^{\ hy}b_j^{\ y}c_{kj}^{\ hx}f_x^{\ \prime}(net_k^{\ x})x$$

$$= c_k^{\ x}(t) + \eta * \delta^{\ ol} * c_{kj}^{\ o} * \delta^{hx} * c_{kj}^{\ hx} * f_x^{\ \prime}(net_k^{\ x}) * x$$

$$= c_k^{\ x}(t) + \eta * \delta^{\ ol} * c_{kj}^{\ o} * \delta^{hx} * c_{kj}^{\ hx}$$

$$* [k[\sin \ (c_k^{\ x}x) \ / \ (c_k^{\ k}x)]^{k-1} * [\cos(c_k^{\ x}x) \ / \ (c_k^{\ x}x) - \sin \ (c_k^{\ x}x) \ / \ (c_k^{\ k}x)^2]] * x$$

$$= c_k^{\ x}(t) + \eta * \delta^{\ ol} * c_{kj}^{\ o} * \delta^{hx} * c_{kj}^{\ hx} * \delta^x * x \qquad (SINCHONN \qquad C. \qquad 17)$$

where :

$$\delta^{\ ol} = (d-z)f^{o\ \prime}(net^o) = (d-z) \qquad (linear \qquad neuron \qquad f^{o\ \prime}(net^{\ o}) = 1)$$

$$\delta^{hx} = f^{h\ \prime}(net_{kj}^{\ h})c_{kj}^{\ hy}b_j^{\ y} = c_{kj}^{\ hy}b_j^{\ y} \qquad (linear \qquad neuron \qquad f^{h\ \prime}(net_{kj}^{\ h}) = 1)$$

$$\delta^x = f_x^{\ \prime}(net_k^{\ x})$$

$$= k[\sin \ (net_k^{\ x}) \ / \ (net_k^{\ x})]^{k-1} * [\cos(net_k^{\ x}) \ / \ (net_k^{\ x}) - \sin \ (net_k^{\ x}) \ / \ (net_k^{\ x})^2]$$

$$= k[\sin \ (c_k^{\ x}x) \ / \ (c_k^{\ x}x)]^{k-1} * [\cos(c_k^{\ x}x) \ / \ (c_k^{\ x}x) - \sin \ (c_k^{\ x}x) \ / \ (c_k^{\ x}x)^2]$$

For a SINC function of y input part:

$$b_j^{\ y} = f_j^{\ y}(net_j^{\ y}) = [\sin(net_j^{\ y}) / (net_j^{\ y})]^j = [\sin(c_j^{\ y}y) / (c_j^{\ y}y)]^j$$

$$f_y'(net_j^{\ y}) = \partial b_j^{\ y} / \partial(net_j^{\ y})$$

$$= j[\sin(net_j^{\ y}) / (net_j^{\ y})]^{j-1} * [\cos(net_j^{\ y}) / (net_j^{\ y}) - \sin(net_j^{\ y}) / (net_j^{\ y})^2]$$

$$= j[\sin(c_j^{\ y}y) / (c_j^{\ y}y)]^{j-1} * [\cos(c_j^{\ y}y) / (c_j^{\ y}y) - \sin(c_j^{\ y}y) / (c_j^{\ y}y)^2] \qquad (SINCHONN \qquad D. \qquad 16)$$

Using above procedure:

$$c_j^{\ y}(t+1) = c_j^{\ y}(t) - \eta(\partial E_p / \partial c_j^{\ y})$$

$$= c_j^{\ y}(t) + \eta(d-z)f^{o}{}'(net^{o})c_{kj}^{\ o} * f^{h}{}'(net_{kj}^{\ h})c_{kj}^{\ hx}b_k^{\ x}c_{kj}^{\ hy}f_y'(net_j^{\ y})y$$

$$= c_j^{\ y}(t) + \eta * \delta^{ol} * c_{kj}^{\ o} * \delta^{hy} * c_{kj}^{\ hy} * f_y'(net_j^{\ y}) * y$$

$$= c_j^{\ y}(t) + \eta * \delta^{ol} * c_{kj}^{\ o} * \delta^{hy} * c_{kj}^{\ hy}$$

$$* [j[\sin(c_j^{\ y}y) / (c_j^{\ y}y)]^{j-1} * [\cos(c_j^{\ y}y) / (c_j^{\ y}y) - \sin(c_j^{\ y}y) / (c_j^{\ y}y)^2]] * y$$

$$= c_j^{\ y}(t) + \eta * \delta^{ol} * c_{kj}^{\ o} * \delta^{hy} * c_{kj}^{\ hy} * \delta^{y} * y \qquad (SINCHONN \qquad D. \qquad 17)$$

where :

$$\delta^{ol} = (d-z)f^{o}{}'(net^{o}) = (d-z) \qquad (linear \qquad neuron \qquad f^{o}{}'(net^{o}) = 1)$$

$$\delta^{hy} = f^{h}{}'(net_{kj}^{\ h})c_{kj}^{\ hx}b_k^{\ x} = c_{kj}^{\ hx}b_k^{\ x} \qquad (linear \qquad neuron \qquad f^{h}{}'(net_{kj}^{\ h}) = 1)$$

$$\delta^{y} = f_y'(net_j^{\ y})$$

$$= j[\sin(net_j^{\ y}) / (net_j^{\ y})]^{j-1} * [\cos(net_j^{\ y}) / (net_j^{\ y}) - \sin(net_j^{\ y}) / (net_j^{\ y})^2]$$

$$= j[\sin(c_j^{\ y}y) / (c_j^{\ y}y)]^{j-1} * [\cos(c_j^{\ y}y) / (c_j^{\ y}y) - \sin(c_j^{\ y}y) / (c_j^{\ y}y)^2]$$

9. SSINCHONN Model First Layer Neuron Weights Learning Formula

Let :

$$f_k^{\ x}(c_k^{\ x}x) = (\sin(c_k^{\ x}x))^k$$

$$f_j^{\ y}(c_j^{\ y}y) = (\sin(c_j^{\ y}y) / (c_k^{\ x}y))^j$$

For a sine function of x input side:

$$b_k^{\ x} = f_k^{\ x}(net_k^{\ x}) = \sin^k(net_k^{\ x}) = \sin^k(c_k^{\ x} * x)^k$$

$$f_x'(net_k^{\ x}) = \partial b_k^{\ x} / \partial(net_k^{\ x})$$

$$= \partial(\sin^k(net_k^{\ x})) / \partial(net_k^{\ x})$$

$$= k * \sin^{k-1}(net_k^{\ x}) * \cos(net_k^{\ x}) = k * \sin^{k-1}(c_k^{\ x} * x) * \cos(c_k^{\ x} * x) \qquad (SSINCHONN \qquad C. \qquad 16)$$

$$c_k{}^x(t+1) = c_k{}^x(t) - \eta(\partial E_p / \partial c_k{}^x)$$
$$= c_k{}^x(t) + \eta(d-z)f^o \,'(net^o)c_{kj}{}^o * f^h \,'(net_{kj}{}^h)c_{kj}{}^{hy}b_j{}^y c_{kj}{}^{hx}f_x \,'(net_k{}^x)x$$
$$= c_k{}^x(t) + \eta * \delta^{ol} * c_{kj}{}^o * \delta^{hx} * c_{kj}{}^{hx} * k * \sin^{k-1}(c_k{}^x * x) * \cos(c_k{}^x * x) * x$$
$$= c_k{}^x(t) + \eta * \delta^{ol} * c_{kj}{}^o * \delta^{hx} * c_{kj}{}^{hx} * \delta^x * x \qquad (SSINCHONN \qquad C. \qquad 17)$$
where :

$$\delta^{ol} = (d-z)f^o \,'(net^o) = d - z \qquad (linear \qquad neuron \qquad f^o \,'(net^o) = 1)$$
$$\delta^{hx} = f^h \,'(net_{kj}{}^h)c_{kj}{}^{hy}b_j{}^y = c_{kj}{}^{hy}b_j{}^y \qquad (linear \qquad neuron \qquad f^h \,'(net_{kj}{}^h) = 1)$$
$$\delta^x = f_x \,'(net_k{}^x) = k * (net_k{}^x)^{k-1} = k * \sin^{k-1}(c_k{}^x * x) * \cos(c_k{}^x * x)$$

For a SINC function of *y* input part:

$$b_j{}^y = f_j{}^y(net_j{}^y) = [\sin(net_j{}^y) / (net_j{}^y)]^j = [\sin(c_j{}^y y) / (c_j{}^y y)]^j$$
$$f_y \,'(net_j{}^y) = \partial b_j{}^y / \partial(net_j{}^y)$$
$$= j[\sin(net_j{}^y) / (net_j{}^y)]^{j-1} * [\cos(net_j{}^y) / (net_j{}^y) - \sin(net_j{}^y) / (net_j{}^y)^2]$$
$$= j[\sin(c_j{}^y y) / (c_j{}^y y)]^{j-1} * [\cos(c_j{}^y y) / (c_j{}^y y) - \sin(c_j{}^y y) / (c_j{}^y y)^2] \qquad (SSINCHONN \qquad D. \qquad 16)$$

Using above procedure:

$$c_j{}^y(t+1) = c_j{}^y(t) - \eta(\partial E_p / \partial c_j{}^y)$$
$$= c_j{}^y(t) + \eta(d-z)f^o \,'(net^o)c_{kj}{}^o * f^h \,'(net_{kj}{}^h)c_{kj}{}^{hx}b_k{}^x c_{kj}{}^{hy}f_y \,'(net_j{}^y)y$$
$$= c_j{}^y(t) + \eta * \delta^{ol} * c_{kj}{}^o * \delta^{hy} * c_{kj}{}^{hy} * f_y \,'(net_j{}^y) * y$$
$$= c_j{}^y(t) + \eta * \delta^{ol} * c_{kj}{}^o * \delta^{hy} * c_{kj}{}^{hy}$$
$$* [j[\sin(c_j{}^y y) / (c_j{}^y y)]^{j-1} * [\cos(c_j{}^y y) / (c_j{}^y y) - \sin(c_j{}^y y) / (c_j{}^y y)^2]] * y$$
$$= c_j{}^y(t) + \eta * \delta^{ol} * c_{kj}{}^o * \delta^{hy} * c_{kj}{}^{hy} * \delta^y * y \qquad (SSINCHONN \qquad D. \qquad 17)$$

where :

$$\delta^{ol} = (d-z)f^o \,'(net^o) = (d-z) \qquad (linear \qquad neuron \qquad f^o \,'(net^o) = 1)$$
$$\delta^{hy} = f^h \,'(net_{kj}{}^h)c_{kj}{}^{hx}b_k{}^x = c_{kj}{}^{hx}b_k{}^x \qquad (linear \qquad neuron \qquad f^h \,'(net_{kj}{}^h) = 1)$$
$$\delta^y = f_y \,'(net_j{}^y)$$
$$= j[\sin(net_j{}^y) / (net_j{}^y)]^{j-1} * [\cos(net_j{}^y) / (net_j{}^y) - \sin(net_j{}^y) / (net_j{}^y)^2]$$
$$= j[\sin(c_j{}^y y) / (c_j{}^y y)]^{j-1} * [\cos(c_j{}^y y) / (c_j{}^y y) - \sin(c_j{}^y y) / (c_j{}^y y)^2]$$

10. CSINCHONN Model First Layer Neuron Weights Learning Formula

Let :

$$f_k^{\ x}(c_k^{\ x}x) = (\cos(c_k^{\ x}x))^k$$

$$f_j^{\ y}(c_j^{\ y}y) = (\sin(c_j^{\ y}y) / (c_k^{\ x}y))^j$$

For a cosine function of *x* input side:

$$b_k^{\ x} = f_k^{\ x}\ (net_k^{\ x}) = \cos^k(net_k^{\ x}) = \cos^k(c_k^{\ x} * x)$$

$$f_x\ '(net_k^{\ x}) = \partial b_k^{\ x} / \partial(net_k^{\ x})$$

$$= \partial(\cos^k(net_k^{\ x})) / \partial(net_k^{\ x})$$

$$= k * \cos^{k-1}(net_k^{\ x}) * (-\sin(net_k^{\ x}))$$

$$= (-k) * \cos^{k-1}(c_k^{\ x} * x) * \sin(c_k^{\ x} * x) \qquad (CSINCHONN \qquad C. \qquad 16)$$

$$c_k^{\ x}(t+1) = c_k^{\ x}(t) - \eta(\partial E_p / \partial c_k^{\ x})$$

$$= c_k^{\ x}(t) + \eta(d-z)f^o\ '(net^o)c_{kj}^{\ o} * f^h\ '(net_{kj}^{\ h})c_{kj}^{\ hy}b_j^{\ y}c_{kj}^{\ hx}f_x\ '(net_k^{\ x})x$$

$$= c_k^{\ x}(t) + \eta * \delta^{\ ol} * c_{kj}^{\ o} * \delta^{\ hx} * c_{kj}^{\ hx} * (-k) * \cos^{k-1}(c_k^{\ x} * x) * \sin(c_k^{\ x} * x) * x$$

$$= c_k^{\ x}(t) + \eta * \delta^{\ ol} * c_{kj}^{\ o} * \delta^{\ hx} * c_{kj}^{\ hx} * \delta^{\ x} * x \qquad (CSINCHONN \qquad C. \qquad 17)$$

where :

$$\delta^{\ ol} = (d-z)f^o\ '(net^o) = d - z \qquad (linear \qquad neuron \qquad f^o\ '(net^o) = 1)$$

$$\delta^{\ hx} = f^h\ '(net_{kj}^{\ h})c_{kj}^{\ hy}b_j^{\ y} \qquad = c_{kj}^{\ hy}b_j^{\ y} \qquad (linear \qquad neuron \qquad f^h\ '(net_{kj}^{\ h}) = 1)$$

$$\delta^{\ x} = f_x\ '(net_k^{\ x}) = (-k) * \cos^{k-1}(net_k^{\ x}) * \sin(net_k^{\ x}) = (-k) * \cos^{k-1}(c_k^{\ x} * x) * \sin(c_k^{\ x} * x)$$

For a SINC function of *y* input part:

$$b_j^{\ y} = f_j^{\ y}(net_j^{\ y}) = [\sin(net_j^{\ y}) / (net_j^{\ y})]^j = [\sin(c_j^{\ y}y) / (c_j^{\ y}y)]^j$$

$$f_y\ '(net_j^{\ y}) = \partial b_j^{\ y} / \partial(net_j^{\ y})$$

$$= j[\sin(net_j^{\ y}) / (net_j^{\ y})]^{j-1} * [\cos(net_j^{\ y}) / (net_j^{\ y}) - \sin(net_j^{\ y}) / (net_j^{\ y})^2]$$

$$= j[\sin(c_j^{\ y}y) / (c_j^{\ y}y)]^{j-1} * [\cos(c_j^{\ y}y) / (c_j^{\ y}y) - \sin(c_j^{\ y}y) / (c_j^{\ y}y)^2] \qquad (CSINCHONN \qquad D. \qquad 16)$$

Using above procedure:

$$c_j^{\ y}(t+1) = c_j^{\ y}(t) - \eta(\partial E_p \,/\, \partial c_j^{\ y})$$

$$= c_j^{\ y}(t) + \eta(d-z)f^o{}'(net^o)c_{kj}^{\ o} * f^h{}'(net_{ki}^{\ h})c_{ki}^{\ hx}b_k^{\ x}c_{ki}^{\ hy}f_y{}'(net_j^{\ y})y$$

$$= c_j^{\ y}(t) + \eta * \delta^{ol} * c_{kj}^{\ o} * \delta^{hy} * c_{kj}^{\ hy} * f_y{}'(net_j^{\ y}) * y$$

$$= c_j^{\ y}(t) + \eta * \delta^{ol} * c_{kj}^{\ o} * \delta^{hy} * c_{kj}^{\ hy}$$
$$\qquad * [j[\sin(c_j^{\ y}y)\,/\,(c_j^{\ y}y)]^{j-1} * [\cos(c_j^{\ y}y)\,/\,(c_j^{\ y}y) - \sin(c_j^{\ y}y)\,/\,(c_j^{\ y}y)^2]] * y$$

$$= c_j^{\ y}(t) + \eta * \delta^{ol} * c_{kj}^{\ o} * \delta^{hy} * c_{kj}^{\ hy} * \delta^y * y \qquad\qquad (CSINCHONN \quad D. \quad 17)$$

where:

$$\delta^{ol} = (d-z)f^o{}'(net^o) = (d-z) \qquad\qquad (linear \quad neuron \quad f^o{}'(net^o)=1)$$

$$\delta^{hy} = f^h{}'(net_{kj}^{\ h})c_{kj}^{\ hx}b_k^{\ x} = c_{kj}^{\ hx}b_k^{\ x} \qquad\qquad (linear \quad neuron \quad f^h{}'(net_{kj}^{\ h})=1)$$

$$\delta^y = f_y{}'(net_j^{\ y})$$
$$= j[\sin(net_j^{\ y})\,/\,(net_j^{\ y})]^{j-1} * [\cos(net_j^{\ y})\,/\,(net_j^{\ y}) - \sin(net_j^{\ y})\,/\,(net_j^{\ y})^2]$$
$$= j[\sin(c_j^{\ y}y)\,/\,(c_j^{\ y}y)]^{j-1} * [\cos(c_j^{\ y}y)\,/\,(c_j^{\ y}y) - \sin(c_j^{\ y}y)\,/\,(c_j^{\ y}y)^2]$$

11. YSINCHONN Model First Layer Neuron Weights Learning Formula

Let:

$$f_k^{\ x}(c_k^{\ x}x) = (c_k^{\ x}x)^k$$

$$f_j^{\ y}(c_j^{\ y}y) = (\sin(c_j^{\ y}y)\,/\,(c_k^{\ x}y))^j$$

For a polynomial function of x input side:

$$b_k^{\ x} = f_k^{\ x}(net_k^{\ x}) = (net_k^{\ x})^k = (c_k^{\ x} * x)^k$$

$$f_x{}'(net_k^{\ x}) = \partial b_k^{\ x} \,/\, \partial(net_k^{\ x})$$

$$= \partial(net_k^{\ x})^k) \,/\, \partial(net_k^{\ x})$$

$$= k(net_k^{\ x})^{k-1} = k * (c_k^{\ x} * x)^{k-1} \qquad\qquad (YSINCHONN \quad C. \quad 16)$$

$$c_k^{\ x}(t+1) = c_k^{\ x}(t) - \eta(\partial E_p \,/\, \partial c_k^{\ x})$$

$$= c_k^{\ x}(t) + \eta(d-z)f^o{}'(net^o)c_{kj}^{\ o} * f^h{}'(net_{kj}^{\ h})c_{kj}^{\ hy}b_j^{\ y}c_{kj}^{\ hx}f_x{}'(net_k^{\ x})x$$

$$= c_k^{\ x}(t) + \eta * \delta^{ol} * c_{kj}^{\ o} * \delta^{hx} * c_{kj}^{\ hx} * k * (c_k^{\ x} * x)^{k-1} * x$$

$$= c_k^{\ x}(t) + \eta * \delta^{ol} * c_{kj}^{\ o} * \delta^{hx} * c_{kj}^{\ hx} * \delta^x * x \qquad\qquad (YSINCHONN \quad C. \quad 17)$$

where:

$$\delta^{ol} = (d-z)f^o{}'(net^o) = d - z \qquad (linear \quad neuron \quad f^o{}'(net^o)=1)$$

$$\delta^{hx} = f^h{}'(net_{kj}^{\ h})c_{kj}^{\ hy}b_j^{\ y} = c_{kj}^{\ hy}b_j^{\ y} \qquad (linear \quad neuron \quad f^h{}'(net_{kj}^{\ h})=1)$$

$$\delta^x = f_x{}'(net_k^{\ x}) = k * (net_k^{\ x})^{k-1} = k * (c_k^{\ x} * x)^{k-1}$$

For a SINC function of y input part:

$$b_j^y = f_j^y(net_j^y) = [\sin(net_j^y)/(net_j^y)]^j = [\sin(c_j^y y)/(c_j^y y)]^j$$

$$f_y'(net_j^y) = \partial b_j^y / \partial(net_j^y)$$

$$= j[\sin(net_j^y)/(net_j^y)]^{j-1} * [\cos(net_j^y)/(net_j^y) - \sin(net_j^y)/(net_j^y)^2]$$

$$= j[\sin(c_j^y y)/(c_j^y y)]^{j-1} * [\cos(c_j^y y)/(c_j^y y) - \sin(c_j^y y)/(c_j^y y)^2] \qquad (YSINCHONN \quad D. \quad 16)$$

Using above procedure:

$$c_j^y(t+1) = c_j^y(t) - \eta(\partial E_p / \partial c_j^y)$$

$$= c_j^y(t) + \eta(d-z)f^o{}'(net^o)c_{kj}^o * f^h{}'(net_{kj}^h)c_{kj}^{hx}b_k^x c_{kj}^{hy}f_y'(net_j^y)y$$

$$= c_j^y(t) + \eta * \delta^{ol} * c_{kj}^o * \delta^{hy} * c_{kj}^{hy} * f_y'(net_j^y) * y$$

$$= c_j^y(t) + \eta * \delta^{ol} * c_{kj}^o * \delta^{hy} * c_{kj}^{hy}$$
$$\qquad * [j[\sin(c_j^y y)/(c_j^y y)]^{j-1} * [\cos(c_j^y y)/(c_j^y y) - \sin(c_j^y y)/(c_j^y y)^2]] * y$$

$$= c_j^y(t) + \eta * \delta^{ol} * c_{kj}^o * \delta^{hy} * c_{kj}^{hy} * \delta^y * y \qquad (YSINCHONN \quad D. \quad 17)$$

where:

$$\delta^{ol} = (d-z)f^o{}'(net^o) = (d-z) \qquad (linear \quad neuron \quad f^o{}'(net^o) = 1)$$

$$\delta^{hy} = f^h{}'(net_{kj}^h)c_{kj}^{hx}b_k^x = c_{kj}^{hx}b_k^x \qquad (linear \quad neuron \quad f^h{}'(net_{kj}^h) = 1)$$

$$\delta^y = f_y'(net_j^y)$$

$$= j[\sin(net_j^y)/(net_j^y)]^{j-1} * [\cos(net_j^y)/(net_j^y) - \sin(net_j^y)/(net_j^y)^2]$$

$$= j[\sin(c_j^y y)/(c_j^y y)]^{j-1} * [\cos(c_j^y y)/(c_j^y y) - \sin(c_j^y y)/(c_j^y y)^2]$$

12. UCSHONN Model First Layer Neuron Weights Learning Formula

Let:

$$f_k^x(c_k^x x) = \cos^k(k * c_k^x x)$$

$$f_j^y(c_j^y y) = \sin^j(j * c_j^y y)$$

For an ultra-high frequency cosine function of x input part:

$$b^x_{\ k} = f_k \ (net_k^{\ x}) = \cos^k(k * net_k^{\ x})$$

$$f_k \ '(net_k^{\ x}) = \partial b^x_{\ k} \, / \, \partial(net_k^{\ x})$$

$$= \partial(\cos^k(k * nct_k^{\ x})) \, / \, \partial(nct_k^{\ x})$$

$$= k \cos^{k-1}(k * net_k^{\ x}) * (-\sin(k * net_k^{\ x})) * k$$

$$= -k^2 \cos^{k-1}(k * net_k^{\ x}) \sin(k * net_k^{\ x})$$

$$= -k^2 \cos^{k-1}(k * c_k^{\ x} * x) \sin(k * c_k^{\ x} * x) \qquad\qquad (UCSHONN \qquad C. \qquad 16)$$

$$c_k^{\ x}(t+1) = c_k^{\ x}(t) - \eta(\partial E_p \, / \, \partial c_k^{\ x})$$

$$= c_k^{\ x}(t) + \eta(d-z)f^o \, '(net^{\ o})c_{kj}^{\ o} * f^h \, '(net_{kj}^{\ h})c_{kj}^{\ hy} b^y_{\ j} c_{kj}^{\ hx} f_x \, '(net_k^{\ x})x$$

$$= c_k^{\ x}(t) + \eta * \delta^{\ ol} * c_{kj}^{\ o} * \delta^{\ hx} * c_{kj}^{\ hx} * (-k^2)\cos^{k-1}(k * c_k^{\ x} * x)\sin(k * c_k^{\ x} * x) * x$$

$$= c_k^{\ x}(t) + \eta * \delta^{\ ol} * c_{kj}^{\ o} * \delta^{\ hx} * c_{kj}^{\ hx} * \delta^{\ x} * x \qquad\qquad (UCSHONN \qquad C. \qquad 17)$$

$$where:$$

$$\delta^{\ ol} = (d-z)f^o \, '(net^{\ o}) = d - z \qquad (linear \qquad neuron \qquad f^o \, '(net^{\ o}) = 1)$$

$$\delta^{\ hx} = f^h \, '(net_{kj}^{\ h})c_{kj}^{\ hy}b^y_{\ j} \qquad = a_{kj}^{\ hy}b_j \qquad (linear \qquad neuron \qquad f^h \, '(net_{kj}^{\ h}) = 1)$$

$$\delta^{\ x} = f_x \, '(net_k^{\ x}) = (-k^2)\cos^{k-1}(k * c_k^{\ x} * x)\sin(k * c_k^{\ x} * x)$$

For an ultra-high frequency sine function of *y* input part:

$$b_j^{\ y} = f_j^{\ y} \ (net_j^{\ y}) = \sin^j(j * net_j^{\ y}) = \sin^j(j * c_j^{\ y} * y)$$

$$f_y \, '(net_j^{\ y}) = \partial b_j^{\ y} \, / \, \partial(net_j^{\ y})$$

$$= \partial(\sin^j(j * net_j^{\ y})) \, / \, \partial(net_j^{\ y})$$

$$= j \sin^{j-1}(j * net_j^{\ y}) * \cos(j * net_j^{\ y}) * j$$

$$= j^2 * \sin^{j-1}(j * net_j^{\ y}) * \cos(j * net_j^{\ y})$$

$$= j^2 * \sin^{j-1}(j * c_j^{\ y} * y) * \cos(j * c_j^{\ y} * y) \qquad\qquad (UCSHONN \qquad D. \qquad 16)$$

Using the above procedure:

$$c_j^{\ y}(t+1) = c_j^{\ y}(t) - \eta(\partial E_p \, / \, \partial c_j^{\ y})$$

$$= c_j^{\ y}(t) + \eta(d-z)f^o \, '(net^{\ o})c_{kj}^{\ o} * f^h \, '(net_{kj}^{\ h})c_{kj}^{\ hx}b_k^{\ x}c_{kj}^{\ hy} f_y \, '(net_j^{\ y})y$$

$$= c_j^{\ y}(t) + \eta * \delta^{\ ol} * c_{kj}^{\ o} * \delta^{\ hy} * c_{kj}^{\ hy} * (j^2)\sin^{j-1}(j * c_j^{\ y} * y)\cos(j * c_j^{\ y} * y) * y$$

$$= c_j^{\ y}(t) + \eta * \delta^{\ ol} * c_{kj}^{\ o} * \delta^{\ hy} * c_{kj}^{\ hy} * \delta^{\ y} * y \qquad\qquad (UCSHONN \qquad D. \qquad 17)$$

$$where:$$

$$\delta^{\ ol} = (d-z)f^o \, '(net^{\ o}) = d - z \qquad (linear \qquad neuron \qquad f^o \, '(net^{\ o}) = 1)$$

$$\delta^{\ hy} = f^h \, '(net_{kj}^{\ hy})c_{kj}^{\ hx}b_k^{\ x} \qquad = c_{kj}^{\ hx}b_k^{\ x} \qquad (linear \qquad neuron \qquad f^h \, '(net_{kj}^{\ hy}) = 1)$$

$$\delta^{\ y} = f_y \, '(net_j^{\ y}) = (j^2)\sin^{j-1}(j * c_j^{\ y} * y)\cos(j * c_j^{\ y} * y)$$

13. UCCHONN Model First Layer Neuron Weights Learning Formula

Let :

$$f_k^x(c_k^x x) = \cos^k(k * c_k^x x)$$

$$f_j^y(c_j^y y) = \cos^j(j * c_j^y y)$$

For an ultra-high frequency cosine function of x input part:

$$b_k^x = f_k \ (net_k^x) = \cos^k(k * net_k^x)$$

$$f_k \ '(net_k^x) = \partial b_k^x / \partial(net_k^x)$$

$$= \partial(\cos^k(k * net_k^x)) / \partial(net_k^x)$$

$$= k \cos^{k-1}(k * net_k^x) * (-\sin(k * net_k^x)) * k$$

$$= -k^2 \cos^{k-1}(k * net_k^x) \sin(k * net_k^x)$$

$$= -k^2 \cos^{k-1}(k * c_k^x * x) \sin(k * c_k^x * x) \qquad\qquad (UCCHONN \quad C. \quad 16)$$

$$c_k^x(t+1) = c_k^x(t) - \eta(\partial E_p / \partial c_k^x)$$

$$= c_k^x(t) + \eta(d - z)f^o{}'(net^o)c_{kj}^o * f^h{}'(net_{kj}^h)c_{kj}^{hy}b_j^y c_{kj}^{hx} f_x{}'(net_k^x)x$$

$$= c_k^x(t) + \eta * \delta^{ol} * c_{kj}^o * \delta^{hx} * c_{kj}^{hx} * (-k^2)\cos^{k-1}(k * c_k^x * x)\sin(k * c_k^x * x) * x$$

$$= c_k^x(t) + \eta * \delta^{ol} * c_{kj}^o * \delta^{hx} * c_{kj}^{hx} * \delta^x * x \qquad\qquad (UCCHONN \quad C. \quad 17)$$

where :

$$\delta^{ol} = (d - z)f^o{}'(net^o) = d - z \qquad (linear \quad neuron \quad f^o{}'(net^o) = 1)$$

$$\delta^{hx} = f^h{}'(net_{kj}^h)c_{kj}^{hy}b_j^y \quad = a_{kj}^{hy}b_j \qquad (linear \quad neuron \quad f^h{}'(net_{kj}^h) = 1)$$

$$\delta^x = f_x{}'(net_k^x) = (-k^2)\cos^{k-1}(k * c_k^x * x)\sin(k * c_k^x * x)$$

For an ultra-high frequency cosine function of y input part:

$$b_j^y = f_y \ (net_j^y) = \cos^j(j * net_j^y) = \cos^j(j * c_j^y * y)$$

$$f_y \ '(net_j^y) = \partial b_j^y / \partial(net_j^y)$$

$$= \partial(\cos^j(j * net_j^y)) / \partial(net_j^y)$$

$$= j \cos^{j-1}(j * net_j^y) * (-\sin(j * net_j^y)) * j$$

$$= -j^2 * \cos^{j-1}(j * net_j^y) * \sin(j * net_j^y)$$

$$= -j^2 * \cos^{j-1}(j * c_j^y * y) * \sin(j * c_j^y * y) \qquad\qquad (UCCHONN \quad D. \quad 16)$$

Using the above procedure:

$$c_j^y(t+1) = c_j^y(t) - \eta(\partial E_p / \partial c_j^y)$$

$$= c_j^y(t) + \eta(d-z)f^o{}'(net^o)c_{kj}^o * f^h{}'(net_{kj}^h)c_{kj}^{hx}b_k^x c_{kj}^{hy}f_y{}'(net_j^y)y$$

$$= c_j^y(t) + \eta * \delta^{ol} * c_{kj}^o * \delta^{hy} * c_{kj}^{hy} * (-j^2) * \cos^{j-1}(j*c_j^y*y)*\sin(j*c_j^y*y)*y$$

$$= c_j^y(t) + \eta * \delta^{ol} * c_{kj}^o * \delta^{hy} * c_{kj}^{hy} * \delta^y * y \qquad\qquad (UCCHONN \qquad D. \qquad 17)$$

where:

$$\delta^{ol} = (d-z)f^o{}'(net^o) = d - z \qquad (linear \qquad neuron \qquad f^o{}'(net^o) = 1)$$

$$\delta^{hy} = f^h{}'(net_{kj}^{hy})c_{kj}^{hx}b_k^x \qquad = c_{kj}^{hx}b_k^x \qquad (linear \qquad neuron \qquad f^h{}'(net_{kj}^{hy}) = 1)$$

$$\delta^y = f_y{}'(net_j^y) = (-j^2) * \cos^{j-1}(j*c_j^y*y)*\sin(j*c_j^y*y)$$

14. USSHONN Model First Layer Neuron Weights Learning Formula

Let :

$$f_k^x(c_k^x x) = \sin^k(k*c_k^x x)$$

$$f_j^y(c_j^y y) = \sin^j(j*c_j^y y)$$

For an ultra-high frequency sine function of *x* input part:

$$b^x{}_k = f_k(net_k^x) = \sin^k(k*net_k^x)$$

$$f_k{}'(net_k^x) = \partial b^x{}_k / \partial(net_k^x)$$

$$= \partial(\sin^k(k*net_k^x)) / \partial(net_k^x)$$

$$= k\sin^{k-1}(k*net_k^x)*\cos(k*net_k^x)*k$$

$$= k^2\sin^{k-1}(k*net_k^x)\cos(k*net_k^x)$$

$$= k^2\sin^{k-1}(k*c_k^x*x)\cos(k*c_k^x*x) \qquad\qquad (USSHONN \qquad C. \qquad 16)$$

For an ultra-high frequency sine function of *y* input part:

$$b_j^y = f_j^y(net_j^y) = \sin^j(j*net_j^y) = \sin^j(j*c_j^y*y)$$

$$f_y{}'(net_j^y) = \partial b_j^y / \partial(net_j^y)$$

$$= \partial(\sin^j(j*net_j^y)) / \partial(net_j^y)$$

$$= j\sin^{j-1}(j*net_j^y)*\cos(j*net_j^y)*j$$

$$= j^2 * \sin^{j-1}(j*net_j^y)*\cos(j*net_j^y)$$

$$= j^2 * \sin^{j-1}(j*c_j^y*y)*\cos(j*c_j^y*y) \qquad\qquad (USSHONN \qquad D. \qquad 16)$$

Using the above procedure:

$$c_j^{\ y}(t+1) = c_j^{\ y}(t) - \eta(\partial E_p / \partial c_j^{\ y})$$

$$= c_j^{\ y}(t) + \eta(d-z)f^{o\,\prime}(net^{\,o})c_{kj}^{\ o} * f^{h\,\prime}(net_{kj}^{\ h})c_{kj}^{\ hx}b_k^{\ x}c_{kj}^{\ hy}f_y^{\,\prime}(net_j^{\ y})y$$

$$= c_j^{\ y}(t) + \eta * \delta^{\,ol} * c_{kj}^{\ o} * \delta^{\,hy} * c_{kj}^{\ hy} * (j^2)\sin^{j-1}(j * c_j^{\ y} * y)\cos(j * c_j^{\ y} * y) * y$$

$$= c_j^{\ y}(t) + \eta * \delta^{\,ol} * c_{kj}^{\ o} * \delta^{\,hy} * c_{kj}^{\ hy} * \delta^{\,y} * y \qquad\qquad (USSHONN \qquad D. \qquad 17)$$

where:

$$\delta^{\,ol} = (d-z)f^{o\,\prime}(net^{\,o}) = d-z \qquad (linear \qquad neuron \qquad f^{o\,\prime}(net^{\,o}) = 1)$$

$$\delta^{\,hy} = f^{h\,\prime}(net_{kj}^{\ hy})c_{kj}^{\ hx}b_k^{\ x} \qquad = c_{kj}^{\ hx}b_k^{\ x} \qquad (linear \qquad neuron \qquad f^{h\,\prime}(net_{kj}^{\ hy}) = 1)$$

$$\delta^{\,y} = f_y^{\,\prime}(net_j^{\ y}) = (j^2)\sin^{j-1}(j * c_j^{\ y} * y)\cos(j * c_j^{\ y} * y)$$

15. SS-HONN Model First Layer Neuron Weights Learning Formula

Let:

$$f_k^{\ x}(c_k^{\ x}x) = \sin^k(c_k^{\ x}x)$$

$$f_j^{\ y}(c_j^{\ y}y) = (1/(1+\exp(c_j^{\ y}(-y))))^j$$

For a sine function of x input side:

$$b_k^{\ x} = f_k^{\ x}(net_k^{\ x}) = \sin^k(net_k^{\ x}) = \sin^k(c_k^{\ x} * x)^k$$

$$f_x^{\,\prime}(net_k^{\ x}) = \partial b_k^{\ x} / \partial(net_k^{\ x})$$

$$= \partial(\sin^k(net_k^{\ x})) / \partial(net_k^{\ x})$$

$$= k * \sin^{k-1}(net_k^{\ x}) * \cos(net_k^{\ x}) = k * \sin^{k-1}(c_k^{\ x} * x) * \cos(c_k^{\ x} * x) \qquad (SS-HONN \qquad C. \qquad 16)$$

$$c_k^{\ x}(t+1) = c_k^{\ x}(t) - \eta(\partial E_p / \partial c_k^{\ x})$$

$$= c_k^{\ x}(t) + \eta(d-z)f^{o\,\prime}(net^{\,o})c_{kj}^{\ o} * f^{h\,\prime}(net_{kj}^{\ h})c_{kj}^{\ hy}b_j^{\ y}c_{kj}^{\ hx}f_x^{\,\prime}(net_k^{\ x})x$$

$$= c_k^{\ x}(t) + \eta * \delta^{\,ol} * c_{kj}^{\ o} * \delta^{\,hx} * c_{kj}^{\ hx} * k * \sin^{k-1}(c_k^{\ x} * x) * \cos(c_k^{\ x} * x) * x$$

$$= c_k^{\ x}(t) + \eta * \delta^{\,ol} * c_{kj}^{\ o} * \delta^{\,hx} * c_{kj}^{\ hx} * \delta^{\,x} * x \qquad\qquad (SS-HONN \qquad C. \qquad 17)$$

where:

$$\delta^{\,ol} = (d-z)f^{o\,\prime}(net^{\,o}) = d-z \qquad (linear \qquad neuron \qquad f^{o\,\prime}(net^{\,o}) = 1)$$

$$\delta^{\,hx} = f^{h\,\prime}(net_{kj}^{\ h})c_{kj}^{\ hy}b_j^{\ y} \qquad = c_{kj}^{\ hy}b_j^{\ y} \qquad (linear \qquad neuron \qquad f^{h\,\prime}(net_{kj}^{\ h}) = 1)$$

$$\delta^{\,x} = f_x^{\,\prime}(net_k^{\ x}) = k * (net_k^{\ x})^{k-1} = k * \sin^{k-1}(c_k^{\ x} * x) * \cos(c_k^{\ x} * x)$$

For a sigmoid function of *y* input side:

$$b_j^y - f_j^y(net_j^y) = [1 / (1 + \exp(-net_j^y))]^j$$
$$= [1 / (1 + \exp(c_j^y * (-y)))]^j$$
$$f_y'(net_j^y) = \partial b_j^y / \partial(net_j^y) \qquad (SS - HONN \qquad D. \qquad 16)$$
$$= \partial[1 / (1 + \exp(-net_j^y))]^k / \partial(net_j^y)$$
$$= j * [1 / (1 + \exp(-net_j^y))]^{j-1} * (1 + \exp(-net_j^y))^{-2} * \exp(-net_j^y)$$
$$= j * [1 / (1 + \exp(-c_j^y * y))]^{j-1} * (1 + \exp(-c_j^y * y))^{-2} * \exp(-c_j^y * y)$$

$$c_j^y(t+1) = c_j^y(t) - \eta(\partial E_p / \partial c_j^y)$$
$$= c_j^y(t) + \eta(d-z) f^o{}'(net^o) c_{kj}^o * f^h{}'(net_{kj}^h) c_{kj}^{hx} b_k^x c_{kj}^{hy} f_y'(net_j^y) y$$
$$= c_j^y(t) + \eta * \delta^{ol} * c_{kj}^o * \delta^{hy} * c_{kj}^{hy} * f_y'(net_j^y) * y$$
$$= c_j^y(t) + \eta * \delta^{ol} * c_{kj}^o * \delta^{hy} * c_{kj}^{hy}$$
$$\qquad * [j * [1 / (1 + \exp(-c_j^y * y))]^{j-1} * (1 + \exp(-c_j^y * y))^{-2} * \exp(-c_j^y * y)] * y$$
$$= c_j^y(t) + \eta * \delta^{ol} * c_{kj}^o * \delta^{hy} * c_{kj}^{hy} * \delta^y * y \qquad (SS - HONN \qquad D. \qquad 17)$$
$$where:$$
$$\delta^{ol} = (d-z) f^o{}'(net^o) = d - z \qquad (linear \qquad neuron \qquad f^o{}'(net^o) = 1)$$
$$\delta^{hy} = f^h{}'(net_{kj}^h) c_{kj}^{hx} b_k^x = c_{kj}^{hx} b_k^x \qquad (linear \qquad neuron \qquad f^h{}'(net_{kj}^h) = 1)$$
$$\delta^y = f_y'(net_j^y)$$
$$\qquad = j * [1 / (1 + \exp(-c_j^y * y))]^{j-1} * (1 + \exp(-c_j^y * y))^{-2} * \exp(-c_j^y * y)$$

16. PS-HONN Model First Layer Neuron Weights Learning Formula

$$Let:$$
$$f_k^x(c_k^x x) = (c_k^x x)^k$$
$$f_j^y(c_j^y y) = (1 / (1 + \exp(c_j^y(-y))))^j$$

For a polynomial function of *x* input side:

$$b_k^x = f_k^x(net_k^x) = (net_k^x)^k = (c_k^x * x)^k$$
$$f_x'(net_k^x) = \partial b_k^x / \partial(net_k^x)$$
$$= \partial(net_k^x)^k) / \partial(net_k^x)$$
$$= k(net_k^x)^{k-1} = k * (c_k^x * x)^{k-1} \qquad (PS - HONN \qquad C. \qquad 16)$$

$$c_k^{\ x}(t+1) = c_k^{\ x}(t) - \eta(\partial E_p / \partial c_k^{\ x})$$

$$= c_k^{\ x}(t) + \eta(d-z)f^{o}{}'(net^{o})c_{kj}^{\ o} * f^{h}{}'(net_{kj}^{\ h})c_{kj}^{\ hy}b_j^{\ y}c_{kj}^{\ hx}f_x{}'(net_k^{\ x})x$$

$$= c_k^{\ x}(t) + \eta * \delta^{ol} * c_{kj}^{\ o} * \delta^{hx} * c_{kj}^{\ hx} * k * (c_k^{\ x} * x)^{k-1} * x$$

$$= c_k^{\ x}(t) + \eta * \delta^{ol} * c_{kj}^{\ o} * \delta^{hx} * c_{kj}^{\ hx} * \delta^{x} * x \qquad\qquad (PS-HONN \qquad C. \qquad 17)$$

where:

$$\delta^{ol} = (d-z)f^{o}{}'(net^{o}) = d-z \qquad (linear \qquad neuron \qquad f^{o}{}'(net^{o}) = 1)$$

$$\delta^{hx} = f^{h}{}'(net_{kj}^{\ h})c_{kj}^{\ hy}b_j^{\ y} \qquad = c_{kj}^{\ hy}b_j^{\ y} \qquad (linear \qquad neuron \qquad f^{h}{}'(net_{kj}^{\ h}) = 1)$$

$$\delta^{x} = f_x{}'(net_k^{\ x}) = k * (net_k^{\ x})^{k-1} = k * (c_k^{\ x} * x)^{k-1}$$

For a sigmoid function of *y* input side:

$$b_j^{\ y} = f_j^{\ y}(net_j^{\ y}) = [1/(1 + \exp(-net_j^{\ y}))]^j$$

$$= [1/(1 + \exp(c_j^{\ y} * (-y)))]^j$$

$$f_y{}'(net_j^{\ y}) = \partial b_j^{\ y} / \partial(net_j^{\ y}) \qquad\qquad (PS-HONN \qquad D. \qquad 16)$$

$$= \partial[1/(1 + \exp(-net_j^{\ y}))]^k / \partial(net_j^{\ y})$$

$$= j * [1/(1 + \exp(-net_j^{\ y}))]^{j-1} * (1 + \exp(-net_j^{\ y}))^{-2} * \exp(-net_j^{\ y})$$

$$= j * [1/(1 + \exp(-c_j^{\ y} * y))]^{j-1} * (1 + \exp(-c_j^{\ y} * y))^{-2} * \exp(-c_j^{\ y} * y)$$

$$c_j^{\ y}(t+1) = c_j^{\ y}(t) - \eta(\partial E_p / \partial c_j^{\ y})$$

$$= c_j^{\ y}(t) + \eta(d-z)f^{o}{}'(net^{o})c_{kj}^{\ o} * f^{h}{}'(net_{kj}^{\ h})c_{kj}^{\ hx}b_k^{\ x}c_{kj}^{\ hy}f_y{}'(net_j^{\ y})y$$

$$= c_j^{\ y}(t) + \eta * \delta^{ol} * c_{kj}^{\ o} * \delta^{hy} * c_{kj}^{\ hy} * f_y{}'(net_j^{\ y}) * y$$

$$= c_j^{\ y}(t) + \eta * \delta^{ol} * c_{kj}^{\ o} * \delta^{hy} * c_{kj}^{\ hy}$$

$$* [j * [1/(1 + \exp(-c_j^{\ y} * y))]^{j-1} * (1 + \exp(-c_j^{\ y} * y))^{-2} * \exp(-c_j^{\ y} * y)] * y$$

$$= c_j^{\ y}(t) + \eta * \delta^{ol} * c_{kj}^{\ o} * \delta^{hy} * c_{kj}^{\ hy} * \delta^{y} * y \qquad (PS-HONN \qquad D. \qquad 17)$$

where:

$$\delta^{ol} = (d-z)f^{o}{}'(net^{o}) = d-z \qquad (linear \qquad neuron \qquad f^{o}{}'(net^{o}) = 1)$$

$$\delta^{hy} = f^{h}{}'(net_{kj}^{\ h})c_{kj}^{\ hx}b_k^{\ x} = c_{kj}^{\ hx}b_k^{\ x} \qquad (linear \qquad neuron \qquad f^{h}{}'(net_{kj}^{\ h}) = 1)$$

$$\delta^{y} = f_y{}'(net_j^{\ y})$$

$$= j * [1/(1 + \exp(-c_j^{\ y} * y))]^{j-1} * (1 + \exp(-c_j^{\ y} * y))^{-2} * \exp(-c_j^{\ y} * y)$$

17. CS-HONN Model First Layer Neuron Weights Learning Formula

Let :

$$f_k^{\ x}(c_k^{\ x}x) = \cos^k(c_k^{\ x}x)$$

$$f_j^{\ y}(c_j^{\ y}y) = (1/(1+\exp(c_j^{\ y}(-y))))^j$$

For a cosine function of x input side:

$$b_k^{\ x} = f_k^{\ x}(net_k^{\ x}) = \cos^k(net_k^{\ x}) = \cos^k(c_k^{\ x}*x)$$

$$f_x{'}(net_k^{\ x}) = \partial b_k^{\ x}/\partial(net_k^{\ x})$$

$$= \partial(\cos^k(net_k^{\ x}))/\partial(net_k^{\ x})$$

$$= k*\cos^{k-1}(net_k^{\ x})*(-\sin(net_k^{\ x}))$$

$$= (-k)*\cos^{k-1}(c_k^{\ x}*x)*\sin(c_k^{\ x}*x) \qquad (CS-HONN \qquad C. \qquad 16)$$

$$c_k^{\ x}(t+1) = c_k^{\ x}(t) - \eta(\partial E_p/\partial c_k^{\ x})$$

$$= c_k^{\ x}(t) + \eta(d-z)f^o{'}(net^o)c_{kj}^{\ o}*f^h{'}(net_{kj}^{\ h})c_{kj}^{\ hy}b_j^{\ y}c_{kj}^{\ hx}f_x{'}(net_k^{\ x})x$$

$$= c_k^{\ x}(t) + \eta*\delta^{\ ol}*c_{kj}^{\ o}*\delta^{\ hx}*c_{kj}^{\ hx}*(-k)*\cos^{k-1}(c_k^{\ x}*x)*\sin(c_k^{\ x}*x)*x$$

$$= c_k^{\ x}(t) + \eta*\delta^{\ ol}*c_{kj}^{\ o}*\delta^{\ hx}*c_{kj}^{\ hx}*\delta^{\ x}*x \qquad (CS-HONN \qquad C. \qquad 17)$$

where :

$$\delta^{\ ol} = (d-z)f^o{'}(net^o) = d-z \qquad (linear \qquad neuron \qquad f^o{'}(net^o) = 1)$$

$$\delta^{\ hx} = f^h{'}(net_{kj}^{\ h})c_{kj}^{\ hy}b_j^{\ y} \qquad = c_{kj}^{\ hy}b_j^{\ y} \qquad (linear \qquad neuron \qquad f^h{'}(net_{kj}^{\ h}) = 1)$$

$$\delta^{\ x} = f_x{'}(net_k^{\ x}) = (-k)*\cos^{k-1}(net_k^{\ x})*\sin(net_k^{\ x}) = (-k)*\cos^{k-1}(c_k^{\ x}*x)*\sin(c_k^{\ x}*x)$$

For a sigmoid function of y input side:

$$b_j^{\ y} = f_j^{\ y}(net_j^{\ y}) = [1/(1+\exp(-net_j^{\ y}))]^j$$

$$= [1/(1+\exp(c_j^{\ y}*(-y)))]^j$$

$$f_y{'}(net_j^{\ y}) = \partial b_j^{\ y}/\partial(net_j^{\ y}) \qquad (PS-HONN \qquad D. \qquad 16)$$

$$= \partial[1/(1+\exp(-net_j^{\ y}))]^k/\partial(net_j^{\ y})$$

$$= j*[1/(1+\exp(-net_j^{\ y}))]^{j-1}*(1+\exp(-net_j^{\ y}))^{-2}*\exp(-net_j^{\ y})$$

$$= j*[1/(1+\exp(-c_j^{\ y}*y))]^{j-1}*(1+\exp(-c_j^{\ y}*y))^{-2}*\exp(-c_j^{\ y}*y)$$

$$c_j^{\ y}(t+1) = c_j^{\ y}(t) - \eta(\partial E_p / \partial c_j^{\ y})$$

$$= c_j^{\ y}(t) + \eta(d-z)f^o{}'(net^o)c_{kj}^{\ o} * f^h{}'(net_{kj}^{\ h})c_{kj}^{\ hx}b_k^{\ x}c_{kj}^{\ hy}f_y{}'(net_j^{\ y})y$$

$$= c_j^{\ y}(t) + \eta * \delta^{\ ol} * c_{kj}^{\ o} * \delta^{hy} * c_{kj}^{\ hy} * f_y{}'(net_j^{\ y}) * y$$

$$= c_j^{\ y}(t) + \eta * \delta^{\ ol} * c_{kj}^{\ o} * \delta^{hy} * c_{kj}^{\ hy}$$

$$\qquad * [j*[1/(1+\exp(-c_j^{\ y} * y))]^{j-1} * (1+\exp(-c_j^{\ y} * y))^{-2} * \exp(-c_j^{\ y} * y)] * y$$

$$= c_j^{\ y}(t) + \eta * \delta^{\ ol} * c_{kj}^{\ o} * \delta^{hy} * c_{kj}^{\ hy} * \delta^y * y \qquad (PS-HONN \qquad D. \qquad 17)$$

where :

$$\delta^{\ ol} = (d-z)f^o{}'(net^o) = d-z \qquad (linear \qquad neuron \qquad f^o{}'(net^o) = 1)$$

$$\delta^{hy} = f^h{}'(net_{kj}^{\ h})c_{kj}^{\ hx}b_k^{\ x} = c_{kj}^{\ hx}b_k^{\ x} \qquad (linear \qquad neuron \qquad f^h{}'(net_{kj}^{\ h}) = 1)$$

$$\delta^y = f_y{}'(net_j^{\ y})$$

$$\qquad = j*[1/(1+\exp(-c_j^{\ y} * y))]^{j-1} * (1+\exp(-c_j^{\ y} * y))^{-2} * \exp(-c_j^{\ y} * y)$$

18. NS-HONN Model First Layer Neuron Weights Learning Formula

Let :

$$f_k^{\ x}(c_k^{\ x}x) = (\sin(c_k^{\ x}x)/(c_k^{\ x}x))^k$$

$$f_j^{\ y}(c_j^{\ y}y) = (1/(1+\exp(c_j^{\ y}(-y))))^j$$

For a SINC function of *x* input part:

$$b_k^{\ x} = f_k^{\ x}(net_k^{\ x}) = [\sin\ (net_k^{\ x})/(net_k^{\ x})]^k = [\sin\ (c_k^{\ x}x)/(c_k^{\ x}x)]^k$$

$$f_x{}'(net_k^{\ x}) = \partial b_k^{\ x} / \partial(net_k^{\ x})$$

$$= k[\sin\ (net_k^{\ x})/(net_k^{\ x})]^{k-1} * [\cos(net_k^{\ x})/(net_k^{\ x}) - \sin\ (net_k^{\ x})/(net_k^{\ x})^2]$$

$$= k[\sin\ (c_k^{\ x}x)/(c_k^{\ k}x)]^{k-1} * [\cos(c_k^{\ x}x)/(c_k^{\ x}x) - \sin\ (c_k^{\ x}x)/(c_k^{\ x}x)^2] \qquad (NS-HONN \qquad C. \qquad 16)$$

$$c_k^{\ x}(t+1) = c_k^{\ x}(t) - \eta(\partial E_p / \partial c_k^{\ x})$$

$$= c_k^{\ x}(t) + \eta(d-z)f^{o}{}'(net^{o})c_{kj}^{\ o} * f^{h}{}'(net_{kj}^{\ h})c_{kj}^{\ hy}b_j^{\ y}c_{kj}^{\ hx}f_x{}'(net_k^{\ x})x$$

$$= c_k^{\ x}(t) + \eta * \delta^{ol} * c_{kj}^{\ o} * \delta^{hx} * c_{kj}^{\ hx} * f_x{}'(net_k^{\ x}) * x$$

$$= c_k^{\ x}(t) + \eta * \delta^{ol} * c_{kj}^{\ o} * \delta^{hx} * c_{kj}^{\ hx}$$

$$\qquad * [k[\sin\ (c_k^{\ x}x)/(c_k^{\ k}x)]^{k-1} * [\cos(c_k^{\ x}x)/(c_k^{\ x}x) - \sin\ (c_k^{\ x}x)/(c_k^{\ k}x)^2]] * x$$

$$= c_k^{\ x}(t) + \eta * \delta^{ol} * c_{kj}^{\ o} * \delta^{hx} * c_{kj}^{\ hx} * \delta^x * x \qquad\qquad (NS-HONN \qquad C. \qquad 17)$$

$where:$

$$\delta^{ol} = (d-z)f^{o}{}'(net^{o}) = (d-z) \qquad (linear \qquad neuron \qquad f^{o}{}'(net^{o}) = 1)$$

$$\delta^{hx} = f^{h}{}'(net_{kj}^{\ h})c_{kj}^{\ hy}b_j^{\ y} = c_{kj}^{\ hy}b_j^{\ y} \qquad (linear \qquad neuron \qquad f^{h}{}'(net_{kj}^{\ h}) = 1)$$

$$\delta^x = f_x{}'(net_k^{\ x})$$

$$\qquad = k[\sin\ (net_k^{\ x})/(net_k^{\ x})]^{k-1} * [\cos(net_k^{\ x})/(net_k^{\ x}) - \sin\ (net_k^{\ x})/(net_k^{\ x})^2]$$

$$\qquad = k[\sin\ (c_k^{\ x}x)/(c_k^{\ x}x)]^{k-1} * [\cos(c_k^{\ x}x)/(c_k^{\ x}x) - \sin\ (c_k^{\ x}x)/(c_k^{\ x}x)^2]$$

For a sigmoid function of y input side:

$$b_j^{\ y} = f_j^{\ y}(net_j^{\ y}) = [1/(1+\exp(-net_j^{\ y}))]^j$$

$$\qquad = [1/(1+\exp(c_j^{\ y} * (-y)))]^j$$

$$f_y{}'(net_j^{\ y}) = \partial b_j^{\ y} / \partial(net_j^{\ y}) \qquad\qquad (NS-HONN \qquad D. \qquad 16)$$

$$= \partial[1/(1+\exp(-net_j^{\ y}))]^k / \partial(net_j^{\ y})$$

$$= j * [1/(1+\exp(-net_j^{\ y}))]^{j-1} * (1+\exp(-net_j^{\ y}))^{-2} * \exp(-net_j^{\ y})$$

$$= j * [1/(1+\exp(-c_j^{\ y} * y))]^{j-1} * (1+\exp(-c_j^{\ y} * y))^{-2} * \exp(-c_j^{\ y} * y)$$

$$c_j^{\ y}(t+1) = c_j^{\ y}(t) - \eta(\partial E_p / \partial c_j^{\ y})$$

$$= c_j^{\ y}(t) + \eta(d-z)f^{o}{}'(net^{o})c_{kj}^{\ o} * f^{h}{}'(net_{kj}^{\ h})c_{kj}^{\ hx}b_k^{\ x}c_{kj}^{\ hy}f_y{}'(net_j^{\ y})y$$

$$= c_j^{\ y}(t) + \eta * \delta^{ol} * c_{kj}^{\ o} * \delta^{hy} * c_{kj}^{\ hy} * f_y{}'(net_j^{\ y}) * y$$

$$= c_j^{\ y}(t) + \eta * \delta^{ol} * c_{kj}^{\ o} * \delta^{hy} * c_{kj}^{\ hy}$$

$$\qquad * [j * [1/(1+\exp(-c_j^{\ y} * y))]^{j-1} * (1+\exp(-c_j^{\ y} * y))^{-2} * \exp(-c_j^{\ y} * y)] * y$$

$$= c_j^{\ y}(t) + \eta * \delta^{ol} * c_{kj}^{\ o} * \delta^{hy} * c_{kj}^{\ hy} * \delta^y * y \qquad (NS-HONN \qquad D. \qquad 17)$$

$where:$

$$\delta^{ol} = (d-z)f^{o}{}'(net^{o}) = d-z \qquad (linear \qquad neuron \qquad f^{o}{}'(net^{o}) = 1)$$

$$\delta^{hy} = f^{h}{}'(net_{kj}^{\ h})c_{kj}^{\ hx}b_k^{\ x} = c_{kj}^{\ hx}b_k^{\ x} \qquad (linear \qquad neuron \qquad f^{h}{}'(net_{kj}^{\ h}) = 1)$$

$$\delta^y = f_y{}'(net_j^{\ y})$$

$$\qquad = j * [1/(1+\exp(-c_j^{\ y} * y))]^{j-1} * (1+\exp(-c_j^{\ y} * y))^{-2} * \exp(-c_j^{\ y} * y)$$

19. UPS-HONN Model First Layer Neuron Weights Learning Formula

Let :

$$f_k^x(c_k^x x) = (c_k^x x)^k$$

$$f_j^y(c_j^y y) = \sin^j(j * c_j^y y)$$

For a polynomial function of *x* input side:

$$b_k^x = f_k^x \ (net_k^x) = (net_k^x)^k = (c_k^x * x)^k$$

$$f_x \ '(net_k^x) = \partial b_k^x / \partial(net_k^x)$$

$$= \partial(net_k^x)^k) / \partial(net_k^x)$$

$$= k(net_k^x)^{k-1} = k * (c_k^x * x)^{k-1} \qquad\qquad (UPS - HONN \qquad C. \qquad 16)$$

$$c_k^x(t+1) = c_k^x(t) - \eta(\partial E_p / \partial c_k^x)$$

$$= c_k^x(t) + \eta(d-z) f^o \ '(net^o) c_{kj}^o * f^h \ '(net_{kj}^h) c_{kj}^{hy} b_j^y c_{kj}^{hx} f_x \ '(net_k^x) x$$

$$= c_k^x(t) + \eta * \delta^{ol} * c_{kj}^o * \delta^{hx} * c_{kj}^{hx} * k * (c_k^x * x)^{k-1} * x$$

$$= c_k^x(t) + \eta * \delta^{ol} * c_{kj}^o * \delta^{hx} * c_{kj}^{hx} * \delta^x * x \qquad\qquad (UPS - HONN \qquad C. \qquad 17)$$

where :

$$\delta^{ol} = (d-z) f^o \ '(net^o) = d-z \qquad (linear \qquad neuron \qquad f^o \ '(net^o) = 1)$$

$$\delta^{hx} = f^h \ '(net_{kj}^h) c_{kj}^{hy} b_j^y \qquad = c_{kj}^{hy} b_j^y \qquad (linear \qquad neuron \qquad f^h \ '(net_{kj}^h) = 1)$$

$$\delta^x = f_x \ '(net_k^x) = k * (net_k^x)^{k-1} = k * (c_k^x * x)^{k-1}$$

For an ultra-high frequency sine function of *y* input part:

$$b_j^y = f_j^y \ (net_j^y) = \sin^j(j * net_j^y) = \sin^j(j * c_j^y * y)$$

$$f_y \ '(net_j^y) = \partial b_j^y / \partial(net_j^y)$$

$$= \partial(\sin^j(j * net_j^y)) / \partial(net_j^y)$$

$$= j \sin^{j-1}(j * net_j^y) * \cos(j * net_j^y) * j$$

$$= j^2 * \sin^{j-1}(j * net_j^y) * \cos(j * net_j^y)$$

$$= j^2 * \sin^{j-1}(j * c_j^y * y) * \cos(j * c_j^y * y) \qquad\qquad (UPS - HONN \qquad D. \qquad 16)$$

Using the above procedure:

$$c_j^{\ y}(t+1) - c_j^{\ y}(t) - \eta(\partial E_p / \partial c_j^{\ y})$$

$$= c_j^{\ y}(t) + \eta(d-z)f^{o\ \prime}(net^{\ o})c_{kj}^{\ o} * f^{h\ \prime}(net_{kj}^{\ h})c_{kj}^{\ hx}b_k^{\ x}c_{kj}^{\ hy}f_y^{\ \prime}(net_j^{\ y})y$$

$$= c_j^{\ y}(t) + \eta * \delta^{\ ol} * c_{kj}^{\ o} * \delta^{\ hy} * c_{kj}^{\ hy} * (j^2)\sin^{j-1}(j*c_j^{\ y}*y)\cos(j*c_j^{\ y}*y)*y$$

$$= c_j^{\ y}(t) + \eta * \delta^{\ ol} * c_{kj}^{\ o} * \delta^{\ hy} * c_{kj}^{\ hy} * \delta^{\ y} * y \qquad\qquad (UPS-HONN \quad D. \quad 17)$$

$where:$

$$\delta^{\ ol} = (d-z)f^{o\ \prime}(net^{\ o}) = d-z \qquad (linear \quad neuron \quad f^{o\ \prime}(net^{\ o}) = 1)$$

$$\delta^{\ hy} = f^{h\ \prime}(net_{kj}^{\ hy})c_{kj}^{\ hx}b_k^{\ x} \quad = c_{kj}^{\ hx}b_k^{\ x} \qquad (linear \quad neuron \quad f^{h\ \prime}(net_{kj}^{\ hy}) = 1)$$

$$\delta^{\ y} = f_y^{\ \prime}(net_j^{\ y}) = (j^2)\sin^{j-1}(j*c_j^{\ y}*y)\cos(j*c_j^{\ y}*y)$$

20. UPC-HONN Model First Layer Neuron Weights Learning Formula

$Let:$

$$f_k^{\ x}(c_k^{\ x}x) = (c_k^{\ x}x)^k$$

$$f_j^{\ y}(c_j^{\ y}y) = \cos^j(j*c_j^{\ y}y)$$

For a polynomial function of x input side:

$$b_k^{\ x} = f_k^{\ x}(net_k^{\ x}) = (net_k^{\ x})^k = (c_k^{\ x}*x)^k$$

$$f_x^{\ \prime}(net_k^{\ x}) = \partial b_k^{\ x} / \partial(net_k^{\ x})$$

$$= \partial(net_k^{\ x})^k) / \partial(net_k^{\ x})$$

$$= k(net_k^{\ x})^{k-1} = k*(c_k^{\ x}*x)^{k-1} \qquad\qquad (UPC-HONN \quad C. \quad 16)$$

$$c_k^{\ x}(t+1) = c_k^{\ x}(t) - \eta(\partial E_p / \partial c_k^{\ x})$$

$$= c_k^{\ x}(t) + \eta(d-z)f^{o\ \prime}(net^{\ o})c_{kj}^{\ o} * f^{h\ \prime}(net_{kj}^{\ h})c_{kj}^{\ hy}b_j^{\ y}c_{kj}^{\ hx}f_x^{\ \prime}(net_k^{\ x})x$$

$$= c_k^{\ x}(t) + \eta * \delta^{\ ol} * c_{kj}^{\ o} * \delta^{\ hx} * c_{kj}^{\ hx} * k*(c_k^{\ x}*x)^{k-1}*x$$

$$= c_k^{\ x}(t) + \eta * \delta^{\ ol} * c_{kj}^{\ o} * \delta^{\ hx} * c_{kj}^{\ hx} * \delta^{\ x} * x \qquad\qquad (UPC-HONN \quad C. \quad 17)$$

$where:$

$$\delta^{\ ol} = (d-z)f^{o\ \prime}(net^{\ o}) = d-z \qquad (linear \quad neuron \quad f^{o\ \prime}(net^{\ o}) = 1)$$

$$\delta^{\ hx} = f^{h\ \prime}(net_{kj}^{\ h})c_{kj}^{\ hy}b_j^{\ y} \quad = c_{kj}^{\ hy}b_j^{\ y} \qquad (linear \quad neuron \quad f^{h\ \prime}(net_{kj}^{\ h}) = 1)$$

$$\delta^{\ x} = f_x^{\ \prime}(net_k^{\ x}) = k*(net_k^{\ x})^{k-1} = k*(c_k^{\ x}*x)^{k-1}$$

For an ultra-high frequency cosine function of y input part:

$$b_j^y = f_y\ (net_j^y) = \cos^j(j * net_j^y) = \cos^j(j * c_j^y * y)$$

$$f_y\ '(net_j^y) = \partial b_j^y / \partial(net_j^y)$$

$$= \partial(\cos^j(j * net_j^y)) / \partial(net_j^y)$$

$$= j\cos^{j-1}(j * net_j^y) * (-\sin(j * net_j^y)) * j$$

$$= -j^2 * \cos^{j-1}(j * net_j^y) * \sin(j * net_j^y)$$

$$= -j^2 * \cos^{j-1}(j * c_j^y * y) * \sin(j * c_j^y * y) \qquad\qquad (UPC-HONN \qquad D. \qquad 16)$$

Using the above procedure:

$$c_j^y(t+1) = c_j^y(t) - \eta(\partial E_p / \partial c_j^y)$$

$$= c_j^y(t) + \eta(d-z)f^o\ '(net^o)c_{kj}^o * f^h\ '(net_{kj}^h)c_{kj}^{hx}b_k^x c_{kj}^{hy}f_y\ '(net_j^y)y$$

$$= c_j^y(t) + \eta * \delta^{ol} * c_{kj}^o * \delta^{hy} * c_{kj}^{hy} * (-j^2) * \cos^{j-1}(j * c_j^y * y) * \sin(j * c_j^y * y) * y$$

$$= c_j^y(t) + \eta * \delta^{ol} * c_{kj}^o * \delta^{hy} * c_{kj}^{hy} * \delta^y * y \qquad\qquad (UPC-HONN \qquad D. \qquad 17)$$

where:

$$\delta^{ol} = (d-z)f^o\ '(net^o) = d - z \qquad (linear \qquad neuron \qquad f^o\ '(net^o) = 1)$$

$$\delta^{hy} = f^h\ '(net_{kj}^{hy})c_{kj}^{hx}b_k^x \qquad = c_{kj}^{hx}b_k^x \qquad (linear \qquad neuron \qquad f^h\ '(net_{kj}^{hy}) = 1)$$

$$\delta^y = f_y\ '(net_j^y) = (-j^2) * \cos^{j-1}(j * c_j^y * y) * \sin(j * c_j^y * y)$$

21. UGS-HONN Model First Layer Neuron Weights Learning Formula

Let :

$$f_k^j(c_k^j x) = (1/(1 + \exp(c_k^x(-x))))^k$$

$$f_j^y(c_j^k y) = \sin^j(j * c_j^k y)$$

For a sigmoid function of x input side:

$$b_k^{\ x} = f_k^{\ x}(net_k^{\ x}) = [1/(1+\exp(-net_k^{\ x}))]^k$$
$$= [1/(1+\exp(c_k^{\ x}*(-x)))]^k$$
$$f_x'(net_k^{\ x}) = \partial b_k^{\ x}/\partial(net_k^{\ x}) \qquad (UGS-HONN \qquad C. \qquad 16)$$
$$= \partial[1/(1+\exp(-net_k^{\ x}))]^k/\partial(net_k^{\ x})$$
$$= k*[1/(1+\exp(-net_k^{\ x}))]^{k-1}*(1+\exp(-net_k^{\ x}))^{-2}*\exp(-net_k^{\ x})$$
$$= k*[1/(1+\exp(-c_k^{\ x}*x))]^{k-1}*(1+\exp(-c_k^{\ x}*x))^{-2}*\exp(-c_k^{\ x}*x)$$

$$c_k^{\ x}(t+1) = c_k^{\ x}(t) - \eta(\partial E_p/\partial c_k^{\ x})$$
$$= c_k^{\ x}(t) + \eta(d-z)f^{o\prime}(net^o)c_{kj}^{\ o}*f^{h\prime}(net_{kj}^{\ h})c_{kj}^{\ hy}b_j^{\ y}c_{kj}^{\ hx}f_x'(net_k^{\ x})x$$
$$= c_k^{\ x}(t) + \eta*\delta^{\ ol}*c_{kj}^{\ o}*\delta^{\ hx}*c_{kj}^{\ hx}*f_x'(net_k^{\ x})*x$$
$$= c_k^{\ x}(t) + \eta*\delta^{\ ol}*c_{kj}^{\ o}*\delta^{\ hx}*c_{kj}^{\ hx}$$
$$\qquad *[k*[1/(1+\exp(-c_k^{\ x}*x))]^{k-1}*(1+\exp(-c_k^{\ x}*x))^{-2}*\exp(-c_k^{\ x}*x)]*x$$
$$= c_k^{\ x}(t) + \eta*\delta^{\ ol}*c_{kj}^{\ o}*\delta^{\ hx}*c_{kj}^{\ hx}*\delta^{\ x}*x \qquad (UGS-HONN \qquad C. \qquad 17)$$
where:
$$\delta^{\ ol} = (d-z)f^{o\prime}(net^o) = d-z \qquad (linear \qquad neuron \qquad f^{o\prime}(net^o)=1)$$
$$\delta^{\ hx} = f^{h\prime}(net_{kj}^{\ h})c_{kj}^{\ hy}b_j^{\ y} = c_{kj}^{\ hy}b_j^{\ y} \qquad (linear \qquad neuron \qquad f^{h\prime}(net_{kj}^{\ h})=1)$$
$$\delta^{\ x} = f_x'(net_k^{\ x})$$
$$\qquad = k*[1/(1+\exp(-c_k^{\ x}*x))]^{k-1}*(1+\exp(-c_k^{\ x}*x))^{-2}*\exp(-c_k^{\ x}*x)$$

For an ultra-high frequency sine function of *y* input part:

$$b_j^{\ y} = f_j^{\ y}(net_j^{\ y}) = \sin^j(j*net_j^{\ y}) = \sin^j(j*c_j^{\ y}*y)$$
$$f_y'(net_j^{\ y}) = \partial b_j^{\ y}/\partial(net_j^{\ y})$$
$$= \partial(\sin^j(j*net_j^{\ y}))/\partial(net_j^{\ y})$$
$$= j\sin^{j-1}(j*net_j^{\ y})*\cos(j*net_j^{\ y})*j$$
$$= j^2*\sin^{j-1}(j*net_j^{\ y})*\cos(j*net_j^{\ y})$$
$$= j^2*\sin^{j-1}(j*c_j^{\ y}*y)*\cos(j*c_j^{\ y}*y) \qquad (UGS-HONN \qquad D. \qquad 16)$$

Using the above procedure:

$$c_j^{\ y}(t+1) = c_j^{\ y}(t) - \eta(\partial E_p \ / \ \partial c_j^{\ y})$$

$$= c_j^{\ y}(t) + \eta(d-z)f^{o\ '}(net^{\ o})c_{kj}^{\ o} * f^{h\ '}(net_{kj}^{\ h})c_{kj}^{\ hx}b_k^{\ x}c_{kj}^{\ hy}f_y^{\ '}(net_j^{\ y})y$$

$$= c_j^{\ y}(t) + \eta * \delta^{\ ol} * c_{kj}^{\ o} * \delta^{\ hy} * c_{kj}^{\ hy} * (j^2)\sin^{j-1}(j*c_j^{\ y}*y)\cos(j*c_j^{\ y}*y)*y$$

$$= c_j^{\ y}(t) + \eta * \delta^{\ ol} * c_{kj}^{\ o} * \delta^{\ hy} * c_{kj}^{\ hy} * \delta^{\ y} * y \qquad\qquad (UGS-HONN \qquad D. \qquad 17)$$

where :

$$\delta^{\ ol} = (d-z)f^{o\ '}(net^{\ o}) = d-z \qquad (linear \qquad neuron \qquad f^{o\ '}(net^{\ o}) = 1)$$

$$\delta^{\ hy} = f^{h\ '}(net_{kj}^{\ hy})c_{kj}^{\ hx}b_k^{\ x} \qquad = c_{kj}^{\ hx}b_k^{\ x} \qquad (linear \qquad neuron \qquad f^{h\ '}(net_{kj}^{\ hy}) = 1)$$

$$\delta^{\ y} = f_y^{\ '}(net_j^{\ y}) = (j^2)\sin^{j-1}(j*c_j^{\ y}*y)\cos(j*c_j^{\ y}*y)$$

22. UGC-HONN Model First Layer Neuron Weights Learning Formula

Let :

$$f_k^{\ j}(c_k^{\ j}x) = (1/(1+\exp(c_k^{\ x}(-x))))^k$$

$$f_j^{\ y}(c_j^{\ k}y) = \cos^j(j*c_j^{\ k}y)$$

For a sigmoid function of *x* input side:

$$b_k^{\ x} = f_k^{\ x}(net_k^{\ x}) = [1/(1+\exp(-net_k^{\ x}))]^k$$

$$= [1/(1+\exp(c_k^{\ x}*(-x)))]^k$$

$$f_x^{\ '}(net_k^{\ x}) = \partial b_k^{\ x} \ / \ \partial(net_k^{\ x}) \qquad\qquad (UGC-HONN \qquad C. \qquad 16)$$

$$= \partial[1/(1+\exp(-net_k^{\ x}))]^k \ / \ \partial(net_k^{\ x})$$

$$= k * [1/(1+\exp(-net_k^{\ x}))]^{k-1} * (1+\exp(-net_k^{\ x}))^{-2} * \exp(-net_k^{\ x})$$

$$= k * [1/(1+\exp(-c_k^{\ x}*x))]^{k-1} * (1+\exp(-c_k^{\ x}*x))^{-2} * \exp(-c_k^{\ x}*x)$$

$$c_k^{\ x}(t+1) = c_k^{\ x}(t) - \eta(\partial E_p / \partial c_k^{\ x})$$

$$= c_k^{\ x}(t) + \eta(d-z)f^o\,'(net^o)c_{kj}^{\ o} * f^h\,'(net_{kj}^{\ h})c_{kj}^{\ hy}b_j^{\ y}c_{kj}^{\ hx}f_x\,'(net_k^{\ x})x$$

$$= c_k^{\ x}(t) + \eta * \delta^{\,ol} * c_{kj}^{\ o} * \delta^{\,hx} * c_{kj}^{\ hx} * f_x\,'(net_k^{\ x}) * x$$

$$= c_k^{\ x}(t) + \eta * \delta^{\,ol} * c_{kj}^{\ o} * \delta^{\,hx} * c_{kj}^{\ hx}$$

$$* [k * [1/(1 + \exp(-c_k^{\ x} * x))]^{k-1} * (1 + \exp(-c_k^{\ x} * x))^{-2} * \exp(-c_k^{\ x} * x)] * x$$

$$= c_k^{\ x}(t) + \eta * \delta^{\,ol} * c_{kj}^{\ o} * \delta^{\,hx} * c_{kj}^{\ hx} * \delta^{\,x} * x \qquad (UGC-HONN \qquad C. \qquad 17)$$

$$where:$$

$$\delta^{\,ol} = (d-z)f^o\,'(net^o) = d-z \qquad (linear \qquad neuron \qquad f^o\,'(net^o) = 1)$$

$$\delta^{\,hx} = f^h\,'(net_{kj}^{\ h})c_{kj}^{\ hy}b_j^{\ y} = c_{kj}^{\ hy}b_j^{\ y} \qquad (linear \qquad neuron \qquad f^h\,'(net_{kj}^{\ h}) = 1)$$

$$\delta^{\,x} = f_x\,'(net_k^{\ x})$$

$$= k * [1/(1 + \exp(-c_k^{\ x} * x))]^{k-1} * (1 + \exp(-c_k^{\ x} * x))^{-2} * \exp(-c_k^{\ x} * x)$$

For an ultra-high frequency cosine function of y input part:

$$b_j^{\ y} = f_y\,(net_j^{\ y}) = \cos^j(j * net_j^{\ y}) = \cos^j(j * c_j^{\ y} * y)$$
$$f_y\,'(net_j^{\ y}) = \partial b^y_{\ j} / \partial(net_j^{\ y})$$
$$= \partial(\cos^j(j * net_j^{\ y})) / \partial(net_j^{\ y})$$
$$= j\cos^{j-1}(j * net_j^{\ y}) * (-\sin(j * net_j^{\ y})) * j$$
$$= -j^2 * \cos^{j-1}(j * net_j^{\ y}) * \sin(j * net_j^{\ y})$$
$$= -j^2 * \cos^{j-1}(j * c_j^{\ y} * y) * \sin(j * c_j^{\ y} * y) \qquad (UGC-HONN \qquad D. \qquad 16)$$

Using the above procedure:

$$c_j^{\ y}(t+1) = c_j^{\ y}(t) - \eta(\partial E_p / \partial c_j^{\ y})$$

$$= c_j^{\ y}(t) + \eta(d-z)f^o\,'(net^o)c_{kj}^{\ o} * f^h\,'(net_{kj}^{\ h})c_{kj}^{\ hx}b_k^{\ x}c_{kj}^{\ hy}f_y\,'(net_j^{\ y})y$$

$$= c_j^{\ y}(t) + \eta * \delta^{\,ol} * c_{kj}^{\ o} * \delta^{\,hy} * c_{kj}^{\ hy} * (-j^2) * \cos^{j-1}(j * c_j^{\ y} * y) * \sin(j * c_j^{\ y} * y) * y$$

$$= c_j^{\ y}(t) + \eta * \delta^{\,ol} * c_{kj}^{\ o} * \delta^{\,hy} * c_{kj}^{\ hy} * \delta^{\,y} * y \qquad (UGC-HONN \qquad D. \qquad 17)$$

$$where:$$

$$\delta^{\,ol} = (d-z)f^o\,'(net^o) = d-z \qquad (linear \qquad neuron \qquad f^o\,'(net^o) = 1)$$

$$\delta^{\,hy} = f^h\,'(net_{kj}^{\ hy})c_{kj}^{\ hx}b_k^{\ x} = c_{kj}^{\ hx}b_k^{\ x} \qquad (linear \qquad neuron \qquad f^h\,'(net_{kj}^{\ hy}) = 1)$$

$$\delta^{\,y} = f_y\,'(net_j^{\ y}) = (-j^2) * \cos^{j-1}(j * c_j^{\ y} * y) * \sin(j * c_j^{\ y} * y)$$

23. UNS-HONN Model First Layer Neuron Weights Learning Formula

Let :

$$f_k^{\ j}(c_k^{\ j}x) = (\sin(c_k^{\ x}x)/(c_k^{\ x}x))^k$$

$$f_j^{\ y}(c_j^{\ k}y) = \sin^j(j*c_j^{\ k}y)$$

For a SINC function of x input part:

$$b_k^{\ x} = f_k^{\ x}(net_k^{\ x}) = [\sin\ (net_k^{\ x})/(net_k^{\ x})]^k = [\sin\ (c_k^{\ x}x)/(c_k^{\ x}x)]^k$$

$$f_x\ '(net_k^{\ x}) = \partial b_k^{\ x}/\partial(net_k^{\ x})$$

$$= k[\sin\ (net_k^{\ x})/(net_k^{\ x})]^{k-1}*[\cos(net_k^{\ x})/(net_k^{\ x}) - \sin\ (net_k^{\ x})/(net_k^{\ x})^2]$$

$$= k[\sin\ (c_k^{\ x}x)/(c_k^{\ x}x)]^{k-1}*[\cos(c_k^{\ x}x)/(c_k^{\ x}x) - \sin\ (c_k^{\ x}x)/(c_k^{\ x}x)^2] \qquad (UNS-HONN \qquad C. \qquad 16)$$

$$c_k^{\ x}(t+1) = c_k^{\ x}(t) - \eta(\partial E_p/\partial c_k^{\ x})$$

$$= c_k^{\ x}(t) + \eta(d-z)f^o\ '(net^o)c_{kj}^{\ o}*f^h\ '(net_{kj}^{\ h})c_{kj}^{\ hy}b_j^{\ y}c_{kj}^{\ hx}f_x\ '(net_k^{\ x})x$$

$$= c_k^{\ x}(t) + \eta*\delta^{\ ol}*c_{kj}^{\ o}*\delta^{\ hx}*c_{kj}^{\ hx}*f_x\ '(net_k^{\ x})*x$$

$$= c_k^{\ x}(t) + \eta*\delta^{\ ol}*c_{kj}^{\ o}*\delta^{\ hx}*c_{kj}^{\ hx}$$

$$*[k[\sin\ (c_k^{\ x}x)/(c_k^{\ x}x)]^{k-1}*[\cos(c_k^{\ x}x)/(c_k^{\ x}x) - \sin\ (c_k^{\ x}x)/(c_k^{\ x}x)^2]]*x$$

$$= c_k^{\ x}(t) + \eta*\delta^{\ ol}*c_{kj}^{\ o}*\delta^{\ hx}*c_{kj}^{\ hx}*\delta^x*x \qquad (UNS-HONN \qquad C. \qquad 17)$$

where :

$$\delta^{\ ol} = (d-z)f^o\ '(net^o) = (d-z) \qquad (linear \qquad neuron \qquad f^o\ '(net^o) = 1)$$

$$\delta^{\ hx} = f^h\ '(net_{kj}^{\ h})c_{kj}^{\ hy}b_j^{\ y} = c_{kj}^{\ hy}b_j^{\ y} \qquad (linear \qquad neuron \qquad f^h\ '(net_{kj}^{\ h}) = 1)$$

$$\delta^x = f_x\ '(net_k^{\ x})$$

$$= k[\sin\ (net_k^{\ x})/(net_k^{\ x})]^{k-1}*[\cos(net_k^{\ x})/(net_k^{\ x}) - \sin\ (net_k^{\ x})/(net_k^{\ x})^2]$$

$$= k[\sin\ (c_k^{\ x}x)/(c_k^{\ x}x)]^{k-1}*[\cos(c_k^{\ x}x)/(c_k^{\ x}x) - \sin\ (c_k^{\ x}x)/(c_k^{\ x}x)^2]$$

For an ultra-high frequency sine function of y input part:

$$b_j^{\ y} = f_j^{\ y}\ (net_j^{\ y}) = \sin^j(j*net_j^{\ y}) = \sin^j(j*c_j^{\ y}*y)$$

$$f_y\ '(net_j^{\ y}) = \partial b_j^{\ y}/\partial(net_j^{\ y})$$

$$= \partial(\sin^j(j*net_j^{\ y}))/\partial(net_j^{\ y})$$

$$= j\sin^{j-1}(j*net_j^{\ y})*\cos(j*net_j^{\ y})*j$$

$$= j^2*\sin^{j-1}(j*net_j^{\ y})*\cos(j*net_j^{\ y})$$

$$= j^2*\sin^{j-1}(j*c_j^{\ y}*y)*\cos(j*c_j^{\ y}*y) \qquad (UNS-HONN \qquad D. \qquad 16)$$

Using the above procedure:

$$c_j^{\ y}(t+1) = c_j^{\ y}(t) - \eta(\partial F_p / \partial c_j^{\ y})$$

$$= c_j^{\ y}(t) + \eta(d-z)f^{o}{}'(net^{o})c_{kj}^{\ o} * f^{h}{}'(net_{kj}^{\ h})c_{kj}^{\ hx}b_k^{\ x}c_{kj}^{\ hy}f_y{}'(net_j^{\ y})y$$

$$= c_j^{\ y}(t) + \eta * \delta^{ol} * c_{kj}^{\ o} * \delta^{hy} * c_{kj}^{\ hy} * (j^2)\sin^{j-1}(j*c_j^{\ y}*y)\cos(j*c_j^{\ y}*y)*y$$

$$= c_j^{\ y}(t) + \eta * \delta^{ol} * c_{kj}^{\ o} * \delta^{hy} * c_{kj}^{\ hy} * \delta^{y} * y \qquad (UNS-HONN \qquad D. \qquad 17)$$

where:

$$\delta^{ol} = (d-z)f^{o}{}'(net^{o}) = d-z \qquad (linear \qquad neuron \qquad f^{o}{}'(net^{o}) = 1)$$

$$\delta^{hy} = f^{h}{}'(net_{kj}^{\ hy})c_{kj}^{\ hx}b_k^{\ x} \quad = c_{kj}^{\ hx}b_k^{\ x} \qquad (linear \qquad neuron \qquad f^{h}{}'(net_{kj}^{\ hy}) = 1)$$

$$\delta^{y} = f_y{}'(net_j^{\ y}) = (j^2)\sin^{j-1}(j*c_j^{\ y}*y)\cos(j*c_j^{\ y}*y)$$

24. UNC-HONN Model First Layer Neuron Weights Learning Formula

Let:

$$f_k^{\ j}(c_k^{\ j}x) = (\sin(c_k^{\ x}x) / (c_k^{\ x}x))^k$$

$$f_j^{\ y}(c_j^{\ k}y) = \cos^j(j*c_j^{\ k}y)$$

For a SINC function of *x* input part:

$$b_k^{\ x} = f_k^{\ x}(net_k^{\ x}) = [\sin (net_k^{\ x}) / (net_k^{\ x})]^k = [\sin (c_k^{\ x}x) / (c_k^{\ x}x)]^k$$

$$f_x{}'(net_k^{\ x}) = \partial b_k^{\ x} / \partial(net_k^{\ x})$$

$$= k[\sin (net_k^{\ x}) / (net_k^{\ x})]^{k-1} * [\cos(net_k^{\ x}) / (net_k^{\ x}) - \sin (net_k^{\ x}) / (net_k^{\ x})^2]$$

$$= k[\sin (c_k^{\ x}x) / (c_k^{\ k}x)]^{k-1} * [\cos(c_k^{\ x}x) / (c_k^{\ x}x) - \sin (c_k^{\ x}x) / (c_k^{\ x}x)^2] \qquad (UNC-HONN \qquad C. \qquad 16)$$

$$c_k^{\ x}(t+1) = c_k^{\ x}(t) - \eta(\partial E_p / \partial c_k^{\ x})$$

$$= c_k^{\ x}(t) + \eta(d-z)f^{o}{}'(net^{o})c_{kj}^{\ o} * f^{h}{}'(net_{kj}^{\ h})c_{kj}^{\ hy}b_j^{\ y}c_{kj}^{\ hx}f_x{}'(net_k^{\ x})x$$

$$= c_k^{\ x}(t) + \eta * \delta^{ol} * c_{kj}^{\ o} * \delta^{hx} * c_{kj}^{\ hx} * f_x{}'(net_k^{\ x}) * x$$

$$= c_k^{\ x}(t) + \eta * \delta^{ol} * c_{kj}^{\ o} * \delta^{hx} * c_{kj}^{\ hx}$$

$$*[k[\sin (c_k^{\ x}x) / (c_k^{\ k}x)]^{k-1} * [\cos(c_k^{\ x}x) / (c_k^{\ x}x) - \sin (c_k^{\ x}x) / (c_k^{\ k}x)^2]] * x$$

$$= c_k^{\ x}(t) + \eta * \delta^{ol} * c_{kj}^{\ o} * \delta^{hx} * c_{kj}^{\ hx} * \delta^{x} * x \qquad (UNC-HONN \qquad C. \qquad 17)$$

where:

$$\delta^{ol} = (d-z)f^{o}{}'(net^{o}) = (d-z) \qquad (linear \qquad neuron \qquad f^{o}{}'(net^{o}) = 1)$$

$$\delta^{hx} = f^{h}{}'(net_{kj}^{\ h})c_{kj}^{\ hy}b_j^{\ y} = c_{kj}^{\ hy}b_j^{\ y} \qquad (linear \qquad neuron \qquad f^{h}{}'(net_{kj}^{\ h}) = 1)$$

$$\delta^{x} = f_x{}'(net_k^{\ x})$$

$$= k[\sin (net_k^{\ x}) / (net_k^{\ x})]^{k-1} * [\cos(net_k^{\ x}) / (net_k^{\ x}) - \sin (net_k^{\ x}) / (net_k^{\ x})^2]$$

$$= k[\sin (c_k^{\ x}x) / (c_k^{\ x}x)]^{k-1} * [\cos(c_k^{\ x}x) / (c_k^{\ x}x) - \sin (c_k^{\ x}x) / (c_k^{\ x}x)^2]$$

For an ultra-high frequency cosine function of y input part:

$$b_j^{\,y} = f_y\,(net_j^{\,y}) = \cos^j(j*net_j^{\,y}) = \cos^j(j*c_j^{\,y}*y)$$

$$f_y\,'(net_j^{\,y}) = \partial b_{\,j}^{\,y} / \partial(net_j^{\,y})$$

$$= \partial(\cos^j(j*net_j^{\,y})) / \partial(net_j^{\,y})$$

$$= j\cos^{j-1}(j*net_j^{\,y})*(-\sin(j*net_j^{\,y}))*j$$

$$= -j^2*\cos^{j-1}(j*net_j^{\,y})*\sin(j*net_j^{\,y})$$

$$= -j^2*\cos^{j-1}(j*c_j^{\,y}*y)*\sin(j*c_j^{\,y}*y) \qquad (UNC-HONN \qquad D. \qquad 16)$$

Using the above procedure:

$$c_j^{\,y}(t+1) = c_j^{\,y}(t) - \eta(\partial E_p / \partial c_j^{\,y})$$

$$= c_j^{\,y}(t) + \eta(d-z)f^o\,'(net^o)c_{kj}^{\,o}*f^h\,'(net_{kj}^{\,h})c_{kj}^{\,hx}b_k^{\,x}c_{kj}^{\,hy}f_y\,'(net_j^{\,y})y$$

$$= c_j^{\,y}(t) + \eta*\delta^{\,ol}*c_{kj}^{\,o}*\delta^{\,hy}*c_{kj}^{\,hy}*(-j^2)*\cos^{j-1}(j*c_j^{\,y}*y)*\sin(j*c_j^{\,y}*y)*y$$

$$= c_j^{\,y}(t) + \eta*\delta^{\,ol}*c_{kj}^{\,o}*\delta^{\,hy}*c_{kj}^{\,hy}*\delta^{\,y}*y \qquad (UNC-HONN \qquad D. \qquad 17)$$

where:

$$\delta^{\,ol} = (d-z)f^o\,'(net^o) = d-z \qquad (linear \qquad neuron \qquad f^o\,'(net^o) = 1)$$

$$\delta^{\,hy} = f^h\,'(net_{kj}^{\,hy})c_{kj}^{\,hx}b_k^{\,x} \quad = c_{kj}^{\,hx}b_k^{\,x} \qquad (linear \qquad neuron \qquad f^h\,'(net_{kj}^{\,hy}) = 1)$$

$$\delta^{\,y} = f_y\,'(net_j^{\,y}) = (-j^2)*\cos^{j-1}(j*c_j^{\,y}*y)*\sin(j*c_j^{\,y}*y)$$

FUTURE RESEARCH DIRECTIONS

As the next step of HONN model research, more HONN models for different data will be built to increase the pool of HONN models. Theoretically, the adaptive HONN models can be built and allow the computer automatically choose the best model, order, and coefficients. Thus, making the adaptive HONN models easier to use is one of the future research topics.

HONNs can automatically select the initial coefficients for nonlinear data analysis. The next step of this study will also focus on how to allow people working in different areas to understand that HONNs are much easier to use and can have better results. Moreover, further research will develop HONNs software packages for people working in the different area. HONNs will challenge classic procedures and change the research methodology that people are currently using in the prediction areas for nonlinear data application.

CONCLUSION

Twenty four nonlinear neural network models are listed in the chapter. This chapter introduces the background of HONN models developing history. This chapter also overviews 24 applied artificial higher order neural network models, and provides 24 HONN Models learning algorithm and weight update formulae. This chapter uses a single uniform HONN architecture for ALL 24 HONN models, and uses a uniform learning algorithm for all 24 HONN models. This chapter provides uniform weight update formulae for all 24 HONN models.

REFERENCES

Crane, J., & Zhang, M. (2005). Data simulation using SINCHONN model. *Proceedings of 2005 IASTED International Conference on Computational Intelligence,* Calgary, Canada (pp. 50 -55).

Fulcher, J., & Zhang, M. (2005). Higher-order neural networks. *Proceedings of 2005 International Conference on Advances in the Internet, Processing, Systems, and Interdisciplinary Research,* Costa Brava, Spain (p. 22).

Fulcher, J., Zhang, M., & Xu, S. (2006). The application of higher-order neural networks to financial time series prediction. In J. Kamruzzaman, R. K. Begg, & R. A. Aarker (Eds.), *Artificial Neural Networks in Finance and Manufacturing* (pp. 80–108). Hershey, PA, USA: Idea Group Publishing. doi:10.4018/978-1-59140-670-9.ch005

Lu, B., Qi, H., Zhang, M., & Scofield, R. A. (2000). Using PT-HONN models for multi-polynomial function simulation. *Proceedings of IASTED International Conference on Neural Networks,* Pittsburg, USA (pp. 1-5).

Qi, H., Zhang, M., & Scofield, R. A. (2001). Rainfall estimation using M-PHONN model. *Proceedings of 2001 International Joint Conference on Neural Networks,* Washington DC, USA (pp.1620 - 1624).

Xu, S., & Zhang, M. (2002). An adaptive activation function for higher order neural networks. *In Proceeding of 15th Australian Joint Conference on Artificial* Intelligence Canberra, Australia(pp. 356-362)..

Zhang, J. C., Zhang, M., & Fulcher, J. (1997). Financial prediction using higher order trigonometric polynomial neural network group models. *Proceedings of ICNN/IEEE International Conference on Neural Networks,* Houston, Texas, USA (pp. 2231-2234). doi:10.1109/ICNN.1997.614373

Zhang, M. (2001). Financial data simulation using A-PHONN model. *Proceedings of 2001 International Joint Conference on Neural Networks,* Washington DC, USA (pp.1823 - 1827).

Zhang, M. (2002a). Rainfall Estimation Using PL-HONN Model. *Proceedings of 2002 IASTED International Conference on Modeling and Simulation,* Marina del Rey, CA, USA (pp. 50-53).

Zhang, M. (2002b). Financial data simulation using PL-HONN model. *Proceedings of 2002 IASTED International Conference on Modeling and Simulation,* Marina del Rey, CA, USA (pp. 229-233).

Zhang, M. (2005). A data simulation system using sinx/x and sinx polynomial higher order neural networks. *Proceedings of 2005 IASTED International Conference on Computational Intelligence*, Calgary, Canada (pp.56 – 61).

Zhang, M. (2006). A data simulation system using CSINC polynomial higher order neural networks. *Proceedings of 2006 International Conference On Artificial Intelligence,* Las Vegas, USA (pp. 91-97).

Zhang, M. (2007). A data simulation system using YSINC polynomial higher order neural networks. *Proceedings of 2007 IASTED International Conference on Modeling and Simulation,* Montreal, Quebec, Canada (pp. 465-470).

Zhang, M. (2008). SAS and higher order neural network nonlinear model. *Proceedings of 2008 International Conference on Modeling, Simulation and Visualization Methods,* Las Vegas, Nevada, USA (pp. 32-38).

Zhang, M. (Ed.). (2009a). *Artificial higher order neural networks for economics and business*. Hershey, PA, USA: IGI Global. doi:10.4018/978-1-59904-897-0

Zhang, M. (2009b). Artificial higher order neural networks for economics and business – SAS NLIN or HONNs. In M. Zhang (Ed.), *Artificial Higher Order Neural Networks for Economics and Business* (pp. 1–47). Hershey, PA, USA: IGI Global. doi:10.4018/978-1-59904-897-0.ch001

Zhang, M. (2009c). Ultra high frequency trigonometric higher order neural networks for time series data analysis. In M. Zhang (Ed.), *Artificial Higher Order Neural Networks for Economics and Business* (pp. 133–163). Hershey, PA, USA: IGI Global. doi:10.4018/978-1-59904-897-0.ch007

Zhang, M. (2009d). Time series simulation using ultra high frequency cosine and cosine higher order neural networks. *Proceedings of International Association of Science and Technology for Development 12th International Conference on Intelligent systems and Control*, Cambridge, Massachusetts, USA (pp. 8-15).

Zhang, M. (Ed.). (2010a). *Higher order neural networks for computer science and engineering: trends for emerging applications.* Hershey, PA, USA: IGI-Global. doi:10.4018/978-1-61520-711-4

Zhang, M. (2010b). Higher order neural network group-based adaptive tolerance tree. In M. Zhang (Ed.), *Higher Order Neural Networks for Computer Science and Engineering: Trends for Emerging Applications* (pp. 1–36). Hershey, PA, USA: IGI- Global. doi:10.4018/978-1-61520-711-4.ch001

Zhang, M. (2010c). Rainfall estimation using neuron-adaptive higher order neural networks. In M. Zhang (Ed.), *Higher Order Neural Networks for Computer Science and Engineering: Trends for Emerging Applications* (pp. 159–186). Hershey, PA, USA: IGI- Global. doi:10.4018/978-1-61520-711-4.ch007

Zhang, M. (2010d). Time series simulation using ultra high frequency sine and sine higher order neural networks. *Proceedings of Seventh International Symposium on Neural Networks,* Shanghai, China (pp. WAD-7).

Zhang, M. (2011). Sine and sigmoid higher order neural networks for data simulation. *Proceedings of 2011 International Conference on Software Engineering, Artificial Intelligence, Networking, and Parallel/Distributed Computing (SNPD),* Sydney, Australia (p. 15).

Zhang, M. (2012). Polynomial and sigmoid higher order neural networks for data simulations and prediction. Proceedings of the 2012 International Journal of Arts & Science Conference, Florence, Italy (p.16).

Zhang, M. (Ed.), (2013a). *Higher order neural networks for modeling and simulation.* Hershey, PA, USA: IGI-Global. doi:10.4018/978-1-4666-2175-6

Zhang, M. (2013b). Artificial multi-polynomial higher order neural network models. In M. Zhang (Ed.), *Higher Order Neural Networks for Modeling and Simulation* (pp. 1–29). Hershey, PA, USA: IGI-Global. doi:10.4018/978-1-4666-2175-6.ch001

Zhang, M. (2013c). Artificial polynomial and trigonometric higher order neural network group models. In M. Zhang (Ed.), *Higher Order Neural Networks for Modeling and Simulation* (pp. 78–102). Hershey, PA, USA: IGI-Global. doi:10.4018/978-1-4666-2175-6.ch005

Zhang, M. (2014a). Sinc and sigmoid higher order neural network for data modeling and simulation. *Proceedings of Second International Conference on Vulnerability and Risk Analysis,* Liverpool, UK (pp. 2608-2617). doi:10.1061/9780784413609.262

Zhang, M. (2014b). Ultra high frequency polynomial and sine artificial higher order neural networks for control signal generator. *Proceedings of 2014 IEEE Symposium Series on Computational Intelligence,* Orlando, Florida, USA (p. 174). doi:10.1109/CICA.2014.7013235

Zhang, M. (2016a). Ultra high frequency polynomial and trigonometric higher order neural networks for control signal generator. In M. Zhang (Ed.), *Applied Artificial Higher Order Neural Networks for Control and Recognition.* Hershey, PA, USA: IGI Global, Information Science Reference.

Zhang, M. (2016b). Ultra high frequency sigmoid and trigonometric higher order neural networks for data pattern recognition. In M. Zhang (Ed.), *Applied Artificial Higher Order Neural Networks for Control and Recognition.* Hershey, PA, USA: IGI Global, Information Science Reference.

Zhang, M. (2016c). Artificial sine and cosine trigonometric higher order neural networks for financial data prediction. In M. Zhang (Ed.), *Applied Artificial Higher Order Neural Networks for Control and Recognition.* Hershey, PA, USA: IGI Global, Information Science Reference.

Zhang, M. (2016d). Ultra high frequency SINC and trigonometric higher order neural networks for data classification. In M. Zhang (Ed.), *Applied Artificial Higher Order Neural Networks for Control and Recognition.* Hershey, PA, USA: IGI Global, Information Science Reference.

Zhang, M. (2016e). Cosine and sigmoid higher order neural networks for date simulations. In M. Zhang (Ed.), *Applied Artificial Higher Order Neural Networks for Control and Recognition.* Hershey, PA, USA: IGI Global.

Zhang, M. (2016f). *Applied artificial higher order neural networks for control and recognition.* Hershey, PA, USA: IGI Global.

Zhang, M., & Crane, J. (2004). Rainfall estimation using SPHONN model. *Proceedings of 2004 International Conference on Artificial Intelligence,* Las Vegas, Nevada, USA (pp.695-701).

Zhang, M., & Fulcher, J. (2004). Higher order neural network for satellite weather predication. In J. Fulcher, & L.C. Jain (Ed.), Applied Intelligent Systems (pp. 17-57). Springer-Verlag Berlin Heidelberg, New York, USA.

Zhang, M., & Lu, B. (2001). Financial data simulation using M-PHONN model. *Proceedings of 2001 International Joint Conference on Neural Networks,* Washington DC, USA (pp. 1828 - 1832).

Zhang, M., Murugesan, S., & Sadeghi, M. (1995). Polynomial higher order neural network for economic data simulation. *Proceedings of International Conference on Neural Information Processing,* Beijing, China (pp. 493-496).

Zhang, M., & Scofield, R. A. (2001). Rainfall estimation using A-PHONN model. *Proceedings of 2001 International Joint Conference on Neural Networks,* Washington DC, USA (pp. 1583 - 1587).

Zhang, M., Xu, S., & Fulcher, F. (2002). Neuron-adaptive higher order neural network models for automated financial data modeling. *IEEE Transactions on Neural Networks, 13*(1), 188–204. doi:10.1109/72.977302 PMID:18244418

Zhang, M., Zhang, J. C., & Fulcher, J. (2000). Higher order neural network group models for financial simulation. *International Journal of Neural Systems, 10*(2), 123–142. doi:10.1142/S0129065700000119 PMID:10939345

Zhang, M., Zhang, J. C., & Keen, S. (1999). Using THONN system for higher frequency non-linear data simulation & prediction. *Proceedings of IASTED International Conference on Artificial Intelligence and Soft Computing,* Honolulu, Hawaii, USA (pp.320-323).

Chapter 13
A Theoretical Framework for Parallel Implementation of Deep Higher Order Neural Networks

Shuxiang Xu
University of Tasmania, Australia

Yunling Liu
China Agricultural University, China

ABSTRACT

This chapter proposes a theoretical framework for parallel implementation of Deep Higher Order Neural Networks (HONNs). First, we develop a new partitioning approach for mapping HONNs to individual computers within a master-slave distributed system (a local area network). This will allow us to use a network of computers (rather than a single computer) to train a HONN to drastically increase its learning speed: all of the computers will be running the HONN simultaneously (parallel implementation). Next, we develop a new learning algorithm so that it can be used for HONN learning in a distributed system environment. Finally, we propose to improve the generalisation ability of the new learning algorithm as used in a distributed system environment. Theoretical analysis of the proposal is thoroughly conducted to verify the soundness of the new approach. Experiments will be performed to test the new algorithm in the future.

INTRODUCTION

HONNs (Higher Order Neural Networks) [Lee et al 1986; Giles et al 1987] are Artificial Neural Networks (ANNs) in which the net input to a computational neuron is a weighted sum of its inputs plus products of its inputs. Such neuron is called a Higher-order Processing Unit (HPU) [Lippman 1989]. It was known that HONNs can implement invariant pattern recognition [Psaltis et al 1988; Reid et al 1989; Wood et al 1996]. It was shown in [Giles et al 1987] that HONNs have impressive computational, storage and generalization capabilities.

DOI: 10.4018/978-1-5225-0063-6.ch013

One of the most important Artificial Intelligence technologies, ANN attempts to mimic the computational power of biological brain, such as the human brain, for image recognition, sound recognition, natural language processing, complicated decision making, etc. by interconnecting simple computational units. Like the human brain, an ANN needs to be trained before it can be used to make decisions. However, nearly all of the current ANN implementations involve using a software program, running on a standalone computer, to learn training examples out of a dataset. Depending on the size of the dataset, this training could take days or even weeks. This is becoming a more serious issue in the current Big-Data era when huge datasets are available for ANNs to learn. Therefore, this chapter proposes a theoretical framework for parallel implementation of Deep HONNs by answering the following research questions:

1. How to develop a new partitioning approach for mapping HONNs to individual computers within a master-slave distributed system (a local area network)? This will allow us to use a network of computers (rather than a single computer) to train a HONN to drastically increase its learning speed: all of the computers will be running the HONN simultaneously (parallel implementation). We will use the master computer to control the overall learning process by distributing learning tasks to the individual slave computers.
2. How to develop a new learning algorithm so that it can be used for HONN learning in a distributed system environment? A HONN model needs to be trained using a learning algorithm before it can be used to make decisions. All the current HONN learning algorithms are intended for use on a standalone computer. We will develop a new algorithm to allow HONN learning/training in a distributed system environment. This involves maintaining communication among individual computers within the system so that they collectively run the same task.
3. How to improve the generalisation ability of the new learning algorithm as used in a distributed system environment? Like the human brain, after a HONN is well trained it may be able to generalise, i.e. producing outputs based on new (previously unseen) inputs. This is the ultimate goal of training a HONN.

BACKGROUND AND LITERATURE REVIEW

Human brain processes information in parallel ways. Parallel processing is the ability of the brain to simultaneously process incoming stimuli of differing quality. For example, in human vision, the brain divides what it sees into several components: colour, motion, shape, and depth. These are individually, but simultaneously analysed, and then combined, and then compared to stored memories, which helps the brain identify what we are viewing [Myers 2001].

Parallel processing in computers is the simultaneous use of more than one CPU to execute a program (such as an ANN learning algorithm). This makes a program run faster because there are more engines (CPUs) running it (with the help of distributed processing software).

To understand why parallel processing is required for ANN implementation, it is necessary to understand how an ANN learns and then makes decisions. Generally speaking, an ANN session consists of two phases: learning (or training) and testing (or recall). In the learning phase, a set of training examples is presented to the network, and weights are adjusted in accordance with input values, their correlation, and output values. By these, an ANN learns a problem or remembers existing patterns (the training examples). In the recall phase, new input sets are presented and an ANN produces appropriate results.

An ANN's ability to recall represents its most important generalisation ability because the new input sets are not presented to the ANN during the learning phase. Given the many weighted summations and weight updates that must be performed and the numerous training examples, the learning phase is the most computationally expensive.

This project focuses on Feedforward Neural Network (FNN), which is made of an input layer, some middle or hidden layers, and an output layer. There is a certain number of neurons for each layer. An FNN with more than two hidden layers of neurons is considered a Deep Neural Network (DNN). It is also a universal approximator [Hinton et al 2006a, Le Roux et al, 2008]. A DNN for a typical speech recognition system usually contains 5 to 7 hidden layers [Han et al, 2014, Zhang et al, 2013]. Compared with shallow FNNs, it can model more complex non-linear relationships. DNNs have been applied to fields like computer vision, speech recognition, natural language processing, where they have been shown to produce remarkable results on various tasks [Hinton et al 2006b, 2009].

The principles of DNNs (with many hidden layers) have been known since the proposal of the back-propagation algorithm for multi-layer perceptrons [Rumelhart et al 1986]. In practice, using more than two hidden layers was not common because it usually resulted in long training time. In 1989, LeCun et al. were able to apply the standard backpropagation algorithm to a DNN with the purpose of recognizing handwritten zip codes on mail. Despite the success of applying the algorithm, the time to train the network on this dataset was approximately 3 days [LeCun et al 1989], making it impractical for general use.

Many factors contribute to the slow speed. An obvious factor is that increasing depth significantly increases training time due to the nature of the backpropagation learning algorithm. Erhan et al. [2009] investigated other reasons for the often unsatisfying performance of DNNs, which conclude that the problem stems from the learning phase, as a) training the lower layers (close to the inputs) is more difficult than training the higher layers (close to the outputs), and b) increasing depth increases the probability of finding poor local minima which affects a DNN's generalisation ability. Another reason might be the so-called vanishing gradients problem [Hochreiter et al 2001], comparable to gradient propagation problems in recurrent neural networks.

Given the inspiration behind DNN models are biological models that are massively parallel, it is natural to develop implementations of DNN models on parallel and distributed computer systems to speed up DNN learning. A typical distributed system is represented by a LAN (Local Area Network) where some general-purpose computers are connected to a centrally located networking device such as a hub or a switch, for communication or information sharing among these computers.

There are some existing parallelization approaches to accelerate training ANNs. Most approaches can be classified into two categories, namely Node Parallelism [Suresh et al, 2005, Seiffert, 2004, Serbedzija 1996], and Data Parallelism [Li et al 2014, Andonie et al 2006]. The Node Parallelism is ANN architecture oriented. An ANN model is partitioned into several parts, with each part allocated to a computer (a node) within a distributed system. For example, if a Feedforward Neural Network (FNN) contains three layers of neurons (which are interconnected with each other), the Node Parallelism approach may allocate each layer of neurons (together with the connection weights) to an individual computer of a LAN. All the nodes process data simultaneously to achieve parallelism, with each computing node only responsible for a part of the computation. Conversely, for Data Parallelism, each computing node has the complete ANN architecture and conducts computation for the entire ANN model. The training dataset is divided into several subsets and the subsets are assigned to different computing nodes, for parallel processing.

This chapter proposes to develop a new partitioning approach for mapping HONNs to individual computers within a master-slave distributed system (a local area network). This will allow us to use a network of computers (rather than a single computer) to train a HONN to drastically increase its learning speed. The chapter will also develop a new learning algorithm so that it can be used for HONN learning in a distributed system environment. This involves maintaining communication among individual computers within the system so that they collectively run the same task. Finally we will attempt to improve the generalisation ability of the new learning algorithm as used in a distributed system environment.

THEORETICAL FRAMEWORK

The first strategy for improving DNN learning is feature engineering which attempts to employ pre-training for each layer of a DNN. Hinton et al [2006b] introduced a significant solution to this. Before minimizing the loss of a DNN with L levels, they optimized a sequence of $L-1$ singe-layer problems using restricted Boltzmann machines (RBM) that can learn a probability distribution over its set of inputs, for reducing the dimensionality of input data (ie, input feature engineering). They showed that the deep learning approach with unsupervised RBM pre-training is useful for compression of handwritten digits and faces. Lee et al. [2009a] extended the RBM to convolutional weights for image recognition. The authors used their model to generate missing parts in images of faces and for classification.

In some related work, Vincent et al (2010) proposed using auto-encoders for input feature engineering. These engineered features could then be used to train DNNs (with reduced training time). The two types of auto-encoder-based DNNs are the stacked auto-encoder (SAE) [Vincent et al 2010] and the stacked denoising auto-encoder (SDAE) [Salakhutdinov et al 2010]. SAEs and SDAEs are created by stacking auto-encoders.

Huang et al [2006a, 2006b, 2012] proposed a new learning algorithm for feedforward neural networks, named Extreme Learning Machine (ELM) algorithm, which randomly chooses hidden layer neuron activation function and analytically determines the output weights. With ELM algorithm, only connection weights between the last hidden layer and the output layer are adjusted. The approach has been independently verified by Widrow et al [2013] who named it as No-Propagation algorithm. ELM algorithm trains multilayer neural networks by training the output layer only, with the advantage of not requiring error backpropagation throughout the network. ELM was initially designed for training feedforward neural networks with a single hidden layer but has now been extended to train DNNs [Kasun et al 2013] – this recent work shows that ELM outperforms various state-of-the-art deep learning methods on the famous MNIST OCR dataset (originally used by LeCun et al in 1989). Numerous other tests have demonstrated the advantages of ELM such as drastically reducing training speed and in the meantime improving generalisation abilities of DNNs [Huang et al, 2006a, 2006b, 2012].

However, most of the current implementations are sequential, and designed to run on a single machine, resulting in long implementation time and low efficiency. A typical DNN implementation involves using C (or Java) programs running on a standalone computer to learn training examples out of a dataset. Depending on the size of the dataset, this training could take days or even weeks. This is becoming a more serious issue in the current Big-Data era when huge datasets are available for DNNs to learn.

This chapter develops novel methods and tools for training Deep HONNs in parallel and distributed environment for drastically speeding up deep learning and effectively improving Deep HONN's generalization abilities.

Step 1. We propose to develop a new partitioning approach for mapping Deep HONNs to individual computers within a master-slave distributed system (a local area network).

We propose a master-slave distributed system, with a new Node Parallelism method - a new vertical partitioning approach where each processor of the distributed system gets a subset of the neurons of a Deep HONN. Our novel approach differs from [Suresh et al 2005] in that our approach deals with Deep HONNs, while the existing work handles multilayer perceptrons with only a single hidden layer. In our new vertical partitioning approach, given a Deep HONN, each hidden layer (l), with n_l neurons, is divided into p partitions, where p is the number of processors in our distributed system which have been allocated to this layer. Each partition of the layer l has n_l/p neurons that are assigned to a processor. Given a Deep HONN, when the total number of hidden layers is known, it's easy to work out the required total number of processors for mapping this Deep HONN. The master computer stores all the input neurons as well as all the output neurons. This makes it easier to implement the new learning algorithm (for calculating connection weights, see Step 3). This partitioning satisfies layer parallelism (concurrent execution of layers within a DNN network), neuron parallelism (parallel execution of neurons), and weight parallelism (simultaneous calculation of connection weights between neurons), because all the individual slave computers as well as the master computer can execute processes in a parallel way.

We use the master computer to control the overall learning process by distributed learning tasks to the slave computers simultaneously. This can be implemented using the Matlab Distributed System Server software. For communication among individual slave computers we use MPICH, a portable implementation of MPI (Message Passing Interface), which is a standard for message-passing for distributed-memory applications used in parallel computing. MPICH is used as the foundation for the vast majority of MPI implementations, including IBM MPI (for Blue Gene), Intel MPI, Cray MPI, Microsoft MPI, and many others.

Step 2. We develop a new learning algorithm so that it can be used for Deep HONN learning in a distributed system environment.

We develop our new learning algorithm based on the idea of Extreme Learning Machine (ELM) algorithm, for feature engineering as well as for calculating connection weights between neurons. ELM algorithm drastically reduces training time (compared with traditional learning algorithm such as back-propagation) and in the meantime improves generalisation abilities. We propose ELM auto-encoder (ELM-AE), which represents features based on singular values.

The ELM for single-layer feed-forward neural networks (SLFNs) shows that hidden nodes can be randomly generated. The input data is mapped to L-dimensional ELM random feature space, and the network output is

$$f_L(\mathrm{X}) = \sum_{i=1}^{L} \beta_i g_i(\mathrm{X}) = h(\mathrm{X})\beta \qquad (1)$$

where $\beta = [\beta_1, \beta_2, ..., \beta_L]^T$ is the output weight matrix between the hidden layer neurons and the output neurons, $h(\mathrm{X}) = [g_1(\mathrm{X}), g_2(\mathrm{X}), ..., g_L(\mathrm{X})]$ are the hidden neuron outputs for input X, and $g_i(\mathrm{X})$ is the output of the *i*th hidden neuron. Given *N* training samples $\left\{\left(X_i, t_i\right)\right\}_{i=1}^{N}$, the ELM can be used to solve the following learning problem:

$$H\beta = T \tag{2}$$

where $T = \left[t_1, t_2, ..., t_N\right]^T$ are target outputs, and $H = \left[h^T(X_1), ..., h^T(X_N)\right]^T$. Then the output weights β can be calculated from:

$$\beta = H^{-1}T \tag{3}$$

where H^{-1} is the Moore-Penrose generalised inverse of matrix *H*. To improve ELM's generalisation ability it is possible to add a regularisation term as below:

$$\beta = \left(\frac{I}{C} + H^T H\right)^{-1} H^T T \tag{4}$$

Based on these, ELM-AE's can be created with the objective of representing input features meaningfully by converting features from a higher dimensional input data space to a lower dimensional feature space, which will reduce training time of a Deep HONN. This can be done by setting input data as output data, with random weights and biases of the hidden nodes chosen to be orthogonal. Widrow et al (2013) introduced a least mean square (LMS) implementation for the ELM and a corresponding ELM-based auto-encoder that uses non-orthogonal random hidden parameters (weights and biases). Orthogonalization of these randomly generated hidden parameters tends to improve ELM-AE's generalization performance. The orthogonal random weights and biases of the hidden nodes project the input data to a reduced dimension space. With extended ELM, a Deep HONN's hidden layer weights are initialized with ELM-AE, which performs layer-wise unsupervised training, which does not require fine tuning. The hidden layer activation functions can be either linear or nonlinear piecewise.

In ELM-AE, the orthogonal random weights and biases of the hidden neurons project the input data to a different dimension space, as calculated as

$$h = g\left(a \cdot X + b\right) \tag{5}$$

where $a = \left[a_1, ..., a_L\right]$ are the orthogonal random weights, and $b = \left[b_1, ..., b_L\right]$ are the orthogonal random biases between the input layer and the hidden layer.

ELM-AE's output weight matrix β is responsible for learning the transformation from the feature space to input data, which can be calculated as follows:

$$\beta = \left(\frac{I}{C} + H^T H\right)^{-1} H^T X \tag{6}$$

where $H = \left[h_1, h_2, ..., h_N \right]$ are ELM-AE's hidden layer outputs, and $X = \left[X_1, X_2, ..., X_N \right]$ are its input and output data. For equal dimension ELM-AE representations, the output weights can be calculated as:

$$\beta = H^{-1}T \tag{7}$$

where $\beta^T \beta = I$. Singular value decomposition (SVD) is a commonly used method for feature representation. Equation (6)'s SVD is:

$$H\beta = \sum_{i=1}^{N} u_i \frac{d_i^2}{d_i^2 + C} u_i^T X \tag{8}$$

Where u are eigenvectors of HH^T, and d are singular values of H, related to the SVD of input data X.

Step 3. Improve the generalisation ability of the new learning algorithm as used in a distributed system environment.

Like the human brain, after a HONN is well trained it may be able to generalise, i.e. producing outputs based on new (previously unseen) inputs. This is the ultimate goal of training a HONN. We target the following aspects for improving HONN generalisation ability: optimal HONN configuration, feature selection, and overfitting.

HONN configuration mainly refers to its architecture, i.e. number of layers, number of neurons for each layer, as well as free parameters such as learning rate. Genetic algorithms can be used to help choose an optimal HONN configuration. Feature selection, also known as variable selection or attribute selection, is the process of selecting a subset of relevant features or variables for the input layer of a HONN. The central assumption is that a dataset usually contains many redundant or irrelevant features. Redundant features are those which provide no more information than the currently selected features, and irrelevant features provide no useful information in any context. Wrappers and filters can be used as feature selection algorithms. Wrapper methods use a predictive model to score feature subsets. Each new subset is used to train a model, which is tested on a hold-out set. Counting the number of mistakes made on that hold-out set (the error rate of the model) gives the score for that subset. As wrapper methods train a new model for each subset, they are very computationally intensive, but usually provide the best performing feature set for that particular type of model. Filter methods use a proxy measure instead of the error rate to score a feature subset. This measure is chosen to be fast to compute, whilst still capturing the usefulness of the feature set. Filters are usually less computationally intensive than wrappers, but they produce a feature set which is not tuned to a specific type of predictive model. This lack of tuning means a feature set from a filter is more general than the set from a wrapper, usually giving lower prediction performance than a wrapper. Combining wrappers and filters will produce better results.

The concept of overfitting is important in machine learning. Usually a learning algorithm is trained using some set of training examples (exemplary situations for which the desired output is known). The learner is assumed to reach a state where it will also be able to predict the correct output for other examples, thus generalizing to situations not presented during training. However, in cases where learning was performed too long, the learner may have no causal relation to the target function. In this process of overfitting, the performance on the training examples still increases while the performance on unseen data becomes worse. We will use techniques such as cross-validation, regularization, and early stopping to overcome overfitting problem.

SUMMARY AND FUTURE RESEARCH DIRECTIONS

This chapter proposes a theoretical framework for parallel implementation of Deep HONNs. First, we propose a new partitioning approach for mapping HONNs to individual computers within a master-slave distributed system (a local area network). This will allow us to use a network of computers (rather than a single computer) to train a HONN to drastically increase its learning speed: all of the computers will be running the HONN simultaneously (parallel implementation). Next, we propose a new learning algorithm so that it can be used for HONN learning in a distributed system environment. Finally, we propose to improve the generalisation ability of the new learning algorithm as used in a distributed system environment. Theoretical analysis of the proposal has been conducted to verify the soundness of the new approach.

This is a report of Stage 1 of our new adventure. In Stage 2, the above new algorithm will be tested by running experiments on large datasets for testing our new methods and tools. We will start with experiments using the well known MNIST digit recognition dataset [LeCun et al 1989], a bench mark dataset for testing deep learning algorithms. We will then conduct experiments using other large datasets which are freely available from the UCI Machine Learning Repository. A Stage 2 report will be produced in the near future.

REFERENCES

Andonie, R., Chronopoulos, A. T., Grosu, D., & Galmeanu, H. (2006). An efficient concurrent implementation of a neural network algorithm. *Concurrency and Computation*, *18*(12), 1559–1573. doi:10.1002/cpe.987

Collobert, R., & Weston, J. (2008). A unified architecture for natural language processing: deep neural networks with multitask learning.*Proceedings of international conference on machine learning (ICML)*, Helsinki, Finland (pp. 160–167). doi:10.1145/1390156.1390177

Dahl, G., Yu, D., Deng, L., & Acero, A. (2012). Context-dependent pretrained deep neural networks for large vocabulary speech recognition. *IEEE Trans. Audio Speech Lang. Process.*, *20*(1), 30–42. doi:10.1109/TASL.2011.2134090

Erhan, D., Manzagol, P., Bengio, Y., Bengio, S., & Vincent, P. (2009). The difficulty of training deep architectures and the effect of unsupervised pre-training.*Proceedings of international conference on artificial intelligence and statistics (AISTATS)*, Clearwater Beach, FL, USA (pp. 153–160).

Fukushima, K. (1980). Neocognitron: A Self-organizing Neural Network Model for a Mechanism of Pattern Recognition Unaffected by Shift in Position. *Biological Cybernetics*, *36*(4), 193–202. doi:10.1007/BF00344251 PMID:7370364

Giles, C. L., & Maxwell, T. (1987). Learning, invariance, and generalization in higher order neural networks. *Applied Optics*, *26*(23), 4972–4978. doi:10.1364/AO.26.004972 PMID:20523475

Grangier, D., Bottou, L., & Collobert, R. (2009). Deep convolutional networks for scene parsing. Proceedings of the ICML deep learning workshop, Montreal, Canada.

Han, K., & Wang, D. L. (2014). Neural Network Based Pitch Tracking in Very Noisy Speech, IEEE/ACM Transactions on Audio. *Speech and Language Processing, 22*(12), 2158–2168.

Hinton, G., Osindero, S., & Teh, Y. (2006a). A fast learning algorithm for deep belief nets. *Neural Computation*, *18*(7), 1527–1554. doi:10.1162/neco.2006.18.7.1527 PMID:16764513

Hinton, G., & Salakhutdinov, R. (2006b). Reducing the dimensionality of data with neural networks. *Science*, *313*(5786), 504–507. doi:10.1126/science.1127647 PMID:16873662

Hinton, G. E. (2009). Deep belief networks. *Scholarpedia*, *4*(5), 5947. doi:10.4249/scholarpedia.5947

Hochreiter, S., Bengio, Y., Frasconi, P., & Schmidhuber, J. (2001). Gradient flow in recurrent nets: the difficulty of learning long-term dependencies. In S. C. Kremer & J. F. Kolen (Eds.), *A field guide to dynamical recurrent neural networks*. New York: Wiley/IEEE Press.

Huang, G. B., Chen, L., & Siew, C. K. (2006a). Universal approximation using incremental constructive feedforward networks with random hidden nodes. *IEEE Transactions on Neural Networks*, *17*(4), 879–892. doi:10.1109/TNN.2006.875977 PMID:16856652

Huang, G. B., Zhou, H., Ding, X., & Zhang, R. (2012). Extreme learning machine for regression and multiclass classification. *IEEE Transactions on Systems, Man, and Cybernetics. Part B, Cybernetics*, *42*(2), 513–529. doi:10.1109/TSMCB.2011.2168604 PMID:21984515

Huang, G. B., Zhu, Q. Y., & Siew, C. K. (2006b). Extreme Learning Machine: Theory and Applications. *Neurocomputing*, *70*(1-3), 489–501. doi:10.1016/j.neucom.2005.12.126

Kasun, L. L. C., Zhou, H., Huang, G. B., & Vong, C. M. (2013). Representational Learning with Extreme Learning Machine for Big Data. *IEEE Intelligent Systems*, *28*(6), 31–34.

Le Roux, N., & Bengio, Y. (2008). Representational power of restricted Boltzmann machines and deep belief networks. *Neural Computation*, *20*(6), 1631–1649. doi:10.1162/neco.2008.04-07-510 PMID:18254699

LeCun, Y., Boser, B., Denker, J. S., Henderson, D., Howard, R. E., Hubbard, W., & Jackel, L. D. (1989). Backpropagation Applied to Handwritten Zip Code Recognition. *Neural Computation*, *1*(4), 541–551. doi:10.1162/neco.1989.1.4.541

Lee, H., Grosse, R., Ranganath, R., & Ng, A. (2009a). Convolutional deep belief networks for scalable unsupervised learning of hierarchical representations. *Proceedings of international conference on machine learning (ICML)*, New York, NY, USA (pp. 609–616). doi:10.1145/1553374.1553453

Lee, H., Pham, P., Largman, Y., & Ng, A. (2009b). Unsupervised feature learning for audio classification using convolutional deep belief networks. In Advances in neural information processing systems (pp. 1096–1104).

Lee, Y. C., Doolen, G., Chen, H., Sun, G., Maxwell, T., Lee, H., & Giles, C. L. (1986). Machine learning using a higher order correlation network. *Physica D. Nonlinear Phenomena, 22*(1-3), 276–306. doi:10.1016/0167-2789(86)90300-6

Li, C., Yang, L. T., & Lin, M. (2014). Parallel Training of An Improved Neural Network for Text Categorization. *International Journal of Parallel Programming, 42*(3), 505–523. doi:10.1007/s10766-013-0245-x

Lippman, R. P. (1989). Pattern classification using neural networks. *IEEE Communications Magazine, 27*(11), 47–64. doi:10.1109/35.41401

Matusugu, M., Mori, K., Mitari, Y., & Kaneda, Y. (2003). Subject independent facial expression recognition with robust face detection using a convolutional neural network. *Neural Networks, 16*(5), 555–559. doi:10.1016/S0893-6080(03)00115-1 PMID:12850007

Mikolov, T. et al.. (2010). *Recurrent neural network based language model* (pp. 1045–1048). Interspeech.

Myers, D. G. (2001). *Psychology* (6th ed.). New York: Worth.

Nordstrom, T., & Svensson, B. (1992). Using and designing massively parallel computers for artificial neural networks. *Journal of Parallel and Distributed Computing, 14*(3), 260–285. doi:10.1016/0743-7315(92)90068-X

Psaltis, D., Park, C. H., & Hong, J. (1988). Higher order associative memories and their optical implementations. *Neural Networks, 1*(2), 149–163. doi:10.1016/0893-6080(88)90017-2

Ranzato, M., & Hinton, G. (2010). Modeling pixel means and covariances using factorized third-order Boltzmann machines. *Proceedings of computer vision and pattern recognition* (pp. 2551–2558). San Francisco, CA, USA: CVPR. doi:10.1109/CVPR.2010.5539962

Reid, M. B., Spirkovska, L., & Ochoa, E. (1989). Simultaneous position, scale, rotation invariant pattern classification using third-order neural networks. *Int. J. Neural Networks, 1,* 154–159.

Rumelhart, D., Hinton, G., & Williams, R. (1986). Learning representations by back-propagating errors. *Nature, 323*(6088), 533–536. doi:10.1038/323533a0

Salakhutdinov, R., & Larochelle, H. (2010). Efficient Learning of Deep Boltzmann Machines. *Journal of Machine Learning Research, 9,* 693–700.

Schmidhuber, J. (1992). Learning complex, extended sequences using the principle of history compression. *Neural Computation, 4*(2), 234–242. doi:10.1162/neco.1992.4.2.234

Schulz, H., & Behnke, S. (2012). Learning object-class segmentation with convolutional neural networks. *Proceedings of the European symposium on artificial neural networks (ESANN),* Bruges, Belgium.

Seiffert, U. (2004). Artificial neural networks on massively parallel computer hardware. *Neurocomputing, 57,* 135–150. doi:10.1016/j.neucom.2004.01.011

Serbedzija, N. B. (1996). Simulating Artificial Neural Networks on Parallel Architectures. *Computer, 29*(3), 56–63. doi:10.1109/2.485893

Sudhakar V, & Murthy, C.S.R. (1998). Efficient Mapping of Backpropagation Algorithm onto a Network of Workstations. *IEEE transactions on systems, man, and cybernetics—part b: cybernetics,* 28(6), 841-848.

Suresh, S., Omkar, S. N., & Mani, V. (2005). Parallel Implementation of Back-propagation Algorithm in Networks of Workstations. *IEEE transactions on parallel and distributed systems, 16*(1), 24–34. doi:10.1109/TPDS.2005.11

Vincent, P., Larochelle, H., Lajoie, I., Bengio, Y., & Manzagol, P. (2010). Stacked Denoising Autoencoders: Learning Useful Representations in a Deep Network with a Local Denoising Criterion. *Journal of Machine Learning Research, 11,* 3371–3408.

Widrow, B., Greenblatt, A., Kim, Y., & Park, D. (2013). The No-Prop algorithm: A new learning algorithm for multilayer neural networks. *Neural Networks, 37,* 182–188. doi:10.1016/j.neunet.2012.09.020 PMID:23140797

Wood, J., & Shawe-Taylor, J. (1996). A unifying framework for invariant pattern recognition. *Pattern Recognition Letters, 17*(14), 1415–1422. doi:10.1016/S0167-8655(96)00103-1

Zhang, S., Zhang, C., You, Z., Zheng, R., & Xu, B. (2013). Asynchronous Stochastic Gradient Descent for DNN Training. Proceedings of *ICASSP '13* (pp. 6660–6663).

KEY TERMS AND DEFINITIONS

Artificial Neural Networks (ANNs): A computational model that simulates the functional aspects of biological neural networks. ANNs are adaptive systems that change their behaviour based on external and/or internal information that flows through the networks during a learning process.

Deep Higher Order Neural Networks: HONNs with more than two hidden layers.

Deep Neural Networks: ANNs with more than two hidden layers.

Extreme Learning Machine: An algorithm for ANNs which randomly chooses hidden neurons and analytically determines the output weights. With ELM algorithm, only the connection weights between hidden layer and output layer are adjusted.

Feedforward Neural Networks: ANNs where connections between the neurons do not form a directed cycle.

Higher Order Neural Networks (HONNs): ANNs in which the net input to a computational neuron is a weighted sum of products of its inputs.

Chapter 14

Ant Colony Optimization Applied to the Training of a High Order Neural Network with Adaptable Exponential Weights

Ashraf M. Abdelbar
Brandon University, Canada

Donald C. Wunsch
Missouri University of Science and Technology, USA

Islam Elnabarawy
Missouri University of Science and Technology, USA

Khalid M. Salama
University of Kent, UK

ABSTRACT

High order neural networks (HONN) are neural networks which employ neurons that combine their inputs non-linearly. The HONEST (High Order Network with Exponential SynapTic links) network is a HONN that uses neurons with product units and adaptable exponents. The output of a trained HONEST network can be expressed in terms of the network inputs by a polynomial-like equation. This makes the structure of the network more transparent and easier to interpret. This study adapts $ACO_{\mathbb{R}}$, an Ant Colony Optimization algorithm, to the training of an HONEST network. Using a collection of 10 widely-used benchmark datasets, we compare $ACO_{\mathbb{R}}$ to the well-known gradient-based Resilient Propagation (R-Prop) algorithm, in the training of HONEST networks. We find that our adaptation of $ACO_{\mathbb{R}}$ has better test set generalization than R-Prop, though not to a statistically significant extent.

1. OVERVIEW

In this work, we present an adaptation of the $ACO_{\mathbb{R}}$ (Socha & Dorigo, 2008) Ant Colony Optimization (ACO) (Dorigo & Stützle, 2004) algorithm applied to the training of the HONEST (Abdelbar, 1998; Abdelbar & Tagliarini, 1996; Abdelbar et al., 2002; Elnabarawy & Abdelbar, 2013; Tsai, 2009; Tsai, 2010) (High Order Network with Exponential SynapTic links) neural network. High Order Neural Networks (HONN) are neural networks which include neurons that combine their inputs nonlinearly,

DOI: 10.4018/978-1-5225-0063-6.ch014

and are thus able to capture nonlinear interactions and codependences among their inputs (Rumelhart *et al.*, 1986). HONEST is a HONN that employs connections with associated adaptable exponents and neurons with product units. In previous work, HONEST has been found to have good generalization capabilities, however, the sensitivity of the adaptable exponents made the network difficult to train and prone to local minima traps (Abdelbar, 1998).

$ACO_{\mathbb{R}}$ (Liao *et al.*, 2014; Socha & Dorigo, 2008) is a fairly-recent Ant Colony Optimization (ACO) algorithm for continuous optimization problems. $ACO_{\mathbb{R}}$ has been applied to several continuous optimization problems, including training MLP neural networks (Socha & Blum, 2007). $ACO_{\mathbb{R}}$ algorithm does not make any use of gradient information, which makes the algorithm robust and applicable to problems where the error function is not differentiable. However, it also means that the algorithm misses out on some important signals that can be obtained from gradient information. Although pure gradient descent methods, such as classical Back-Propagation (Werbos, 1994), can suffer from many problems, including local minima traps, there are methods that perform well by making limited use of gradient information. An example is the Resilient Propagation (R-Prop) algorithm (Reidmiller and Braun, 1993), a robust and powerful technique, that uses only the sign of the partial derivative, and ignores the magnitude.

We present an adaptation of $ACO_{\mathbb{R}}$, called Gradient-based $ACO_{\mathbb{R}}$ ($\mathcal{G}\text{-}ACO_{\mathbb{R}}$), that uses gradient information to help steer the evolutionary direction of the $ACO_{\mathbb{R}}$ algorithm.

We begin by introducing the HONEST network more fully in Section 2, and presenting the standard $ACO_{\mathbb{R}}$ algorithm in Section 3. Then, in Section 4, we present our $\mathcal{G}\text{-}ACO_{\mathbb{R}}$ applied to the HONEST network. Experimental results are presented in Section 5, and final remarks are offered in Section 6.

2. THE HONEST NEURAL NETWORK

The HONEST network can be considered to be a generalization of the sigma-pi model (Rumelhart *et al.*, 1986), and is also similar in some ways to the ExpoNet (Narayan, 1993) and GMDH (Ivakhnenko, 1971; Puig *et al.*, 2007) networks. An HONEST network is a feedforward network that always contains exactly three layers—although Tsai (2009; 2010) has considered variations of HONEST that use more layers. Let the external inputs to the network be denoted $x_1, x_2, \ldots, x_n$, let the output of the hidden layer neurons be denoted $h_1, \ldots, h_r$, and let the external output of the network be denoted $y_1, \ldots, y_m$. A connection from an input unit x_j to a hidden neuron h_k does not have an associated weight as in MLP networks, but rather has an associated adaptable exponent p_{kj}. Each hidden unit h_k computes the product of its inputs after first raising each input to the power of the exponent associated with its incoming connection:

$$h_k = \prod_{j=1}^{n} x_j^{p_{kj}} \tag{1}$$

as illustrated in Fig. 1. Hidden layer neurons do not have associated biases.

Output layer neurons are simple linear MLP-like neurons that have an identity activation function—although Tsai (2009; 2010) has explored variations that use sigmoidal activation functions. Connections between hidden neurons and output neurons have associated adaptable weights. Each output layer neuron *i* computes its output according to:

Figure 1. Hidden Layer Neuron in the HONEST Architecture.

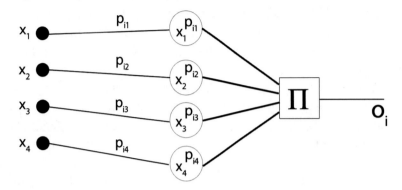

$$y_i = \sum_{k=1}^{r} w_{ik} h_k + \theta_i \qquad (2)$$

where θ_i is the bias associated with output neuron i, and w_{ik} is the weight from hidden neuron k to output neuron i. Fig. 2 illustrates the network as a whole: the connections from the input to hidden layers have associated adaptable exponents, while the connections from the hidden to output layers have associated multiplicative weights. Hidden layer neurons compute the product of their inputs, after each is raised to its associated power, while output layer neurons compute the sum of their weighted inputs. All layers have identity activation functions. The advantage of this is that each of the outputs y_i of an HONEST network can be expressed in terms of the network inputs by a polynomial-like expression of the form:

$$y_i = \sum_{k} \left(w_{ik} \prod_{j} x_j^{P_{kj}} \right) + \theta_i \qquad (3)$$

Figure 2. The HONEST Network Architecture.

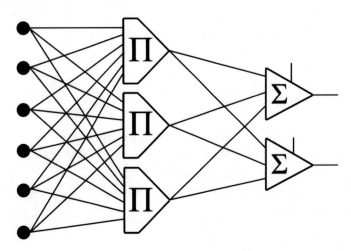

For example, the equation

$$y_i = 0.8x_1^{1.5}x_2^{3.1}x_3^{-2.4} - 4.7x_1^{-3.5}x_2^{0.8}x_3^{-1.1} - 3.7 \tag{4}$$

is represented by the network shown in Fig. 3. Thus, an advantage of HONEST is that the structure of a trained network is more transparent and easier to interpret by human experts.

Previous work on training HONEST networks has used ordinary stochastic gradient-descent (Back-Propagation) (Abdelbar, 1998), R-Prop (Elnabarawy *et al.*, 2013; Elnabarawy & Abdelbar, 2014), high-order gradient-based methods such as conjugate gradient and Levenberg-Marquardt (Elnabarawy and Abdelbar, 2014), as well as particle swarm optimization (Tsai, 2010). Hybrid approaches (Abdelbar *et al.*, 2002) have also been considered where statistical learning is used to learn an initial quadratic mapping that is used to initialize an HONEST network, which is then trained with a small learning rate to "fine-tune" the initial mapping. Other work has considered adding a regularization term in HONEST's training that penalizes exponents of high-magnitude (Elnabarawy & Abdelbar, 2014), which are often a sign of overfitting the training set.

Variations of HONEST that use nonlinear activation functions and allow more than one hidden layer have been investigated by Tsai (2009; 2010), however this approach comes at the expense of the transparency of the trained networks.

We will use the generic term *weight* to refer to any of HONEST's adaptable parameters, including the exponential weights from the input to hidden layer, the multiplicative weights from the hidden to output layers, and the bias weights associated with output layer units. Let $w=(w_1,\ldots,w_{|w|})$ denote a *weight vector* that comprises all the weights of the network. In Back-Propagation, each weight is iteratively adapted according to:

$$\Delta w_i = -\eta \frac{\partial E}{\partial w_i} \tag{5}$$

where η is the learning rate.

It is straightforward to derive that:

Figure 3. Example of an HONEST Network.

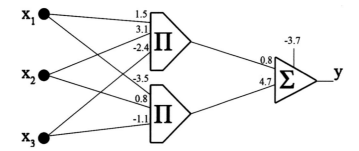

$$\frac{\partial h_k}{\partial p_{kj}} = -\delta_k h_k \ln\left(x_j\right) \tag{6}$$

for a hidden layer neuron k and input unit j. The rest of HONEST's BackPropagation equations are the same as for MLP networks.

A better-performing alternative to Back-Propagation is Resilient-Propagation (R-Prop) (Reidmiller & Braun, 1993), which uses only the sign of the partial derivative and neglects the magnitude. At each iteration t of R-Prop, the following is applied:

$$\Delta w_i(t) = \begin{cases} -s_i(t) & \text{if } \dfrac{\partial E}{\partial w_i}(t) > 0 \\[2mm] +s_i(t) & \text{if } \dfrac{\partial E}{\partial w_i}(t) < 0 \\[2mm] 0 & \text{if } \dfrac{\partial E}{\partial w_i}(t) = 0 \end{cases} \tag{7}$$

where each weight w_i has its own adaptable step size s_i. In other words, if $\dfrac{\partial E}{\partial w_i}(t)$ is positive, then this means that a decrease in the value of $w_i(t)$ will result in a decrease in E—thus $w_i(t)$ is decreased by $s_i(t)$. Similarly, if $\dfrac{\partial E}{\partial w_i}(t)$ is negative, then an increase in $w_i(t)$ will decrease E, and thus, $w_i(t)$ is increased by $s_i(t)$.

Each step size $s_i(t)$ is always positive and is individually adapted according to:

$$s_i(t) = \begin{cases} b \cdot s_i(t-1) & \text{if } \dfrac{\partial E}{\partial w_i}(t) \cdot \dfrac{\partial E}{\partial w_i}(t-1) > 0 \\[2mm] a \cdot s_i(t-1) & \text{if } \dfrac{\partial E}{\partial w_i}(t) \cdot \dfrac{\partial E}{\partial w_i}(t-1) < 0 \\[2mm] s_i(t-1) & \text{if } \dfrac{\partial E}{\partial w_i}(t) \cdot \dfrac{\partial E}{\partial w_i}(t-1) = 0 \end{cases} \tag{8}$$

where a and b are the only external parameters of the R-Prop algorithm, with $0 < a < 1 < b$. This means that if the two partial derivatives $\dfrac{\partial E}{\partial w_i}(t-1)$ and $\dfrac{\partial E}{\partial w_i}(t)$ have the same sign, in which case their product will be positive, then $s_i(t)$ will be increased by a factor of b. On the other hand, if the two partial derivatives $\dfrac{\partial E}{\partial w_i}(t-1)$ and $\dfrac{\partial E}{\partial w_i}(t)$ have opposite signs, in which case their product will be negative, then this change in sign indicates that a minimum has been missed, and thus the step size $s_i(t)$ will be decreased by a factor of a.

Furthermore, if the two partial derivatives $\frac{\partial E}{\partial w_i}(t-1)$ and $\frac{\partial E}{\partial w_i}(t)$ have opposite signs, then the previous weight change is undone:

$$\Delta w_i(t) = -\Delta w_i(t-1) \qquad \text{if } \frac{\partial E}{\partial w_i}(t) \cdot \frac{\partial E}{\partial w_i}(t-1) < 0 \tag{9}$$

and an internal flag is set that prevents the step size $s_i(t)$ from being updated in the next iteration.

3. THE ACO$_R$ ALGORITHM

Ant Colony Optimization (Dorigo & Stützle, 2004) (ACO) algorithms are AI (Artificial Intelligence) algorithms that are inspired by various aspects of the behavior of natural ant colonies. Like neural networks, computation in ACO is based on a number of simple and primitive processing elements called *ants*, where the collection of processing elements is called a *colony*. In most ACO algorithms, there is typically a central *pheromone* data structure, analogous to pheromone in natural ant colonies, that represents the time-varying collective wisdom of the colony. Historically, ACO researchers have been more focused on discrete optimization problems. ACO$_R$ (Socha & Dorigo, 2008) is a recently-introduced ACO algorithm for continuous optimization. An extension (Liao *et al.*, 2014) of ACO$_R$ has recently been introduced that can be applied to optimization problems that contain a mixture of discrete and continuous variables.

Suppose the ACO$_R$ algorithm is to be applied to optimizing a neural network weight vector w, where $|w|=n$. The central data structure, analogous to pheromone information in natural ant colonies, that is maintained by ACO$_R$ is an archive τ of L previously-generated candidate solutions (weight vectors).

Each element w_a in the archive, for $a=1, 2,..., L$, is an n-dimensional real-valued weight vector, $w_a=(w_{a1}, w_{a2},..., w_{an})$. For example, w_{aj} refers to the value of the j-th weight in the a-th vector in the archive—where for the HONEST network the j-th weight could be an exponent, a multiplicative weight, or a self-bias. The archive is ranked and sorted by solution quality, so that

$$Q(s_1) \geq Q(s_2) \geq ... \geq Q(s_L) \tag{10}$$

Each solution w_a in the archive has an associated utility coefficient ω_a that is computed according to:

$$\omega_a = g(a;1,\sigma_\omega) \tag{11}$$

where g is the Gaussian function:

$$g(y;\mu,\sigma) = \frac{1}{\sigma\sqrt{2\pi}} e^{\frac{-(y-\mu)^2}{2\sigma^2}} \tag{12}$$

Thus, Eq. (11) assigns the weight ω_a to be the value of the Gaussian function with argument a, mean 1.0, and standard deviation σ_ω. The value of σ_ω is set to:

$$\sigma_\omega = qL \tag{13}$$

where q is an external parameter of the algorithm. Smaller values of q will cause the better ranked solutions to have higher weights ω (and thus makes the algorithm more exploitative), while larger values of q will result in a more uniform distribution.

Note that Eqs. (10-11) imply that:

$$\omega_1 \geq \omega_2 \geq \ldots \geq \omega_L \tag{14}$$

The ACO$_\mathbb{R}$ algorithm consists of repeated generations until some termination criteria is reached, where the termination criteria could be that some maximum number of generations has elapsed, or that the solution quality has reached a desired value, or any other criteria. In each generation, there are two phases: the *solution construction* phase, and the *pheromone update* phase.

In the *solution construction* phase, each ant probabilistically constructs a solution based on the solution archive τ (representing pheromone information). The solution archive τ is initialized with L randomly-generated solutions, where the size L is an external parameter of the ACO$_\mathbb{R}$ algorithm. Then, in the *pheromone update* phase, the m constructed solutions (where m is the number of ants) are added to τ. The archive τ is then sorted by solution quality, and the m worst solutions are discarded, so that the size of τ returns to being L.

The heart of the algorithm is the solution construction phase. In this phase, each ant i generates a candidate solution w_i, where w_i is an n-dimensional weight vector, and w_{ij} represents an assignment to the j-th element of w_i. In constructing its solution w_i, ant i is influenced by one of the L solutions in the archive τ. The ant first probabilistically selects one of the L solutions in the archive according to the "roulette wheel" equation:

$$\Pr\left(\text{select } s_a\right) = \frac{\omega_a}{\sum_{k=1}^{L} \omega_k} \tag{15}$$

Thus, the probability of selecting the a-th solution is proportional to its weight ω_a.

Recall that the archive τ is sorted by quality, so that solution w_a has rank a, and the weights ω_a that are used in Eq. (15) are constructed in each generation according to Eq. (11).

Let w_a be the solution of τ that is selected by ant i according to Eq. (15) in a given generation. Ant i then generates each solution element w_{ij} by sampling the Gaussian probability density function (PDF) $N(w_{aj}, \sigma_{aj})$:

$$w_{ij} \sim N\left(w_{aj}, \sigma_{aj}\right) \tag{16}$$

where $N(\mu, \sigma)$ denotes the Gaussian PDF with mean μ and standard deviation σ.

The standard deviation σ_{aj} is computed according to:

$$\sigma_{aj} = \xi \cdot \mu\left[\left\{w_r \in \tau\right\}\right] \tag{17}$$

where $\mu[.]$ is the set-mean operator and ξ is an external parameter of the algorithm. The effect of Eq. (17) is that the average distance from w_a to other solutions in the archive, for the j-th dimension, is computed, and is then multiplied by ξ. The parameter ξ plays a role in $ACO_{\mathbb{R}}$ similar to that of evaporation rate in other ACO algorithms (Socha & Dorigo, 2008). Once each ant constructs its solution, the archive τ is updated as described above. The process repeats until the desired termination criteria are met.

4. PROPOSAL

$ACO_{\mathbb{R}}$ is an algorithm that does not make use of gradient information at all. This makes the algorithm more robust, and applicable to problems where the error function is not differentiable. However, it also means that the algorithm misses out on some important signals that can be obtained from gradient information. We present an adaptation of $ACO_{\mathbb{R}}$, that we call Gradient-based $ACO_{\mathbb{R}}$ ($\mathcal{G}$-$ACO_{\mathbb{R}}$), that uses gradient information to guide the $ACO_{\mathbb{R}}$ algorithm to an extent that is controlled by an external parameter ρ.

When $ACO_{\mathbb{R}}$ is applied to training HONEST, in order to obtain the fitness of a candidate weight vector, an HONEST network would be initialized with the weight vector under evaluation. The training set would then be applied to the network once, and the total mean-squared-error would be obtained over the entire training set. The fitness of the solution vector would be set inversely to the value of the network error. This is similar to the way that the test set is processed in classical Back-Propagation.

In our proposed $\mathcal{G}$-$ACO_{\mathbb{R}}$ algorithm, for each pattern, we would make a backward pass as well as a forward pass, and would compute the partial derivative $\dfrac{\partial E}{\partial w_j}$ for each network weight w_j. In the solution construction phase, rather than apply Eq. (17), we instead apply the following procedure.

1. As before, let w_a be the solution of τ that is selected by ant i according to Eq. (15) in a given generation. Rather than compute the average distance, in the j-th dimension, between w_a and every other weight vector in the archive τ, we instead compute the average distance between w_a and those vectors in τ that would move w_{aj} in the direction indicated by gradient information. Specifically:

$$\sigma_{aj} = \begin{cases} \xi \bullet \mu[\{w_r \in \tau \mid w_{rj} < w_{aj}\}] & \text{if } \dfrac{\partial E}{\partial w_a} > 0 \\[4mm] \xi \bullet \mu[\{w_r \in \tau \mid w_{rj} > w_{aj}\}] & \text{if } \dfrac{\partial E}{\partial w_a} < 0 \end{cases} \tag{18}$$

In other words, if the partial derivative $\dfrac{\partial E}{\partial w_a}$ is positive suggesting that a decrease in w_a would result in a decrease in E, then we are influenced in the computation of σ_{aj} only by weight vectors w_r for which $(w_{aj} - w_{rj})$ is negative. Similarly, if the partial derivative is negative, then we include in the computation of σ_{aj} only those weight vectors w_r which would result in an increase in w_{aj}.

Further, rather than apply Eq. (16), we generate a temporary variable t by sampling the Gaussian PDF:

$$t \sim N(w_{aj}, \sigma_{aj}) \tag{19}$$

then we compute Δ as the absolute value of the difference between t and w_{aj}:

$$\Delta = | t - w_{aj} | \tag{20}$$

The positive quantity Δ is then added or subtracted from w_{aj}, depending on the sign of the partial derivative:

$$w_{ij} = \begin{cases} w_{aj} + \Delta & \text{if } \dfrac{\partial E}{\partial w_a} < 0 \\[2em] w_{aj} - \Delta & \text{if } \dfrac{\partial E}{\partial w_a} > 0 \end{cases} \tag{21}$$

This will ensure that, as in the R-Prop algorithm, each dimension w_{ij} of the weight vector w_i will move in the direction indicated by the gradient, but the step size for each dimension will be different and dependent on the archive τ.

3. To inject an additional element of randomness, with a small probability ρ, we do not apply gradient guidance, and instead apply the standard solution construction mechanisms of $ACO_\mathbb{R}$. This is applied for each dimension separately. So, if $\rho=0.05$, then roughly 5% of the dimensions for a given weight vector will be constructed without regard for gradient information, while the rest of the weight vector will be constructed with gradient guidance.

We also apply an additional mechanism in $\mathcal{G}$-$ACO_\mathbb{R}$ that is specific to HONEST. We do not allow the magnitude of adaptable exponents to exceed p_m, where we use $p_m =3.0$ in our experimental results. This is because we have found in previous work (Elnabarawy and Abdelbar, 2014) that large exponent magnitudes are usually symptomatic of overfitting of the training set, and typically result in poor test set performance. Previous work explored adding terms to the network error function to penalize high-magnitude exponents (Elnabarawy and Abdelbar, 2014), but this can be accomplished more easily in $ACO_\mathbb{R}$ by simple clipping. After the application of Eq. (21), we apply:

$$p_{ij} = \begin{cases} +p_m & \text{if} & p_{ij} > p_m \\ -p_m & \text{if} & p_{ij} < -p_m \\ p_{ij} & \text{if} & -p_m \leq p_{ij} \leq p_m \end{cases} \qquad (22)$$

This will ensure that all exponents remain in the range $[-p_m, p_m]$.

5. EXPERIMENTAL METHODOLOGY AND RESULTS

We compare our proposed $\mathcal{G}\text{-ACO}_{\mathbb{R}}$ to the well-known R-Prop (Reidmiller & Braun, 1993) algorithm using 10 popular benchmark datasets (Asuncion & Newman, 2007). The R-Prop results are taken from previous published work (Elnabarawy & Abdelbar, 2014) and are based on the R-Prop parameter settings shown in Table 1; that table also reports the parameter settings for our $\mathcal{G}\text{-ACO}_{\mathbb{R}}$ algorithm, which were determined through initial *ad hoc* experimentation. The termination criteria for $\mathcal{G}\text{-ACO}_{\mathbb{R}}$ were set to be either reaching 5000 generations, or proceeding for 100 generations without improvement in the quality of the best solution in the archive.

The experiments were carried out using the *stratified* ten-fold cross validation procedure. This means that a dataset is divided into ten mutually exclusive partitions (folds), with approximately the same number of instances and roughly the same class distribution in each fold. Then, each algorithm (R-Prop or $\mathcal{G}\text{-ACO}_{\mathbb{R}}$) is run ten times, where each time a different fold is used as the test set and the other nine folds are used as the training set. Performance on each of the test set folds is recorded, and the average test set performance, aggregated over all 10 folds, is reported as representative of the performance of each algorithm.

Table 1. Parameter values used in experimental results.

Algorithm	Parameter	Value
R-Prop	a	0.7
	b	1.2
$\mathcal{G}\text{-ACO}_{\mathbb{R}}$	m	5
	L	40
	q	0.05
	ξ	0.30
	ρ	0.05
	ρ_m	3.0

Table 2. Characteristics of the datasets used in the experimental results.

Dataset	Instances	Classes	Attributes
balance	625	3	4
breast-tissue	106	6	9
breast-cancer-wisconsin-diagnostic	569	2	30
ecoli	336	8	7
glass	214	7	9
iris	150	3	4
transfusion	722	2	4
vertebral-column-2c	310	2	6
vertebral-column-3c	310	3	6
wine	101	3	13

We used 10 datasets, obtained from the publicly-available University of California Irvine (UCI) dataset repository (Asuncion & Newman, 2007). Table 2 reports the main characteristics of these datasets. Each dataset went through the following preprocessing steps before being presented to the HONEST network:

1. Each continuous (numeric) attribute was scaled to the range [0.1, 0.9].
2. Each categorical attribute with *c* category labels was transformed to *c* network inputs, one input for each category label. For each pattern, the input corresponding to the category label for each categorical attribute was set to 0.9, and all the others were set to 0.1.
3. Any missing value for a continuous attribute was set to the mean value for that attribute. Any missing value for a categorical attribute was set to the mode (the most popular category) for that attribute.
4. If the number of classes is *m*, then the network will have *m* output neurons, one corresponding to each class. For each pattern, the target value for the output neuron corresponding to the correct class was set to 0.9, and for all other output neurons was set to 0.1.

For each dataset, the number of hidden neurons used in the present study was set to be the same as the number of hidden neurons that was used for that dataset in (Elnabarawy & Asuncion, 2007). Table 3 summarizes the network topology for each dataset.

The results are shown in Table 4. For each dataset, the table reports the average test set MSE (averaged over the 10 cross-validations folds) for each of the two algorithms; the better MSE value for each row is shown in boldface, and the last row of the table shows the average MSE over all datasets. As the table indicates, $\mathcal{G}$-ACO$_R$ had better test set performance on 7 out of the 10 datasets, and R-Prop had better test set performance on 3 out of the 10 datasets.

Table 5 shows the results of applying a (two-tailed) non-parameteric Wilcoxon signed-ranks test to the MSE results. As the table shows, the computed value of the Wilcoxon statistic W is 18, while the critical value W^{crit}, for the conventional 0.05 significance level, is 10. This indicates that there is no observed

Table 3. HONEST network topology for each dataset.

Dataset	Input	Hidden	Output
balance	20	5	3
breast-tissue	9	11	6
breast-cancer-wisconsin-diagnostic	30	21	2
ecoli	7	10	8
glass	9	10	7
iris	4	5	3
transfusion	4	5	2
vertebral-column-2c	6	5	2
vertebral-column-3c	6	6	3
wine	13	11	3

Table 4. Experimental Results

Dataset	R-Prop	$\mathcal{G}$-ACO$_R$
balance	0.0807	0.0447
breast-cancer-wisconsin-diagnostic	0.2530	0.1250
breast-tissue	0.1130	0.1358
ecoli	0.0482	0.0978
glass	0.1360	0.1687
iris	0.0578	0.0275
transfusion	0.1540	0.1295
vertebral-column-2c	0.1490	0.1216
vertebral-column-3c	0.1340	0.1245
wine	0.1060	0.0760
Avg	0.1232	0.1051

Table 5. Results of Wilcoxon signed-ranks test (at 0.05 threshold).

Statistic	Value
N	10
(W+,W-)	(37,18)
W	18
W^{crit}	10

statistically significant difference between the two algorithms. This is noteworthy because R-Prop is well-established and is generally considered to be a very powerful neural network training algorithm.

6. CONCLUDING REMARKS

The present work adapted the ACO_R Ant Colony Optimization algorithm to the HONEST high order neural network. Our experimental results indicate that our proposed adaptation, called $\mathcal{G}\text{-}ACO_R$, is an effective method for training the HONEST network, and has test set generalization that is competitive with the well-established R-Prop algorithm.

In an experimental comparison using 10 popular benchmark UCI datasets, $\mathcal{G}\text{-}ACO_R$ had better test set performance than R-Prop on 70% of the datasets, although the Wilcoxon signed-rank test did not detect a statistically significant difference between the two.

In future work, we would like to consider a further variation of the ACO_R algorithm where the Cauchy function is used in Eq. (11) in place of the Gaussian function. Like the Gaussian, the Cauchy function is also symmetric and bell-shaped. However, it has a much wider tail than the Gaussian, which means that it would result in greater search diversity than the Gaussian. It is possible to also use a Cauchy PDF in place of a Gaussian PDF in Eq. (16), but the use of the wider-tail Cauchy in Eq. (11) is likely to have a greater positive impact on diversity.

REFERENCES

Abdelbar, A. M. (1998). Achieving superior generalisation with a high order neural network. *Neural Computing & Applications*, *7*(2), 141–146. doi:10.1007/BF01414166

Abdelbar, A. M., Attia, S., & Tagliarini, G. A. (2002). A hybridization of Bayesian and neural learning. *Neurocomputing*, *48*(1), 443–453. doi:10.1016/S0925-2312(01)00608-7

Abdelbar, A. M., & Tagliarini, G. (1996). HONEST: A new high order feedforward neural network, *Proceedings of the IEEE International Conference on Neural Networks* (Vol. 2, pp. 1257-1262). doi:10.1109/ICNN.1996.549078

Asuncion, A., & Newman, D. (2007). University of California at Irvine Machine Learning Repository. Retrieved from http://www.ics.uci.edu/~mlearn/MLRepository.html, 2007.

Dorigo, M., & Stützle, T. (2004). *Ant Colony Optimization*. Cambridge, MA, USA: MIT Press. doi:10.1007/b99492

El-Nabarawy, I., & Abdelbar, A. M. (2014). Advanced learning methods and exponent regularization applied to a high order neural network. *Neural Computing & Applications*, *25*(3), 897–910. doi:10.1007/s00521-014-1563-7

El-Nabarawy, I., Abdelbar, A. M., & Wunsch, D. (2013). Levenberg-Marquardt and conjugate gradient methods applied to a high order neural network. *Proceedings IEEE International Joint Conference on Neural Networks* (pp. 2162-2132). doi:10.1109/IJCNN.2013.6707004

Ivakhnenko, A. (1971). Polynomial theory of complex systems. *IEEE Transactions on Systems, Man, and Cybernetics*, *SMC-1*(4), 364–378. doi:10.1109/TSMC.1971.4308320

Liao, T., Socha, K., Montes de Oca, M., Stützle, T., & Dorigo, M. (2014). Ant colony optimization for mixed-variable optimization problems. *IEEE Transactions on Evolutionary Computation*, *18*(4), 503–518. doi:10.1109/TEVC.2013.2281531

Narayan, S. (1993). ExpoNet: A generalization of the multi-layer perceptron model. *Proceedings World Congress on Neural Networks* (Vol. 3, pp. 494-497).

Puig, V., Witczak, M., Nejjari, F., Quevedo, J., & Korbicz, J. (2007). A GMDH neural network-based approach to passive robust fault detection using a constraint satisfaction backward test. *Engineering Applications of Artificial Intelligence*, *20*(7), 886–897. doi:10.1016/j.engappai.2006.12.005

Riedmiller, M., & Braun, H. (1993). A direct adaptive method for faster backpropagation learning: The RPROP algorithm. *Proceedings IEEE International Conference on Neural Networks* (pp. 586-591). doi:10.1109/ICNN.1993.298623

Rumelhart, D. E., & Hinton, G. E.PDP Research Group. (1986). *Parallel Distributed Processing: Explorations in the Microstructure of Cognition*. Cambridge, MA, USA: MIT Press.

Socha, K., & Blum, C. (2007). An ant colony optimization algorithm for continuous optimization: Application to feed-forward neural network training. *Neural Computing & Applications*, *16*(3), 235–247. doi:10.1007/s00521-007-0084-z

Socha, K., & Dorigo, M. (2008). Ant colony optimization for continuous domains. *European Journal of Operational Research*, *185*(3), 1155–1173. doi:10.1016/j.ejor.2006.06.046

Tsai, H.-C. (2009). Hybrid high order neural networks. *Applied Soft Computing*, *9*(3), 874–881. doi:10.1016/j.asoc.2008.11.007

Tsai, H.-C. (2010). Predicting strengths of concrete-type specimens using hybrid multilayer perceptrons with center-unified particle swarm optimization. *Expert Systems with Applications*, *37*(2), 1104–1112. doi:10.1016/j.eswa.2009.06.093

Werbos, P. J. (1994). *The Roots of Backpropagation: From Ordered Derivatives to Neural Networks and Political Forecasting*. New York, NY: Wiley-Interscience.

Chapter 15
Utilizing Feature Selection on Higher Order Neural Networks

Zongyuan Zhao
University of Tasmania, Australia

Mir Md Jahangir Kabir
University of Tasmania, Australia

Shuxiang Xu
University of Tasmania, Australia

Yunling Liu
China Agricultural University, China

Byeong Ho Kang
University of Tasmania, Australia

Rainer Wasinger
University of Tasmania, Australia

ABSTRACT

Artificial Neural Network has shown its impressive ability on many real world problems such as pattern recognition, classification and function approximation. An extension of ANN, higher order neural network (HONN), improves ANN's computational and learning capabilities. However, the large number of higher order attributes leads to long learning time and complex network structure. Some irrelevant higher order attributes can also hinder the performance of HONN. In this chapter, feature selection algorithms will be used to simplify HONN architecture. Comparisons of fully connected HONN with feature selected HONN demonstrate that proper feature selection can be effective on decreasing number of inputs, reducing computational time, and improving prediction accuracy of HONN.

INTRODUCTION

Artificial Neural Network (ANN) is a massively parallel distributed processor made up of simple processing units, which has a natural propensity for storing experiential knowledge and making it available for use (Haykin, 1999). It was motivated by inspecting the human brain, which has high efficiency in computing and recognizing (West, 2000). ANN has been successfully applied to applications involving pattern classification and function approximation (Shin & Ghosh, 1991).

Although some training algorithms of ANN, such as back propagation (BP) have shown great performance, ANNs often take long time to converge and may stuck in local minima (Fulcher, Zhang, & Xu, 2006). Also, ANNs are not suitable for discontinuous data (Zhang, 2008). Moreover, the explanations

DOI: 10.4018/978-1-5225-0063-6.ch015

for ANNs' output is not obvious (Spirkovska & Reid, 1990). These shortages of ANNs are the motivations of the development of Higher Order Neural Network (HONN).

At first, HONN was designed to promote ANN's computational, storage and learning capabilities, as the order or structure of HONN can be tailored to the order or structure of a problem (Giles & Maxwell, 1987). They also prove that when a priori knowledge, such as geometric invariances, is encoded in HONN, the network becomes more efficient in solving problems that utilize this knowledge.

This character of HONN provides a solution for invariant pattern recognition problems (Redding, Kowalczyk, & Downs, 1993). As a preprocessing for BP ANN, HONN can be designed to be invariant to changes in scale, translation, and in-plane rotation (Schmidt & Davis, 1993). As invariances are built directly into the architecture of HONN and do not need to be learned, the training time can be shortened and a smaller training set is required (Spirkovska & Reid, 1993). Some researchers also provide pruning algorithms to decrease the complexity of HONN by reducing the number of network weights (Kosmatopoulos, Polycarpou, Christodoulou, & Ioannou, 1995; Li, Wang, Li, Zhang, & Jinyan, 1998).

Unfortunately, proper higher order attributes can only be chosen manually by expert knowledge. This can be achieved in visual object recognition, but not fit for other tasks such as function approximation and stock prediction, as the higher order features in these dataset are meaningless. Feature Selection methods for ANN provides a solution of this problem by reducing the number of attributes of HONN.

Feature Selection (FS), also known as attribute selection, or variable selection, is the process of selecting a subset of relevant features for use in computational model construction (Chakraborty & Pal, 2015). Actually, it can be treated as a searching procedure: search for an acceptable feature subset evaluated by certain criterion from the original dataset (Yukyee & Yeungsam, 2010). Benefits provided by FS include improved model interpretability, shorter training times, and enhanced generalization by reducing over-fitting (Luping, Lei, & Chunhua, 2010).

Feature Selection models can be divided into filters and wrappers according to whether it depends on data mining structure or purely by datasets. Filters focus on general characters of instances and take no consider about data mining algorithms (Huan & Lei, 2005). Filters choose only "good" features which are more representative or contain more information. It is commonly used as a pre-process of large scale data. Wrappers use predetermined data mining algorithm to evaluate the performance of each feature subsets. They are more time consuming than filters but also has greater influence on the data mining performance (Kohavi & John, 1997).

In this paper, we will present the utilization of FS filters on HONN by comparing the networks' performance. The second and third sections describe the background research of HONN and FS respectively. After that we will present our experiment and the end the conclusion and some future research will be discussed.

BACKGROUND OF HIGHER ORDER NEURAL NETWORK

Among ANNs, Multilayer Perceptron (MLP) has been shown to be capable of approximating generic classes of functions. The research in paper (Leshno, Lin, Pinkus, & Schocken, 1993) has proved that a three layer MLP with one hidden layer can perform well enough as a universal approximation. A typical three layer MLP can be described in Figure 1.

Figure 1. A typical three layer MLP structure

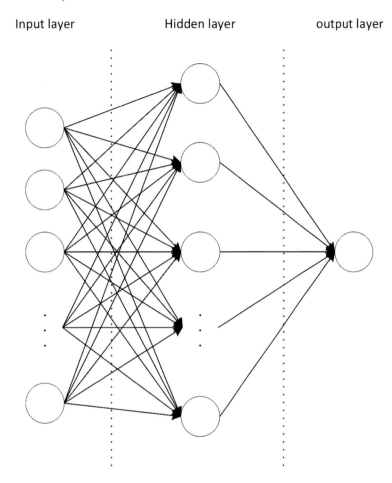

We use the following notations

$w_{i,j,k}$: The weight that connects the *j*th neuron in layer k-1 and the *i*th neuron in layer *k*.
f_i: The activation function of the *i*th neuron in the hidden layer.
X: The number of input neurons (equals to the number of attributes in dataset).
x_i: The *i*th input.
H: The number of hidden neurons

Usually there is no activation function for neurons in the input layer and the output neurons are summing units. Then the output of a three layer MLP is

$$y = \sum_{i=0}^{H} w_{0,i,3} f_i \left(\sum_{j=0}^{X} w_{i,j,2} x_j \right)$$

The HONN also uses three layer MLP structure, but is added into the higher order neurons and weights. The output of HONN can be represented by equation:

$$y = \sum_{i=0}^{H} w_{0,i,3} f_i \left(\sum_{j=0}^{X} w_{i,j,2} x_j + \sum_{j=0}^{X}\sum_{k=0}^{X} w_{i,j*k,2} x_j x_k + ... \right)$$

As we can see, the ordinary MLP can be regarded as a first order neural network. Usually, only second order neural network is used because the networks with more orders have too long training time but little improvement. The structure of a second order neural network is described in Figure 2.

Accordingly, the output of second order neural network can be calculated by:

$$y = \sum_{i=0}^{H} w_{0,i,3} f_i \left(\sum_{j=0}^{X} w_{i,j,2} x_j + \sum_{j=0}^{X}\sum_{k=0}^{X} w_{i,j*k,2} x_j x_k \right)$$

Other structures of ANN can also be used for HONN. For instance, a higher order Hopfield-type neural network was designed in (Xinzhi, Kok Lay, & Bingji, 2005). It solved the problems of global exponential stability and exponential convergence rate for impulsive higher order Hopfield-type neural networks with time-varying delays.

Figure 2. Structure of a second order neural network

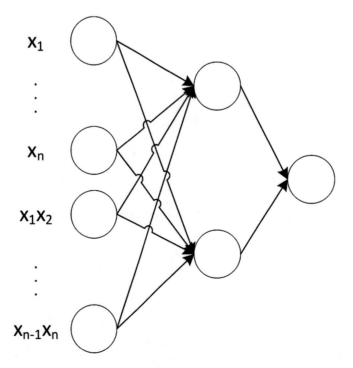

Recurrent HONN was designed and applied to the identification of dynamic systems in paper (Kosmatopoulos et al., 1995). The dynamic components were distributed throughout the network in the form of dynamic neurons. This recurrent HONN structure can approximate arbitrary dynamical systems.

HONN Learning Algorithm

As HONN has the same structure with MLP, the learning algorithm of MLP is available for HONN as well. Back Propagation has proved to be effective for MLP learning and is often used for HONN. However, as the number of weights in HONN is much larger than ordinary MLP, some learning algorithms that can promote learning speed of HONN are designed.

Ming Zhang (Ming, Shuxiang, & Fulcher, 2002) developed neuron-adaptive higher order neural-network (NAHONN) and an appropriate learning algorithm for it. The learning algorithm was based on the steepest descent gradient rule. As the variables in the hidden layer activation functions can be adjusted, NAHONN provides more flexibility and more accurate approximation than traditional HONN.

A HONN training method using differential evolution (DE) was designed in paper (Epitropakis, Plagianakos, & Vrahatis, 2006). DE, as an Evolutionary Algorithm, was proven to be an effective and efficient optimization method on numerous hard real-life problems.

To decrease the training time of HONN, some pruning algorithms were developed. In paper (Li et al., 1998), a pruning algorithm of eliminating the redundant connection weights is proposed. This algorithm can be applied to the implementation of sparselized HONN and other networks. Paper (Schmidt & Davis, 1993) explored alternatives that reduce the number of network weights while maintaining geometric invariant properties for recognizing patterns in real-time processing applications.

Applications of HONN

HONN for Pattern Recognition

An important function of HONN is achieving invariances for pattern recognition. HONN can handcraft the units such that their output is invariant under the action of an arbitrary finite group of transformations on the input space. As the invariances are built directly into the architecture of a HONN and do not need to be learned, objects with position, scale and rotation changes can be detected with higher accuracy than using the ordinary ANN. Most researches in this field focus on simplifying the structure and learning process of HONN for pattern recognition.

In paper (Giles & Maxwell, 1987) the implementation of invariances for HONN was proposed for both pattern recognition and associative memory applications. Authors of that paper proved that their implementation of translation invariance is equivalent to redefining the correlation matrices such that they depend only on relative position and not absolute position. Some other invariances can be implemented in the same manner.

Different strategies for nun-fully connected HONN were explored in paper (Spirkovska & Reid, 1990). As only a subset of input pixel triplets were connected to the output node, an input field of 128*128 pixels can be attained while still achieving in-plain rotation and translation invariant recognition. These techniques allow HONN to be used with the larger input scenes required for practical pattern recognition applications.

The input field size was increased to allow the larger input scenes for practical object recognition problems by coarse coding the input image (Spirkovska & Reid, 1993). Simulations show that HONN can be trained to distinguish between two objects in a 4096*4096 pixel input field independent of transformations in translation, in-plane rotation and scale less than ten passes through the training set.

HONN for Finance and Other Applications

Real world financial data often comprises high-frequency multi polynomial components, and is discontinues. Traditional ANN has shown good performance on finance data, but cannot handle with problems that involve higher order data.

A trigonometric polynomial higher order neural network (THONN) group model is developed for financial data prediction (Ming, Shuxiang, & Bo, 1999). Results show that THONN group models can handle nonlinear data that has discontinuous points. Neuron –adaptive higher order neural network is developed to address the problem of automatically determining the optimum model and appropriate order for financial data approximation (Ming et al., 2002). To make financial time series prediction, polynomial and trigonometric HONN (PTHONN) is developed in paper (Fulcher et al., 2006). All these researches demonstrate that HONN is able to better approximate real world economic data (Zhang, 2008).

As to other applications, in paper (Song, Saraf, & Gupta, 2013) HONN is used to forecast the oil production of a petroleum reservoir. In order to reduce noise in the measured data from the oil field a pre-processing procedure that consists of a low pass filter was used. Also an autocorrelation function and cross-correlation function was employed for selecting the optimal input variables. Test results from real world data showed that the HONN models have enhanced forecasting capability with higher accuracy in the prediction of oil production.

FEATURE SELECTION

The rationale with using a Feature Selection technique is that a lot of datasets contain many redundant or irrelevant features. Redundant features are those which provide no more information than the currently selected features, and irrelevant features provide no useful information for establishing models. Benefits provided by Feature Selection techniques include improved model interpretability, shorter training times, and enhanced generalization by reducing over-fitting (Luping et al., 2010; Mingkui, Tsang, & Li, 2013).

Traditional Feature Selection was achieved by experts in special fields who have empirical knowledge. As data accumulated in a speed unmatchable by human's capacity of data processing, automatic Feature Selection is essential to data mining since it can have great affection on reducing computation time and improving mining performance(Guyon & Elisseeff, 2003). Basically, Feature Selection methods can eliminate irrelevant features or find out important features, which decrease the amount of features in some extent.

Feature Selection is utilized in many data mining areas such as classification, clustering, association rules and regression. Applications include text categorization, image retrieval, financial prediction, genomic analysis and so on (Ting, D'Souza, Vijayakumar, & Schaal, 2010). Actually, it can be treated as a search procedure: search for an acceptable feature subset evaluated by certain criterion from the original dataset. Thus, utilizing an effective searching strategy is essential for Feature Selection methods.

In this section, some well-known Feature Selection algorithms will be introduced briefly.

Correlation based Feature Subset Selection (CFS)

CFS is an algorithm that evaluate subsets of attributes rather than individual attributes (Mark Andrew Hall & Holmes, 2003). It was first proposed by Mark Hall in his PhD thesis (Mark A. Hall, 1999). In his paper, an evaluation heuristic is designed to assign high scores to subsets containing attributes that are highly correlated with the class and have low inter correlation with each other. The heuristic he uses below takes into account the usefulness of individual features for predicting the class along with the level of inter correlation among them:

$$\text{Merit}_s = \frac{k\overline{r_{cf}}}{\sqrt{k + k(k-1)\overline{r_{ff}}}}$$

where Merits is the heuristic "merit" of a feature subset S containing k features, $\overline{r_{cf}}$ the average feature-class correlation, and $\overline{r_{ff}}$ the average feature inter correlation. The heuristic handles irrelevant features as they will be poor predictors of the class. Redundant attributes are discriminated against as they will be highly correlated with one or more of the other features (Mark Andrew Hall & Holmes, 2003).

Mutual Information based Feature Selection (MIFS)

Let X and Y be two discrete random variables. p(x, y) is the joint probability distribution function of X and Y, and p(x) and p(y) are the marginal probability distribution functions of X and Y respectively. The Mutual Information (MI) between X and Y can be defined as:

$$I(X;Y) = \sum_{y \in Y}\sum_{x \in X} p(x,y)\log\left(\frac{p(x,y)}{p(x)p(y)}\right)$$

The MI has two main properties that distinguish it from other dependency measures: first, the capacity of measuring any kind of relationship between variables; second, its invariance under space transformations (Bolón-Canedo, Porto-Díaz, Sánchez-Maroño, & Alonso-Betanzos, 2014).

Based on MI, a filter for Feature Selection was posed: Given an initial set F with n features, find subset S⊆F with k features that maximizes the MI I(C; S) between the class variable C, and the subset of selected feature S. The Mutual Information Feature Selection (MIFS) algorithm is as follows (Estevez, Tesmer, Perez, & Zurada, 2009):

- **Initialization:** Set F as the original feature set, and set S empty.
- **Computation of the MI with the output class:** For each $f_i \in F$ compute $I(C; f_i)$.
- **Selection of the first feature:** Find the feature f_i that maximizes $I(C; f_i)$; set F as F\{ f_i }; set S as { f_i }.
- **Greedy selection:** Repeat until ISI=k.

- **Computation of the MI between variables:** for all pairs (f_i, f_s) with $f_i \in F$ and $f_s \in S$, compute $I(f_i; f_s)$, if it is not yet available.
- **Selection of the next feature:** Choose the feature $f_i \in F$ that maximizes

- $$I(C; f_i) - \beta \sum_{f \in S} I(f_i; f_s)$$

- The parameter β is a user-defined parameter that regulates the relative importance of the redundancy between the candidate feature and the set of selected features. Then set F as F\{ f_i }; set S as { f_i }.

- Output the set S containing the selected features

ReliefF

Relief was first developed by Kira and Rendell in (Kira & Rendell, 1992), and improved by Kononenko in (Kononenko, 1994), extending it with multi-class datasets and noise datasets. The main procedure of ReliefF is randomly sampling an instance from the data and then locating its nearest neighbor from the same and opposite class (Mark Andrew Hall & Holmes, 2003). The weight of attribute is updated by each instances such that:

$$W_i = W_i - (x_i - nearHit_i)^2 + (x_i - nearMiss_i)^2$$

Thus the weight of any given feature decrease if it differs from that feature in nearby instances of the same class more than nearby instances of the other class, and increases in the reverse case. After m iterations, divide each element of the weight vector my m and it becomes the relevance vector. Features can be ranked by their relevance vector (Kira & Rendell, 1992).

The strengths of Relief are that it is not dependent on heuristics, requires only liner time in the number of given features and training instances, and is nose-tolerant and robust to feature interactions, as well as being applicable for binary or continuous data (Kononenko, 1994).

Consistency-Concentration Feature Selection (CCBFS)

Consistency-Concentration Based Feature Selection (CCBFS) is more suitable for datasets that contains both nominal and numeric features. The main idea of CCBFS is to calculate the Consistency Concentration Rate (CCR) for each attribute. CCR is proposed based on the hypothesis of CBFS, enhancing the consistency rate by improving the calculation of it. At the same time, CCBFS inducts the idea of concentration rate of data. For numeric attributes and nominal attributes with lots of values, if instances with similar condition values have the same class label, then the attribute will be considered more concentrative, because it has a tendency of concentration and therefore may be more relevant to the class attribute.

In general, the algorithm of CCBFS can be described as follows:

- For each attribute Ai
- If Ai is nominal
- Then turn nominal to numeric

- Rank all instances according to the value of Ai
- Find all Patterns in (Ai, D)
- Calculate the CCR of each attribute
- Rank all attributes with their CCR

EXPERIMENTS

To decrease the number of attributes in HONN, we utilize several well-known feature selection methods as a pre-processing step for HONN. In this section, a comparison of prediction ability between traditional ANN, full HONN and HONN with feature selection will be demonstrated. Real world dataset in different fields will be used to test the overwhelming effects of feature selection methods. All datasets are from UCI Machine Learning Dataset. Weka is used in these experiments. AUC (Area Under Curve) is used to evaluate the performance of networks, as it can reduce the effects of class imbalance problem. All networks are trained with 10-fold validation to avoid over training.

Calculation of Area Under Curve (AUC) in ROC Space

Receiver Operating Characteristic (ROC) is a graphical plot that demonstrates the performance of a classifier as its discrimination threshold is varied (Greiner, Pfeiffer, & Smith, 2000). ROC graphics are able to provide a richer measure of classification performance than scalar measures such as accuracy, error rate or error cost (Fawcett, 2006). Define an experiment from P positive instances and N negative instances for some condition. The four outcomes can be formulated in a 2*2 contingency table or confusion matrix, as in Table 1

A receiver operating characteristic (ROC) space is defined by false positive rate (FPR) and true positive rate (TPR) as x and y axes respectively. Each prediction result or instance of a confusion matrix represents one point in the ROC space. The best possible prediction method would yield a point in the

Table 1. Four outcomes of an experiment

		Condition		
		Positive	Negative	
Test outcome	Positive	**True positive**	False positive (**Type 1 error**)	Precision= $\dfrac{\sum Ture\,positve}{\sum Test\,outcome\,positive}$
	Negative	**False negative** (**Type 2 error**)	**True negative**	Negative predictive value= $\dfrac{\sum True\,negative}{\sum Test\,outcome\,negative}$
		Sensitivity= $\dfrac{\sum True\,positive}{\sum Condition\,positive}$	Specificity= $\dfrac{\sum Ture\,negative}{\sum Condition\,negative}$	Accuracy

upper left corner or coordinate (0,1) of the ROC space, representing 100% sensitivity (no false negatives) and 100% specificity (no false positives).

Classifications are often based on a continuous random variable, or a Threshold T. Then the probability for belonging in the class as a function of a decision/threshold parameter T as $P_1(T)$ and the probability of not belonging to the class as $P_0(T)$. The false positive rate FPR is given by $FPR(T) = \int_T^\infty P_0(T)dT$ and the true positive rate is $TPR(T) = \int_T^\infty P_1(T)dT$. The ROC curve plots parametrically TPR(T) versus FPR(T) with T as the varying parameter.

The area under the curve (AUC) of ROC is equal to the probability that a classifier will rank a randomly chosen positive instance higher than a randomly chosen negative one (assuming 'positive' ranks higher than 'negative') (Fawcett, 2006). The value of AUC can be calculated by

$$AUC = \int_\infty^{-\infty} y(T)x'(T)dT = \int_\infty^{-\infty} TPR(T)FPR'(T)dT = \int_\infty^{-\infty} TPR(T)P_0(T)dT$$

An effective way of calculating AUC is given by (Fawcett, 2006). Any instance that is classified positive with respect to a given threshold will be classified positive for all lower thresholds as well. In this way an ROC graph can be created from a linear scan. Some researches calculate AUC by the related Mann-Whitney U test, which tests whether positives are ranked higher than negatives.

Haberman's Survival Data Set

The dataset contains cases from a study that was conducted between 1958 and 1970 at the University of Chicago's Billings Hospital on the survival of patients who had undergone surgery for breast cancer. It has 3 attributes and 306 instances. First, the higher order attributes are created and their values of all instances are calculated. Then we apply feature selection on the extended dataset, together with the original first order dataset. Test results are listed in Table 2.

For this dataset, HONN improves prediction accuracy by 4 percent, which indicates that there are some second order contents in the dataset. All feature selection methods decrease the number of attributes, but only ReliefF and CCBFS can maintain or improve the network performance.

Table 2. Test results of Haberman's Survival dataset

	Attributes	Number of Attributes	Average Training Time	AUC
ANN	1,2,3	3	2.4	66.5%
HONN	1,2,3,4,5,6	6	5.9	70.2%
CFS	4,5,6	3	2.5	69.2%
ReliefF	1,2,6	3	2.3	70.2%
MIFS	4,5,6	3	2.5	69.2%
CCBFS	**3,5,6**	**3**	**2.7**	**70.5%**

However, this dataset only contains 3 attributes. The effect of feature selection is not so obvious.

Liver Disorders Dataset

This dataset is made of 345 instances, with 6 attributes and 1 class attribute which shows recurrence or no-recurrence of the disease. The experiment is similar with the above dataset. Test results is in Table 3.

This dataset gets a similar result as the last one. HONN, again, surpasses ANN regarding to the prediction accuracy. One feature selection algorithm decreased the number of inputs while keeps the same AUC of network. One interesting fact of this experiment is the selected features are all second order ones. This also explains why HONN performs better than ANN.

German Credit Dataset

The German dataset is a real world dataset with 21 features including 20 attributes recording personal information and financial history of applicants. The last feature is labelled as approved (marked as 1) or rejected (marked as 2). This dataset contains 1000 instances, with 700 approved application cases and 300 rejected ones. These instances are presented randomly.

As HONN is not fit for nominal datasets, nominal attributes in this dataset are not transferred into the second order. Thus, HONN of this dataset contents 26 attributes. Test results are shown in Table 4.

Table 3. Test results of Liver Disorders dataset

	Attributes	Number of Attributes	Average Training Time	AUC
ANN	1-6	6	5.9	74.3%
HONN	1-21	21	8.1	76.2%
CFS	1,2,4,7,9,10	6	4.8	63.2%
ReliefF	6,11,14,15,18,20	6	5.2	68.7%
MIFS	7,8,10,12,14,17	6	5.6	72.2%
CCBFS	**7,8,9,10,12,13,14,17,19**	**9**	**6.4**	**76.2%**

Table 4. Test results of German Credit dataset

	Attributes	Number of Attributes	Average Training Time	AUC
ANN	1-20	20	7.9	73.4%
HONN	1-26	26	8.4	74.4%
CFS	22,24,26	3	2.5	62.8%
ReliefF	1,2,3,6,7,9,11,21	8	6.3	73.8%
MIFS	1,2,5,21-26	9	6.5	73.4%
CCBFS	**1,2,3,5,6,22,24,26**	**8**	**6.7**	**75.5%**

The improvement made by HONN is not as obvious as that in the first two datasets. That's because there are some irrelevant features distract the network. Thus, feature selection performs better, with a big improvement for HONN.

Australian Credit Dataset

The Australian Credit dataset contains 14 attributes, in which 8 of them are numeric. So the HONN model has 42 inputs for the similar reason as German Credit dataset. Test results are shown in Table 5.

In this test, HONN improves ANN by 0.6% but with much more attributes. One feature selection method (ReliefF) decreases the attribute number while at the same time keeps the networks performance. The number of selected features is even smaller than the original dataset, and contains many second order attributes.

Blood Transfusion Service Center Data Set

This dataset contains 4 numeric attributes. So the HONN model has 10 inputs. Test results are shown in Table 6.

In this test, HONN improves ANN by 0.6% but with much more attributes. CCBFS can enhance AUC to 74.7% with 4 features. With fewer features than HONN, CCBFS has shorter training time.

Table 5. Test results of Australian Credit dataset

	Attributes	Number of Attributes	Average Training Time	AUC
ANN	1-14	14	7.4	92%
HONN	1-42	42	14.6	92.6%
CFS	8,19	2	1.6	90.4%
ReliefF	**5-10,12,28,32-34,36**	**12**	**6.9**	**92.6%**
MIFS	2,15,16,20,21,26,27,32,36,38	10	6.2	81.4%
CCBFS	4,8,9,10,19-21,25,30,32,34,37,41	13	7.6	92.3%

Table 6. Test results of Blood Transfusion Service Center dataset

	Attributes	Number of Attributes	Average Training Time	AUC
ANN	1-4	4	2.4	72.4%
HONN	1-10	10	5.2	73%
CFS	1,2,9	3	3.2	74.3%
ReliefF	2,3,8,9,10	5	3.8	67.9%
MIFS	1,5,6,7,9,10	6	3.4	70.9%
CCBFS	**1,2,3,9**	**4**	**3.8**	**74.7%**

FUTURE RESEARCH DIRECTIONS

The experiments demonstrate that proper feature selection methods can enhance the performance of HONN by eliminating irrelevant features. But it is still not clear which feature selection method should be used. The choice of feature selection methods should be based on the characters of dataset, such as the number of attributes, if the attributes are nominal or numeric.

This chapter only focuses on the second order neural network. Feature selection utilized on networks higher than two orders should be researched in the future.

As the second order of nominal attributes have no clear meaning, this research just ignored those features. Information contained in these features may have high value and should be researched.

CONCLUSION

In this chapter, the backgrounds of HONN and feature selection are researched. As an improvement of ANN, HONN can be applied on many fields and researches show that it is more effective. Applications such as pattern recognition and financial prediction benefit from HONN as it can reveal and learn important information in dataset. Its disadvantages, complex structure and irrelevant second order attributes, can be partly solved by feature selection. As a pre-processing step of HONN, proper feature selection methods can remove irrelevant features and simplify network structure.

Five dataset are used in experiments and made comparison. Three of them are for medical diagnose and the other two are for credit rating. HONN improved the prediction accuracy for all these dataset. That indicates these dataset has second order maps to the class label, or some second order attributes are more relevant to the decision class.

Four feature selection methods are used for HONNs and the prediction accuracies are compared. 3 of the 5 datasets have improvements when using feature selection methods. As to the other two datasets, feature selection achieves equal AUC with pure HONN, but with fewer features. That means the feature selection methods can simplify HONN structure and remove irrelevant features without affecting the prediction ability of the network.

In conclusion, the experiments prove that HONN can improve the prediction ability comparing with ANN for some kinds of datasets. By proper choosing feature selection methods, accuracy of HONN can be again improved by removing irrelevant features and simplifying network structure.

ACKNOWLEDGMENT

Supported by the Fundamental Research Funds Project (arranged by college): Automatic Detecting and Controlling Technology in Agricultural Manufacturing Process. Project number: 2015XD004

REFERENCES

Bolón-Canedo, V., Porto-Díaz, I., Sánchez-Maroño, N., & Alonso-Betanzos, A. (2014). A framework for cost-based feature selection. *Pattern Recognition*, *47*(7), 2481–2489. doi:10.1016/j.patcog.2014.01.008

Chakraborty, R., & Pal, N. R. (2015). Feature selection using a neural framework with controlled redundancy. *IEEE Transactions on* Neural Networks and Learning Systems, *26*(1), 35–50.

Epitropakis, M. G., Plagianakos, V. P., & Vrahatis, M. N. (2006). Higher-order neural networks training using differential evolution. *Paper presented at theInternational Conference of Numerical Analysis and Applied Mathematics*, Crete, Greece. Wiley-VCH.

Estevez, P. A., Tesmer, M., Perez, C. A., & Zurada, J. M. (2009). Normalized Mutual Information Feature Selection. *IEEE Transactions on* Neural Networks, *20*(2), 189–201. doi:10.1109/TNN.2008.2005601

Fawcett, T. (2006). An introduction to ROC analysis. *Pattern Recognition Letters*, *27*(8), 861–874. doi:10.1016/j.patrec.2005.10.010

Fulcher, J., Zhang, M., & Xu, S. (2006). Application of higher-order neural networks to financial time-series prediction. In *Artificial neural networks in finance and manufacturing* (pp. 80-108).

Giles, C. L., & Maxwell, T. (1987). Learning, invariance, and generalization in high-order neural networks. *Applied Optics*, *26*(23), 4972–4978. doi:10.1364/AO.26.004972 PMID:20523475

Greiner, M., Pfeiffer, D., & Smith, R. D. (2000). Principles and practical application of the receiver-operating characteristic analysis for diagnostic tests. *Preventive Veterinary Medicine*, *45*(1–2), 23–41. doi:10.1016/S0167-5877(00)00115-X PMID:10802332

Guyon, I., & Elisseeff, A. (2003). An Introduction to Variable and Feature Selection. *Journal of Machine Learning Research*, *3*(7/8), 1157–1182.

Hall, M. A. (1999). *Correlation-based feature selection for machine learning*. The University of Waikato.

Hall, M. A., & Holmes, G. (2003). Benchmarking attribute selection techniques for discrete class data mining. *IEEE Transactions on* Knowledge and Data Engineering, *15*(6), 1437–1447.

Haykin, S. S. (1999). *Neural networks: a comprehensive foundation / Simon Haykin* (2nd ed.). Upper Saddle River, N.J.: Prentice Hall, c.

Huan, L., & Lei, Y. (2005). Toward integrating feature selection algorithms for classification and clustering. *IEEE Transactions on* Knowledge and Data Engineering, *17*(4), 491–502. doi:10.1109/TKDE.2005.66

Kira, K., & Rendell, L. A. (1992). A practical approach to feature selection. *Paper presented at theninth international workshop on Machine learning*.

Kohavi, R., & John, G. H. (1997). Wrappers for feature subset selection. *Artificial Intelligence*, *97*(1–2), 273–324. doi:10.1016/S0004-3702(97)00043-X

Kononenko, I. (1994). Estimating attributes: Analysis and extensions of RELIEF. In F. Bergadano & L. De Raedt (Eds.), *Machine Learning: ECML-94* (Vol. 784, pp. 171–182). Springer Berlin Heidelberg. doi:10.1007/3-540-57868-4_57

Kosmatopoulos, E. B., Polycarpou, M. M., Christodoulou, M. A., & Ioannou, P. A. (1995). High-order neural network structures for identification of dynamical systems. *IEEE Transactions on* Neural Networks, *6*(2), 422–431. doi:10.1109/72.363477

Leshno, M., Lin, V. Y., Pinkus, A., & Schocken, S. (1993). Multilayer feedforward networks with a nonpolynomial activation function can approximate any function. *Neural Networks, 6*(6), 861–867. doi:10.1016/S0893-6080(05)80131-5

Li, W., Wang, Y., Li, W., Zhang, J., & Jinyan, L. (1998, May 4-8). Sparselized higher-order neural network and its pruning algorithm. *Paper presented at the 1998 IEEE World Congress on Computational Intelligence on Neural Networks.*

Luping, Z., Lei, W., & Chunhua, S. (2010). Feature Selection with Redundancy-Constrained Class Separability. *IEEE Transactions on* Neural Networks, *21*(5), 853–858. doi:10.1109/TNN.2010.2044189

Ming, Z., Shuxiang, X., & Bo, L. (1999). Neuron-adaptive higher order neural network group models. *Paper presented at the International Joint Conference on Neural Networks IJCNN '99.*

Ming, Z., Shuxiang, X., & Fulcher, J. (2002). Neuron-adaptive higher order neural-network models for automated financial data modeling. *IEEE Transactions on* Neural Networks, *13*(1), 188–204. doi:10.1109/72.977302

Mingkui, T., Tsang, I. W., & Li, W. (2013). Minimax Sparse Logistic Regression for Very High-Dimensional Feature Selection. *IEEE Transactions on* Neural Networks and Learning Systems., *24*(10), 1609–1622. doi:10.1109/tnnls.2013.2263427

Redding, N. J., Kowalczyk, A., & Downs, T. (1993). Constructive higher-order network that is polynomial time. *Neural Networks, 6*(7), 997–1010. doi:10.1016/S0893-6080(09)80009-9

Schmidt, W. A. C., & Davis, J. P. (1993). Pattern recognition properties of various feature spaces for higher order neural networks. *Pattern Analysis and Machine Intelligence. IEEE Transactions on, 15*(8), 795–801. doi:10.1109/34.236250

Shin, Y., & Ghosh, J. (1991, July 8-14). The pi-sigma network: an efficient higher-order neural network for pattern classification and function approximation. *Paper presented at the Seattle International Joint Conference on Neural Networks IJCNN '91.*

Song, K.-Y., Saraf, D. N., & Gupta, M. M. (2013). Production forecasting of petroleum reservoir applying higher-order neural networks (HONN) with limited reservoir data. *Neural Networks, 72*(2).

Spirkovska, L., & Reid, M. B. (1990, June 17-21). Connectivity strategies for higher-order neural networks applied to pattern recognition. *Paper presented at the International Joint Conference on Neural Networks IJCNN '90.*

Spirkovska, L., & Reid, M. B. (1993). Coarse-coded higher-order neural networks for PSRI object recognition. *IEEE Transactions on* Neural Networks, *4*(2), 276–283. doi:10.1109/72.207615 PMID:18267727

Ting, J. A., D'Souza, A., Vijayakumar, S., & Schaal, S. (2010). Efficient Learning and Feature Selection in High-Dimensional Regression. *Neural Computation, 22*(4), 831–886. doi:10.1162/neco.2009.02-08-702 PMID:20028222

West, D. (2000). Neural network credit scoring models. *Computers & Operations Research, 27*(11-12), 1131–1152. doi:10.1016/S0305-0548(99)00149-5

Xinzhi, L., Kok Lay, T., & Bingji, X. (2005). Exponential stability of impulsive high-order Hopfield-type neural networks with time-varying delays. *IEEE Transactions on* Neural Networks, *16*(6), 1329–1339. doi:10.1109/TNN.2005.857949 PMID:16342478

Yukyee, L., & Yeungsam, H. (2010). A Multiple-Filter-Multiple-Wrapper Approach to Gene Selection and Microarray Data Classification. *IEEE/ACM Transactions on Computational Biology and Bioinformatics*, *7*(1), 108–117. doi:10.1109/TCBB.2008.46 PMID:20150673

Zhang, M. (2008). *Artificial higher order neural networks for economics and business*. IGI Global.

KEY TERMS AND DEFINITIONS

Area Under the Curve: A metric for binary classification that replace accuracy. It is defined as the area under the receiver operating characteristic curve, which can partly avoid class imbalance problem.

Artificial Neural Network: A massively parallel distributed processor made up of simple processing units, which has a natural propensity for storing experiential knowledge and making it available for use.

Credit Rating: The set of decision models and their underlying techniques that help lenders judge whether an application of credit should be approved or rejected.

Feature Selection: The process of selecting a subset of relevant features for use in computational model construction.

Higher Order Neural Network: Network in which the net input to a computational neuron is a weighted sum of products of its inputs.

Machine Learning: Algorithms that can learn from and make predictions on data.

Medical Diagnosis: In machine learning, medical diagnosis is the process of identifying a disease by inputting symptoms into a pre learned computation model.

Chapter 16
Some Properties on the Capability of Associative Memory for Higher Order Neural Networks

Hiromi Miyajima
Kagoshima University, Japan

Noritaka Shigei
Kagoshima University, Japan

Shuji Yatsuki
Yatsuki Information System, Inc., Japan

Hirofumi Miyajima
Kagoshima University, Japan

ABSTRACT

Higher order neural networks (HONNs) have been proposed as new systems. In this paper, we show some theoretical results of associative capability of HONNs. As one of them, memory capacity of HONNs is much larger than one of the conventional neural networks. Further, we show some theoretical results on homogeneous higher order neural networks (HHONNs), in which each neuron has identical weights. HHONNs can realize shift-invariant associative memory, that is, HHONNs can associate not only a memorized pattern but also its shifted ones.

1. INTRODUCTION

Numerous advances have been made in developing some intelligent systems inspired by biological neural networks (Rumelhart, McClelland, & the PDP Research Group, 1986; Hertz, Krogh, & Palmer 1991; Kasabov, 1996; Mehrotra, Mohan, & Ranka, 1997; Gupta, Jin, & Homma, 2003). Scientific studies have been done with designing artificial neural networks to solve a variety of problems in pattern recognition, prediction, optimization, associative memory, and control (Hopfield, & Tnak, 1985; Reid, Spirkovska, & Ochoa, 1989; Meir, & Domany, 1987; Gupta, Jin, & Homma, 2003). Associative memory is one of the well-studied applications of neural networks. Numerous associative memory models processing static and sequential patterns have been studied such as auto, mutual and multidirectional associative memory (Amari, & Maginu, 1988; McEliece, Posner, Rodemich, & Venkatesh, 1987; Yanai, & Sawada,

DOI: 10.4018/978-1-5225-0063-6.ch016

1990; Amari, 1990; Okada, 1996; Oda, & Miyajima, 2001; Amit, Gutfreund, & Sompolinsky, 1985; Kohonen, 1972; Kosko, 1987; Yoshizawa, Morita, & Amari, 1993; Morita, 1996; Abbott, & Arian, 1987; Amari, & Yanai, H., 1993; Hattori, & Hagiwara, 1995). However, it is known that the capability of the conventional associative memory using neural networks is not so high. Therefore, many associative memory models are proposed such as HONNs, in which the potential of a neuron is represented as the weighted sum of products of input variables, and have been applied to associative memory. It has been shown that HONNs have higher associative capability than the conventional neural networks, in which the potential of a neuron is represented as the weighted sum of input variables (Chan, & Michael, 1988; Reid, Spirkovska, & Ochoa, 1989; Abbott, & Arian, 1987; Cheung, & Lee, 1993; Miyajima, Shigei, & Yatsuki, 2012). However, there are little theoretical studies for the reason why HONNs are effective and the capability of HONNs. Further, from the practical points of view, associative memory should be invariant to pattern transformation such as shift, scaling and rotation. However, the conventional neural networks, cannot inherently acquire any transformation invariant property. Therefore, the conventional neural networks require pre-processing of input patterns to support transformed patterns; a transformed pattern is converted into a standard one, and then the standard pattern is inputted to the network. In order that neural networks inherently acquire shift-invariant properties, their structure should be homogeneous like cellular automata (Wolfram, 1984). Then, how many patterns can HONNs memorize and how about HHONNs?

In this paper, the authors show the basic results about them. As for the conventional neural networks, theoretical results have been shown in (Amari, & Maginu, 1988; McEliece, Posner, Rodemich, & Venkatesh, 1987; and Yanai, & Sawada, 1990). The authors generalize their results and analyze memory capacity of HONNs. As one of them, memory capacity of HONNs is much larger than one of the conventional neural networks. Further, the authors show some theoretical results on homogeneous higher order neural networks (HHONNs), in which each neuron has identical weights. HHONNs can realize essentially shift-invariant associative memory, that is, without any pre-processing of input patterns HHONNs can associate not only a memorized pattern but also its shifted ones (Miyajima, Shigei, & Yatsuki, 2005). HHONNs need $k \geq 2$ for associative memory. The transition property of HHONNs is analyzed by the statistical method. The authors show the probability that each neuron outputs correctly, and the error-correcting capability. Lastly, the relation between this chapter and other studies and the future works are discussed.

2. HIGHER ORDER NEURONS

Let us explain the conventional neuron. Let $I_i=\{1, \ldots, i\}$ for a positive integer i. The output y for each neuron is given by

$$u = \sum_{j=0}^{n} w_j x_j \tag{1}$$

$$y = f(u), \tag{2}$$

where x_j is the j-th input, u is the internal potential of the neuron, $f(u)$ is the output function, w_j is the weight for the *j*-th input, w_0 is the threshold and $x_0=1$. (See Figure 1).

Figure 1. The conventional neuron

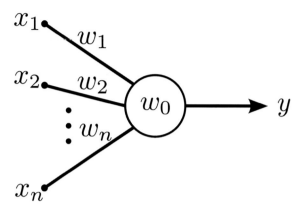

The internal potential for a higher order neuron is represented by

$$u = \sum_{j=0}^{n} w_j x_j + \sum_{j=1}^{n} \sum_{k=j+1}^{n} v_{jk} x_j x_k + \cdots, \tag{3}$$

where the second term of the right hand side is the weighted sums of products for combinations of two input, x_j and x_k, and v_{jk} is the weight for them. The *k*-th term is represented by

$$\sum_{L_k} v_{L_k} x_{l_1} x_{l_2} \cdots x_{l_k}, \tag{4}$$

$$\sum_{L_k} = \sum_{l_1=1}^{n} \sum_{l_2=l_1+1}^{n} \cdots \sum_{l_k=l_{k-1}+1}^{n} \tag{5}$$

where v_{L_k} is the weight for products of input to the neuron.

The Equation 3 is rewritten as follows:

$$u = \sum_{k'=1}^{k} \sum_{L_{k'}} v_{L_{k'}} x_{l_1'} x_{l_2'} \cdots x_{l_k'} + v_0 \tag{6}$$

where k is the order of the network. In this paper, the following element with the order k is used (See Figure 2).

$$u = \sum_{L_k} v_{L_k} x_{l_1} \cdots x_{l_k} + v_0 \tag{7}$$

$$y = f(u). \tag{8}$$

It is called the k-th order neural network whose components are composed of the k-th order neurons.

Figure 2. A higher order neuron

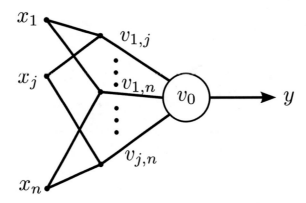

3. ASSOCIATIVE MEMORY FOR THE CONVENTIONAL NEURAL NETWORKS

In this section, let us explain associative memory the conventional neural networks and the capability of them.

3.1 Associative Memory for Neural Networks

Let $\{X^{(s)}, Y^{(s)}\}$ be P pairs of memory patterns for $s \in I_P$, where $X^{(s)}$ and $Y^{(s)}$ are m and n dimensional vectors, respectively, as follows:

$$\begin{cases} X^{(s)} &= \left(x_1^{(s)}, \cdots, x_m^{(s)}\right)^{\mathrm{T}} \\ Y^{(s)} &= \left(y_1^{(s)}, \cdots, y_n^{(s)}\right)^{\mathrm{T}} \end{cases} \tag{9}$$

where T represents the transposition of a vector and each element of $X^{(s)}$ and $Y^{(s)}$ takes 1 or -1.

Let us consider a two-layered network composed of the input and output layers as shown in Figure 3. All input elements are connected to only output layer, and there are no any mutual connections among neurons. In the case of correlation learning, the weight w_{ij} is determined as follows:

Figure 3. A two-layered neural network

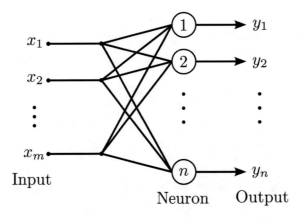

$$w_{ij} = \frac{1}{m} \sum_s y_i^{(s)} x_j^{(s)}. \tag{10}$$

Likewise, as for the HONNs, the weight $v_j^{(k)}$ is determined by

$$w_{i,L_k} = \frac{1}{\binom{m}{k}} \sum_s y_i^{(s)} x_{l_1}^{(s)} \cdots x_{l_k}^{(s)}, \tag{11}$$

where $\binom{m}{k}$ represents the number of the combination between m and k. The following function is used as output one:

$$f(u) = \mathrm{sgn}(u) = \begin{cases} 1 & u \geq 0 \\ -1 & u < 0. \end{cases} \tag{12}$$

In order to show the transition property of the network, three assumptions for the model are made as follows:

1. Each element of memory patterns, $x_j^{(s)}$ and $y_i^{(s)}$, takes the values 1 or -1 with the probability 1/2.
2. P and m are sufficiently large.
3. All states, $x_j^{(s)}$ and $y_i^{(s)}$, with different values of i and j are mutually independent.

In order to obtain the results on HONNs, the process of the results on the conventional neural networks is introduced based on Ref. [Uesaka, 1972] as follows.

3.2 The Capability of the Conventional Models

Let us consider mutual correlation learning for the conventional neural networks. The weights w_{ij} and the threshold w_{i0} for any i, j are defined as follows:

$$w_{ij} = \frac{1}{m} \sum_{s=1}^{P} y_i^{(s)} x_j^{(s)}, \tag{13}$$

where $w_{i0} = 0$.

If a pattern X is input, then each element of Y is computed as follows:

$$y_i = \mathrm{sgn}(u_j)$$
$$u_i = \sum_{j=1}^{m} w_{ij} x_j \tag{14}$$

If $X = X^{(r)}$, then the following relation is obtained:

$$
\begin{aligned}
u_i &= \sum_j w_{ij} x_j^{(r)} \\
&= \sum_{j=1}^{m} \frac{1}{m} \sum_{s=1}^{P} y_i^{(s)} x_j^{(s)} x_j^{(r)} \\
&= \frac{1}{m} \sum_{j=1}^{m} y_i^{(r)} x_j^{(r)} x_j^{(r)} + \frac{1}{m} \sum_{j=1}^{m} \sum_{s \neq r} y_j^{(s)} x_j^{(s)} x_j^{(r)} \\
&= y_i^{(r)} + \frac{1}{m} \sum_{j=1}^{m} \sum_{s \neq r} y_j^{(s)} x_j^{(s)} x_j^{(r)}
\end{aligned}
\tag{15}
$$

Let $v_j^{(s)} = \dfrac{y_i^{(s)} x_j^{(s)} x_j^{(r)}}{m}$ and $h_i = \displaystyle\sum_{j=1}^{m} \sum_{s \neq r} v_j^{(s)}$.

Then, we have

$$
u_i = y_i^{(r)} + h_i .
$$

Each term $v_j^{(s)}$ of h_i is independent to each other and h_i is the sum of $v_j^{(s)}$ with the same property. Let t and k be the numbers of $v_j^{(s)}$ with $1/m$ and $-1/m$, respectively. Let $h=(t-k)/m$. The probability(Pr) of h_i is computed as follows:

$$
\mathrm{Pr}\,ob(h_i = \frac{2t-(P-1)m}{m}) = (\frac{1}{2})^{(P-1)m} \; {}_{(P-1)m}C_t
\tag{16}
$$

From the assumptions of the model, P and m are sufficiently large, so h_i is approximated by the normal distribution with the average 0 and the variance P/m (See Appendix A-2.).

Let us show the probability $\mathrm{Pr}\left(y_i = y_i^{(r)}\right)$ that the output y_i of the i-th element for input $X^{(r)}$ equals to $y_i^{(r)}$ is computed as follows:

$$
\begin{aligned}
\mathrm{Pr}\left(y_i = y_i^{(r)}\right) &= \mathrm{Pr}\left(h > -1\right) \\
&= \frac{1}{\sqrt{2\pi}\sigma} \int_{-1}^{\infty} \exp\left(-\frac{s^2}{2\sigma^2}\right) ds \\
&= \frac{1}{\sqrt{2\pi}} \int_{-\sqrt{m/P}}^{\infty} \exp\left(-\frac{s^2}{2}\right) ds
\end{aligned}
\tag{17}
$$

Let $\Phi(u)$ be the error integral function defined by

$$
\Phi(u) = \frac{1}{\sqrt{2\pi}} \int_{-\infty}^{u} \exp\left(-\frac{s^2}{2}\right) ds.
\tag{18}
$$

The result for mutual correlation model is shown as follow [Uesaka, & Ozeki, 1972; Hertz, Krogh, & Palmer, 1991]:

$$\Pr\left(y_i = y_i^{(r)}\right) = \Phi\left(\sqrt{m/P}\right) \tag{19}$$

Generally speaking, the capacity of neural networks is proportional to the number of input dimension(corresponding to the number of neurons) and inversely proportional to the number of patterns.

Likewise, the result for auto correlation learning for networks ($Y^{(r)} = X^{(r)}$) is obtained as follows [Uesaka, & Ozeki, 1972; Hertz, Krogh, & Palmer, 1991]:

$$\Pr\left(y_i = x_i^{(r)}\right) = \Phi\left(\frac{1 + P/m}{\sqrt{P/m}}\right) \tag{20}$$

Figure 4 shows the results of the associative capability for mutual and auto correlation neural networks.

Further, the error correcting capability for the mutual correlation neural networks has been shown in the following. Let $X^{(r)'}$ be defined as an input pattern which d bits of $X^{(r)}$ are reversed. Then, $X^{(r)'}$ is input, the probability that the correct output is given is shown as follows [Uesaka, & Ozeki, 1972; Hertz, Krogh, & Palmer, 1991]:

$$\Pr\left(y_i = y_i^{(r)}\right) = \Phi\left(\frac{1 - 2d/m}{\sqrt{P/m}}\right) \tag{21}$$

Figure 4. The capabilities of auto and mutual correlation learning for the conventional neural networks

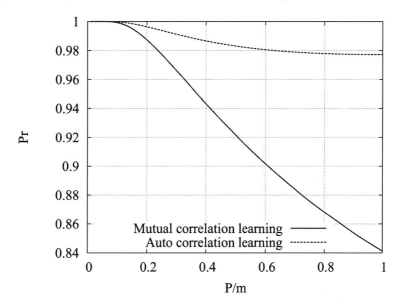

Likewise, the error correcting capability for auto correlation learning for neural networks has been shown as follows [Uesaka, & Ozeki, 1972; Hertz, Krogh, & Palmer, 1991]:

$$\Pr\left(y_i = y_i^{(r)}\right) = \frac{d}{m}A + \left(1 - \frac{d}{m}\right)B \tag{22}$$

where

$$\begin{cases} A = \Phi\left(\dfrac{1 - 2\dfrac{d}{m} - \dfrac{P}{m}}{\sqrt{P/m}}\right) & for\ i = 1, ---, d \\[3em] B = \Phi\left(\dfrac{1 - 2\dfrac{d}{m} + \dfrac{P}{m}}{\sqrt{P/m}}\right) & for\ i = d+1, ---, m \end{cases} \tag{23}$$

Equation 22 means the average probability for $i \in I_m$.

Figures 5 and 6 show the results of the error correcting capability for mutual and auto correlation learning for the conventional neural networks, respectively.

Figure 5. Error correcting capabilities of mutual correlation learning for the conventional neural networks

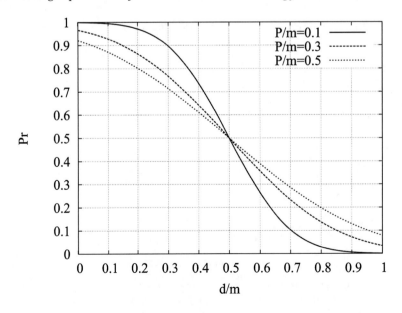

Figure 6. Error correcting capabilities of auto correlation learning for the conventional neural networks

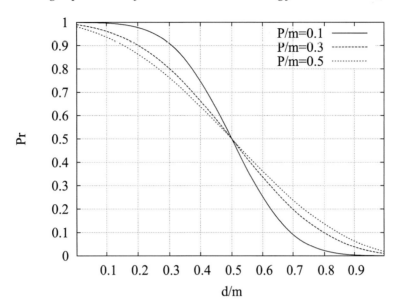

Example 1: Let us show an example of auto associative memory for $k=1$. Let $A =(-1,-1,1,-1,-1)^{T}$ and $B=(-1,1,1,-1,-1)^T$ be two patterns. Then the authors have the following weights based on Equation 10:

$$W = (w_{ij}) = \frac{1}{5}(A \bullet A^T + B \bullet B^T)$$

$$= \frac{1}{5}\begin{pmatrix} 1 & 0 & -1 & 1 & 1 \\ 0 & 1 & 0 & 0 & 0 \\ -1 & 0 & 1 & -1 & -1 \\ 1 & 0 & -1 & 1 & 1 \\ 1 & 0 & -1 & 1 & 1 \end{pmatrix}$$

Therefore, it holds for sgn(WA)=A and sgn(WB)=B. Further, let C=(-1, 1, 1, 1, -1)^{T} and D=(-1, -1, -1, -1, -1)^{T} that are similar to the patterns A and B, respectively. It holds for sgn(WC)=B and sgn(WD)=A.

4. ASSOCIATIVE CAPABILITIES FOR HONNs

In the previous section, the associative capability for the conventional neural networks has been shown. Then, how is the capability for HONNs. In the following section, the associative capability of correlation learning for HONNs has been shown using the same method as the case of $k=1$.

4.1 Mutual Associative Capability

The authors will evaluate the probability that each neuron outputs correctly, in other words, the output of the i-th neuron is $y_i^{(r)}$ for the r-th input pattern $X^{(r)}$. Then the potential u_i for an input pattern $X^{(r)}$ is given by

$$
u_i = \sum_{L_k} w_{i,L_k} x_{l_1}^{(r)} \cdots x_{l_k}^{(r)}
$$

$$
= y_i^{(r)} + \frac{\displaystyle\sum_{s \neq r} y_i^{(s)} \left(\sum_{L_k} x_{l_1}^{(s)} x_{l_1}^{(r)} \cdots x_{l_k}^{(s)} x_{l_k}^{(r)} \right)}{\displaystyle \binom{m}{k}}.
\tag{24}
$$

Let h_i and $h_1^{(s)}$ be defined as follows:

$$
h_1^{(s)} = \sum_{L_k} x_{l_1}^{(s)} x_{l_1}^{(r)} \cdots x_{l_k}^{(s)} x_{l_k}^{(r)},
\tag{25}
$$

$$
h_i = \frac{\displaystyle\sum_{s \neq r} y_i^{(s)} h_1^{(s)}}{\displaystyle\binom{m}{k}}.
\tag{26}
$$

The term h_i is called the interference term and it means the noise for $y_i^{(r)}$. Let us estimate the statistical property. Let the expectation of $h_1^{(s)}$ be denoted by $\mathrm{E}[h_1^{(s)}]$. Then, the authors have

$$
E[h_1^{(s)}] = E\left[\sum_{L_k} x_{l_1}^{(s)} x_{l_1}^{(r)} \cdots x_{l_k}^{(s)} x_{l_k}^{(r)} \right] = 0,
\tag{27}
$$

because of $s \neq r$, $l_1 \neq l_2 \neq - - - \neq l_k$, and three assumptions of the model. Let the variance of $h_1^{(s)}$ be denoted by $\mathrm{Var}[h_1^{(s)}]$. The authors have

$$
Var[h_1^{(s)}] = E\left[\left(\sum_{L_k} x_{l_1}^{(s)} x_{l_1}^{(r)} \cdots x_{l_k}^{(s)} x_{l_k}^{(r)} \right)^2 \right]
$$

$$
= \binom{m}{k} + \sum_{L_k} \sum_{L_k' \neq L_k} E\left[\left(x_{l_1}^{(s)} x_{l_1}^{(r)} \cdots x_{l_k}^{(r)} \right) \left(x_{l_1'}^{(s)} x_{l_1'}^{(r)} \cdots x_{l_k'}^{(r)} \right) \right]
\tag{28}
$$

$$
= \binom{m}{k}
$$

where $\displaystyle\sum_{L_k}\sum_{L'_k \neq L_k}$ means the sum for all combinations of $l_1, ---, l_k$ and $l'_1, ---, l'_k$ such that $l'_\alpha \neq l_\alpha$

for at least one α. In the Equation 26, $y_i^{(s)}$ is 1 or -1 independently of h_1. Hence, from the Central Limit

Theorem, $h_1^{(s)}$ is regarded as the normal distribution with mean 0 and variance $\dfrac{P-1}{\binom{m}{k}} \approx \dfrac{P}{\binom{m}{k}}$ (See Ap-

pendix A-2.). If $y_i^{(s)} = 1$, the output of the i-th neuron is correct for $u_i \geq 0$ and if $y_i^{(r)} = -1$, the output
is correct for $u_i < 0$. Therefore, the probability that each neuron outputs correctly, is given as follows
[Yatsuki, Miyajima, & Murashima, 1996, p.1933];

$$\Pr(y_i = y_i^{(r)}) = \Pr(h \leq 1) = \Pr(h > -1) = \Phi\left(\sqrt{\frac{\binom{m}{k}}{P}}\right). \tag{29}$$

If $k=1$, then the Equation 19 is obtained.

Generally speaking, the capacity of HONNs with the order k is proportional to the number m to the power of k and inversely proportional to the number of patterns.

Example 2: Let us consider two patterns A and B of the Example 1. The weights for the model for $k=2$ are defined based on Equation 11 as follows:

$$\text{w}_{1, l_1 l_2} = \frac{1}{10}(0,2,-2,-2,-1,0,0,2,2,-2)$$

$$\text{w}_{2, l_1 l_2} = \frac{1}{10}(-2,0,0,0,2,-2,-2,0,0,0)$$

$$\text{w}_{3, l_1 l_2} = \frac{1}{10}(0,-2,2,2,0,0,0,-2,-2,2)$$

$$\text{w}_{4, l_1 l_2} = \frac{1}{10}(0,2,-2,-2,-1,0,0,2,2,-2)$$

$$\text{w}_{5, l_1 l_2} = \frac{1}{10}(0,2,-2,-2,-1,0,0,2,2,-2)$$

Then, sgn(WA^*)=A and sgn(WB^*)=B hold, where

$A^* = (1,-1,1,1,-1,1,1,-1,-1,1)^{\mathrm{T}}$,
$B^* = (-1,-1,1,1,1,-1,-1,-1,-1,1)^{\mathrm{T}}$.

4.2 Auto Associative Ability for HONNs

Let us consider auto associative memory in the case where $Y^{(s)} = X^{(s)}$. Let us compute $\Pr(y_i = x_i^{(r)})$ assuming that $k \geq 2$. Then the weight w_{i,L_k} is determined by

$$w_{i,L_k} = \frac{1}{\binom{m}{k}} \sum_s x_i^{(s)} x_{l_1}^{(s)} \cdots x_{l_k}^{(s)}. \tag{30}$$

The potential u_i for input pattern $X^{(r)}$ is given by

$$
\begin{aligned}
u_i &= \sum_{[L_k]} w_{i,L_k} x_{l_1}^{(r)} \cdots x_{l_k}^{(r)} \\
&= x_i^{(r)} + \frac{x_i^{(r)}}{\binom{m}{k}} \sum_{s \neq r} \sum_{l_i \notin L_{k-1}} x_{l_1}^{(s)} x_{l_1}^{(r)} \cdots x_{l_{k-1}}^{(s)} x_{l_{k-1}}^{(r)} \\
&+ \frac{1}{\binom{m}{k}} \sum_{s \neq r} \sum_{l_i \notin L_{k-1}} x_i^{(s)} x_{l_1}^{(s)} x_{l_1}^{(r)} \cdots x_{l_k}^{(s)} x_{l_k}^{(r)}
\end{aligned} \tag{31}
$$

where

$$l_i \notin L_{k-1} \text{ means } L_{k-1} = l_1 - - - l_{i-1} l_{i+1} - - - l_{k-1}.$$

If $k = 1$, the second order term of the Equation 31 is not the interference term. Using the same method as 3.1, the authors can calculate the expectations and the variances of the second and third terms, and the second term and the third term are regarded as the normal distribution. Further, the authors can calculate the covariance of the second and third terms. By their results, the interference term is regarded as the normal distribution. Therefore, the authors can obtain the following result [Yatsuki, Miyajima, & Murashima, 1996];

$$\Pr(y_i = x_i^{(r)}) = \Phi\left(\sqrt{\frac{\binom{m}{k}}{P}} \right). \tag{32}$$

As a result, it is shown that the result of auto associative memory is the same as one of mutual associative memory.

Figure 7 shows the results of Equation 32. The result of the experiment accords with theory [Yatsuki, Miyajima, & Murashima, 1996].

Example 3: In the case of $m = 1000$ and $P = 100000$, the probabilities of the Equation (32) are shown in Table 1.

Figure 7. Associative capability by HONNs with the order k

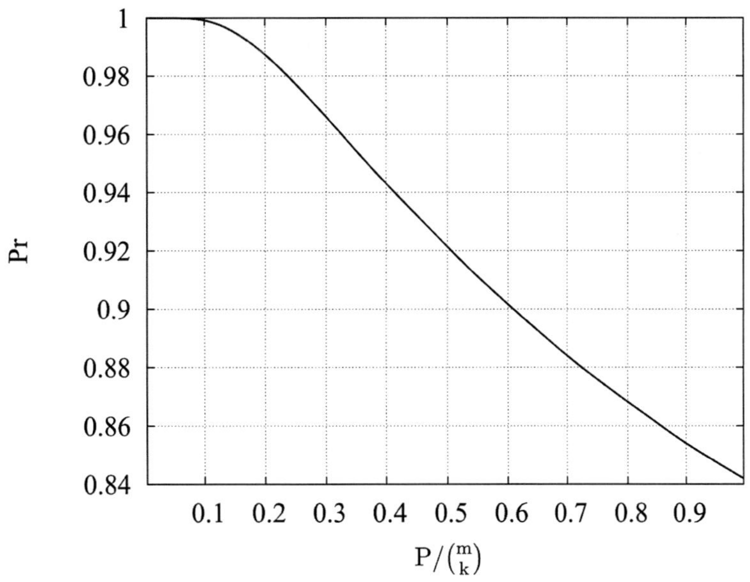

The numbers of memory patterns P satisfying $\Pr(y_i = y_i^{(r)}) > 0.99$ and $m = 1000$, are shown in Table 2.

As a result, it is shown that memory capacity of HONNs is greater than one of the conventional neural networks.

Table 1. Associative probabilities by HONNs with the order k for m = 1000 and P = 100000

k	1	2	3
$\dfrac{P}{\begin{pmatrix} m \\ k \end{pmatrix}}$	100	0.2002	0.0006
Prob	0.540	0.9872	1.000

Table 2. Capacity of associative memory by HONNs with the order k for Prob > 0.99 and m = 1000

k	1	2	3
P	180	89910	2991006

4.3 Error Correcting Capability

Let us show the error correcting ability of mutual associative memory. Let $\bar{X}^{(r)}$ be defined as an input pattern which d bits of $X^{(r)}$ are reversed. Without loss of generality, the authors assume that $\bar{x}_1^{(r)} = -x_1^{(r)}, ----, \bar{x}_d^{(r)} = -x_d^{(r)} \; \bar{x}_{d+1}^{(r)} = x_{d+1}^{(r)}, ----, \bar{x}_m^{(r)} = x_m^{(r)}$ and $k \leq d$. Then the potential u_i is given by

$$
u_i = \sum_{L_k} w_{i,L_k} \bar{x}_{l_1}^{(r)} \cdots \bar{x}_{l_k}^{(r)}
$$

$$
= y_i^{(r)} \cdot \frac{\displaystyle\sum_{L_k} (x_{l_1}^{(r)} \bar{x}_{l_1}^{(r)}) \cdots (x_{l_k}^{(r)} \bar{x}_{l_k}^{(r)})}{\binom{m}{k}}
$$

$$
+ \frac{1}{\binom{m}{k}} \sum_{L_k} \sum_{s \neq r} y_i^{(s)} x_{l_1}^{(s)} \bar{x}_{l_1}^{(r)} \cdots x_{l_k}^{(s)} \bar{x}_{l_k}^{(r)} \tag{33}
$$

$$
= y_i^{(r)} \cdot \frac{\displaystyle\sum_{a=0}^{k} (-1)^a \binom{d}{a}\binom{m-d}{k-a}}{\binom{m}{k}} + h
$$

The interference term h is regarded as the normal distribution with mean 0 and variance $\dfrac{P}{\binom{m}{k}}$ as shown already in 3.1. Therefore, the authors have the probability that each neuron outputs correctly for an input $\bar{X}^{(r)'}$ as follows [Yatsuki, Miyajima, & Murashima, 1996, p.1935]:

$$
\Pr(y_i = y_i^{(r)}) = \Phi\left(\frac{\displaystyle\sum_{a=0}^{k} (-1)^a \frac{\binom{d}{a}\binom{m-d}{k-a}}{\binom{m}{k}}}{\sqrt{\dfrac{P}{\binom{m}{k}}}} \right). \tag{34}
$$

Likewise, we can get the results for the case of $k > d$. The numerical examples of the Equation 34 are shown in Figures 8 and 9 for k=2 and 3, respectively. The horizontal axis is the rate of error-bits of an input pattern. For $\dfrac{P}{\binom{m}{k}} = 0.1, 0.2$ and 0.3, the probabilities are shown. Let $-X^{(s)}$ and $-Y^{(s)}$ be defined as patterns which reverse all bits of $X^{(s)}$ and $Y^{(s)}$, respectively. In the case where k is odd, $\{-X^{(s)}, -Y^{(s)}\}$ is also memorized. On the other hand, in the case where k is even, $\{-X^{(s)}, Y^{(s)}\}$ is also memorized.

Figure 8. Error-correcting capability by HONNs with k=2 and m=100

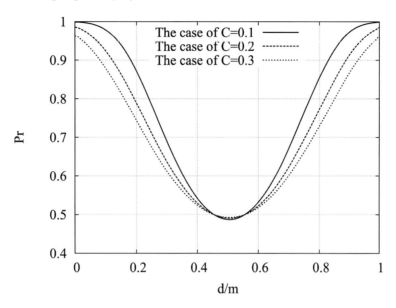

Figure 9. Error correcting capability by HONNs with k=3 and m=100

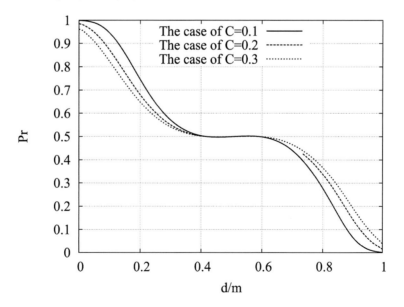

4.4 Associative Capability for Non-Orthogonal Memory Patterns

The authors have assumed that memory patterns are orthogonal approximately to each other in the previous section. Here, the authors will generalize Assumption 1 for the model in 3.1. As for mutual associative memory, the probability that each element of memory patterns, $y_i^{(s)}$ and $x_j^{(s)}$, is ± 1, is generalized as follows:

$$\Pr(x_j^{(s)} = -1) = p, \quad \Pr(x_j^{(s)} = 1) = 1 - p \,, \tag{35}$$

$$\Pr(y_i^{(s)} = -1) = q, \quad \Pr(y_i^{(s)} = 1) = 1 - q \tag{36}$$

Let c_1 and c_1 be defined as

$$c_1 = 1 - 2p, \quad c_2 = 1 - 2q \tag{37}$$

Assuming that $|c_1|$ and $|c_2|$ are not always near 1. The weight w_{i,L_k} is determined as

$$w_{i,L_k} = \sum_{s=1}^{P} (y_i^{(s)} - c_2)(x_{l_1}^{(s)} - c_1) - - - (x_{l_k}^{(s)} - c_1). \tag{38}$$

Then, the potential u_i for $X^{(r)}$ is given by

$$u_i = y_i^{(r)} - c_2 + \left\{ \sum_{s \neq r} \left(y_i^{(s)} - c_2 \right) \frac{\sum_{L_k} \left(x_{l_1}^{(s)} - c_1 \right) \cdots \left(x_{l_k}^{(s)} - c_1 \right) x_{l_1}^{(r)} \cdots x_{l_k}^{(r)}}{\sum_{L_k} \left(1 - x_{l_1}^{(r)} c_1 \right) \cdots \left(1 - x_{l_k}^{(r)} c \right)_1} \right\}$$

$$= y_i^{(r)} - c_2 + h \tag{39}$$

The authors can regard the interference term h as the normal distribution with the following mean and variance:

$$\mathrm{E}[h] = 0, \tag{40}$$

$$\mathrm{Var}[h] = \frac{(1 - c_2^2)P}{\sum_{t=0}^{k} \binom{k}{t} \binom{m-k}{t} (1 - c_1^2)^t}. \tag{41}$$

Therefore, the authors have [Yatsuki, Miyajima, & Murashima, 1996, p.1937]

$$\Pr(y_i = y_i^{(r)})$$
$$= \frac{1 + c_2}{2} \Phi\left(\frac{1 - c_2}{\sigma}\right) + \frac{1 - c_2}{2} \Phi\left(\frac{1 + c_2}{\sigma}\right), \tag{42}$$

because each probability of $y_i^{(r)} = \pm 1$ is $\dfrac{1 \pm c_2}{2}$, where $\sigma^2 = \mathrm{Var}[h]$. If $m >> k$, σ^2 can be approximated as

$$\sigma^2 \approx \frac{(1-c_2^{\,2})P}{\dbinom{m}{k}(1-c_1^{\,2})^k} \tag{43}$$

Figures 10 and 11 show the graphs of the Equation 42 for $c_2 = 0, 0.5$ and Figures 12 and 13 show the graphs of Equation 42 for $c_1 = 0, 0.5$, where $\dfrac{P}{\binom{m}{k}} = 1$. These results mean that if $\dfrac{P}{\binom{m}{k}}$ is constant, then HONNs receive greater influence for inputs patterns which are not orthogonal to each other. If P is the same for each k, then it is negligible.

5. HOMOGENEOUS NEURAL NETWORKS

When the shifted pattern $\mathrm{shift}(X^{(s)}, \alpha)$ of $X^{(s)}$ is input, in the correlation learning by Equation 11, the pattern $Y^{(s)}$ is not always recalled, where

$$shift\left(X^{(s)}, \alpha\right) =$$
$$\left(x_{\left((1+\alpha)\bmod(m+1)\right)^*}^{(s)}, - - -, x_{\left((m+\alpha)\bmod(m+1)\right)^*}^{(s)}\right)^T \text{ for } \alpha \in \{0, - - -, m-1\}$$

where $\left((i+\alpha)\bmod(m+1)\right)^*$ means that $i+\alpha \ge m+1$ then $\left((i+\alpha)\bmod(m+1)\right)+1$ and $i+\alpha < m+1$ then $\left((i+\alpha)\bmod(m+1)\right)$.

Figure 10. Associative abilities at $c_2=0$

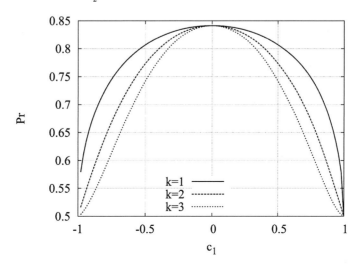

Figure 11. Associative capabilities for $c_2=0.5$

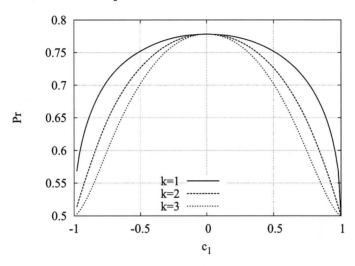

Figure 12. Associative capabilities for $c_1=0$

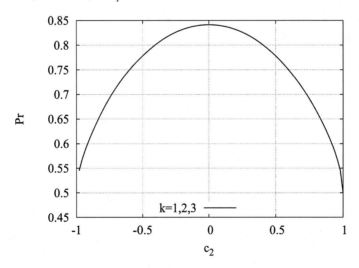

In order to recall the shifted patterns, the conventional correlation learning needs to explicitly memorize all the shifted patterns in neural networks.

Based on the Ref. [Miyajima, 2005], the authors explain correlation learning for HHONNs that when the memorized $X^{(s)}$ and its shifted pattern shift $(X^{(s)}, \alpha)$ are input, $Y^{(s)}$ is recalled (See Figure 14). In the proposed method, the weight w is defined as follows:

$$w_{L_k} = \frac{1}{\binom{m}{k}} \sum_{j=1}^{m} \sum_{s=1}^{P} y_j^{(s)} x_{j+l_1}^{(s)} \cdots x_{j+l_k}^{(s)}, \tag{44}$$

where $L_k = l_1 \cdots l_k$ and $l_i \in I_n$. Note that the suffixes $j+l_1, ---, j+l_k$ are cyclical.

Figure 13. Associative capabilities for c_1=0.5

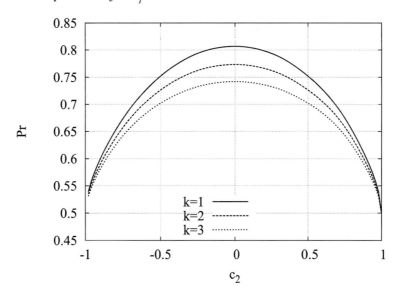

Figure 14. Shift invariant association

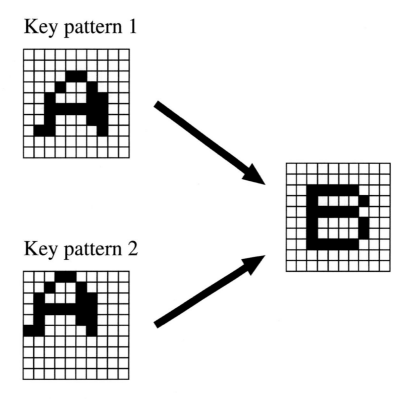

For the sake of briefness, the authors abbreviate the suffixes as in Equation 44. The neural networks with the weights defined by Equation 44 are called homogeneous higher order neural networks (HHONNs).

Example 4: For $k=1,2$, the following weights are obtained:

$$w_{L_1} = w_\alpha = \frac{1}{m}\sum_j\sum_s y_j^{(s)} x_{j+\alpha}^{(s)}$$

$$w_{L_2} = w_{\alpha,\beta} = \frac{1}{\binom{m}{2}}\sum_j\sum_s y_j^{(s)} x_{j+\alpha}^{(s)} x_{j+\beta}^{(s)} ,$$

where $\alpha, \beta \in I_m$ and $\alpha < \beta$. Let us consider the case of patterns A and B of Example 1.

$$w_\alpha = \frac{1}{5}\sum_{j=1}^5 \left(A_j A_{j+\alpha} + B_j B_{j+\alpha}\right), for\ \alpha = \{0,1,---,4\}\ \text{Then it holds as follows:}$$

$$w = \frac{1}{5}(10,2,-2,-2,2)\ and\ \text{sgn}(w\tilde{A})$$

$$= \frac{1}{5}(10,2,-2,-2,2)\begin{pmatrix}-1 & -1 & 1 & -1 & -1\\ -1 & 1 & -1 & -1 & -1\\ 1 & -1 & -1 & -1 & -1\\ -1 & -1 & -1 & -1 & 1\\ -1 & -1 & -1 & 1 & -1\end{pmatrix} = A \quad \text{where } \tilde{A} = \begin{pmatrix} shift(A,0)\\ \vdots \\ shift(A,4)\end{pmatrix}.$$

When the r-th pattern $X^{(r)}$ is input, the potential u_i of the i-th neuron is defined as follows:

$$u_i = \sum_{L_k}\left(\frac{1}{\binom{m}{k}}\sum_j\sum_s y_j^{(s)} x_{j+l_1}^{(s)} \cdots x_{j+l_k}^{(s)}\right)\cdot x_{i+l_1}^{(r)} \cdots x_{i+l_k}^{(r)} \tag{45}$$

$$y_i = f(u_i) \tag{46}$$

where $\sum_{L_k}$ is defined as $\sum_{l_1=1}^{m-k}\sum_{l_2=l_1+1}^{m-k+1}\cdots\sum_{l_k=l_{k-1}+1}^{m-1}$.

By considering the rough transition property of HOHNNs, let us show that HOHNNs can realize associative memory. If an input pattern $Y = (y_1,\cdots,y_m)^T$ similar to the memorized pattern $X^{(r)}$ is given, then the internal potential of $Y^{(r)} = (y_1^{(r)},\cdots,y_m^{(r)})^T$ is obtained as follows:

$$u_i = y_i^r + N_i,$$

where N_i is the crosstalk term for the pattern $Y^{(r)}$. If the absolute value of N_i is sufficiently small, then $y_i = y_i^{(r)}$ for $i \in I_m$. That is, the pattern is correctly recalled. Specifically, if sequential patterns are mutually orthogonal, perfect recalling is performed. Likewise, if an shifted pattern $\text{shift}(Y, \alpha)$ of Y is input, then a shifted pattern $\text{shift}(Y^{(r)}, \alpha)$ of $Y^{(r)}$ is output. It means that HHONNs can realize shift-invariant associative memory.

Let us consider the associative capability of HHONNs for mutual and auto associative memory. In particular, the authors examine the probability that each neuron outputs correctly, in other words, the output of the i-th neuron is $y_i^{(r)}$ for an input pattern $X^{(r)}$. In the following, without loss of generality, the author assume $r = 1$. Further, the authors show the error correcting ability of HHONNs. See Ref. [Miyajima, Shigei, & Yatsuki, 2005] about the detailed derivation.

5.1 Capability of Mutual Associative Memory

In this section, we consider mutual associative case $Y^{(s)} \neq X^{(s)}$. Let us evaluate $\Pr(y_i = y_i^{(1)})$ by using the same method as the section 4.1. The potential u_i for an input pattern $X^{(1)}$ is given by

$$
\begin{aligned}
u_i &= \sum_{L_k} w_{L_k} x_{i+l_1}^{(1)} \cdots x_{i+l_k}^{(1)} = y_i^{(1)} \\
&+ \frac{\displaystyle\sum_{j \neq i \, or \, s \neq 1} \sum_s y_i^{(s)} \left(\sum_{L_k} x_{j+l_1}^{(s)} x_{i+l_1}^{(1)} \cdots x_{j+l_k}^{(s)} x_{i+l_k}^{(1)} \right)}{\binom{m}{k}}.
\end{aligned}
\tag{47}
$$

When $y_i^{(1)} = 1$ and $y_i^{(1)} = -1$, the output of the i-th neuron are correct for $u_i \geq 0$ and $u_i < 0$, respectively. Therefore, the probability that each neuron outputs correctly, is given as follows [Miyajima, Shigei, & Yatsuki, 2005]

$$
\begin{aligned}
\Pr(y_i = y_i^{(1)}) &= \Pr(h \leq 1) = \Pr(h > -1) \\
&= \Phi\left(\sqrt{\frac{\left\lfloor \binom{m}{k} \right\rfloor}{mP}} \right).
\end{aligned}
\tag{48}
$$

By the Equation 48, the number of memory patterns is in proportion to the total number of weights. In the case of mutual associative memory, the results in numerical simulations are in fairly general agreement with the theoretical ones. If $k = 1$, then $\Pr(y_i = y_i^{(1)}) = \Phi(\sqrt{\frac{1}{P}})$. It means that it is impossible to perform associative memory by using HHONNs for $k = 1$.

5.2 Auto Associative Capability

In this section, the authors consider auto associative case $Y^{(s)} = X^{(s)}$. Let us evaluate $\Pr(y_i = x_i^{(1)})$. The weight w_{L_k} is determined by

$$w_{L_k} = \frac{1}{\binom{m}{k}} \sum_{j=1}^{m} \sum_{s=1}^{P} x_j^{(s)} x_{j+l_1}^{(s)} \cdots x_{j+k_k}^{(s)}. \tag{49}$$

The potential u_i for an input pattern $X^{(1)}$ is given by

$$
\begin{aligned}
u_i &= \sum_{L_k} w_{L_k} x_{i+l_1}^{(1)} \cdots x_{i+l_k}^{(1)} = x_i^{(1)} \\
&+ \frac{x_i^{(1)}}{\binom{m}{k}} \sum_{j \neq i} \sum_{L_k} x_j^{(1)} x_{j+l_1}^{(1)} \cdots x_{j+l_{k-1}}^{(1)} x_{i+l_1}^{(1)} \cdots x_{i+l_k}^{(1)}, \\
&+ \frac{1}{\binom{m}{k}} \sum_{s \neq 1} \sum_{j} \sum_{L_k} x_j^{(s)} x_{j+l_1}^{(s)} \cdots x_{j+l_k}^{(s)} x_{i+l_1}^{(1)} \cdots x_{i+l_k}^{(1)}
\end{aligned} \tag{50}
$$

Using the same method as section 4.2, the authors can calculate the expectations and the variances of the second and third terms, which are regarded as the normal distribution. Further, the authors can calculate the covariance of the second and third terms. By their results, the interference term is regarded as the normal distribution. Therefore, we have [Miyajima, Shigei, & Yatsuki, 2005]

$$\Pr(y_i = x_i^{(1)}) = \Phi\left(\sqrt{\frac{\binom{m}{k}}{mP}} \right). \tag{51}$$

As a result, it is shown that the result of auto associative memory is the same as one of mutual associative memory. Fig.15 shows theoretical results. The experimental results are in fairly general agreement with the theoretical ones.

5.3 Error Correcting Capability

Let us show the error correcting capability. Let $X^{(1)'}$ be defined as an input pattern which d bits of $X^{(1)}$ are reversed. Without loss of generality, the authors assume that $x_{i+l_t}^{(1)''} = -x_{i+l_t}^{(1)}$ for $l_t \in I_d$, $x_{i+l_t}^{(1)''} = x_{i+l_t}^{(1)}$ for $l_t > d$. Then, the authors have the probability that each neuron outputs correctly for an input $X^{(1)'}$ as follows [Miyajima, Shigei, & Yatsuki, 2005]:

Figure 15. The probability that each neuron outputs correctly

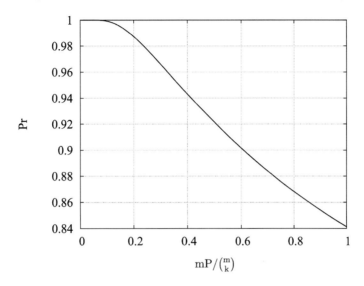

$$\Pr(y_i = y_i^{(1)}) = \Phi\left(\frac{\sum_{a=0}^{\min\{k,d\}} (-1)^a \binom{d}{a}\binom{m-d}{k-a} / \binom{m}{k}}{\sqrt{mP / \binom{m}{k}}}\right) \tag{52}$$

The Figure 16 and Figure 17 show theoretical results on the error correcting capability of HHONNs for $k=2$ and $k=3$, respectively. The simulation results are in fairly good agreement with the theoretical ones.

Figure 16. Simulation and theoretical results on the probability that each neuron outputs correctly for k=2

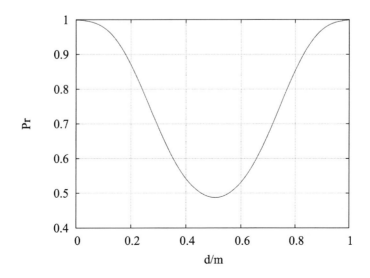

Figure 17. Simulation and theoretical results on the probability that each neuron outputs correctly for k=3

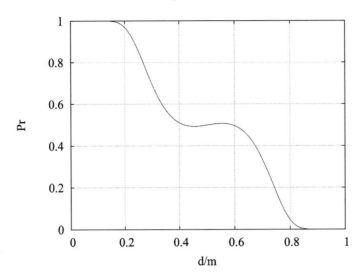

6. CONCLUDING REMARKS AND FUTURE TREND

In this paper, the authors have analyzed the basic capability of associative memory for HONNs and HHONNs. As a result, for HONNs, the authors have shown that the associative capability depends upon $\dfrac{P}{\binom{m}{k}}$, and the memory capacity is in proportion to $\binom{m}{k}$, where m is the dimension of input vectors, k is the order of connections and P is the number of memory patterns. For example, when the memory capacity of the conventional neural networks is P, the memory capacity of HONNs with $k=2$, is $P \times \dfrac{\binom{m}{2}}{m} \approx \dfrac{Pm}{2}$.

That is, the memory capacity is in proportion to $O(m^k)$.

Further, the authors have shown the associative capability of HHONNs. The main feature of HHONNs is that they can realize essentially shift-invariant associative memory. Under the condition of $k \geq 2$, HHONNs are possible to perform associative memory. The transition property of HHONNs has also been analyzed by the statistical method. The authors have evaluated, for two cases of auto and mutual associative memory, the probability that each neuron outputs correctly, and the error-correcting capability. As a result, the authors have shown that, for both cases, HHONNs have the same capability.

Table 3 shows the summarized results of associative capacity for HONNs. It shows how HONNs and HHONNs against neural networks has high capability of associative memory.

This paper deals with associative memory for static patterns of HONNs, thoretically. The authors also have discussed with associative memory for sequential patterns of HONNs [Hamakawa, Miyajima, Shigei, & Tsuruta, 2004; Miyajima, Shigei, & Hamakawa, 2004-I; Miyajima, Shigei, & Hamakawa, 2004-II; Miyajima, Shigei, & Hamakawa,2004-III; Miyajima, & Shigei, 2005-I; Miyajima, & Shigei, 2005-II; Miyajima, & Shigei, 2006]. Further, the studies on associative memory for Hopfield HONNs have been done[Yatsuki, Matsuoka, & Miyajima, 1999; Yatsuki, & Miyajima, 2000; Miyajima, Shigei, & Yatsuki, 2009]. In other words, the authors deal with the capability for associative memory for static and sequential patterns of Hopfield HONNs. In these studies, it is shown that HONNs are superior to

Table 3. The summarized results on the capability of associative memory for HONNs and HHONNs against NNs

		Associative Capability		Error-Correcting Capability	
		Mutual Model	Auto Model	Mutual Model	Auto Model
NNs	k=1	$\Phi\left(\sqrt{m/P}\right)$	$\Phi\left(\dfrac{1+P/m}{\sqrt{P/m}}\right)$	$\Phi\left(\dfrac{1-2d/m}{\sqrt{P/m}}\right)$	$\dfrac{d}{m}\Phi\left(\dfrac{1-2\frac{d}{m}-\frac{P}{m}}{\sqrt{P/m}}\right)+\left(1-\dfrac{d}{m}\right)\Phi\left(\dfrac{1-2\frac{d}{m}+\frac{P}{m}}{\sqrt{P/m}}\right)$
HONNs	$k\geq2$	$\Phi\left(\sqrt{\dfrac{\left\lfloor\frac{m}{k}\right\rfloor}{P}}\right)$		$\Phi\left(\dfrac{\sum\limits_{a=0}^{k}(-1)^a\dfrac{\binom{d}{a}\binom{m-d}{k-a}}{\binom{m}{k}}}{\sqrt{\dfrac{P}{\binom{m}{k}}}}\right)$	
HNNs	k=1	$\Phi\left(\dfrac{1}{\sqrt{P}}\right)$		$\Phi\left(\dfrac{m-2d}{m\sqrt{P}}\right)$	
HHONNs	$k\geq2$	$\Phi\left(\sqrt{\dfrac{\left\lfloor\frac{m}{k}\right\rfloor}{mP}}\right)$		$\Phi\left(\dfrac{\sum\limits_{a=0}^{\min\{k,d\}}(-1)^a\binom{d}{a}\binom{m-d}{k-a}/\binom{m}{k}}{\sqrt{mP/\binom{m}{k}}}\right)$	

the conventional neural networks. Furthermore, the studies of associative memory have been done with multi-dimensional HONNs [Miyajima, Shigei, & Kiriki, 2004].

The studies on associative memory using sparse models [Koulakov, & Rinberg, 2011; Palm, 2013] are future works for HONNs.

REFERENCES

Abbott, L. F., & Arian, Y. (1987). Storage capacity of generalized networks. *Physical Review A., 36*(10), 5091–5094. doi:10.1103/PhysRevA.36.5091 PMID:9898773

Amari, S. (1990). Mathematical foundations of neurocomputing. *Proceedings of the IEEE, 79*(9), 1443–1463. doi:10.1109/5.58324

Amari, S., & Maginu, K. (1988). Statistical neurodynamics of associative memory. *Neural Networks, 1*(1), 63–73. doi:10.1016/0893-6080(88)90022-6

Amari, S., & Yanai, H. (1993). Statistical neurodynamics of various types of associative memories. In M. H. Hassoun (Ed.), *Associative Neural Memories: Theory and Implementations*. Oxford University Press.

Amit, D., Gutfreund, H., & Sompolinsky, H. (1985). Storing infinite numbers of patterns in a spin-glass model of neural networks. *Physical Review Letters*, *55*(14), 1530–1533. doi:10.1103/PhysRevLett.55.1530 PMID:10031847

Chan, S. B., & Michael. (1988). Memory capacity of artificial neural networks with high order node connections. *Proc. of IEEE International Conference on Neural Networks* (pp. 207-216).

Cheung, K.-W., & Lee, T. (1993). On the convergence of neural network for higher order programming. *Proc. of International Joint Conference on Neural Networks* (Vol. 2, pp. 1507-1511).

Gupta, M. M., Jin, L., & Homma, N. (2003). *Static and Dynamic Neural Networks*. Los Alamitos: IEEE Press. doi:10.1002/0471427950

Hamakawa, Y., Miyajima, H., Shigei, N., & Tsuruta, T. (2004). On Some Properties of Higher Order Correlation Associative Memory of Sequential Patterns. *Journal of Signal Processing*, *8*(3), 225–234. doi:10.2299/jsp.8.225

Hattori, M., & Hagiwara, M. (1995). Quick learning for multidirectional associative memories. *Proceedings of the IEEE International Conference on Neural Networks* (pp. 1949-1954).

Hertz, J., Krogh, A., & Palmer, R. G. (1991). *Introduction to the Theory of Neural Computation*. Perseus Books.

Hopfield, J. J., & Tnak, D. W. (1985). Neural computation of decisions in optimization problems. *Biological Cybernetics*, *52*, 141–152. PMID:4027280

Kasabov, N. K. (1996). *Foundations of Neural Networks, Fuzzy Systems and Knowledge Engineering*. The MIT Press.

Kohonen, T. (1972). Correlation matrix memories. *IEEE Transactions on Computers*, *C-21*(4), 353–359. doi:10.1109/TC.1972.5008975

Kosko, B. (1987). Adaptive bidirectional associative memory. *Applied Optics*, *26*(23), 4947–4960. doi:10.1364/AO.26.004947 PMID:20523473

Koulakov, A. A., & Rinberg, D. (2011). Sparse incomplete representations: A potential role for olfactory granule cells. *Neuron*, *72*(1), 124–136. doi:10.1016/j.neuron.2011.07.031 PMID:21982374

McEliece, R. J., Posner, E. C., Rodemich, E. R., & Venkatesh, S. S. (1987). The capacity of the Hopfield associative memory. *IEEE Transactions on Information Theory*, *33*(4), 461–482. doi:10.1109/TIT.1987.1057328

Mehrotra, K., Mohan, C. K., & Ranka, S. (1997). *Elements of Artificial Neural Networks*. The MIT Press.

Meir, R., & Domany, E. (1987). Exact solution of a layered neural network memory. *Physical Review Letters*, *59*(3), 359–362. doi:10.1103/PhysRevLett.59.359 PMID:10035740

Miyajima, H., Shigei, H., & Hamakawa, Y. (2004-I). Higher order differential correlation associative memory of sequential patterns. *Proceedings of the International Joint Conference on Neural Networks* (Vol. 2, pp. 891-896).

Miyajima, H., & Shigei, N. (2005). -II) Absolute Capacities for Higher Order Associative Memory of Sequential Patterns. *Proceedings of KES '04, LNAI* (Vol. *3683*, pp. 547–553).

Miyajima, H., & Shigei, N. (2006). Associative ability of higher order correlation models for sequential patterns. *Journal of Knowledge-Based and Intelligent Engineering Systems, 10*(6), 403–416.

Miyajima, H., & Shigei, N. (2005). Robustness and Capacity of Higher Order Correlation Associative Memory for Sequential Patterns. *Proc. of the 12th ICONIP* (Vol. 1, pp. 388-393).

Miyajima, H., Shigei, N., & Hamakawa, Y. (2004). -II) Transition Properties of Higher Order Associative Memory of Sequential Patterns. *Proceedings of KES '04, LNAI* (Vol. *3215*, 855–861.

Miyajima, H., Shigei, N, Hamakawa, Y. (2004) Higher Order Differential Correlation Associative Memory of Sequential Patterns. Proceedings of IJCNN '04 (Vol. II, pp. 891-896).

Miyajima, H., Shigei, N., & Kiriki, N. (2004) Higher Order Multidirectional Associative Memory with Decreasing Energy Function. In Rajapakse, J.C., & Wang, L. (Eds.), Neural Information Processing: Research and Development (Vol. 152, pp. 128-149).

Miyajima, H., Shigei, N., & Yatsuki, S. (2005). Shift-Invariant Associative Memory Based on Homogeneous Neural Networks. *IEICE Trans. Fundamentals, E88-A*(10), 2600–2606. doi:10.1093/ietfec/e88-a.10.2600

Miyajima, H., Shigei, N., & Yatsuki, S. (2009). Higher Order Neurodynamics of Associative Memory for Sequential Patterns. *Proc. of Int. symposium on Neural Networks, LNCS* (Vol. 55552, pp. 886-891). doi:10.1007/978-3-642-01510-6_100

Miyajima, H., Shigei, N., & Yatsuki, S. (2012). *On Some Dynamical Properties of Randomly Connected Higher Order Neural Networks*. IGI.

Miyajima, H., Yatsuki, S., & Kubota, J. (1995). Dynamical properties of neural networks with product connections. *Proc. of IEEE International Conference on Neural Networks* (Vol. 6, pp. 3198-3203). doi:10.1109/ICNN.1995.487297

Morita, M. (1996). Memory and learning of sequential patterns by non-monotone neural networks. *Neural Networks, 9*(8), 1447–1489. doi:10.1016/S0893-6080(96)00021-4 PMID:12662546

Oda, M., & Miyajima, H. (2001). Autoassociative memory using refractory period of neurons and its on-line learning. *Proc. of IEEE International Conference on Electronics, Circuits and Systems* (Vol. 2, pp. 623-626). doi:10.1109/ICECS.2001.957553

Okada, M. (1996). Notions of associative memory and sparse coding. *Neural Networks, 9*(8), 1429–1458. doi:10.1016/S0893-6080(96)00044-5 PMID:12662544

Palm, G. (2013). Neural associative memories and sparse coding. *Neural Networks, 37*, 165–171. doi:10.1016/j.neunet.2012.08.013 PMID:23043727

Reid, M. B., Spirkovska, L., & Ochoa, L. (1989). Rapid training of higher-order neural networks for invariant pattern recognition. *Proc. of International Joint Conference on Neural Nets* (pp. 689-692).

Ross, S. M. (1970). *Applied Probability Models with Optimization Applications*. Dover Publications, INC.

Rumelhart, D. E., & McClelland, J. L.PDP Research Group. (1986). *Parallel Distributed Processing.* Cambridge: The MIT Press.

Uesaka, Y., & Ozeki, K. (1972). Two or three Properties of associative memory, IEICE Trans. Fundamentals of Electronics[in Japanese]. *Communications and Computer Sciences, D-II, 55-D*, 323–330.

Wolfram, S. (1984). Universality and complexity in cellular automata. *Physica D. Nonlinear Phenomena, 10*(1-2), 1–35. doi:10.1016/0167-2789(84)90245-8

Yanai, H., & Sawada, Y. (1990). On some properties of sequence-association type model neural networks (in Japanese). IEICE Trans. on Information & Systems II (Japanese Edition), J73-DII(8), 1192-1197.

Yatsuki, S., Matsuoka, N., & Miyajima, H. (1999). Dynamic Properties of Association Memory for Higher Order Neural Networks, IEICE Trans. Fundamentals of Electronics. *Communications and Computer Sciences, D-II, J82*(5), 919–929.

Yatsuki, S., & Miyajima, H. (1997). Associative ability of higher order neural networks.*Proc. of IEEE International Conference on Neural Networks* (Vol. 2, pp. 1299-1304).

Yatsuki, S., & Miyajima, H. (2000). Statistical dynamics of associative memory for higher order neural networks.*Proc. of IEEE International Symposium on Circuits and Systems* (Vol. 3, pp. 670-673). doi:10.1109/ISCAS.2000.856149

Yatsuki, S., Miyajima, H., & Murashima, S. (1996). Ability of associative memory by higher order neural networks. IEICE Trans. on Information & Systems II (Japanese Edition), J79-D-II(11), 1929-1939.

Yoshizawa, S., Morita, M., & Amari, S. (1993). Capacity of associative memory using a nonmonotonic neuron model. *Neural Networks, 6*(2), 167–176. doi:10.1016/0893-6080(93)90014-N

APPENDIX

In this appendix, a few basic theorems in probability theory (Ross, 1970) are introduced. These theorems are often used in this chapter.

Let X_i for $i \in I_n$ be random variables. Then, the following results hold:

$$\mathrm{E}\left(\sum_{i=1}^{n} X_i\right) = \sum_{i=1}^{n} \mathrm{E}\left(X_i\right),$$

where $E(X)$ means the mathematical expectation of X.

When random variables $X_1, X_2, ---, X_n$ are independent and n is sufficient large, the mean of these random variables is approximately normally distributed. This phenomenon is well known as the following theorem.

Central Limit Theorem

If $X_1, X_2, ---$ are independent and identically distributed with mean μ and variance σ^2 then

$$\lim_{n \to \infty} \mathrm{Pr}\left\{\frac{X_1 + \cdots + X_n - n\mu}{\sigma\sqrt{n}} \le a\right\}$$
$$= \int_{-\infty}^{a} \frac{1}{\sqrt{2\pi}} e^{\frac{-x^2}{2}} \, dx.$$

that is, the mean of a sufficiently large number of independent random variables will be approximately normally distributed.

Chapter 17

Discrete–Time Decentralized Inverse Optimal Higher Order Neural Network Control for a Multi–Agent Omnidirectional Mobile Robot

Michel Lopez-Franco
CINVESTAV, Unidad Guadalajara, Mexico

Alma Y. Alanis
CUCEI, Universidad de Guadalajara, Mexico

Edgar N. Sanchez
CINVESTAV, Unidad Guadalajara, Mexico

Carlos Lopez-Franco
CUCEI, Universidad de Guadalajara, Mexico

Nancy Arana-Daniel
CUCEI, Universidad de Guadalajara, Mexico

ABSTRACT

This chapter presents a new approach to multi- agent control of complex systems with unknown parameters and dynamic uncertainties. A key strategy is to use of neural inverse optimal control. This approach consists in synthesizing a suitable controller for each subsystem, which is approximated by an identifier based on a recurrent high order neural network (RHONN), trained with an extended Kalman filter (EKF) algorithm. On the basis of this neural model and the knowledge of a control Lyapunov function, then an inverse optimal controller is synthesized to avoid solving the Hamilton Jacobi Bellman (HJB) equation. We have adopted an omnidirectional mobile robot, KUKA youBot, as robotic platform for our experiments. Computer simulations are presented which confirm the effectiveness of the proposed tracking control law.

INTRODUCTION

The study of multi-agent systems has become an important aspect of systems architecture in order to deal successfully with the complexity and large-scale systems. Each agent system has special functions to solve the problems. In addition, in the multi-agent system the agents can work together to solve problems,

DOI: 10.4018/978-1-5225-0063-6.ch017

which are beyond the capabilities or knowledge of an individual agent. One of the main characteristics of multi-agent systems is that each agent takes decisions solely on the basis of its local perception of the environment. As a result, a challenging task is to synthesize a decentralized control approach for certain global goals in presence of limited information exchanges. On many occasions, agents need to reach certain quantities of interest. For example, flocks of birds tend to synchronize during migration in order to avoid predators and to reach their destination (Zeng-Guang et al., 2009).

Multi-agent system is basically defined as any system composed of more than two subsystems or agents. For these systems a local control station directly considers the state of its subsystem (agent), without considering the state of the other subsystems (agents). As an advantage of this technique, even though the whole system is large scale and complex, the subsystem (agent) controllers are simple (Kageyama & Ohnishi, 2002; Mahajan, 2011).

Many of today technological and social problems involve very complex and large-scale systems. For such systems, it is usually recommended to avoid centralized controllers due to the cost of implementation, complexity of on-line computations, complexity of controller design, and reliability. In such a situation, a multi-agent or partially decentralized feedback structure may be imposed (Iftar, 1991).

For real-world applications, uncertainties are due to the imprecise measurements, external disturbances, and interactions with the unknown environment. Hence, the questions arise naturally: How to design the tracking algorithm for multi-agent systems with uncertain dynamics (Gourdeau, 1997)?

Neural networks have grown to be a well-established methodology, which allows for solving very difficult problems in engineering, as exemplified by their applications to identification and control of general nonlinear and complex systems. In particular, the use of recurrent neural networks for modeling and learning has rapidly increased in recent years (Sanchez & Ricalde, 2003) and references there in).

There exist different training algorithms for neural networks, which normally encounter some technical problems such as local minima, slow learning, and high sensitivity to initial conditions, among others. As a viable alternative, new training algorithms, e.g., those based on Kalman filtering, have been proposed (Grover and Hwang, 1992; Haykin, 2001; Singhal & Wu, 1989). Due to the fact that training a neural network typically results in a nonlinear problem, the Extended Kalman Filter (EKF) is a common tool to use, instead of a linear Kalman filter (Haykin, 2001).

This fact motivates the need to derive a model based on recurrent high order neural networks (RHONN) in order to identify the dynamics of the plant to be controlled. The RHONN model advantages are: easy implementation, relative simple structure, robustness, capacity to on-line adjust its parameters (Rovithakis & Chistodoulou, 2000; Sanchez et al., 2008), and incorporation of a priory information about the system structure (Ornelas-Tellez et al., 2012).

This RHONN is used to identify each subsystem (agent), under the assumption that for all of them the state is available for measurement. The learning algorithm for the local RHONN is implemented using an Extended Kalman Filter (EKF). The objective of optimal control theory is to determine the control signals which will force a process to satisfy physical constraints and at the same time to minimize a performance criterion (Kirk, 2004). Unfortunately, for nonlinear systems, it is required to solve the associated Hamilton Jacobi Bellman (HJB) equation, which is not an easy task. The aim of the inverse optimal control is to avoid the solution of such equation (Krstic et al., 1995). For the inverse approach, a stabilizing feedback control law is developed and then it is established that this control law optimizes a cost function. The main characteristic of the inverse approach is that the cost function is a posteriori determined for the stabilizing feedback control law (Do et al., 2004; Feldkamp et al., 2003; Park et al., 2010).

When a vehicle has non-holonomic constraints, it can travel in every direction under any orientation. The term omnidirectional is used to describe the ability of a system to move instantaneously in any direction from any configuration (Doroftei et al., 2007). There are two types of omnidirectional wheeled platforms: one type is uses special wheels, and the other one includes conventional wheels. Special wheels are called Mecanum or Swedish wheel, which have been mostly studied for the omnidirectional mobile platforms. Conventional wheels can be broken into two types, caster wheels and steering wheels. Using four Swedish wheels provides omnidirectional movement for a vehicle without needing a conventional steering system (Doroftei et al., 2007; Muir & Neuman, 1990).

The holonomic motion offers exceptional mobility. There is no need of starts and stops to change the direction of motion of the robot, and to reach restricted spaces in factories and plants will be easier. These will save time and difficulties (Cuellar, 2006). The non-holonomic constraints on their wheel mechanisms prevent sideways movements (also termed "crab motion") without preliminary maneuvering; these vehicles are quite restricted in their motion, particularly when operating in tight environments (Cuellar, 2006). We apply our methodology to the control to KUKA youBot. It provides omnidirectional mobility (i.e., independent and simultaneous X and Y translations and Z rotation) with a stable, rectangular wheelbase.

This chapter proposes a discrete-time decentralized inverse optimal neural control for a multi-agent omnidirectional mobile robot. This approach consists in synthesizing a suitable controller for each agent; accordingly, each local controller is approximated by an identifier using a discrete-time recurrent high order neural network (RHONN), trained with an extended Kalman filter (EKF) algorithm. The neural identifier scheme is used to model each uncertain nonlinear subsystem, and based on this neural model and the knowledge of a control Lyapunov function, and then an inverse optimal controller is synthesized to avoid solving the Hamilton Jacobi Bellman (HJB) equation. The stability of this neural-network-based controller is guaranteed by the Lyapunov synthesis method, and the synaptic weights of neural networks are tuned online.

BACKGROUND

Inverse Optimal Control

This section closely follows (Sanchez & Ornelas- Tellez, 2013). Its main goal is the synthesis of an inverse optimal control. First, we give briefly details about optimal control methodology and their limitations. Let consider the discrete-time affine-in-the- input nonlinear system:

$$\chi_{k+1} = f\left(\chi_k\right) + g\left(\chi_k\right)u_k, \chi(0) = \chi_0 \tag{1}$$

where $\chi_k \in \mathbb{R}^n$ is the state of the system, $u_k \in \mathbb{R}^m$ is the control input, $f(\chi_k) : \mathbb{R}^n \to \mathbb{R}^n$ and $g(\chi_k) : \mathbb{R}^n \to \mathbb{R}^{n \times m}$ are smooth maps, the subscript $k \in \mathbb{Z}^+ \cup 0 = \{0, 1, 2, ...\}$ stands for the value of the functions and/or variables at time k, $f(0)=0$ and $rank\{g(\chi_k)\} = m \; \forall \chi_k \neq 0$. For system 1, it is desired to determine a control law $u_k = \bar{u}(x_k)$ which minimizes a cost functional. The following cost functional is associated with trajectory tracking for system 1:

$$\chi_{k+1} = f\left(\chi_k\right) + g\left(\chi_k\right)u_k, \chi\left(0\right) = \chi_0 \tag{2}$$

where $z_k = \chi_k - \chi_{\delta,k}$ with $\chi_{\delta,k}$ as the desired trajectory for χ_k; $z_k \in \mathbb{R}^n$; $\mathcal{J}(z_k): \mathbb{R}^n \to \mathbb{R}^+$; $l(z_k): \mathbb{R}^n \to \mathbb{R}^+$ is a positive semidefinite function and $R: \mathbb{R}^n \to \mathbb{R}^{m \times m}$ is a real symmetric positive definite weighting matrix. The meaningful cost functional (2) is a performance measure (Kirk, 2004). The entries of R may be functions of the system state in order to vary the weighting on control efforts according to the state value (Kirk, 2004). Considering the state feedback control approach, we assume that the full state χ_k is available.

Equation (2) can be rewritten as

$$\mathcal{J}\left(z_k\right) = l\left(z_k\right) + u_k^T R u_k + \sum_{n=k+1}^{\infty} l\left(z_n\right) + u_n^T R u_n = l\left(z_k\right) + u_k^T R u_k + \mathcal{J}\left(z_{k+1}\right) \tag{3}$$

where we require the boundary condition $\mathcal{J}(0) = 0$ so that $\mathcal{J}(z_k)$ becomes a Lyapunov function (Sepulchre et al., 1997; Al-Tamimi et al., 2008). The value of $\mathcal{J}(z_k)$ if finite, then it is a function of the initial state z_0. When $\mathcal{J}(z_k)$ is at its minimum, which is denoted as $\mathcal{J}^*(z_k)$, it is named the optimal value function, and it will be used as a Lyapunov function, i.e., $\mathcal{J}(z_k) \triangleq V(z_k)$.

From Bellman's optimality principle (Lewis & Syrmos, 1995; Basar & Olsder, 1995), it is known that, for the infinite horizon optimization case, the value function $V(z_k)$ becomes time invariant and satisfies the discrete-time (DT) Bellman equation (Al- Tamimi et al., 2008; Basar & Olsder, 1995; Ohsawa et al., 2010)

$$V\left(z_k\right) = \min_{u_k} \left\{ l\left(z_k\right) + u_k^T R u_k + V\left(z_{k+1}\right) \right\} \tag{4}$$

where $V(z_{k+1})$ depends on both z_k and u_k by means of z_{k+1} in (1). Note that the DT Bellman equation is solved backward in time (Al-Tamimi et al., 2008). In order to establish the conditions that the optimal control law must satisfy, we define the discrete-time Hamiltonian $\mathcal{H}(z_k, u_k)$ (Haddad et al., 1998a) as

$$\mathcal{H}\left(z_k, u_k\right) = l\left(z_k\right) + u_k^T R u_k + V\left(z_{k+1}\right) - V\left(z_k\right) \tag{5}$$

The Hamiltonian is a method to adjoin constraint (1) to the performance index (2), and then, solving the optimal control problem by minimizing the Hamiltonian without constraints (Lewis & Syrmos, 1995).

A necessary condition that the optimal control law u_k should satisfy is $\dfrac{\partial \mathcal{H}\left(z_k, u_k\right)}{\partial u_k} = 0$ (Kirk, 2004), which is equivalent to calculate the gradient of (4) right-hand side with respect to u_k, then

$$0 = 2R u_k + g^T\left(\chi_k\right) \frac{\partial V\left(z_{k+1}\right)}{\partial z_{k+1}} \tag{6}$$

Therefore, the optimal control law is formulated as

$$u_k^* = -\frac{1}{2} R^{-1} g^T \left(\chi_k \right) \frac{\partial V \left(z_{k+1} \right)}{\partial z_{k+1}} \tag{7}$$

with the boundary condition $V(0) = 0$; u_k^* is used when we want to emphasize that u_k is optimal. Moreover, if $\mathcal{H}(z_k, u_k)$ has a quadratic form in u_k and $R > 0$, then

$$\frac{\partial^2 \mathcal{H}(z_k, u_k)}{\partial u_k^2} > 0$$

holds as a sufficient condition such that optimal control law (7) (globally (Kirk, 2004)) minimizes $\mathcal{H}(z_k, u_k)$ and the performance index (2) (Lewis and Syrmos, 1995).

Substituting (7) into (4), we obtain the discrete-time Hamilton-Jacobi-Bellman (HJB) equation described by

$$0 = l\left(z_k \right) + V \left(z_{k+1} \right) - V \left(z_k \right) + \frac{1}{4} \frac{\partial V^T \left(z_{k+1} \right)}{\partial z_{k+1}} g \left(\chi_k \right) R^{-1} g^T \left(\chi_k \right) \frac{\partial V \left(z_{k+1} \right)}{\partial z_{k+1}} \tag{8}$$

Solving the HJB partial-differential Equation (8) is not straightforward; this is one of the main disadvantages of discrete-time optimal control for nonlinear systems. To overcome this problem, we propose the inverse optimal control. Due to the fact that the inverse optimal control is based on a Lyapunov function, we establish the following

Definition 1: A function $V(\chi_k)$ satisfying $V(\chi_k) \to \infty$ as $\|\chi_k\| \to \infty$ is said to be radially unbounded.

Theorem 1: The equilibrium $\chi_k = 0$ of (1) is globally asymptotically stable if there is a function $V : \mathbb{R}^n \to \mathbb{R}$ such that (I) V is a positive definite function, radially unbounded, and (II) $-\Delta V(\chi_k)$ is a positive definite function, where $\Delta V(\chi_k) = V(\chi_{k+1}) - V(\chi_k)$.

Theorem 2: Suppose that there exists a positive definite function $V : \mathbb{R}^n \to \mathbb{R}$ and constants $c_1, c_2, c_3 > 0$ such $p > 1$ that

$$c_1 \|\chi_k\|^p \le V(\chi_k) \le c_2 \|\chi_k\|^p \tag{9}$$

$$\Delta V \left(\chi_k \right) \le -c_3 \|\chi_k\|^p, \quad \forall k \ge 0, \ \forall \chi \in \mathbb{R}^n \tag{10}$$

Then $\chi_k = 0$ is an exponentially stable equilibrium for system (1).

Clearly, exponential stability implies asymptotic stability. The converse is, however, not true.

Definition 2: Let $V(\chi_k)$ be a radially unbounded function, with $V(\chi_k) > 0, \forall \chi_k \neq 0$ and $V(0)=0$. If for any $\chi_k \in \mathbb{R}^n$, there exist real values u_k such that

$$\Delta V(\chi_k, u_k) < 0 \tag{11}$$

where the Lyapunov difference $\Delta V(\chi_k, u_k)$ is defined as $V(\chi_{k+1}) - V(\chi_k) = V(f(\chi_k) + g(\chi_k)u_k) - V(\chi_k)$. Then $V(\bullet)$ is said to be a "discrete-time control Lyapunov function" (CLF) for system (1).

INVERSE OPTIMAL CONTROL: A CLF APPROACH

Let consider a class of disturbed discrete-time nonlinear and interconnected system

$$\chi^j_{i,k+1} = f^j_i\left(\chi^j_{i,k}\right) + g^j_i\left(\chi^j_{i,k}\right)u_{i,k} + \Gamma^j_{i\ell,k}\left(\chi_\ell\right) \tag{12}$$

where $i = 1,\ldots,\gamma$, $j = 1,\ldots,n_i$, $\chi_i \in \mathbb{R}^{n_i}$, $\chi_i = \left[\chi^{1T}_i \chi^{2T}_i \ldots \chi^{rT}_i\right]^T$, $\chi^j_i \in \mathbb{R}^{n_{ij} \times 1}$, $u_i \in \mathbb{R}^{m_i}$; γ is the number of subsystems (agents), χ_ℓ reflection between the i-th and the ℓ-th subsystem (agent) with $1 \leq \ell \leq \gamma$. We assume that f_i, B_i and Γ_i are smooth and bounded functions, $f^j_i(0) = 0$ and $B^j_i(0) = 0$. Without loss of generality, $\chi = 0$ is an equilibrium point of (12), which is of be used later.

For the inverse optimal control approach, let consider the discrete-time affine-in-the-input nonlinear system:

$$\chi_{i,k+1} = f_i\left(\chi_{i,k}\right) + g_i\left(\chi_{i,k}\right)u_{i,k}, \quad \chi_{i,0} = \chi_i\left(0\right) \tag{13}$$

with $i = 1,\ldots,\gamma$; γ is the number of subsystems (agents). Where $\chi_{i,k} \in \mathbb{R}^{n_i}$ are the states of the systems, $u_{i,k} \in \mathbb{R}^{m_i}$ are the control inputs, $f_i(\chi_{i,k}): \mathbb{R}^{n_i} \to \mathbb{R}^{n_i}$ and $g(\chi_k): \mathbb{R}^{n_i} \to \mathbb{R}^{n_i \times m_i}$ are smooth maps, the subscript $k \in \mathbb{Z}^+ \cup 0 = \{0,1,2,\ldots\}$ will stand for the value of the functions and/or variables at the time k. We establish the following assumptions and definitions, which allow the inverse optimal control solution via the CLF approach.

Assumption 1: The full state of system (13) is measurable.

Definition 3: Consider the tracking error $z_{i,k} = \chi_{i,k} - \chi_{i\delta,k}$ with $\chi_{i\delta,k}$ as the desired trajectory for $\chi_{i,k}$ (Sanchez and Ornelas-Tellez, 2013).

Let define the control law

$$u^*_{i,k} = -\frac{1}{2}R^{-1}_i g^T_i\left(\chi_{i,k}\right)\frac{\partial V_i\left(z_{i,k+1}\right)}{\partial z_{i,k+1}} \tag{14}$$

425

which will be inverse optimal stabilizing along the desired trajectory $\chi_{i\delta,k}$ if:

1. It achieves (global) asymptotic stability for system (13) along reference $\chi_{i\delta,k}$; $V_i(z_{i,k})$ is (radially unbounded) positive definite function such that inequality

$$\bar{V}_i := V_i(z_{i,k+1}) - V_i(z_{i,k}) + u_{i,k}^{*T} R_i u_{i,k}^{*} \leq 0 \tag{15}$$

is satisfied.

2. When $l_i(z_{i,k}) := -\bar{V}_i \leq 0$ is selected, then $V_i(z_{i,k})$ is a solution for the HJB equation

$$0 = l_i\left(z_{i,k}\right) + V_i\left(z_{i,k+1}\right) - V_i\left(z_{i,k}\right) + \frac{1}{4} \frac{\partial V_i^T\left(z_{i,k+1}\right)}{\partial z_{i,k+1}} g_i\left(\chi_{i,k}\right) R^{-1} g_i^T\left(\chi_{i,k}\right) \frac{\partial V_i\left(z_{i,k+1}\right)}{\partial z_{i,k+1}} \tag{16}$$

and the cost functional (2) is minimized. It is possible to establish the main conceptual differences between optimal control and inverse optimal control as follows:

- For optimal control, the meaningful cost indexes $l_i(z_{i,k}) \leq 0$ and $R_i > 0$ are given a priori; then, they are used to calculate $u_i(z_{i,k})$ and $V_i(z_{i,k})$ by means of the HJB equation solution.
- For inverse optimal control, a candidate CLF $V_i(z_{i,k})$ and the meaningful cost index R_i are given a priori, and then these functions are used to calculate the inverse control law $u_i^*(z_{i,k})$ and the meaningful cost index $l_i(z_{i,k})$, defined as $l_i(z_i) := -\bar{V}_i$.

As established in Definition 3, the inverse optimal control law for trajectory tracking is based on the knowledge of $V_i(z_{i,k})$. Thus, we propose a CLF $V_i(z_{i,k})$, such that 1 and 2 are guaranteed. That is, instead of solving (8) for $V_i(z_{i,k})$, a quadratic CLF candidate $V_i(z_{i,k})$ is proposed with the form:

$$V_i(z_{i,k}) = \frac{1}{2} z_{i,k}^T P_i z_{i,k}, \quad P_i = P_i^T > 0 \tag{17}$$

for control law (14) in order to ensure stability of the tracking error $z_{i,k}$, where

$$z_{i,k} = \chi_{i,k} - \chi_{i\delta,k} \tag{18}$$

$$= \begin{bmatrix} \left(\chi_{i,k}^1 - \chi_{i\delta,k}^1\right) \\ \left(\chi_{i,k}^2 - \chi_{i\delta,k}^2\right) \\ \vdots \\ \left(\chi_{i,k}^n - \chi_{i\delta,k}^n\right) \end{bmatrix} \tag{19}$$

Moreover, it will be established that control law (14) with (17), which is referred to as the inverse optimal control law, optimizes a cost functional of the form (2).

Consequently, by considering $V_i\left(\chi_{i,k}\right)$ as in (17), control law (14) takes the following form:

$$\alpha_i\left(\chi_{i,k}\right) := u_{i,k}^* = -\frac{1}{2}\left[R_i\left(\chi_{i,k}\right) + \frac{1}{2}g_i^T\left(\chi_{i,k}\right)P_ig_i\left(\chi_{i,k}\right)\right]^{-1}g_i^T\left(\chi_{i,k}\right)P_i\left(f_i\left(\chi_{i,k}\right) - \chi_{i\delta,k+1}\right) \tag{19}$$

It is worth to point out that P_i and R_i are positive definite and symmetric matrices; thus, the existence of the inverse in (20) is ensured.

Once we have proposed a CLF for solving the inverse optimal control in accordance with Definition 3. Which allows establishing the following theorem.

Theorem 3: Consider the affine discrete-time non-linear system (13) with $i = 1, \ldots, \gamma; \gamma$ is the number of subsystems. If there exists a matrixes $P_i = P_i^T > 0$ such that the following inequality holds:

$$\sum_{i=0}^{\gamma}\left[\begin{matrix} \frac{1}{2}f_i^T\left(\chi_{i,k}\right)P_if_i\left(\chi_{i,k}\right) + \frac{1}{2}\chi_{i\delta,k+1}^T P_i\chi_{i\delta,k+1} - \chi_{i,k}^T P_i\chi_{i\delta,k}^T - \frac{1}{2}\chi_{i\delta,k}^T P_i\chi_{i\delta,k} \\ -\frac{1}{4}P_{i1}^T\left(\chi_{i,k}, \chi_{i\delta,k}\right)\left(R_i + P_{i2}\left(\chi_{i,k}\right)\right)^{-1}P_{i1}\left(\chi_{i,k}, \chi_{i\delta,k}\right) \end{matrix}\right] \tag{21}$$

$$\leq \sum_{i=0}^{\gamma}\left[-\frac{1}{2}\|P_i\|\|f_i(\chi_{i,k})\|^2 - \frac{1}{2}\|P_i\|\|\chi_{i\delta,k+1}\|^2 - \frac{1}{2}\|P_i\|\|\chi_{i,k}\|^2 - \frac{1}{2}\|P_i\|\|\chi_{i\delta,k}\|^2\right]$$

where $\sum_{i=0}^{\gamma}\left[P_{i,1}(\chi_{i,k}, \chi_{i\delta,k})\right]$ and $\sum_{i=0}^{\gamma}\left[P_{i,2}(\chi_{i,k})\right]$ are defined as

$$\sum_{i=0}^{\gamma}\left[P_{i,1}(\chi_{i,k}, \chi_{i\delta,k})\right] = \sum_{i=0}^{\gamma}\left[g_i^T(\chi_{i,k})P_i(f_i(\chi_{i,k}) - \chi_{i\delta,k+1})\right] \tag{22}$$

are

$$\sum_{i=0}^{\gamma}\left[P_{i,2}(\chi_{i,k})\right] = \sum_{i=0}^{\gamma}\left[\frac{1}{2}g_i^T(\chi_{i,k})P_ig_i(\chi_{i,k})\right] \tag{23}$$

respectively, then system (13) with control law (20) guarantees asymptotic trajectory tracking along the desired trajectory $\chi_{i\delta,k}$, where $z_{i,k+1} = \chi_{i,k+1} - \chi_{i\delta,k+1}$.

Moreover, with (17) as a CLF, this control law is inverse optimal in the sense that it minimizes the meaningful functional given by

$$\sum_{i=0}^{\gamma}\mathcal{J}_i\left(z_{i,k}\right) = \sum_{i=0}^{\gamma}\sum_{k=0}^{\infty}\left(l_i\left(z_{i,k}\right) + u_{i,k}^T R_i\left(z_{i,k}\right)u_{i,k}\right) \tag{24}$$

with

$$\sum_{i=0}^{\gamma} l_i\left(z_{i,k}\right) = -\sum_{i=0}^{\gamma} \overline{V}_i \left.\right|_{u_{i,k}^* = \alpha_i\left(z_{i,k}\right)} \tag{25}$$

and optimal value function $\displaystyle\sum_{i=0}^{\gamma}\left[\mathcal{J}_i\left(z_{i,k}\right)\right] = \sum_{i=0}^{\gamma}\left[V_i\left(z_0\right)\right]$

Optimal control will be in general of the form (14) and the minimum value of the performance index will be function of the initial state $z_{i,0}$. If system (13) and the control law (14) are given, we shall say that the pair $\{V_i(z_{i,k}), l_i(z_{i,k})\}$ is a solution to *the inverse optimal control problem* if the performance index (2) is minimized by (14), with the minimum value being $V_i(z_{i,0})$.

NEURAL IDENTIFICATION

To identify system (12) when $i=1$, let consider the following discrete-time recurrent high order neural network (RHONN):

$$x_{j,k+1} = w_{j,k}^{\top} \Phi_j\left(x_k, u_{j,k}\right), \quad j = 1, \cdots, n_i \tag{26}$$

where x_j is the state of the j-th neuron, L_j is the respective number of high-order connections, $\{I_1, I_2, \cdots, I_{L_p}\}$ is a collection of non-ordered sub-sets of $\{1, 2, \cdots, n_i + m_i\}$, n_j is the state dimension, m_j is the number of external inputs, w_j is the respective on-line adapted weight vector, and $\Phi_j(x_k, u_k)$ is given by

$$\Phi_j\left(x_k, u_k\right) = \begin{bmatrix} \Phi_{j_1,k} \\ \Phi_{j_2,k} \\ \vdots \\ \Phi_{j_{L_j},k} \end{bmatrix} = \begin{bmatrix} \prod_{\ell \in I_1} \xi_{j_\ell}^{d_{j\ell}(1)} \\ \prod_{\ell \in I_2} \xi_{j_\ell}^{d_{j\ell}(2)} \\ \vdots \\ \prod_{\ell \in I_{L_p}} \xi_{j_\ell}^{dj\ell(L_p)} \end{bmatrix} \tag{27}$$

with d_{j_ℓ} being nonnegative integers, and ξ_j defined as follows:

$$\xi_j = \begin{bmatrix} \xi_{j_1} \\ \vdots \\ \xi_{j_{n_i}} \\ \xi_{j_{n_i+1}} \\ \vdots \\ \xi_{j_{n_i+m_i}} \end{bmatrix} = \begin{bmatrix} S\left(x_{1,k}\right) \\ \vdots \\ S\left(x_{j,k}\right) \\ u_{1,k} \\ \vdots \\ u_{m_i,k} \end{bmatrix} \tag{28}$$

where $u_i = [u_{i_1}, u_{i_2}, \ldots, u_{im_i}]^\top$ is the input vector to the neural network, and $S(\bullet)$ is defined by

$$S(\varsigma) = \frac{1}{1 + \exp(-\beta\varsigma)}, \beta > 0 \tag{29}$$

where ς is any real value variable.

Using the structure of system (13), we propose the following neural networks model:

$$x_{i,k+1}^j = W_{i,k}^j \Phi_i \left(\chi_k, u_k \right) + W_i'^j \psi_i^j \left(\chi_{i,k}^{j+1}, u_{i,k} \right) \tag{30}$$

where $x_i = [x_i^{1\top}, x_i^{2\top}, \ldots, x_i^{n_i\top}]$ is the i-th block neuron state with the same properties that (12), $W_{i,k}^j = [w_{1,k}^{jT} w_{2,k}^{jT} \ldots w_{n\theta_{k+1,1},k}^{jT}]$ are the adjustable weight matrices, $W_{i,k}'^j$ are matrices with fixed parameters and $rank(W_{i,k}'^j) = n_{ij}$, with $j = 1, \ldots, n_i$, $i = 1, \ldots, \gamma$; ; ψ denotes a linear function of x or u corresponding to the plant structure (12) or external inputs to the network, respectively.

It is worth to note that, (30) constitutes a series-parallel identifier (Felix, 2003; Ioannou & Sun, 1996) and does not consider explicitly the interconnection terms of (12), whose effects are compensated by the neural network weights update.

THE EKF TRAINING ALGORITHM

The best well-known training approach for recurrent neural networks (RNN) is the back propagation through time learning (Haddad et al., 1998b). However, it is a first order gradient descent method and hence its learning speed can be very slow (Chi-Sing & Lai-Wan, 2003). Extended Kalman Filter (EKF) based algorithms have been introduced to train neural networks (Feldkamp et al., 2003; Alanis et al., 2009). With the EKF based algorithm, the learning convergence is improved (Chi-Sing and Lai- Wan, 2003). The EKF training of neural networks, both feed forward and recurrent ones, has proven to be reliable and practical for many applications over the past ten years (Feldkamp et al., 2003). The training goal is to determine the optimal weight values, which minimize the prediction error. The EKF- based training algorithm is described by (Grover & Hwang, 1992):

$$K_{iq,k}^j = P_{iq,k}^j H_{iq,k}^j M_{iq,k}^j \tag{31}$$

$$w_{iq,k+1}^j = w_{iq,k}^j + \eta_{iq}^j K_{iq,k}^j e_{iq,k}^j$$

$$P_{iq,k+1}^j = P_{iq,k}^j - K_{iq,k}^j H_{iq,k}^{j\top} P_{iq,k}^j + Q_{iq,k}^j$$

with

$$M_{iq,k}^j = \left[R_{iq,k}^j + H_{iq,k}^{j\top} P_{iq,k}^j H_{iq,k}^j \right]^{-1} \tag{32}$$

$$e_{iq,k}^{j} = \chi_{iq,k}^{j} - x_{iq,k}^{j} \tag{33}$$

where $e_{iq,k}^{j}$ is the identification error, $P_{iq,k+1}^{j}$ is the state estimation prediction error covariance matrix, $w_{iq,k}^{j}$ is the jq-th weight (state) of the i-th subsystem, η_{iq}^{j} is a design parameter such that $0 \leq \eta_{iq}^{j} \leq 1$, $\chi_{iq,k}^{j}$ is the jq-th plant state, $x_{iq,k}^{j}$ is the jq-th neural network state q is the number of states, $K_{iq,k}^{j}$ is the Kalman gain matrix, $Q_{iq,k}^{j}$ is the measurement noise covariance matrix, $R_{iq,k}^{j}$ is the state noise covariance matrix, and $H_{iq,k}^{j}$ is a matrix, in which each entry of. $\left(H_{q,k}^{j}\right)$. is the derivative of jq-th neural network state $\left(x_{iq,k}^{j}\right)$, with respect to all adjustable weights $\left(w_{iq,k}^{j}\right)$ as follows

$$H_{q,k}^{j} = \left[\frac{\partial x_{iq,k}^{j}}{\partial w_{iq,k}^{j}}\right]_{w_{iq,k}^{j}=w_{iq,k+1}^{j}}^{T} \tag{34}$$

$$i = 1,...,\gamma \text{ and } j = 1,...,n_i \tag{35}$$

Usually P_{iq}^{j}, Q_{iq}^{j} and R_{iq}^{j} are initialized as diagonal matrices, with entries $P_{iq}^{j}(0)$, $Q_{iq}^{j}(0)$ and $R_{iq}^{j}(0)$, respectively (Haykin, 2001). It is important to note that $H_{iq,k}^{j}$, $K_{iq,k}^{j}$ and $P_{iq,k}^{j}$ for the EKF are bounded (Song and Grizzle, 1995). Then the dynamics of (33) can be expressed as

$$e_{iq,k}^{j} = w_{iq,k}^{j} \Phi_{iq,k}^{j}\left(x_k, u_k\right) + \epsilon_{\Phi_{iq,k}^{j}} \tag{36}$$

For the case when i is fixed, the stability analysis for the i-th subsystem of RHONN (26) to identify the -th subsystem of nonlinear plant (13), is based on the following theorem.

Theorem 4: The i-th subsystem of RHONN (30) trained with the EKF-based algorithm (31) to identify the i-subsystem of nonlinear plant (12) in absence of interconnections, ensures that the identification error (33) is semiglobally uniformly ultimately bounded (SGUUB); moreover, the RHONN weights remain bounded (Garcia-Hernandez, 2005).

Let consider the RHONN (30) which identify the nonlinear plant (12) in presence of interconnections.

Theorem 5: Assume that the solution of i-th subsystem (agent) of RHONN (30) is satisfied by the bounds b_1 and b_2, respectively of Theorem 4, then RHONN (30) with $i = 1,...,\gamma$ trained with the EKF-based algorithm (31) to identify the nonlinear plant (12) in presence of interconnections, ensures that the identification error (33) and the RHONN weights are semi globally uniformly bounded (SGUUB) (Garcia-Hernandez, 2005).

Proposition 1: The tracking of a desired trajectory x_{id}^{j}, defined in terms of the plant state χ_i^{j} formulated as (12) can be established as the following inequality (Felix et al., 2005)

$$\left\| x_{i\delta}^{j} - \chi_{i}^{j} \right\| \le \left\| x_{i}^{j} - \chi_{i}^{j} \right\| + \left\| x_{i\delta}^{j} - x_{i}^{j} \right\| \tag{38}$$

where $\left\| \bullet \right\|$ stands for the Euclidean norm, $i = 1, \dots, \gamma, j = 1, \dots, n_{i}; x_{i\delta}^{j} - \chi_{i}^{j}$ is the system output tracking error; $x_{i}^{j} - \chi_{i}^{j}$ is the output identification error; and $x_{i\delta}^{j} - x_{i}^{j}$ is the RHONN output tracking error.

We establish the following requirements for the tracking solution:

Requirement 1:

$$\lim_{t \to \infty} \left\| x_{i}^{j} - \chi_{i}^{j} \right\| \le \zeta_{i}^{j} \tag{39}$$

with ζ_{i}^{j} a small positive constant.

Requirement 2:

$$\lim_{t \to \infty} \left\| x_{i\delta}^{j} - x_{i}^{j} \right\| = 0 \tag{40}$$

An on-line multi-agent neural identifier based on (30) ensures (39), while (40) is guaranteed by a discrete-time multi-agent inverse optimal control. It is possible to establish Proposition 1 due to separation principle for discrete-time nonlinear systems (Lin & Byrnes, 1994).

KUKA YOUBOT APPLICATION

Applicability of the scheme is illustrated via simulation implementation for an omnidirectional mobile robot, whose model is considered to be unknown as well as all its parameters and disturbances.

Omnidirectional Mobile Robot

We consider a KUKA youBot omnidirectional mobile robot with 4 actuated wheels as shown in (Figure 1). The dynamic of a DC motor can be expressed in the following state-space model (Ch et al., 2011):

$$x_{i,k+1}^{1} = x_{i,k}^{1} + T\left(-\frac{b}{J} x_{i,k}^{1} + \frac{K_{t}}{J} x_{i,k}^{2} \right)$$

$$x_{i,k+1}^{2} = x_{i,k}^{2} + T\left(-\frac{K_{b}}{L_{a}} x_{i,k}^{1} - \frac{R_{a}}{L_{a}} x_{i,k}^{2} + \frac{1}{L_{a}} u_{i,k} \right) \tag{41}$$

$$R_{a} = 0.6\Omega \; J = 0.0167 \frac{kgm^{2}}{s^{2}}$$

$$K_b = 0.8 \frac{Vs}{rad} \quad K_t = 0.8 \frac{Nm}{A} \tag{42}$$

$$L_a = 0.012H \quad b = 0.0167 Nms \frac{kgm^2}{s^2}$$

where x_i^1 represent the angular velocity in $\frac{rad}{s}$ for each motor respectively with $i = 1...4$. x_i^2 is the armature current in *Amp*. The input terminal voltage u_j is taken to be the controlling variable. R_a and L_a are the armature inductance in *H* and resistance in *ohm* respectively. K_t is the torque factor constant in $\frac{Nm}{Amp}$. K_b is the back emf constant in $\frac{Vs}{rad}$. J represent the moment of inertia in $\frac{kgm^2}{s^2}$ and b is the coefficient of viscous friction which opposes the direction of motion in *Nms*.

Neural Identification Design

We apply the neural identifier, developed in previous section, to obtain a discrete-time neural model for the electrically driven Shrimp robot (41) which is trained with the EKF (31) respectively, as follows:

$$x_{i,k+1}^1 = x_{i,k}^1 + T\left(-\frac{b}{J} x_{i,k}^1 + \frac{K_t}{J} x_{i,k}^2\right)$$

$$x_{i,k+1}^2 = x_{i,k}^2 + T\left(-\frac{K_b}{L_a} x_{i,k}^1 - \frac{R_a}{L_a} x_{i,k}^2 + \frac{1}{L_a} u_{i,k}\right) \tag{43}$$

where x_i^1 and x_i^2 identify the angular velocities χ_i^1 and the motor currents χ_i^2, respectively. The NN training is performed on-line, and all of its states are initialized, randomly. The RHONN parameters are heuristically selected as:

$$P_{iq}^1(0) = 1 \times 10^{10} I \quad R_{iq}^1(0) = 1 \times 10^8 \quad Q_{iq}^1(0) = 1 \times 10^7 I$$

$$P_{iq}^2(0) = 1 \times 10^{10} I \quad R_{iq}^2(0) = 5 \times 10^3 \quad Q_{iq}^2(0) = 5 \times 10^3 I$$

$$w_{1i}' = 1 \quad w_{2i}' = 1$$

where *I* is the identity matrix. It is important to consider that for the EKF-learning algorithm the covariances are used as design parameters (Feldkamp et al., 2003; Haykin, 2001). The neural network structure (43) is determined heuristically in order to minimize the state estimation error.

Figure 1. KUKA youBot

Control Design

The goal is to force the state $x_{1i,k}$ to track a desired reference signal $\chi_{1i\delta,k}$, which is achieved by a control law as described in previous section. First the tracking error is defined as

$$z_{1i,k} = x_{1i,k} - \chi_{1i\delta,k}$$

Then using (43) and introducing the desired dynamics for $z_{1i,k}$ results in

$$z_{1i,k+1} = w_{1i,k}\varphi_1(\chi_{1i,k}) + w'_{1i,k}\chi_{2i,k} - \chi_{1i\delta,k+1} = K_{1i}z_{1i,k}$$

$$= K_{1i}z_{1i,k} \tag{44}$$

where $\left|K_{1i}\right| < 1$. The desired value $\chi_{2i\delta,k}$ for the pseudo-control input $\chi_{2i,k}$ is calculated from (44) as

$$\chi_{2i\delta,k} = \left(w'_{1i,k}\right)^{-1}\left(-w_{1i,k}\varphi_{1i}\left(\chi_{1i,k}\right) + \chi_{1i\delta,k+1} + K_{1i}z_{1i,k}\right) \tag{45}$$

At the second step, we introduce a new variable as

$$z_{2i_k} = x_{2i,k} - \chi_{2i\delta,k}$$

Taking one-step ahead, we have

$$z_{2i,k+1} = w_{2i,k}\varphi_{2i}\left(\chi_{1i,k}, \chi_{2i,k}\right) + w'_{2i,k}\, u_{i,k} - \chi_{2i\delta,k+1} \tag{46}$$

where $u_{i,k}$ is defined as

$$u_{i,k} = -\frac{1}{2}\left(R_i\left(z_k\right) + g_i^T\left(x_{i,k}\right)P_i g_i\left(z_k\right)\right)^{-1} g_i^T\left(x_k\right)P_i\left(f_i\left(x_{i,k}\right) - x_{i\delta,k+1}\right) \tag{47}$$

the controllers parameters are shown below:

$$P_i = \begin{bmatrix} 1.6577 & 0.6299 \\ 0.6299 & 2.8701 \end{bmatrix}$$

SIMULATION RESULTS

The reference trajectories are selected as shown in the pictures below. where results are displayed as follows: Figure 2 to Figure 5 present on the top the trajectory tracking performance for the angular velocities of i-th motor and on the bottom the error trajectory tracking performance for the currents of i-th motor respectively.

Figure 2. Tracking performance of the front right motor

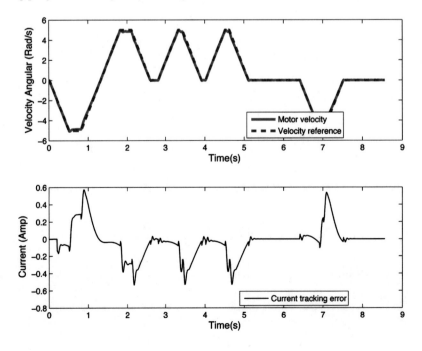

Figure 3. Tracking performance of the front left motor

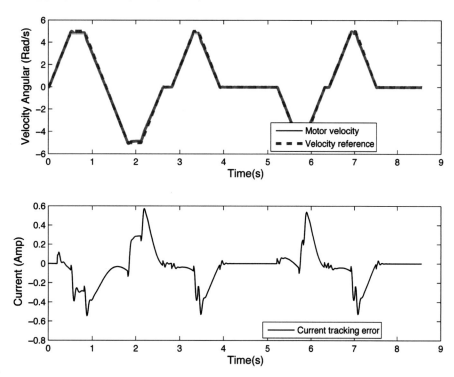

Figure 4. Tracking performance of the back right motor

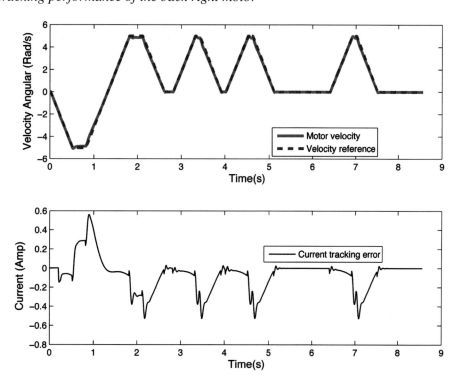

Figure 5. Tracking performance of the back left motor

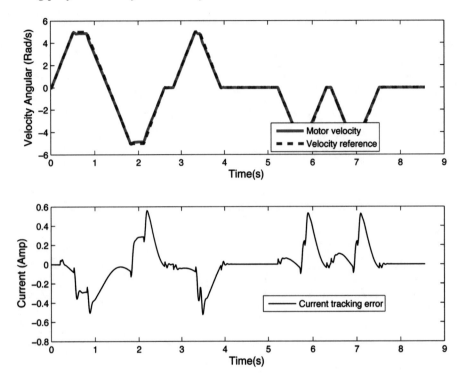

CONCLUSION

This chapter has presented a discrete-time decentralized inverse optimal neural control, which achieve tracking for nonlinear systems and is inverse optimal in the sense that, a posteriori, minimizes a meaningful cost functional. The training of the neural network is performed on-line using an extended Kalman filter. The proposed scheme stabilizes the system (41) along a desired trajectory. Considering these successful results, real-time application is proposed as future work.

REFERENCES

Al-Tamimi, A., Lewis, F., & Abu-Khalaf, M. (2008). Discrete-time nonlinear hjb solution using approximate dynamic programming: Convergence proof. *IEEE Transactions on* Systems, Man, and Cybernetics, Part B: Cybernetics, *38*(4), 943–949.

Alanis, A. Y., Sanchez, E. N., & Loukianov, A. G. (2009). Real-time output tracking for induction motors by recurrent high-order neural network control. *Proceedings of the 17th Mediterranean Conference on Control and Automation MED '09*, Thessaloniki, Greece (pp. 868–873). doi:10.1109/MED.2009.5164654

Basar, T., & Olsder, G. J. (1995). *Dynamic Non-cooperative Game Theory* (2nd ed.). New York, New York, USA: Academic Press.

Ch, U. M., Babu, Y., & Amaresh, K. (2011). *Sliding Mode Speed Control of a DC Motor. Communication Systems and Network Technologies*. CSNT: Katra, Jammu, India.

Chi-Sing, L., & Lai-Wan, C. (2003). Dual extended Kalman filtering in recurrent neural networks. *Neural Networks*, *16*(2), 223–239. doi:10.1016/S0893-6080(02)00230-7 PMID:12628608

Cuellar, F. (2006). Analysis and design of a wheeled holonomic omnidirectional robot. *Proceedings of the IEEE 3rd Latin American Robotics Symposium LARS '06* (pp. 41–46). IEEE. doi:10.1109/LARS.2006.334341

Do, K., Jiang, Z., & Pan, J. (2004). Simultaneous tracking and stabilization of mobile robots: An adaptive approach. *IEEE Transactions on* Automatic Control, *49*(7), 1147–1151.

Doroftei, I., Grosu, V., & Spinu, V. (2007). *Omnidirectional mobile robot–design and implementation*. INTECH Open Access Publisher.

Feldkamp, L. A., Prokhorov, D. V., & Feldkamp, T. M. (2003). Simple and conditioned adaptive behavior from Kalman. *Neural Networks*, *16*(5-6), 683–689. doi:10.1016/S0893-6080(03)00127-8 PMID:12850023

Felix, R. A. (2003). Variable Structure Neural Control [Ph.D thesis]. Cinvestav, Unidad Guadalajara, Guadalajara, Jalisco, Mexico.

Felix, R. A., Sanchez, E. N., & Loukianov, A. G. (2005). Avoiding controller singularities in adaptive recurrent neural control. *Proceedings of the 16th IFAC World Congress*, Prague, Czech Republic.

Garcia-Hernandez, R. (2005). *Control Neuronal Decentralizado Discreto para Manipuladores Robuticos* [Ph.D thesis]. Cinvestav, Unidad Guadalajara, Guadalajara, Jalisco, Mexico.

Gourdeau, R. (1997). Object-oriented programming for robotic manipulator simulation. *Robotics Automation Magazine, IEEE*, *4*(3), 21–29. doi:10.1109/100.618020

Grover, R., & Hwang, P. Y. C. (1992). *Introduction to Random Signals and Applied Kalman Filtering*. New York, NY, USA: John Wiley and Sons.

Haddad, W. M., Chellaboina, V.-S., Fausz, J. L., & Abdallah, C. (1998a). Optimal discrete-time control for non-linear cascade systems. *Journal of the Franklin Institute*, *335*(5), 827–839. doi:10.1016/S0016-0032(97)00013-6

Haddad, W. M., Chellaboina, V.-S., Fausz, J. L., & Abdallah, C. (1998b). Optimal discrete-time control for non-linear cascade systems. *Journal of the Franklin Institute*, *335*(5), 827–839. doi:10.1016/S0016-0032(97)00013-6

Haykin, S. (2001). *Kalman Filtering and Neural Networks*. New York, NY, USA: John Wiley and Sons. doi:10.1002/0471221546

Iftar, A. (1991). Decentralized optimal control with overlapping decompositions. Proceedings of the 1991 IEEE International Conference on Systems Engineering, Dayton, OH, USA (pp. 299–302). doi:10.1109/ICSYSE.1991.161138

Ioannou, P. A., & Sun, J. (1996). *Robust Adaptive Control*. New Jersey, USA: Prentice Hall, Inc.

Kageyama, T., & Ohnishi, K. (2002). An architecture of decentralized control for multi-degrees of freedom parallel manipulator. *Proceedings of the 7th International Workshop on Advanced Motion Control*, Maribor, Slovenia (pp. 74–79).

Kirk, D. E. (2004). *Optimal Control Theory: An Introduction*. Englewood Cliffs, NJ, USA: Dover Publications.

Krstic, M., Kokotovic, P. V., & Kanellakopoulos, I. (1995). *Nonlinear and Adaptive Control Design* (1st ed.). New York, NY, USA: John Wiley and Sons, Inc.

Lewis, F. L., & Syrmos, V. L. (1995). *Optimal Control*. New York, New York, USA: John Wiley and Sons.

Lin, W., & Byrnes, C. I. (1994). Design of discrete- time nonlinear control systems via smooth feedback. *IEEE Transactions on* Automatic Control, *39*(11), 2340–2346.

Mahajan, A. (2011). Optimal decentralized control of coupled subsystems with control sharing. *Proceedings of the 2011 50th IEEE Conference on Decision and Control and European Control Conference (CDC-ECC)*, Orlando, FL, USA (pp. 5726–5731).

Muir, P. F., & Neuman, C. P. (1990). Kinematic modeling for feedback control of an omnidirectional wheeled mobile robot. In *Autonomous robot vehicles* (pp. 25–31). Springer. doi:10.1007/978-1-4613-8997-2_2

Ohsawa, T., Bloch, A. M., & Leok, M. (2010). Discrete Hamilton-Jacobi theory and discrete optimal control. *Proceedings of the 2010 49th IEEE Conference on Decision and Control (CDC)*, Atlanta, GA, USA (pp. 5438–5443). doi:10.1109/CDC.2010.5717665

Ornelas-Tellez, F., Sanchez, E. N. Garcia- Hernandez, R., Ruz-Hernandez, J., & Rullan-Lara, J. (2012). Neural inverse optimal control for discrete-time uncertain nonlinear systems stabilization. *Proceedings of the 2012 International Joint Conference on Neural Networks (IJCNN)* (pp. 1–6).

Park, B. S., Yoo, S. J., Park, J. B., & Choi, Y. H. (2010). A simple adaptive control approach for trajectory tracking of electrically driven non-holonomic mobile robots. *IEEE Transactions on Control Systems Technology*, *18*(5), 1199–1206. doi:10.1109/TCST.2009.2034639

Rovithakis, G. A., & Chistodoulou, M. A. (2000). Adaptive Control with Recurrent High-Order Neural Networks. London, UK.

Sanchez, E. N., Alanis, A. Y., & Loukianov, A. G. (2008). *Discrete-time High Order Neural Control*. Berlin, Germany: Springer-Verlag. doi:10.1007/978-3-540-78289-6

Sanchez, E. N., & Ornelas-Tellez, F. (2013). *Discrete-Time Inverse Optimal Control for Nonlinear Systems*. Boca Raton, FL, USA: CRC Press.

Sanchez, E. N., & Ricalde, L. J. (2003). Trajec- tory tracking via adaptive recurrent control with input saturation. *Proceedings of the 2003 International Joint Conference on Neural Networks* (Vol. 1, pp. 359–364). IEEE.

Sepulchre, R., Jankovic, M., & Kokotovi, P. V. (1997). *Constructive Nonlinear Control*. Berlin, Germany: Springer-Verlag. doi:10.1007/978-1-4471-0967-9

Singhal, S., & Wu, L. (1989). Advances in neural information processing systems. Morgan San Francisco, CA, USA: Kaufmann Publishers Inc.

Song, Y., & Grizzle, J. W. (1995). The extended Kalman filter as a local asymptotic observer for discrete-time nonlinear systems. *Journal of Mathematical Systems, Estimation and Control, 5,* 59–78.

Zeng-Guang, H., Long, C., & Min, T. (2009). De- centralized robust adaptive control for the multiagent system consensus problem using neural networks. *IEEE Transactions on* Systems, Man, and Cybernetics, Part B: Cybernetics, *39*(3), 636–647.

Chapter 18
Higher Order Neural Network for Financial Modeling and Simulation

Partha Sarathi Mishra
North Orissa University, India

Satchidananda Dehuri
Fakir Mohan University, India

ABSTRACT

Financial market creates a complex and ever changing environment in which population of investors are competing for profit. Predicting the future for financial gain is a difficult and challenging task, however at the same time it is a profitable activity. Hence, the ability to obtain the highly efficient financial model has become increasingly important in the competitive world. To cope with this, we consider functional link artificial neural networks (FLANNs) trained by particle swarm optimization (PSO) for stock index prediction (PSO-FLANN). Our strong experimental conviction confirms that the performance of PSO tuned FLANN model for the case of lower number of ahead prediction task is promising. In most cases LMS updated algorithm based FLANN model proved to be as good as or better than the RLS updated algorithm based FLANN but at the same time RLS updated FLANN model for the prediction of stock index system cannot be ignored.

1. INTRODUCTION

The higher order neural network has re-awakened the scientific and engineering community to the modeling and processing of numerous quantitative phenomenons specifically in the field of financial domain using neural network. These networks are specifically designed for handling linearly non-separable problems using appropriate input representation. Thus, suitable enhanced representation of input data has to be found out. This can be achieved by increasing the dimensions of the input space. The input data which is expanded is used for training instead of the actual input data. In this case, higher order

DOI: 10.4018/978-1-5225-0063-6.ch018

input terms are chosen so that they are linearly independent of the original pattern components. Thus, the input representation has been enhanced and linear-separability can be achieved in the extended space.

The increasing development in the field of NN has made their structure more complex in nature. This complexity has been raised as a result of combining a large number of hidden layers and a large number of neurons in those layers, making the NN model behavior more impracticable in the length of their training time. On the other hand HONN alleviate this problem by providing simpler NNs with all of the possible higher order multiplicative or functional interactions between the elements of the input vectors being provided explicitly.

HONN is a different type of neural network with the presence of expanded input space in it single layer feed-forward architecture. HONN contains summing units and product units that multiply their inputs. These high order terms or product units can increase the information capacity for the input features and provides nonlinear decision boundaries to give a better classification and prediction capability than the linear neuron (Sahin, 1994). A major advantage of HONNs is that only one layer of trainable weight is needed to achieve nonlinear separable, unlike the typical MLP or feed-forward neural network (Mishra and Dehuri, 2007).

Although most neural networks models share a common goal in performing functional mapping, different network architecture may vary significantly in their ability to handle different types of problems. For some tasks, higher order architecture of some of the inputs or activations may be appropriate to help good representation for solving the problems. HONNs are needed because ordinary feed-forward network like MLP cannot avoid the problem of slow learning, especially when involving highly complex nonlinear problems (Chen and Leung, 2004).

1.1 Related Work

HONNs have traditionally recognitions of being the input to a computational neuron which is a weighted sum of the products of its inputs (Lee et al., 1986). Such neurons are refereed as the higher-order processing units (HPUs) (Lippmann, 1989). It has been shown that HONNs can successfully perform invariant pattern recognition (Psaltis, Park, and Hong, 1988; Reid, Spirkovska, and Ochoa, 1989; Wood and Shawe-Taylor, 1996). Giles and Maxwell (1987) have showed that, HONNs have impressive computational storage, and learning capabilities. Redding, Kowalski and Downs (1993) proved that HONNs were at least as powerful as any other (similar order) FNN. Kosmatopoulos, Polycarpou, Christodoulou, and Ioannou (1995) have studied the approximation and learning properties of one class of recurrent HONNs and applied these architectures to the identification of dynamical systems. Thimm and Fiesler (1997) proposed a suitable initialization method for HONNs and compared this with FNN-weight initialization.

Though the HONNs have been extensively used in pattern recognition, classifications, non-linear simulations, identification of dynamic systems and other fields as mentioned, but applications in financial modeling and prediction are limited. Hence, the motivation behind this chapter is to explore the key issues and to specifically develop potential indicators based HONN for financial modeling and simulations purpose. Experimentally, it has been justified that the potential indicators used as an input to the HONN model gives better performance with less effort with a capable of simulating higher frequency and higher order nonlinear data, thus producing superior financial data simulations, compared with those derived from traditional ANN based models trained with back-propagation (Mishra and Dehuri, 2012; Mishra and Dehuri, 2014). Most important aspect is that, HONN is trained using evolutionary algorithms like PSO which is based on directed random searches. The beauties of this evolutionary algorithms is that, it will train the HONN irrespective of the network connections and structure which overcomes the drawback of the back-propagation algorithm which trains certain restricted topologies and types of network. It is also found that, a little work has been done in the field of financial modeling and prediction using evolutionary algorithms to train the HONNs. Hence in all, the care has been taken to develop a financial model using HONN specifically FLANN trained by PSO which have the predictive ability, that the structure detected by the models is persistent and the result is compared with other benchmarking NN architectures like MLP-BP and Psi-Sigma models. Therefore, we believe that this effort can make a springboard for the researchers who are working in the field of financial domain specifically for the prediction as well as trading system.

The rest of the chapter is organized as follows: In Section 2, we have discussed the background materials along with the different HONNs used for financial modeling and simulations. Section 3 provides our proposed PSO-FLANN as HONN. In Section 4 we have presented the experimental studies and simulation results. Section 5 concludes the chapter.

2. PRELIMINARIES

2.1 Technical Analysis and Efficient Market Contend

Technical analysts do not think that the securities industry is ineffective in processing available information into prices; rather they agree that the prediction of market prices is difficult. For reasons of market efficiency, a priori, one would assume that there is no privileged market. Due to risk aversion, investors require a small positive expected return in risky markets. In long-only markets—like a stock market—this signifies a positive upward movement. In symmetric markets, which traders are as likely to go as they are short, like futures and foreign exchange markets, the implication is that one would expect the monetary value to be predictable to some level. Furthermore, government interference in foreign exchange markets may make them more predictable still. Thus, for theoretical understandings, one may anticipate that foreign exchange markets should be the most predictable, futures markets intermediate and stock markets the least predictable as discussed by Sewell (2007).The empirical evidence found in the Park and Irwin (2004) and Jessica (2006) corroborates this hypothesis. With all a buy-and-hold strategy in the stock market should create money because stock markets are positive sum games, whilst the same cannot be said for futures or foreign exchange markets Sweeney.

2.2 Potential Indicators for Financial Modeling

Trading decision allows using a variety of categories of technical analysis indicators. Each class contains several indexes, all of which serve the same main function, but the methodology and parameters of which are dissimilar as suggested in financial literature by Murphy (1999) and Pring (1991). Although there are potentially an infinite act of technical indicators which can be formed from historic cost and volume information, the potential indicators shown in Table 1 has been widely used in this chapter for strengthening the HONNs for the purpose of financial modeling and simulations (Mishra and Dehuri, 2012).

Table 1. Potential indicators and respective formulae

Technical Indicators	Interpretation	Formula
Simple Moving Average (SMA)	Go long (short) when the difference between the short and long moving averages crosses a moving average of intermediate length from below(above).	$$\frac{1}{N}\sum_{k=0}^{n}X \quad \frac{1}{N}\sum_{K=0}^{n}x_k$$ N=No. of Days Xk= today's price
Exponential Moving Average (EMA)	Go long (short) when the short EMA of past prices exceeds (falls short of) the long EMA.	**SMA:** 10 period sum / 10 **Multiplier:** (2 / (Time periods + 1)) = (2 / (10 + 1)) = 0.1818 (18.18%) **EMA:** (Close – EMA(previous day)) * multiplier + EMA(previous day)
Accumulation Distribution Osciilator (ADO)	Chartists can use this indicator to affirm a security's underlying trend or anticipate reversals when the indicator diverges from the security price	Money Flow Multiplier = [(Close - Low) - (High - Close)] / (High - Low) Money Flow Volume = Money Flow Multiplier x Volume for the Period ADL = Previous ADL + Current Period's Money Flow Volume
Stochastic Oscillator (STOC)	Here critical points may be set at 20 and 80, with values greater than 80 triggering a sell signal and values less than 20 triggering a buy signal.	%K = (Current Close - Lowest Low) / (Highest High - Lowest Low) * 100 %D = 3-day SMA of %K Lowest Low = lowest low for the look-back period Highest High = highest high for the look-back period %K is multiplied by 100 to move the decimal point two places
On Balance Volume (OBV)	Chartists can look for divergences between OBV and price to predict price movements or use OBV to confirm price trends.	If the closing price is above the prior close price then: Current OBV = Previous OBV + Current Volume If the closing price is below the prior close price then: Current OBV = Previous OBV - Current Volume If the closing prices equals the prior close price then: Current OBV = Previous OBV (no change)
Relative Strength Index (RSI)	Go long if the RSI is less than 30; go short if the RSI is greater than 70. RS is the ratio of average gain and average loss over the last n days	RSI = 100 – (100/(1+RS)) RS = Average Gain / Average Loss
Price Rate of Change (PROC)	Go long (short) when the rate of change crosses the predetermined oversold (overbought) level from below (above).	ROC = [(Close - Close n periods ago) / (Close n periods ago)] * 100
Williams %R (WILLIAMS)	Traditional settings use -20 as the overbought threshold and -80 as the oversold threshold. These levels can be adjusted to suit analytical needs and security characteristics.	%R = (Highest High - Close)/(Highest High - Lowest Low) * -100 Lowest Low = lowest low for the look-back period Highest High = highest high for the look-back period %R is multiplied by -100 correct the inversion and move the decimal.
Closing Price Acceleration (CPACC)	It is the acceleration of the closing price during a given period of time.	[(Close Price- Close Price N-period ago) / (Close Price N-period ago)]*100
High Price Acceleration (HPACC)	It is the acceleration of the high prices during a given period of time.	[(High Price- High Price N-period ago) / (High Price N-period ago)]*100

2.3 Artificial Neural Networks (ANNs)

Neural networks are an emergent technology with an increasing number of real-world applications including Finance (Lisboa et al., 2000). However their numerous limitations are often creating skepticism about their use among practitioners. When we talk of ANNs, they are most likely referring to feed-forward Multilayer Perceptrons (MLPs), which incorporates the back-propagation (BP) training algorithm (Lapedes and Farber, 1987; Refenes, 1994; Schoneberg, 1990). But in the more recent comparative study, the ANNs along with the state-space reconstruction techniques are fared well. At beginning, it is observed that MLP-BPs give promising results at financial modeling. More specifically, a single hidden layer MLP-BP can approximate, arbitrarily closely to any suitable smooth function (Hecht-Nielsen, 1987; Hornik, Stinchcombe, & White, 1989). Furthermore, when this approximation improves as the number of nodes in the hidden layer increases, it demands for a suitable network structure. The determination of the best size of the hidden layer is complex, Nabhan and Zomaya (1994). Studies showed that the smaller size of the hidden layer leads to faster training but gives us fewer feature detectors (Dayhoff (1990). Increasing the number of hidden neurons presents a trade-off between the smoothness of the function and closeness of fit (Barnard and Wessel, 1992). One major problem with the freedom with the hidden-layer is that it induces Over-fitting (Walczak and Cerpa (1999).

So most researchers view that the "black-box" nature of NN training as a primary disadvantage due to the lack of understanding of the reasons that allow NNs to reach their decisions regarding the functions they are trained to model. Sometimes the data has higher order correlations requiring more complex NNs, Psaltis et al. (1988). Hence, the increased complexity in the already complex NN design process as well as the numerous limitations of the more classic neural architectures motivated us to explore new types of NN such as HONNs specifically HONNs trained by evolutionary algorithms like PSO as an alternative tools.

2.4 Higher-Order Neural Networks (HONNs)

Ivakhnenko (1971) have proposed that neural network architecture is capable of approximating higher-order functions such as polynomial equations. In order to obtain similar complex decision regions, ordinary NNs need to incorporate increasing number of neurons and hidden layers. A simple HONN could be thought of as describing elliptical curved regions as Higher Order functions (HO) which include squared terms, cubic terms, and higher orders. Giles and Maxwell (1987) were the first to publish a paper on HONNs in 1987 and the first book on HONN was by Bengtsson (1990). HONNs contain processing units that are capable of performing functions such as polynomial, multiplicative, smoothing or trigonometric functions Giles and Maxwell (1987); Selviah et al. (1991) which generate more complex decision regions which are multiply connected.

It has been demonstrated that HONNs are always faster, more accurate, and easier to explain, Bengtsson (1990). The exclusion of hidden layers allows for easier training methods to be used such as the Hebbian and Perceptron learning rules. HONNs lead to faster convergence, reduced network size and more accurate curve fitting, compared to other types of more complex NNs, Zhang et al. (2002).

First-order neural networks can be formulated as follows, assuming simple McCullough and Pitts-type neurons (Giles & Maxwell, 1987):

$$y_i(x) = f\left[\sum_j^N W(i,j)x(j)\right] \tag{1}$$

where $\{x(j)\}$ = an N-element input vector, $W(i,j)$ = adaptable weights from all other neurons to neuron-i, and f = neuron threshold function (e.g., sigmoid). Such neurons are said to be linear, since they are only capable of capturing first-order correlations in the training data. In this sense, they can be likened to Least Mean Squared or Delta learning. HONNs also contain high order nodes, i.e., nodes in which more than one input are involved in some of the terms of the summation. So, a second-order node can be described as shown in Equation 2.

$$y_i = f_i\left(\sum_{j,k=1}^n w_{ijk}x_j x_k - \theta_i\right) \tag{2}$$

Higher-order correlations in the training data require more complex neuron activation functions, characterized as shown in Equation 3 (Barron, Gilstrap, & Shrier, 1987; Giles & Maxwell, 1987; Psaltis, Park, & Hong, 1988).

$$y_i(x) = f\left[W_0(i)\sum_j^N W_i(i,j)x(j) + \sum_j^N \sum_k^M W_i(i,j,k)x(j)x(k) + ...\right] \tag{3}$$

The other types of HONNs are discussed as follows:

1. **Sigma-Pi Networks:** The hidden of a sigma-pi neural network is to calculate a product (or conjunct) of the inputs. In sigma-pi neural networks a weight is applied, not only to each input, but also to second and possibly higher order products or conjuncts of the inputs. The connections in sigma-pi neural networks allow one unit to get another. Thus, if one unit of a multiplicative pair of units is zero, then the other members have no effect on the output. On the other hand, if one unit of a pair has a value 1, the output of the unit is passed unchanged to the receiving unit. In this way a polynomial function of the inputs is presented as input to the transfer function of the output layer, i.e. the value of the output unit O_k is shown in Equation 4.

$$O_k = f\left(\sum_{q \in conjunct} W_{qk}\prod_{k=1}^N Z_{qk}\right) \tag{4}$$

where, f is the activation function, W_{qk} a synaptic weight, $Z_{q1}, Z_{q2, ...} Z_{qN}$ are the N input signals combined to form the product or conjunct, and q indexes the conjuncts or products that are used in unit k; the conjunct is the set of all conjuncts of subscripts for the inputs. The Figure 1 shows the architecture of the Sigma-Pi Networks.

Figure 1. Sigma-Pi networks

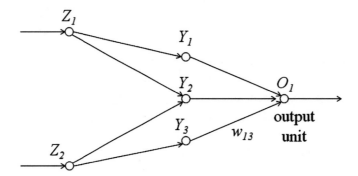

2. **Psi-Sigma Networks:** Ghosh and Nag (2002) have introduced a higher-order network called the 'Psi-sigma' network, which avoids the exponential increase in the number of weights and processing units normally associated with higher-order networks. A Psi-sigma network (PSN) consists of an input layer, a single hidden layer of liner summation units and product units in the output layer. The term pi-sigma comes from the fact that these networks use products of sums of input components. PSNs have only one layer of adjustable weights, the weights of the output layer is normally fixed at 1, as shown in Figure 2.

The output of a pi-sigma network is computed as follows:

$$O_k = f\left(\prod_{j=1}^{j} y_{kj}\right) \tag{5}$$

where,

$$y_{kj} = \left(\sum_{i=1}^{I+1} W_{kji} Z_i\right) \tag{6}$$

Figure 2. Pi-Sigma network

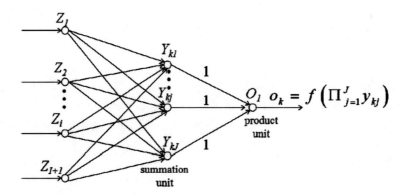

where, f is the activation function, $Z_1,...Z_{I+1}$ are the input signals, Z_{I+1} an input to the bias unit, W_{kji} the weight between input unit Z_I. The hidden unit Y_{kj} for the K_{th} output unit O_k, W_{kj}; $I+1$ is the threshold (or bias), y_{kj} is the output of hidden unit. $Y_{kj \, and} \, O_k$ is the output of output unit O_k. Each hidden unit is connected to only one output unit, as indicated to by the subscript k in y_{kj}. Thus equation shows that for multiple output PSNs as independent summing unit is required for each output unit.

3. **Second-Order Neural Networks:** Another type of higher-order neural network is the second order neural network, developed by Milenkovic et al. The research of Milenkovic et al was inspired by a greedy constructive neural network algorithm called the hyper plane determination from examples (HDE) that suggested a discrete approach to neural network optimization suitable for parallel and distributed implementation (Fletcher et al., 1995).

The objective of the neural network architecture developed by Milenkovic et al. was to overcome the HDE local minima problem by allowing hidden units with higher representational power. The higher representational power was achieved by allowing neurons with input interactions of the following forms.

$$f(\vec{z}) = \left(\sum_{i=1}^{I} W_i^1 Z_i \right) \tag{7}$$

$$f(\vec{z}) = \left(\sum_{i=1}^{I} W_i^1 Z_i + \sum_{i=1}^{I} W_i^2 Z_i Z_i \right) \tag{8}$$

$$f(\vec{z}) = \left(\sum_{i=1}^{I} W_i^1 Z_i + \sum_{i=1}^{I} W_i^2 Z_i Z_i + \sum_{i=1}^{I-1} \sum_{j=1+1}^{I} W_{ij}^3 Z_i Z_i \right) \tag{9}$$

where, f is the activation function, $\vec{z}$ is the input vector to the network, $W_i^{(1)}$, $W_i^{(2)}$ are weight parameters associated with the ith input value Z_i, while $W_i^{(3)}$ is a weight associated with the product of the ith and j^{th} input values z_i and z_j. First-order neural networks contain neurons only constructed with interaction functions described by Equation (7). Feed-forward neural networks that are constructed using neurons are described by all three interaction functions above, i.e. as described by Equations (7), (8) and (9) are referred to as second order neural network.

4. **Functional Link Artificial Neural Network:** FLANN is a class of Higher Order Neural Networks (HONNs) that utilize higher combination of its inputs (Pao and Takefuji, 1992). It was created by Pao (1989) and has been successfully used in many applications such as classification (Dehuri and Cho, 2010), pattern recognition (Klaseen and Pao, 1990) and prediction (Majhi, et al., 2009; Ghazali, et al., 2011). FLANN is much more modest than MLP since it has a single-layer network compared to the MLP but still is able to handle a non-linear separable prediction task with faster convergence rate and lesser computational load. The FLANN architecture is basically a flat network without any

hidden layer which has make the learning algorithm used in the network less complicated (Mishra and Dehuri, 2007). The functional expansion of the input to the network effectively increases the dimensionality of the input vector and hence the hyper-planes generated by the FLANN provide greater discrimination capability in the input pattern space. In this chapter, emphasis is given to trace the prediction of stock index using the potential indicators based computational model on historical data using the FLANN architecture. The FLANN network is shown in Figure 3(c.f.).

Computational Model of a FLANN

The most popular model used to solve complex prediction problems is multilayer neural network. There are many algorithms to train neural network models. However, for models being complex in nature, one single algorithm cannot be claimed to be the best for training to suite different scenarios of complexities of real life problems. Depending on the complexities of the problems, number of layers and number of neurons in the hidden layer need to be changed. As the number of layers and the number of neurons in the hidden layers increases, training the model becomes more complex.

To overcome the complexities associated with multi-layer neural network, a single layer neural network can be considered as an alternative approach. But the single layer neural network being linear in nature often fails to solve the complex non-linear problems. The prediction task in stock market is highly non-linear in nature. Therefore, a single layer NN cannot solve this problem.

In order to bridge the gap between linearity in the single layer neural network and the highly complex and computationally intensive multi-layer neural network, the FLANN architecture with back propagation learning for classification was proposed (Mishra and Dehuri, 2007; Pao, 1989; Pao et al., 1992). FLANN architecture can be viewed as a non-linear network. In contrast to the linear weighting of the input pattern produced by the linear links of the artificial neural network, the functional link acts on an element of a pattern or on the entire pattern by generating a set of linearly independent functions, then evaluating these functions with the inputs as the argument. A simple FLANN model with a pattern of eleven (11) inputs for the purpose of stock index tracing system is shown in Figure 4.

Figure 3. Architecture of functional link artificial neural network

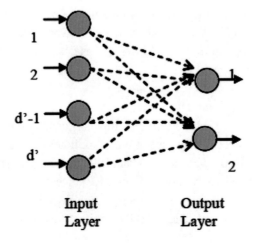

Figure 4. Proposed model for stock index tracing system using FLANN

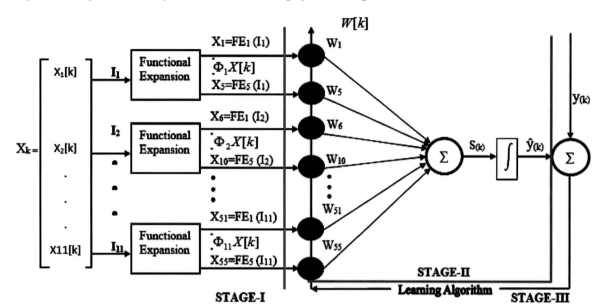

Let k training patterns denoted by $\left(X_i : Y_i \right)$, $1 \leq i \leq k$ be applied to the FLANN and let the weight matrix be W. At the ith instant $1 \leq i \leq k$, the Q-dimensional input pattern and the FLANN output are given by $X_i = [x_{i1}, x_{i2}, \dots x_{iQ}]$, $1 \leq i \leq k$ and $\hat{y}_i = \left[\hat{y}_i \right]$, $1 \leq i \leq k$. Hence $X = [X_1, X2, \dots \dots \dots X_k]$. The augmented matrix of Q-dimensional input pattern and the FLANN output are given by:

$$\left\langle X : \hat{Y} \right\rangle = \begin{pmatrix} x_{1,1} & x_{1,2} & \cdot & x_{1,Q} & : & \hat{y}_1 \\ x_{2,1} & x_{2,2} & \cdot & x_{2,Q} & : & \hat{y}_2 \\ \cdot & \cdot & \cdot & \cdot & : & \cdot \\ x_{k,1} & x_{k,2} & \cdot & x_{k,Q} & : & \hat{y}_k \end{pmatrix}$$

As the dimension of the input pattern is increased from Q to Q' by a set of basis functions Φ given by:

$$\Phi(X_i) = \begin{bmatrix} \Phi_1(x_{i1}), \Phi_2(x_{i1}), \dots, \Phi_1(x_{i2}), \Phi_2(x_{i2}), \dots, \Phi_1(x_{iQ}), \Phi_2(x_{iQ}), \dots \\ = \left[\Phi_1(x_{i1}), \Phi_2(x_{i2}), \dots, \Phi_Q(x_{iQ}) \right] \end{bmatrix}$$

The $k \times Q$ dimensional weight matrix is given by $W = [W_1, W_2, \dots \dots W_k]^T$, where W_i is the weight vector associated with the ith output and is given by $W_1 = \left[w_{i1,} w_{i2,}, \dots, w_{iQ} \right]$. The ith output of the FLANN is given by

$$\hat{y}_i(t) = \phi \left(\sum_{j=1}^{Q'} \Phi_j \left(x_{ij} \right) \cdot w_{ij} \right) = \phi \left(W_i \cdot \Phi^T \left(X_i \right) \right), \forall i .$$

The error associated with the ith output is given by $e_i(t) = y_i(t) - \hat{y}_i(t)$. Using adaptive learning; weights of the FLANN can be updated as:

$$w_{ij}(t+1) = w_{ij}(t) + \mu \cdot \Delta(t)$$
$$\Delta(t) = \delta(t) \cdot \left[\Phi(X_i) \right]$$

$$(10)$$

where,

$$\delta(t) = \left[\delta_1(t), \delta_2(t), ..., \delta_k(t) \right], \delta_i(t) = \left(1 - \hat{y}_i^2(t) \right) \cdot e_i(t), \mu$$

is known as the learning parameter.

The set of function considered for expansion may not always be suitable for mapping the non-linearity of the complex task. In such cases a few more function may be incorporated to the set of functions considered for expansion of the input data. The non-linear function considered in this case $\rho(\bullet) = \tanh(\bullet)$. However, dimensionalities of many problems are very high and further increasing the dimensionality to a large extent may not be an appropriate choice. So, it is advisable to choose a small set of alternative functions, which can map the function to the desired extent with significant improvement in output.

Learning of FLANN

The hardware structures of MLP and FLANN differ in the sense that FLANN has only input and output layers and the hidden layers are completely replaced by the nonlinear mappings. In fact, the task performed by the hidden layers in an MLP is carried out by functional expansions in FLANN. Being similar to a MLP, the FLANN also uses BP algorithm to train the neural networks. A shown in Figure 4, the STAGE-1 describes the 11 potential indicators (Table 1) as the input factors of the validated datasets taken as the input of the network. These eleven potential indicators are then mapped to a higher dimensional space by functional expansion using trigonometric functions as given below:

$$\Phi = \begin{bmatrix} \left(x_1, \sin px_1, \sin 2px_1, \cos px_1, \cos 2px_1 \right), \\ \left(x_2, \sin px_2, \sin 2px_2, \cos px_2, \cos 2px_2 \right), ..., \\ \left(x_{55}, \sin px_{55}, \sin 2px_{55}, \cos px_{55}, \cos 2px_{55} \right) \end{bmatrix}$$

$$(11)$$

The weighted sum is defined by

$$\hat{y} = \sum_{i,j=1...55} w_i x_j + \sum_{i,j=1...55} w_i \sin_i \pi x_j + \sum_{i,i=1...55} w_i \cos_i \pi x_j$$

$$(12)$$

The motivations for using trigonometric polynomials in the functional expansion stage is that, of all the polynomials of N-th order with respect to an orthonormal system $\{\Phi_i(x)\}_{i=1}^N$ the best approximation in the metric space L^2 is given by the Nth partial sum of its Fourier series with respect to this system.

Thus, the trigonometric polynomial basis functions given by $\{1, \cos(\pi\,x), \sin(\pi\,x), \cos(2\pi\,x), \sin(2\pi\,x),....,\cos(N\pi\,x), \sin(N\pi\,x)\}$ provide a compact representation of the function in the mean square sense. However, when the outer product terms are used along with the trigonometric polynomials for function expansion, better results were obtained in the case of learning of a two-variable function. The trigonometric polynomial expansion of the original data set is shown in Table 5 which is done in the STAGE-II of the proposed FLANN architecture which is represented in the Figure 4.

The STAGE-III of the FLANN architecture describes the training of the datasets and the learning of the FLANN network. The learning of ANN can be described as approximating a continuous, multivariate function f(X) by an approximating function *fw(X)*.Given a function the objective of the learning algorithm is to find the optimum weights such that $f_w(X)$ obtained approximates f(X) within an error e. This is achieved by recursively updating the weights. Let the training sequence be denoted by $\{X_k, y_k\}$ and the weight of the network be W(k), where k is the discrete time index given by $k = \kappa + \lambda K$ where $\lambda = 0,1,2,.....,$ and $\kappa = 0,1,2,...,K$. From Equation (12) the jth output of FLANN at given time k is given as below:

$$\hat{y}_j = \rho\left(\sum_{i=1}^{N} w_{ji}\left(k\right)\varphi_i\left(X_k\right)\right) = \rho\left(w_j\left(k\right)\varphi^T\left(X_k\right)\right) \tag{13}$$

For all $X \in A$ and $j = 1, 2, 3... m$ where $\varphi = \left[\varphi_1\left(X_k\right)\varphi_2\left(X_k\right)...\varphi_N\left(X_k\right)\right]$. Let the corresponding error be denoted by $e_j\left(k\right) = y_j\left(k\right) - \hat{y}_j\left(k\right)$. *The Least Mean Square (LMS)* update rule for all the weights of the FLANN is given by,

$$W\left(k+1\right) = W\left(k\right) + \mu\delta\left(k\right)\varphi\left(X_k\right) \tag{14}$$

Table 5. The trigonometric polynomial expansion of the original dataset

	10-day EMA					20-day EMA					30-day EMA					ADO	STI	RSI9	RSI14	CPACC	HPACC	14-day William's %R				
2	sin(pi*x)	sin(2*pi*x)	x	cos(pi*x)	cos(2*pi*x)	sin(pi*x)	sin(2*pi*x)	x	cos(pi*x)	cos(2*pi*x)	sin(pi*x)	sin(2*pi*x)	x	cos(pi*x)	cos(2*pi*x)							sin(pi*x)	sin(2*pi*x)	x	cos(pi*x)	cos(2*pi*x)
3	-0.69222	0.999132	10610.62	-0.72168	0.041653	0.53928	0.90829	10635.57	0.84213	0.418351	0.30901	0.58778128	10671.51	0.9511	0.80902	.	.	.	.	.	.	-0.80502	-0.95515	-68.33	0.59325	-0.296119822
4	-0.60126	-0.96088	10639.19	0.79905	0.276977	0.68873	-0.99868	10648.16	-0.72501	0.051293	0.81694	0.94229361	10677.72	0.5767	-0.334788	.	.	.	.	.	.	-0.99128	-0.26121	-34.48	0.13175	-0.965281307
5	0.95893	0.543969	10709.84	0.28363	-0.839105	0.3625	-0.67569	10684.30	-0.93198	0.737183	0.38788	-0.7150253	10700.30	-0.9217	0.699099	.	.	.	.	.	.	-0.77892	-0.97696	-10.72	-0.62713	-0.213418057
6	-0.96938	-0.47607	10771.04	0.24555	-0.879409	-0.88248	0.83014	10718.78	-0.47034	-0.55755	-0.56374	0.93124832	10722.63	-0.8259	0.364385	.	.	.	.	.	.	0.94356	-0.62501	-17.40	-0.3312	-0.7806132
7	0.54976	0.918451	10847.68	0.83533	0.395536	0.97724	0.41459	10763.89	0.21212	-0.91001	-0.99955	0.05969682	10752.94	-0.0299	-0.998217	.	.	.	.	.	.	0.92356	0.70829	-9.63	0.38346	-0.705919906
8	-0.70795	0.999997	10918.79	-0.70626	-0.002382	-0.93129	-0.6785	10809.10	0.36428	-0.7346	0.55903	-0.9270395	10784.28	-0.8291	0.374964	.	.	.	.	.	.	-0.36523	-0.68	-14.13	0.93092	0.733210771
9	0.31344	0.595286	10973.66	0.94961	0.803514	0.64097	-0.98397	10848.28	-0.76757	0.178313	0.1785	-0.3512665	10812.42	-0.9839	0.936276	.	.	.	.	.	.	0.1342	0.26697	-21.97	0.99095	0.963980595
10	-0.92727	-0.69431	10965.18	0.37438	-0.719672	0.74814	0.99284	10855.77	0.66354	-0.11943	0.85956	0.87853467	10819.81	0.511	-0.477679	.	.	.	.	.	.	0.96801	0.48577	-43.60	0.25091	-0.874087129
11	0.62514	0.975862	10943.76	0.78051	0.21839	-0.99543	0.1902	10854.97	-0.09554	-0.98175	0.32598	0.616342	10821.59	0.9454	0.787479	.	.	.	.	.	.	0.98482	-0.3419	-49.47	-0.17359	-0.93973458
12	-0.00972	0.019449	10890.52	-0.99995	0.999811	0.16756	0.33038	10835.55	0.98586	0.943847	-0.3178	0.60264911	10810.58	-0.9482	0.798006	.	.	.	.	.	.	0.27748	0.53317	-63.94	0.96073	0.846009085
13	-0.96548	-0.50295	10837.08	0.26047	-0.864315	-0.83004	0.92584	10812.79	-0.55771	-0.37793	-0.81659	0.94269626	10796.78	-0.5772	-0.333652	.	.	.	.	.	.	0.49319	0.85807	-75.87	0.86992	0.513526257
14	0.95192	0.583248	10719.84	0.30635	-0.812294	0.72735	0.99831	10753.71	0.68627	-0.05807	0.85649	0.88417126	10757.78	0.5162	-0.467163	.	.	.	.	.	.	-0.95279	0.57861	-80.64	-0.30364	-0.815604399
15	0.65103	-0.98833	10630.16	-0.75906	0.152329	0.3173	0.6018	10703.53	0.84833	0.798645	0.25752	0.49766941	10723.52	0.9663	0.867367	.	.	.	.	.	.	-0.84856	-0.89794	-66.36	0.52909	-0.440121013
16	-0.96117	-0.5305	10622.97	0.27596	-0.847688	-0.90387	0.77336	10692.78	-0.42781	-0.63397	-0.99885	-0.095659	10714.95	0.0479	-0.995414	.	.	.	.	.	.	0.90594	0.76717	-47.66	0.42341	-0.641446248
17	-0.05524	0.110312	10658.42	0.99847	0.993897	-0.74891	0.99256	10704.70	-0.66267	-0.12174	0.46947	0.82903902	10721.59	0.8829	0.559191	.	.	.	.	.	.	0.08863	0.17656	-35.99	0.99606	0.984290056
18	0.19329	-0.37929	10648.34	0.98114	0.92528	-0.96195	-0.52566	10695.01	0.27323	-0.85069	0.99975	-0.0045606	10713.94	-0.0223	-0.999007	.	.	.	.	.	.	0.01994	-0.03986	-47.03	-0.9998	0.999205123
19	-0.96651	-0.49604	10644.98	0.25661	-0.868299	0.94078	0.63768	10688.81	-0.33901	-0.77014	-0.27119	0.52206092	10693.15	0.6512	0.852908	.	.	.	.	.	.	0.92423	0.70583	-45.65	0.38185	-0.708383747
20	-0.51089	-0.87837	10613.21	0.85965	0.477981	0.95873	-0.54516	10668.00	-0.28431	-0.83833	-0.75887	-0.9884159	10693.15	0.6512	-0.15177	.	.	.	.	.	.	0.54105	0.91004	-53.85	0.84099	0.414530347
21	0.7694	0.982938	10569.64	0.63877	-0.183938	0.97354	-0.44493	10639.97	-0.22851	-0.89556	-0.3727	0.69169843	10672.53	-0.928	0.722186	.	.	.	.	.	.	-0.63618	0.98168	-58.81	-0.77154	0.190559966
22	0.83256	0.922372	10595.68	0.55394	-0.386302	-0.99903	-0.08786	10646.91	0.04397	-0.99613	-0.76117	-0.9873157	10675.14	0.6485	-0.158769	.	.	.	.	.	.	0.90853	-0.75921	-41.38	-0.41782	-0.650845165
23	-0.33338	0.628617	10566.46	-0.94279	0.777715	-0.88588	0.82194	10626.73	-0.46391	-0.56957	0.68705	0.99849055	10659.65	0.7266	0.055921	.	.	.	.	.	.	0.3547	0.66327	-51.91	0.93498	0.748380483
24	-0.87126	-0.88527	10579.03	0.49082	-0.518186	0.55237	0.92091	10627.57	0.8336	0.389764	0.8299	-0.9260172	10658.09	-0.5579	-0.377481	.	.	.	.	.	.	-0.87938	0.83738	-32.67	0.47612	-0.546628311
25	-0.91317	-0.74436	10617.02	0.40757	-0.667774	-0.98776	0.30819	10642.85	-0.156	-0.95133	-0.19538	0.38323879	10666.47	-0.9807	0.923651	.	.	.	.	.	.	0.06016	-0.1201	-23.03	-0.99819	0.99276211
26	-0.56368	-0.93119	10625.20	0.826	0.364536	-0.75767	0.98897	10644.67	-0.65263	-0.14814	0.64929	-0.9876214	10666.18	-0.7605	0.156857	.	.	.	.	.	.	-0.01739	-0.03477	-34.02	0.99985	0.999395418
27	-0.85744	-0.88245	10607.05	0.51458	-0.470406	-0.23953	-0.46511	10633.31	0.97089	0.885254	-0.81284	0.9469356	10657.10	0.5825	-0.321423	.	.	.	.	.	.	-0.74358	-0.99439	-42.29	0.66865	-0.105811738
28	0.41476	0.754799	10603.51	0.90993	0.655957	-0.9743	-0.43894	10628.96	0.22526	-0.89851	-0.62954	0.97826623	10652.62	-0.777	0.207353	.	.	.	.	.	.	-0.99986	0.03356	-38.52	-0.01678	-0.999436684
29	0.94797	0.603569	10613.78	0.31835	-0.79731	0.99719	-0.14935	10631.91	-0.07488	-0.98878	-0.82457	-0.933021	10653.09	0.5658	-0.359822	.	.	.	.	.	.	0.63721	-0.98218	-49.24	-0.77069	0.187928357

where,

$$W = \left[w_1\left(k\right) w_2\left(k\right) \dots w_m\left(k\right) \right]^T$$

is the M x N dimensional weight matrix of the FLANN at the kth time instant is,

$$\delta\left(k\right) = \left[\delta_1\left(k\right) \delta_2\left(k\right) \dots \delta_m\left(k\right) \right]^T \tag{15}$$

and

$$\delta_j\left(k\right) = \left(1 - \hat{y}_j\left(k\right)^2\right) e_j(k) \tag{16}$$

Similarly, the *Recursive Least Square (RLS)* update rule for all weights of the FLANN is given by:

$$W\left(k+1\right) = W(k) + e_j(k) zzk'(k) \tag{17}$$

where,

$$zzk\left(k\right) = z\left(k\right) / \left(1+q\right),$$
$$q = X(k) \cdot zk(k) \ and \ zk(k) = R(k) \cdot X(k)) \tag{18}$$

The autocorrelation matrix R (k) is updated with the equation,

$$R\left(k+1\right) = R\left(k\right) - zzk\left(k\right) \cdot zk(k)' \tag{19}$$

which is initialized using the expression, $R(0) = \eta.I$, where I is the identity matrix and η is the constant.

Basics of Particle Swarm Algorithms

Particle swarm optimization (PSO) is a nature inspired algorithm invented by Kennedy and Eberhart (1995). Like Leonardo DaVincis work modeling flying machines from watching bird flight, PSO received its inspiration from bird flocking, fish schooling, and herds of animals. In PSO, a set of randomly generated solutions (initial swarm) propagates in the design space towards the optimal solution over a number of iterations (moves) based on large amount of information about the design space that is assimilates and shared by all members of the swarm. A complete chronicle of the development of the PSO algorithm from merely a motion simulator to heuristic optimization of the PSO algorithm is described in Kennedy and Eberhart (2001, 1995). The standard PSO algorithm broadly consists of three computational steps:

1.   Generation of particles' positions and velocities;
2.   Updating the velocity of each particle;
3.   Updating the position of each particle.

Here, a particle refers to a potential solution to a problem. A particle $\vec{x}_k$ in d-dimensional design space is represented as $\vec{x}_k = (x_{k1}, x_{k2}, x_{k3},........x_{kd})$, where k = 1, 2,..., N, N is the number of particles in a swarm. Each particle has its own velocity and maintains a memory of its previous best position, $P_k = P_{k1}, P_{k2}, P_{k3}......P_{kd}$. Let the velocity $\vec{P}_g = (P_{g1}, P_{g2}, P_{g3},...,P_{gd})$ refer to the position found by the kth member of the neighborhood that has the best performance so far. The particle changes its position from iteration to iteration based on the velocity updates. In each iteration $\vec{P}_g$ and $\vec{P}_k$ of the current swarm are combined with some weighting coefficients to adjust the velocities of the particles in the swarm. The position of the velocity adjustment influenced by the particle's previous best position is considered as the cognition component, and the position influenced by the best in the neighborhood is the social component.

The weight vector between hidden layer and output layer is multiplied with the resultant sets of non-linear outputs and are fed to the output neuron as input. Hence weighted sum is computed as follows:

$$s = \sum_{j=1}^{m} y_{ij} \cdot w_j, i = 1, 2, ..., N$$

and m be the total number of expanded features.

The network has the ability to learn through training by PSO. The training requires a set of training data, i.e., a series of input and associated output vectors. During the training, the network is repeatedly presented with the training data and the weights adjusted by PSO from time to time till the desired input–output mapping occurs. The estimated output is then computed by the following metric:

$$\hat{y}_i(t) = f(s_i), i = 1, 2, ..., N,$$

The error $e_i(t) = y_i(t) - \hat{y}_i(t), i = 1, 2, ..., N$ is the error obtained from the ith pattern of the training set. Therefore the error criterion function can be written as,

$$E(t) = \sum_{i=1}^{N} e_i(t),$$ (20)

and our objective is to minimize this function with an optimal set of weights.

In a minimization optimization problem, problems are formulated so that "best" simply means the position with the smallest objective value. Members of a swarm communicate good positions to each other and adjust their own position and velocity based on these good positions. So a particle has the following information to make a suitable change in its position and velocity:

- A global best that is known to all and immediately updated when a new best position is found by any particle in the swarm.
- Neighborhood best that the particle obtains by communicating with a subset of the swarm.
- The local best, which is the best solution that the particle has seen.

The particle position and velocity update equations in the simplest form that govern the PSO are given by:

$$v\left(t+1\right) = v\left(t\right) + c1 * rand * \left(pbest - x\left(t\right)\right) + c2 * rand \left(gbest - x\left(t\right)\right), \tag{21}$$

and

$$x\left(t+1\right) = x\left(t\right) + v(t+1). \tag{22}$$

As the swarm iterates, the fitness of the global best solution improves (decreases for minimization problem). It could happen that all particles being influenced by the global best eventually approach the global best, and from there on the fitness never improves despite however many runs the PSO is iterated thereafter. The particles also move about in the search space in close proximity to the global best and not exploring the rest of search space. This phenomenon is called 'convergence'. If the inertial coefficient of the velocity is small, all particles could slow down until they approach zero velocity at the global best. The selection of coefficients in the velocity update equations affects the convergence and the ability of the swarm to find the optimum. One way to come out of the situation is to reinitialize the particles positions at intervals or when convergence is detected. A single particle by itself is unable to accomplish anything. The power is in interactive collaboration. The algorithm adopted for tracing of stock index system using PSO is given below.

Algorithm

Let $f(x)$: $R^n \rightarrow R$ be the fitness function that takes a particle's solution with several components in higher dimensional space and maps it to a single dimension metric. Let there be n particles, each with associated positions $X_i \in R^n$ and velocities $v_i \in R^n$. Let $\hat{X}_i$ be the current best position of each particle and let $\hat{g}$ be the global best.

- Initialize X_i and V_i for all i. One common choice is to take $X_{ij} \in U$ [a_j, b_j] and $V_i = 0$ for all i and j= 1,......,m, where a_j, b_j are the limits of the search domain in each dimension, and U represents the uniform distribution (continuous).

$\hat{X}_i \leftarrow X_i$ and $\hat{g} \leftarrow$ arg min $f(X_i)$, i=1,..............,n.

- While not converged: For each particle $1 \leq i \leq n$:
  - Create random vectors r_1, r_2: r_{1j} and r_{2j} for all j, by taking r_{1j}, $r_{2j} \in U [0, 1]$ for j=1,.....m.
- Update the particle positions: $x_i \leftarrow x_i + v_i$.
- Update the particle velocities: $v_i \leftarrow \omega v_i + c_1 r_1 o(\hat{X}_i - Xi) + c_2 r_2 o(\hat{g} - x_i)$.
- Update the local bests: if $f(x_i) < f(\hat{x}_i)$, $\hat{x}_i \leftarrow x_i$.
- Update the global best: if $f(x_i) < f(\hat{g})$, $\hat{g} \leftarrow x_i$
- $\hat{g}$ is the optimal solution with fitness $f(\hat{g})$.

Note the following about the above algorithm:

- ω is an inertial constant. Good values are usually slightly less than 1.
- C_1 and C_2 are constants that say how much the particle is directed towards good positions. They represent a "cognitive" and a "social" component, respectively, in that they affect how much the particle's personal best and the global best (respectively) influence its movement. Usually we take $c_1, c_2 \approx 2$.
- r_1, r_2 are two random vectors with each component generally a uniform random number between 0 and 1.
- O operator indicates element-by-element multiplication.

3. PSO-FLANN AS HONN FOR FINANCIAL MODELING

PSO-FLANN is a typical three layer feed forward neural network consists of an input layer, a hidden layer and an output layer. The only difference from FLANN is that, the weight vector is evolved by the proposed PSO during the training of the network. Even though many heuristic approaches exist (Goldberg, 1989) for optimizing the weight vector, we use PSO because of its characteristics like rapid convergence to global solutions and less number of parameters to be optimized. In other words, here we are trying to reduce the local optimal solution of weight vector by PSO. The nodes between input and hidden layers are connected without weight vector, but the nodes between hidden layer and output layer are connected by weights. The signal of the output node is based on a function of the sum of the inputs to the node.

In PSO-FLANN architecture, there are d input nodes (i.e., equal to the number of inputs of the dataset) and m nodes in the hidden layer, where m is the number of functionally expanded node and one output neuron in the output layer. The connection between hidden layer and output layer is assigned with the weight vector. In this work, we have used the orthonormal trigonometric function for mapping the input feature from one form to another form of higher dimension. However, one can use a function that is very close to the underlying distribution of the data, but it requires some prior domain knowledge. In this work we are taking five functions out of which four are trigonometric and one is linear (i.e., keeping the original form of the feature value). Out of the four trigonometric functions, two are sine and two are cosine functions. In the case of trigonometric functions the domain is the given input values and range lies between $[-1, 1]$. It can be written as

$$f : D \to R^{[-1,1] \cup [x]},$$

(23)

where, $D = \{x_{i1}, x_{i2}, ..., x_{id}\}$, and d is the number of inputs.

In general let us take $f_1, f_2, ..., f_k$ as the number of functions to be used to expand each feature value of the pattern. Therefore, each input pattern can now be expressed as

$$\vec{x} = \{x_{i1}, x_{i2}, ..., x_{id}\} \rightarrow \{\{f_1(x_{i1}), f_2(x_{i1}), ..., f_k(x_{i1})\}, ..., \{f_1(x_{id}), f_2(x_{id}), ..., f_k(x_{id})\}\}$$
$$= \{\{y_{11}, y_{21}, ..., y_{k1}\}, ..., \{y_{1d}, y_{2d}, ..., y_{kd}\}\}.$$

The weight vector between hidden layer and output layer is multiplied with the resultant sets of non-linear outputs and are fed to the output neuron as an input. Hence the weighted sum is computed as follows:

$$s = \sum_{j=1}^{m} y_{ij}.w_j, i = 1, 2, ..., N \tag{24}$$

and m be the total number of expanded inputs.

The network has the ability to learn through training by PSO. The training requires a set of training data, i.e., a series of input and associated output vectors. During the training, the network is repeatedly presented with the training data and the weights adjusted by PSO from time to time till the desired input–output mapping occurs. The estimated output is then computed by the following metric:

$$\hat{y}_i(t) = f(s_i), i = 1, 2, ..., N .$$

The error $e_i(t) = y_i(t) - \hat{y}_i(t), i = 1, 2, ..., N$ is the error obtained from the ith pattern of the training set. Therefore the error criterion function can be written as,

$$E(t) = \sum_{i=1}^{N} e_i(t), \tag{25}$$

and our objective is to minimize this function with an optimal set of weights.

3.1 Representation of a Particle

For the evolutionary process, the length of each and every particle is m and it is fixed (i.e., the number of connection between expanded inputs of the hidden layer and the output neuron of the output layer), but one can go for variable length particle also. The variable length particle representation is highly useful for simultaneous evolution of architectures and weights. In this work our focus is on fixed length particle, the variable length particle is beyond the scope of our study. A particle can be represented as a vector of m weights, i.e., $(w_1, w_2, w_3, ..., w_m)$. In PSO-FLANN the weight values lie between $[-1, 1]$. Hence the velocity of the particle also lies between $[-1, 1]$. In case of extreme values like $w_i = 0$, one can believe that the connection between the expanded features and output node corresponding to w_i is not an informative one and is virtually deleted from the network.

3.2 Steps of PSO-FLANN

The steps involved in the process of PSO-FLANN financial modeling as follows:

1. The dataset is divided into two parts such as training set and testing set.
2. Then the each pattern is mapped from lower dimension to higher dimension using predefined functions.
3. Then each particle initialized randomly with small values from the domain [-1, 1].
4. While not converged:

```
For entire swarm
                        For each particle in the swarm
For each sample of training sample
                Calculate the weighted sum and feed as an input to the node
of the
                Output layer.
                Calculate the error and accumulate it.
End
        It is found that the fitness of the particle is equal to the accu-
mulated error.
                        If fitness value is better than the best fitness
value, then current value is set as the new personal best.
                End
                        Choose the particle with best fitness value of
all the particles as the global best.
                End
```

Update the Update the particle positions: $x_i \leftarrow x_i + v_i$.
Update the particle velocities: $v_i \leftarrow \omega v_i + c_1 r_1 o(\hat{X}_i - Xi) + c_2 r_2 o(\hat{g} - x_i)$.
Update the local bests: if $f(x_i) < f(\hat{x}_i)$, $\hat{x}_i \leftarrow x_i$.
Update the global best: if $f(x_i) < f(\hat{g})$, $\hat{g} \leftarrow x_i \hat{g}$ is the optimal solution with fitness $f(\hat{g})$.

5. While End.

The PSO algorithm is vastly different from the other traditional methods of training. It not only trains one network, but also trains a network of networks. PSO builds a set number of FLANN and initializes all network weights to random values and starts training each one. On each pass through a data set, PSO compares each network's fitness. The network with the highest fitness is considered the global best. The other networks are updated based on the global best network rather than on their personal error or fitness. Each neuron is assigned a position and velocity. The position corresponds to the weight of a neuron. The velocity is used to update the weight along with control power to know how much the position is updated. If a neuron is further away from the global best position, then it will adjust its weight more than a neuron that is closer to the global best position.

The particles in this context are considered as the individual networks not the neurons. The particles reside in the dimension of the hyperspace and are marked by the number of neurons in the network. A network is placed at a certain location in the problem hyperspace by the positions of each neuron in a network. Particles fly around the hyperspace containing maxima and minima by updating their position according to the best position found by their fellow particles. When particle come across the optima of sorts, it continues to climb the hill towards the optima. This is observed by the fellow particles and accordingly they adjust their positions to swarm towards the optima. The network stops training when the associated fitness at this optimum is acceptable and PSO assures that the network will never get stuck trying to converge to a false maxima.

4. EXPERIMENTAL DETAILS

Even though the proposed algorithms is primarily intended for prediction of datasets with large number of records and a moderate number of inputs, it can also be used very well on more conventional datasets. To exhibit this fact we evaluated our algorithm using a dataset consists of historical prices of the daily closing price, opening price, and lowest value in the day, highest value in the day and the total volume of stocks traded in each day obtained from the yahoo finance website: http://finance.yahoo.com/. We collected daily closing price of the index in each day values for DJIA starting from 3rd January 2000 to 22nd October 2007for a period of seven years which amounted to about 408 data points (shown in Figure 5). Each input is split into five branches each being distinct function of the primary input. Thus effectively, now the five times the primary inputs are considered which goes as inputs to the single neuron.

We have compared results of PSO-FLANN with other competing financial prediction methods such as MLP with gradient descent, FLANN with LMS update, FLANN with RLS update and Psi Sigma with the same set of orthonormal basis functions.

Figure 5. Graph showing daily price change of DJIA

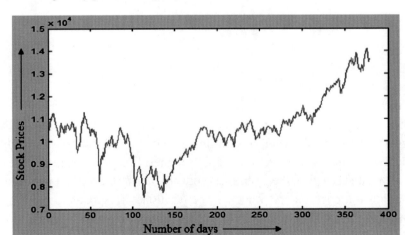

4.1 Environments

In order to evaluate the performance of the proposed learning scheme such as LMS and RLS algorithm updated FLANN as well as PSO optimized FLANN for tracing of stock index system problem, simulation experiments were carried out on a personal computer having, 2.30 GHz Core i5-2410M Intel CPU with 4.0 GB RAM in a 64-bitOperating System. The comparison of standard LMS, RLS training and PSO algorithms is discussed based on the simulation results implemented in Matlab 2010b. The dataset is divided into training and testing set as shown in Table 2.

4.2 Parameters

For our experiment, we have taken eleven input parameters for each pattern. For an eleven different statistical parameters of the stock index lag values, the total input to the single neuron FLANN is fifty five plus a bias. This gives us fifty six weights that are to be trained using the proposed adaptive algorithm for a particular stock index. The neurons add up the input weight products and bias. The sum is then taken up by a suitable activation function, specifically tan hyperbolic to give the output of the network. An optimum value of the convergence coefficient of 0.1 is considered for our all prediction experiments. The inputs of the network have been normalized for the proper training of the network. The inputs are normalized to values between +1 and -1 which has been done by the normalization technique shown below by considering the maximum and minimum of the data set. All the values have been normalized by using the following equation:

$$Y = \frac{2 * X - [Max(X) + Min(X)]}{[Max(X) + Min(X)]} \tag{26}$$

where, Y is the normalized values and X is the present value. The activation function used for the network output for both MLP as well as FLANN is Tangent Hyperbolic Sigmoid function. Table 3 summarizes the parameters considered in this simulation.

In PSO-FLANN, the quality of each particle is measured by the error criterion function E. It is also very important for the user to set a priori the values of the parameters of the proposed PSO algorithm. These parameters are presented in the Table 5. Researchers use different values for n for swarm size. In this work we have set n=10 X d to avoid under-fit and over-fit during the training of the algorithm. The larger the number of particles more is the computation time. Length of the particle is fixed to m, where, m depends on the functionally expanded features of the hidden layer. Although the parameters are quite

Table 2. The HONN datasets

Name of Period	Training Days	Beginning	End
Total Dataset	408	3rd January 2000	22nd October 2007
Training Dataset	265	24th July 2000	22nd August 2005
Testing Dataset	113	29th August 2005	22nd October 2007
Out-of-Sample Dataset (Validation Dataset)	30	3rd January 2000	17th July 2000

Table 3. Parameters considered for MLP-BP, 2nd FLANN with RLS & LMS and PSO-FLANN simulation

Parameters	MLP-BP	2nd FLANN-BP	PSO-FLANN
Learning Algorithms	Gradient Descent	LMS & RLS	-
Learning Rate	0.03	0.03	-
Momentum	0.07	0.07	-
Maximum Epoch	1000	1000	-
Minimum Error	0.001	0.001	0.001
Maximum Generations	-	-	100
Parameters Range	[-1,1]	[-1,1]	[-1,1]

restricted and there are no such standard rule to assign systematic parameter values to c_1, c_2 and ω but in this experimental study the value of ω is restricted to 0.5. The values of c_1, c_2 chosen as 1.6 and 1.7 respectively. The set of parameters are assigned after extensive set of trial and error process. The initial position and the velocity range of the particles in PSO lies in the interval [-1, +1] and if the global best position p_k is not improved for successive generations (100), then it goes for next iterations for finding the global optimum. Table 4 describes the symbols and parameters set for the PSO-FLANN Algorithm.

4.3 Training Process

The training of the proposed FLANN model network takes place in the following manner. The weight update is epoch based. The initial weights of the network are taken as 56 random values between -1 to +1. The input data set are also normalized prior to the network training. The weights remain unchanged till all of the training data set is fed into the network, compared with the desired output and their respective error stored is shown in the Figure 6. The mean error for the entire epoch is calculated, and then the adaptive weight update takes place. The Least Mean Square (LMS) update algorithm used in our experiment updates the weights by adding the product of the convergence constant, the respective input with the mean error for the epoch to the weights of the previous epoch.

The cost function for the training process is the Mean Square Error (MSE). It is suitable to end the training of the network when the minimum level of the cost function is observed. Thus for each iteration (epoch), the mean square error is calculated and plotted (shown in Figure 7). Each of the iterations involves training the network with the 378 odd patterns, calculation of mean error, weight update and representing the MSE. The number of iteration is decided upon by gradient of the MSE curve. It is

Table 4. Parameters set in the PSO-FLANN algorithm

Symbol	Name and Purpose of the Parameter
N	Size of the Swarm
Ω	Inertial constant(Always less than 1)
C_1	Cognitive Parameter (Here 1.6)
C_2	Social Parameter(Here 1.7)
O	Operator indicates element by element multiplication

Figure 6. Plot of predicted vs. actual price at the last iteration of training for DJIA

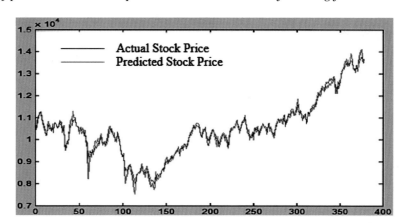

observed that at the 10000 iterations, there is no significant decrease in the MSE, hence the training experiment is stopped (shown in Figure 7). It is also observed that the high number of iterations tends to give better training of the network.

4.4 Testing Process

After the training process to the proposed FLANN is over, the weights are frozen for testing the network on inputs that were set apart from the training set. The testing set patterns are the input to the network and the output, the predicted index close price is compared with actual closing price of the DJIA index. The percentage of error is recorded for each data set and the mean of all the percentage error of the testing data set is calculated. The Mean Absolute Percentage Error (MAPE) is used to evaluate the

Figure 7. FLANN showing mean square error during training

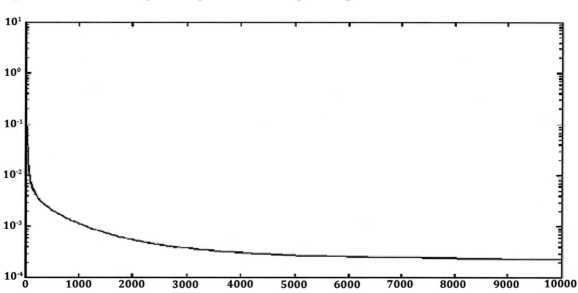

performance of the trained prediction model for the test data. The effort is to minimize the MAPE for testing patterns in the quest for finding a better model for forecasting stock index price movements The MAPE formula is given below:

$$MAPE = \frac{1}{n} \sum_{j=1}^{n} \left| \frac{Y_j - \hat{Y}_j}{Y_j} \right| \times 100 \tag{27}$$

4.5 Simulation Results

The experiments have been performed to study the one day, 30-days, and 60-days in advance prediction using FLANN with LMS and RLS updated algorithms and the results obtained is shown in Table 6.

The same experiment has been carried out with PSO-FLANN model using the parameter mentioned in the Table 4 and the results obtained are shown in Table 7.

Table 6. Comparative status of the both the LMS and RLS updated FLANN model

Stock Index	FLANN Inputs	Testing Periods	Advance Prediction Period(s)	MAPE (LMS)	MAPE (RLS)
DJIA	10-day EMA, 20-day EMA, 30-day EMA, ADO,STI,RSI9,RSI14,POROC27, CPACC,HPACC, 14-day William's %R	100 days	1- day	0.61%	0.54%
DJIA	10-day EMA, 20-day EMA, 30-day EMA, ADO,STI,RSI9,RSI14,POROC27, CPACC,HPACC, 14-day William's %R	100 days	30-days	2.73%	2.81%
DJIA	10-day EMA, 20-day EMA, 30-day EMA, ADO,STI,RSI9,RSI14,POROC27, CPACC,HPACC, 14-day William's %R	100 days	60-days	2.23%	2.32%

Table 7. Model Comparison for DJIA stock index using MAPE

Stock Index	FLANN Inputs	Testing Periods	Advance Prediction Period(s)	MAPE (LMS)	MAPE (RLS)	MAPE (PSO)
DJIA	10-day EMA, 20-day EMA, 30-day EMA, ADO,STI,RSI9,RSI14,POROC27, CPACC,HPACC, 14-day William's %R	100 days	1- day	0.61%	0.54%	2.19%
DJIA	10-day EMA, 20-day EMA, 30-day EMA, ADO,STI,RSI9,RSI14,POROC27, CPACC,HPACC, 14-day William's %R	100 days	30-days	2.73%	2.81%	7.31%
DJIA	10-day EMA, 20-day EMA, 30-day EMA, ADO,STI,RSI9,RSI14,POROC27, CPACC,HPACC, 14-day William's %R	100 days	60-days	2.23%	2.32%	8.19%

4.6 Comparisons with Other Models

The results obtained from the LMS and RLS updated FLANN model and PSO tuned FLANN model for performing the one day, 30-days, and 60-days in advance prediction of DJIA were compared with the MLP-BP as well as with the Psi Sigma model. Table 8 represents a summary of the comparative results of PSO-FLANN with other financial models like FLANN-LMS, FLANN-RLS, MLP-BP and Psi-Sigma on both the training set and testing set respectively.

4.7 Discussions

From the Table 8 it is clear that the RLS algorithm is faster computationally but less stable than LMS algorithm. It is also found that in case of lower number of ahead prediction, PSO tuned FLANN model gives the best result as compared to other HONN like Psi Sigma model as well as MLP-BP model. It is also marked that the LMS has the advantage of faster convergence but the probability of getting stuck in local optima is high. On the other hand, PSO is a derivative free technique but slower compared to LMS.

5. CONCLUSION AND FUTURE RESEARCH DIRECTIONS

Though the large numbers of applications of HONNs are found in pattern recognition and classifications, still then the applications of HONNs in the financial modeling and simulations cannot be neglected. In this chapter, experimental studies have demonstrated that the performance of PSO tuned FLANN model for the case of lower number of ahead prediction task is promising and PSO is marked as competitors for other top training algorithms. In most cases FLANN trained by LMS updated algorithm proved to be as good as or better than the RLS updated algorithm based FLANN but at the same time RLS updated FLANN model for the prediction of stock index system cannot be ignored. FLANN model has made

Table 8. Comparison of the HONN financial model with other models

Stock Index	FLANN Inputs	Testing Periods	Advance Prediction Period(s)	MAPE (LMS)	MAPE (RLS)	MAPE (PSO)	MAPE MLP-BP	MAPE Psi Sigma
DJIA	10-day EMA, 20-day EMA, 30-day EMA, ADO,STI,RSI9,RSI14,POROC27, CPACC,HPACC, 14-day William's %R	100 days	1- day	0.61%	0.54%	2.19%	0.75%	1.82%
DJIA	10-day EMA, 20-day EMA, 30-day EMA, ADO,STI,RSI9,RSI14,POROC27, CPACC,HPACC, 14-day William's %R	100 days	30-days	2.73%	2.81%	7.31%	0.85%	5.87%
DJIA	10-day EMA, 20-day EMA, 30-day EMA, ADO,STI,RSI9,RSI14,POROC27, CPACC,HPACC, 14-day William's %R	100 days	60-days	2.23%	2.32%	8.19%	0.91%	7.92%

prediction of the stock market indices simpler and involves lesser computation as compared to other such model used by the researchers. Hence, FLANN model tuned with LMS, RLS as well as PSO can attract the researchers working in financial domain for prediction task. Future research includes simultaneous evolution of architecture tuned by the evolutionary approaches. The expanded inputs will be chosen using an evolutionary technique, which will makes use of GA and gradually evolve inputs of the FLANN to achieve the desired model. A rigorous study on the convergence and stability analysis of the proposed model will also be made.

REFERENCES

Barnard, E., & Wessels, L. (1992). Extrapolation and interpolation in neural network classifiers. *IEEE Control Systems*, *12*(5), 50–53. doi:10.1109/37.158898

Barron, R., Gilstrap, L., & Shrier, S. (1987). Polynomial and neural networks: Analogies and engineering applications. *Proceedings of the International Conference on Neural Networks*, New York, (Vol. 2, pp. 431-439).

Bengtsson, M. (1990). *Higher Order Artificial Neural Networks*. Darby, PA, USA: Diane Publishing Company.

Chen, A. S., & Leung, M. T. (2004). Regression neural network for error correction in foreign exchange forecasting and trading, *Computers & Operations Research*, *31*, 1049–1068.

Dayhoff, H. E. (1990). *Neural Network Architectures: An Introduction*. New York: Van Nostrand Rein-hold.

Dehuri, S., & Cho, S. B. (2010). Evolutionarily optimized features in functional link neural network for classification. *Expert Systems with Applications*, *37*(6), 4379–4391. doi:10.1016/j.eswa.2009.11.090

Fletcher, R., & Reeves, C. M. (1964). Function Minimization by conjugate gradients. *The Computer Journal*, *7*(2), 149–154. doi:10.1093/comjnl/7.2.149

Ghosh, J., & Nag, A. C. (2002). Knowledge enhancement and reuse with radial basis function networks. *Proceedings of the 2002 International Joint Conference onNeural Networks IJCNN '02* (Vol. 2, pp. 1322–1327).

Giles, L., & Maxwell, T. (1987). Learning, invariance and generalisation in high-order neural networks. *Applied Optics*, *26*(23), 4972–4978. doi:10.1364/AO.26.004972 PMID:20523475

Goldberg, D. E. (1989). *Genetic Algorithms in Search, Optimization and Machine Learning* (1st ed.). Boston, MA, USA: Addison-Wesley Longman Publishing Co., Inc.

Hecht-Nielsen, R. (1987). Kolmogorov's mapping neural network existence theorem. *Proceedings of the International Conference on Neural Networks* (Vol. 3, pp. 11-13) New York: IEEE Press.

Hornik, K., Stinchcombe, M., & White, H. (1989). Multi-layer feed-forward networks are universal approximators. *Neural Networks*, *2*(5), 359–366. doi:10.1016/0893-6080(89)90020-8

Jessica, J. (2006). FX markets the most inefficient. *The Technical Analyst*, *19*(4).

Kennedy, J., & Eberhart, R. C. (1995). Particle swarm optimization. *Proceedings of the IEEE International Conference on Neural Networks*, Perth, Australia (pp. 1942–1948). doi:10.1109/ICNN.1995.488968

Kennedy, J., & Eberhart, R. C. (2001). *Swarm Intelligence Morgan Kaufmann* (3rd ed.). New Delhi, India: Academic Press.

Klaseen, M., & Pao, Y. H. (1990).The functional link net in structural pattern recognition. *Proceedings of the IEEE Region 10 Conference on Computer and Communication Systems TENCON '90* (Vol. 2, pp. 567-571).

Kosmatopoulos, E. B., Polycarpou, M. M., Christodoulou, M. A., & Ioannou, P. A. (1995). High-order neural network structures for identification of dynamical systems. *IEEE Transactions on Neural Networks*, *6*(2), 422–431. doi:10.1109/72.363477 PMID:18263324

Lapedes, A. S., & Farber, R. (1987). Non-linear signal processing using neural networks: Prediction and system modeling (Technical Report LA-UR-87). *Los Alamos National Laboratory*.

Lee, Y. C., Doolen, G., Chen, H., Sun, G., Maxwell, T., Lee, H., & Giles, C. L. (1986). Machine learning using a higher order correlation network. *Physica D. Nonlinear Phenomena*, *22*(1-3), 276–306. doi:10.1016/0167-2789(86)90300-6

Lippmann, R. P. (1989). Pattern classification using neural networks. *IEEE Communications Magazine*, *27*(11), 47–64. doi:10.1109/35.41401

Lisboa, P.J.G., & Vellido, A. (2000). Business Applications of Neural Networks. In P.J.G. Lisboa, B. Edisbury & A. Vellido (Eds.), Business Applications of Neural Networks: The State-of-the-Art of Real-World Applications (pp. vii-xxii). Singapore: World Scientific.

Mishra, B.B., & Dehuri, S. (2007). Functional Link Artificial Neural Network for Classification Task in Data Mining. *Journal of Computer Science*, *3*(12), 948–955. doi:10.3844/jcssp.2007.948.955

Mishra, P. S., & Dehuri, S. (2012). Potential indictors for stock index prediction: A Perspective. *International Journal of Electronic Finance*, *6*(2), 157–183. doi:10.1504/IJEF.2012.048465

Mishra, P.S. & Dehuri, S. (2014). Potential Indicators Based Neural Networks for Cash Forecasting of an ATM. *International Journal of Information Systems and Social Change, 5*(4), 41-57. DOI:10.4018/ijissc.2014100103

Murphy, J.J. (1999).Technical Analysis of the Financial Markets. New York: New York Institute of Finance.

Nabhan, T. M., & Zomaya, A. Y. (1994). Towards generating neural-network structures for function approximation. *Neural Networks*, *7*(1), 89–99. doi:10.1016/0893-6080(94)90058-2

Pao, Y. H. (1989). *Adaptive Pattern Recognition and Neural Networks*. Reading, MA: Addison-Wesley.

Pao, Y. H., & Takefuji, Y. (1992). Functional-link net computing: Theory, system architecture, and functionalities. *Computer*, *25*(5), 76–79. doi:10.1109/2.144401

Park, C. H., & Irwin, S. H. (2004). *The Profitability of Technical Analysis: A Review* (AgMAS Project Research Report 2004-04). University of Illinois at Urbana-Champaign, Urbana.

Pring, M. (1991). *Technical Analysis Explained: The successful Investor's Guide to Spotting Investment Trends and Turning points*. New York: McGraw Hill.

Psaltis, D., Brady, D., & Wagner, K. (1988). Adaptive optical networks using photorefractive crystals. *Applied Optics*, 27(9), 1752-1759.

Psaltis, D., Park, C., & Hong, J. (1988). Higher order associative memories and their optical implementations. *Neural Networks*, 1(2), 149–163. doi:10.1016/0893-6080(88)90017-2

Redding, N., Kowalczyk, A., & Downs, T. (1993). Constructive higher-order network algorithm that is polynomial time. *Neural Networks*, 6(7), 997–1010. doi:10.1016/S0893-6080(09)80009-9

Refenes, A. N. (Ed.). (1994). *Neural networks in the capital markets*. Chichester, UK: Wiley.

Reid, M. B., Spirkovska, L., & Ochoa, E. (1989). Simultaneous position, scale, rotation invariant pattern classification using third-order neural networks, International. *Journal of Neural Networks*, 1, 154–159.

Sahin, E. (1994). *A New Higher-order Binary-input Neural Unit: Learning and Generalizing Effectively via Using Minimal Number of Monomials, Master*. Middle East Technical University of Ankara.

Schoneburg, E. (1990). Stock market prediction using neural networks: A project report. *Neurocomputing*, 2(1), 17–27. doi:10.1016/0925-2312(90)90013-H

Selviah, D. R., Mao, Z. Q., & Midwinter, J. E. (1991). A high order feedback net (HOFNET) with variable non-linearity. IEEE, 11, 59-63.

Sewell, M. (2007). *Technical Analysis*. Department of Computer Science, University College London.

Thimm, G., & Fiesler, E. (1997). High-order and multilayer perceptron initialization. *IEEE Transactions on Neural Networks*, 8(2), 349–359. doi:10.1109/72.557673 PMID:18255638

Walczak, S., & Cerpa, N. (1999). Heuristic principles for the design of artificial neural Networks. *Information and Software Technology*, 41(2), 107–117. doi:10.1016/S0950-5849(98)00116-5

Wood, J., & Shawe-Taylor, J. (1996). A unifying framework for invariant pattern recognition. *Pattern Recognition Letters*, 17(14), 1415–1422. doi:10.1016/S0167-8655(96)00103-1

Compilation of References

Abbott, L. F., & Arian, Y. (1987). Storage capacity of generalized networks. *Physical Review A.*, *36*(10), 5091–5094. doi:10.1103/PhysRevA.36.5091 PMID:9898773

Abdelbar, A. M. (1998). Achieving superior generalisation with a high order neural network. *Neural Computing & Applications*, *7*(2), 141–146. doi:10.1007/BF01414166

Abdelbar, A. M., Attia, S., & Tagliarini, G. A. (2002). A hybridization of Bayesian and neural learning. *Neurocomputing*, *48*(1), 443–453. doi:10.1016/S0925-2312(01)00608-7

Abdelbar, A. M., & Tagliarini, G. (1996). HONEST: A new high order feedforward neural network, *Proceedings of the IEEE International Conference on Neural Networks* (Vol. 2, pp. 1257-1262). doi:10.1109/ICNN.1996.549078

Abdel-Galil, T. K., El-Saadany, E. F., & Salama, M. M. A. (2003). Power quality event detection using adaline. *Electric Power Systems Research*, *64*(2), 137–144. doi:10.1016/S0378-7796(02)00173-6

Abraham, A., Nath, B., & Mahanti, P. K. (2001). Hybrid intelligent systems for stock market analysis. In *Computational science-ICCS 2001* (pp. 337–345). Springer Berlin Heidelberg. doi:10.1007/3-540-45718-6_38

Agüera-Pérez, A., Palomares-Salas, J. C., De la Rosa, J. J. G., Sierra-Fernández, J. M., Ayora-Sedeño, D., & Moreno-Muñoz, A. (2011). Characterization of electrical sags and swells using higher-order statistical estimators. *Journal of the International Measurement Confederation*, *44*(8), 1453–1460.

Aiken, M. W., & Bsat, M. (1999). Forecasting Market Trends with Neural Networks. *IS Management*, *16*(4), 1–7.

Alanis, A. Y., Sanchez, E. N., & Loukianov, A. G. (2006). Discrete- Time Recurrent Neural Induction Motor Control using Kalman Learning. *Proceedings of International Joint Conference on Neural Networks*, Vancouver, Canada (pp. 1993 – 2000). doi:10.1109/IJCNN.2006.246946

Alanis, A. Y., Sanchez, E. N., & Loukianov, A. G. (2009). Real-time output tracking for induction motors by recurrent high-order neural network control. *Proceedings of the 17th Mediterranean Conference on Control and Automation MED '09*, Thessaloniki, Greece (pp. 868–873). doi:10.1109/MED.2009.5164654

Alanis, A. Y., Sanchez, E. N., Loukianov, A. G., & Perez-Cisneros, M. A. (2010). Real-Time Discrete Neural Block Control Using Sliding Modes for Electric Induction Motors. *IEEE Transactions on Control Systems Technology*, *18*(1), 11–21. doi:10.1109/TCST.2008.2009466

Alatas, B. (2011). ACROA: Artificial chemical reaction optimization algorithm for global optimization. *Expert Systems with Applications*, *38*(10), 13170–13180. doi:10.1016/j.eswa.2011.04.126

Alatas, B. (2012). A novel chemistry based metaheuristic optimization method for mining of classification rules. *Expert Systems with Applications*, *39*(12), 11080–11088. doi:10.1016/j.eswa.2012.03.066

Alexandrov, A. G., & Palenov, M. V. (2014). Adaptive PID controllers: State of the art and development prospects. *Automation and Remote Control, 75*(2), 188–199. doi:10.1134/S0005117914020027

Alippi, C., Boracchi, G., & Roveri, M. (2013). Just-In-Time Classifiers for Recurrent Concepts. *IEEE Transactions on Neural Networks and Learning Systems, 24*(4), 620–634. doi:10.1109/TNNLS.2013.2239309 PMID:24808382

AlRashidi, M. R., & El-Hawary, M. E. (2009). A survey of particle swarm optimization applications in electric power systems. *IEEE Transactions on* Evolutionary Computation, *13*(4), 913–918.

Al-Tamimi, A., Lewis, F., & Abu-Khalaf, M. (2008). Discrete-time nonlinear hjb solution using approximate dynamic programming: Convergence proof. *IEEE Transactions on* Systems, Man, and Cybernetics, Part B: Cybernetics, *38*(4), 943–949.

Amari, S. (1990). Mathematical foundations of neurocomputing. *Proceedings of the IEEE, 79*(9), 1443–1463. doi:10.1109/5.58324

Amari, S., & Maginu, K. (1988). Statistical neurodynamics of associative memory. *Neural Networks, 1*(1), 63–73. doi:10.1016/0893-6080(88)90022-6

Amari, S., & Yanai, H. (1993). Statistical neurodynamics of various types of associative memories. In M. H. Hassoun (Ed.), *Associative Neural Memories: Theory and Implementations*. Oxford University Press.

Aminian, F., Suarez, E. D., Aminian, M., & Walz, D. T. (2006). Forecasting economic data with neural networks. *Computational Economics, 28*(1), 71–88. doi:10.1007/s10614-006-9041-7

Amit, D., Gutfreund, H., & Sompolinsky, H. (1985). Storing infinite numbers of patterns in a spin-glass model of neural networks. *Physical Review Letters, 55*(14), 1530–1533. doi:10.1103/PhysRevLett.55.1530 PMID:10031847

Andonie, R., Chronopoulos, A. T., Grosu, D., & Galmeanu, H. (2006). An efficient concurrent implementation of a neural network algorithm. *Concurrency and Computation, 18*(12), 1559–1573. doi:10.1002/cpe.987

Angrisani, L., Daponte, P., & D'Apuzzo, M. (2001). Wavelet Network-based detection and classification of transients. *IEEE Transactions on Instrumentation and Measurement, 50*(5), 1425–1435. doi:10.1109/19.963220

Arai, M., Kohon, R., & Imai, H. (1991). Adaptive control of a neural network with a variable function of a unit and its application. *Transactions of the Institute of Electronics, Information and Communication Engineers, J74-A*, 551–559.

Aristoklis D Anastasiadis, G. D. M. (2003). *An efficient improvement of the Rprop algorithm.* 10.13140/2.1.5157.7282

Arteaga, C., & Marrero, I. (2013). Universal approximation by radial basis function networks of delsarte translates. *Neural Networks, 46*, 299–305. doi:10.1016/j.neunet.2013.06.011 PMID:23876407

Arteaga, C., & Marrero, I. (2014). Approximation in weighted p-mean by RBF networks of Delsarte translates. *Journal of Mathematical Analysis and Applications, 414*(1), 450–460. doi:10.1016/j.jmaa.2014.01.012

Artyomov, E., & Yadid-Pecht, O. (2005). Modified High-Order Neural Network for Invariant Pattern Recognition. *Pattern Recognition Letters, 26*(6), 843–851. doi:10.1016/j.patrec.2004.09.029

Asuncion, A., & Newman, D. (2007). University of California at Irvine Machine Learning Repository. Retrieved from http://www.ics.uci.edu/~mlearn/MLRepository.html, 2007.

Atiya, A.F. (2001). Bankruptcy prediction for credit risk using neural networks: A survey and new results. *IEEE Transactions on Neural Networks*, 12(4), 929-935.

Babaei, M. (2013). A general approach to approximate solutions of nonlinear differential equations using particle swarm optimization. *Applied Soft Computing*, *13*(7), 3354–3365. doi:10.1016/j.asoc.2013.02.005

Barnard, E., & Wessels, L. (1992). Extrapolation and interpolation in neural network classifiers. *IEEE Control Systems*, *12*(5), 50–53. doi:10.1109/37.158898

Barron, R., Gilstrap, L., & Shrier, S. (1987). Polynomial and neural networks: Analogies and engineering applications. *Proceedings of the International Conference on Neural Networks*, New York, (Vol. 2, pp. 431-439).

Barron, R., Gilstrap, L., & Shrier, S. (1987). Polynomial and neural networks: analogies and engineering applications. *Proceedings of International Conference of Neural Networks*New York, USA (Vol. 2, pp. 431-439).

Baruch, I. S., Galvan-Guerra, R., & Nenkova, B. (2008). Centralized Indirect Control of an Anaerobic Digestion Bioprocess Using Recurrent Neural Identifier.Artificial Intelligence: Methodology, sytems and applications,*LNCS* (Vol. *5253*, pp. 297–310). doi:10.1007/978-3-540-85776-1_25

Basar, T., & Olsder, G. J. (1995). *Dynamic Non-cooperative Game Theory* (2nd ed.). New York, New York, USA: Academic Press.

Behnke, S., & Karayiannis, N. B. (1998). CNeT: Competitive neural trees for pattern classifications. *IEEE Transactions on Neural Networks*, *9*(6), 1352–1369. doi:10.1109/72.728387 PMID:18255815

Benes, P., & Bukovsky, I. (2014). Neural network approach to hoist deceleration control. *Proceedings of the 2014 International Joint Conference on Neural Networks (IJCNN)* (pp. 1864–1869). IEEE. Retrieved from http://ieeexplore.ieee.org/xpls/abs_all.jsp?arnumber=6889831

Bengtsson, M. (1990). *Higher Order Artificial Neural Networks*. Darby, PA, USA: Diane Publishing Company.

Blum, E., & Li, K. (1991). Approximation theory and feed-forward networks. *Neural Networks*, *4*(4), 511–515. doi:10.1016/0893-6080(91)90047-9

Bollen, M. H. J., Bahramirad, S., & Khodaei, A. (2014). Is there a place for power quality in the smart grid? *Proceedings of 2014 IEEE 16th International Conference on Harmonics and Quality of Power* Bucharest, Romania, University Politehnica of Bucharest (pp. 713-717). doi:10.1109/ICHQP.2014.6842865

Bollen, M.H.J., & Gu, I.Y.H., Axelber, P.G.V., & Styvaktakis, E. (2007). Classification of underlying causes of power quality disturbances: Deterministic versus statistical methods. *EURASIP Journal on Advances in Signal Processing*, *1*(1), 172.

Bolón-Canedo, V., Porto-Díaz, I., Sánchez-Maroño, N., & Alonso-Betanzos, A. (2014). A framework for cost-based feature selection. *Pattern Recognition*, *47*(7), 2481–2489. doi:10.1016/j.patcog.2014.01.008

Bouaziz, S., Alimi, A. M., & Abraham, A. (2014) Universal approximation propriety of flexible beta basis function neural tree. *Proceedings of theInternational Joint Conference on Neural Networks (IJCNN)* (pp. 573-580). doi:10.1109/IJCNN.2014.6889671

Boutalis, Y. S., Christodoulou, M. A., & Theodoridis, D. C. (2010). Identification of nonlinear systems using a new neuro-fuzzy dynamical system definition based on high order neural network function approximators. In M. Zhang (Ed.), *Artificial Higher Order Neural Networks for Computer Science and Engineering – Trends for Emerging Applications* (pp. 423–449). Hershey, PA, USA: IGI Global, Information Science Reference. doi:10.4018/978-1-61520-711-4.ch018

Boutalis, Y. S., Theodoridis, D. C., & Christodoulou, M. A. (2009). A new Neuro FDS definition for indirect adaptive control of unknown nonlinear systems using a method of parameter hopping. *IEEE Transactions on Neural Networks*, *20*(4), 609–625. doi:10.1109/TNN.2008.2010772 PMID:19273046

Bukovsky, I., & Bila, J. (2010). Adaptive Evaluation of Complex Dynamical Systems Using Low-Dimensional Neural Architectures. In Y. Wang, D. Zhang, & W. Kinsner (Eds.), Advances in Cognitive Informatics and Cognitive Computing (Vol. 323, pp. 33–57). Berlin, Heidelberg: Springer Berlin Heidelberg; Retrieved from http://link.springer.com/10.1007/978-3-642-16083-7_3 doi:10.1007/978-3-642-16083-7_3

Bukovsky, I., Bila, J., & Gupta, M. M, Hou, Z-G., & Homma, N. (2010a). Foundation and classification of nonconventional neural units and paradigm of nonsynaptic neural interaction. In Y. Wang (Ed.), Discoveries and Breakthroughs in Cognitive Informatics and Natural Intelligence (pp.508-523). Hershey, PA, USA: IGI Publishing.

Bukovsky, I., Bila, J., & Gupta, M. M. (2005). Linear Dynamic Neural Units with Time Delay for Identification and Control (in Czech). *Automatizace*, 48(10), 628-635.

Bukovsky, I., Hou, Z.-G., Bila, J., & Gupta, M. M. (2007). Foundation of Notation and Classification of Nonconventional Static and Dynamic Neural Units. *Proceedings of the6th IEEE International Conference on Cognitive Informatics* (pp. 401–407). http://doi.org/ doi:10.1109/COGINF.2007.4341916

Bukovsky, I., Redlapalli, S., & Gupta, M. M. (2003). Quadratic and cubic neural units for identification and fast state feedback control of unknown nonlinear dynamic systems. *Proceedings of theFourth International Symposium on Uncertainty Modeling and Analysis, 2003. ISUMA 2003* (pp. 330–334). http://doi.org/ doi:10.1109/ISUMA.2003.1236182

Bukovsky, I. (2013). Learning Entropy: Multiscale Measure for Incremental Learning. *Entropy*, 15(10), 4159–4187. doi:10.3390/e15104159

Bukovsky, I., Benes, P., & Slama, M. (2015). Laboratory Systems Control with Adaptively Tuned Higher Order Neural Units. In R. Silhavy, R. Senkerik, Z. K. Oplatkova, Z. Prokopova, & P. Silhavy (Eds.), *Intelligent Systems in Cybernetics and Automation Theory* (pp. 275–284). Springer International Publishing; doi:10.1007/978-3-319-18503-3_27

Bukovsky, I., Kinsner, W., & Bila, J. (2012). Multiscale analysis approach for novelty detection in adaptation plot. In *Sensor Signal Processing for Defence* (pp. 1–6). SSPD; doi:10.1049/ic.2012.0114

Bukovsky, I., & Oswald, C. (2015). *Case Study of Learning Entropy for Adaptive Novelty Detection in Solid-fuel Combustion Control*. Advances in Intelligent Systems and Computing.

Bukovsky, I., Oswald, C., Cejnek, M., & Benes, P. M. (2014). Learning entropy for novelty detection a cognitive approach for adaptive filters. In *Sensor Signal Processing for Defence* (pp. 1–5). SSPD. doi:10.1109/SSPD.2014.6943329

Butt, N. R., & Shafiq, M. (2006). Higher-Order Neural Network Based Root-Solving Controller for Adaptive Tracking of Stable Nonlinear Plants.*Proceedings of IEEE International Conference on Engineering of Intelligent Systems,*Islamabad, Pakistan (pp. 1–6). doi:10.1109/ICEIS.2006.1703175

Calderon, T. G., & Cheh, J. J. (2002). A roadmap for future neural networks research in auditing and risk assessment. *International Journal of Accounting Information Systems*, 3(4), 203–236. doi:10.1016/S1467-0895(02)00068-4

Campolucci, P., Capparelli, F., Guarnieri, S., Piazza, F., & Uncini, A. (1996). Neural networks with adaptive spline activation function. *Proceedings of IEEE MELECON '96*, Bari, Italy (pp. 1442-1445). doi:10.1109/MELCON.1996.551220

Campos, J., Loukianov, A. G., & Sanchez, E. N. (2003). Synchronous motor VSS control using recurrent high order neural networks.*Proceedings of 42nd IEEE Conference on Decision and Control*, Maui, Hawaii, USA (Vol. 4, pp. 3894–3899). doi:10.1109/CDC.2003.1271757

Cejnek, M., Benes, P. M., & Bukovsky, I. (2014). Another Adaptive Approach to Novelty Detection in Time Series. In Computer Science & Information Technology (Vol. 4, pp. 341–351). Academy & Industry Research Collaboration Center (AIRCC). http://doi.org/ doi:10.5121/csit.2014.4229

Chakraborty, R., & Pal, N. R. (2015). Feature selection using a neural framework with controlled redundancy. *IEEE Transactions on* Neural Networks and Learning Systems, *26*(1), 35–50.

Chan, S. B., & Michael. (1988). Memory capacity of artificial neural networks with high order node connections. *Proc. of IEEE International Conference on Neural Networks* (pp. 207-216).

Charitou, A., & Charalambous, C. (1996). The prediction of earnings using financial statement information: Empirical evidence with logit models and artificial neural networks. *Intelligent Systems in Accounting, Finance & Management*, *5*(4), 199–215. doi:10.1002/(SICI)1099-1174(199612)5:4<199::AID-ISAF114>3.0.CO;2-C

Chauhan, R. S., & Arya, S. K. (2013). An application of swarm intelligence for the design of IIR digital filters. *International Journal of Swarm Intelligence*, *1*(1), 3–18. doi:10.1504/IJSI.2013.055799

Chen, G., & Lewis, F. L. (2013). Cooperative Control of Unknown Networked Lagrange Systems Using Higher Order Neural Networks. In M. Zhang (Ed.), Artificial Higher Order Neural Networks for Modeling and Simulation (pp. 214-236). Hershey, PA, USA: IGI Global.

Chen, Y., Wu, P., & Wu, Q. (2009). Foreign Exchange Rate Forecasting Using Higher Order Flexible Neural Tree. In M. Zhang (Ed.), Artificial Higher Order Neural Networks for Economics and Business (pp. 94-112). Hershey, PA, USA: IGI Global.

Chen, A. S., & Leung, M. T. (2004). Regression neural network for error correction in foreign exchange forecasting and trading, *Computers & Operations Research*, *31*, 1049–1068.

Chen, F. C., & Khalil, H. K. (1992). Adaptive control of nonlinear systems using neural networks. *International Journal of Control*, *55*(6), 1299–1317. doi:10.1080/00207179208934286

Chen, L., & Narendra, K. S. (2002, June). Nonlinear Adaptive Control Using Neural Networks and Multiple Models. *Proceedings of the 2000 American Control Conference,* Chicago, Illinois (pp. 4199-4203).

Cheung, K.-W., & Lee, T. (1993). On the convergence of neural network for higher order programming. *Proc. of International Joint Conference on Neural Networks* (Vol. 2, pp. 1507-1511).

Chiang, W. C., Urban, T. L., & Baldridge, G. W. (1996). A neural network approach to mutual fund net asset value forecasting. *Omega*, *24*(2), 205–215. doi:10.1016/0305-0483(95)00059-3

Chi-Sing, L., & Lai-Wan, C. (2003). Dual extended Kalman filtering in recurrent neural networks. *Neural Networks*, *16*(2), 223–239. doi:10.1016/S0893-6080(02)00230-7 PMID:12628608

Choi, J. H., Lee, M. K., & Rhee, M. W. (1995, June). Trading S&P 500 stock index futures using a neural network. *Proceedings of the third annual international conference on artificial intelligence applications on Wall Street* (pp. 63-72).

Ch, U. M., Babu, Y., & Amaresh, K. (2011). *Sliding Mode Speed Control of a DC Motor. Communication Systems and Network Technologies.* CSNT: Katra, Jammu, India.

Chun Liu, H., Hsien Lee, Y., & Chih Lee, M. (2009). Forecasting China Stock Markets Volatility via GARCH Models Under Skewed-GED Distribution.

Collobert, R., & Weston, J. (2008). A unified architecture for natural language processing: deep neural networks with multitask learning. *Proceedings of international conference on machine learning (ICML),* Helsinki, Finland (pp. 160–167). doi:10.1145/1390156.1390177

Costa, M., Goldberger, A. L., & Peng, C.-K. (2002). Multiscale Entropy Analysis of Complex Physiologic Time Series. *Physical Review Letters*, *89*(6), 068102. doi:10.1103/PhysRevLett.89.068102 PMID:12190613

Costarelli, D. (2014). Interpolation by neural network operators activated by ramp functions. *Journal of Mathematical Analysis and Applications*, *419*(1), 574–582. doi:10.1016/j.jmaa.2014.05.013

Crane, J., & Zhang, M. (2005). Data simulation using SINCHONN model. *Proceedings of 2005 IASTED International Conference on Computational Intelligence,*Calgary, Canada (pp. 50 -55).

Cuellar, F. (2006). Analysis and design of a wheeled holonomic omnidirectional robot. *Proceedings of the IEEE 3rd Latin American Robotics Symposium LARS '06* (pp. 41–46). IEEE. doi:10.1109/LARS.2006.334341

Cybenko, G. (1989). Approximation by superpositions of a sigmoidal function. *Mathematics of Control, Signals, and Systems*, *2*(4), 303–314. doi:10.1007/BF02551274

Dahl, G., Yu, D., Deng, L., & Acero, A. (2012). Context-dependent pretrained deep neural networks for large vocabulary speech recognition. *IEEE Trans. Audio Speech Lang. Process.*, *20*(1), 30–42. doi:10.1109/TASL.2011.2134090

Darbellay, G. A., & Slama, M. (2000). Forecasting the short-term demand for electricity: Do neural networks stand a better chance? *International Journal of Forecasting*, *16*(1), 71–83. doi:10.1016/S0169-2070(99)00045-X

Das, A., & Lewis, F. (2013). Distributed Adaptive Control for Multi-Agent Systems with Pseudo Higher Order Neural Net. In M. Zhang (Ed.), Artificial Higher Order Neural Networks for Modeling and Simulation (pp. 194-213). Hershey, PA, USA: IGI Global.

Das, A., Lewis, F. L., & Subbarao, K. (2010). Back-Stepping Control of Quadrotor: A Dynamically Tuned Higher Order Like Neural Network Approach. In M. Zhang (Ed.), Artificial Higher Order Neural Networks for Computer Science and Engineering – Trends for Emerging Applications (pp. 484-513). Hershey, PA, USA: IGI Global.

Dayhoff, H. E. (1990). *Neural Network Architectures: An Introduction*. New York: Van Nostrand Rein-hold.

De la Rosa, J. J. G., Agüera-Pérez, A., Palomares-Salas, J. C., Sierra-Fernández, J. M., & Moreno-Muñoz, A. (2012). A novel virtual instrument for power quality surveillance based in higher-order statistics and case-based reasoning. *Journal of the International Measurement Confederation*, *45*(7), 1824–1835.

De la Rosa, J. J. G., Lloret, I., Puntonet, C. G., & Górriz, J. M. (2004). Higher-order statistics to detect and characterize termite emissions. *Electronics Letters*, *40*(20), 1316–1317. doi:10.1049/el:20045664

De la Rosa, J. J. G., Moreno-Muñoz, A., Gallego, A., Piotrkowski, R., & Castro, E. (2010). Higher-order characterization of power quality transients and their classification using competitive layers. *Journal of the International Measurement Confederation*, *42*(3), 478–484.

De la Rosa, J. J. G., Sierra-Fernández, J. M., Agüera-Pérez, A., Palomares-Salas, J. C., Jiménez-Montero, A., & Moreno-Muñoz, A. (2013). Power quality events' measurement criteria based in higher-order statistics: towards new measurement indices.*Proceedings on the IEEE International Workshop on the Applied Measurements for Power Systems,*Aachen, Germany, RWTH Aachen University (pp. 73-79).

De la Rosa, J. J. G., Sierra-Fernández, J. M., Agüera-Pérez, A., Palomares-Salas, J. C., & Moreno-Muñoz, A. (2013). An application of the spectral kurtosis to characterize power quality events. *International Journal of Electrical Power & Energy Systems*, *49*, 386–398. doi:10.1016/j.ijepes.2013.02.002

Dehuri, S., & Cho, S. B. (2010a). Evolutionarily optimized features in functional link neural network for classification. *Expert Systems with Applications*, *37*(6), 4379–4391. doi:10.1016/j.eswa.2009.11.090

Dehuri, S., & Cho, S. B. (2010b). A hybrid genetic based functional link artificial neural network with a statistical comparison of classifiers over multiple datasets. *Neural Computing & Applications*, *19*(2), 317–328. doi:10.1007/s00521-009-0310-y

Demetriou, M. A., & Polycarpou, M. M. (1998). Incipient fault diagnosis of dynamical systems using online approximators. *IEEE Transactions on Automatic Control*, *43*(11), 1612–1617. doi:10.1109/9.728881

Di Ruscio, D. (2010). On Tuning PI Controllers for Integrating Plus Time Delay Systems. Retrieved from https://teora.hit.no/handle/2282/1044

Diao, Y., & Passino, K. M. (2002). Adaptive Neural/Fuzzy Control for Interpolated Nonlinear Systems. *IEEE Transactions on Fuzzy Systems*, *10*(5), 583–595. doi:10.1109/TFUZZ.2002.803493

Do, K., Jiang, Z., & Pan, J. (2004). Simultaneous tracking and stabilization of mobile robots: An adaptive approach. *IEEE Transactions on* Automatic Control, *49*(7), 1147–1151.

Dorigo, M., & Stützle, T. (2004). *Ant Colony Optimization*. Cambridge, MA, USA: MIT Press. doi:10.1007/b99492

Doroftei, I., Grosu, V., & Spinu, V. (2007). *Omnidirectional mobile robot–design and implementation*. INTECH Open Access Publisher.

Doulamis, A. D., Doulamis, N. D., & Kollias, S. D. (2000). Recursive nonlinear models for online traffic prediction of VBR MPEG Coded video sources.Proceedings of IEEE-INNS-ENNS international joint conference on neural networks IJCNN, Como, Italy (pp. 114-119).

Doulamis, A. D., Doulamis, N. D., & Kollias, S. D. (2003). An adaptable neural network model for recursive nonlinear traffic prediction and modeling of MPEG video sources. *IEEE Transactions on Neural Networks*, *14*(1), 150–166. doi:10.1109/TNN.2002.806645 PMID:18237998

Drossu, R., & Obradovic, Z. (1996). Rapid design of neural networks for time series prediction. *Computational Science & Engineering, IEEE*, *3*(2), 78–89. doi:10.1109/99.503317

Duque, C. A., Ribeiro, M. V., Ramos, F. R., & Szczupak, J. (2005). Power quality event detection based on the principle divided to conquer and innovation concept. *IEEE Transactions on Power Delivery*, *20*(4), 2361–2369. doi:10.1109/TPWRD.2005.855478

Durbin, R., & Rumelhart, D. E. (1989). Product units: A computationally powerful and biologically plausible extension to backpropagation networks. *Neural Computation*, *1*(1), 133–142. doi:10.1162/neco.1989.1.1.133

Eberhart, R., Simpson, P., & Dobbins, R. (1996). *Computational intelligence PC tools*. Academic Press Professional, Inc.

Ece, D. G., & Gerek, O. N. (2004). Power quality event detection using joint 2D wavelet subspaces. *IEEE Transactions on Instrumentation and Measurement*, *53*(4), 1040–1046. doi:10.1109/TIM.2004.831137

El-Nabarawy, I., & Abdelbar, A. M. (2014). Advanced learning methods and exponent regularization applied to a high order neural network. *Neural Computing & Applications*, *25*(3), 897–910. doi:10.1007/s00521-014-1563-7

El-Nabarawy, I., Abdelbar, A. M., & Wunsch, D. (2013). Levenberg-Marquardt and conjugate gradient methods applied to a high order neural network. *Proceedings IEEE International Joint Conference on Neural Networks* (pp. 2162-2132). doi:10.1109/IJCNN.2013.6707004

Epitropakis, M. G., Plagianakos, V. P., & Vrahatis, M. N. (2006). Higher-order neural networks training using differential evolution. *Paper presented at theInternational Conference of Numerical Analysis and Applied Mathematics*, Crete, Greece. Wiley-VCH.

Epitropakis, M. G., Plagianakos, V. P., & Vrahatis, M. N. (2010). Hardware-friendly higher-order neural network training using distributed evolutionary algorithms. *Applied Soft Computing*, *10*(2), 398–408. doi:10.1016/j.asoc.2009.08.010

Erhan, D., Manzagol, P., Bengio, Y., Bengio, S., & Vincent, P. (2009). The difficulty of training deep architectures and the effect of unsupervised pre-training.*Proceedings of international conference on artificial intelligence and statistics (AISTATS)*, Clearwater Beach, FL, USA (pp. 153–160).

Eskander, G. S., & Atiya, A. (2013). Symbolic Function Networks: Application to Telecommunication Networks Prediction. In M. Zhang (Ed.), Artificial Higher Order Neural Networks for Modeling and Simulation (pp. 237-253). Hershey, PA, USA: IGI Global.

Estevez, P. A., Tesmer, M., Perez, C. A., & Zurada, J. M. (2009). Normalized Mutual Information Feature Selection. *IEEE Transactions on* Neural Networks, 20(2), 189–201. doi:10.1109/TNN.2008.2005601

Fallahnezhad, M., & Zaferanlouei, S. (2013). A Hybrid Higher Order Neural Structure for Pattern Recognition. In M. Zhang (Ed.), Artificial Higher Order Neural Networks for Modeling and Simulation (pp. 364-387). Hershey, PA, USA: IGI Global.

Fallahnezhad, M., Moradi, M. H., & Zaferanlouei, S. (2011). A hybrid higher order neural classifier for handling classification problems. *International Journal of Expert System and Application*, 38(1), 386–393. doi:10.1016/j.eswa.2010.06.077

Farrell, J. A., & Polycarpou, M. M. (2006). *Adaptive approximation Based Control: Unifying Neural, Fuzzy and Traditional Adaptive Approximation Approaches*. N. Y., USA: John Wiley and Sons. doi:10.1002/0471781819

Fawcett, T. (2006). An introduction to ROC analysis. *Pattern Recognition Letters*, 27(8), 861–874. doi:10.1016/j.patrec.2005.10.010

Feldkamp, L. A., Prokhorov, D. V., & Feldkamp, T. M. (2003). Simple and conditioned adaptive behavior from Kalman. *Neural Networks*, 16(5-6), 683–689. doi:10.1016/S0893-6080(03)00127-8 PMID:12850023

Felix, R. A. (2003). Variable Structure Neural Control [Ph.D thesis]. Cinvestav, Unidad Guadalajara, Guadalajara, Jalisco, Mexico.

Felix, R. A., Sanchez, E. N., & Loukianov, A. G. (2005). Avoiding controller singularities in adaptive recurrent neural control. *Proceedings of the 16th IFAC World Congress*, Prague, Czech Republic.

Ferreira, D. D., Marques, C. A. G., Seixas, J. M., Cerqueira, A. S., Ribeiro, M. V., & Duque, C. A. (2011). *Exploiting Higher-Order Statistics Information for Power Quality Monitoring*. Rijeka, Croatia: InTech Open Science.

Fletcher, R., & Reeves, C. M. (1964). Function Minimization by conjugate gradients. *The Computer Journal*, 7(2), 149–154. doi:10.1093/comjnl/7.2.149

Foresti, G. L., & Dolso, T. (2004). An adaptive high-order neural tree for pattern recognition. *IEEE Transactions on Systems, Man, and Cybernetics. Part B, Cybernetics*, 34(2), 988–996. doi:10.1109/TSMCB.2003.818538 PMID:15376845

Frank, P. M. (1990). Fault diagnosis in dynamic systems using analytical and knowledge-based redundancy: A survey and some new results. *Automatica*, 26(3), 459–474. doi:10.1016/0005-1098(90)90018-D

Fukushima, K. (1980). Neocognitron: A Self-organizing Neural Network Model for a Mechanism of Pattern Recognition Unaffected by Shift in Position. *Biological Cybernetics*, 36(4), 193–202. doi:10.1007/BF00344251 PMID:7370364

Fulcher, J., Zhang, M., & Shuxiang, Xu. (2006). Application of higher-order neural networks to financial time series prediction. In J. B. Kamruzzaman (Ed.), *Artificial neural networks in finance and manufacturing* (pp. 80-108). Hershey, PA, USA: IGI Global.

Fulcher, J., Zhang, M., & Xu, S. (2006). Application of higher-order neural networks to financial time-series prediction. In *Artificial neural networks in finance and manufacturing* (pp. 80-108).

Fulcher, J., & Zhang, M. (2005). Higher-order neural networks. *Proceedings of 2005 International Conference on Advances in the Internet, Processing, Systems, and Interdisciplinary Research,* Costa Brava, Spain (p. 22).

Fulcher, J., Zhang, M., & Xu, S. (2006). The application of higher-order neural networks to financial time series prediction. In J. Kamruzzaman, R. K. Begg, & R. A. Aarker (Eds.), *Artificial Neural Networks in Finance and Manufacturing* (pp. 80–108). Hershey, PA, USA: Idea Group Publishing. doi:10.4018/978-1-59140-670-9.ch005

Functionalities of smart grids and smart meters (2009). *European Union.* Retrieved from http://ec.europa.eu/energy/en/topics/markets-and-consumers/smartgrids-and-meters

Funuhashi, K. (1989). On the approximate realization of continuous mapping by neural networks. *Neural Networks, 2,* 359–366.

Garcia-Hernandez, R. (2005). *Control Neuronal Decentralizado Discreto para Manipuladores Robuticos* [Ph.D thesis]. Cinvestav, Unidad Guadalajara, Guadalajara, Jalisco, Mexico.

Gately, E. (1995). *Neural networks for financial forecasting.* John Wiley & Sons, Inc.

Gerek, O. N., & Ece, D. G. (2004). 2-D analysis and compression of power quality event data. *IEEE Transactions on Power Delivery, 19*(2), 791–798. doi:10.1109/TPWRD.2003.823197

Gerek, O. N., & Ece, D. G. (2006). Power-quality event analysis using higher order cumulants and quadratic classifiers. *IEEE Transactions on Power Delivery, 21*(2), 883–889. doi:10.1109/TPWRD.2006.870989

Ge, S. S., Zhang, J., & Lee, T. H. (2004). Adaptive neural network control for a class of MIMO nonlinear systems with disturbances in discrete-time. *IEEE Transactions on Systems, Man, and Cybernetics, 34,* 1630-1634. PMID:15462431

Ghazali, R. (2007). *Higher order neural networks for financial time series prediction* [Doctoral dissertation]. Liverpool John Moores University.

Ghazali, R., & Al-Jumeily, D. (2009). Application of Pi-Sigma Neural Networks and Ridge Polynomial Neural Networks to Financial Time Series Prediction. In M. Zhang (Ed.), Artificial Higher Order Neural Networks for Economics and Business (pp. 271-294). Hershey, PA, USA: IGI Global.

Ghazali, R., Hussain, A., & El-Deredy, W. (2006, July). Application of ridge polynomial neural networks to financial time series prediction. *Proceedings of the International Joint Conference on Neural Networks IJCNN '06* (pp. 913-920). IEEE.

Ghazali, R., Hussain, A. J., & Liatsis, P. (2011). Dynamic Ridge Polynomial Neural Network: Forecasting the univariate non-stationary and stationary trading signals. *Expert Systems with Applications, 38*(4), 3765–3776. doi:10.1016/j.eswa.2010.09.037

Ghazali, R., Hussain, A., & Nawi, N. (2010). Dynamic ridge polynomial higher order neural network. In M. Zhang (Ed.), *Artificial Higher Order Neural Networks for Computer Science and Engineering* (pp. 255–268). Hershey, PA, USA: IGI Global.

Ghazali, R., Ismail, L. H., Husaini, N. A., & Samsuddin, N. A. (2012). *An Application of jordan pi-sigma neural network for the prediction of temperature time series signal.* INTECH Open Access Publisher. doi:10.5772/36026

Ghosh, J., & Nag, A. C. (2002). Knowledge enhancement and reuse with radial basis function networks. *Proceedings of the 2002 International Joint Conference on Neural Networks IJCNN '02* (Vol. 2, pp. 1322–1327).

Ghosh, J., & Shin, Y. (1992). Efficient Higher-order Neural Networks for Function Approximation and Classification. *International Journal of Neural Systems, 3*(4), 323–350. doi:10.1142/S0129065792000255

Giles, C. L., & Maxwell, T. (1987). Learning, invariance, and generalization in high-order neural networks. *Applied Optics*, *26*(23), 4972–4978. doi:10.1364/AO.26.004972 PMID:20523475

Goldberg, D. E. (1989). *Genetic Algorithms in Search, Optimization and Machine Learning* (1st ed.). Boston, MA, USA: Addison-Wesley Longman Publishing Co., Inc.

Goldberg, D. E., & Holland, J. H. (1988). Genetic algorithms and machine learning. *Machine Learning*, *3*(2), 95–99. doi:10.1023/A:1022602019183

Gorr, W. L. (1994). Research prospective on neural network forecasting. *International Journal of Forecasting*, *10*(1), 1–4. doi:10.4018/978-1-61520-711-4.ch011

Gourdeau, R. (1997). Object-oriented programming for robotic manipulator simulation. *Robotics Automation Magazine, IEEE*, *4*(3), 21–29. doi:10.1109/100.618020

Granger, C. W. J., & Lee, T. H. (1990). Multicointegration. In G. F. Rhodes, Jr & T. B. Fomby (Eds.), Advances in Econometrics: Cointegration, Spurious Regressions and Unit Roots (pp. 17-84). New York, USA: JAI Press.

Granger, C. W. J., & Weiss, A. A. (1983). Time series analysis of error-correction models. In S. Karlin, T. Amemiya & L. A. Goodman (Eds), Studies in Econometrics, Time Series and Multivariate Statistics (pp. 255-278). San Diego, USA: Academic Press. doi:10.1016/B978-0-12-398750-1.50018-8

Granger, C. W. J. (1981). Some properties of time series data and their use in econometric model specification. *Journal of Econometrics*, *16*(1), 121–130. doi:10.1016/0304-4076(81)90079-8

Granger, C. W. J., & Swanson, N. R. (1996). Further developments in study of cointegrated variables. *Oxford Bulletin of Economics and Statistics*, *58*, 374–386.

Grangier, D., Bottou, L., & Collobert, R. (2009). Deep convolutional networks for scene parsing. Proceedings of the ICML deep learning workshop, Montreal, Canada.

Greiner, M., Pfeiffer, D., & Smith, R. D. (2000). Principles and practical application of the receiver-operating characteristic analysis for diagnostic tests. *Preventive Veterinary Medicine*, *45*(1–2), 23–41. doi:10.1016/S0167-5877(00)00115-X PMID:10802332

Grossberg, S. (2013). Adaptive Resonance Theory: How a Brain Learns to Consciously Attend, Learn, and Recognize a Changing World. *Neural Networks*, *37*, 1–47. doi:10.1016/j.neunet.2012.09.017 PMID:23149242

Grover, R., & Hwang, P. Y. C. (1992). *Introduction to Random Signals and Applied Kalman Filtering*. New York, NY, USA: John Wiley and Sons.

Gu, I. Y. H., & Bollen, M. H. J. (2000). Time-frequency and time-scale domain analysis of voltage disturbances. *IEEE Transactions on Power Delivery*, *15*(4), 1279–1283. doi:10.1109/61.891515

Guler, M., & Sahin, E. (1994). A new higher-order binary-input neural unit: learning and generalizing effectively via using minimal number of monomials.*Proceedings of third Turkish symposium on artificial intelligence and neural networks* (pp. 51-60).

Gupta, M. M., Jin, L., & Homma, N. (2003). *Static and Dynamic Neural Networks*. Los Alamitos: IEEE Press. doi:10.1002/0471427950

Guresen, E., Kayakutlu, G., & Daim, T. U. (2011). Using artificial neural network models in stock market index prediction. *Expert Systems with Applications*, *38*(8), 10389–10397. doi:10.1016/j.eswa.2011.02.068

Guyon, I., & Elisseeff, A. (2003). An Introduction to Variable and Feature Selection. *Journal of Machine Learning Research*, *3*(7/8), 1157–1182.

Haddad, W. M., Chellaboina, V.-S., Fausz, J. L., & Abdallah, C. (1998a). Optimal discrete-time control for non-linear cascade systems. *Journal of the Franklin Institute*, *335*(5), 827–839. doi:10.1016/S0016-0032(97)00013-6

Hahm, N., & Hong, B. I. (2004). An approximation by neural networks with a fixed weight. *Computers & Mathematics with Applications (Oxford, England)*, *47*(12), 1897–1903. doi:10.1016/j.camwa.2003.06.008

Hall, M. A. (1999). *Correlation-based feature selection for machine learning*. The University of Waikato.

Hall, M. A., & Holmes, G. (2003). Benchmarking attribute selection techniques for discrete class data mining. *IEEE Transactions on* Knowledge and Data Engineering, *15*(6), 1437–1447.

Hamakawa, Y., Miyajima, H., Shigei, N., & Tsuruta, T. (2004). On Some Properties of Higher Order Correlation Associative Memory of Sequential Patterns. *Journal of Signal Processing*, *8*(3), 225–234. doi:10.2299/jsp.8.225

Han, K., & Wang, D. L. (2014). Neural Network Based Pitch Tracking in Very Noisy Speech, IEEE/ACM Transactions on Audio. *Speech and Language Processing, 22*(12), 2158–2168.

Hattori, M., & Hagiwara, M. (1995). Quick learning for multidirectional associative memories. *Proceedings of theIEEE International Conference on Neural Networks* (pp. 1949-1954).

Hayes, M. H. (1996). Recursive least squares. *Statistical Digital Signal Processing and Modeling*, 541.

Haykin, S. (1994). *Neural Networks*. Englewood Cliffs, NJ: Prentice Hall.

Haykin, S. (2001). *Kalman Filtering and Neural Networks*. New York, NY, USA: John Wiley and Sons. doi:10.1002/0471221546

Haykin, S. S. (1999). *Neural networks: a comprehensive foundation / Simon Haykin* (2nd ed.). Upper Saddle River, N.J.: Prentice Hall, c.

Hecht-Nielsen, R. (1987). Kolmogorov's mapping neural network existence theorem. *Proceedings of the International Conference on Neural Networks* (Vol. 3, pp. 11-13) New York: IEEE Press.

Hertz, J., Krogh, A., & Palmer, R. G. (1991). *Introduction to the Theory of Neural Computation*. Perseus Books.

He, Z., & Siyal, M. Y. (1999, August). Improvement on higher-order neural networks for invariant object recognition. *Neural Processing Letters*, *10*(1), 49–55. doi:10.1023/A:1018610829733

Hinton, G. E. (2009). Deep belief networks. *Scholarpedia*, *4*(5), 5947. doi:10.4249/scholarpedia.5947

Hinton, G., Osindero, S., & Teh, Y. (2006a). A fast learning algorithm for deep belief nets. *Neural Computation*, *18*(7), 1527–1554. doi:10.1162/neco.2006.18.7.1527 PMID:16764513

Hinton, G., & Salakhutdinov, R. (2006b). Reducing the dimensionality of data with neural networks. *Science*, *313*(5786), 504–507. doi:10.1126/science.1127647 PMID:16873662

Hochreiter, S., Bengio, Y., Frasconi, P., & Schmidhuber, J. (2001). Gradient flow in recurrent nets: the difficulty of learning long-term dependencies. In S. C. Kremer & J. F. Kolen (Eds.), *A field guide to dynamical recurrent neural networks*. New York: Wiley/IEEE Press.

Holland, J. H. (1975). *Adaptation in natural and artificial systems: an introductory analysis with applications to biology, control, and artificial intelligence*. U Michigan Press.

Holubar, P., Zani, L., Hager, M., Froschl, W., Radak, Z., & Braun, R. (2002). Advanced controlling of anaerobic digestion by means of hierarchical neural networks. *Water Research*, *36*(10), 2582–2588. doi:10.1016/S0043-1354(01)00487-0 PMID:12153025

Hopfield, J. J., & Tnak, D. W. (1985). Neural computation of decisions in optimization problems. *Biological Cybernetics*, *52*, 141–152. PMID:4027280

Hornik, K., Stinchcombe, M., & White, H. (1989). Multi-layer feed-forward networks are universal approximators. *Neural Networks*, *2*(5), 359–366. doi:10.1016/0893-6080(89)90020-8

Hou, Z. G., Cheng, L., & Tan, M. (2009). Decentralized robust adaptive control for the multiagent system consensus problem using neural networks. *IEEE Transactions on Systems, Man, and Cybernetics. Part B, Cybernetics*, *39*(3), 636–647. doi:10.1109/TSMCB.2008.2007810 PMID:19174350

Huang, D.S., Ip, H.H., Law, K.C.K., & Chi, Z. (2005). Zeroing polynomials using modified constrained neural network approach. *IEEE Transactions on* Neural Networks, *16*(3), 721–732.

Huang, G. B., Chen, L., & Siew, C. K. (2006a). Universal approximation using incremental constructive feedforward networks with random hidden nodes. *IEEE Transactions on Neural Networks*, *17*(4), 879–892. doi:10.1109/TNN.2006.875977 PMID:16856652

Huang, G. B., Zhou, H., Ding, X., & Zhang, R. (2012). Extreme learning machine for regression and multiclass classification. *IEEE Transactions on Systems, Man, and Cybernetics. Part B, Cybernetics*, *42*(2), 513–529. doi:10.1109/TSMCB.2011.2168604 PMID:21984515

Huang, G. B., Zhu, Q. Y., & Siew, C. K. (2006b). Extreme Learning Machine: Theory and Applications. *Neurocomputing*, *70*(1-3), 489–501. doi:10.1016/j.neucom.2005.12.126

Huan, L., & Lei, Y. (2005). Toward integrating feature selection algorithms for classification and clustering. *IEEE Transactions on* Knowledge and Data Engineering, *17*(4), 491–502. doi:10.1109/TKDE.2005.66

Husken, M., & Stagge, P. (2003). Recurrent neural networks for time series classification. *Neurocomputing*, *50*, 223–235. doi:10.1016/S0925-2312(01)00706-8

Hussain, A., & Liatsis, P. (2009). A Novel Recurrent Polynomial Neural Network for Financial Time Series Prediction. In M. Zhang (Ed.), Artificial Higher Order Neural Networks for Economics and Business (pp. 190-211). Hershey, PA, USA: IGI Global.

Hu, Z., & Shao, H. (1992). The study of neural network adaptive control systems. *Control and Decision*, *7*, 361–366.

Iftar, A. (1991). Decentralized optimal control with overlapping decompositions. Proceedings of the 1991 IEEE International Conference on Systems Engineering, Dayton, OH, USA (pp. 299–302). doi:10.1109/ICSYSE.1991.161138

Ioannou, P. A., & Sun, J. (1996). *Robust Adaptive Control*. New Jersey, USA: Prentice Hall, Inc.

Ismailov, V. E. (2012). Approximation by neural networks with weights varying on a finite set of directions. *Journal of Mathematical Analysis and Applications*, *398*(1), 72–83. doi:10.1016/j.jmaa.2011.11.037

Ismailov, V. E. (2014). On the approximation by neural networks with bounded number of neurons in hidden layers. *Journal of Mathematical Analysis and Applications*, *417*(2), 963–969. doi:10.1016/j.jmaa.2014.03.092

Ivakhnenko, A. G. (1971). Polynomial Theory of Complex Systems. *IEEE Transactions on Systems, Man, and Cybernetics*, *SMC-1*(4), 364–378. doi:10.1109/TSMC.1971.4308320

Jakubowski, J., Kwiatos, K., Chwaleba, A., & Osowski, S. (2002). Higher order statistics and neural network for tremor recognition. *IEEE Transactions on Bio-Medical Engineering, 49*(2), 152–159. doi:10.1109/10.979354 PMID:12066882

Jessica, J. (2006). FX markets the most inefficient. *The Technical Analyst,* 19(4).

Jiang, M., Gielen, G., & Wang, L. (2010). Analysis of quantization effects of higher order function and multilayer feedforward neural networks. In M. Zhang (Ed.), *Artificial Higher Order Neural Networks for Computer Science and Engineering* (pp. 187–222). Hershey, PA, USA: IGI Global. doi:10.4018/978-1-61520-711-4.ch008

John, G. H., Miller, P., & Kerber, R. (1996). Stock selection using rule induction. *IEEE Intelligent Systems, 5,* 52–58.

Jones, F. (1993). *Lebesgue integration on Euclidean space*. Jones and Bartlett.

Kageyama, T., & Ohnishi, K. (2002). An architecture of decentralized control for multi-degrees of freedom parallel manipulator. *Proceedings of the 7th International Workshop on Advanced Motion Control*, Maribor, Slovenia (pp. 74–79).

Kaita, T., Tomita, S., & Yamanaka, J. (2002, June). On a higher-order neural network for distortion invariant pattern recognition. *Pattern Recognition Letters, 23*(8), 977 – 984, New York, NY, USA: Elsevier Science Inc.

Kanaoka, T., Chellappa, R., Yoshitaka, M., & Tomita, S. (1992). A Higher-order neural network for distortion unvariant pattern recognition. *Pattern Recognition Letters, 13*(12), 837–841. doi:10.1016/0167-8655(92)90082-B

Karci, A., & Arslan, A. (2002). Uniform population in genetic algorithms. *IU-Journal of Electrical & Electronics Engineering, 2*(2), 495–504.

Karnavas, Y. L. (2010). Electrical Machines Excitation Control via Higher Order Neural Networks, In M. Zhang (Ed.), Artificial Higher Order Neural Networks for Computer Science and Engineering – Trends for Emerging Applications (pp. 366-396). Hershey, PA, USA: IGI Global.

Kasabov, N. K. (1996). *Foundations of Neural Networks, Fuzzy Systems and Knowledge Engineering*. The MIT Press.

Kasun, L. L. C., Zhou, H., Huang, G. B., & Vong, C. M. (2013). Representational Learning with Extreme Learning Machine for Big Data. *IEEE Intelligent Systems, 28*(6), 31–34.

Kennedy, J. (2011). Particle swarm optimization. In Encyclopedia of machine learning (pp. 760-766). Springer US.

Kennedy, J., & Eberhart, R. C. (1995). Particle swarm optimization. *Proceedings of the IEEE International Conference on Neural Networks*, Perth, Australia (pp. 1942–1948). doi:10.1109/ICNN.1995.488968

Kennedy, J., & Eberhart, R. C. (2001). *Swarm Intelligence Morgan Kaufmann* (3rd ed.). New Delhi, India: Academic Press.

Kira, K., & Rendell, L. A. (1992). A practical approach to feature selection. *Paper presented at theninth international workshop on Machine learning.*

Kirk, D. E. (2004). *Optimal Control Theory: An Introduction*. Englewood Cliffs, NJ, USA: Dover Publications.

Klaseen, M., & Pao, Y. H. (1990).The functional link net in structural pattern recognition. *Proceedings of the IEEE Region 10 Conference on Computer and Communication Systems TENCON '90* (Vol. 2, pp. 567-571).

Knowles, A., & Hussain, A. Dereby, Wal El, Lisboa, P G. J. & Dunis, C L. (2009). Higher Order Neural Networks with Bayesian Confidence Measure for the Prediction of the EUR/USD Exchange Rate. In M. Zhang (Ed.), Artificial Higher Order Neural Networks for Economics and Business (pp. 48-59). Hershey, PA, USA: IGI Global.

Knowles, A., Hussein, A., Deredy, W., Lisboa, P., & Dunis, C. L. (2005). Higher-order neural networks with Bayesian confidence measure for prediction of EUR/USD exchange rate. In M. Zhang (Ed.), Artificial Higher Order Neural networks for Economics and Business (pp. 48-59). Hershey, PA, USA: Idea Group.

Knowles, A., Hussein, A., Deredy, W., Lisboa, P., & Dunis, C. L. (2009). Higher-order neural networks with Bayesian confidence measure for prediction of EUR/USD exchange rate. In M. Zhang (Ed.), Artificial Higher Order Neural networks for Economics and Business (pp. 48-59). Hershey, PA, USA: IGI Global.

Kohavi, R., & John, G. H. (1997). Wrappers for feature subset selection. *Artificial Intelligence*, *97*(1–2), 273–324. doi:10.1016/S0004-3702(97)00043-X

Kohonen, T. (1972). Correlation matrix memories. *IEEE Transactions on Computers*, *C-21*(4), 353–359. doi:10.1109/TC.1972.5008975

Kohonen, T. (1990). The self-organizing map. *Proceedings of the IEEE*, *78*(9), 1464–1480. doi:10.1109/5.58325

Kononenko, I. (1994). Estimating attributes: Analysis and extensions of RELIEF. In F. Bergadano & L. De Raedt (Eds.), *Machine Learning: ECML-94* (Vol. 784, pp. 171–182). Springer Berlin Heidelberg. doi:10.1007/3-540-57868-4_57

Kosko, B. (1987). Adaptive bidirectional associative memory. *Applied Optics*, *26*(23), 4947–4960. doi:10.1364/AO.26.004947 PMID:20523473

Kosmatopoulos, E. B., Polycarpou, M. M., Christodoulou, M. A., & Ioannou, P. A. (1995). High-order neural network structures for identification of dynamical systems. *IEEE Transactions on* Neural Networks, *6*(2), 422–431. doi:10.1109/72.363477

Koulakov, A. A., & Rinberg, D. (2011). Sparse incomplete representations: A potential role for olfactory granule cells. *Neuron*, *72*(1), 124–136. doi:10.1016/j.neuron.2011.07.031 PMID:21982374

Krstic, M., Kokotovic, P. V., & Kanellakopoulos, I. (1995). *Nonlinear and Adaptive Control Design* (1st ed.). New York, NY, USA: John Wiley and Sons, Inc.

Kryzanowski, L., Galler, M., & Wright, D. W. (1993). Using artificial neural networks to pick stocks. *Financial Analysts Journal*, *49*(4), 21–27. doi:10.2469/faj.v49.n4.21

Kumar, A. S., Subba Rao, M., & Babu, Y. S. K. (2008). Model reference linear adaptive control of DC motor using fuzzy controller. Proceedings of the 2008 IEEE Region 10 Conference TENCON '08 (pp. 1–5). doi:10.1109/TENCON.2008.4766484

Kumar, N., Panwar, V., Sukavanam, N., Sharma, S. P., & Borm, J. H. (2011). Neural Network-Based Nonlinear Tracking Control of Kinematically Redundant Robot Manipulators. *Mathematical and Computer Modelling*, *53*(9), 1889–1901. doi:10.1016/j.mcm.2011.01.014

Kung, L. M., & Yu, S. W. (2008). Prediction of index futures returns and the analysis of financial spillovers—A comparison between GARCH and the grey theorem. *European Journal of Operational Research*, *186*(3), 1184–1200. doi:10.1016/j.ejor.2007.02.046

Kwon, Y. K., & Moon, B. R. (2007). A hybrid neurogenetic approach for stock forecasting. *IEEE Transactions on* Neural Networks, *18*(3), 851–864.

Lam, A., & Li, V. O. (2010, December). Chemical reaction optimization for cognitive radio spectrum allocation. *Proceedings of the Global Telecommunications Conference GLOBECOM '10* (pp. 1-5). IEEE. doi:10.1109/GLOCOM.2010.5684065

Lam, A., Xu, J., & Li, V. O. (2010, July). Chemical reaction optimization for population transition in peer-to-peer live streaming. *Proceedings of the 2010 IEEE Congress on Evolutionary Computation (CEC)* (pp. 1-8). IEEE. doi:10.1109/CEC.2010.5585933

Lam, A., & Li, V. O. (2010). Chemical-reaction-inspired metaheuristic for optimization. *IEEE Transactions on* Evolutionary Computation, *14*(3), 381–399.

Lam, A., Li, V. O., & Yu, J. J. (2012). Real-coded chemical reaction optimization. *IEEE Transactions on* Evolutionary Computation, *16*(3), 339–353.

Lam, A.Y., & Li, V.O. (2012). Chemical reaction optimization: A tutorial. *Memetic Computing, 4*(1), 3–17. doi:10.1007/s12293-012-0075-1

Lapedes, A. S., & Farber, R. (1987). Non-linear signal processing using neural networks: Prediction and system modeling (Technical Report LA-UR-87). *Los Alamos National Laboratory*.

Le Roux, N., & Bengio, Y. (2008). Representational power of restricted Boltzmann machines and deep belief networks. *Neural Computation, 20*(6), 1631–1649. doi:10.1162/neco.2008.04-07-510 PMID:18254699

Lebedev, V. (1997). *An introduction to functional analysis and computational mathematics*. Boston: Brikhauser.

LeCun, Y., Boser, B., Denker, J. S., Henderson, D., Howard, R. E., Hubbard, W., & Jackel, L. D. (1989). Backpropagation Applied to Handwritten Zip Code Recognition. *Neural Computation, 1*(4), 541–551. doi:10.1162/neco.1989.1.4.541

Lee, H., Pham, P., Largman, Y., & Ng, A. (2009b). Unsupervised feature learning for audio classification using convolutional deep belief networks. In Advances in neural information processing systems (pp. 1096–1104).

Lee, W.-K., Hyun, C.-H., Kim, E., & Park, M. (2006). Adaptive Synchronization of Discrete-Time T-S Fuzzy Chaotic Systems Using Output Tracking Control. *Proceedings of theInternational Joint ConferenceSICE-ICASE '06* (pp. 3816–3820). http://doi.org/ doi:10.1109/SICE.2006.314668

Lee, H., Grosse, R., Ranganath, R., & Ng, A. (2009a). Convolutional deep belief networks for scalable unsupervised learning of hierarchical representations.*Proceedings of international conference on machine learning (ICML)*, New York, NY, USA (pp. 609–616). doi:10.1145/1553374.1553453

Lee, M., Lee, S. Y., & Park, C. H. (1992). Neural controller of nonlinear dynamic systems using higher order neural networks. *Electronics Letters, 28*(3), 276–277. doi:10.1049/el:19920170

Leerink, L. R., Giles, C. L., Horne, B. G., & Jabri, M. A. (1995). Learning with product units, In G. Tesaro, D. Touretzky, & T. Leen (Eds.), Advances in Neural Information Processing Systems (Vol. 7, pp. 537-544). Cambridge, MA: MIT Press.

Leerink, L. R., Giles, C. L., Horne, B. G., & Jabri, M. A. (1995). Learning with Product Units. *Advances in Neural Information Processing Systems*, 1995, 537–544.

Lee, T. T., & Jeng, J. T. (1998). The Chebyshev-polynomials-based unified model neural networks for function approximation. *IEEE Transactions on* Systems, Man, and Cybernetics, Part B: Cybernetics, *28*(6), 925–935.

Lee, Y. C., Doolen, G., Chen, H., Sun, G., Maxwell, T., Lee, H., & Giles, C. L. (1986). Machine learning using a higher order correlation network. *Physica D. Nonlinear Phenomena, 22*(1-3), 276–306. doi:10.1016/0167-2789(86)90300-6

Leshno, M., Pinkus, A., & Schocken, S. (1993). Multilayer feedforward neural networks with a polynomial activation function can approximate any function. *Neural Networks, 6*(6), 861–867. doi:10.1016/S0893-6080(05)80131-5

Leu, Y.-G., Wang, W.-Y., & Lee, T.-T. (2005). Observer-based direct adaptive fuzzy-neural control for nonaffine nonlinear systems. *IEEE Transactions on Neural Networks, 16*(4), 853–861. doi:10.1109/TNN.2005.849824 PMID:16121727

Lewis, F. L., Jagannathan, S., & Yesildirek, A. (1998). *Neural Network Control of Robot Manipulators and Non-Linear Systems*. New York: Taylor & Francis.

Lewis, F. L., & Syrmos, V. L. (1995). *Optimal Control.* New York, New York, USA: John Wiley and Sons.

Lewis, F. L., Yesildirek, A., & Liu, K. (1996). Multilayer neural-net robot controller with guaranteed tracking performance. *IEEE Transactions on Neural Networks, 7*(2), 388–399. doi:10.1109/72.485674 PMID:18255592

Li, F. (2008). Function approximation by neural networks. *Proceedings of the 5th International symposium on Neural Networks, LNCS* (Vol. 5263, pp. 384–390). doi:10.1007/978-3-540-87732-5_43

Li, W., Wang, Y., Li, W., Zhang, J., & Jinyan, L. (1998, May 4-8). Sparselized higher-order neural network and its pruning algorithm. *Paper presented at the 1998 IEEE World Congress on Computational Intelligence on Neural Networks.*

Liao, T., Socha, K., Montes de Oca, M., Stützle, T., & Dorigo, M. (2014). Ant colony optimization for mixed-variable optimization problems. *IEEE Transactions on Evolutionary Computation, 18*(4), 503–518. doi:10.1109/TEVC.2013.2281531

Li, C., Yang, L. T., & Lin, M. (2014). Parallel Training of An Improved Neural Network for Text Categorization. *International Journal of Parallel Programming, 42*(3), 505–523. doi:10.1007/s10766-013-0245-x

Lin, S., Guo, X., Cao, F., & Xu, Z. (2013). Approximation by neural networks with scattered data. *Applied Mathematics and Computation, 224*, 29–35. doi:10.1016/j.amc.2013.08.014

Lin, W., & Byrnes, C. I. (1994). Design of discrete- time nonlinear control systems via smooth feedback. *IEEE Transactions on* Automatic Control, *39*(11), 2340–2346.

Lin, Y. H., & Cunningham, G. A. (1995). A new approach to fuzzy-neural system modelling. *IEEE Transactions on Fuzzy Systems, 3*(2), 190–198. doi:10.1109/91.388173

Lippman, R. P. (1989). Pattern classification using neural networks. *IEEE Communications Magazine, 27*(11), 47–64. doi:10.1109/35.41401

Lisboa, P.J.G., & Vellido, A. (2000). Business Applications of Neural Networks. In P.J.G. Lisboa, B. Edisbury & A. Vellido (Eds.), Business Applications of Neural Networks: The State-of-the-Art of Real-World Applications (pp. vii-xxii). Singapore: World Scientific.

Lisboa, P., & Perantonis, S. (1991). Invariant pattern recognition using third-order networks and zernlike moments. *Proceedings of the IEEE International Joint Conference on Neural Networks,* Singapore (Vol. II, pp. 1421-1425).

Liu, Z., Zhang, Q., Han, Z., & Chen, G. (2014). A new classification method for transient power quality combining spectral kurtosis with neural network. *Neurocomputing, 125*, 95–101. doi:10.1016/j.neucom.2012.09.037

Li, X., Chen, Z. Q., & Yuan, Z. Z. (2002). Simple Recurrent Neural Network-Based Adaptive Predictive Control for Nonlinear Systems. *Asian Journal of Control, 4*(2), 31–239.

Long, J., Wu, W., & Nan, D. (2007). Lp approximation capabilities of sum-of-product and sigma-pi-sigma neural networks. *International Journal of Neural Systems, 17*(05), 419–424. doi:10.1142/S0129065707001251 PMID:18098373

Long, J., Wu, W., & Nan, D. (2007a). Uniform approximation capabilities of sum-of product and sigma-pi-sigma neural networks. In Advances in Neural Networks, *LNCS* (Vol. *4491*, pp. 1110–1116). doi:10.1007/978-3-540-72383-7_130

Lu, B., Qi, H., Zhang, M., & Scofield, R. A. (2000). Using PT-HONN models for multi-polynomial function simulation. *Proceedings of IASTED International Conference on Neural Networks,* Pittsburg, USA (pp. 1-5).

Lu, H., Han, J., & Feng, L. (1998, June). Stock movement prediction and n-dimensional inter-transaction association rules. *Proceedings of the ACM SIGMOD workshop on research issues in data mining and knowledge discovery* (p. 12).

Luping, Z., Lei, W., & Chunhua, S. (2010). Feature Selection with Redundancy-Constrained Class Separability. *IEEE Transactions on* Neural Networks, *21*(5), 853–858. doi:10.1109/TNN.2010.2044189

Lu, Z., Song, G., & Shieh, L. (2010). Improving sparsity in kernelized nonlinear feature extraction algorithms by polynomial kernel higher order neural networks. In M. Zhang (Ed.), *Artificial Higher Order Neural Networks for Computer Science and Engineering* (pp. 223–238). Hershey, PA, USA: IGI Global. doi:10.4018/978-1-61520-711-4.ch009

M. Solo, G. (2012). Fundamentals of Higher Order Neural Networks for Modeling and Simulation. *Artificial Higher Order Neural Networks for Modeling and Simulation.* 10.4018/978-1-4666-2175-6.ch006

Mahajan, A. (2011). Optimal decentralized control of coupled subsystems with control sharing. *Proceedings of the 2011 50th IEEE Conference on Decision and Control and European Control Conference (CDC-ECC)*, Orlando, FL, USA (pp. 5726–5731).

Majhi, R., Majhi, B., & Panda, G. (2012). Development and performance evaluation of neural network classifiers for Indian internet shoppers. *Expert Systems with Applications, 39*(2), 2112–2118. doi:10.1016/j.eswa.2011.07.128

Majhi, R., Panda, G., & Sahoo, G. (2009a). Development and performance evaluation of FLANN based model for forecasting of stock markets. *Expert Systems with Applications, 36*(3), 6800–6808. doi:10.1016/j.eswa.2008.08.008

Mandic, D., & Goh, V. S. L. (2009). *Complex Valued Nonlinear Adaptive Filters: Noncircularity, Widely Linear and Neural Models.* Wiley Publishing. doi:10.1002/9780470742624

Markou, M., & Singh, S. (2003a). Novelty detection: a review—part 1: statistical approaches. *Signal Processing, 83*(12), 2481–2497. doi:10.1016/j.sigpro.2003.07.018

Markou, M., & Singh, S. (2003b). Novelty detection: a review—part 2: neural network based approaches. *Signal Processing, 83*(12), 2499–2521. doi:10.1016/j.sigpro.2003.07.019

Matusugu, M., Mori, K., Mitari, Y., & Kaneda, Y. (2003). Subject independent facial expression recognition with robust face detection using a convolutional neural network. *Neural Networks, 16*(5), 555–559. doi:10.1016/S0893-6080(03)00115-1 PMID:12850007

McEliece, R. J., Posner, E. C., Rodemich, E. R., & Venkatesh, S. S. (1987). The capacity of the Hopfield associative memory. *IEEE Transactions on Information Theory, 33*(4), 461–482. doi:10.1109/TIT.1987.1057328

Mehrotra, K., Mohan, C. K., & Ranka, S. (1997). *Elements of Artificial Neural Networks.* The MIT Press.

Meir, R., & Domany, E. (1987). Exact solution of a layered neural network memory. *Physical Review Letters, 59*(3), 359–362. doi:10.1103/PhysRevLett.59.359 PMID:10035740

Mhaskar, H. N. (1993). Approximation properties of a multilayered feedforward artificial neural network. *Advances in Computational Mathematics, 1*(1), 61–80. doi:10.1007/BF02070821

Mikolov, T. et al.. (2010). *Recurrent neural network based language model* (pp. 1045–1048). Interspeech.

Milone, D. H. (2007). Adaptive learning of polynomial networks, genetic programming, backpropagation and Bayesian methods, series on genetic and evolutionary computation. *Genetic Programming and Evolvable Machines, 8*(3), 289–291. doi:10.1007/s10710-007-9034-x

Ming, Z., Shuxiang, X., & Bo, L. (1999). Neuron-adaptive higher order neural network group models. *Paper presented at the International Joint Conference on Neural Networks IJCNN '99.*

Mingkui, T., Tsang, I. W., & Li, W. (2013). Minimax Sparse Logistic Regression for Very High-Dimensional Feature Selection. *IEEE Transactions on* Neural Networks and Learning Systems., *24*(10), 1609–1622. doi:10.1109/tnnls.2013.2263427

Mishra, P.S. & Dehuri, S. (2014). Potential Indicators Based Neural Networks for Cash Forecasting of an ATM. *International Journal of Information Systems and Social Change, 5*(4), 41-57. DOI:10.4018/ijissc.2014100103

Mishra, B. B., Dehuri, S., Panda, G., & Dash, P. K. (2008). Fuzzy swarm net (FSN) for classification in data mining. *The CSI Journal of Computer Science and Engineering, 5*(2 & 4 (b)), 1–8.

Mishra, B.B., & Dehuri, S. (2007). Functional Link Artificial Neural Network for Classification Task in Data Mining. *Journal of Computer Science, 3*(12), 948–955. doi:10.3844/jcssp.2007.948.955

Mishra, P. S., & Dehuri, S. (2012). Potential indictors for stock index prediction: A Perspective. *International Journal of Electronic Finance, 6*(2), 157–183. doi:10.1504/IJEF.2012.048465

Misra, B. B., & Dehuri, S. (2007). Functional Link Artificial Neural Network for Classification Task in Data Mining 1.

Miyajima, H., Shigei, H., & Hamakawa, Y. (2004-I). Higher order differential correlation associative memory of sequential patterns. *Proceedings of theInternational Joint Conference on Neural Networks* (Vol. 2, pp. 891-896).

Miyajima, H., Shigei, N, Hamakawa, Y. (2004) Higher Order Differential Correlation Associative Memory of Sequential Patterns. Proceedings of IJCNN '04 (Vol. II, pp. 891-896).

Miyajima, H., Shigei, N., & Kiriki, N. (2004) Higher Order Multidirectional Associative Memory with Decreasing Energy Function. In Rajapakse, J.C., & Wang, L. (Eds.), Neural Information Processing: Research and Development (Vol. 152, pp. 128-149).

Miyajima, H., Shigei, N., & Yatsuki, S. (2009). Higher Order Neurodynamics of Associative Memory for Sequential Patterns. *Proc. of Int. symposium on Neural Networks, LNCS* (Vol. 55552, pp. 886-891). doi:10.1007/978-3-642-01510-6_100

Miyajima, H., & Shigei, N. (2005). -II) Absolute Capacities for Higher Order Associative Memory of Sequential Patterns. *Proceedings of KES '04, LNAI* (Vol. *3683*, pp. 547–553).

Miyajima, H., & Shigei, N. (2005). Robustness and Capacity of Higher Order Correlation Associative Memory for Sequential Patterns. *Proc. of the 12th ICONIP* (Vol. 1, pp. 388-393).

Miyajima, H., & Shigei, N. (2006). Associative ability of higher order correlation models for sequential patterns. *Journal of Knowledge-Based and Intelligent Engineering Systems, 10*(6), 403–416.

Miyajima, H., Shigei, N., & Hamakawa, Y. (2004). -II) Transition Properties of Higher Order Associative Memory of Sequential Patterns. *Proceedings of KES '04, LNAI* (Vol. *3215*, 855–861.

Miyajima, H., Shigei, N., & Yatsuki, S. (2005). Shift-Invariant Associative Memory Based on Homogeneous Neural Networks. *IEICE Trans. Fundamentals, E88-A*(10), 2600–2606. doi:10.1093/ietfec/e88-a.10.2600

Miyajima, H., Shigei, N., & Yatsuki, S. (2012). *On Some Dynamical Properties of Randomly Connected Higher Order Neural Networks*. IGI.

Miyajima, H., Yatsuki, S., & Kubota, J. (1995). Dynamical properties of neural networks with product connections. *Proc. of IEEE International Conference on Neural Networks* (Vol. 6, pp. 3198-3203). doi:10.1109/ICNN.1995.487297

Monedero, I., Leon, C., Ropero, J., Garcia, A., Elena, J. M., & Montano, J. C. (2007). Classification of electrical disturbances in real time using neural networks. *IEEE Transactions on Power Delivery, 22*(3), 1288–1296. doi:10.1109/TPWRD.2007.899522

Moon, S., & Chang, S. H. (1994). Classification and prediction of the critical heat flux using fuzzy clustering and artificial neural networks. *Nuclear Engineering and Design, 150*(1), 151–161. doi:10.1016/0029-5493(94)90059-0

Morita, M. (1996). Memory and learning of sequential patterns by non-monotone neural networks. *Neural Networks*, *9*(8), 1447–1489. doi:10.1016/S0893-6080(96)00021-4 PMID:12662546

Mostafa, M. M. (2004). Forecasting the Suez Canal traffic: A neural network analysis. *Maritime Policy & Management*, *31*(2), 139–156. doi:10.1080/0308883032000174463

Mostafa, M. M. (2010). Forecasting stock exchange movements using neural networks: Empirical evidence from Kuwait. *Expert Systems with Applications*, *37*(9), 6302–6309. doi:10.1016/j.eswa.2010.02.091

Muir, P. F., & Neuman, C. P. (1990). Kinematic modeling for feedback control of an omnidirectional wheeled mobile robot. In *Autonomous robot vehicles* (pp. 25–31). Springer. doi:10.1007/978-1-4613-8997-2_2

Murata, J. (2010). Analysis and Improvement of Function Approximation Capabilities of Pi-Sigma Higher Order Neural Networks. In M. Zhang (Ed.), Artificial Higher Order Neural Networks for Computer Science and Engineering – Trends for Emerging Applications (pp. 239-254). Hershey, PA, USA: IGI Global.

Murata, J. (2010). Analysis and improvement of function approximation capabilities of pi-sigma higher order neural networks. In M. Zhang (Ed.), *Artificial Higher Order Neural Networks for Computer Science and Engineering* (pp. 239–254). Hershey, PA, USA: IGI Global. doi:10.4018/978-1-61520-711-4.ch010

Murphy, J.J. (1999).Technical Analysis of the Financial Markets. New York: New York Institute of Finance.

Murphy, J. J. (1999). *Technical analysis of the financial markets: A comprehensive guide to trading methods and applications*. Penguin.

Myers, D. G. (2001). *Psychology* (6th ed.). New York: Worth.

Nabhan, T. M., & Zomaya, A. Y. (1994). Towards generating neural-network structures for function approximation. *Neural Networks*, *7*(1), 89–99. doi:10.1016/0893-6080(94)90058-2

Najarian, S., Hosseini, S. M., & Fallahnezhad, M. (2010). Artificial tactile sensing and robotic surgery using higher order neural networks. In M. Zhang (Ed.), *Artificial Higher Order Neural Networks for Computer Science and Engineering – Trends for Emerging Applications* (pp. 514–544). Hershey, PA, USA: IGI Global. doi:10.4018/978-1-61520-711-4.ch021

Nam, K., Yi, J., & Prybutok, V. R. (1997). Predicting airline passenger volume. *The Journal of Business Forecasting*, *16*(1), 14.

Narayan, S. (1993). ExpoNet: A generalization of the multi-layer perceptron model. *Proceedings World Congress on Neural Networks* (Vol. 3, pp. 494-497).

Narendra, K. S., & Parthasarathy, K. (1990). Identification and Control of Dynamical Systems Using Neural Networks. *IEEE Transactions on Neural Networks*, *1*(1), 4–27. doi:10.1109/72.80202 PMID:18282820

Nayak, S. C., Misra, B. B., & Behera, H. S. (2012, February). Index prediction with neuro-genetic hybrid network: A comparative analysis of performance. *Proceedings of the 2012 International Conference on Computing Communication and Applications (ICCCA)* (pp. 1-6). IEEE. doi:10.1109/ICCCA.2012.6179215

Nayak, J., Naik, B., & Behera, H. S. (2015). A novel chemical reaction optimization based higher order neural network (CRO-HONN) for nonlinear classification. *Ain Shams Engineering Journal*, *6*(3), 1069–1091. doi:10.1016/j.asej.2014.12.013

Nayak, S. C., Misra, B. B., & Behera, H. S. (2012). Stock index prediction with neuro-genetic hybrid techniques. *Int. J. Comput. Sci. Inform*, *2*, 27–34.

Nie, Y., & Deng, W. (2008, October). A hybrid genetic learning algorithm for Pi-sigma neural network and the analysis of its convergence. *Proceedings of the Fourth International Conference on Natural Computation ICNC '08* (Vol. 3, pp. 19-23). IEEE. doi:10.1109/ICNC.2008.896

Nikolaev, N. Y., & Iba, H. (2006). Adaptive learning of polynomial networks genetic programming, backpropagation and Bayesian methods. New York: Springer. Retrieved from http://public.eblib.com/choice/publicfullrecord.aspx?p=303002

Nikolaev, N. Y., & Iba, H. (2003). Learning polynomial feedforward neural networks by genetic programming and back-propagation. *IEEE Transactions on Neural Networks*, *14*(2), 337–350. doi:10.1109/TNN.2003.809405 PMID:18238017

Nong, J. (2013) Conditions for radial basis function neural networks to universal approximation and numerical experiments. *Proceedings of the 25th Chinese Control and Decision Conference CCDC '13* (pp. 2193-2197). IEEE. doi:10.1109/CCDC.2013.6561299

Nordstrom, T., & Svensson, B. (1992). Using and designing massively parallel computers for artificial neural networks. *Journal of Parallel and Distributed Computing*, *14*(3), 260–285. doi:10.1016/0743-7315(92)90068-X

Norgaard, M., Ravn, O., Poulsen, N. K., & Hansen, L. K. (2000). *Neural Networks for Modelling and Control of Dynamic Systems: A practitioner's Handbook*. London, Great Britain: Springer-Verlag. doi:10.1007/978-1-4471-0453-7

Oda, M., & Miyajima, H. (2001). Autoassociative memory using refractory period of neurons and its on-line learning.*Proc. of IEEE International Conference on Electronics, Circuits and Systems* (Vol. 2, pp. 623-626). doi:10.1109/ICECS.2001.957553

Ohsawa, T., Bloch, A. M., & Leok, M. (2010). Discrete Hamilton-Jacobi theory and discrete optimal control. *Proceedings of the 2010 49th IEEE Conference on Decision and Control (CDC)*, Atlanta, GA, USA (pp. 5438–5443). doi:10.1109/CDC.2010.5717665

Okada, M. (1996). Notions of associative memory and sparse coding. *Neural Networks*, *9*(8), 1429–1458. doi:10.1016/S0893-6080(96)00044-5 PMID:12662544

Onwubolu, G. C. (2009). Artificial Higher Order Neural Networks in Time Series Prediction. In M. Zhang (Ed.), Artificial Higher Order Neural Networks for Economics and Business (pp. 250-270). Hershey, PA, USA: IGI Global.

Ornelas-Tellez, F., Sanchez, E. N. Garcia- Hernandez, R., Ruz-Hernandez, J., & Rullan-Lara, J. (2012). Neural inverse optimal control for discrete-time uncertain nonlinear systems stabilization. *Proceedings of the 2012 International Joint Conference on Neural Networks (IJCNN)* (pp. 1–6).

Palm, G. (2013). Neural associative memories and sparse coding. *Neural Networks*, *37*, 165–171. doi:10.1016/j.neunet.2012.08.013 PMID:23043727

Palomares-Salas, J. C., De la Rosa, J. J. G., Agüera-Pérez, A., & Moreno-Muñoz, A. (2012). Intelligent methods for characterization of electrical power quality signals using higher order statistical features. *Przeglad Elektrotechniczny*, *8*, 236–243.

Pan, B., Lam, A., & Li, V. O. (2011, December). Network coding optimization based on chemical reaction optimization. *Proceedings of theGlobal Telecommunications Conference GLOBECOM '11* (pp. 1-5). IEEE.

Panahian Fard, S., & Zainuddin, Z. (2014b) The universal approximation capabilities of pi-periodic approximate identity neural networks. *Proceedings of the 2013 International Conference on Information Science and Cloud Computing (ISCC)* (pp. 793-798). IEEE. doi:10.1007/s00500-014-1449-8

Panahian Fard, S., & Zainuddin, Z. (2013). On the universal approximation capability of flexible approximate identity neural networks. In Emerging technologies for Information systems, computing and management,*LNEE* (Vol. *236*, pp. 201 207). doi:10.1007/978 1 4614 7010 6_23

Panahian Fard, S., & Zainuddin, Z. (2013a). The universal approximation capabilities of Mellin approximate identity neural networks. In Advances in Neural Networks,*LNCS* (Vol. *7951*, pp. 205–213). doi:10.1007/978-3-642-39065-4_26

Panahian Fard, S., & Zainuddin, Z. (2014). Analyses for Lp[a, b]-norm approximation capability of flexible approximate identity neural networks. *Neural Computing & Applications*, *24*(1), 45–50. doi:10.1007/s00521-013-1493-9

Panahian Fard, S., & Zainuddin, Z. (2014a). The Universal Approximation Capability of Double Flexible Approximate Identity Neural Networks. In Computer Engineering and Networking, *LNEE* (Vol. *277*, pp. 125–133). doi:10.1007/978-3-319-01766-2_15

Panahian Fard, S., & Zainuddin, Z. (2014d). Toroidal approximate identity neural networks are universal approximators. In Neural Information Processing, *LNCS* (Vol. *8834*, pp. 135–142). doi:10.1007/978-3-319-12637-1_17

Pao, Y. (1989) Adaptive Pattern Recognition and Neural Networks. Addison-Wesley, USA, ISBN: 0 201012584-6

Pao, Y. (1989). Adaptive pattern recognition and neural networks.

Pao, Y. H. (1989). *Adaptive Pattern Recognition and Neural Networks*. Reading, MA: Addison-Wesley.

Pao, Y. H., & Takefji, Y. (1992). Functional-link net computing. *IEEE Computer Journal*, *25*(5), 76–79. doi:10.1109/2.144401

Park, C. H., & Irwin, S. H. (2004). *The Profitability of Technical Analysis: A Review* (AgMAS Project Research Report 2004-04). University of Illinois at Urbana-Champaign, Urbana.

Park, B. S., Yoo, S. J., Park, J. B., & Choi, Y. H. (2010). A simple adaptive control approach for trajectory tracking of electrically driven non-holonomic mobile robots. *IEEE Transactions on Control Systems Technology*, *18*(5), 1199–1206. doi:10.1109/TCST.2009.2034639

Park, J., & Sandberg, I. W. (1991). Universal approximation using radial-basis-function networks. *Neural Computation*, *3*(2), 246–257. doi:10.1162/neco.1991.3.2.246

Park, J., & Sandberg, I. W. (1993). Approximation and radial-basis-functions networks. *Neural Computation*, *5*(2), 305–316. doi:10.1162/neco.1993.5.2.305

Park, S., Smith, M. J. T., & Mersereau, R. M. (2000, October). Target Recognition Based on Directional Filter Banks and higher-order neural network. *Digital Signal Processing*, *10*(4), 297–308. doi:10.1006/dspr.2000.0376

Patino, H. D., & Liu, D. (2000). Neural network-based model reference adaptive control system. *IEEE Transactions on Systems, Man, and Cybernetics. Part B, Cybernetics*, *30*(1), 198–204. doi:10.1109/3477.826961 PMID:18244743

Patra, J. C., Lim, W., Meher, P. K., & Ang, E. L. (2006, July). Financial prediction of major indices using computational efficient artificial neural networks. *Proceedings of the International Joint Conference on Neural Networks IJCNN '06* (pp. 2114-2120). IEEE.

Patra, J. C., Pal, R. N., Baliarsingh, R., & Panda, G. (1999b). Nonlinear channel equalization for QAM signal constellation using artificial neural networks. *IEEE Transactions on* Systems, Man, and Cybernetics, Part B: Cybernetics, *29*(2), 262–271.

Patra, J. C., Pal, R. N., Chatterji, B. N., & Panda, G. (1999a). Identification of nonlinear dynamic systems using functional link artificial neural networks. *IEEE Transactions on* Systems, Man, and Cybernetics, Part B: Cybernetics, *29*(2), 254–262.

Patra, J. C., Panda, G., & Baliarsingh, R. (1994). Artificial neural network-based nonlinearity estimation of pressure sensors. *IEEE Transactions on* Instrumentation and Measurement, *43*(6), 874–881.

Patra, J. C., & Van den Bos, A. (2000). Modeling of an intelligent pressure sensor using functional link artificial neural networks. *ISA Transactions*, *39*(1), 15–27. doi:10.1016/S0019-0578(99)00035-X PMID:10826282

Pedro, J., & Dahunsi, O. (2011). Neural Network Based Feedback Linearization Control of a Servo-Hydraulic Vehicle Suspension System. *International Journal of Applied Mathematics and Computer Science*, *21*(1), 137–147. doi:10.2478/v10006-011-0010-5

Perantonis, S. J., & Lisboa, P. J. G. (1992). Translation, rotation and scale invariant pattern recognition by high-order neural networks and moment classifiers. *IEEE Transactions on Neural Networks*, *3*(2), 241–251. doi:10.1109/72.125865 PMID:18276425

Perantonis, S., Ampazis, N., Varoufakis, S., & Antoniou, G. (1998). Constrained learning in neural networks: Application to stable factorization of 2-D polynomials. *Neural Processing Letters*, *7*(1), 5–14. doi:10.1023/A:1009655902122

Pincus, S. M. (1991). Approximate entropy as a measure of system complexity. *Proceedings of the National Academy of Sciences of the United States of America*, *88*(6), 2297–2301. doi:10.1073/pnas.88.6.2297 PMID:11607165

Plett, G. L. (2003). Adaptive Inverse Control of Linear and Nonlinear Systems Using Dynamic Neural Networks. *IEEE Transactions on Neural Networks*, *14*(2), 360–376. doi:10.1109/TNN.2003.809412 PMID:18238019

Poisson, O., Rioual, P., & Meunier, M. (2000). Detection and measurement of power quality disturbances using wavelet transform. *IEEE Transactions on Power Delivery*, *15*(3), 1039–1044. doi:10.1109/61.871372

Polycarpou, M. M. (1996). Stable adaptive neural control scheme for nonlinear systems. *IEEE Transactions on Automatic Control*, *41*(3), 447–451. doi:10.1109/9.486648

Polycarpou, M. M., & Trunov, A. B. (2000). Learning approach to nonlinear fault diagnosis: Detectability analysis. *IEEE Transactions on Automatic Control*, *45*(4), 806–812. doi:10.1109/9.847127

Poznyak, A. S., Sanchez, E. N., & Yu, W. (2000). *Differential Neural Networks for Robust Nonlinear Control*. USA: World Scientific.

Principe, J. C., & Chen, B. (2015). Universal approximation with convex optimization: Gimmic or reality? *IEEE Computational Intelligence Magazine*, *10*, 68–77. doi:10.1109/MCI.2015.2405352

Pring, M. (1991). *Technical Analysis Explained: The successful Investor's Guide to Spotting Investment Trends and Turning points*. New York: McGraw Hill.

Psaltis, D., Brady, D., & Wagner, K. (1988). Adaptive optical networks using photorefractive crystals. *Applied Optics*, *27*(9), 1752-1759.

Psaltis, D., Park, C., & Hong, J. (1988). Higher order associative memories and their optical implementations. *Neural Networks*, *1*(2), 149–163. doi:10.1016/0893-6080(88)90017-2

Puig, V., Witczak, M., Nejjari, F., Quevedo, J., & Korbicz, J. (2007). A GMDH neural network-based approach to passive robust fault detection using a constraint satisfaction backward test. *Engineering Applications of Artificial Intelligence*, *20*(7), 886–897. doi:10.1016/j.engappai.2006.12.005

Purwar, S., Kar, I. N., & Jha, A. N. (2007). On-line system identification of complex systems using Chebyshev neural networks. *Applied Soft Computing*, *7*(1), 364–372. doi:10.1016/j.asoc.2005.08.001

Qi, H., Zhang, M., & Scofield, R. A. (2001). Rainfall estimation using M-PHONN model.*Proceedings of 2001 International Joint Conference on Neural Networks*, Washington DC, USA (pp.1620 - 1624).

Ragothaman, S., & Lavin, A. (2008). Restatements Due to Improper Revenue Recognition: A Neural Networks Perspective. *Journal of Emerging Technologies in Accounting, 5*(1), 129–142. doi:10.2308/jeta.2008.5.1.129

Ranzato, M., & Hinton, G. (2010). Modeling pixel means and covariances using factorized third-order Boltzmann machines. *Proceedings of computer vision and pattern recognition* (pp. 2551–2558). San Francisco, CA, USA: CVPR. doi:10.1109/CVPR.2010.5539962

Redding, N., Kowalczyk, A., & Downs, T. (1993). Constructive high-order network algorithm that is polynomial time. *Neural Networks, 6*(7), 997–1010. doi:10.1016/S0893-6080(09)80009-9

Refenes, A. N. (Ed.). (1994). *Neural networks in the capital markets*. Chichester, UK: Wiley.

Refenes, A. N., Zapranis, A., & Francis, G. (1994). Stock performance modeling using neural networks: A comparative study with regression models. *Neural Networks, 7*(2), 375–388. doi:10.1016/0893-6080(94)90030-2

Reid, M. B., Spirkovska, L., & Ochoa, E. (1989). Rapid training of higher-order neural networks for invariant pattern recognition. *Proceedings of International Joint Conference on Neural Networks,* Washington, DC, USA (Vol.1, pp. 689-692).

Reid, M. B., Spirkovska, L., & Ochoa, E. (1989). Simultaneous position, scale, rotation invariant pattern classification using third-order neural networks, International. *Journal of Neural Networks, 1*, 154–159.

Reid, M. B., Spirkovska, L., & Ochoa, E. (1989). Simultaneous position, scale, rotation invariant pattern classification using third-order neural networks. *Int. J. Neural Networks, 1*, 154–159.

Reid, M. B., Spirkovska, L., & Ochoa, L. (1989). Rapid training of higher-order neural networks for invariant pattern recognition.*Proc. of International Joint Conference on Neural Nets* (pp. 689-692).

Ribeiro, M. V., Marques, C. A. G., Duque, C. A., Cerqueira, A. S., & Pereira, J. L. R. (2007). Detection of disturbances in voltage signals for power quality analysis using HOS. *EURASIP Journal on Advances in Signal Processing, 2007*(1), 1–13.

Ribeiro, M. V., & Pereira, J. L. R. (2007). Classification of single and multiple disturbances in electric signals. *EURASIP Journal on Advances in Signal Processing,* (1): 1–18.

Ricalde, L. J., Catzin, G. A., Alanis, A. Y., & Sanchez, E. N. (2013). Time Series Forecasting via a Higher Order Neural Network trained with the Extended Kalman Filter for Smart Grid Applications. In M. Zhang (Ed.), Artificial Higher Order Neural Networks for Modeling and Simulation (pp. 254-275). Information Science Reference, Hershey, PA, USA: IGI Global.

Ricalde, L. J., Sanchez, E. N., & Alanis, A. Y. (2010). Recurrent Higher Order Neural Network Control for Output Trajectory Tracking with Neural Observers and Constrained Inputs. In M. Zhang (Ed.), Artificial Higher Order Neural Networks for Computer Science and Engineering – Trends for Emerging Applications (pp. 286-311). Hershey, PA, USA: IGI Global.

Richman, J. S., & Moorman, J. R. (2000). Physiological time-series analysis using approximate entropy and sample entropy. *American Journal of Physiology. Heart and Circulatory Physiology, 278*(6), H2039–H2049. PMID:10843903

Riedmiller, M., & Braun, H. (1993). A direct adaptive method for faster backpropagation learning: The RPROP algorithm. *Proceedings IEEE International Conference on Neural Networks* (pp. 586-591). doi:10.1109/ICNN.1993.298623

Romahi, Y., & Shen, Q. (2000, May). Dynamic financial forecasting with automatically induced fuzzy associations. *Proceedings of the Ninth IEEE International Conference on Fuzzy Systems FUZZ '00* (Vol. 1, pp. 493-498). IEEE. doi:10.1109/FUZZY.2000.838709

Ross, S. M. (1970). *Applied Probability Models with Optimization Applications*. Dover Publications, INC.

Rovithakis, G. A., & Chistodoulou, M. A. (2000). Adaptive Control with Recurrent High-Order Neural Networks. London, UK.

Rovithakis, G. A., & Chistodoulou, M. A. (2000). *Adaptive Control with Recurrent High -Order Neural Networks*. Berlin, Germany: Springer Verlag. doi:10.1007/978-1-4471-0785-9

Rovithakis, G. A., Kosmatopoulos, E. B., & Christodoulou, M. A. (1993). Robust adaptive control of unknown plants using recurrent high order neural networks-application to mechanical systems. In *Proceedings of International Conference on Systems, Man and Cybernetics,*Le Touquet, France (Vol. 4, pp. 57 – 62). doi:10.1109/ICSMC.1993.390683

Rovithakis, G., Gaganis, V., Perrakis, S., & Christodoulou, M. (1996). A recurrent neural network model to describe manufacturing cell dynamics.*Proceedings of the 35th IEEE Conference on Decision and Control*, Kobe, Japan (Vol. 2, pp.1728 – 1733). doi:10.1109/CDC.1996.572808

Rumelhart, D. E., & Hinton, G. E.PDP Research Group. (1986). *Parallel Distributed Processing: Explorations in the Microstructure of Cognition*. Cambridge, MA, USA: MIT Press.

Rumelhart, D. E., & McClelland, J. L.PDP Research Group. (1986). *Parallel Distributed Processing*. Cambridge: The MIT Press.

Rumelhart, D., Hinton, G., & Williams, R. (1986). Learning representations by back-propagating errors.*Nature, 323*(6088), 533–536. doi:10.1038/323533a0

Saad, E. W., Prokhorov, D. V., & Wunsch, D. C. II. (1998). Comparative Study of Stock Trend Prediction Using Time Delay Recurrent and Probabilistic Neural Networks. *IEEE Transactions on Neural Networks, 9*(6), 1456–1470. doi:10.1109/72.728395 PMID:18255823

Sahin, E. (1994). A New Higher-order Binary-input Neural Unit: Learning and Generalizing Effectively via Using Minimal Number of Monomials.

Sahin, E. (1994). *A New Higher-order Binary-input Neural Unit: Learning and Generalizing Effectively via Using Minimal Number of Monomials, Master*. Middle East Technical University of Ankara.

Salakhutdinov, R., & Larochelle, H. (2010). Efficient Learning of Deep Boltzmann Machines. *Journal of Machine Learning Research, 9*, 693–700.

Sanchez, E. N., & Ricalde, L. J. (2003). Trajec- tory tracking via adaptive recurrent control with input saturation. *Proceedings of the 2003 International Joint Conference on Neural Networks* (Vol. 1, pp. 359–364). IEEE.

Sanchez, E. N., Alanis, A. Y., & Rico, J. (2009). Electric Load Demand and Electricity Prices Forecasting Using Higher Order Networks Trained by Kalman Filtering. In M. Zhang (Ed.), Artificial Higher Order Neural Networks for Economics and Business (pp. 295-313). Hershey, PA, USA: IGI Global.

Sanchez, E. N., Alanis, A. Y., & Loukianov, A. G. (2008). *Discrete Time High Order Neural Control Trained with Kalman Filtering*. Germany: Springer-Verlag. doi:10.1007/978-3-540-78289-6

Sanchez, E. N., Alanis, A. Y., & Rico, J. (2004). Electric Load Demand Prediction Using Neural Networks Trained by Kalman Filtering.*Proceedings of the IEEE International Joint Conference on Neural Networks,*Budapest, Hungary (pp. 2771-2775). doi:10.1109/IJCNN.2004.1381093

Sanchez, E. N., & Ornelas-Tellez, F. (2013). *Discrete-Time Inverse Optimal Control for Nonlinear Systems*. Boca Raton, FL, USA: CRC Press.

Sanchez, E. N., Urrego, D. A., Alanis, A. Y., & Carlos-Hernandez, S. (2010). Recurrent higher order neural observers for anaerobic processes. In M. Zhang (Ed.), *Artificial Higher Order Neural Networks for Computer Science and Engineering – Trends for Emerging Applications* (pp. 333–365). Hershey, PA, USA: IGI Global. doi:10.4018/978-1-61520-711-4.ch015

Sankar, A., & Mammone, R. J. (1991). Speaker Independent Vowel Recognition using Neural Tree Networks.*Proceedings of International Joint Conference on Neural Networks*, Seattle, WA (pp. 809-814).

Santoso, S., Grady, W. M., Powers, E. J., Lamoree, J., & Bhatt, S. C. (2000). Characterization of distribution power quality events with Fourier and wavelet transforms. *IEEE Transactions on Power Delivery, 15*(1), 247–254. doi:10.1109/61.847259

Schmidhuber, J. (1992). Learning complex, extended sequences using the principle of history compression. *Neural Computation, 4*(2), 234–242. doi:10.1162/neco.1992.4.2.234

Schmidt, W., & Davis, J. (1993). Pattern recognition properties of various feature spaces for higher order neural networks. *IEEE Transactions on Pattern Analysis and Machine Intelligence, 15*, 795–801.

Schmidt, W. A. C., & Davis, J. P. (1993). Pattern recognition properties of various feature spaces for higher order neural networks. *Pattern Analysis and Machine Intelligence. IEEE Transactions on, 15*(8), 795–801. doi:10.1109/34.236250

Schmidt, W. A. C., & Davis, J. P. (1993). Pattern recognition properties of various feature spaces for higher order neural networks. *IEEE Transactions on Pattern Analysis and Machine Intelligence, 1993, 15*.

Schöneburg, E. (1990). Stock price prediction using neural networks: A project report. *Neurocomputing, 2*(1), 17–27. doi:10.1016/0925-2312(90)90013-H

Schulz, H., & Behnke, S. (2012). Learning object-class segmentation with convolutional neural networks.*Proceedings of the European symposium on artificial neural networks (ESANN)*, Bruges, Belgium.

Seiffert, U. (2004). Artificial neural networks on massively parallel computer hardware. *Neurocomputing, 57*, 135–150. doi:10.1016/j.neucom.2004.01.011

Selviah, D. R. (2009). High Speed Optical Higher Order Neural Networks for Discovering Data Trends and Patterns in Very Large Databases. In M. Zhang (Ed.), Artificial Higher Order Neural Networks for Economics and Business (pp. 442-465). Hershey, PA, USA: IGI Global.

Selviah, D. R., & Shawash, J. (2009). Generalized Correlation Higher Order Neural Networks for Financial Time Series Prediction. In M. Zhang (Ed.), Artificial Higher Order Neural Networks for Economics and Business (pp. 212-249). Hershey, PA, USA: IGI Global.

Selviah, D. R., Mao, Z. Q., & Midwinter, J. E. (1991). A high order feedback net (HOFNET) with variable non-linearity. IEEE, 11, 59-63.

Sepulchre, R., Jankovic, M., & Kokotovi, P. V. (1997). *Constructive Nonlinear Control*. Berlin, Germany: Springer-Verlag. doi:10.1007/978-1-4471-0967-9

Serbedzija, N. B. (1996). Simulating Artificial Neural Networks on Parallel Architectures. *Computer, 29*(3), 56–63. doi:10.1109/2.485893

Sethi, I. K., & Jan, A. K. (1991). Decision Tree Performance Enhancement Using an Artificial Neural Networks Implementation. In *Artificial Neural Networks and Statistical Pattern Recognition* (pp. 71–88). Amsterdam, the Netherlands: Elsevier.

Sewell, M. (2007). *Technical Analysis*. Department of Computer Science, University College London.

Shannon, C. E. (1998). Communication in the presence of noise, *Proceedings of IEEE, 86*(2).

Shannon, C. E. (1998, February). Communication in the presence of noise. In *Proceedings of Institute of Radio Engineers* (vol 37 (1), pp. 10–21, Jan. 1949). Reprint as classic paper in. *Proceedings of the IEEE, 86*(2).

Shannon, C. E. (1998, February). Communication in the presence of noise. *Proceedings of the IEEE, 86*(2).

Sharma, R., Nayak, S. K., Rout, P. K., & Krishnanand, K. R. (2013). Solution to dynamic economic dispatch problem using modified invasive weed optimisation with dual mutation strategy. *International Journal of Swarm Intelligence, 1*(1), 70–90. doi:10.1504/IJSI.2013.055803

Shawash, J., & Selviah, D. R. (2010). Artificial higher order neural network training on limited precision processors. In M. Zhang (Ed.), *Artificial Higher Order Neural Networks for Computer Science and Engineering – Trends for Emerging Applications* (pp. 312–332). Hershey, PA, USA: IGI Global. doi:10.4018/978-1-61520-711-4.ch014

Shawver, T. (2005). Merger premium predictions using neural network approach. *Journal of Emerging Technologies in Accounting, 1*(1), 61–72. doi:10.2308/jeta.2005.2.1.61

Shi, Da, Tan, Shaohua, & Ge Shuzhi Sam (2009). Automatically Identifying Predictor Variables for Stock Return Prediction. In M. Zhang (Ed.), *Artificial Higher Order Neural Networks for Economics and Business* (pp. 60-78). Hershey, PA, USA: IGI Global.

Shi, K. L., & Li, H. (2004). A Novel Control of a Small Wind Turbine Driven Generator Based on Neural Networks. *IEEE Power Engineering Society General Meeting, 2*, 1999-2005.

Shin, Y., & Ghosh, J. (1991, July 8-14). The pi-sigma network: an efficient higher-order neural network for pattern classification and function approximation. *Paper presented at the Seattle International Joint Conference on Neural Networks IJCNN '91.*

Shin, Y., & Ghosh, J. (1991, July). The pi-sigma network: An efficient higher-order neural network for pattern classification and function approximation. *Proceedings of the Seattle International Joint Conference on Neural Networks IJCNN '91* (Vol. 1, pp. 13-18). IEEE.

Shin, Y., Ghosh, J., & Samani, D. (1992). Computationally efficient invariant pattern classification with higher-order pi-sigma networks. In Burke, & Shin (Ed.), Intelligent Engineering Systems through Artificial Neural Networks (Vol II, pp. 379-384). ASME Press.

Shin, S. Y., Lee, I. H., Kim, D., & Zhang, B. T. (2005). Multiobjective evolutionary optimization of DNA sequences for reliable DNA computing. *IEEE Transactions on* Evolutionary Computation, *9*(2), 143–158.

Shin, Y. (1991). The pi-sigma network: an efficient higher-order neural network for pattern classification and function approximation.*Proceedings of the International Joint Conference on Neural Networks,*Seattle, WA, USA (Vol. I, pp.13-18). doi:10.1109/IJCNN.1991.155142

Shin, Y., & Ghosh, J. (1995). Ridge polynomial networks. *IEEE Transactions on* Neural Networks, *6*(3), 610–622.

Singhal, S., & Wu, L. (1989). Advances in neural information processing systems. Morgan San Francisco, CA, USA: Kaufmann Publishers Inc.

Singh, M. R., Mahapatra, S. S., & Mishra, K. (2013). A novel swarm optimiser for flexible flow shop scheduling. *International Journal of Swarm Intelligence*, *1*(1), 51–69. doi:10.1504/IJSI.2013.055802

Skogestad, S. (2003). Simple analytic rules for model reduction and PID controller tuning. *Journal of Process Control*, *13*(4), 291–309. doi:10.1016/S0959-1524(02)00062-8

Socha, K., & Blum, C. (2007). An ant colony optimization algorithm for continuous optimization: Application to feed-forward neural network training. *Neural Computing & Applications*, *16*(3), 235–247. doi:10.1007/s00521-007-0084-z

Socha, K., & Dorigo, M. (2008). Ant colony optimization for continuous domains. *European Journal of Operational Research*, *185*(3), 1155–1173. doi:10.1016/j.ejor.2006.06.046

Softky, W. R., & Kammen, D. M. (1991). Correlations in high dimensional or asymmetric data sets: Hebbian neuronal processing. *Neural Networks*, *4*(3), 337–347. doi:10.1016/0893-6080(91)90070-L

Song, K.-Y., Saraf, D. N., & Gupta, M. M. (2013). Production forecasting of petroleum reservoir applying higher-order neural networks (HONN) with limited reservoir data. *Neural Networks*, *72*(2).

Song, Y., & Grizzle, J. W. (1995). The extended Kalman filter as a local asymptotic observer for discrete-time nonlinear systems. *Journal of Mathematical Systems, Estimation and Control*, *5*, 59–78.

Spirkovska L., & Reid, M. B. (1994, May). Higher-order neural networks applied to 2D and 3D object recognition. *Machine Learning*, 15(2), 169-199.

Spirkovska, L., & Reid, M. B. (1990, June 17-21). Connectivity strategies for higher-order neural networks applied to pattern recognition. *Paper presented at the International Joint Conference on Neural Networks IJCNN '90.*

Spirkovska, L., & Reid, M. B. (1990). Connectivity strategies for higher-order neural networks applied to pattern recognition. *Proceedings of International Joint Conference on Neural Networks,* San Diego, CA, USA (Vol. 1, pp. 21-26). doi:10.1109/IJCNN.1990.137538

Spirkovska, L., & Reid, M. B. (1993). Coarse-coded higher-order neural networks for PSRI object recognition. *IEEE Transactions on* Neural Networks, *4*(2), 276–283. doi:10.1109/72.207615 PMID:18267727

Su, M.-C., Zhao, Y.-X., & Lee, J. (2004). SOM-based optimization. *Proceedings of the 2004 IEEE International Joint Conference on Neural Networks, 2004. Proceedings* (Vol. 1, p. -786). http://doi.org/ doi:<ALIGNMENT.qj></ALIGNMENT>10.1109/IJCNN.2004.1380019

Sudhakar V, & Murthy, C.S.R. (1998). Efficient Mapping of Backpropagation Algorithm onto a Network of Workstations. *IEEE transactions on systems, man, and cybernetics—part b: cybernetics*, 28(6), 841-848.

Su, G., Fukuda, K., Jia, D., & Morita, K. (2002). Application of an artificial neural network in reactor thermo hydraulic problem: Prediction of critical heat flux. *Journal of Nuclear Science and Technology*, *39*(5), 564–571. doi:10.1080/18811248.2002.9715235

Suresh, S., Omkar, S. N., & Mani, V. (2005). Parallel Implementation of Back-propagation Algorithm in Networks of Workstations. *IEEE transactions on parallel and distributed systems*, 16(1), 24–34. doi:10.1109/TPDS.2005.11

Suzuki, S. (1998). Constructive function approximation by three-layer artificial neural networks. *Neural Networks*, *11*(6), 1049–1058. doi:10.1016/S0893-6080(98)00068-9 PMID:12662774

Swicegood, P., & Clark, J. A. (2001). Off-site monitoring systems for predicting bank underperformance: A comparison of neural networks, discriminant analysis, and professional human judgment. *Intelligent Systems in Accounting, Finance & Management*, *10*(3), 169–186. doi:10.1002/isaf.201

Tan, W., Liu, J., Chen, T., & Marquez, H. J. (2006). Comparison of some well-known PID tuning formulas. *Computers & Chemical Engineering*, *30*(9), 1416–1423. doi:10.1016/j.compchemeng.2006.04.001

Taylor, J. G., & Coombes, S. (1993). Learning higher order correlations. *Neural Networks*, *6*(3), 423–427. doi:10.1016/0893-6080(93)90009-L

Theodoridis, D. C., Boutalis, Y. S., & Christodoulou, M. A. (2009, August 23 – 26). A new Neuro-Fuzzy Dynamical System Definition Based on High Order Neural Network Function Approximators. *Proceedings of the European Control Conference ECC-09,* Budapest, Hungary (pp. 3305-3310).

Theodoridis, D. C., Christodoulou, M. A., & Boutalis, Y. S. (2010). Neuro-Fuzzy Control Schemes Based on High Order Neural Network Function Approximators. In M. Zhang (Ed.), Artificial Higher Order Neural Networks for Computer Science and Engineering – Trends for Emerging Applications (pp. 450-383). Hershey, PA, USA: IGI Global.

Thimm, G., & Fiesler, E. (1997). High-order and multilayer perceptron initialization. *IEEE Transactions on Neural Networks*, *8*(2), 349–359. doi:10.1109/72.557673 PMID:18255638

Tikk, D., Koczy, L. T., & Gedeon, T. D. (2003). A survey on universal approximation and its limits in soft computing techniques. *International Journal of Approximate Reasoning*, *33*(2), 185–202. doi:10.1016/S0888-613X(03)00021-5

Ting, J. A., D'Souza, A., Vijayakumar, S., & Schaal, S. (2010). Efficient Learning and Feature Selection in High-Dimensional Regression. *Neural Computation*, *22*(4), 831–886. doi:10.1162/neco.2009.02-08-702 PMID:20028222

Trippi, R. R., & DeSieno, D. (1992). Trading equity index futures with a neural network. *Journal of Portfolio Management*, *19*(1), 27–33. doi:10.3905/jpm.1992.409432

Trunov, A. B., & Polycarpou, M. M. (2000). Automated fault diagnosis in nonlinear multivariable systems using a learning methodology. *IEEE Transactions on Neural Networks*, *11*(1), 91–101. doi:10.1109/72.822513 PMID:18249742

Truong, T. K., Li, K., & Xu, Y. (2013). Chemical reaction optimization with greedy strategy for the 0–1 knapsack problem. *Applied Soft Computing*, *13*(4), 1774–1780. doi:10.1016/j.asoc.2012.11.048

Tsai, H.-C. (2009). Hybrid high order neural networks. *Applied Soft Computing*, *9*(3), 874–881. doi:10.1016/j.asoc.2008.11.007

Tsai, H.-C. (2010). Predicting strengths of concrete-type specimens using hybrid multilayer perceptrons with center-unified particle swarm optimization. *Expert Systems with Applications*, *37*(2), 1104–1112. doi:10.1016/j.eswa.2009.06.093

Turchetti, C., Conti, M., Crippa, P., & Orcioni, S. (1998). On the approximation of stochastic processes by approximate identity neural networks. *IEEE Transactions on Neural Networks*, *9*(6), 1069–1085. doi:10.1109/72.728353 PMID:18255793

Uesaka, Y., & Ozeki, K. (1972). Two or three Properties of associative memory, IEICE Trans. Fundamentals of Electronics[in Japanese]. *Communications and Computer Sciences, D-II*, *55-D*, 323–330.

Valtierra-Rodriguez, M., Romero-Troncoso, R. J., Osornio-Ríos, R. A., & García-Pérez, A. (2014). Detection and classification of single and combined power quality disturbances using neural networks. *IEEE Transactions on Industrial Electronics*, *61*(5), 2473–2482. doi:10.1109/TIE.2013.2272276

Vaziri, N., Hojabri, A., Erfani, A., Monsey, M., & Nilforooshan, N. (2007). Critical heat flux prediction by using radial basis function and multilayer perceptron neural networks: A comparison study. *Nuclear Engineering and Design*, *237*(4), 377–385. doi:10.1016/j.nucengdes.2006.05.005

Videnova, I., Nedialkov, D., Dimitrova, M., & Popova, S. (2006). Neural networks for air pollution nowcasting. *Applied Artificial Intelligence*, *20*(6), 493–506. doi:10.1080/08839510600753741

Vincent, P., Larochelle, H., Lajoie, I., Bengio, Y., & Manzagol, P. (2010). Stacked Denoising Autoencoders: Learning Useful Representations in a Deep Network with a Local Denoising Criterion. *Journal of Machine Learning Research,* *11,* 3371–3408.

Vorburger, P., & Bernstein, A. (2006). Entropy-based Concept Shift Detection. *Proceedings of theSixth International Conference on Data Mining, 2006. ICDM '06* (pp. 1113–1118). http://doi.org/ doi:<ALIGNMENT.qj></ALIGN-MENT>10.1109/ICDM.2006.66

Voutriaridis, C., Boutalis, Y. S., & Mertzios, G. (2003). Ridge Polynomial Networks in pattern recognition. *Proceedings of 4th EURASIP Conference focused on Video/Image Processing and Multimedia Communications,* Croatia, Republic of Croatia (pp. 519-524).

Walczak, S., & Cerpa, N. (1999). Heuristic principles for the design of artificial neural Networks. *Information and Software Technology,* *41*(2), 107–117. doi:10.1016/S0950-5849(98)00116-5

Wang, Z., Liu, Y., & Liu, X. (2009). On Complex Artificial Higher Order Neural Networks: Dealing with Stochasticity Jumps and Delays. In M. Zhang (Ed.), Artificial Higher Order Neural Networks for Economics and Business (pp. 466-483). Hershey, PA, USA: IGI Global.

Wang, J., Chen, B., & Yang, C. (2012). Approximation of algebraic and trigonometric polynomials by feedforward neural networks. *Neural Computing & Applications,* *21*(1), 73–80. doi:10.1007/s00521-011-0617-3

Wang, J., & Xu, Z. (2010). New study on neural networks: The essential order of approximation. *Neural Networks,* *23*(5), 618–624. doi:10.1016/j.neunet.2010.01.004 PMID:20138734

Wang, Z., Fang, J. A., & Liu, X. (2008). Global stability of stochastic high-order neural networks with discrete and distributed delays. *Chaos, Solitons, and Fractals,* *36*(2), 388–396. doi:10.1016/j.chaos.2006.06.063

Weidong, X., Yubing, L., & Xingpei, L. (2010). Short-Term Forecasting of Wind Turbine Power Generation Based on Genetic Neural Network. *Proceedings ofEighth World Congress on Intelligent Control and Automation,* Jinan, China (pp. 5943-5946).

Welch, R. L., Ruffing, S. M., & Venayagamoorthy, G. K. (2009). Comparison of Feedforward and Feedback Neural Network Architectures for Short Term Wind Speed Prediction. *Paper presented at theIEEE International Joint Conference on Neural Networks,* Atlanta, Georgia, USA (pp. 3335-3340). doi:10.1109/IJCNN.2009.5179034

Werbos, P. J. (1990). Backpropagation through time: What it does and how to do it. *Proceedings of the IEEE,* *78*(10), 1550–1560. doi:10.1109/5.58337

Werbos, P. J. (1994). *The Roots of Backpropagation: From Ordered Derivatives to Neural Networks and Political Forecasting.* New York, NY: Wiley-Interscience.

West, D. (2000). Neural network credit scoring models. *Computers & Operations Research,* *27*(11-12), 1131–1152. doi:10.1016/S0305-0548(99)00149-5

White, H. (1988, July). Economic prediction using neural networks: The case of IBM daily stock returns. *Proceedings of the IEEE International Conference on Neural Networks '88* (pp. 451-458). IEEE.

Widmer, G., & Kubat, M. (1996). Learning in the presence of concept drift and hidden contexts. *Machine Learning,* *23*(1), 69–101. doi:10.1007/BF00116900

Widrow, B., & Stearns, S. D. (1985). *Adaptive signal processing.* Retrieved from http://adsabs.harvard.edu/abs/1985ph...book.....W

Widrow, B., Greenblatt, A., Kim, Y., & Park, D. (2013). The No-Prop algorithm: A new learning algorithm for multilayer neural networks. *Neural Networks*, *37*, 182–188. doi:10.1016/j.neunet.2012.09.020 PMID:23140797

Widrow, B., & Stearns, S. D. (1985). *Adaptive signal processing*. Englewood Cliffs, N.J: Prentice Hall.

Williams, R. J., & Zipser, D. (1989). A Learning Algorithm for Continually Running Fully Recurrent Neural Networks. *Neural Computation*, *1*(2), 270–280. doi:10.1162/neco.1989.1.2.270

Willsky, A. S. (1976). A survey of design methods for failure detection in dynamic systems. *Automatica*, *12*(6), 601–611. doi:10.1016/0005-1098(76)90041-8

Wolfram, S. (1984). Universality and complexity in cellular automata. *Physica D. Nonlinear Phenomena*, *10*(1-2), 1–35. doi:10.1016/0167-2789(84)90245-8

Wood, J., & Shawe-Taylor, J. (1996). A unifying framework for invariant pattern recognition. *Pattern Recognition Letters*, *17*(14), 1415–1422. doi:10.1016/S0167-8655(96)00103-1

Wu, W., Nan, D., Li, Z., & Long, J. (2007) Approximation to compact set of functions by feedforward neural networks.*Proceedings of the International Joint Conference on Neural Networks (Vol. 20*, pp. 1222-1225). doi:10.1109/IJCNN.2007.4371132

Wu, X., Wu, X., Luo, X., Zhu, Q., & Guan, X. (2012). Neural network-based adaptive tracking control for nonlinearly parameterized systems with unknown input nonlinearities.*Neurocomputing*, *82*, 127–142. doi:10.1016/j.neucom.2011.10.019

Xiao, Y. (2012). *Communication and networking in smart grids. Broken Sound Parkway NW*. USA: CRC Press. doi:10.1201/b11897

Xinzhi, L., Kok Lay, T., & Bingji, X. (2005). Exponential stability of impulsive high-order Hopfield-type neural networks with time-varying delays. *IEEE Transactions on* Neural Networks, *16*(6), 1329–1339. doi:10.1109/TNN.2005.857949 PMID:16342478

Xu, J., Lam, A., & Li, V. O. (2010, May). Chemical reaction optimization for the grid scheduling problem. *Proceedings of the 2010 IEEE International Conference on Communications (ICC)* (pp. 1-5). IEEE. doi:10.1109/ICC.2010.5502406

Xu, S., & Zhang, M. (2002). An adaptive activation function for higher order neural networks. *In Proceeding of 15*th *Australian Joint Conference on Artificial* Intelligence Canberra, Australia(pp. 356-362). .

Xu, J., Lam, A. Y., & Li, V. O. (2011, June). Stock portfolio selection using chemical reaction optimization.*Proceedings of the international conference on operations research and financial engineering, Paris, France*.

Xu, J., Lam, A., & Li, V. O. (2011). Chemical reaction optimization for task scheduling in grid computing. *IEEE Transactions on* Parallel and Distributed Systems, *22*(10), 1624–1631.

Yamada, T., & Yabuta, T. (1992). Remarks on a neural network controller which uses an auto-tuning method for nonlinear functions. *IJCNN*, *2*, 775–780.

Yanai, H., & Sawada, Y. (1990). On some properties of sequence-association type model neural networks (in Japanese). IEICE Trans. on Information & Systems II (Japanese Edition), J73-DII(8), 1192-1197.

Yang, S. S., & Tseng, C. S. (1996). An orthogonal neural network for function approximation. *IEEE Transactions on* Systems, Man, and Cybernetics, Part B: Cybernetics, *26*(5), 779–785.

Yang, X. S., & He, X. (2013). Firefly algorithm: Recent advances and applications. *International Journal of Swarm Intelligence*, *1*(1), 36–50. doi:10.1504/IJSI.2013.055801

Yang, Y., Zhou, C., & Ren, J. (2003). Model reference adaptive robust fuzzy control for ship steering autopilot with uncertain nonlinear systems. *Applied Soft Computing, 3*(4), 305–316. doi:10.1016/j.asoc.2003.05.001

Yao, Y., Freeman, W. J., Burke, B., & Yang, Q. (1991). Pattern recognition by a distributed neural network: An industrial application. *Neural Networks, 4*(1), 103–121. doi:10.1016/0893-6080(91)90036-5

Yapo, T., Embrechets, S. T., & Cathey, S. T. (1992). Prediction of critical heat using a hybrid kohon-backpropagation neural network intelligent. Eng. *Systems through Artificial Neural Networks-proc. Artificial Neural Networks in Eng., 2*, 853–858.

Yatsuki, S., Miyajima, H., & Murashima, S. (1996). Ability of associative memory by higher order neural networks. IEICE Trans. on Information & Systems II (Japanese Edition), J79-D-II(11), 1929-1939.

Yatsuki, S., Matsuoka, N., & Miyajima, H. (1999). Dynamic Properties of Association Memory for Higher Order Neural Networks, IEICE Trans. Fundamentals of Electronics. *Communications and Computer Sciences, D-II, J82*(5), 919–929.

Yatsuki, S., & Miyajima, H. (1997). Associative ability of higher order neural networks.*Proc. of IEEE International Conference on Neural Networks* (Vol. 2, pp. 1299-1304).

Yatsuki, S., & Miyajima, H. (2000). Statistical dynamics of associative memory for higher order neural networks.*Proc. of IEEE International Symposium on Circuits and Systems* (Vol. 3, pp. 670-673). doi:10.1109/ISCAS.2000.856149

Yin, L., & Zhou, L. (2012). Function Based Fault Detection for Uncertain Multivariate Nonlinear Non-Gaussian Stochastic Systems Using Entropy Optimization Principle. *Entropy, 15*(1), 32–52. doi:10.3390/e15010032

Yoon, Y., & Swales, G. (1991, January). Predicting stock price performance: A neural network approach. *Proceedings of the Twenty-Fourth Annual Hawaii International Conference onSystem Sciences* (Vol. 4, pp. 156-162). IEEE. doi:10.1109/HICSS.1991.184055

Yoon, Y., Guimaraes, T., & Swales, G. (1994). Integrating artificial neural networks with rule-based expert systems. *Decision Support Systems, 11*(5), 497–507. doi:10.1016/0167-9236(94)90021-3

Yoshizawa, S., Morita, M., & Amari, S. (1993). Capacity of associative memory using a nonmonotonic neuron model. *Neural Networks, 6*(2), 167–176. doi:10.1016/0893-6080(93)90014-N

Yu, J. J., Lam, A., & Li, V. O. (2011, June). Evolutionary artificial neural network based on chemical reaction optimization. *Proceedings of the 2011 IEEE Congress on Evolutionary Computation (CEC)* (pp. 2083-2090). IEEE. doi:10.1109/CEC.2011.5949872

Yu, W. (2010). Robust Adaptive Control Using Higher Order Neural Networks and Projection. In M. Zhang (Ed.), Artificial Higher Order Neural Networks for Computer Science and Engineering – Trends for Emerging Applications (pp. 99-137). Hershey, PA, USA: IGI Global.

Yukyee, L., & Yeungsam, H. (2010). A Multiple-Filter-Multiple-Wrapper Approach to Gene Selection and Microarray Data Classification. *IEEE/ACM Transactions on Computational Biology and Bioinformatics, 7*(1), 108–117. doi:10.1109/TCBB.2008.46 PMID:20150673

Yu, L., Chen, H., Wang, S., & Lai, K. K. (2009). Evolving least squares support vector machines for stock market trend mining. *IEEE Transactions on* Evolutionary Computation, *13*(1), 87–102.

Yu, L., Wang, S., & Lai, K. K. (2009). A neural-network-based nonlinear metamodeling approach to financial time series forecasting. *Applied Soft Computing, 9*(2), 563–574. doi:10.1016/j.asoc.2008.08.001

Yu, L., & Zhang, Y. Q. (2005). Evolutionary fuzzy neural networks for hybrid financial prediction. *Proceedings of the IEEE Transactions on* Systems, Man, and Cybernetics, Part C: Applications and Reviews, *35*(2), 244–249.

Zainuddin, Z., & Panahian Fard, S. (2014c) Spherical approximate identity neural networks are universal approximators. *Proceedings of the 10th International Conference on Natural Computation (ICNC)* (pp. 72-76). IEEE. doi:10.1109/ICNC.2014.6975812

Zainuddin, Z., & Panahian Fard, S. (2012). Double approximate identity neural networks universal approximation in real Lebesgue space. In Neural Information Processing,*LNCS* (Vol. *7663*, pp. 409–415). doi:10.1007/978-3-642-34475-6_49

Zeng-Guang, H., Long, C., & Min, T. (2009). De- centralized robust adaptive control for the multiagent system consensus problem using neural networks. *IEEE Transactions on* Systems, Man, and Cybernetics, Part B: Cybernetics, *39*(3), 636–647.

Zhang, M. (2006). A data simulation system using CSINC polynomial higher order neural networks. *Proceedings of 2006 International Conference On Artificial Intelligence,* Las Vegas, USA (pp. 91-97).

Zhang, M. (2008). Artificial Higher Order Neural Networks for Economics and Business. Hershey, PA, USA: IGI Global.

Zhang, M. (2008). SAS and higher order neural network nonlinear model. *Proceedings of 2008 International Conference on Modeling, Simulation and Visualization Methods,* Las Vegas, Nevada, USA (pp. 32-38).

Zhang, M. (2010). Rainfall Estimation Using Neuron-Adaptive Artificial Higher Order Neural Networks. In M. Zhang (Ed.), Artificial Higher Order Neural Networks for Computer Science and Engineering – Trends for Emerging Applications (pp. 159-186). Hershey, PA, USA: IGI Global.

Zhang, M. (2012). Polynomial and sigmoid higher order neural networks for data simulations and prediction. Proceedings of the 2012 International Journal of Arts & Science Conference, Florence, Italy (p.16).

Zhang, M., & Fulcher, J. (2004). Higher order neural network for satellite weather predication. In J. Fulcher, & L.C. Jain (Ed.), Applied Intelligent Systems (pp. 17-57). Springer-Verlag Berlin Heidelberg, New York, USA.

Zhang, M., & Fulcher, J. (2004). Higher Order Neural Networks for Satellite Weather Prediction. In J. Fulcher, & L.C. Jain (Eds.), Applied Intelligent Systems (Vol. 153, pp. 17-57). Springer. doi:10.1007/978-3-540-39972-8_2

Zhang, J. C., Zhang, M., & Fulcher, J. (1997). Financial prediction using higher order trigonometric polynomial neural network group models.*Proceedings of ICNN/IEEE International Conference on Neural Networks,*Houston, Texas, USA (pp. 2231-2234). doi:10.1109/ICNN.1997.614373

Zhang, M. (2001). Financial data simulation using A-PHONN model. *Proceedings of 2001 International Joint Conference on Neural Networks,*Washington DC, USA (pp.1823 - 1827).

Zhang, M. (2002a). Rainfall Estimation Using PL-HONN Model. *Proceedings of 2002 IASTED International Conference on Modeling and Simulation,*Marina del Rey, CA, USA (pp. 50-53).

Zhang, M. (2002b). Financial data simulation using PL-HONN model. *Proceedings of 2002 IASTED International Conference on Modeling and Simulation,*Marina del Rey, CA, USA (pp. 229-233).

Zhang, M. (2005). A data simulation system using sinx/x and sinx polynomial higher order neural networks.*Proceedings of 2005 IASTED International Conference on Computational Intelligence*, Calgary, Canada (pp.56 – 61).

Zhang, M. (2007). A data simulation system using YSINC polynomial higher order neural networks.*Proceedings of 2007 IASTED International Conference on Modeling and Simulation,*Montreal, Quebec, Canada (pp. 465-470).

Zhang, M. (2009A). *Artificial higher order neural networks for economics and business*. Hershey, PA, USA: IGI Global. doi:10.4018/978-1-59904-897-0

Zhang, M. (2009B). Artificial higher order neural network nonlinear models: SAS NLIN or HONNs. In M. Zhang (Ed.), *Artificial higher order neural networks for economics and business* (pp. 1–47). Hershey, PA, USA: IGI Global. doi:10.4018/978-1-59904-897-0.ch001

Zhang, M. (2009C). Ultra high frequency trigonometric higher order neural networks. In M. Zhang (Ed.), *Artificial higher order neural networks for economics and business* (pp. 133–163). Hershey, PA, USA: IGI Global. doi:10.4018/978-1-59904-897-0.ch007

Zhang, M. (2009d). Time series simulation using ultra high frequency cosine and cosine higher order neural networks. *Proceedings of International Association of Science and Technology for Development 12th International Conference on Intelligent systems and Control*, Cambridge, Massachusetts, USA (pp. 8-15).

Zhang, M. (2010b). Higher order neural network group-based adaptive tolerance tree. In M. Zhang (Ed.), *Higher Order Neural Networks for Computer Science and Engineering: Trends for Emerging Applications* (pp. 1–36). Hershey, PA, USA: IGI- Global. doi:10.4018/978-1-61520-711-4.ch001

Zhang, M. (2010c). Rainfall estimation using neuron-adaptive higher order neural networks. In M. Zhang (Ed.), *Higher Order Neural Networks for Computer Science and Engineering: Trends for Emerging Applications* (pp. 159–186). Hershey, PA, USA: IGI- Global. doi:10.4018/978-1-61520-711-4.ch007

Zhang, M. (2010d). Time series simulation using ultra high frequency sine and sine higher order neural networks. *Proceedings of Seventh International Symposium on Neural Networks,* Shanghai, China (pp. WAD-7).

Zhang, M. (2011). Sine and sigmoid higher order neural networks for data simulation. *Proceedings of 2011 International Conference on Software Engineering, Artificial Intelligence, Networking, and Parallel/Distributed Computing (SNPD),* Sydney, Australia (p. 15).

Zhang, M. (2013b). Artificial multi-polynomial higher order neural network models. In M. Zhang (Ed.), *Higher Order Neural Networks for Modeling and Simulation* (pp. 1–29). Hershey, PA, USA: IGI-Global. doi:10.4018/978-1-4666-2175-6.ch001

Zhang, M. (2013c). Artificial polynomial and trigonometric higher order neural network group models. In M. Zhang (Ed.), *Higher Order Neural Networks for Modeling and Simulation* (pp. 78–102). Hershey, PA, USA: IGI-Global. doi:10.4018/978-1-4666-2175-6.ch005

Zhang, M. (2014a). Sinc and sigmoid higher order neural network for data modeling and simulation. *Proceedings of Second International Conference on Vulnerability and Risk Analysis,* Liverpool, UK (pp. 2608-2617). doi:10.1061/9780784413609.262

Zhang, M. (2014b). Ultra high frequency polynomial and sine artificial higher order neural networks for control signal generator. *Proceedings of 2014 IEEE Symposium Series on Computational Intelligence,* Orlando, Florida, USA (p. 174). doi:10.1109/CICA.2014.7013235

Zhang, M. (2016a). Ultra high frequency polynomial and trigonometric higher order neural networks for control signal generator. In M. Zhang (Ed.), *Applied Artificial Higher Order Neural Networks for Control and Recognition.* Hershey, PA, USA: IGI Global, Information Science Reference.

Zhang, M. (2016b). Ultra high frequency sigmoid and trigonometric higher order neural networks for data pattern recognition. In M. Zhang (Ed.), *Applied Artificial Higher Order Neural Networks for Control and Recognition.* Hershey, PA, USA: IGI Global, Information Science Reference.

Zhang, M. (2016c). Artificial sine and cosine trigonometric higher order neural networks for financial data prediction. In M. Zhang (Ed.), *Applied Artificial Higher Order Neural Networks for Control and Recognition.* Hershey, PA, USA: IGI Global, Information Science Reference.

Zhang, M. (2016d). Ultra high frequency SINC and trigonometric higher order neural networks for data classification. In M. Zhang (Ed.), *Applied Artificial Higher Order Neural Networks for Control and Recognition*. Hershey, PA, USA: IGI Global, Information Science Reference.

Zhang, M. (2016e). Cosine and sigmoid higher order neural networks for date simulations. In M. Zhang (Ed.), *Applied Artificial Higher Order Neural Networks for Control and Recognition*. Hershey, PA, USA: IGI Global.

Zhang, M. (2016f). *Applied artificial higher order neural networks for control and recognition*. Hershey, PA, USA: IGI Global.

Zhang, M. (Ed.), (2013a). *Higher order neural networks for modeling and simulation*. Hershey, PA, USA: IGI-Global. doi:10.4018/978-1-4666-2175-6

Zhang, M. (Ed.). (2010a). *Higher order neural networks for computer science and engineering: trends for emerging applications*. Hershey, PA, USA: IGI-Global. doi:10.4018/978-1-61520-711-4

Zhang, M., & Crane, J. (2004). Rainfall estimation using SPHONN model. *Proceedings of 2004 International Conference on Artificial Intelligence,*Las Vegas, Nevada, USA (pp.695-701).

Zhang, M., Fulcher, J., & Scofield, R. A. (1996). Neural network group models for estimating rainfall from satellite images.*Proceedings of World Congress on Neural Networks,*San Diego, CA, USA (pp. 897-900).

Zhang, M., & Lu, B. (2001). Financial data simulation using M-PHONN model.*Proceedings of 2001International Joint Conference on Neural Networks,*Washington DC, USA (pp. 1828 - 1832).

Zhang, M., Murugesan, S., & Sadeghi, M. (1995). Polynomial higher order neural network for economic data simulation, *Proceedings of International Conference on Neural Information Processing,*Beijing, China (pp. 493-496).

Zhang, M., Murugesan, S., & Sadeghi, M. (1995). Polynomial higher order neural network for economic data simulation. *Proceedings of International Conference on Neural Information Processing,*Beijing, China (pp. 493-496).

Zhang, M., & Scofield, R. A. (2001). Rainfall estimation using A-PHONN model. *Proceedings of 2001 International Joint Conference on Neural Networks,*Washington DC, USA (pp. 1583 - 1587).

Zhang, M., Xu, S., & Fulcher, J. (2002). Neuron-adaptive higher order neural-network models for automated financial data modeling. *IEEE Transactions on* Neural Networks, *13*(1), 188–204.

Zhang, M., Xu, S., & Fulcher, J. (2002). Neuron-adaptive higher order neural-network models for automated financial data modeling. *IEEE Transactions on Neural Networks, 13*(1), 188–204. doi:10.1109/72.977302 PMID:18244418

Zhang, M., Zhang, J. C., & Fulcher, J. (2000). Higher order neural network group models for data approximation. *International Journal of Neural Systems, 10*(2), 123–142. doi:10.1142/S0129065700000119 PMID:10939345

Zhang, M., Zhang, J. C., & Keen, S. (1999). Using THONN system for higher frequency non-linear data simulation & prediction, *Proceedings of IASTED, International Conference on Artificial Intelligence and Soft Computing,*Honolulu, Hawaii, USA (pp. 320-323).

Zhang, M., Zhang, J. C., & Keen, S. (1999). Using THONN system for higher frequency non-linear data simulation & prediction.*Proceedings of IASTED International Conference on Artificial Intelligence and Soft Computing,*Honolulu, Hawaii, USA (pp.320-323).

Zhang, S., Zhang, C., You, Z., Zheng, R., & Xu, B. (2013). Asynchronous Stochastic Gradient Descent for DNN Training. Proceedings of*ICASSP '13* (pp. 6660–6663).

Zhuo, W., Li-Min, J., Yong, Q., & Yan-Hui, W. (2007). Railway passenger traffic volume prediction based on neural network. *Applied Artificial Intelligence, 21*(1), 1–10. doi:10.1080/08839510600938409

About the Contributors

Ming Zhang received a M.S. degree in information processing and a Ph.D. degree in the research area of computer vision from the East China Normal University, Shanghai, China, in 1982 and 1989, respectively. He held Postdoctoral Fellowships in artificial neural networks with the Shanghai Institute of Technical Physics, Chinese Academy of the Sciences in 1989 and the National Oceanic and Atmospheric Administration, USA National Research Council in 1991. He was a face recognition airport security system project manager and was a Ph.D. co-supervisor at the University of Wollongong, Australia in 1992. Since 1994, he has been a lecturer at the Monash University, Australia. From 1995 to 1999, he was a lecturer and a senior lecturer and a Ph.D. supervisor at the University of Western Sydney, Australia. He also held a Senior Research Associate Fellowship in artificial neural networks with the National Oceanic and Atmospheric Administration, USA National Research Council in 1999. Since 2000, he has been an associate professor at Christopher Newport University, VA, USA. He is currently a full Professor and a graduate student supervisor in computer science at the Christopher Newport University, VA, USA.

***

Ashraf Abdelbar received his M.Sc. and Ph.D. in Computer Science from Clemson University in 1994 and 1996, respectively. He has published more than 70 publications in various fields of artificial intelligence, including neural networks, Bayesian belief networks, and swarm intelligence.

Agustín Agüera-Pérez received a M.S. degree in Physics in 2004, from the University of Sevilla, Spain, and his Ph.D. in Industrial Engineering in 2013 (summa cum laude), from the University of Cádiz, Spain. Actually, he is a Professor of Electronics in the Department of Automatic Engineering, Electronics, Architecture and Computer Networks at the University of Cádiz and researcher of the research group ICEI-PAIDI-TIC-168. His research interests include signal processing, virtual instruments and environmental monitoring.

Alma Y. Alanis, received a B. Sc degree from Instituto Tecnologico de Durango (ITD), Durango Campus, in 2002, a M.Sc. and a Ph.D. degree both in electrical engineering from the Advanced Studies and Research Center of the National Polytechnic Institute (CINVESTAV-IPN), Guadalajara Campus, Mexico, in 2004 and 2007, respectively. Since 2008, she has been with the University of Guadalajara, where she is currently a Chair Professor in the Department of Computer Science and a member of the Intelligent Systems Research Group. She is also a member of the Mexican National Research System (SNI-1). Her research interest centers on neural control, backstepping control, block control, and their applications to electrical machines, power systems and robotics.

Nancy Arana-Daniel received a M. S. degree in Computer Science in 2003 and a Ph.D. in Computer Science in 2007, both from Center of Research and Advanced Studies, CINVESTAV, Unidad Guadalajara, México. She is currently a research fellow at Department of Computer Science in the University of Guadalajara, México, where she is working, with other researchers, on the Intelligent Systems Research Group. Her research interests focuses on the application of geometric algebra, machine learning, optimization, computer vision, pattern recognition and visually guided robot navigation.

H. S. Behera has completed his M. E (Computer Science & Engineering) from the National Institute of Technology, Rourkela, India, and a Ph.D. (Engineering) from Biju Pattanaik University of Technology. His area of interests include data mining and soft-computing, machine intelligence, evolutionary computation, and distributed systems. Dr. Behera has more than 80 research publications in national and international journals and conferences. Currently, he is working as an associate Professor in the Department of computer science engineering and information technology, VSS University of Technology, Burla, India. He has more than 18 years of experiences in teaching as well as research.

Peter Mark Beneš received his Bachelor's and Master's degrees with honour from the Czech Technical University (CTU) in Prague in 2012 and 2014, respectively. Currently, he is a PhD student, with an expected graduation to Fellow in 2016. His research focuses are on non-conventional neural networks for adaptive identification and control of industrial systems, including hoist mechanisms and skew control of rail-based mechanisms such as cranes and railway vehicles. Peter's work has been awarded in both local and international student competitions along with an industrial BOSCH award in 2013.

Ivo Bukovsky was born in Prague in the Czech Republic in 1975. Ivo graduated from the Czech Technical University (CTU) in Prague where he received his Ph.D. in the field of Control and System Engineering in 2007. His research interests include higher-order neural networks, adaptive evaluation of time series and systems, multiscale-analysis approaches, control and biomedical applications. He was a visiting researcher at the Research Laboratory at the University of Saskatchewan (2003), at the Cybersicence Center at the Tohoku University in Japan (2009), and at the Manitoba University in Canada (2010), and recently he was a visiting professor at the Tohoku University in 2011.

Matous Cejnek is a PhD student in the Department of Instrumentation and Control Engineering, Faculty of Mechanical Engineering at CTU in Prague.

Satchidananda Dehuri is a member of the faculty of the Department of Information and Communication Technology, Fakir Mohan University, Vyasa Vihar, Balasore. He received his M. Tech. and Ph.D. degrees in Computer Science from Utkal University, Vani Vihar, Odisha in 2001 and 2006, respectively. He completed his Post-Doctoral Research in the Soft Computing Laboratory, Yonsei University, Seoul, South Korea under the BOYSCAST Fellowship Program of DST, Govt. of India. In 2010, he received a Young Scientist Award in Engineering and Technology for the year 2008 from Odisha Vigyan Academy, Department of Science and Technology, Govt. of Odisha. He has published about 180 research papers in reputed journals and referred conferences, has published four text books for undergraduate and Postgraduate students and edited eight books. As a part of academic collaboration, he has visited Ireland, New Zealand, Hong Kong, and France.

Islam Elnabarawy received his Master's degree in Computer Science from The American University in Cairo in 2013. He is currently working towards a PhD in Computer Science at the Missouri University of Science and Technology, where he enrolled in the Fall 2014 semester. His Master's research was in the area of neural networks, and he has some experience with other areas of computational intelligence such as ant colony optimization and particle swarm optimization. His current research interest is in Adaptive Resonance Theory and its application in supervised, unsupervised, and reinforcement learning, as well as blending it with other computational intelligence approaches.

Miroslav Erben graduated in 2007 from CTU in Prague, was a member of the Faculty of Mechanical Engineering 2011-2014 Dept. of Applied Physics FME, CERN group from 2015 Dept. of Instrumentation and Control Engineering, ASPICC group.

Saeed Panahian Fard received his B.S. from the Iran University of Science and Technology with a first-class honor degree in Applied Mathematics in 2000. He was awarded a M.Sc. degree in Applied Mathematics from Ferdowsi University of Mashhad of Iran in 2003. He is currently a postdoctoral fellow at Universiti Sains Malaysia (USM) under the supervision of Prof. Zarita Zainuddin and his research interests are in the area of Neural Networks, Fuzzy and Bioinformatics.

Álvaro Jiménez-Montero received a M.S. degree in Industrial Engineering in 2013, from University of Cádiz, Spain. Currently, he is completing a Ph.D. at the University of Cádiz, in the Research Group in Computational Instrumentation and Industrial Electronics (PAIDI-TIC168), Electronics Area. His research interests include time-series analysis, power quality, higher-order statistics, intelligent systems, forecasting and modeling of wind speeds.

Mir Md Jahangir Kabir is currently a doctoral student in the School of Engineering and ICT, University of Tasmania, Australia. He received B.Sc. and M.Sc. degrees, from the Rajshahi University of Engineering and Technology, Bangladesh and the University of Stuttgart, Germany in 2004 and 2009, respectively. He received an Overseas Postgraduate Research Award from the Australian Government in 2013 to research in Ph.D. After working as a lecturer (from 2004), he became an assistant professor (from 2010) in the Dept. of Computer Science and Engineering, Rajshahi University of Engineering and Technology, Bangladesh. His research interests include the theory and applications of data mining, evolutionary algorithms, machine learning and artificial intelligence.

Byeong Ho Kang, computer scientist, is the Associate Professor of Computing and Information Systems, University of Tasmania, Australia. Over his 25-year professional career, he received his Ph.D from the University of New South Wales, Sydney, in 1996, and has worked as a visiting researcher in the Advanced Research Lab HITACHI situated in Japan. He has also taken part in major research and development projects with industries and research organizations. Dr Kang has published more than 200 papers in journals and international conferences, and was an editor for several books of proceedings and has been a guest editor for special issues in journals. He has served as a chair and steering committee member of many international organizations and conferences.

Ondrej Liska is at the Technical University of Kosice, Letna 9, Kosice.

Yunling Liu, Associate Professor, College of Information and Electrical Engineering, China Agricultural University. Education: 2008 Ph.D., China Agricultural University, Agricultural Electrification and Automation, 2003 M.S., China Agricultural University, Agricultural Electrification and Automation, 1997 B.S., China Agricultural University, Power System and its Automation. Research Interests: Applications of Intelligent optimization technologies, Machine learning, Data mining, Bioinformatics. Employment: 2011.1- Present, Associate professor, China Agricultural University, Beijing, China. 2008.12-Present, Researcher of EU-China Centre for Information & Communication Technologies, China Agricultural University, Beijing, China. 2002.12-2011.1, Lecturer, China Agricultural University, Beijing, China. 1997.7-2002.12, Assistant, China Agricultural University, Beijing, China.

Carlos López-Franco received a Ph.D. degree in Computer Science in 2007 from the Center of Research and Advanced Studies, CINVESTAV, Mexico. He is currently a professor at the University of Guadalajara, Mexico, Computer Science Department, and a member of the Intelligent Systems group. His research interests include geometric algebra, computer vision, robotics and intelligent systems.

Michel Lopez-Franco was born in 1986, in Guadalajara, Jalisco, Mexico. He received the B. E. Degree in Computer Engineering from the University of Guadalajara, Guadalajara, Mexico, in 2008, and a M. S. degree in Computer and Electrical Engineering from the University of Guadalajara, Guadalajara, Mexico, in 2011. He is a Ph. D. student in Automatic Control from CINVESTAV-IPN (Advanced Studies and Research Center of the National Polytechnic Institute), Guadalajara, Mexico. His current research interests include optimal control, decentralized control, and adaptive and neural networks controllers for dynamic systems.

Partha Sarathi Mishra is currently working as a Lecturer in the Department of Computer Science and Engineering at North Orissa University, Odisha, India. He received his M. Tech degree in Computer Science from Fakir Mohan University, and a Ph.D. degree in Computer Science and Information Technology from North Orissa University. His research interests include neural networks, high order neural networks, evolutionary algorithms and creation of computational intelligent systems that incorporate robustness, adaptation and creativity in their approaches for solving computationally intensive financial problems. He has already published about fifteen research papers in reputed journals and referred conferences, and has published one textbook for undergraduate and post graduate students.

B. B. Misra is currently working as a Dean (Research) at the Silicon Institute of Technology, Bhubaneswar, India. He received a Bachelor's degree in Textiles from Kanpur University, India in 1984, a Master of Technology in Computer Science from Utkal University, Bhubaneswar, India in 2002 and a Ph.D. in Engineering from the Biju Pattanaik University of Technology, Rourkela, India, in 2011. His areas of interests include data mining, sensor network, bioinformatics, evolutionary computation, bioinspired computation and computational intelligence. He has published one book, three book chapters and seventy five papers in different journals and conferences of national and international repute. He has been a keynote speaker and session chair of several different national and international conferences. Dr. Misra has more than 25 years of industrial as well as academics experiences.

Hirofumi Miyajima received a B.E. degree in Electronics and Information Engineering from Hokkaido University, Japan, in 2010, and a M.E. degree in Information Science and Technology from Osaka University, Japan, in 2012. He is currently working toward his Dr. Eng. Degree at Kagoshima University. His current research interests include fuzzy modeling and neural networks.

Hiromi Miyajima received a B.E. degree in electrical engineering from Yamanashi University, Japan, in 1974, and a M.E. and D.E. degrees in electrical and communication engineering from the Tohoku University, in 1976 and 1979, respectively. He is currently a Professor in the Graduate School of Science and Engineering at Kagoshima University. His current research interests include fuzzy modeling, neural networks, quantum computing, and parallel computing.

S. C. Nayak has received a M. Tech (Computer Science) degree from Utkal University, Bhubaneswar, India in 2011. He is pursuing a Ph.D. (Engineering) at Veer Surendra Sai University of Technology, Burla, India. Currently, he is working in the Computer Science & Engineering department at Silicon Institute of Technology, Bhubaneswar, India. His area of research interest include data mining, soft computing, evolutionary computation, and financial time series forecasting. He has published 15 research papers in various journals and conferences of national and international repute.

Cyril Oswald is at the Czech Technical University in Prague, Czech Republic.

José Carlos Palomares-Salas received a M.S. degree in Industrial Engineering in 2008, from the University of Cádiz, Spain, and his Ph.D. in Industrial Engineering in 2013 (summa cum laude), from the University of Cádiz, Spain. Currently, he is a Professor at the University of Cádiz, in the Research Group in Computational Instrumentation and Industrial Electronics (PAIDI-TIC168), Electronics Area. His research interests include time-series analysis, power quality, higher-order statistics, intelligent systems, forecasting and modeling of wind speeds.

Rosa Piotrkowski is a graduate and a Ph.D. in Physics from the University of Buenos Aires, Argentina. She is an Associate Professor at the National University of San Martin, School of Science and Technology and an Associate Professor at the University of Buenos Aires, Faculty of Engineering. She integrates and directs interdisciplinary research projects on topics of applied mathematics and applied physics. She is the author of book chapters and over 60 articles with a broad international impact, and usually acts as a referee for international journals and as a director and an evaluator of university researchers and teachers. She has been a visiting researcher at the University of Granada, Spain and participated in prestigious international conferences.

Juan José González de la Rosa is an accredited Full Professor by the Spanish National Agency for Quality Assessment (ANECA). He received his M.S. Degree in Physics-Electronics in 1992, from the University of Granada, Spain, and his Ph.D. in Industrial Engineering in 1999 (summa cum laude), from the University of Cádiz, Spain. Currently, he is a Full Professor at the University of Cádiz, in the Research Group in Computational Instrumentation and Industrial Electronics (PAIDI-TIC-168), Electronics Area. He is an IEEE Senior Member and the author of a number of JCR research articles, an attendant of multiple conferences and international research meetings, which are the result of his leadership in research projects. He has also visited and attended Universities (invited professor), research institutes and companies. His research interests can be summarized by computational intelligence for enhancing measurement systems and applications.

Khalid M. Salama is a Data scientist at Hitachi Consulting UK and an Honorary Research Fellow at School of Computing, University of Kent, UK.

Edgar N. Sanchez was born in 1949, in Sardinata, Colombia, South America. He obtained a BSEE, majoring in Power Systems, from the Universidad Industrial de Santander (UIS), Bucaramanga, Colombia in 1971, a MSEE from CINVESTAV-IPN (Advanced Studies and Research Center of the National Polytechnic Institute), majoring in Automatic Control from Mexico City, Mexico, in 1974 and a Docteur Ingenieur degree in Automatic Control from the Institut Nationale Polytechnique de Grenoble, France in 1980. In 1971, 1972, 1975 and 1976, he worked for different Electrical Engineering consulting companies in Bogota, Colombia. In 1974, he was a professor of Electrical Engineering in the Department of UIS, Colombia. From January 1981 to November 1990, he worked as a researcher at the Electrical Research Institute, Cuernavaca, Mexico. He was a professor of the graduate program in Electrical Engineering of the Universidad Autonoma de Nuevo Leon (UANL), Monterrey, Mexico, from December 1990 to December 1996. Since January 1997, he has been with CINVESTAV-IPN, Guadalajara Campus, Mexico, as a Professor of Electrical Engineering graduate programs. His research interests center on Neural Networks and Fuzzy Logic as applied to Automatic Control systems. He has been the advisor of 18 Ph.D. theses and 40 M. Sc Theses. He was granted a USA National Research Council Award as a research associate at the NASA Langley Research Center, Hampton, Virginia, USA (January 1985 to March 1987). He is also a member of the Mexican National Research System (promoted to highest rank, III, in 2005), a member of the Mexican Academy of Science and a member of the Mexican Academy of Engineering. He has published 4 books, more than 150 technical papers in international journals and conferences, and has served as reviewer for different international journals and conferences. He has also been a member of many international conferences IPCs, both for the IEEE and IFAC.

Noritaka Shigei received B.E., M.E., and D.E. degrees from Kagoshima University, Japan, in 1992, 1994, and 1997, respectively. He is currently an Associate Professor in the Graduate School of Science and Engineering at Kagoshima University. His current research interests include neural networks, wireless sensor networks, digital communication systems, digital circuit design, and parallel computing systems.

Jose María Sierra-Fernandez received a degree in Industrial Engineering, specialized in Industrial electronics and electricity in 2009 from the University of Cádiz, Spain and completed his Master's degree in Computational Modelling on Engineering in 2012 from the University of Cádiz, Spain. Currently, he is a Granted Pre-doctoral Researcher and a Professor at the University of Cádiz, where he continues to develop his Ph.D., in the Research Group in Computational Instrumentation and Industrial Electronics (PAIDI-TIC168), Electronics Area. His research interests include time-series analysis, power quality, higher-order statistics, intelligent systems, forecasting and modeling of wind speeds.

Martin Vesely was a student from 2006 to 2012 in the Department of Fluid Dynamics and Thermo-dynamics. Since 2013, he has been a Ph.D. student in the Department of Instrumentation and Control Engineering at the Czech Technical University in Prague, Faculty of Mechanical as an Engineering student.

Jan Vrba is at the Czech Technical University in Prague (CTU), Technicka 4, Czech Republic.

Rainer Wasinger is a senior lecturer in the HIT Lab at the University of Tasmania, Australia. Predominantly his research interests are in mobile and ubiquitous computing and the broader fields of Software Engineering and HCI.

Donald Wunsch is the M.K. Finley Missouri Distinguished Professor at Missouri University of Science & Technology (Missouri S&T). Earlier employers were: Texas Tech University, Boeing, Rockwell International, and International Laser Systems. His education includes: Executive MBA - Washington University in St. Louis; Ph.D., Electrical Engineering - University of Washington (Seattle); M.S., Applied Mathematics (same institution); B.S., Applied Mathematics - University of New Mexico. Key research contributions are: Clustering, including hierarchical clustering and biclustering; Adaptive resonance and Reinforcement Learning architectures, hardware and applications; Neurofuzzy regression; Traveling Salesman Problem heuristics; Smart Grid; Robotic Swarms; and Bioinformatics. He has produced 16 Ph.D. recipients in Computer Engineering, Electrical Engineering, and Computer Science; has attracted over $8 million in sponsored research; and has over 300 publications including nine books. He is an IEEE Fellow and previous INNS President, INNS Fellow and Senior Fellow 07 - present, and served as IJCNN General Chair, and on several Boards, including the IEEE Neural Net Council, International Neural Networks Society, and the University of Missouri Bioinformatics Consortium. He chairs the Missouri S&T Information Technology and Computing Committee, a Faculty Senate Standing Committee.

Shuxiang Xu is currently a lecturer of Computing within the School of Engineering and ICT, University of Tasmania, Australia. He received a Bachelor of Applied Mathematics from the University of Electronic Science and Technology of China (1986), China, a Master of Applied Mathematics from Sichuan Normal University (1989), China, and a PhD in Computing from the University of Western Sydney (2000), Australia. He received an Overseas Postgraduate Research Award from the Australian government in 1996 to research his Computing PhD. His current interests include the theory and applications of Artificial Neural Networks, Genetic Algorithms, and Data Mining.

Shuji Yatsuki received B.E., M.E., and Ph.D. degrees in System Information Engineering from Kagoshima University, Japan, in 1993, 1995, and 1998, respectively. He is currently working at Yatsuki Information System, Inc. His research interests are neural networks, artificial intelligence systems and 3D computer graphics systems.

Zarita Zainuddin is a Professor in the School of Mathematical Sciences at Universiti Sains Malaysia (USM). She graduated from Monmouth College, Illinois with a B.Sc. in Mathematics (Departmental Honours and Cum Laude) and subsequently obtained an M.Sc.in Applied Mathematics from Ohio University, USA. She holds a Ph.D. with specialization in Neural Networks from USM. Her research interests center on optimization methods in learning algorithms of neural networks, applications of neural networks, mathematical modeling and the integration of technology in the teaching of mathematics.

Zongyuan Zhao is currently a PhD student in Computing within the School of Computing and Information Systems, University of Tasmania, Australia. He received a Bachelor of Computer Science and Technology from Beihang University, China (2010), and a Master of Computer Science and Technology from China Agriculture University, China (2012). His current interests include the theory and applications of Artificial Neural Networks and Data Mining.

Index

Become an IRMA Member

Members of the **Information Resources Management Association (IRMA)** understand the importance of community within their field of study. The Information Resources Management Association is an ideal venue through which professionals, students, and academicians can convene and share the latest industry innovations and scholarly research that is changing the field of information science and technology. Become a member today and enjoy the benefits of membership as well as the opportunity to collaborate and network with fellow experts in the field.

IRMA Membership Benefits:

- **One FREE Journal Subscription**

- **30% Off Additional Journal Subscriptions**

- **20% Off Book Purchases**

- Updates on the latest events and research on Information Resources Management through the IRMA-L listserv.

- Updates on new open access and downloadable content added to Research IRM.

- A copy of the Information Technology Management Newsletter twice a year.

- A certificate of membership.

IRMA Membership $195

Scan code to visit irma-international.org and begin by selecting your free journal subscription.

Membership is good for one full year.